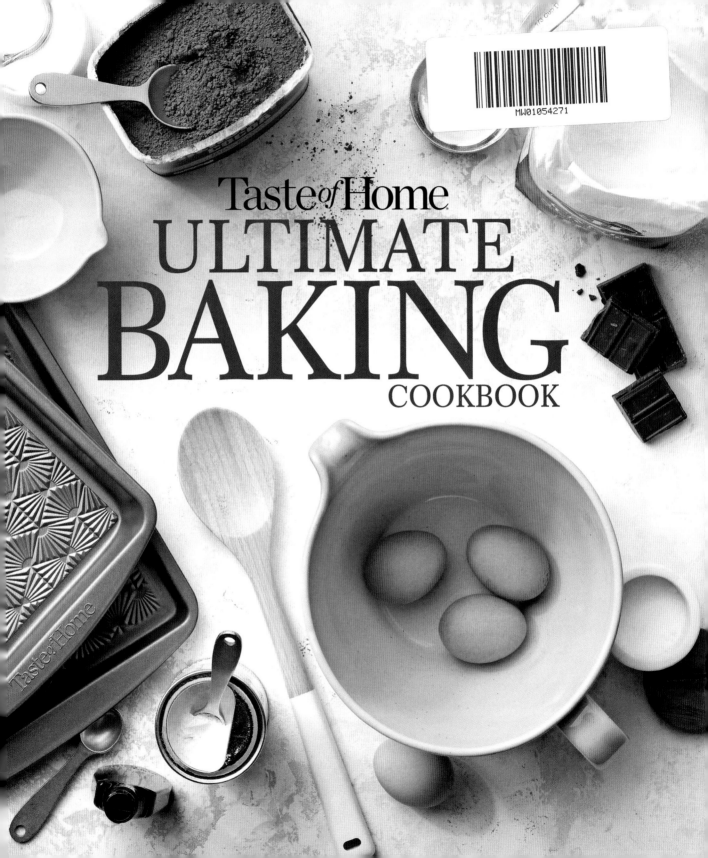

Taste of Home

ULTIMATE BAKING COOKBOOK

Visit us at **tasteofhome.com** for other Taste of Home
books and products.

International Standard Book Number:
WIRO: 978-1-62145-731-2
PB: 978-1-62145-739-8
HC: 978-1-62145-740-4

LOCC: 2021933637

Executive Editor: Mark Hagen
Senior Art Director: Raeann Thompson
Editor: Hazel Wheaton
Art Director: Courtney Lovetere
Designer: Arielle Anttonen
Deputy Editor, Copy Desk: Dulcie Shoener
Senior Copy Editor: Ann Walter

Cover:
Photographer: Mark Derse
Set Stylist: Melissa Franco
Food Stylist: Josh Rink

Pictured on front cover:
Rhubarb Strawberry Pie, p. 213; Fluffy Biscuits, p. 113; Linzer
Cookies, p. 140; White Velvet Cutouts, p. 149; Yellow Layer Cake
with Chocolate Buttercream, p. 286; Challah, p. 38; Mexican
Wedding Cakes, p. 167; Wild Blueberry Muffins, p. 97
Pictured on back cover:
Ginger-Glazed Lemon Bundt, p. 311; Peanut Caramel
Brownie Bites, p. 184; New York Cheesecake with Shortbread
Crust, p. 364; Peach Cream Puffs, p. 420; Skillet Rolls, p. 55;
Coastal Coconut Cream Cake, p. 278; Strawberry-Pecan Yeast
Rolls, p. 398; Chai Cupcakes, p. 290; Plum Good Crisp, p. 263;
Classic Lemon Bars, p. 197

Printed in China
1 3 5 7 9 10 8 6 4 2

CONTENTS

· · · · · · · · · · · ·

EVERYTHING THE HOME BAKER NEEDS IN ONE HANDY REFERENCE

In times of celebration and times of comfort, there's nothing like home-baked treats to warm the heart and share the love. If you've ever wanted to learn the traditional, timeless art of baking, this comprehensive book is just the place to start. And if you're already an experienced baker looking for new recipes to add to your repertoire, here are more than 500 to choose from.

Want to bake crescent rolls like Grandma's? Follow the how-to photos for a truly delicious result. Wondering how to make the perfect pie crust? See the step-by-step directions for sweet success. Want to master sourdough bread? We show you how, from the care and feeding of sourdough starter to the perfect rise and the best bake. Entire chapters walk you through the basics of yeast and quick breads, cheesecakes, brownies, coffee cakes, cobblers, cookies, pies, cakes for every occasion and many other mouthwatering favorites.

LOOK INSIDE FOR:

- Clear, detailed photographs demonstrating how to make some of our favorite recipes.

- A special BAKING 101 icon spotlighting recipes perfect for beginner bakers.

BAKING 101

- Introductory sections to every chapter packed with must-have information and advice.

- A handy reference section with a guide to ingredient weights, pan conversions and substitutions for both!

From apple pie to zucchini bread, from measuring ingredients through the final decorative touches on your three-layer cake, the *Ultimate Baking Cookbook* has all the answers you're looking for.

INGREDIENTS

THE WELL-STOCKED PANTRY

ESSENTIAL BAKING INGREDIENTS

- Flour
- Old-fashioned oats
- Sugar (confectioners', granulated and light brown)
- Oil (canola or vegetable)
- Shortening
- Salt
- Baking chocolate bars (bittersweet)
- Baking powder and baking soda
- Cream of tartar
- Chocolate chips (semisweet)
- Cocoa powder
- Cinnamon
- Extracts (almond and vanilla)
- Shredded coconut
- Raisins
- Peanut butter
- Applesauce

FLOUR

Flours are made from the finely ground meal of edible grains. Wheat flour, the most commonly used flour, contains gluten—an elastic protein that traps the gases produced by leaveners. The trapped gases push against the protein, causing the product to rise. During baking, the protein is set by the heat and gives the baked good its structure. The amount of gluten will affect the texture of the baked product.

- **All-purpose flour** is a blend of hard (high-gluten) wheat and soft (low-gluten) wheat flours. It is a general purpose flour, suitable for all types of baking.

- **Bread flour** is made from hard wheat and is specifically formulated for yeast breads.

- **Cake flour** is made from low-gluten wheat and has a fine texture. It gives a tender, delicate crumb to cakes.

- **Rye flour** contains less gluten than wheat flours and should be used in combination with wheat flour. Rye flour produces breads with a darker color, denser texture and more distinctive flavor. Medium rye flour is available in most grocery stores; light and dark rye flours are sold in specialty stores.

- **Self-rising flour** is all-purpose flour to which salt and baking powder have been added. It is used as a shortcut in some biscuit and cake recipes.

- **Whole wheat flour,** also called graham flour, is a wheat flour processed from the entire wheat kernel, which contains the bran and the germ. Whole wheat flour has more fiber, nutrients and fat than all-purpose flour. Because of the fat from the bran and germ, whole wheat flour has a shorter shelf life than white flours. Store whole wheat flour in the refrigerator for up to 6 months.

EGGS

Eggs perform many functions in baking. They add color, flavor, texture and structure and help leaven. Yolks add fat and act as an emulsifier, which helps blend the shortening, oil or butter into the liquid ingredients. The whites are used for their drying properties, especially for meringues. The recipes in this cookbook were tested with large eggs.

To make sure your eggs are still good to use, try this easy test: Place them in a bowl of water deep enough to cover. If the eggs lie flat on the bottom of the bowl, they are fresh and perfect for cooking. If they tilt up slightly or stand on one end, they are less fresh, but still usable for baking. (Eggs that are less than perfectly fresh actually work better for recipes that call for beaten egg whites or meringue.) If the eggs float to the top of the water, they are no longer usable and should be discarded.

THE STAGES OF BEATING EGGS

LIGHTLY BEATEN

LEMON-COLORED

THICK & PALE YELLOW

FATS

Fats in baked goods tenderize, add moisture, carry flavors and provide richness. They act as a leavener when creamed (see "What is Creaming?," p. 15), and help keep baked goods fresh. In baking, a fat usually means butter, shortening, lard, oil or margarine.

Unsalted butter is most commonly called for in baking recipes. Unsalted butter has a neutral, creamy flavor, making it a great base for many baked goods. Because the salt levels varies in different brands of butter, using unsalted guarantees control over how much salt is in the recipe.

However, the only difference between salted and unsalted butter is the salt content, so you can use salted and still have your recipe work—just use less of any added salt the recipe calls for.

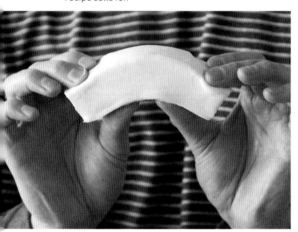

SOFTENING BUTTER

Unless the recipe specifies otherwise, butter should be softened before being used in a recipe. It takes about 45 minutes for butter left on the kitchen counter to soften to the right state—you should be able to make an indentation in the butter with your finger, but the surface shouldn't be melted or greasy. There are also ways to soften butter quickly (see below), which is more convenient and also better in hot climates, where butter left out is liable to sweat liquid and melt quickly.

DAIRY

Dairy products add moisture to baked goods. They also impart flavor and tenderness and aid in browning. Unless otherwise stated, the recipes in this book were tested with 2% milk. You may substitute whole or fat-free milk, but the texture of the final product may be affected.

MAKE YOUR OWN BUTTERMILK

Sour or fermented dairy—yogurt, sour cream and buttermilk—have acidity that breaks down the gluten in baked goods, creating a more tender end product. If you don't have buttermilk, you can easily make your own. Combine 1 Tbsp. of either white vinegar or lemon juice plus enough milk to measure 1 cup. Stir, then let stand for 5 minutes.

Cut the butter into cubes, and they'll be ready in about 15 minutes. The smaller the pieces, the more quickly they will come to room temperature.

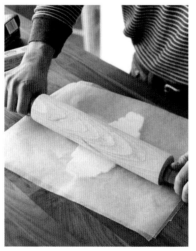

Place the butter between two sheets of waxed or parchment paper and, with a rolling pin, roll or pound the butter out flat.

LEAVENERS

Leaveners cause baked goods to rise and have a light texture. Baking powder, baking soda, yeast and eggs are leavening agents. **Baking powder** is available in single-acting and double-acting varieties—double-acting is more common and is the type used in this cookbook. **Baking soda** is an alkaline substance used in batters that have acidic ingredients (such as buttermilk, molasses and sour cream). Batters that use only baking soda as a leavener should be baked immediately. **Yeast** is a microorganism that becomes activated when combined with warm water and sugar. (For more about yeast, see p. 18.) **Eggs** are whipped to incorporate air to create a foam; the the air expands when heated. Foam cakes, such as angel foods and chiffons, use egg whites as a leavening agent.

SWEETENERS

Other than the obvious—adding sweetness and flavor—sweeteners also tenderize, promote browning, and enhance the keeping quality of baked goods. Common baking sweeteners are granulated sugar, brown sugar, confectioners' sugar, corn syrup, honey and molasses. In baking, sugars are classified as liquids, as they dissolve when heated.

CHOCOLATE

Chocolate is one of the most popular flavorings in baked goods. Chocolate comes from cocoa beans, which are processed to produce cocoa powder, cocoa butter and chocolate liquor (the liquid created when the meat of the cocoa bean nibs are crushed). Commercially available chocolate comes in a range of forms, such as cocoa powder, chocolate bars, chips and chunks, and concentrations—from sweet milk chocolate to unsweetened. (For more about different types of chocolate, see p. 183.)

NUTS

Because of their high fat content, nuts spoil easily. Store shelled nuts in airtight containers in a dry, cool location for up to 3 months. Shelled or unshelled nuts can be stored in the refrigerator for up to 6 months, or in the freezer for up to a year.

Toasting nuts brings out their flavor and adds a depth and richness to baked goods. To toast nuts, bake them in a single layer in a shallow pan at 350° for 5-10 minutes, stirring or shaking halfway through. Or, cook in a skillet over low heat until lightly browned, stirring occasionally.

BAKING SPICES

- Store spices in a dark, cool and dry place.

- Spices lose color and flavor as they age. Write the date on spice jars when you buy them. Toss ground spices after 1-3 years; whole spices after 3-4 years.

- To make spices last longer, buy whole spices whenever possible, and grind them as needed.

- Toasting spices enhances their flavor.

- To avoid spilling, don't measure spices directly over the bowl; pour them into your hand or another small bowl first.

METHODS & EQUIPMENT

THE WELL-STOCKED KITCHEN

MEASURING TOOLS
- Liquid measuring cups (Pyrex or transparent plastic)
- Dry measuring cups
- Measuring spoons
- Kitchen scale

BAKEWARE
- 9x1½-in. round baking pans (2-3)
- 9x13-in. baking pan (3 qt.)
- 11x7-in. baking dish (2 qt.)
- 10-in. fluted tube pan
- 15x10x1-in. baking pan (jelly-roll pan)
- Baking sheets (assorted sizes)
- 9-in. springform pan
- Pie plates: 9-in. and 9-in. deep dish
- 12-cup muffin pan (standard size)
- Miniature muffin pans
- 6-oz. custard cups (set of 6)
- Loaf pans: 9x5-in. (two), 8x4-in. (two), 5¾x3x2-in. mini loaf pans (3-4)
- 8- and 9-in. square baking pans
- 10-in. tube pan
- 9-in. fluted tart pan with removable bottom

MIXING TOOLS
- Stand mixer
- Hand mixer
- Glass mixing bowls
- Food processor
- Spatulas (silicone, rubber or plastic)
- Dough cutter/scraper
- Wire whisk
- Wooden spoons
- Pastry blender
- Mesh strainers

MISCELLANOUS TOOLS
- Juicer
- Kitchen timers
- Rolling pin
- Wire racks
- Pastry brushes
- Metal spatula and offset spatula
- Grater
- Pastry bag and tips
- Cookie cutters

CHOOSING BAKEWARE

The recipes in this book call for standard-size baking pans and dishes. For best results, use the pan size called for in the recipe. However, there are some practical substitutions (see p. 439).

Baking pans are made of metal. Aluminum pans with dull finishes give the best overall baking results. Pans with dark finishes tend to cook and brown foods more quickly—If you use a pan with a dark finish, you may need to adjust the baking time and cover tops of baked goods with foil to prevent overbrowning. Insulated pans generally take longer to bake and brown foods.

Baking dishes are made of ovenproof glass or ceramic. If you substitute a glass baking dish in a recipe calling for a metal baking pan, reduce the oven temperature by 25° to avoid overbaking and overbrowning.

To measure your bakeware's diameter, length or width, use a ruler to measure from one inside top edge to the opposite inside top edge. To measure the height, place a ruler on the outside of the dish and measure from the bottom to a top edge. To find the volume without doing math, fill the pan or dish full to the rim with water, then pour the water into a liquid measuring cup.

MEASURING

To ensure good and consistent results in your baking, it is important to accurately measure ingredients. Get a good set of measuring tools—not all measuring cups and spoons are the same, so prioritize accuracy over aesthetics. Also, not all ingredients should be measured in the same way.

DRY INGREDIENTS

Lightly sprinkle dry ingredients such as flour, sugar or cornmeal into a dry measuring cup—do not scoop out the ingredient from its container. Fill the cup to overflowing, then level by sweeping a metal spatula or the flat side of a knife across the top. Do not press down to pack the dry ingredient or tap the cup against the counter to get it to settle.

LIQUIDS

Place a liquid measuring cup on a level surface. Pour in the liquid and view the amount at eye level to be sure of an accurate measure. Do not lift the cup to check the level. If measuring sticky liquids such as molasses, corn syrup or honey, first spray the measuring cup with cooking spray to make it easier to pour out the liquid and clean the cup.

MEASURING STICK BUTTER

The wrappers for sticks of butter come with markings for tablespoons, ¼ cup, ⅓ cup and ½ cup. Use a sharp knife to cut off the desired amount.

SOUR CREAM AND YOGURT

Spoon sour cream and yogurt into a dry measuring cup, then level the top by sweeping a metal spatula or flat side of a knife across the top of the cup.

BROWN SUGAR AND SHORTENING

These ingredients are exceptions to the usual rule, as they both should be compressed into the measuring cup. Firmly press brown sugar into the cup with your fingers or the back of a spoon, then level the top. The sugar should hold the shape of the cup when it is turned out.

For shortening (or lard), use a spatula to press the ingredient into a dry measuring cup to make sure it is solidly packed without air pockets, then level it. Some shortenings come in sticks and may be measured like butter.

USING MEASURING SPOONS

Measuring spoons use the same rules as measuring cups. Heap dry ingredients into the spoon rather than scooping, spread shortening or butter into the spoon, and pour liquids into the spoon. Never measure over the batter, because some may spill.

WEIGHING FLOUR

For the most precise measurement for dry ingredients, use a kitchen scale (preferably one with a tare function). This is most important for flour, as the most common baking mistake is using too much (or too little) flour. Even the experts in the *Taste of Home* Test Kitchen can measure out "standard" cups of flour that weigh anywhere from 3 oz. to 5½ oz.—a variance that can have a noticeable impact on the texture of the finished baked good.

To accurately measure flour, place a bowl on the scale, zero the tare and then add the flour. A cup of all-purpose flour should weigh 120 g or very close to it. (For a chart of the weights of some of the most common baking ingredients, including various types of flour, see p. 436.)

SEPARATING EGGS

You can separate egg yolks from whites using the two halves of a broken shell, a specially designed egg separator or a slotted spoon. It is easier to separate eggs when they are cold, so it's best to separate them and then let the yolks and whites sit to come to room temperature before using in the recipe.

BEATING EGG WHITES

For maximum volume, egg whites should be allowed to stand at room temperature for 30 minutes before beating. Use a small mixer bowl for up to three egg whites and a large bowl for four or more. For best results, use a clean metal or glass bowl—plastic is more likely to have oily residue which will inhibit the beating of the egg whites. Be careful not to get any of the yolk in with the whites.

An acidic ingredient (most commonly cream of tartar, but this could also be lemon juice or vinegar) stabilizes the egg whites so they don't deflate quickly after beating. A good rule of thumb is ⅛ tsp. of cream of tartar per egg white.

Beat eggs on medium speed until soft peaks form, then continue beating until stiff peaks form. Overbeaten whites look grainy with liquid pooling in the bottom of the bowl. If you do overbeat your egg whites, you may be able to recover them by mixing in one more room-temperature egg white.

SOFT PEAKS

STIFF PEAKS

OVERBEATEN

FOLDING INGREDIENTS

Folding is a gentle mixing technique to incorporate light and airy ingredients (such as egg whites and whipped cream) into heavier batters without deflating the lighter mixture. Nuts and fruit are also often folded into a batter as the final step to avoid overmixing.

Use a large bowl to give you space to maneuver and use a wide, flexible spatula. Always fold the lighter mixture into the heavier batter. Starting in the center of the bowl, cut straight down through the center to the bottom of the bowl. Scrape along the bottom of the bowl toward you, continue up the side of the bowl and then fold the mixture over on top. Rotate the bowl a quarter turn and continue until combined.

If the batter is particularly thick, fold a small portion of the lighter mixture in first to help lighten it, then fold in the remaining amount.

The process may take several minutes—resist the urge to stir to speed things up. Fold until the mixture is just combined. It should be homogenous, without any obvious streaks or separation of ingredients. Stop at this point; continued folding will increase deflation.

WHAT IS CREAMING?

One instruction you'll see a lot is to cream the butter and sugar. This vital step is more than just beating butter and sugar together until they're combined; creaming takes the ingredients through several stages until they form a light and fluffy mixture.

Unless otherwise directed, start with butter at a cool room temperature (64-68°)—not too soft, or your mixture will be more liquid and greasy than light and fluffy. Creaming will take anywhere from 3 to 10 minutes, depending on the mixer, mixing speed and ingredient quantities, but typically takes 5 to 7 minutes. This can be done with either a hand mixer or a stand mixer; if your mixer has both a whisk and a paddle attachment, use the paddle.

MELTING CHOCOLATE

There are two rules to melting chocolate: Don't get it too hot and don't get it wet. Even small amounts of water will cause the chocolate to seize (become thick and lumpy), making it unusable.

Break or chop large pieces of chocolate so it will melt evenly; heat in a double boiler and stir until smooth.

To melt chocolate in the microwave, use a microwave-safe bowl. Stir frequently until the chocolate is melted; do not overheat.

NOTES ON GLUTEN-FREE BAKING

To make your recipes gluten-free, you can substitute an equal amount of commercially available all-purpose gluten-free flour for the all-purpose regular flour the recipe calls for. (Check the ingredients on the gluten-free flour—if it doesn't already contain a binder, add 1 tsp. xanthan gum or ½ tsp. arrowroot powder.)

If you want to mix your own gluten-free flour mixture, combine:

- 3 parts white or brown rice flour
- 2 parts potato starch
- 1 part tapioca flour/starch
- 1 tsp. xanthan gum for every 1½ cups flour mixture

Gluten-free flours are finer than wheat flours, so it's more important than ever to measure properly, preferably by weight.

Mix your batters longer. The standard rule of thumb that overmixing will turn the end product tough and rubbery doesn't apply when there is no gluten in the flour. Instead, mix the batter longer to develop more structure.

Let the batter sit. Another rule that doesn't apply is baking quick breads as soon as possible. Batters made with gluten-free flour benefit from sitting up to 30 minutes before going in the oven—batters firm up, develop more structure, are less sticky and the end product has less of a gritty texture.

Use an oven thermometer—gluten-free baked goods often appear underdone, as the starches set as the baked good cools.

Pie crusts made with gluten-free flours may be drier or more prone to cracking than a traditional crust. Add water sparingly. Some gluten-free crusts may brown more quickly; cover the pie with foil for the last half of the baking time to prevent burning.

YEAST BREADS

There's nothing that matches the aroma of freshly baked bread—and there are so many mouthwatering ways to create flavors that live up to the scent!

. . . .

YEAST BREADS

Yeast breads depend on a living organism for their height and texture. Yeast breads fall into two main categories: kneaded breads and batter breads.

Kneaded breads are traditionally worked by hand to develop the gluten in the dough. Modern gadgets—a bread machine or a stand mixer with a dough hook—make the process easier, but the dough itself is still kneaded.

Batter breads, or stirred breads, are beaten with a mixer to develop the gluten. Because they use less flour, their dough is stickier than kneaded yeast breads. The finished breads have a coarser texture and a rugged, textured crust.

There are also two categories of sweet yeast breads: loaves and rolls. Sweet loaves include fruit-filled breads and a variety of coffee cakes. Sweet rolls refer to fruit-filled rolls, sticky buns, cinnamon rolls, doughnuts, kolaches and Danishes (see Chapter 9 for recipes for breakfast rolls, pastries and coffee cakes).

YEAST BREAD INGREDIENTS

Ingredients and their qualities affect the texture, density and crust of bread. Understanding the job of each ingredient will help you to understand the science of yeast breads.

Fats (and eggs) tenderize, add moisture, carry flavor and give richness to breads.

Flours: Gluten, an elastic protein in wheat flour, gives bread its structure. Flours with high gluten content (hard flours), such as bread flour or all-purpose flour, yield the best results. Whole wheat and rye flours (soft flours) have less gluten; used alone, they make a very dense loaf, so they're often used in combination with hard flour for lighter, airier results.

Liquids: Water and milk are the primary liquids used in bread. Water gives a crunchy crust; milk gives a softer crust and a more tender crumb. Always warm liquid to the temperature stated in the recipe. Too cold, and the yeast will be slow to activate; too hot, and it will kill the yeast.

Yeast: Once activated, this microorganism produces carbon dioxide gas that stretches gluten strands to give breads a light, airy texture. Store yeast in the refrigerator or freezer.

Sweeteners provide food for the yeast; they also tenderize, add flavor, promote browning and lengthen shelf life. White or brown sugar, molasses, honey and maple syrup are some common sweeteners.

Salt controls the yeast's growth. Use the amount given in the recipe—do not omit it.

TYPES OF YEAST

Active dry yeast is the most commonly used type of yeast. It must be proofed before using (see proofing steps, opposite page) to activate the dormant organism. A standard packet of yeast contains approximately 2½ tsp. To use active dry yeast in recipes that call for Instant yeast, increase yeast amount by 25%.

Instant and rapid-rise yeasts are finely granulated and cut the rising time for dough by up to half. They can be added directly to the dry ingredients and do not need proofing. Instant and Rapid-Rise yeast can be used interchangeably; Rapid-Rise yeast may contain dough conditioners, like ascorbic acid, to produce the quick rise. To use instant yeast in recipes that call for Active Dry yeast, use 25% less than what the recipe calls for.

Bread machine yeast has fine, small granules that can be mixed easily into the dough. Like Rapid-Rise yeast, this type of yeast may contain dough conditioners.

Vintage cookbooks may call for **Cake yeast** (also known as fresh yeast or compressed yeast). It has a short shelf life and may be difficult to find—check the dairy case in your grocery store. Cake yeast is proofed at a lower temperature (80-90°), and is most suitable for breads with a long, cool rise time.

There is also a type of yeast—**osmotolerant yeast**—designed for sugar-heavy doughs. It's not as common as the dry yeasts but is becoming more readily available. Look for it at your grocer or specialty food store.

STEPS IN MAKING BREAD

PROOFING YEAST

When discussing yeast breads, "proof" is used two ways: proofing yeast, and proofing dough. Proofing the dough comes after kneading; proofing yeast ensures it is alive and ready to create carbon dioxide.

Dissolve active dry yeast in a dish with ½ tsp. sugar and ¼ cup warm water (between 105° and 115°). When, after 5-10 minutes, it starts to bubble and foam, you know it's alive and ready for bread.

Proofing may already be included as the first step in bread recipes that use the traditional mixing method (see below), but it's a handy method to know when you find an older jar of yeast in your fridge or pantry; proof a sample of it before you start making your baking plans to prevent false starts.

If your recipe uses the rapid mixing method, subtract liquid from the recipe to compensate for the liquid you used to proof the yeast.

MIXING

There are two basic ways to mix bread ingredients. In the **traditional mixing** method, yeast is activated by being dissolved in warm liquid before being mixed with the remaining ingredients. In **rapid mixing**, the yeast is mixed with the dry ingredients first. Your recipe will give specific instructions for mixing. Be aware, however, if the recipe uses the traditional mixing method, you should not use instant yeast.

KNEADING

Kneading dough helps develop gluten, which gives yeast bread its structure. Turn the dough out onto a lightly floured surface. Dust your hands with flour, then shape the dough into a ball. Push the bread away from you with your palms, using a rolling motion. After every push, fold the dough over on itself, give it a quarter turn and repeat. If the dough sticks, add a little more flour, but be careful not to add too much. Try using your bench scraper first, then add flour to the work surface as needed.

To determine if you've kneaded the dough long enough, you're looking for smoothness and elasticity. After mixing, the dough can look a little sticky and rough; kneading gives it a nice, smooth texture. To test the dough's elasticity, let it rest for about a minute and then press it with your finger. If the indentation stays, it's not yet ready. If the indentation springs back slightly, it's ready.

PROOFING DOUGH

Proofing dough is letting the yeast work—creating bubbles that push outward to expand the dough. Place the dough in large bowl greased with butter, oil or cooking spray; turn it over once to grease the top so it won't dry out. Cover the bowl—a clean tea towel is traditional, although cling film is best to prevent moisture from escaping. If the dough is sticky, rub a tiny bit of oil onto the film so the dough won't stick to it as it rises.

To proof bread, you need to create a warm (75° or above), humid and stable environment. If you bake regularly, you may want to invest in a proofing box. Some ovens have a proofing setting. There are other ways you can use your oven:

- Place a glass baking dish on the bottom rack and fill it with boiling water. Place your bowl of dough on the middle or top rack and shut the oven door. Refresh the hot water every 30 to 45 minutes.

- Some oven lights radiate enough heat to proof dough. Turn on your oven light. Then, after 30 minutes, check the oven's temperature with an oven thermometer. If it's above 75°, set your dough in the oven and shut the door with the light on.

- If your oven has a top vent, set the oven to its lowest temperature and place your dough on the stovetop.

Finally, use the windowpane test. Tear off a piece of dough and stretch it between your fingers. If you can stretch it until you can see light through it when your hold it up, it's ready; if it tears, it needs more work.

It is possible to over-knead dough, resulting in tough, chewy bread. If you're kneading by hand, you'll be tired long before the dough is overworked, but it can happen with stand mixers or food processors. If you're kneading with a dough hook, stop when the dough clears the sides of the bowl, then turn it out onto your work surface and finish kneading by hand.

You can also fill a slow cooker halfway with water and set it to low (which will heat the water to about 200°F). Put the lid on upside down, lay a towel over it, and set your bowl of dough on top of that.

Proofing can take 1-3 hours. When it's ready, your dough should have expanded to roughly twice its original size and have a full, puffed appearance. To test it, press two fingers ½ inch into the dough. It should feel soft and supple, and your fingers should leave an indentation.

STEPS *(CONTINUED)*

PUNCHING DOWN

After the initial proofing stage, you'll need to punch down the dough before shaping it. That sounds violent, but the action isn't an actual fast punch—just press your fist firmly into the center of the dough to remove some of the air. Gather the edge of the dough to the center and shape it into a ball, then follow the recipe for dividing the dough for loaves or rolls. After punching down the dough, let it rest for 10 minutes; this lets the dough relax, which makes it easier to shape.

SCORING

Slashing or scoring the top of a bread loaf allows the steam to vent, helps to prevent cracking and gives bread a decorative appearance. You can use a sharp knife, a razor blade, or a special tool called a lame to make shallow slashes across the top of the loaf. Some bakers create elaborate patterns with their lame when making crusty, rustic loaves.

SHAPING

To shape a loaf, roll out the dough onto a lightly floured surface into a 12x8-in. rectangle. Air bubbles will pop as you roll out the dough. Dust off any loose flour, then roll up the dough from the short end. If the roll is too loose, there will be air pockets in the bread; too tight, and the top will crack during baking. Pinch the seam and ends to seal, and place seam side down in a greased pan, tucking the ends under if necessary. Then cover the pan and let the dough rise for its second proofing.

SECOND RISE

Underproofed dough won't rise properly during baking and you'll wind up with a flat, dense doorstop. If the dough looks stretched across the top and springs back instantly when pressed with a fingertip, it's overproofed. Like a balloon inflated to bursting, this spells trouble—the dough will crack and collapse when baked. To fix overproofed dough, punch it down, knead it briefly and then reshape it and let it proof again, for a shorter period of time or at a cooler temperature, until it's the correct size.

TESTING DONENESS

The best way to tell if your bread is done is to take the internal temperature with a quick-read thermometer; yeast breads are done when they reach 160-185° inside. You can also test the loaf by tapping the bottom—it should sound hollow. If it doesn't, put it back in the loaf pan and let it bake a little longer.

BAKING BREAD AT HIGH ALTITUDES

At elevations over 3,000 feet, lower air pressure makes yeast rise in as little as half the time. Use about a third less yeast—for each package of active dry yeast the recipe calls for, use 1½ tsp. Add flour slowly; use only enough to make the dough easy to handle. If the dough is sticky, use greased rather than floured hands for kneading. Start checking your dough halfway through the recommended rise time to prevent over-rising. While shaping the loaf, keep any extra dough oiled and covered with plastic wrap. Check for doneness a few minutes before the minimum baking time given in the recipe.

UNDERPROOFED | JUST RIGHT | OVERPROOFED

REASONS YOUR BREAD ISN'T RISING
(AND WHAT TO DO ABOUT IT)

The little organisms that help your bread rise need extra care—warm temperatures, some kind of food (usually a sugar) and just-right conditions. If any of these variables are off, the dough may not rise. Here are some of the most common reasons your bread isn't getting the right lift:

1. The yeast is too old. To make sure your yeast is ready to go, proof it before adding to your dough.

2. The liquid is the wrong temperature. Too hot and the yeast will die; too cool and the yeast won't grow. Be sure that the liquid you use is between 105° and 115°.

3. Too much salt. Salt controls the yeast so it doesn't ferment too quickly—too much salt means too much control, which can keep the yeast from doing its job. Measure carefully and never pour yeast and salt directly on top of one another in your mixing bowl.

4. Too much sugar. Sweet doughs take longer to rise because sugar absorbs the liquid in the dough so the yeast isn't as efficient. Measure carefully, don't add extra sugar, and allow your sweet doughs plenty of time to rise. (Sweet doughs often proof overnight in the refrigerator). There's also a type of yeast—called osmotolerant yeast—designed for sugar-heavy doughs.

5. Too much flour. Be mindful of how much flour your dough picks up during the kneading process—too much can turn the dough stiff and dry instead of slightly sticky and elastic. Use a bench scraper to scrape the dough off your work surface in the early stages of kneading, then than add more flour only when you're sure it's needed.

6. You're using whole grains. White flour creates wonderful gluten strands that give bread an airy texture, while whole wheat and other alternative flours don't develop gluten as easily or at all. Use a recipe specially formulated for those flours. If you want to add wheat flour into a recipe you already love, keep some all-purpose flour in the equation.

7. The crust is too dry. The dough should be nice and moist; if it develops a crust during proofing, it can be difficult for the bread to rise in the oven later. If your dough tends to dry out, use plastic wrap to cover it, not a tea towel.

ABOUT BREAD MACHINES
TIPS FOR USING A BREAD MACHINE

- Before you begin, carefully read your bread machine's manual.

- All liquid ingredients should be at room temperature (70° to 80°). This includes water, milk, yogurt, juice, cottage cheese, eggs and applesauce.

- Use bread flour and either active dry yeast or bread machine yeast. Bread machine yeast is finer, allowing for better dispersion during mixing and kneading. As a general guideline, for each cup of flour, use ¾ tsp. active dry yeast or ½ tsp. bread machine yeast.

- Check the dough after 5 minutes of mixing; it should feel smooth, soft and slightly tacky. If it's moist or sticky, add 1 Tbsp. flour and check again after a few more minutes of mixing. If it's dry and crumbly, add 1 Tbsp. liquid, then check again in 5 minutes.

- Recipes containing eggs, milk, sour cream, cottage cheese and other perishable foods should never be used on the delay-bake cycle.

CONVERTING RECIPES

Adapting a bread machine recipe to make by hand is simple. Start by dissolving the yeast in warm water (105° to 115°). Add any wet ingredients (such as eggs, additional liquid, sugar, honey), then dry ingredients—herbs, salt and most of the flour. Beat until smooth; it will be a sticky dough to start. Add enough remaining flour to form a soft dough that pulls away from the sides of the bowl. Then follow the steps for a traditional recipe (such as Basic Homemade Bread, page 29) to knead, proof, shape and bake the bread.

Converting a standard recipe for use with a bread machine requires experimentation, as bread machines usually make smaller loaves. Check the size of your appliance and look at the recipes that came with it. Note the amount of dry and liquid ingredients those recipes call for, and their proportion to sweeteners and fat.

Begin with a standard recipe that has given you good results. Adjust the amount of flour to match a typical recipe for the bread machine, then adjust the other ingredients to keep the proportions the same. (It may be as simple as taking a recipe that makes two loaves and cutting it in half.) Make notes about the conversion for reference. If it wasn't quite right, adjust one ingredient and try again. Once you're happy with the result, look for other recipes that use the amount of flour your bread machine requires.

Sourdough and refrigerated dough recipes are not suitable for bread machines.

For breads with toppings, filling or special shaping, mix, knead and proof the dough in the bread machine, then punch dough down and finish shaping, rising and baking the traditional way.

The chart below is a guideline for bread machines yielding 1-pound, 1½-pound and 2-pound loaves.

BREAD MACHINE SIZE	1 lb.	1½ lbs.	2 lbs.
FLOUR	2 to 2½ cups	3 to 3½ cups	4 to 4½ cups
LIQUID	⅔ cup	1 cup	1⅓ cups
ACTIVE DRY YEAST	1½ tsp.	2½ tsp.	3 tsp.
SUGAR	2 Tbsp.	3 Tbsp.	4 Tbsp.
SALT	1 tsp.	1½ tsp.	2 tsp.
FAT	4 tsp.	6 tsp.	8 tsp.

LOAVES

CRUSTY HOMEMADE BREAD

Crackling homemade bread makes an average day extraordinary. Enjoy this beautiful crusty bread recipe as is, or stir in a few favorites like cheese, garlic, herbs and dried fruits.

—Megumi Garcia, Milwaukee, WI

PREP: 20 MIN. + RISING • **BAKE:** 50 MIN.
MAKES: 1 LOAF (16 PIECES)

1½	tsp. active dry yeast
1¾	cups warm water (105° to 115°)
3½	cups plus 1 Tbsp. all-purpose flour, divided
2	tsp. salt
1	Tbsp. cornmeal or additional flour

1. In a large bowl, dissolve yeast in warm water. Using a rubber spatula, stir in 3½ cups flour and salt to form a soft, sticky dough. Do not knead. Cover and let rise at room temperature for 1 hour.
2. Stir down dough (dough will be sticky). Turn onto a floured surface; with floured hands pat dough into a 9-in. square. Fold square into thirds, forming a 9x3-in. rectangle. Fold rectangle into thirds, forming a 3-in. square. Place in a large greased bowl, turning once to grease the top. Cover and let rise at room temperature until almost doubled, about 1 hour.
3. Punch down dough and repeat the folding process. Return dough to bowl; refrigerate, covered, overnight.
4. Grease the bottom of a disposable foil roasting pan with sides at least 4 in. high; dust pan with cornmeal. Turn the dough onto a floured surface. Knead gently 6-8 times; shape into a 6-in. round loaf. Place into prepared pan; dust top with remaining 1 Tbsp. flour. Cover and let rise at room temperature until dough expands to a 7½-in. loaf, about 1¼ hours.
5. Preheat oven to 500°. Using a sharp knife, make a slash (¼ in. deep) across top of loaf. Cover pan tightly with foil. Bake on lowest oven rack 25 minutes.
6. Reduce oven setting to 450°. Remove foil; bake bread until the crust is a deep golden brown, 25-30 minutes. Remove loaf to a wire rack to cool.

1 piece: 105 cal., 0 fat (0 sat. fat), 0 chol., 296mg sod., 22g carb. (0 sugars, 1g fiber), 3g pro.

DID YOU KNOW?

The key to a beautifully crisp crust is the presence of steam during the baking process. A closed container helps capture the moisture of the dough as it escapes. Covering a pan with foil, as in this recipe, is the easiest method; other crusty bread recipes are baked in a Dutch oven.

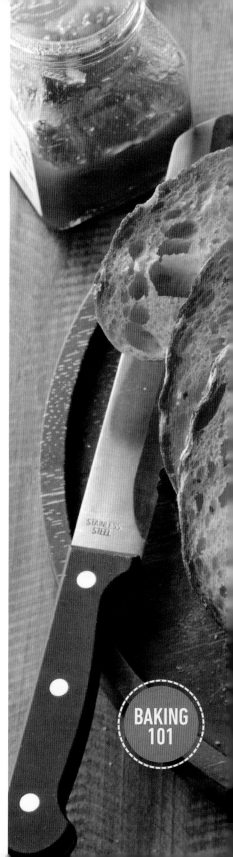

BAKING 101

CRUSTY
HOMEMADE BREAD

DILL BATTER
BREAD

BAKING 101

SUNFLOWER SEED & HONEY WHEAT BREAD

I've tried other bread recipes, but this one is a staple in our home. I once won $50 in a baking contest with a loaf that I had stored in the freezer!
—Mickey Turner, Grants Pass, OR

PREP: 40 MIN. + RISING • **BAKE:** 35 MIN.
MAKES: 3 LOAVES (12 PIECES EACH)

2	pkg. (¼ oz. each) active dry yeast
3¼	cups warm water (105° to 115°)
¼	cup bread flour
⅓	cup canola oil
⅓	cup honey
3	tsp. salt
6½ to 7½	cups whole wheat flour
½	cup sunflower kernels
3	Tbsp. butter, melted

1. In a large bowl, dissolve yeast in warm water. Add the bread flour, oil, honey, salt and 4 cups whole wheat flour. Beat until smooth. Stir in the sunflower kernels and enough of the remaining flour to form a firm dough.
2. Turn onto a floured surface; knead until smooth and elastic, 6-8 minutes. Place in a greased bowl, turning once to grease the top. Cover and let rise in a warm place until doubled, about 1 hour.
3. Punch dough down; divide into 3 portions. Shape into loaves; place in 3 greased 8x4-in. loaf pans. Cover loaves and let rise until doubled, about 30 minutes.
4. Bake at 350° until golden brown, 35-40 minutes. Brush with melted butter. Remove from pans to wire racks to cool.
1 piece: 125 cal., 4g fat (1g sat. fat), 3mg chol., 212mg sod., 19g carb. (3g sugars, 3g fiber), 4g pro. **Diabetic exchanges:** 1 starch, 1 fat.

DILL BATTER BREAD

Even those who don't consider themselves bakers can make this bread with success. And your guests will be delighted!
—Donna Lindecamp, Morganton, NC

PREP: 15 MIN. + RISING
BAKE: 45 MIN. + COOLING
MAKES: 1 LOAF (16 PIECES)

¼	cup sugar
2	pkg. (¼ oz. each) active dry yeast
2	tsp. dill weed
1½	tsp. salt
4½	cups all-purpose flour
1	cup water
1	cup 2% milk
¼	cup canola oil
1	large egg, room temperature
2	tsp. butter, melted
½	tsp. kosher salt

1. In a large bowl, mix sugar, yeast, dill weed, salt and 2 cups flour. In a small saucepan, heat water, milk and oil to 120°-130°. Add to dry ingredients; beat on medium speed 2 minutes. Add egg; beat on high 2 minutes. Stir in remaining 2½ cups flour to form a stiff batter. Cover and let rise until doubled, about 1 hour.
2. Preheat oven to 375°. Stir down batter. Transfer to a greased 2½-qt. round baking dish. Bake until bread is deep golden brown and sounds hollow when tapped, 45-50 minutes.
3. Cool 5 minutes before removing to a wire rack. Brush with butter; sprinkle with salt. Cool completely.
1 piece: 191 cal., 5g fat (1g sat. fat), 14mg chol., 298mg sod., 31g carb. (4g sugars, 1g fiber), 5g pro.

SWEDISH LIMPA BREAD

I've entered my bread in several fairs, and it has won every time! Orange and anise give it a subtle but wonderful flavor.
—Beryl Parrott, Franklin, MB

PREP: 30 MIN. + RISING • **BAKE:** 30 MIN.
MAKES: 2 LOAVES (12 PIECES EACH)

- ½ cup packed light brown sugar
- ¼ cup dark molasses
- ¼ cup butter, cubed
- 2 Tbsp. grated orange zest
- 1½ tsp. salt
- 1 tsp. aniseed, lightly crushed
- 1 cup boiling water
- 1 cup cold water
- 2 pkg. (¼ oz. each) active dry yeast
- ½ cup warm water (105° to 115°)
- 4½ cups all-purpose flour
- 3 to 4 cups rye flour
- 2 Tbsp. cornmeal
- 2 Tbsp. butter, melted

1. In a large bowl, combine brown sugar, molasses, butter, orange zest, salt, aniseed and boiling water; stir until brown sugar is dissolved and butter is melted. Stir in cold water; let stand until mixture cools to 105° to 115°.
2. Meanwhile, in a large bowl, dissolve yeast in warm water. Stir in molasses mixture; mix well. Add the all-purpose flour and 1 cup of the rye flour. Beat on medium speed 3 minutes. Stir in enough remaining rye flour to form a stiff dough.
3. Turn dough onto a floured surface; knead 6-8 minutes or until smooth and elastic. Place in a greased bowl, turning once to grease the top. Cover and let rise in a warm place until doubled, about 1 hour.
4. Punch dough down. Turn onto a lightly floured surface; divide in half. Shape dough into 2 oval loaves. Grease 2 baking sheets and sprinkle lightly with cornmeal. Place loaves on prepared pans. Cover and let rise until doubled, about 30 minutes.
5. Preheat oven to 350°. With a sharp knife, make 4 shallow slashes across top of each loaf. Bake 30-35 minutes or until golden brown. Remove to wire racks; brush with butter.
1 piece: 186 cal., 3g fat (2g sat. fat), 8mg chol., 172mg sod., 35g carb. (7g sugars, 3g fiber), 4g pro.

SOUR CREAM CHIVE BREAD

This savory loaf mildly flavored with chives is delicious when served warm with a meal, soup, salad or stew. It also tastes fantastic toasted the next day for breakfast.
—Deborah Plank, West Salem, OH

PREP: 10 MIN. • **BAKE:** 3 HOURS
MAKES: 1 LOAF (1½ LBS., 16 PIECES)

- ⅔ cup 2% milk (70° to 80°)
- ¼ cup water (70° to 80°)
- ¼ cup sour cream
- 2 Tbsp. butter
- 1½ tsp. sugar
- 1½ tsp. salt
- 3 cups bread flour
- ⅛ tsp. baking soda
- ¼ cup minced chives
- 2¼ tsp. active dry yeast

In a bread machine pan, place all the ingredients in the order suggested by manufacturer. Select basic bread setting. Choose crust color and loaf size if available. Bake according to the bread machine directions (check dough after 5 minutes of mixing; add 1 to 2 Tbsp. water or flour if needed).
1 piece: 105 cal., 2g fat (2g sat. fat), 8mg chol., 253mg sod., 18g carb. (1g sugars, 1g fiber), 4g pro.

DUTCH-OVEN RAISIN WALNUT BREAD

On a cold day there's nothing better than a warm, crusty bread filled with raisins and walnuts!

—Catherine Ward, Mequon, WI

PREP: 15 MIN. + RISING
BAKE: 50 MIN. + COOLING
MAKES: 1 LOAF (32 PIECES)

- 6 to 7 cups all-purpose flour
- ¼ cup sugar
- 2 tsp. active dry yeast
- 2 tsp. ground cinnamon
- 2 tsp. salt
- 1 cup raisins
- 1 cup chopped walnuts
- 3 cups cool water (70° to 75°)

1. In a large bowl, whisk 6 cups flour, the sugar, yeast, cinnamon and salt. Stir in raisins and walnuts; add water and enough of the remaining flour to form a moist, shaggy dough. Do not knead. Cover and let rise in a cool place until doubled, 7-8 hours.

2. Preheat oven to 450°; place a Dutch oven with lid onto center rack and heat for at least 30 minutes. Once Dutch oven is heated, turn dough onto a generously floured surface. Using a metal scraper or spatula, quickly shape dough into a round loaf. Gently place on top of a piece of parchment.

3. Using a sharp knife, make a slash (¼ in. deep) across top of loaf. Using the parchment, immediately lower bread into the heated Dutch oven. Cover; bake for 30 minutes. Uncover and bake until loaf is deep golden brown and sounds hollow when tapped, 20-30 minutes longer, partially covering if browning too much. Remove loaf from pan and cool completely on wire rack.

1 piece: 130 cal., 3g fat (0 sat. fat), 0 chol., 149mg sod., 24g carb. (4g sugars, 1g fiber), 3g pro.

DUTCH-OVEN RAISIN WALNUT BREAD

HAZELNUT WHEAT BREAD

I developed this recipe in an effort to match the flavors of our favorite store-bought bread, adapting it to a recipe in my bread machine manual. It's a hearty, great-tasting loaf!
—Ruth Fanger, Monroe, OR

PREP: 20 MIN. • **BAKE:** 3 HOURS
MAKES: 1 LOAF (1½ LBS., 12 PIECES)

- 1   cup water (70° to 80°)
- 1   Tbsp. honey
- 1   Tbsp. butter, softened
- 3   Tbsp. toasted wheat germ
- 2   Tbsp. mashed potato flakes
- 1   Tbsp. nonfat dry milk powder
- 1   Tbsp. ground flaxseed
- 1   Tbsp. sesame seeds
- 1   Tbsp. poppy seeds
- 1   tsp. salt
- 1¼ cups whole wheat flour
- 1   cup bread flour
- ¼   cup chopped hazelnuts
- 1½ tsp. active dry yeast

In a bread machine pan, place all the ingredients in the order suggested by manufacturer. Choose crust color and loaf size if available. Bake according to bread machine directions (check the dough after 5 minutes of mixing; add 1 to 2 Tbsp. water or flour if needed).
1 piece: 127 cal., 4g fat (1g sat. fat), 3mg chol., 213mg sod., 21g carb. (2g sugars, 3g fiber), 5g pro. **Diabetic exchanges:** 1 starch, ½ fat.

MOM'S ITALIAN BREAD

I think Mom used to bake at least four of these tender loaves at once, and they never lasted long. She served this bread with every Italian meal. I love it toasted, too.
—Linda Harrington, Windham, NH

BAKING 101

PREP: 30 MIN. + RISING • **BAKE:** 20 MIN.
MAKES: 2 LOAVES (12 PIECES EACH)

- 1   pkg. (¼ oz.) active dry yeast
- 2   cups warm water (105° to 115°)
- 1   tsp. sugar
- 2   tsp. salt
- 5½ cups all-purpose flour

1. In a large bowl, dissolve yeast in warm water. Add the sugar, salt and 3 cups flour. Beat on medium speed for 3 minutes. Stir in remaining 2½ cups flour to form a soft dough.
2. Turn dough onto a floured surface; knead 6-8 minutes or until smooth and elastic. Place in a greased bowl, turning once to grease the top. Cover and let rise in a warm place until doubled, about 1 hour.
3. Punch dough down. Turn onto a floured surface; divide in half. Shape each portion into a loaf. Place each loaf seam side down on a greased baking sheet. Cover and let rise until doubled, about 30 minutes.
4. Meanwhile, preheat oven to 400°. With a sharp knife, make 4 shallow slashes across top of each loaf. Bake 20-25 minutes or until golden brown. Remove from pans to wire racks to cool.
1 piece: 106 cal., 0 fat (0 sat. fat), 0 chol., 197mg sod., 22g carb. (1g sugars, 1g fiber), 3g pro. **Diabetic exchanges:** 1½ starch.

BRAIDED MULTIGRAIN LOAF

Use oats, rye flour, rice and sunflower seeds for this hearty bread. It's so robust, you could almost make a meal out of it! It makes a beautiful addition to a holiday table.
—Jane Thomas, Burnsville, MN

PREP: 40 MIN. + RISING • **BAKE:** 30 MIN.
MAKES: 1 LOAF (24 PIECES)

- 2 cups whole wheat flour
- 1 cup quick-cooking oats
- ½ cup rye flour
- 2 pkg. (¼ oz. each) active dry yeast
- 2 tsp. salt
- 3 cups all-purpose flour
- 2 cups 2% milk
- ½ cup honey
- ⅓ cup water
- 2 Tbsp. butter
- 1 cup cooked long grain rice, cooled

TOPPING
- 1 large egg
- 1 Tbsp. water
- ⅓ cup sunflower kernels

1. In a large bowl, mix whole wheat flour, oats, rye flour, yeast, salt and 1 cup all-purpose flour. In a small saucepan, heat milk, honey, water and butter to 120°-130°. Add to dry ingredients; beat on medium speed for 2 minutes. Add 1 cup all-purpose flour; beat 2 minutes longer. Stir in the rice and enough of the remaining 1 cup all-purpose flour to form a stiff dough.

2. Turn dough onto a floured surface; knead 6-8 minutes or until smooth and elastic. Place in a greased bowl, turning once to grease the top. Cover and let rise in a warm place until doubled, about 1 hour.

3. Punch down dough. Turn onto a lightly floured surface; divide into thirds. Cover and let rest 5 minutes. Roll each portion into an 18-in. rope. Place the ropes on a greased baking sheet and braid. Shape the braid into a ring. Pinch ends to seal; tuck ends under.

4. Cover with a kitchen towel; let rise in a warm place until doubled, about 30 minutes. Preheat oven to 375°.

5. For topping, in a small bowl, whisk egg and water; brush over dough. Sprinkle with sunflower kernels. Bake 30-40 minutes or until golden brown. Remove to a wire rack to cool.

1 piece: 177 cal., 4g fat (1g sat. fat), 12mg chol., 231mg sod., 32g carb. (7g sugars, 2g fiber), 5g pro.

PEPPERONI CHEESE BREAD

As a stay-at-home mother of two little girls, I pack a lot of activity into my days. The bread machine makes it a snap for me to turn out this attractive loaf that gets its zip from cayenne pepper, pepperoni and Mexican cheese.
—Dusti Christensen, Goodridge, MN

PREP: 10 MIN. • **BAKE:** 4 HOURS
MAKES: 1 LOAF (16 PIECES)

- 1 cup water (70° to 80°)
- 1 Tbsp. butter
- 2 Tbsp. sugar
- 2 tsp. ground mustard
- ½ tsp. salt
- ½ tsp. cayenne pepper
- ¼ tsp. garlic powder
- 3 cups bread flour
- 2¼ tsp. active dry yeast
- 1½ cups shredded Mexican cheese blend
- 1 cup chopped pepperoni

1. In bread machine pan, place the first 9 ingredients in the order suggested by manufacturer. Select basic bread setting. Choose crust color and loaf size if available. Bake according to bread machine directions (check dough after 5 minutes of mixing; add 1 to 2 Tbsp. water or flour if needed).

2. Just before the final kneading (your machine may audibly signal this), add the cheese and pepperoni.

1 piece: 177 cal., 8g fat (4g sat. fat), 19mg chol., 329mg sod., 19g carb. (2g sugars, 1g fiber), 7g pro.

BASIC
HOMEMADE
BREAD

BASIC HOMEMADE BREAD

If you'd like to learn how to make bread, here's a wonderful place to start. This easy bread recipe bakes up deliciously golden brown. There's nothing like the aroma wafting through my kitchen as it bakes.
—Sandra Anderson, New York, NY

PREP: 20 MIN. + RISING • **BAKE:** 30 MIN.
MAKES: 2 LOAVES (16 PIECES EACH)

1	pkg. (¼ oz.) active dry yeast
3	Tbsp. sugar plus ½ tsp. sugar
2¼	cups warm water (105° to 115°)
1	Tbsp. salt
6¼	to 6¾ cups bread flour
2	Tbsp. canola oil

1. In a large bowl, dissolve yeast and ½ tsp. sugar in warm water; let stand until bubbles form on surface. Whisk together the remaining 3 Tbsp. sugar, salt and 3 cups flour. Stir oil into yeast mixture; pour into the flour mixture and beat until smooth. Stir in enough of the remaining flour, ½ cup at a time, to form a soft dough.

2. Turn dough onto a floured surface; knead 8-10 minutes or until smooth and elastic. Place in a greased bowl, turning once to grease the top. Cover and let the dough rise in a warm place until doubled, 1½-2 hours.

3. Punch dough down. Turn onto a lightly floured surface; divide dough in half. Shape each into a loaf. Place in 2 greased 9x5-in. loaf pans. Cover and let rise until doubled, 1-1½ hours.

4. Bake at 375° until golden brown and bread sounds hollow when tapped or has reached an internal temperature of 200°, 30-35 minutes. Remove from pans to wire racks to cool.

1 piece: 102 cal., 1g fat (0 sat. fat), 0 chol., 222mg sod., 20g carb. (1g sugars, 1g fiber), 3g pro.

. . . .
TEST KITCHEN TIP

One of the major advantages of homemade bread is also one of its potential drawbacks—no preservatives. Fresh bread lasts 3-4 days when properly stored in a bread box. Otherwise, wrap it in foil, place it in a freezer bag and freeze it; bread lasts for up to 6 months in the freezer.

GARLIC FONTINA BREAD

With its golden brown color and soft texture, this bread is a must at our family meals. It's a modified version of a traditional white bread recipe my brother gave me. Try it as garlic bread toast, for grilled sandwiches or enjoy as is.

—Cindy Ryan, St. Johns, MI

PREP: 30 MIN. + RISING • **BAKE:** 30 MIN.
MAKES: 2 LOAVES (16 PIECES EACH)

- 2 pkg. (¼ oz. each) active dry yeast
- 2 cups warm water (105° to 115°)
- 3 Tbsp. sugar
- 2 Tbsp. shortening
- 1 Tbsp. garlic powder
- 2 tsp. salt
- 5 to 5½ cups all-purpose flour
- 1½ cups plus 2 Tbsp. shredded fontina cheese, divided
- 1½ tsp. canola oil

1. In a large bowl, dissolve yeast in warm water. Add the sugar, shortening, garlic powder, salt and 3 cups flour. Beat until smooth. Stir in enough of the remaining flour to form a firm dough. Stir in 1½ cups cheese.
2. Turn onto a floured surface; knead until smooth and elastic, 6-8 minutes. Place in a greased bowl, turning once to grease the top. Cover and let rise in a warm place until doubled, about 1 hour.
3. Punch the dough down. Shape into 2 loaves. Place in 2 greased 9x5-in. loaf pans. Cover and let rise in a warm place until doubled, about 30 minutes. Brush with oil and sprinkle with the remaining 2 Tbsp. cheese.
4. Bake at 375° for 30-35 minutes or until golden brown. Cool on a wire rack.
1 piece: 119 cal., 4g fat (2g sat. fat), 10mg chol., 215mg sod., 17g carb. (2g sugars, 1g fiber), 4g pro.

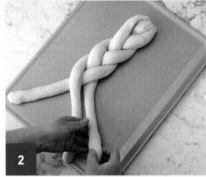

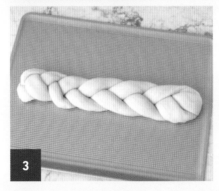

HOW TO BRAID BREAD DOUGH

STEP 1
On a lightly floured surface, divide dough into thirds. Roll each into a rope.

Add just enough flour so the dough doesn't stick. Too much flour, and the dough will just slide back and forth on the counter.

Use even pressure so the ropes are the same width from end to end. All three ropes should be the same length.

STEP 2
Arrange ropes on a greased baking sheet. Pinch the three ropes together at one end and tuck that end under.

To braid, cross the right rope over the center rope then the left rope over the center rope. Continue alternating left and right over center until the braid is done.

Braiding directly on the sheet means you won't have to move the finished braid and risk stretching it out of shape.

STEP 3
Pinch the ropes together at the other end and tuck it under for a clean look.

ROASTED RED PEPPER BREAD

These savory loaves are moist, tender and loaded with flavor from grated Parmesan cheese and roasted sweet red peppers. They're fantastic at dinner or as an appetizer.
—Cheryl Perry, Hertford, NC

PREP: 45 MIN. + RISING • **BAKE:** 20 MIN.
MAKES: 2 LOAVES (12 PIECES EACH)

- 1½ cups roasted sweet red peppers, drained
- 1 pkg. (¼ oz.) active dry yeast
- 2 Tbsp. warm water (105° to 115°)
- 1¼ cups grated Parmesan cheese, divided
- ⅓ cup warm 2% milk (105° to 115°)
- 2 Tbsp. butter, softened
- 1¼ tsp. salt
- 3¼ to 3¾ cups all-purpose flour
- 1 large egg
- 1 Tbsp. water
- 1½ tsp. coarsely ground pepper

1. Place the red peppers in a food processor; cover and process until pureed. In a large bowl, dissolve yeast in warm water. Add the red peppers, 1 cup cheese, milk, butter, salt and 1½ cups flour. Beat until smooth. Stir in enough of the remaining flour to form a firm dough.
2. Turn onto a floured surface; knead until smooth and elastic, 6-8 minutes. Place in a greased bowl, turning once to grease the top. Cover and let rise in a warm place until doubled, about 1 hour.
3. Punch dough down. Turn onto a lightly floured surface; divide the dough into 6 pieces. Shape each into an 18-in. rope. Place 3 ropes on a greased baking sheet and braid; pinch ends to seal and tuck under. Repeat with the remaining dough. Cover and let rise until doubled, about 1 hour.
4. Preheat oven to 350°. In a small bowl, combine egg and water; brush over the braids. Sprinkle with pepper and the remaining ¼ cup cheese. Bake for 18-22 minutes or until golden brown.
1 piece: 99 cal., 3g fat (1g sat. fat), 15mg chol., 254mg sod., 14g carb. (1g sugars, 1g fiber), 4g pro. **Diabetic exchanges:** 1 starch.

COUNTRY WHITE BREAD

Everyone loves a good slice of homemade bread, especially when it's spread with butter or jam. These loaves are especially nice because the crust stays tender. My husband makes most of the bread at our house, and this recipe is his favorite.
—Joanne Shew Chuk, St. Benedict, , SK

PREP: 20 MIN. + RISING • **BAKE:** 25 MIN.
MAKES: 2 LOAVES (16 PIECES EACH)

- 2 pkg. (¼ oz. each) active dry yeast
- 2 cups warm water (105° to 115°)
- ½ cup sugar
- 2 tsp. salt
- 2 large eggs, room temperature
- ¼ cup canola oil
- 6½ to 7 cups all-purpose flour

1. In a large bowl, dissolve yeast in warm water. Add sugar, salt, eggs, oil and 3 cups flour; beat on medium speed until smooth. Stir in enough of the remaining flour to form a soft dough.
2. Turn onto a floured surface; knead until smooth and elastic, 6-8 minutes. Place in a greased bowl, turning once to grease the top. Cover and let rise in a warm place until doubled, about 1 hour.
3. Punch down dough. Divide in half and shape each half into a loaf. Place in 2 greased 9x5-in. loaf pans. Cover with kitchen towels; let rise in a warm place until doubled, about 1 hour.
4. Bake at 375° until golden brown, 25-30 minutes. Remove from pans to wire racks to cool.
1 piece: 125 cal., 2g fat (0 sat. fat), 13mg chol., 226mg sod., 23g carb. (3g sugars, 1g fiber), 3g pro.
Herbed Country White Bread: Along with the 3 cups of flour, stir in 2 Tbsp. dried parsley flakes, 1 Tbsp. dried basil, 1 tsp. each dried oregano and thyme and ½ tsp. garlic powder.

RUSTIC RYE BREAD

This gorgeous rye bread has just a touch of sweetness and the perfect amount of caraway seeds. With a crusty top and firm texture, it holds up well for sandwiches.
—Holly Wade, Harrisonburg, VA

PREP: 25 MIN. + RISING
BAKE: 30 MIN.
MAKES: 2 LOAVES (12 PIECES EACH)

- 1 pkg. (¼ oz.) active dry yeast
- 1¾ cups warm water (105° to 115°), divided
- ¼ cup packed brown sugar
- ¼ cup light molasses
- 3 Tbsp. caraway seeds
- 2 Tbsp. canola oil
- 1 Tbsp. salt
- 1¾ cups rye flour
- ¾ cup whole wheat flour
- 2½ to 3 cups all-purpose flour
  Optional: Large egg white beaten lightly with water, additional caraway seeds

1. In a large bowl, dissolve yeast in ¼ cup warm water. Stir in brown sugar, molasses, caraway seeds, oil, salt and remaining 1½ cups water. Add rye flour, whole wheat flour and 1 cup of the all-purpose flour; beat on medium speed until smooth. Stir in enough remaining all-purpose flour to form a firm dough.

2. Turn onto a floured surface; knead until smooth and elastic, 6-8 minutes. Place in a greased bowl, turning once to grease the top. Cover and let rise in a warm place until doubled, about 1½ hours.

3. Punch down dough. Turn onto a lightly floured surface; divide in half. Shape each into a round loaf; place on a baking sheet coated with cooking spray. Cover with kitchen towels; let rise in a warm place until almost doubled, about 1½ hours. Preheat oven to 350°.

4. If desired, brush loaves with an egg white beaten lightly with water; sprinkle with caraway seeds. Bake until golden brown, 30-35 minutes. Remove from pan to wire racks to cool.

1 piece: 118 cal., 2g fat (0 sat. fat), 0 chol., 298mg sod., 24g carb. (5g sugars, 2g fiber), 3g pro.

CRUSTY FRENCH LOAF

I love the delicate texture of this wonderful bread. I sometimes use the dough to make breadsticks, which I brush with melted butter and sprinkle with garlic powder.
—Deanna Naivar, Temple, TX

PREP: 20 MIN. + RISING
BAKE: 25 MIN.
MAKES: 1 LOAF (16 PIECES)

- 1 pkg. (¼ oz.) active dry yeast
- 1 cup warm water (105° to 115°)
- 2 Tbsp. sugar
- 2 Tbsp. canola oil
- 1½ tsp. salt
- 3 to 3¼ cups all-purpose flour
  Cornmeal
- 1 large egg white
- 1 tsp. cold water

1. In a large bowl, dissolve yeast in warm water. Add sugar, oil, salt and 2 cups flour. Beat until blended. Stir in enough remaining flour to form a stiff dough.

2. Turn onto a floured surface; knead until smooth and elastic, 6-8 minutes. Place in a greased bowl, turning once to grease top. Cover and let rise in a warm place until doubled, about 1 hour. Punch dough down; return to bowl. Cover and let rise for 30 minutes.

3. Punch dough down. Turn onto a lightly floured surface. Shape into a 16x2½-in. loaf with tapered ends. Sprinkle cornmeal over a greased baking sheet; place loaf on baking sheet. Cover and let rise until doubled, about 25 minutes. Preheat oven to 375°.

4. Beat egg white and cold water; brush over dough. With a sharp knife, make diagonal slashes 2 in. apart across the top of the loaf. Bake until golden brown, 25-30 minutes. Remove from pan to a wire rack to cool.

1 piece: 109 cal., 2g fat (0 sat. fat), 0 chol., 225mg sod., 20g carb. (2g sugars, 1g fiber), 3g pro.

. . . .
TEST KITCHEN TIP

When making French bread, it's customary to sprinkle cornmeal on the pan to prevent the dough from sticking, as well as to add texture. If your dough isn't sticky, the cornmeal is optional; the greased pan should be enough. If your dough is sticky, however, the extra measures are helpful. If you don't have cornmeal, use parchment instead.

CRUSTY
FRENCH LOAF

QUICK & EASY
BREAD BOWLS

QUICK & EASY BREAD BOWLS

Impress your family and friends by serving cream soups or dips in bread bowls. It's one of the most popular recipes on my blog, yammiesnoshery.com.
—Rachel Preus, Marshall, MI

PREP: 35 MIN. + RISING
BAKE: 20 MIN+ COOLING
MAKES: 6 SERVINGS

- 2 **Tbsp. active dry yeast**
- 3 **cups warm water (105° to 115°)**
- 2 **Tbsp. sugar**
- 2 **tsp. salt**
- 6½ **to 7½ cups bread flour**
   Optional: Cornmeal and sesame seeds

1. In a small bowl, dissolve yeast in warm water. In a large bowl, combine sugar, salt, yeast mixture and 3 cups flour; beat on medium speed 3 minutes. Stir in enough of the remaining flour to form a soft dough (dough will be sticky).
2. Turn onto a floured surface; knead until smooth and elastic, 6-8 minutes. Place in a greased bowl, turning once to grease the top. Cover with a kitchen towel and let rise in a warm place until doubled, about 30 minutes.
3. Preheat oven to 500°. Punch dough down. Divide and shape into 6 balls. Place 3 in. apart on 2 baking sheets that have been generously sprinkled with cornmeal or greased. Cover with a kitchen towel; let rise in a warm place until doubled, about 15 minutes. Spray loaves with water; if desired, generously sprinkle with sesame seeds. Using a sharp knife, score surface with shallow cuts in an "X" pattern. Bake 2 minutes. Reduce oven setting to 425°. Bake until golden brown and internal temperature reaches 190°-200°. Remove from pans to wire racks to cool completely.
4. Cut a thin slice off the top of bread. Hollow out the bottom portion of the loaf, leaving a ½-in. shell. Discard the removed bread or save for another use, such as croutons.

1 bread bowl: 283 cal., 1g fat (0 sat. fat), 0 chol., 396mg sod., 57g carb. (2g sugars, 2g fiber), 10g pro.

SAVORY STUFFING BREAD

Poultry seasoning and celery salt make this hearty loaf taste like just like stuffing. It's the perfect bread to serve with turkey during the holidays, and it's nice for making sandwiches with the leftovers.
—Elizabeth King, Duluth, MN

PREP: 30 MIN. + RISING
BAKE: 20 MIN. + COOLING
MAKES: 2 LOAVES (16 PIECES EACH)

 2 Tbsp. sugar
 2 pkg. (¼ oz. each) active dry yeast
1½ tsp. poultry seasoning
 ½ tsp. salt
 ½ tsp. celery salt
 ½ tsp. pepper
5½ to 6 cups all-purpose flour
 ¼ cup butter, cubed
 1 small onion, finely chopped
 1 can (14½ oz.) chicken broth
 2 large eggs, room temperature

1. In a large bowl, mix sugar, yeast, seasonings and 2 cups flour. In a small saucepan, heat butter over medium-high heat. Add onion; cook and stir 2-3 minutes or until tender. Stir in broth; heat to 120°-130°. Add to dry ingredients; beat on medium speed 2 minutes. Add eggs; beat on high for 2 minutes longer. Stir in enough of the remaining flour to form a soft dough (dough will be sticky).
2. Turn the dough onto a well-floured surface; knead until smooth and elastic, 6-8 minutes. Place in a greased bowl, turning once to grease the top. Cover dough and let rise in a warm place until doubled, about 1 hour.
3. Punch down dough. Turn onto a lightly floured surface; divide in half. Shape into 2 loaves. Place in 2 greased 9x5-in. loaf pans, seam side down. Cover with kitchen towels; let rise in a warm place until doubled, about 30 minutes.
4. Preheat oven to 375°. Bake until golden brown, 18-22 minutes. Remove loaves from pans to wire racks to cool completely.

1 piece: 102 cal., 2g fat (1g sat. fat), 16mg chol., 127mg sod., 18g carb. (1g sugars, 1g fiber), 3g pro.

OLD-WORLD RYE BREAD

Rye and caraway lend to this bread's flavor, while the surprise ingredient of baking cocoa gives it a rich, dark color. I sometimes stir in a cup each of raisins and chopped walnuts to make this hearty bread even more substantial.
—Perlene Hoekema, Lynden, WA

PREP: 25 MIN. + RISING
BAKE: 35 MIN.
MAKES: 2 LOAVES (12 PIECES EACH)

 2 pkg. (¼ oz. each) active dry yeast
1½ cups warm water (105° to 115°)
 ½ cup molasses
 6 Tbsp. butter, softened
 2 cups rye flour
 ¼ cup baking cocoa
 2 Tbsp. caraway seeds
 2 tsp. salt
3½ to 4 cups all-purpose flour
    Cornmeal

1. In a large bowl, dissolve yeast in warm water. Beat in molasses, butter, rye flour, cocoa, caraway seeds, salt and 2 cups all-purpose flour until smooth. Stir in enough remaining all-purpose flour to form a stiff dough.
2. Turn onto a floured surface; knead until smooth and elastic, 6-8 minutes. Place in a greased bowl, turning once to grease top. Cover and let rise in a warm place until doubled, about 1½ hours.
3. Punch dough down. Turn onto a lightly floured surface; divide in half. Shape each piece into a loaf about 10 in. long. Grease 2 baking sheets and sprinkle with cornmeal. Place loaves on the prepared pans. Cover and let rise until doubled, about 1 hour.
4. Bake at 350° for 35-40 minutes or until bread sounds hollow when tapped. Remove from pans to wire racks to cool.

1 piece: 146 cal., 3g fat (2g sat. fat), 8mg chol., 229mg sod., 26g carb. (5g sugars, 2g fiber), 3g pro.

GOLDEN
SANTA BREAD

EGG BREADS

GOLDEN SANTA BREAD

A friend shared this fun idea. She originally made it with premade frozen dough, but I used one of my own recipes. It makes an amazing impression at the holidays!
—Vicki Melies, Elkhorn, NE

PREP: 30 MIN. + RISING
BAKE: 25 MIN.
MAKES: 1 LOAF (18 SERVINGS)

- 4 to 4½ cups bread flour
- ½ cup sugar
- 2 pkg. (¼ oz. each) active dry yeast
- 1½ tsp. salt
- ½ cup 2% milk
- ¼ cup water
- ¼ cup butter, cubed
- 2 large eggs, room temperature
- 2 raisins
- 2 large egg yolks
- 2 to 3 drops red food coloring

1. In a large bowl, combine 2 cups flour, sugar, yeast and salt. In a small saucepan, heat milk, water and butter to 120°-130°. Add to dry ingredients; beat just until moistened. Beat in eggs until smooth. Stir in enough remaining flour to form a stiff dough.
2. Turn onto a floured surface; knead until smooth and elastic, 6-8 minutes. Place in a greased bowl, turning once to grease top. Cover and let rise in a warm place until doubled, about 1 hour.
3. Preheat oven to 350°. Punch dough down. Turn dough onto a lightly floured surface; divide into 2 portions, 1 slightly larger than the other.
4. Shape the larger portion into an elongated triangle with rounded corners for Santa's head and hat.

5. Divide the smaller portion in half. Shape and flatten 1 half into a beard. Lay the beard over the face; use a sharp knife to cut deep slits to resemble hair.
6. Use the remaining dough to make the rest of the details. Shape a portion of the dough into a mustache; flatten it and place it on the face over the beard. Cut slits to resemble hair. Place a small ball of dough above mustache for the nose. With scissors, cut 2 slits for the eyes; insert raisins into the slits. Form another small portion of dough into eyebrows; flatten and place above the eyes. Roll out a narrow strip of dough to create the hat brim. Fold the tip of the hat over and add a dough ball for the pompom. If desired, using scissors or sharp knife, cut small lines along edges of brim and pompom to resemble fur.
7. Beat each egg yolk in a separate small bowl. Add red food coloring to 1 yolk; carefully brush over hat. Brush plain yolk over the remaining dough.
8. Cover loosely with foil. Bake for 15 minutes. Uncover; bake until golden brown, 10-12 minutes longer. Cool on a wire rack.
1 piece: 175 cal., 4g fat (2g sat. fat), 49mg chol., 230mg sod., 29g carb. (6g sugars, 1g fiber), 5g pro.

HOMEMADE EGG BREAD

People rave about this tender, delicate bread every time I serve it!
—June Mullins, Livonia, MO

PREP: 30 MIN. + RISING • **BAKE:** 30 MIN.
MAKES: 2 LOAVES (16 PIECES EACH)

- 2 pkg. (¼ oz. each) active dry yeast
- ½ cup warm water (105° to 115°)
- 1½ cups warm 2% milk (105° to 115°)
- 3 large eggs, room temperature
- ¼ cup butter, softened
- ¼ cup sugar
- 1 Tbsp. salt
- 7 to 7½ cups all-purpose flour

- 1 large egg yolk, room temperature
- 2 Tbsp. water
  Sesame seeds

1. In a large bowl, dissolve yeast in warm water. Add milk, eggs, butter, sugar, salt and 3 cups flour; beat on medium speed until smooth. Stir in enough remaining flour to form a soft dough.
2. Turn onto a floured surface; knead until smooth and elastic, 6-8 minutes. Place in a greased bowl, turning once to grease the top. Cover dough and let rise in a warm place until doubled, 1½-2 hours.
3. Punch down dough. Turn onto a lightly floured surface; divide into 6 portions. Roll each portion into a 14-in. rope. For each loaf, braid 3 ropes together on a greased baking sheet; pinch ends to seal and tuck under. Cover with kitchen towels; let rise in a warm place until doubled, about 50 minutes. Preheat oven to 375°.
4. Beat together egg yolk and water; brush over the loaves. Sprinkle with sesame seeds. Bake until golden brown, 30-35 minutes. Remove from pans to wire racks to cool.
1 piece: 135 cal., 3g fat (1g sat. fat), 28mg chol., 245mg sod., 23g carb. (2g sugars, 1g fiber), 4g pro.

CHALLAH

Eggs lend to the richness of this traditional challah bread recipe. The attractive golden color and delicious flavor make it hard to resist.
—*Taste of Home* Test Kitchen

PREP: 30 MIN. + RISING • **BAKE:** 30 MIN.
MAKES: 2 LOAVES (16 PIECES EACH)

- 2 pkg. (¼ oz. each) active dry yeast
- 1 cup warm water (105° to 115°)
- ½ cup canola oil
- ⅓ cup sugar
- 1 Tbsp. salt
- 4 large eggs, room temperature
- 6 to 6½ cups all-purpose flour
TOPPING
- 1 large egg
- 1 tsp. cold water
- 1 Tbsp. sesame or poppy seeds, optional

1. In a large bowl, dissolve yeast in warm water. Add the oil, sugar, salt, eggs and 4 cups of flour. Beat until smooth. Stir in enough of the remaining flour to form a firm dough. Turn onto a floured surface; knead until smooth and elastic, 6-8 minutes. Place in a greased bowl, turning once to grease top. Cover dough and let rise in a warm place until doubled, about 1 hour.

2. Punch dough down. Turn onto a lightly floured surface; divide in half. Divide each portion into thirds. Shape each piece into a 15-in. rope.

3. Place 3 ropes on a greased baking sheet and braid; pinch ends to seal and tuck under. Repeat with the remaining dough. Cover and let rise until doubled, about 1 hour.

4. Preheat oven to 350°. Beat egg and cold water; brush over braids. Sprinkle with sesame or poppy seeds if desired. Bake until crusts are golden brown, 30-40 minutes. Remove to wire racks to cool.

1 piece: 139 cal., 5g fat (1g sat. fat), 29mg chol., 233mg sod., 20g carb. (2g sugars, 1g fiber), 4g pro.

PASKA EASTER BREAD

Paska is a traditional Easter bread prepared with lots of eggs, making it much richer than ordinary sweet breads.
—Millie Cherniwchan, Smoky Lake, AB

PREP: 40 MIN. + RISING • **BAKE:** 50 MIN.
MAKES: 2 LOAVES (12 PIECES EACH)

- 2 pkg. (¼ oz. each) active dry yeast
- 1 tsp. plus ⅓ cup sugar, divided
- 4 cups warm water (105° to 115°), divided
- 1 cup nonfat dry milk powder
- 13½ to 14½ cups all-purpose flour, divided
- 6 large eggs, room temperature, beaten
- ½ cup butter, melted
- 1 Tbsp. salt
EGG GLAZE
- 1 large egg
- 2 Tbsp. water

1. In a large bowl, dissolve yeast and 1 tsp. sugar in 1 cup warm water. Let stand for 5 minutes. Add remaining 3 cups water. Beat in the milk powder and 5 cups flour until smooth. Cover and let rise in a warm place until bubbly, about 20 minutes.

2. Add eggs, butter, salt and remaining ⅓ cup sugar; mix well. Stir in enough remaining flour to form a soft dough. Turn onto a floured surface; knead until smooth and elastic, about 8-10 minutes. Place in a greased bowl, turning once to grease top. Cover and let rise in a warm place until doubled, about 1 hour.

3. Punch dough down. Turn onto a lightly floured surface; divide in half and set 1 portion aside. Divide the remaining portion in half; press each portion into a well-greased 10-in. springform pan. Divide the reserved dough into 6 balls. Shape each ball into a 30-in. rope; make 2 braids of 3 ropes each. Place a braid around the edge of each pan, forming a circle. Trim ends of braids, reserving dough scraps. Pinch ends of braids to seal. Shape scraps into 2 long thin ropes; form into rosettes or crosses. Place 1 decoration on the center of each loaf. Cover and let rise until doubled, about 1 hour.

4. In a small bowl, beat egg and water; brush over dough. Bake at 350° for 50-60 minutes or until golden brown. Remove from pans to wire racks to cool.

1 piece: 342 cal., 6g fat (3g sat. fat), 73mg chol., 380mg sod., 60g carb. (7g sugars, 2g fiber), 11g pro.

CHOCOLATE BABKA

CHOCOLATE BABKA

I love this chocolate babka. It's a rewarding recipe for taking the next step in your bread baking. Even if it's slightly imperfect going into the oven, it turns out gorgeous. Look at those swirls!
—Lisa Kaminski, Wauwatosa, WI

PREP: 20 MIN. + CHILLING
BAKE: 35 MIN. + COOLING
MAKES: 2 LOAVES (16 PIECES EACH)

4¼ to 4¾ cups all-purpose flour
½ cup sugar
2½ tsp. quick-rise yeast
¾ tsp. salt
⅔ cup butter
½ cup water
3 large eggs plus 1 large egg yolk, room temperature, beaten
2 Tbsp. grated orange zest
FILLING
½ cup butter, cubed
5 oz. dark chocolate chips
½ cup confectioners' sugar
⅓ cup baking cocoa
¼ tsp. salt
GLAZE
¼ cup sugar
¼ cup water

1. In a large bowl, mix 2 cups flour, sugar, yeast and salt. Cut in butter until crumbly. In a small saucepan, heat water to 120°-130°; stir into dry ingredients. Stir in eggs and yolk, orange zest and enough remaining flour to form a soft dough (dough will be sticky).
2. Turn onto a floured surface; knead until smooth and elastic, 6-8 minutes. Place in a greased bowl, turning once to grease the top. Cover and refrigerate 8 hours or overnight.
3. Turn out dough onto a lightly floured surface; divide in half. Roll each half into a 12x10-in. rectangle. For filling, in a microwave, melt butter and chocolate chips; stir until smooth. Stir in the confectioners' sugar, cocoa and salt. Spread filling to within ½ in. of edges. Roll up each rectangle jelly-roll style, starting with a long side; pinch seam and ends to seal.
4. Using a sharp knife, cut each roll lengthwise in half; carefully turn each half cut side up. Loosely twist strips around each other, keeping cut surfaces facing up; pinch ends together to seal. Place in 2 greased 9x5-in. loaf pans, cut side up. Cover with kitchen towels; let rise in a warm place until almost doubled, about 1 hour.
5. Bake at 375° until golden brown, 35-45 minutes, tenting with foil halfway through baking.
6. Meanwhile, in a saucepan, combine sugar and water; bring to a boil. Reduce heat; simmer, uncovered, 10 minutes. Brush syrup over warm babka. Cool for 10 minutes before removing from pans to wire racks.

1 piece: 181 cal., 9g fat (5g sat. fat), 41mg chol., 136mg sod., 23g carb. (10g sugars, 1g fiber), 3g pro.

FOCACCIA

HERB FOCACCIA ROLLS

Yeast rolls speckled with fresh thyme and rosemary are a breeze to make without kneading and long wait times. Splurge on the best-quality butter for these adorable rolls.
—Linda Schend, Kenosha, WI

PREP: 15 MIN. + RISING • **BAKE:** 20 MIN.
MAKES: 1½ DOZEN

- 3 cups all-purpose flour
- 1 pkg. (¼ oz.) quick-rise yeast
- 2 Tbsp. minced fresh thyme, divided
- 2 Tbsp. minced fresh rosemary, divided
- 1 Tbsp. sugar
- 1½ tsp. kosher salt, divided
- 1½ cups warm water (105° to 115°)
- 6 Tbsp. extra-virgin olive oil, divided

1. Combine flour, yeast, 1 Tbsp. thyme, 1 Tbsp. rosemary, the sugar and 1 tsp. salt. Add water and 2 Tbsp. oil; beat 1 minute (dough will be very sticky).
2. Divide dough among 18 greased muffin cups. Let rise in a warm place until doubled, about 30 minutes.
3. Preheat oven to 375°. In a small saucepan over medium-low heat, stir together remaining 1 Tbsp. thyme, 1 Tbsp. rosemary, ½ tsp. salt and 4 Tbsp. olive oil just until the herbs are fragrant and the oil is hot, about 1½ minutes. Remove from heat; cool.
4. Gently spoon cooled herb mixture over each roll. Bake until golden brown, 20-25 minutes.
1 roll: 120 cal., 5g fat (1g sat. fat), 0 chol., 161mg sod., 17g carb. (1g sugars, 1g fiber), 2g pro.

BAKING 101

HERB FOCACCIA ROLLS

CHIPOTLE FOCACCIA WITH GARLIC-ONION TOPPING

Chipotle peppers make some people grab their water glasses; others can't get enough of the smoky heat. I came up with this recipe to fit right in the middle. Add more chipotle if you crave spiciness.

—Frances Kay Bouma, Trail, BC

PREP: 1¼ HOURS + RISING • **BAKE:** 20 MIN.
MAKES: 1 LOAF (16 PIECES)

- 1 cup water (70° to 80°)
- 2 Tbsp. olive oil
- 2½ cups all-purpose flour
- 1 tsp. salt
- 1 Tbsp. chopped chipotle pepper in adobo sauce
- 1½ tsp. active dry yeast

TOPPING
- 6 garlic cloves, peeled
- ¼ tsp. plus 7 Tbsp. olive oil, divided
- 2 large onions, cut into ¼-in. slices
- 2 Tbsp. chopped chipotle peppers in adobo sauce
- ¼ tsp. salt
  Chopped chives, optional

1. In bread machine pan, place the first 6 ingredients in the order suggested by the manufacturer. Select dough setting (check dough after 5 minutes of mixing; add 1-2 Tbsp. water or flour if needed).
2. When cycle is completed, turn the dough onto a lightly floured surface. Punch down dough; cover and let rest for 15 minutes.
3. Place garlic in a small microwave-safe bowl. Drizzle with ¼ tsp. oil. Microwave on high for 20-60 seconds or until softened. Mash the garlic.
4. Roll dough into a 12x10-in. rectangle. Transfer to a well-greased baking sheet. Cover and let rise in a warm place until slightly risen, about 20 minutes. Preheat oven to 400°.
5. With your fingertips, make several dimples over top of dough. Brush dough with 1 Tbsp. oil. Bake for 10 minutes or until lightly browned.
6. Meanwhile, in a large skillet, saute onions in the remaining 6 Tbsp. oil until tender. Add the chipotle peppers, salt and mashed garlic; saute 2-3 minutes longer. Sprinkle over dough.
7. Bake 10-15 minutes longer or until golden brown. If desired, top with chopped chives. Cut into serving portions; serve warm.

Freeze option: Freeze cooled focaccia squares in freezer containers; separate layers with waxed paper. Reheat on an ungreased baking sheet in a preheated 400° oven until heated through.

1 piece: 159 cal., 8g fat (1g sat. fat), 0 chol., 206mg sod., 19g carb. (2g sugars, 1g fiber), 3g pro.

. . . .

TEST KITCHEN TIP

To make the dough by hand, in a large bowl, dissolve yeast in warm water (105° to 115°). Stir in oil, chipotle pepper, salt and 2 cups flour; beat until smooth. Stir in enough remaining flour to form a soft dough. Turn dough onto a floured surface; knead until smooth and elastic, 6-8 minutes. Place in a greased bowl, turning once to grease the top. Cover and let rise in a warm place until doubled, about 1 hour. Punch dough down. Proceed with recipe as written.

**CHERRY TOMATO
& BASIL FOCACCIA**

CHERRY TOMATO
& BASIL FOCACCIA

When I had 80 pounds of tomatoes, I got creative incorporating them into meals. Sometimes I slice this loaf into squares to make sandwiches with fresh mozzarella cheese and deli meats.
—Katie Ferrier, Houston, TX

PREP: 45 MIN. + RISING • **BAKE:** 15 MIN.
MAKES: 2 LOAVES (20 PIECES EACH)

1   **pkg. (¼ oz.) active dry yeast**
2   **cups warm 2% milk (105° to 115°)**
¼   **cup canola oil**
4½ **tsp. sugar**
1   **tsp. salt**
5   **to 5½ cups all-purpose flour**
2   **cups cherry tomatoes**
⅓   **cup olive oil**
2   **Tbsp. cornmeal**
3   **Tbsp. thinly sliced fresh basil**
1   **tsp. coarse salt**
⅛   **tsp. pepper**

1. In a small bowl, dissolve the yeast in warm milk. In a large bowl, combine the canola oil, sugar, salt, yeast mixture and 2 cups flour; beat on medium speed until smooth. Stir in enough remaining flour to form a stiff dough (dough will be sticky).

2. Turn onto a floured surface; knead until smooth and elastic, 6-8 minutes. Place in a greased bowl, turning once to grease the top. Cover and let rise in a warm place until doubled, about 45 minutes.

3. Meanwhile, fill a large saucepan two-thirds with water; bring to a boil. Cut a shallow "X" on the bottom of each tomato. Using a slotted spoon, place tomatoes, a cup at a time, in boiling water for 30 seconds or just until the skin at the "X" begins to loosen.

4. Remove tomatoes and immediately drop them into ice water. Pull off and discard skins. Place the tomatoes in a small bowl; drizzle with oil.

5. Sprinkle 2 greased baking sheets with cornmeal; set aside. Punch down dough. Turn onto a lightly floured surface. Cover; let rest 10 minutes. Divide dough in half. Shape each into a 12x8-in. rectangle and place on prepared baking sheets.

6. Using your fingertips, press several dimples into dough. Pour the tomato mixture over the dough; sprinkle with basil, coarse salt and pepper. Let rise in a warm place until doubled, about 30 minutes.

7. Bake at 425° until golden brown, 15-18 minutes.

1 piece: 97 cal., 4g fat (1g sat. fat), 1mg chol., 125mg sod., 14g carb. (1g sugars, 1g fiber), 2g pro.

. . . .
DID YOU KNOW?
The name focaccia comes from Latin *panis focacius,* which translates to "hearth bread." This ancient bread was once baked in coals; the modern equivalent is a very hot oven. The customary indentations in the bread's surface are made to prevent bubbles from forming.

OLIVE FOCACCIA

After adding my own special touches to a basic focaccia recipe—including sun-dried tomatoes, olives and roasted sweet red peppers—the results were delectable. The flavorful, chewy loaf makes a wonderful accompaniment to nearly any meal.
—Dee Froemel, Hayward, WI

PREP: 30 MIN. + RISING • **BAKE:** 15 MIN.
MAKES: 1 LOAF (8 WEDGES)

- 1⅛ tsp. active dry yeast
- ½ cup warm water (105° to 115°)
- 1 Tbsp. sugar
- 1 Tbsp. Italian seasoning
- ¼ tsp. salt
- ¼ tsp. pepper
- 1⅓ to 1⅔ cups all-purpose flour
- 2 Tbsp. oil-packed sun-dried tomatoes, chopped
- 2 Tbsp. roasted sweet red peppers, drained and chopped
- 2 Tbsp. sliced ripe olives, drained
- 5 Greek olives, sliced
- 5 sliced green olives with pimientos, drained
- 2 Tbsp. minced fresh parsley
- 1 Tbsp. olive oil
- 1 tsp. kosher salt
- 1 tsp. shredded Parmesan cheese
- 1 tsp. shredded Romano cheese

1. In a large bowl, dissolve yeast in warm water. Add the sugar, Italian seasoning, salt, pepper and 1 cup flour. Beat until smooth. Stir in enough of the remaining flour to form a firm dough. Stir in the tomatoes, peppers, olives and parsley.
2. Turn onto a floured surface; knead until smooth and elastic, 6-8 minutes. Place in a greased bowl, turning once to grease the top. Cover and let rise in a warm place until doubled, about 50 minutes.
3. Punch dough down. Shape into a 9-in. circle on a greased baking sheet. Cover and let rise in a warm place until doubled, about 25 minutes. With your fingertips, make several dimples over the top of the dough. Brush with oil. Sprinkle with kosher salt and cheeses.
4. Bake at 400° until golden brown, 14-18 minutes. Remove to a wire rack.
1 wedge: 118 cal., 3g fat (0 sat. fat), 0 chol., 418mg sod., 19g carb. (2g sugars, 1g fiber), 3g pro.

SAGE FONTINA FOCACCIA

These rustic loaves have plenty of sage flavor—a tasty addition to any feast.
—Beth Dauenhauer, Pueblo, CO

PREP: 30 MIN. + RISING • **BAKE:** 15 MIN.
MAKES: 1 LOAF (8 WEDGES)

- 1¼ tsp. active dry yeast
- ½ cup warm water (105° to 115°)
- ½ tsp. honey
- ¾ to 1 cup all-purpose flour
- ¼ cup whole wheat flour
- 1 Tbsp. olive oil
- 2 tsp. minced fresh sage
- ¼ tsp. salt
TOPPING
- 1½ tsp. olive oil, divided
- 8 fresh sage leaves
- ½ cup shredded fontina cheese

1. In a large bowl, dissolve the yeast in warm water. Stir in honey; let stand for 5 minutes. Add ¾ cup all-purpose flour, the whole wheat flour, oil, minced sage and salt. Beat on medium speed for 3 minutes or until smooth. Stir in enough of the remaining flour to form a soft dough (dough will be sticky).
2. Turn dough onto a lightly floured surface; knead until smooth and elastic, 6-8 minutes. Place in a greased bowl, turning once to grease the top. Cover and let rise in a warm place until doubled, about 1 hour.
3. Punch dough down. Cover and let rest for 5 minutes. Place 1 Tbsp. olive oil in a 10-in. cast-iron or other ovenproof skillet; tilt pan to evenly coat. Add the dough; shape to fit pan. Cover and let rise until doubled, about 30 minutes.
4. With fingertips, make several dimples over top of dough. For topping, brush dough with 1 tsp. oil. Top with sage leaves; brush leaves with remaining ½ tsp. oil. Sprinkle with cheese. Bake at 400° until golden brown, 10-15 minutes. Remove to a wire rack. Serve warm.
1 wedge: 112 cal., 5g fat (2g sat. fat), 8mg chol., 131mg sod., 12g carb. (1g sugars, 1g fiber), 4g pro.

ROLLS

BAKING 101

CHEDDAR-SQUASH CLOVERLEAF ROLLS

My rolls started out as a basic bread recipe. I just adapted it to our taste. They're great with a meal anytime, but especially in fall. Our son-in-law (we have two grown children) can't stand squash—he loves these, though!

—DeDe Waldmann, Monona, WI

PREP: 25 MIN. + RISING • **BAKE:** 20 MIN.
MAKES: 2 DOZEN

- 2 Tbsp. sugar
- ¼ cup warm water (105° to 115°)
- 1 pkg. (¼ oz.) active dry yeast
- 1 cup warm 2% milk (105° to 115°)
- 4 Tbsp. butter, melted, divided
- 1 tsp. salt
- 1 cup mashed cooked winter squash
- ¾ cup shredded cheddar cheese
- 4 to 4½ cups all-purpose flour
  Sesame seeds, optional

1. In a large bowl, dissolve sugar in water. Sprinkle the yeast over the water and stir gently. Let stand until light and foamy. Stir in milk, 3 Tbsp. butter, salt, squash and cheese. Add enough flour to form a soft dough.

2. Turn out onto a lightly floured surface; knead until the dough is no longer sticky, about 5 minutes. Form into a ball and place in a greased bowl, turning once to grease top. Cover and let rise in a warm place until doubled, about 1 hour.

3. Meanwhile, lightly grease 24 muffin cups. Punch down dough. Break off small portions and roll into 1-in. balls. Put 3 balls into each cup. Cover and let rise in a warm place until doubled, about 30 minutes. Preheat oven to 375°.

4. Brush tops of rolls with remaining butter; sprinkle with sesame seeds if desired. Bake for 16-18 minutes or until golden. Serve warm.

1 roll: 120 cal., 3g fat (2g sat. fat), 10mg chol., 145mg sod., 19g carb. (2g sugars, 1g fiber), 3g pro.

HOLIDAY HERB-CHEESE ROLLS

These low-fat rolls are flavored with garlic, dill and cheese, and they're yummy even without butter! They also make delicious little sandwiches.

—Nancy Boyd, Midlothian, VA

PREP: 45 MIN. + RISING • **BAKE:** 20 MIN.
MAKES: 2 DOZEN

- 4 to 4½ cups all-purpose flour
- ¼ cup sugar
- 2 Tbsp. mashed potato flakes
- 1 pkg. (¼ oz.) active dry yeast
- 2 tsp. salt
- ½ tsp. dill weed
- ¼ tsp. garlic powder
- 2 cups water
- 4½ tsp. butter
- 1 cup old-fashioned oats
- 1 large egg, room temperature
- ¾ cup shredded part-skim mozzarella cheese

TOPPING
- 2 Tbsp. fat-free milk
- 4½ tsp. grated Parmesan cheese
- ½ tsp. garlic powder
- ½ tsp. dill weed
- ½ tsp. dried basil

1. In a large bowl, combine 1½ cups flour, the sugar, potato flakes, yeast, salt, dill and garlic powder. In a small saucepan, bring water and butter just to a boil.

2. In a small bowl, pour boiling liquid over oats. Let stand until the mixture cools to 120°-130°, stirring occasionally. Add to the dry ingredients; beat just until moistened. Add egg; beat until smooth. Stir in enough of the remaining flour to form a firm dough (dough will be sticky).

3. Turn dough onto a floured surface; knead until smooth and elastic, 6-8 minutes. Knead in mozzarella cheese. Place in a large bowl coated with cooking spray, turning once to coat the top. Cover and let rise in a warm place until doubled, about 1¼ hours.

4. Punch dough down. Turn onto a lightly floured surface; divide into 24 pieces. Shape each piece into a ball. Place in a 13x9-in. baking pan coated with cooking spray; brush milk over rolls.

5. In a small bowl, combine remaining ingredients; sprinkle over tops. Cover and let rise until nearly doubled, about 45 minutes.

6. Bake at 375° for 20-25 minutes or until golden brown. Remove from pan to a wire rack. Refrigerate leftovers.

1 roll: 119 cal., 2g fat (1g sat. fat), 13mg chol., 228mg sod., 21g carb. (3g sugars, 1g fiber), 4g pro. **Diabetic exchanges:** 1½ starch.

HOLIDAY
HERB-CHEESE
ROLLS

BEST EVER CRESCENT ROLLS

BEST EVER CRESCENT ROLLS

My daughter and I have cranked out dozens of homemade crescent rolls. It's a real team effort. I cut the dough into pie-shaped wedges; she rolls.

—Irene Yeh, Mequon, WI

PREP: 40 MIN. + CHILLING
BAKE: 10 MIN./BATCH
MAKES: 32 ROLLS

- 3¾ to 4¼ cups all-purpose flour
- 2 pkg. (¼ oz. each) active dry yeast
- 1 tsp. salt
- 1 cup 2% milk
- ½ cup butter, cubed
- ¼ cup honey
- 3 large egg yolks. room temperature
- 2 Tbsp. butter, melted

1. Combine 1½ cups flour, yeast and salt. In a small saucepan, heat milk, cubed butter and honey to 120°-130°. Add to dry ingredients; beat on medium speed 2 minutes. Add egg yolks; beat on high 2 minutes. Stir in enough of the remaining flour to form a soft dough (dough will be sticky).

2. Turn onto a floured surface; knead until smooth and elastic, 6-8 minutes. Place in a greased bowl, turning once to grease the top. Cover and let rise in a warm place until doubled, about 45 minutes.

3. Punch down dough. Cover and refrigerate overnight.

4. To bake, turn dough onto a lightly floured surface; divide in half. Roll each portion into a 14-in. circle; cut each circle into 16 wedges. Lightly brush wedges with melted butter. Roll up each wedge from the wide end, pinching pointed end to seal. Place 2 in. apart on parchment-lined baking sheets, point side down. Cover with lightly greased plastic wrap; let rise in a warm place until doubled, about 45 minutes.

5. Preheat oven to 375°. Bake until golden brown, 9-11 minutes. Remove from pans to wire racks; serve warm.

Freeze option: Immediately after shaping, freeze rolls on parchment-lined baking sheets until firm. Transfer to a freezer container; return to freezer. Freeze up to 4 weeks. To use, let rise and bake as directed, increasing rise time to 2½-3 hours.

1 roll: 104 cal., 4g fat (3g sat. fat), 28mg chol., 107mg sod., 14g carb. (3g sugars, 1g fiber), 2g pro.

HOW TO MAKE FILLED CRESCENT ROLLS

Sprinkle dough with your filling of choice immediately after brushing with butter (Step 4); cut, shape and bake as directed.

CHIVE CRESCENTS
Divide ⅔ cup minced fresh chives between the 2 circles of dough.

ORANGE-PECAN CRESCENTS
Toss 1 cup finely chopped pecans with ⅓ cup sugar and 4 tsp. grated orange zest; divide mixture between the 2 circles of dough.

CRANBERRY-THYME CRESCENTS
Toss 1 cup finely chopped dried cranberries with ⅔ cup finely chopped walnuts and 2 tsp. minced fresh thyme leaves; divide mixture between the 2 circles of dough.

**JUMBO
JALAPENO
CHEDDAR
ROLLS**

CRUSTY FRENCH ROLLS

Save time by letting your bread machine knead the dough for these hearty, chewy rolls with a wonderful golden crust. They're best eaten the day that they're baked, or frozen for later.
—Donna Washburn and Heather Butt, Mallorytown, ON

PREP: 20 MIN. + RISING • **BAKE:** 25 MIN.
MAKES: 1½ DOZEN

- 1¼ cups water (70° to 80°)
- 2 tsp. sugar
- 1 tsp. salt
- 3½ cups bread flour
- 1¼ tsp. active dry yeast
- 1 Tbsp. cornmeal
- 1 egg white
- 1 Tbsp. water

1. In bread machine pan, place the first 5 ingredients in the order suggested by manufacturer. Select dough setting (check the dough after 5 minutes of mixing; add 1-2 Tbsp. of water or flour if needed). When cycle is completed, turn the dough onto a lightly floured surface. Divide into 18 portions; shape each into a round ball.
2. Place on a lightly greased baking sheets; sprinkle with cornmeal. Cover rolls and let rise in a warm place until doubled, about 45 minutes.
3. Beat egg white and water; brush over dough. Bake at 375° for 15 minutes; brush again with glaze. Bake 10 minutes longer or until golden brown.
1 roll: 101 cal., 1g fat (0 sat. fat), 0 chol., 133mg sod., 20g carb. (0 sugars, 0 fiber), 4g pro. **Diabetic exchanges:** 1½ starch.

JUMBO JALAPENO CHEDDAR ROLLS

Add some excitement to your Christmas or New Year's spread with these colorful rolls. The cheddar and jalapeno flavors are mild, but everyone loves the zesty taste.
—Linda Foreman, Locust Grove, OK

PREP: 35 MIN. + RISING • **BAKE:** 20 MIN.
MAKES: 1 DOZEN

- 2 pkg. (¼ oz. each) active dry yeast
- 2 Tbsp. sugar
- 2 cups warm 2% milk (105° to 115°)
- 2 large eggs, room temperature
- 2 tsp. salt
- 6½ to 7½ cups all-purpose flour
- 2 cups shredded cheddar cheese
- ¼ cup chopped seeded jalapeno pepper

EGG WASH
- 1 large egg
- 2 tsp. water

1. In a large bowl, dissolve yeast and sugar in warm milk. Add the eggs, salt and 4 cups flour. Beat on medium speed for 3 minutes. Add cheese and jalapeno. Stir in enough of the remaining flour to form a firm dough.
2. Turn onto a floured surface; knead until smooth and elastic, 6-8 minutes. Place in a greased bowl, turning once to grease top. Cover and let rise in a warm place until doubled, about 1 hour.
3. Punch dough down. Turn onto a lightly floured surface; divide into 12 pieces. Shape each into a roll. Place 3 in. apart on lightly greased baking sheets. Cover rolls and let rise until doubled, about 30 minutes.
4. Combine egg and water; brush over rolls. Bake at 375° for 16-20 minutes or until golden brown. Remove from pans to wire racks. Serve warm.
1 roll: 368 cal., 9g fat (5g sat. fat), 77mg chol., 542mg sod., 57g carb. (5g sugars, 2g fiber), 14g pro.

SOUR CREAM FAN ROLLS

I received this recipe from an email pen pal in Canada. The dough is so easy to work with, and it makes the lightest yeast rolls. I haven't used another white bread recipe since I started making this one.
—Carrie Ormsby, West Jordan, UT

PREP: 30 MIN. + RISING
BAKE: 20 MIN./BATCH
MAKES: ABOUT 2½ DOZEN

    7   to 8 cups all-purpose flour
    ½   cup sugar
    2   Tbsp. active dry yeast
    1½ tsp. salt
    ¼   tsp. baking powder
    2   cups sour cream
    1   cup water
    6   Tbsp. butter, cubed
    2   large eggs, room temperature, lightly beaten

1. In a large bowl, combine 3½ cups flour, sugar, yeast, salt and baking powder. In a small saucepan, heat the sour cream, water and butter to 120°-130°; add to dry ingredients. Beat on medium speed for 2 minutes. Add eggs and ½ cup flour; beat 2 minutes longer. Stir in enough remaining flour to form a soft dough.

2. Turn onto a floured surface; knead until smooth and elastic, 6-8 minutes. Place in a greased bowl, turning once to grease top. Cover and let rise in a warm place until doubled, about 1 hour.

3. Punch dough down. Turn onto a lightly floured surface; divide in half. Roll each portion into a 23x9-in. rectangle. Cut rectangles into 1½-in. strips. Stack 5 strips together; cut into 1½-in. pieces and place cut side up in a greased muffin cup. Repeat with the remaining strips. Cover and let rise until doubled, about 20 minutes.

4. Bake at 350° for 20-25 minutes or until golden brown. Remove from pans to wire racks.

1 roll: 182 cal., 6g fat (3g sat. fat), 31mg chol., 158mg sod., 27g carb. (5g sugars, 1g fiber), 4g pro.

PUMPKIN KNOT ROLLS

These rolls are the lightest, most delicious ones I've ever tasted...and everyone else seems to agree. The pumpkin gives them mild flavor, moist texture and a pretty golden color. At our house, it wouldn't be the holidays without them.
—Dianna Shimizu, Issaquah, WA

PREP: 30 MIN. + RISING • **BAKE:** 15 MIN.
MAKES: 2 DOZEN

    2   pkg. (¼ oz. each) active dry yeast
    1   cup warm 2% milk (105° to 115°)
    ⅓   cup butter, softened
    ½   cup sugar
    1   cup canned pumpkin
    3   large eggs, room temperature, divided use
    1½ tsp. salt
    5½ to 6 cups all-purpose flour
    1   Tbsp. cold water
        Sesame or poppy seeds, optional

1. In a bowl, dissolve yeast in warm milk. Add the butter, sugar, pumpkin, 2 eggs, salt and 3 cups flour. Beat until smooth. Stir in enough remaining flour to form a soft dough. Turn onto a lightly floured surface; knead until smooth and elastic, 6-8 minutes. Place in a greased bowl, turning once to grease top. Cover and let dough rise in a warm place until doubled, about 1 hour.

2. Punch dough down. Turn onto a lightly floured surface; divide in half. Shape each portion into 12 balls. Roll each ball into a 10-in. rope; tie into a knot and tuck ends under. Place 2 in. apart on greased baking sheets. Cover and let rise until doubled, about 30 minutes.

3. Preheat oven to 350°. In a small bowl, beat water and the remaining egg. Brush over rolls. Sprinkle with sesame or poppy seeds if desired. Bake for 15-17 minutes or until golden brown. Remove from pans to wire racks.

1 roll: 165 cal., 4g fat (2g sat. fat), 35mg chol., 188mg sod., 28g carb. (5g sugars, 1g fiber), 5g pro.

ZUCCHINI DINNER ROLLS

Grated squash gives these golden dinner rolls wonderful moistness. They're scrumptious warm from the oven.
—Robert Keith, Rochester, MN

PREP: 25 MIN. + RISING • **BAKE:** 20 MIN.
MAKES: 2 DOZEN

ZUCCHINI
DINNER ROLLS

- 1 cup shredded peeled zucchini
- 1 tsp. salt, divided
- 3½ cups all-purpose flour, divided
- 1 pkg. (¼ oz.) quick-rise yeast
- 5 Tbsp. grated Parmesan cheese, divided
- 1 tsp. sugar
- 1 cup warm water (120° to 130°)
- ¼ cup butter, softened

1. Place zucchini in a small bowl; sprinkle with ½ tsp. salt. Let stand for 5 minutes; drain.

2. Meanwhile, in another bowl, combine 3 cups flour, yeast, 2 Tbsp. cheese, sugar and remaining salt. Add zucchini; toss to combine. Combine water and butter; add to dry ingredients. Stir in remaining flour to form a soft dough.

3. Turn onto a floured surface; knead until smooth and elastic, 6-8 minutes. Place in a greased bowl, turning once to grease top. Cover and let rise in a warm place until doubled, about 1 hour.

4. Divide dough in half; shape each portion into 12 balls. Place in a greased 13x9-in. baking pan. Sprinkle with remaining cheese. Repeat. Cover and let rise in a warm place until doubled, about 45 minutes.

5. Bake at 375° until golden brown, 20-25 minutes. Remove from pan to a wire rack.

1 roll: 90 cal., 2g fat (1g sat. fat), 6mg chol., 133mg sod., 15g carb. (0 sugars, 1g fiber), 2g pro.

HONEY-SQUASH DINNER ROLLS

These puffy dinner rolls take on rich color when you add squash to the dough. Any squash variety works. I've even used cooked carrots.
—Marcia Whitney, Gainesville, FL

PREP: 40 MIN. + RISING • **BAKE:** 20 MIN.
MAKES: 2 DOZEN

- 2 pkg. (¼ oz. each) active dry yeast
- 2 tsp. salt
- ¼ tsp. ground nutmeg
- 6 to 6½ cups all-purpose flour
- 1¼ cups 2% milk
- ½ cup butter, cubed
- ½ cup honey
- 1 pkg. (12 oz.) frozen mashed winter squash, thawed (about 1⅓ cups)
- 1 large egg, lightly beaten
  Poppy seeds, salted pumpkin seeds or pepitas, or sesame seeds

1. In a large bowl, mix yeast, salt, nutmeg and 3 cups flour. In a small saucepan, heat milk, butter and honey to 120°-130°. Add to dry ingredients; beat on medium speed 2 minutes. Add squash; beat on high 2 minutes. Stir in enough remaining flour to form a soft dough (dough will be sticky).
2. Turn onto a floured surface; knead until smooth and elastic, 6-8 minutes. Place in a greased bowl, turning once to greasetop. Cover and let rise in a warm place until doubled, about 1 hour.
3. Punch down dough. Turn onto a lightly floured surface; divide and shape into 24 balls. Divide between 2 greased 9-in. cast-iron skillets or round baking pans. Cover pans with kitchen towels; let rise in a warm place until doubled, about 45 minutes.

4. Preheat oven to 375°. Brush tops of rolls with beaten egg; sprinkle with seeds. Bake until dark golden brown, 20-25 minutes. Cover loosely with foil during the last 5-7 minutes if needed to prevent overbrowning. Remove from pans to wire racks; serve warm.
1 roll: 186 cal., 5g fat (3g sat. fat), 19mg chol., 238mg sod., 32g carb. (6g sugars, 1g fiber), 4g pro. **Diabetic exchanges:** 2 starch, 1 fat.

TEST KITCHEN TIP

Feel free to substitute 1⅓ cups canned pumpkin or your own mashed butternut or acorn squash for the frozen version. Try baking these in a cast-iron skillet for a beautiful, rustic presentation.

GRANDMA'S ROSEMARY DINNER ROLLS

My grandma (I called her Baba) made these in her coal oven. How she regulated the temperature is beyond me! She always made extra rolls for the neighbors to bake in their own ovens. At lunchtime, my mom and aunts delivered the formed rolls.
—Charlotte Hendershot, Hudson, PA

PREP: 35 MIN. + RISING • **BAKE:** 20 MIN.
MAKES: 1 DOZEN

- 1 pkg. (¼ oz.) active dry yeast
- ¼ cup warm water (105° to 115°)
- 3 cups bread flour
- 2 Tbsp. sugar
- 1 Tbsp. minced fresh rosemary, divided
- ¾ tsp. salt
- ⅔ cup warm 2% milk (110° to 115°)
- 1 large egg, room temperature
- ¼ to ⅓ cup canola oil

EGG WASH
- 1 large egg yolk
- 2 Tbsp. 2% milk

1. In a small bowl, dissolve yeast in warm water. Place the flour, sugar, 2 tsp. rosemary and the salt in a food processor; pulse until blended. Add the warm milk, egg and yeast mixture; cover and pulse 10 times or until almost blended.

2. While processing, gradually add oil just until the dough pulls away from the sides and begins to form a ball. Process 2 minutes longer to knead dough (dough will be very soft).

3. Transfer dough to a greased bowl, turning once to grease the top. Cover and let rise in a warm place until doubled, about 1 hour.

4. Punch down dough. Turn onto a lightly floured surface; divide and shape into 12 balls. Roll each ball into a 15-in. rope. Starting at 1 end, loosely wrap dough around itself to form a coil. Tuck end under; pinch to seal.

5. Place 2 in. apart on greased baking sheets. Cover and let rise until doubled, about 30 minutes.

6. Preheat oven to 350°. For egg wash, in a small bowl, whisk egg yolk and milk; brush over rolls. Sprinkle with remaining rosemary. Bake until golden brown, 18-22 minutes. Remove from pans to wire racks; serve warm.

1 roll: 194 cal., 6g fat (1g sat. fat), 32mg chol., 163mg sod., 28g carb. (3g sugars, 1g fiber), 6g pro.

HAWAIIAN DINNER ROLLS

Pineapple and coconut give a subtle sweetness to these golden homemade rolls. If you have any leftovers, they're great for sandwiches.
—Kathy Kurtz, Glendora, CA

PREP: 35 MIN. + RISING • **BAKE:** 15 MIN.
MAKES: 15 ROLLS

- 1 can (8 oz.) crushed pineapple, undrained
- ¼ cup warm pineapple juice (70° to 80°)
- ¼ cup water (70° to 80°)
- 1 large egg, room temperature
- ¼ cup butter, cubed
- ¼ cup nonfat dry milk powder
- 1 Tbsp. sugar
- 1½ tsp. salt
- 3¼ cups bread flour
- 2¼ tsp. active dry yeast
- ¾ cup sweetened shredded coconut

1. In bread machine pan, place the first 10 ingredients in order suggested by manufacturer. Select dough setting (check the dough after 5 minutes of mixing; add 1-2 Tbsp. of water or flour if needed). Just before final kneading (your machine may audibly signal this), add coconut.

2. When cycle is complete, turn dough onto a lightly floured surface. Cover and let rest for 10 minutes. Divide into 15 portions; roll each into a ball. Place in a greased 13x9-in. baking pan.

3. Cover and let rise in a warm place for 45 minutes or until doubled. Bake at 375° for 15-20 minutes or until rolls are golden brown.

1 roll: 165 cal., 5g fat (3g sat. fat), 23mg chol., 294mg sod., 26g carb. (6g sugars, 1g fiber), 5g pro.

SCOTTISH OATMEAL ROLLS

My family likes rolls that can hold up to scooping gravies, sauces and more. This recipe is a favorite. The oatmeal in the dough gives it a Scottish touch.
—Peggy Goodrich, Enid, OK

PREP: 30 MIN. + RISING • **BAKE:** 20 MIN.
MAKES: 2 DOZEN

- 1½ cups boiling water
- 1½ cups old-fashioned oats
- ⅓ cup packed brown sugar
- 1½ tsp. salt
- 1 Tbsp. canola oil
- 1 pkg. (¼ oz.) active dry yeast
- ¼ cup warm water (105° to 115°)
- 2¾ to 3¼ cups all-purpose flour
  Optional: Butter and honey

1. Pour boiling water over oats in a large bowl. Add brown sugar, salt and oil. Cool to 110°-115°, stirring occasionally. Meanwhile, in a small bowl, dissolve yeast in warm water; let stand 5 minutes. Add to oat mixture. Beat in enough flour to form a stiff dough (dough will be sticky).
2. Turn onto a floured surface; knead until smooth and elastic, 6-8 minutes. Place in a greased bowl, turning once to grease the top. Cover dough and let rise in a warm place until doubled, about 1 hour.
3. Punch dough down. Turn onto a lightly floured surface; divide and shape into 24 balls. Place in a greased 13x9-in. baking pan. Cover with a kitchen towel; let rise in a warm place until doubled, about 30 minutes.
4. Preheat oven to 350°. Bake until lightly browned, 20-25 minutes. Remove rolls from pan to a wire rack to cool. If desired, serve with butter and honey.
1 roll: 89 cal., 1g fat (0 sat. fat), 0 chol., 149mg sod., 17g carb. (3g sugars, 1g fiber), 2g pro. **Diabetic exchanges:** 1 starch.

YOGURT
YEAST ROLLS

YOGURT YEAST ROLLS

Bring these fluffy, golden rolls to a potluck and people will snap them up in a hurry. It's a nice contribution because rolls are easy to transport and one batch goes a long way.
—Carol Forcum, Marion, IL

PREP: 30 MIN. + RISING • **BAKE:** 15 MIN.
MAKES: 2 DOZEN

- 1½ cups whole wheat flour
- 3¼ cups all-purpose flour, divided
- 2 pkg. (¼ oz. each) active dry yeast
- 2 tsp. salt
- ½ tsp. baking soda
- 1½ cups plain yogurt
- ½ cup water
- 3 Tbsp. butter
- 2 Tbsp. honey
  Additional melted butter, optional

1. In a large bowl, combine whole wheat flour, ½ cup all-purpose flour, the yeast, salt and baking soda. In a saucepan over low heat, heat yogurt, water, butter and honey to 120°-130°. Pour over the dry ingredients; blend well. Beat on medium speed for 3 minutes. Add enough of the remaining all-purpose flour to form a soft dough.
2. Turn onto a floured surface; knead until smooth and elastic, 6-8 minutes. Place in a greased bowl, turning once to grease top. Cover and let rise in a warm place until doubled, about 1 hour.
3. Punch dough down. Turn onto a lightly floured surface; divide into 24 portions. Roll each into a 10-in. rope. Shape each rope into an S, then coil each end until it touches the center. Place rolls 3 in. apart on greased baking sheets. Cover dough and let rise until doubled, about 30 minutes. Preheat oven to 400°.
4. Bake until golden brown, about 15 minutes. If desired, brush tops with additional butter while warm. Remove from pans to wire racks to cool.
1 roll: 115 cal., 2g fat (1g sat. fat), 6mg chol., 245mg sod., 21g carb. (3g sugars, 1g fiber), 3g pro. **Diabetic exchanges:** 1½ starch, ½ fat.

BAKING 101

BEST DINNER ROLLS

If you can't decide which enticing topping to choose, just use them all.
—Christina Pittman, Parkville, MO

PREP: 35 MIN. + RISING • **BAKE:** 10 MIN.
MAKES: 2 DOZEN

- ¼ cup sugar
- 1 pkg. (¼ oz.) active dry yeast
- 1¼ tsp. salt
- 4½ to 5 cups all-purpose flour
- 1 cup 2% milk
- ½ cup water
- 2 Tbsp. butter
- 2 large eggs, room temperature
- 1 large egg, lightly beaten

FOR EVERYTHING DINNER ROLLS
- 1 tsp. kosher salt
- 1 tsp. dried minced garlic
- 1 tsp. dried minced onion
- 1 tsp. poppy seeds
- 1 tsp. sesame seeds

FOR PARMESAN-GARLIC DINNER ROLLS
- 2 Tbsp. grated Parmesan cheese
- ½ tsp. dried minced garlic

FOR ALMOND-HERB DINNER ROLLS
- 2 Tbsp. chopped sliced almonds
- ½ tsp. kosher salt
- ½ tsp. dried basil
- ½ tsp. dried oregano

1. In a large bowl, mix sugar, yeast, salt and 2 cups flour. In a small saucepan, heat milk, water and butter to 120°-130°. Add to dry ingredients; beat on medium speed 3 minutes. Add 2 eggs; beat on high 2 minutes. Stir in enough remaining flour to form a soft dough (dough will be sticky).
2. Turn onto a floured surface; knead until smooth and elastic, 6-8 minutes. Place in a greased bowl, turning once to grease top. Cover and let rise in a warm place until doubled, about 1 hour.
3. Punch down dough. Turn onto a lightly floured surface; divide and shape dough into 24 balls. Place in 2 greased 13x9-in. baking pans. Cover with kitchen towels; let rise in a warm place until doubled, about 30 minutes.
4. Preheat oven to 375°. Brush rolls with lightly beaten egg. Sprinkle with toppings for rolls of your choice. Bake until golden brown, 10-15 minutes. Remove from pans to wire racks; serve warm.

1 roll: 118 cal., 2g fat (1g sat. fat), 30mg chol., 143mg sod., 21g carb. (3g sugars, 1g fiber), 4g pro.

THREE WAYS TO SHAPE DINNER ROLLS

A good basic dough can be shaped into any number of different rolls. Round rolls are a classic for a reason, but to try something a little different, here are three easy and elegant variations. Follow the recipe for the Best Dinner Rolls (left) or use your own favorite roll recipe.

CLOVERLEAF
Divide dough into 24 portions (or as many rolls as your recipe yields), then divide each portion into 3 equal pieces. Roll each piece into a ball. Place 3 balls in each cup of a greased muffin tin. Let rise, then top and bake as directed.

TWIST
Divide dough into 24 portions (or as many rolls as your recipe yields), roll each portion into a ball, then roll each ball into a 10-in. rope. Fold each rope in half and twist 2 or 3 times, holding both ends. Pinch the rope ends to seal. Let rise; top and bake as directed.

ROSETTE
Divide dough into 24 portions (or as many rolls as your recipe yields), roll each into a ball, then roll each ball into a 10-in. rope. Tie a loose knot in the center of the rope. Bring the bottom end up and tuck into the center of the roll; wrap top end around and tuck under the roll. Let rise; top and bake as directed.

BAKING 101

SKILLET ROLLS

Baking these rolls in a skillet makes them soft and tender. My family requests them for holiday dinners and other special occasions. I most enjoy them split and spread with butter and black raspberry jelly.
—Susan Baughman, Houston, PA

PREP: 25 MIN. + RISING • **BAKE:** 20 MIN.
MAKES: 2 DOZEN

- 1 pkg. (¼ oz.) active dry yeast
- ¼ cup warm water (105° to 115°)
- 1 cup warm buttermilk (105° to 115°)
- ¼ cup butter, softened
- ¼ cup sugar
- 1 tsp. salt
- ¼ tsp. baking soda
- 1 large egg, room temperature
- 4 to 4½ cups all-purpose flour
- 1 Tbsp. cornmeal
- 1 Tbsp. butter, melted

1. In a large bowl, dissolve yeast in warm water. Add the buttermilk, butter, sugar, salt, baking soda and egg. Beat until blended. Stir in enough flour to form a soft dough.

2. Turn onto a floured surface; knead until smooth and elastic, 6-8 minutes. Place in a greased bowl, turning once to grease top. Cover and let rise in a warm place until doubled, about 1 hour.
3. Punch dough down. Turn onto a lightly floured surface; knead for 5 minutes. Divide into 24 pieces. Shape each into a ball. Grease a 12-in. cast-iron or other ovenproof skillet and sprinkle with cornmeal. Place rolls in prepared pan. Cover and let rise until doubled, about 40 minutes.
4. Preheat oven to 375°. Drizzle butter over rolls. Bake until golden brown, 18-20 minutes. Remove from skillet to a wire rack to cool.
1 roll: 114 cal., 3g fat (2g sat. fat), 16mg chol., 149mg sod., 19g carb. (3g sugars, 1g fiber), 3g pro.

ICEBOX ROLLS

I remember my mom making these rolls almost every Saturday so they'd be ready to bake on Sunday for company or someone just dropping by. Of course, when we did have company, we'd get to enjoy these rolls, too! Although they take a little time to prepare, they're not difficult to make. And there's nothing in the stores that can compare with them!
—Jean Fox, Welch, MN

PREP: 30 MIN. + RISING • **BAKE:** 15 MIN.
MAKES: 36 ROLLS

- 1 pkg. (¼ oz.) active dry yeast
- 2½ cups water, divided
- ½ cup shortening
- 2 large eggs, beaten
- 1½ tsp. salt
- ½ cup sugar
- 8½ to 9 cups all-purpose flour
- ⅓ cup butter, melted

1. Dissolve yeast in ½ cup warm water (105°-115°). In another bowl, combine 1 cup boiling water and shortening. Add remaining 1 cup (room-temperature) water, the eggs, salt, sugar and the yeast mixture.
2. Stir in flour 1 cup at a time, mixing well after each addition, until soft dough forms. Turn onto floured surface; knead until smooth and elastic, 6-8 minutes. Place in a greased bowl, turning once to grease top. Cover; refrigerate overnight.
3. Turn onto a lightly floured surface; divide dough into 9 portions. Divide and shape each portion into 12 balls. Place 3 balls in each cup of 3 greased muffin tins. Cover with kitchen towels; let rise in a warm place until doubled, about 1 hour.
4. Preheat oven to 375°. Brush rolls with half of the melted butter; bake until golden brown, 15-20 minutes. Remove from oven; brush with remaining butter.
1 roll: 162 cal., 5g fat (2g sat. fat), 15mg chol., 117mg sod., 25g carb. (3g sugars, 1g fiber), 4g pro.

SWEET BREADS

CHAI-SPICED STAR BREAD

My chai star bread is great for potlucks or parties because it's easy to share and looks beautiful. Prepare it ahead of time, refrigerate, then just pop it in the oven before serving. Try using this recipe with other fruits, too, like persimmons or apples.
—Elizabeth Ding, El Cerrito, CA

PREP: 45 MIN. + RISING
BAKE: 20 MIN. + COOLING
MAKES: 16 SERVINGS

- 2 tsp. active dry yeast
- ½ cup warm water (105° to 115°)
- ½ cup warm 2% milk (105° to 115°)
- ¼ cup sugar
- 2¾ to 3¼ cups all-purpose flour

FILLING
- 5 Tbsp. butter, softened
- ¾ cup packed brown sugar
- 2 tsp. vanilla extract
- 1 tsp. ground ginger
- 1 tsp. ground cinnamon
- ½ tsp. ground nutmeg
- ½ tsp. ground allspice
- ¼ tsp. ground cloves
- 1 medium Bartlett pear, peeled and chopped
- 1 large egg, beaten

1. In a small bowl, dissolve yeast in warm water. In a large bowl, combine milk, sugar, the yeast mixture and 1½ cups flour; beat on medium speed until smooth. Stir in enough of the remaining flour to form a soft dough (dough will be sticky).

2. Turn onto a floured surface; knead until smooth and elastic, 6-8 minutes. Place in a greased bowl, turning once to grease top. Cover and let rise in a warm place until doubled, about 1 hour.

3. Punch down dough. Turn onto a lightly floured surface; divide into 4 portions. Roll each into a 12-in. circle. Place 1 circle on a parchment-lined 14-in. pizza pan. For filling, combine butter, brown sugar, vanilla and spices. Spread circle with a third of the filling. Repeat twice, layering dough and filling; top with pears. Top with the final portion of dough.

4. Cut and shape the dough into a star (see opposite page). Cover with a kitchen towel; let rise until almost doubled, about 30 minutes.

5. Preheat oven to 375°. Brush with beaten egg. Bake until golden brown, 20-25 minutes. Cool completely on a wire rack.

1 piece: 178 cal., 4g fat (3g sat. fat), 13mg chol., 37mg sod., 32g carb. (15g sugars, 1g fiber), 3g pro.

CHAI-SPICED
STAR BREAD

HOW TO SHAPE STAR BREAD

You can make star bread filled with anything from a simple spread of preserves to a more substantial filling of fruit, nuts and spices.

STEP 1
Layer the circles of dough with the filling of your choice.

STEP 2
Place a 2½-in. round cutter in the center of the circle (do not press down). With a sharp knife, make 16 evenly spaced cuts from the cutter to the edge of the dough.

STEP 3
Grasp 2 strips and rotate outward twice. Pinch the ends of the strips together to seal. Repeat with the remaining strips.

CHOCOLATE YEAST BREAD

BANANA WHEAT BREAD

A subtle banana flavor comes through in this moist whole wheat loaf. Flecked with poppy seeds, the sweet slices are wonderful warm or toasted and spread with butter.
—Louise Myers, Pomeroy, OH

PREP: 15 MIN. • **BAKE:** 4 HOURS
MAKES: 1 LOAF (16 PIECES)

- ¾ cup water (70° to 80°)
- ¼ cup honey
- 1 large egg, room temperature, lightly beaten
- 4½ tsp. canola oil
- ½ tsp. vanilla extract
- 1 medium ripe banana, sliced
- 2 tsp. poppy seeds
- 1 tsp. salt
- 1¾ cups bread flour
- 1½ cups whole wheat flour
- 2¼ tsp. active dry yeast

In bread machine pan, place all ingredients in order suggested by manufacturer. Select basic bread setting. Choose crust color and loaf size if available. Bake according to the bread machine directions (check dough after 5 minutes of mixing; add 1-2 Tbsp. of water or flour if needed).
1 piece: 125 cal., 2g fat (0 sat. fat), 13mg chol., 153mg sod., 24g carb. (6g sugars, 2g fiber), 4g pro. **Diabetic exchanges:** 1½ starch, ½ fat.

1 slice: 124 cal., 3g fat (1g sat. fat), 11mg chol., 125mg sod., 22g carb. (3g sugars, 1g fiber), 3g pro.

CHOCOLATE YEAST BREAD

Your family will love this tender loaf of chocolate bread. Try slices toasted and spread them with butter, cream cheese or peanut butter.
—Laura Cryts, Derry, NH

PREP: 30 MIN. + RISING • **BAKE:** 25 MIN.
MAKES: 2 LOAVES (12 PIECES EACH)

- 4½ cups all-purpose flour
- ⅓ cup baking cocoa
- 2 Tbsp. sugar
- 1 pkg. (¼ oz.) active dry yeast
- 1 tsp. salt
- ¼ tsp. baking soda
- 1 cup water
- ½ cup 2% milk
- ½ cup semisweet chocolate chips
- 2 Tbsp. butter
- 1 large egg, room temperature
  Optional: Baking cocoa and/or confectioners' sugar

1. Combine 1¼ cups flour, the cocoa, sugar, yeast, salt and baking soda. In a saucepan, heat water, milk, chocolate chips and butter; stir until chocolate is melted. Cool to 120°-130°. Add to dry ingredients; beat on medium speed for 2 minutes. Add ½ cup flour and egg; beat on high for 2 minutes. Stir in enough of the remaining flour to form a stiff dough.
2. Turn onto a floured surface; knead until smooth and elastic, 6-8 minutes. Place in a greased bowl, turning once to grease top. Cover and let rise in a warm place until doubled, about 1 hour.
3. Punch dough down. Turn onto a lightly floured surface; divide in half. Shape into loaves. Place in 2 greased 8x4-in. loaf pans. Cover and let rise until doubled, about 1 hour.
4. Bake at 375° until browned, 25-30 minutes. Remove from pans to cool on wire racks. Dust with baking cocoa and/or confectioners' sugar if desired.

ROSEMARY ORANGE BREAD

Of all the herbs, rosemary is my favorite. This bread is great with a roast, chicken or lasagna. It's especially festive to serve at holiday time.
—Deidre Fallavollita, Vienna, VA

PREP: 20 MIN. + RISING
BAKE: 45 MIN. + COOLING
MAKES: 1 LOAF (16 PIECES)

    1   pkg. (¼ oz.) active dry yeast
    ¾   cup warm water (105° to 115°)
    ¾   cup orange juice
    2   Tbsp. honey
    1   Tbsp. vegetable oil
    1   Tbsp. minced fresh rosemary or
        1 tsp. dried rosemary, crushed
    2   tsp. salt
    1   tsp. grated orange zest
    3¾ to 4½ cups all-purpose flour
    1   large egg white
        Optional: Additional fresh
        rosemary and whole peppercorns

1. In a large bowl, dissolve yeast in warm water. Add orange juice, honey, oil, rosemary, salt, orange zest and 2 cups flour; beat until smooth. Stir in enough remaining flour to form a soft dough.

2. Turn onto a floured surface; knead until smooth and elastic, 6-8 minutes. Place in a greased bowl, turning once to grease top. Cover and let rise in a warm place until doubled, about 1 hour.

3. Punch dough down. Roll into a 15x1-in. rectangle. Starting at a short end, roll up jelly-roll style. Pinch edges to seal and shape into an oval. Place seam side down on a greased baking sheet. Cover and let rise until nearly doubled, about 30 minutes.

4. Bake at 375° for 20 minutes. Whisk egg white; brush over loaf. Place small sprigs of rosemary and peppercorns on top if desired. Bake 25 minutes longer or until browned. Remove from pan to wire rack to cool.

1 piece: 130 cal., 1g fat (0 sat. fat), 0 chol., 299mg sod., 26g carb. (4g sugars, 1g fiber), 3g pro.

FRENCH CRESCENT ROLLS

Layers of buttered dough result in the richest sweet rolls you've ever tasted.
—Betty Ann Wolery, Joplin, MT

PREP: 25 MIN. + CHILLING • **BAKE:** 10 MIN.
MAKES: 16 ROLLS

    1   pkg. (¼ oz.) active dry yeast
    ¼   cup warm water (105° to 115°)
    ¾   cup warm 2% milk (105° to 115°)
    1   large egg, room temperature
    2   Tbsp. sugar
    1   Tbsp. shortening
    1   tsp. salt
    3   cups all-purpose flour
    3   Tbsp. butter, softened, divided
    ICING
    1½ cups confectioners' sugar
    2   Tbsp. 2% milk
    3   Tbsp. butter
    ½   tsp. almond extract
    ½   tsp. vanilla extract
    ½   cup chopped walnuts

1. Dissolve yeast in warm water. Add milk, egg, sugar, shortening and salt; mix well. Add flour; mix until smooth. Place in a greased bowl, turning once to grease top. Cover and refrigerate at least 1 hour.

2. Turn dough onto a floured surface; roll to a ¼-in.-thick square. Spread with 1 Tbsp. softened butter. Fold corners to the middle and then fold in half. Wrap dough in waxed paper; chill for 30 minutes. Repeat rolling, buttering, folding and chilling steps twice.

3. Turn dough onto a floured surface; roll into a 34x5-in. rectangle. Cut into 16 triangles; roll up each triangle from wide edge to tip and pinch to seal. Place rolls, tip down, on greased baking sheets and curve to form crescents. Cover and let rise in a warm place until doubled, about 30 minutes.

4. Bake at 400° for 10 minutes or until lightly browned. For icing, combine sugar, milk, butter and extracts; spread over warm rolls. Sprinkle with nuts.

1 roll: 204 cal., 8g fat (3g sat. fat), 27mg chol., 202mg sod., 29g carb. (13g sugars, 1g fiber), 4g pro.

TRADITIONAL
NEW ORLEANS
KING CAKE

TRADITIONAL NEW ORLEANS KING CAKE

Get in on the fun of king cake by hiding a little toy baby inside. According to the tradition, whoever finds it will enjoy one year of good luck!
—Rebecca Baird, Salt Lake City, UT

PREP: 40 MIN. + RISING
BAKE: 25 MIN. + COOLING
MAKES: 1 CAKE (12 PIECES)

- 2 pkg. (¼ oz. each) active dry yeast
- ½ cup warm water (105° to 115°)
- ¾ cup sugar, divided
- ½ cup butter, softened
- ½ cup warm 2% milk (110° to 115°)
- 2 large egg yolks, room temperature
- 1¼ tsp. salt
- 1 tsp. grated lemon zest
- ¼ tsp. ground nutmeg
- 3¼ to 3¾ cups all-purpose flour
- 1 tsp. ground cinnamon
- 1 large egg, beaten

GLAZE
- 1½ cups confectioners' sugar
- 2 tsp. lemon juice
- 2 to 3 Tbsp. water
  Green, purple and yellow sugars

1. In a large bowl, dissolve yeast in warm water. Add ½ cup sugar, the butter, milk, egg yolks, salt, lemon zest, nutmeg and 2 cups flour. Beat until smooth. Stir in enough of the remaining flour to form a soft dough (dough will be sticky).
2. Turn onto a floured surface; knead until smooth and elastic, 6-8 minutes. Place in a greased bowl, turning once to grease the top. Cover; let rise in a warm place until doubled, about 1 hour.
3. Punch dough down. Turn onto a lightly floured surface. Roll into a 16x10-in. rectangle. Combine cinnamon and remaining sugar; sprinkle over dough to within ½ in. of edges. Roll up jelly-roll style, starting with a long side; pinch seam to seal. Place seam side down on a greased baking sheet; pinch ends together to form a ring. Cover and let rise until doubled, about 1 hour. Brush with egg.
4. Bake at 375° for 25-30 minutes or until golden brown. Cool completely on a wire rack. For glaze, combine the confectioners' sugar, lemon juice and enough water to achieve desired consistency. Spread over cake. Sprinkle with colored sugars.

1 piece: 321 cal., 9g fat (5g sat. fat), 73mg chol., 313mg sod., 55g carb. (28g sugars, 1g fiber), 5g pro.

STOLLEN BUTTER ROLLS

Our family enjoys my stollen so much they say it's just too good to be served only as a holiday sweet bread. I created this buttery, less sweet dinner roll so we can satisfy our stollen cravings anytime.
—Mindy White, Nashville, TN

PREP: 45 MIN. + RISING • **BAKE:** 15 MIN.
MAKES: 2 DOZEN

- 1 pkg. (¼ oz.) active dry yeast
- ¼ cup warm water (105° to 115°)
- 1 cup warm 2% milk (105° to 115°)
- 2 large eggs, room temperature
- ½ cup butter, softened
- 1 Tbsp. sugar
- 1 tsp. salt
- 4¼ to 4¾ cups all-purpose flour
- ¾ cup chopped mixed candied fruit
- ¾ cup dried currants
- ½ cup cold butter, cut into 24 pieces (1 tsp. each)

1. In a small bowl, dissolve yeast in warm water. In a large bowl, combine milk, eggs, butter, sugar, salt, yeast mixture and 3 cups flour; beat on medium speed until smooth. Stir in enough remaining flour to form a soft dough (dough will be sticky).

2. Turn onto a floured surface; knead until smooth and elastic, 6-8 minutes. Place in a greased bowl, turning once to grease the top. Cover and let rise in a warm place until doubled, about 1 hour.
3. Punch dough down; turn onto a floured surface. Knead candied fruit and currants into dough (knead in more flour if necessary). Divide and shape into 24 balls; flatten slightly. Place 1 tsp. cold butter in center of each circle. Fold circles in half over butter; press edges to seal. Place in a greased 15x10x1-in. baking pan. Cover and let rise in a warm place until doubled, about 45 minutes.
4. Preheat oven to 375°. Bake until golden brown, 15-20 minutes. Cool in pan 5 minutes; serve warm.
Freeze option: Freeze baked and cooled rolls in airtight containers. To use, microwave each roll on high until warmed, 30-45 seconds.

1 roll: 198 cal., 9g fat (5g sat. fat), 37mg chol., 178mg sod., 28g carb. (9g sugars, 1g fiber), 4g pro.

CINNAMON SWIRL BREAD

Your family will be impressed with the soft texture and appealing swirls of cinnamon in these lovely breakfast loaves.
—Diane Armstrong, Elm Grove, WI

PREP: 25 MIN. + RISING • **BAKE:** 30 MIN.
MAKES: 2 LOAVES (16 PIECES EACH)

- 2 pkg. (¼ oz. each) active dry yeast
- ⅓ cup warm water (105° to 115°)
- 1 cup warm 2% milk (105° to 115°)
- 1 cup sugar, divided
- 2 large eggs, room temperature
- 6 Tbsp. butter, softened
- 1½ tsp. salt
- 5½ to 6 cups all-purpose flour
- 2 Tbsp. ground cinnamon

1. In a large bowl, dissolve yeast in warm water. Add milk, ½ cup sugar, eggs, butter, salt and 3 cups flour; beat on medium speed until smooth. Stir in enough remaining flour to form a soft dough.
2. Turn onto a floured surface; knead until smooth and elastic, 6-8 minutes. Place in a greased bowl, turning once to grease the top. Cover; let rise in a warm place until doubled, about 1 hour.
3. Mix cinnamon and the remaining ½ cup sugar. Punch down dough. Turn onto a lightly floured surface; divide in half. Roll each portion into an 18x8-in. rectangle; sprinkle each with about ¼ cup cinnamon sugar to within ½ in. of edges. Roll up jelly-roll style, starting with a short side; pinch seam to seal. Place in 2 greased 9x5-in. loaf pans, seam side down.
4. Cover with kitchen towels; let rise in a warm place until doubled, about 1½ hours. .
5. Bake at 350° until golden brown, 30-35 minutes. Remove from pans to wire racks to cool.

1 piece: 132 cal., 3g fat (2g sat. fat), 20mg chol., 141mg sod., 23g carb. (7g sugars, 1g fiber), 3g pro.

APPLE RAISIN BREAD

I've been making this bread for many years. It smells so good in the oven and tastes even better. I make bread almost every Saturday, and it doesn't stay around long when our sons are home from college in the summer.
—Perlene Hoekema, Lynden, WA

PREP: 25 MIN. + RISING • **BAKE:** 30 MIN.
MAKES: 3 LOAVES (16 PIECES EACH)

- 2 pkg. (¼ oz. each) active dry yeast
- 1½ cups warm water (110° to 115°), divided
- 1 tsp. sugar
- 3 large eggs, room temperature, beaten
- 1 cup applesauce
- ½ cup honey
- ½ cup canola oil
- 2 tsp. salt
- 8 to 9 cups all-purpose flour
- 1½ cups diced peeled apples
- 1½ cups raisins
- 2 Tbsp. lemon juice
- 2 Tbsp. cornmeal

GLAZE
- 1 large egg, beaten
  Sugar

1. In a small bowl, combine yeast, ½ cup water and sugar; set aside. In a large bowl, combine eggs, applesauce, honey, oil, salt and remaining 1 cup water; mix well. Stir in yeast mixture. Gradually add enough flour to form a soft dough.
2. Turn onto a lightly floured surface and knead until smooth and elastic, about 10 minutes. Place dough in a greased bowl, turning once to grease top. Cover and let rise in a warm place until doubled, about 1 hour.
3. Punch dough down and turn over in bowl. Cover and let rise 30 minutes.
4. In a small bowl, combine the apples, raisins and lemon juice. Divide dough into 3 parts; knead a third of the apple mixture into each part. Shape each into a round flat ball. Place each ball in a greased 8-in. round baking pan that has been sprinkled with cornmeal. Cover and let rise until doubled, about 1 hour.
5. Brush each loaf with egg and sprinkle with sugar. Bake at 350° for 30-35 minutes or until bread sounds hollow when tapped.

1 piece: 135 cal., 3g fat (0 sat. fat), 18mg chol., 105mg sod., 25g carb. (8g sugars, 1g fiber), 3g pro.

· · · · · · · · · · · · · · · · · · · ·

TEST KITCHEN TIP

If your baking day gets interrupted, you can hit "pause" on your bread. After your dough has been shaped and is ready for the final rise, you can put it in the refrigerator overnight; this will slow down the proofing stage while still allowing the bread to rise. The next day, let the dough come to room temperature before baking as instructed.

BLACK RASPBERRY
BUBBLE RING

BLACK RASPBERRY BUBBLE RING

I first made this pretty bread years ago for a 4-H project. It helped me win grand champion for my county and took me to the Ohio State Fair. It takes some time to make, but I pull out this recipe anytime I want a breakfast or dessert that will really impress.
—Kila Frank, Reedsville, OH

PREP: 35 MIN. + RISING • **BAKE:** 25 MIN.
MAKES: 1 LOAF (16 PIECES)

1   pkg. (¼ oz.) active dry yeast
¼   cup warm water (105° to 115°)
1   cup warm 2% milk (105° to 115°)
¼   cup plus 2 Tbsp. sugar, divided
½   cup butter, melted, divided
1   large egg, room temperature
1   tsp. salt
4   cups all-purpose flour
1   jar (10 oz.) seedless black
      raspberry preserves
SYRUP
⅓   cup corn syrup
2   Tbsp. butter, melted
½   tsp. vanilla extract

1. In a large bowl, dissolve yeast in warm water. Add the milk, ¼ cup sugar, ¼ cup butter, egg, salt and 3½ cups flour. Beat until smooth. Stir in enough remaining flour to form a soft dough.
2. Turn onto a floured surface; knead until smooth and elastic, 6-8 minutes. Place in a greased bowl, turning once to grease top. Cover and let rise in a warm place until doubled, about 1¼ hours.
3. Punch dough down. Turn onto a lightly floured surface; divide into 32 pieces.

Flatten each piece into a 3-in. disk. Place about 1 tsp. of preserves on the center of each piece; bring edges together and seal.
4. Place 16 dough balls in a greased 10-in. fluted tube pan. Brush with half the remaining ¼ cup butter; sprinkle with 1 Tbsp. sugar. Top with the remaining balls, ⅛ cup butter and 1 Tbsp. sugar. Cover and let rise until doubled, about 35 minutes.
5. Preheat oven to 350°. Bake until golden brown, 25-30 minutes. Combine syrup ingredients; pour over warm bread. Cool bread for 5 minutes before inverting onto a serving plate.

1 piece: 274 cal., 8g fat (5g sat. fat), 34mg chol., 220mg sod., 46g carb. (18g sugars, 1g fiber), 4g pro.

ITALIAN SWEET BREAD

This golden brown bread offers satisfying sweetness in every slice. The hearty round loaves rise well and cut beautifully. With an egg wash and a sprinkling of Italian seasoning, the bread looks pretty, too.
—Kim Ooms, Cottage Grove, MN

PREP: 10 MIN. + RISING
BAKE: 20 MIN. + COOLING
MAKES: 2 LOAVES (16 PIECES EACH)

- 1 cup warm 2% milk (70° to 80°)
- 1 large egg, lightly beaten
- 2 Tbsp. butter, softened
- ¼ cup sugar
- 1 tsp. salt
- 3 cups all-purpose flour
- 2 tsp. active dry yeast

EGG WASH
- 1 large egg
- 1 Tbsp. water
- Italian seasoning, optional

1. In bread machine pan, place the first 7 ingredients in the order suggested by the manufacturer. Select dough setting (check the dough after 5 minutes of mixing; add 1 to 2 Tbsp. of water or flour if needed).

2. When the cycle is completed, turn dough onto a floured surface. Divide in half. Shape each portion into a ball; flatten slightly. Place in 2 greased 9-in. round baking pans. Cover and let rise until doubled, about 45 minutes.

3. Preheat oven to 350°. Beat egg and water; brush over the dough. Sprinkle with Italian seasoning if desired. Bake for 20-25 minutes or until golden brown. Remove from pans to wire racks to cool.

1 piece: 87 cal., 2g fat (1g sat. fat), 22mg chol., 119mg sod., 15g carb. (3g sugars, 0 fiber), 3g pro.

CRANBERRY
SWIRL LOAF

CRANBERRY SWIRL LOAF

My mother made this bread for years, but she uses date filling. I loved her bread so much that I made my own, with cranberries for a slightly tart filling and a sweet streusel topping. Each slice shows off the enticing ruby swirl.

—Darlene Brenden, Salem, OR

PREP: 30 MIN. + RISING
BAKE: 40 MIN. + COOLING
MAKES: 1 LOAF (16 PIECES)

- ⅓ cup sugar
- 1 pkg. (¼ oz.) quick-rise yeast
- ½ tsp. salt
- 3 to 3½ cups all-purpose flour
- ½ cup water
- ½ cup 2% milk
- ⅓ cup butter, cubed

FILLING
- 1 cup chopped fresh or frozen cranberries
- ¼ cup packed brown sugar
- ¼ cup water
- 1 Tbsp. butter
- 1 Tbsp. lemon juice
- ½ cup chopped walnuts, optional

TOPPING
- 2 Tbsp. all-purpose flour
- 2 Tbsp. sugar
- 2 Tbsp. cold butter, divided

GLAZE (OPTIONAL)
- ½ cup confectioners' sugar
- 2 tsp. 2% milk

1. In a large bowl, mix sugar, yeast, salt and 1 cup flour. In a small saucepan, heat water, milk and butter to 120°-130°. Add to dry ingredients; beat on medium speed 2 minutes. Stir in enough of the remaining flour to form a soft dough.
2. Turn onto a floured surface; knead until smooth and elastic, 6-8 minutes. Place in a greased bowl, turning once to grease top. Cover and let rise in a warm place until doubled, about 1 hour.

3. Meanwhile, in a small saucepan, combine cranberries, brown sugar and water. Cook over medium heat until cranberries are soft, about 15 minutes. Remove from heat; stir in butter, lemon juice and, if desired, walnuts. Cool.
4. Punch down dough. Turn onto a lightly floured surface; roll into a 20x10-in. rectangle. Spread filling to within ½ in. of edges. Roll up jelly-roll style, starting with a long side; pinch seam to seal. Transfer to a greased 9x5-in. loaf pan, arranging in a slight zigzag fashion to fit.
5. For topping, in a small bowl, combine flour and sugar; cut in 1 Tbsp. butter until crumbly. Melt remaining butter; brush over dough. Sprinkle with crumb mixture. Cover with a towel; let rise in a warm place until doubled, about 40 minutes.
6. Bake at 350°until crust is golden brown and bread is cooked through, 40-45 minutes. Carefully remove bread from pan to a wire rack to cool. If desired, combine glaze ingredients; drizzle over bread.

1 piece: 210 cal., 9g fat (4g sat. fat), 17mg chol.,140mg sod., 30g carb. (10g sugars, 1g fiber), 4g pro.
Confectioners' Sugar Icing: Mix ¾ cup confectioners' sugar and 1 Tbsp. milk. Drizzle over cooled bread.
Cranberry-Caramel Icing: Combine 1½ cups cranberry juice and a cinnamon stick in a small saucepan; bring to a boil. Cook until liquid is reduced to ½ cup. Reduce heat; remove cinnamon stick. Whisk in 1 cup Kraft caramel bits, ½ cup at a time, until melted. Remove from heat and stir in 1 Tbsp. heavy whipping cream; cool. Drizzle over cooled bread.

SOURDOUGH

BAKING 101

SOURDOUGH FRENCH BREAD

These loaves rival any found in stores and can be made with relative ease.
—Delila George, Junction City, OR

PREP: 15 MIN. + RISING • **BAKE:** 20 MIN.
MAKES: 2 LOAVES (10 PIECES EACH)

- 1   pkg. (¼ oz.) active dry yeast
- 1¾ cups warm water (105° to 115°)
- ¼   cup Sourdough Starter (p. 67)
- 2   Tbsp. canola oil
- 2   Tbsp. sugar
- 2   tsp. salt
- 4¼ cups all-purpose flour

CORNSTARCH WASH
- ½   cup water
- 1½ tsp. cornstarch

1. In a large mixing bowl, dissolve yeast in warm water. Add the Sourdough Starter, oil, sugar, salt and 3 cups flour. Beat until smooth. Stir in enough additional flour to form a soft dough.
2. Turn onto a floured surface; knead gently 20-30 times (dough will be slightly sticky). Place in a greased bowl, turning once to grease top. Cover and let rise in a warm place until doubled, 1-1½ hours.
3. Punch dough down. Turn onto a lightly floured surface; divide in half. Roll each into a 12x8-in. rectangle. Roll up, jelly-roll style, starting with a long side; pinch ends to seal. Place seam side down on 2 greased baking sheets; tuck ends under. Cover and let rise until doubled, about 30 minutes.
4. Preheat oven to 400°. With a sharp knife, make 4 shallow diagonal slashes across top of each loaf. In a small saucepan, combine the water and cornstarch. Cook and stir over medium heat until thickened. Brush some over loaves.
5. Bake for 15 minutes. Brush loaves with remaining cornstarch wash. Bake until lightly browned, 5-10 minutes. Remove from pans to wire racks to cool.
1 piece: 116 cal., 2g fat (0 sat. fat), 0 chol., 237mg sod., 22g carb. (1g sugars, 1g fiber), 3g pro.

HONEY WHEAT SOURDOUGH BREAD

Honey adds a slightly sweet taste to this bread, which nicely complements the tang of the sourdough.
—Evelyn Newlands, Sun Lakes, AZ

PREP: 20 MIN. + RISING
BAKE: 25 MIN. + COOLING
MAKES: 2 LOAVES (12 PIECES EACH)

- 1   Tbsp. active dry yeast
- 1   cup warm water (105° to 115°)
- 3   Tbsp. butter, softened
- 2   Tbsp. honey
- 2   Tbsp. molasses
- 2   cups Sourdough Starter (p. 67)
- 3   Tbsp. toasted wheat germ
- 1   Tbsp. sugar
- 1   tsp. baking soda
- 1   tsp. salt
- 1   cup whole wheat flour
- 3¼ to 3¾ cups all-purpose flour
      Canola oil

1. In a large bowl, dissolve yeast in warm water. Add the butter, honey, molasses, Sourdough Starter, wheat germ, sugar, baking soda, salt, whole wheat flour and 2 cups all-purpose flour. Beat until smooth. Stir in enough remaining all-purpose flour to form a soft dough.
2. Turn dough onto a floured surface; knead until smooth and elastic, 6-8 minutes. Place in a greased bowl, turning once to grease top. Cover and let rise in a warm place until doubled, about 1 hour.
3. Punch dough down. Turn onto a lightly floured surface; divide in half. Shape into loaves. Place in 2 greased 8x4-in. loaf pans. Cover and let rise until doubled, about 1 hour.
4. Brush with oil. Bake at 375° until browned, 25-30 minutes. Remove from pans to wire racks to cool.
1 piece: 109 cal., 2g fat (1g sat. fat), 4mg chol., 164mg sod., 20g carb. (3g sugars, 1g fiber), 3g pro.

DID YOU KNOW?

Sourdough starter, properly nourished and kept in the fridge, can live indefinitely. Always bring your starter to room temperature before using in your recipe.

SOURDOUGH
STARTER

To nourish starter: Remove half of the starter. Stir in equal parts of flour and warm water; cover loosely and let stand in a warm place 1-2 days or until light and bubbly. Stir; cover tightly and refrigerate.
1 Tbsp.: 19 cal., 0 fat (0 sat. fat), 0 chol., 0 sod., 4g carb. (0 sugars, 0 fiber), 1g pro.

SOURDOUGH STARTER

I received this recipe and some starter from a friend years ago. I've used it many times to make my Sourdough French Bread (p. 66).
—Delila George, Junction City, OR

PREP: 10 MIN. + STANDING
MAKES: ABOUT 3 CUPS

- 2   cups all-purpose flour
- 1   pkg. (¼ oz.) active dry yeast
- 2   cups warm water (105° to 115°)

1. In a covered 4-qt. glass or ceramic container, mix flour and yeast. Gradually stir in warm water until smooth. Cover loosely with a kitchen towel; let stand in a warm place 2-4 days or until mixture is bubbly and sour smelling and a clear liquid has formed on top. (Starter may darken, but if it turns another color or develops an offensive odor or mold, discard it and start over.)
2. Cover tightly and refrigerate until ready to use. Use and replenish starter, or nourish it, once every 1-2 weeks.
To use and replenish starter: Stir to blend in any liquid on top. Remove amount of starter needed; always bring starter to room temperature before using. For each ½ cup starter removed, add ½ cup flour and ½ cup warm water to the remaining starter and stir until smooth. Cover loosely and let stand in a warm place 1-2 days or until light and bubbly. Stir; cover tightly and refrigerate.

COUNTRY CRUST
SOURDOUGH BREAD

BAKING
101

3. Punch dough down. Turn onto a lightly floured surface; divide in half. Shape into loaves. Place in 2 greased 8x4-in. loaf pans. Cover and let rise until doubled, about 45 minutes.

4. Bake at 375° for 30-35 minutes or until golden brown. Remove from pans to wire racks to cool. Brush with butter.

1 piece: 113 cal., 2g fat (0 sat. fat), 12mg chol., 79mg sod., 20g carb. (2g sugars, 1g fiber), 3g pro.

GOLDEN SOURDOUGH BISCUITS

These soft sourdough biscuits are best enjoyed straight from the oven.
—Stephanie Church, Delaware, OH

TAKES: 30 MIN. • **MAKES:** 1 DOZEN

- 2 cups all-purpose flour
- 1 tsp. baking powder
- 1 tsp. salt
- ½ tsp. baking soda
- ½ cup cold butter
- 1 cup Sourdough Starter (p. 67)
- ½ cup buttermilk
   Additional butter, melted

1. In a large bowl, combine the flour, baking powder, salt and baking soda; cut in butter until mixture resembles coarse crumbs. Combine Sourdough Starter and buttermilk; stir into the crumb mixture with a fork until dough forms a ball. Preheat oven to 425°.

2. Turn dough onto a well-floured surface; knead 10-12 times. Roll to ½-in. thickness. Cut with a floured 2½-in. biscuit cutter. Place 2 in. apart on a greased baking sheet.

3. Bake until golden brown, 12-15 minutes. Brush with melted butter. Remove biscuits from pan to a wire rack to cool.

1 biscuit: 148 cal., 8g fat (5g sat. fat), 21mg chol., 370mg sod., 17g carb. (1g sugars, 1g fiber), 3g pro.

COUNTRY CRUST SOURDOUGH BREAD

For many years, I've been making 45 loaves of this bread for an annual Christmas bazaar, where we feed bread and soup to over 300 folks.
—Beverley Whaley, Camano Island, WA

PREP: 20 MIN. + RISING • **BAKE:** 30 MIN.
MAKES: 2 LOAVES (16 PIECES EACH)

- 2 pkg. (¼ oz. each) active dry yeast
- 1¼ cups warm water (105° to 115°)
- 1 cup Sourdough Starter (p. 67)
- 2 large eggs. room temperature
- ¼ cup sugar
- ¼ cup vegetable oil
- 1 tsp. salt
- 6 to 6½ cups all-purpose flour
   Melted butter

1. In a large bowl, dissolve yeast in warm water. Add the Sourdough Starter, eggs, sugar, oil, salt and 3 cups flour. Beat until smooth. Stir in enough remaining flour to form a soft dough.

2. Turn onto a floured surface; knead until smooth and elastic, 6-8 minutes. Place in a greased bowl, turning once to grease top. Cover and let rise in a warm place until doubled, about 1 hour.

SAGE & GRUYERE SOURDOUGH BREAD

A sourdough starter gives loaves extra flavor and helps the rising process. This bread with sage and Gruyere cheese comes out so well that I'm thrilled to share it.
—Debra Kramer, Boca Raton, FL

PREP: 35 MIN. + RISING • **BAKE:** 25 MIN.
MAKES: 1 LOAF (16 PIECES)

1⅛ tsp. active dry yeast
⅓ cup warm water (105° to 115°)
½ cup Sourdough Starter (p. 67)
½ cup canned pumpkin
½ cup shredded Gruyere cheese, divided
4 tsp. butter, softened
1 Tbsp. sugar
1 Tbsp. minced fresh sage
1 tsp. salt
2¼ to 2¾ cups all-purpose flour
1 large egg, lightly beaten

1. In a small bowl, dissolve yeast in warm water. In a large bowl, combine Sourdough Starter, pumpkin, ¼ cup cheese, butter, sugar, sage, salt, the yeast mixture and 1 cup flour; beat on medium speed until smooth. Stir in enough remaining flour to form a stiff dough (dough will be slightly sticky).
2. Turn onto a floured surface; knead until smooth and elastic, 6-8 minutes. Place in a greased bowl, turning once to grease the top. Cover and let rise in a warm place until doubled, about 1 hour.
3. Punch down dough. Turn onto a lightly floured surface; shape into a round loaf. Place on a greased baking sheet. Cover; let rise in a warm place until doubled, about 30 minutes. Preheat oven to 375°.
4. Brush egg over loaf; sprinkle with remaining ¼ cup cheese. Bake until golden brown, 25-30 minutes. Remove from pan to a wire rack to cool.
1 piece: 98 cal., 3g fat (1g sat. fat), 18mg chol., 186mg sod., 15g carb. (1g sugars, 1g fiber), 3g pro.

TEST KITCHEN TIP

Because sourdough starter has a strong smell and can look separated or discolored, it can be hard to tell if it's gone bad. Look for signs of fuzzy mold or for orange or pink streaks—those indicate that the starter should be discarded. If the starter is merely dark and separated, it may just be hungry—try nourishing it (p. 67) and check back to see if it has recovered.

PIZZA CRUST & MORE

PERFECT PIZZA CRUST

I have spent years trying different recipes and techniques, looking for the perfect pizza crust recipe—and this is it! I'm amazed I finally found a crust recipe my family prefers over the pizza parlor's!
—Lesli Dustin, Nibley, UT

PREP: 20 MIN. + RISING • **BAKE:** 20 MIN.
MAKES: 8 SERVINGS

- 1 Tbsp. active dry yeast
- 1½ cups warm water (105° to 115°)
- 2 Tbsp. sugar
- ½ tsp. salt
- 2 cups bread flour
- 1½ cups whole wheat flour
  Cornmeal
  Pizza toppings of your choice

1. In a large bowl, dissolve yeast in warm water. Add sugar, salt, 1 cup bread flour and the whole wheat flour. Beat until smooth. Stir in enough of the remaining bread flour to form a soft dough (dough will be sticky).
2. Turn onto a floured surface; knead until smooth and elastic, 6-8 minutes. Place in a greased bowl, turning once to grease the top. Cover and let rise in a warm place until doubled, about 1 hour.
3. Preheat oven to 425°. Punch dough down; roll into a 15-in. circle. Grease a 14-in. pizza pan and sprinkle with cornmeal. Transfer dough to the prepared pan; build up edges slightly. Add toppings of your choice.
4. Bake until the crust is golden brown and toppings are lightly browned and heated through, 20-25 minutes.

1 piece: 193 cal., 0 fat (0 sat. fat), 0 chol., 149mg sod., 42g carb. (3g sugars, 4g fiber), 8g pro.

SOFT ONION BREADSTICKS

These breadsticks bake up golden and chewy. They make the perfect complement to your favorite pasta dish.
—Maryellen Hays, Wolcottville, IN

PREP: 30 MIN. + RISING • **BAKE:** 20 MIN.
MAKES: 2 DOZEN

- ¾ cup chopped onion
- 1 Tbsp. canola oil
- 1 pkg. (¼ oz.) active dry yeast
- ½ cup warm water (105° to 115°)
- ½ cup warm 2% milk (105° to 115°)
- ¼ cup butter, softened
- 2 large eggs, room temperature, divided use
- 1 Tbsp. sugar
- 1½ tsp. salt
- 3½ to 4 cups all-purpose flour
- 2 Tbsp. cold water
- 2 Tbsp. sesame seeds
- 1 Tbsp. poppy seeds

1. In a small skillet, saute onion in oil until tender; cool. In a large bowl, dissolve yeast in warm water. Add the warm milk, butter, 1 egg, sugar, salt and 1 cup flour. Beat on medium speed for 2 minutes. Stir in onion and enough remaining flour to form a soft dough.
2. Turn onto a floured surface; knead until smooth and elastic, 6-8 minutes. Place in a greased bowl, turning once to grease top. Cover and let rise in a warm place until doubled, about 1 hour.
3. Punch dough down. Let stand for 10 minutes. Turn onto a lightly floured surface; divide into 32 pieces. Shape each piece into an 8-in. rope. Place 2 in. apart on greased baking sheets. Cover and let rise for 15 minutes. Preheat oven to 350°.
4. Beat cold water and remaining egg; brush over breadsticks. Sprinkle half with sesame seeds and half with poppy seeds. Bake 16-22 minutes or until golden brown. Remove to wire racks.

1 breadstick: 82 cal., 3g fat (1g sat. fat), 16mg chol., 129mg sod., 12g carb. (1g sugars, 1g fiber), 2g pro.

Garlic Parmesan Breadsticks: Prepare breadsticks as directed. Omit brushing with the egg mixture and sprinkling with sesame and poppy seeds. Brush with ¼ cup melted butter and sprinkle with garlic salt and grated Parmesan cheese. Bake as directed.

HERBED ONION BAGELS

I created my delightful bagels by combining elements from several recipes. I enjoy them spread with plain cream cheese or with onion and chive cream cheese.

—Pam Kaiser, Mansfield, MO

PREP: 30 MIN. + CHILLING • **BAKE:** 15 MIN.
MAKES: 9 BAGELS

- ½ cup finely chopped sweet onion
- 2 Tbsp. butter
- ¾ cup warm water (70° to 80°)
- ¼ cup sour cream
- 3 Tbsp. sugar, divided
- 3½ tsp. salt, divided
- 1½ tsp. minced chives
- 1½ tsp. dried basil
- 1½ tsp. dried parsley flakes
- ¾ tsp. dried oregano
- ¾ tsp. dill weed
- ¾ tsp. dried minced garlic
- 3 cups bread flour
- 1 pkg. (¼ oz.) active dry yeast
- 3 qt. water
- 2 Tbsp. yellow cornmeal

1. In a large skillet, saute onion in butter until tender. In bread machine pan, place the water, sour cream, onion mixture, 2 Tbsp. sugar, 1½ tsp. salt, herbs, garlic, flour and yeast in order suggested by manufacturer. Select dough setting (check the dough after 5 minutes of mixing; add 1-2 Tbsp. of water or flour if needed).
2. When cycle is completed, turn the dough onto a lightly floured surface. Shape into 9 balls. Push thumb through centers to form a 1½-in. hole. Place on parchment-lined baking sheets. Cover and let rest for 30 minutes, then refrigerate overnight.
3. Let stand at room temperature for 30 minutes; flatten bagels slightly. In a non-aluminum Dutch oven, bring water to a boil with remaining sugar and salt. Drop bagels, 1 at a time, into boiling water. Cook for 30 seconds; turn and cook 30 seconds longer. Remove with a slotted spoon; drain well on paper towels.
4. Sprinkle 2 greased baking sheets with cornmeal; place bagels 2 in. apart on prepared pans. Bake at 425° until golden brown, 12-15 minutes. Remove to wire racks to cool.

1 bagel: 195 cal., 4g fat (2g sat. fat), 11mg chol., 415mg sod., 35g carb. (3g sugars, 2g fiber), 6g pro. **Diabetic exchanges:** 2 starch, ½ fat.

CINNAMON BAGELS WITH CRUNCHY TOPPING

Once you get the hang of it, you won't believe how simple it is to make these bakery-quality bagels right in your kitchen.

—Kristen Streepey, Geneva, IL

PREP: 40 MIN. + RISING
BAKE: 15 MIN. + COOLING
MAKES: 1 DOZEN

- 2 tsp. active dry yeast
- 1½ cups warm water (105° to 115°)
- 4 Tbsp. brown sugar, divided
- 3 tsp. ground cinnamon
- 1½ tsp. salt
- 2¾ to 3¼ cups all-purpose flour
- TOPPING
- ¼ cup sugar
- ¼ cup packed brown sugar
- 3 tsp. ground cinnamon

1. In a large bowl, dissolve yeast in warm water. Add 3 Tbsp. brown sugar, cinnamon and salt; mix well. Stir in enough flour to form a soft dough.
2. Turn dough onto a lightly floured surface; knead until smooth and elastic, 6-8 minutes. Place in a bowl coated with cooking spray, turning once to coat the top. Cover and let rise in a warm place until doubled, about 1 hour.
3. Punch dough down. Shape into 12 balls. Push thumb through each center to form a 1½-in. hole. Stretch and shape dough to form an even ring. Place on a floured surface. Cover and let rest for 10 minutes.
4. Fill a Dutch oven two-thirds full with water and remaining brown sugar; bring to a boil. Drop bagels, 2 at a time, into boiling water. Cook for 45 seconds; turn and cook for another 45 seconds. Remove with a slotted spoon; drain well on paper towels.
5. In a small bowl, mix the topping ingredients; sprinkle over bagels. Place 2 in. apart on baking sheets coated with cooking spray. Bake at 400° until golden brown, 15-20 minutes. Remove to wire racks to cool.

1 bagel: 164 cal., 0 fat (0 sat. fat), 0 chol., 300mg sod., 37g carb. (14g sugars, 2g fiber), 4g pro.

BOIL + BAKE = BAGELS

The key to dense, chewy bagels is putting them in hot water before baking—and you can control the texture of your bagel with this important step.

STEP 1
To shape bagels, use your thumb to make a 1½-in. hole in the center of each ball of dough, then stretch the dough into an even ring.

STEP 2
The first step in cooking bagels is to boil them; this sets the crust before the bagel goes in the oven, and prevents the dough from rising.

STEP 3
Boil the bagels 30-60 seconds on each side before removing them with a slotted spoon. You can adjust this time to suit your tastes. A shorter boil gives a thinner crust that allows the bagels to rise a bit; a longer boil gives a thicker, chewier crust and results in a denser bagel.

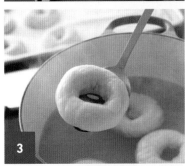

STEP 4
Sprinkle your toppings on the bagels before they're completely dry. Or, brush the bagels with a bit of beaten egg white to help the toppings stick. If you find your toppings starting to get too dark before the bagels are done, brush them with a little beaten egg white in the last minute or two of baking time.

GLUTEN-FREE PIZZA CRUST

You don't necessarily need to visit a health food store to find the flours for this recipe. I am able to buy both at two local grocery stores here in my small town in Wyoming.
—Sylvia Girmus, Torrington, WY

PREP: 20 MIN. + STANDING • **BAKE:** 20 MIN.
MAKES: 6 SERVINGS

- 1 Tbsp. active dry yeast
- ⅔ cup warm water (105° to 115°)
- ½ cup tapioca flour
- 2 Tbsp. nonfat dry milk powder
- 2 tsp. xanthan gum
- 1 tsp. unflavored gelatin
- 1 tsp. Italian seasoning
- 1 tsp. cider vinegar
- 1 tsp. olive oil
- ½ tsp. salt
- ½ tsp. sugar
- 1 to 1⅓ cups brown rice flour
  Pizza toppings of your choice

1. In a small bowl, dissolve yeast in warm water. Add the tapioca flour, milk powder, xanthan gum, gelatin, Italian seasoning, vinegar, oil, salt, sugar and ⅔ cup brown rice flour. Beat until smooth. Stir in enough remaining brown rice flour to form a soft dough (dough will be sticky).

2. On a floured surface, roll dough into a 13-in. circle. Transfer to a 12-in. pizza pan coated with cooking spray; build up edges slightly. Cover and let rest for 10 minutes.

3. Bake at 425° for 10-12 minutes or until golden brown. Add toppings of your choice. Bake 10-15 minutes longer or until the crust is golden brown and the toppings are lightly browned and heated through.

1 piece: 142 cal., 2g fat (0 sat. fat), 1mg chol., 223mg sod., 30g carb. (2g sugars, 3g fiber), 4g pro. **Diabetic exchanges:** 2 starch.

SOFT BEER PRETZELS

I'm always looking for new ways to combine fun flavors, and what goes together better than beer and pretzels? Not much that I can think of. That's why I put them together into one delicious recipe.

—Alyssa Wilhite, Whitehouse, TX

PREP: 1 HOUR + RISING • **BAKE:** 10 MIN.
MAKES: 8 PRETZELS

- 1 bottle (12 oz.) amber beer or nonalcoholic beer
- 1 pkg. (¼ oz.) active dry yeast
- 2 Tbsp. unsalted butter, melted
- 2 Tbsp. sugar
- 1½ tsp. salt
- 4 to 4½ cups all-purpose flour
- 10 cups water
- ⅔ cup baking soda

TOPPING

- 1 large egg yolk
- 1 Tbsp. water
  Coarse salt, optional

1. In a small saucepan, heat beer to 105°-115°; remove from heat. Stir in yeast until dissolved. In a large bowl, combine butter, sugar, 1½ tsp. salt, yeast mixture and 3 cups flour; beat on medium speed until smooth. Stir in enough remaining flour to form a soft dough (dough will be sticky).
2. Turn onto a floured surface; knead until smooth and elastic, 6-8 minutes. Place in a greased bowl, turning once to grease the top. Cover and let rise in a warm place until doubled, about 1 hour.
3. Preheat oven to 425°. Punch dough down. Turn onto a lightly floured surface; divide and shape into 8 balls. Roll each into a 24-in. rope. Curve ends of each rope to form a circle; twist ends once and lay over opposite side of circle, pinching ends to seal.
4. In a Dutch oven, bring water and baking soda to a boil. Drop pretzels, 2 at a time, into boiling water. Cook 30 seconds. Remove with a slotted spoon; drain well on paper towels.
5. Place 2 in. apart on greased baking sheets. In a small bowl, whisk egg yolk and water; brush over pretzels. Sprinkle with coarse salt if desired. Bake until golden brown. 10-12 minutes. Remove from pans to a wire rack to cool.

Freeze option: Freeze cooled pretzels in freezer containers. To use, thaw at room temperature or microwave each pretzel on high until heated through, 20-30 seconds.

1 pretzel: 288 cal., 4g fat (2g sat. fat), 16mg chol., 604mg sod., 53g carb. (6g sugars, 2g fiber), 7g pro.

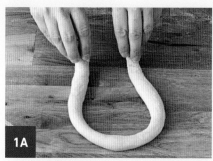

CLASSIC TWIST OR BITES—YOU CHOOSE!

TRADITIONAL PRETZELS

Divide and shape dough into 8 balls; roll each ball into a 24-in. rope. Curve ends of rope to form a circle (**1A**). Twist ends once and lay over opposite side of circle, pinching ends to seal (**1B**).

Bake at 425° until golden brown, 10-12 minutes.

PRETZEL BITES

For pretzel bites, divide and shape the dough into 8 balls; roll each ball into a 12-in. rope. Use a bench scraper or a sharp knife to cut each rope into 1-in. pieces (**2**). Boil and top as directed in the recipe.

Bake at 400° until golden brown, 6-8 minutes.

SOUTHWEST PRETZELS

These fun pretzels with mild southwest spices are the perfect snack for watching football games. And they score just as high with kids as they do with the adults!
—Cathy Tang, Redmond, WA

PREP: 30 MIN. + STANDING • **BAKE:** 25 MIN.
MAKES: 16 PRETZELS

4	cups all-purpose flour
1	Tbsp. sugar
1	pkg. (¼ oz.) quick-rise yeast
1½	tsp. salt
1	tsp. dried minced onion
½	tsp. chili powder
¼	tsp. ground cumin
¼	tsp. cayenne pepper
1½	cups warm water (105° to 115°)
1	large egg, lightly beaten
	Coarse salt
	Salsa con queso dip

1. In a large bowl, combine 2 cups flour, sugar, yeast, salt, minced onion and spices. Add water. Beat just until moistened. Stir in enough remaining flour to form a soft dough.
2. Turn dough onto a floured surface; knead until smooth and elastic, 4-6 minutes. Cover and let rest 10 minutes. Divide dough into 16 equal portions; roll each into a 15-in. rope. Cover and let rest 10 minutes longer. Preheat oven to 350°.
3. Twist into pretzel shapes. Place on greased baking sheets; brush with egg. Bake for 15 minutes. Brush again with egg; sprinkle with coarse salt. Bake until golden brown, 10-13 minutes longer. Remove to wire racks. Serve pretzels warm with dip.
1 pretzel: 120 cal., 0 fat (0 sat. fat), 4mg chol., 224mg sod., 25g carb. (1g sugars, 1g fiber), 4g pro. **Diabetic exchanges:** 1½ starch.

SOFT GIANT PRETZELS

SOFT GIANT PRETZELS

My husband, friends and family love these soft, chewy pretzels. Let your machine mix the dough; then all you have to do is shape and bake these fun snacks.
—Sherry Peterson, Fort Collins, CO

PREP: 20 MIN. + RISING • **BAKE:** 10 MIN.
MAKES: 8 PRETZELS

1	cup plus 2 Tbsp. water (70° to 80°), divided
3	cups all-purpose flour
3	Tbsp. brown sugar
1½	tsp. active dry yeast
2	qt. water
½	cup baking soda
	Coarse salt

1. In a bread machine pan, place 1 cup water and the next 3 ingredients in the order suggested by manufacturer.
Select dough setting. Check dough after 5 minutes of mixing; add 1-2 Tbsp. water or flour if needed.
2. When cycle is completed, turn dough onto a lightly floured surface. Divide dough into 8 balls. Roll each into a 20-in. rope; form into pretzel shape.
3. Preheat oven to 425°. In a large saucepan, bring 2 qt. water and the baking soda to a boil. Drop pretzels into boiling water, 2 at a time; boil for 10-15 seconds. Remove with a slotted spoon; drain on paper towels.
4. Place pretzels on greased baking sheets. Bake until golden brown, 8-10 minutes. Spritz or lightly brush with remaining 2 Tbsp. water. Sprinkle warm pretzels with salt.
1 pretzel: 193 cal., 1g fat (0 sat. fat), 0 chol., 380mg sod., 41g carb. (5g sugars, 1g fiber), 5g pro.

QUICK BREADS

Banana bread and cornbread, biscuits and scones, popovers, soda bread and more! Quick breads are just what their name says—quick, delicious and always welcome!

. . . .

QUICK BREADS

Quick breads are a great place to start baking, as they're fast and easy to make. A quick bread is one that rises with baking soda or baking powder, rather than living yeast (some quick breads also may use eggs to leaven them). Quick breads can be either sweet or savory, and this large group includes loaves, muffins, biscuits, scones, soda bread, popovers and some kinds of coffee cakes (for coffee cakes, see chapter 9).

The beauty of quick breads is that they have a shorter prep time than yeast breads—they're ready to pop in the oven and start baking right away rather than needing time to rise. In fact, most quick breads suffer in quality if not baked immediately.

LOAVES & MUFFINS

Quick bread loaves are loved for their simplicity. They're a great option for morning coffee breaks, afternoon snacks or late-night nibbles. Standard loaves are great housewarming presents, while mini loaves make great gifts at the holidays, bagged up in colorful cellophane and given to teachers, neighbors and co-workers.

Loaf pans come in various sizes, from large to miniature. The two most popular loaf pan sizes are 9x5 and 8½x4½ inches; both are typically 2½ inches tall. The difference seems small, but it equals a 15% difference in capacity. That can really affect outcome—especially in quick breads and those that use less than 3 cups of flour—so pay attention to your recipe.

If the recipe doesn't specify, use the pans you have—just be sure not to fill them more than two-thirds full, as quick breads rise during baking. If you have too much batter for your pans, use the extra to make a few muffins.

PAN SIZE	BATTER VOLUME
5¾ to 3¼ inches	2 cups
8 x 4 inches	4 cups
8½ x 4½ inches	6 cups
9 x 5 inches	8 cups

Most quick bread recipes can also be made as muffins; one 9x5-in. loaf is roughly equal to 12 muffins. Use the temperature and bake time for a favorite muffin recipe as a starting point, then start testing for doneness. (Muffins generally bake at a higher temperature than loaves.) Muffin tins come in mini, standard and jumbo sizes. Standard muffin tins hold ¼ to ⅓ cup batter in each cup—fill each cup two-thirds to three-fourths full.

To uniformly fill muffin cups, use an ice cream scoop or a ¼ cup measuring cup. Fill any unused cups with water; this will help the muffins bake more evenly.

Quick bread batter is usually sweet, and the sugar content makes it prone to sticking, so either use a nonstick pan or grease the pan. If you're making muffins, paper tin liners work well.

When baking loaves or muffins, set your timer for the minimum time stated in the recipe, and check for doneness with a toothpick inserted in the center. If it comes out clean, the bread is done; if it comes out with moist crumbs or wet batter clinging to it, bake longer. If your quick bread or muffins have a filling, be sure you're checking the batter portion and not the filling.

When finished baking, let the bread or muffins cool in their pans for 5-10 minutes. Then, let loaves cool on a wire rack before cutting—many quick breads will crumble if cut when they're still warm. Muffins, on the other hand, are best served warm.

BISCUITS & SCONES

Flaky, buttery, crumbly and tender, these breads owe their delicate crumb to the technique of cutting fat into the flour mixture. Use cold fat to get the best texture, one where the flour mixture resembles coarse crumbs. For fat, you can use butter, margarine (with at least 80% oil), shortening or lard. Lard produces an even more tender and flaky biscuit than butter; replace the butter called for in the recipe with an equal amount of lard.

Biscuits are usually formed in one of two ways: rolled out and cut, or dropped on a baking sheet.

Scones are similar to biscuits but are usually sweeter. The secret of tender, flaky scones is to keep the butter in large flakes rather than small pieces. Scones are generally patted into a circle and then cut into wedges. Separate the wedges on the baking sheet to get a crisper crust; leave them cut but unseparated if you want a softer crust.

To test for doneness, check that biscuits and scones are golden brown on both top and bottom (the sides will always be a little light). Remove to wire racks right away; they may otherwise burn on the pan. Biscuits are best served warm and scones are best the day they are made.

Store leftovers in an airtight container at room temperature. Store foods made with perishable ingredients, such as cream cheese, in the refrigerator, or freeze for up to 3 months.

CORNBREAD

There's no better partner for a bowl of chili than a big piece of cornbread—perhaps smeared with butter and drizzled with honey— but that's not its only purpose. Cornbreads can be baked in a preheated cast-iron skillet, in loaf pans, in a round or rectangular baking pan or in muffin tins. Cornbread is best eaten the day it is made; if you're planning for leftovers, muffins stay moist longer than a loaf will and also freeze well. Cornbread's rustic appeal makes it a great option for using up rendered bacon grease—use it to grease your pan (especially if you're cooking in cast iron) or as the fat in the bread itself.

White or Yellow?

Cornmeal gets its color from the corn that was ground to make it; there's little difference between the flavor of white and yellow cornmeal. Some white cornmeals come in a finer grain than yellow, giving the end product a finer texture. Preferences for white or yellow tend to vary according to geographical region, and the two can be used interchangeably in most recipes.

SODA BREAD

As may be apparent from the name, soda bread is leavened by baking soda. It's a dense but tender quick bread that is usually savory and is a great partner for soups and stews.
The batter for soda bread is thick and is usually baked free-form on a baking sheet.

POPOVERS

Unlike muffins and scones, popovers use steam rather than baking powder or baking soda as a leavener. The high proportion of liquid in the batter creates steam as the popovers bake; the steam causes the batter to rise and "pop over" the sides of the pan. The end result is light, airy puffs with a crispy crust and hollow center. Popover pans are generally deeper than muffin tins, with more widely spaced cups, but muffin tins will do well as a substitute. To use a muffin tin for popovers, leave every other cup empty—skipping cups will give the batter the necessary space to expand. Fill cups two-thirds full.

QUICK TIPS FOR SUCCESSFUL QUICK BREADS

- Use cold fat.

- Use fats like butter, stick margarine with at least 80% oil, shortening or lard. Unless a recipe specifically calls for it, do not use whipped, tub, soft, liquid or reduced-fat butter or margarine.

- Stir dry ingredients (flour, leaveners, salt and any spices) together with a fork or a whisk to evenly distribute the baking powder or soda.

- Mix liquid and dry ingredients together just until moistened. A few lumps in the batter are fine. Overmixed or (with biscuits and scones) over-kneaded dough leads to a tough texture.

- When reworking biscuit trimmings, handle dough as little as possible and use as little additional flour as needed.

- A pan's material and finish can affect cook time and browning. Aluminum pans with a dull finish give the best results. Dark finishes can cause overbrowning; shiny finishes or air-cushioned pans may result in lightly colored baked goods or longer bake times.

- Grease pans only if the recipe dictates.

- Fill pans two-thirds full; batters will rise during baking. Fill muffin tins two-thirds to three-fourths full, depending on how large you like your muffin top.

- Bake shortly after combining the ingredients.

TROUBLESHOOTING

LOAF, MUFFINS, BISCUITS OR SCONES:
Tough and dense: Batter was overmixed. Mix just until combined.

LOAF OR MUFFINS:
Tunnels: Batter was overmixed.

Thick brown crust: Batter had too much sugar.

Soggy: Batter had too much liquid or fat.

Bitter aftertaste: Batter had too much leavener.

Nuts, fruit or chocolate chips sink to bottom: Either the batter was too thin to hold the solid ingredients, or—in the case of fruit—the add-ins were wet. Chop nuts,

chocolate or fruit into smaller pieces. Make sure fruit pieces are well dried and toss them in a little flour before adding to the batter.

LOAF:
Center has sunk: Too little or too much leavening, the bread was underbaked, or the batter stood too long before baking.

Crumbles while being cut: Bread was still warm; cool completely before slicing.

BISCUITS:
Baked unevenly: Batter was not patted or rolled out evenly. Next time, use a ruler to double-check thickness.

QUICK BREADS

AMISH ONION CAKE

This rich, moist bread with an onion-poppy seed topping is a wonderful break from your everyday bread routine. You can serve it with any meat, and it's especially nice paired with soup or salad. I've made it many times and have often been asked to share the recipe.

—Mitzi Sentiff, Annapolis, MD

PREP: 25 MIN. • **BAKE:** 35 MIN.
MAKES: 12 SERVINGS

3   to 4 medium onions, chopped
2   cups cold butter, divided
1   Tbsp. poppy seeds
1½ tsp. salt
1½ tsp. paprika
1   tsp. coarsely ground pepper
4   cups all-purpose flour
½   cup cornstarch
1   Tbsp. baking powder
1   Tbsp. sugar
1   Tbsp. brown sugar
5   large eggs, room temperature
¾   cup 2% milk
¾   cup sour cream

1. Preheat oven to 350°. In a large skillet, cook onions in ½ cup butter over low heat for 10 minutes. Stir in the poppy seeds, salt, paprika and pepper; cook until onions are golden brown, stirring occasionally. Remove from heat; set aside.
2. In a large bowl, combine the flour, cornstarch, baking powder and sugars. Cut in 1¼ cups butter until mixture resembles coarse crumbs.
3. Melt the remaining ¼ cup butter. In a small bowl, whisk the eggs, milk, sour cream and melted butter. Make a well in dry ingredients; stir in the egg mixture just until moistened.
4. Spread into a greased 10-in. cast-iron skillet or springform pan. Spoon onion mixture over the batter. Place pan on a baking sheet. Bake until a toothpick inserted in the center comes out clean, 35-40 minutes. Serve warm.
1 piece: 539 cal., 36g fat (22g sat. fat), 182mg chol., 748mg sod., 44g carb. (7g sugars, 2g fiber), 9g pro.

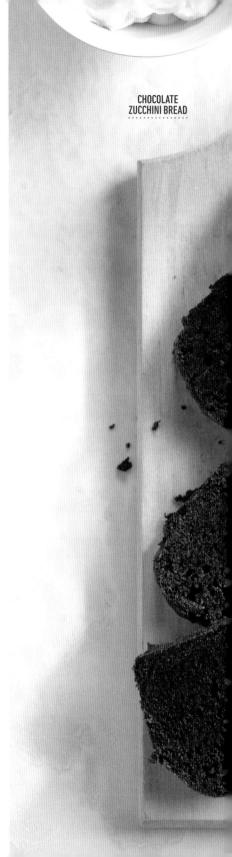

CHOCOLATE
ZUCCHINI BREAD

CHOCOLATE ZUCCHINI BREAD

I shred and freeze zucchini from my garden each summer so that I can make this bread all winter long. Our family loves this lovely chocolaty treat.
—Shari McKinney, Birney, MT

PREP: 15 MIN. • **BAKE:** 50 MIN. + COOLING
MAKES: 2 LOAVES (12 PIECES EACH)

- 2 cups sugar
- 1 cup canola oil
- 3 large eggs, room temperature
- 3 tsp. vanilla extract
- 2½ cups all-purpose flour
- ½ cup baking cocoa
- 1 tsp. salt
- 1 tsp. baking soda
- 1 tsp. ground cinnamon
- ¼ tsp. baking powder
- 2 cups shredded peeled zucchini

1. In a large bowl, beat the sugar, oil, eggs and vanilla until well blended. Combine the flour, cocoa, salt, baking soda, cinnamon and baking powder; gradually beat into sugar mixture until blended. Stir in zucchini. Transfer to 2 greased 8x4-in. loaf pans.
2. Bake at 350° for 50-55 minutes or until a toothpick inserted in the center comes out clean. Cool for 10 minutes before removing from pans to wire racks to cool completely.
1 piece: 209 cal., 10g fat (1g sat. fat), 26mg chol., 165mg sod., 28g carb. (17g sugars, 1g fiber), 3g pro.

Gluten-Free Banana Bread

Best Ever Banana Bread

Makeover Banana Nut Bread

Moist Banana Nut Bread

MORE BANANA BREAD!

Every home baker has a favorite banana bread— why not try a few to find yours?

GLUTEN-FREE BANANA BREAD

Combine 2 cups gluten-free all-purpose flour, 1 tsp. baking soda and ¼ tsp. salt. Whisk 4 eggs, 2 cups mashed bananas, 1 cup sugar, ½ cup unsweetened applesauce, ⅓ cup canola oil and 1 tsp. vanilla. Stir into dry ingredients until moistened. Pour into greased 8x4-in. pans. Sprinkle with ½ cup chopped walnuts. Bake at 350° for 45-55 minutes.

MAKEOVER BANANA NUT BREAD

Beat 2 Tbsp. butter and ¾ cup sugar until crumbly. Add 1 egg, then 1 egg white; beat after each addition. Beat on high speed until light and fluffy. Stir in 2 cups mashed bananas, ¼ cup unsweetened applesauce, ¼ cup honey and 1 tsp. vanilla. Combine 1⅓ cups all-purpose flour, ⅔ cup whole wheat flour, 1 tsp. baking soda and ½ tsp. salt; add to banana mixture just until moistened. Pour into greased 9x5-in. pan; sprinkle with ¼ cup chopped pecans. Bake at 325° for 60-65 minutes.

MOIST BANANA NUT BREAD

Combine 1 cup all-purpose flour, 1 cup whole wheat flour, 1 tsp. baking powder, ½ tsp. baking soda and ¼ tsp. salt. Beat 1 cup sugar, 1 cup mashed bananas, ¾ cup silken soft tofu, ¼ cup canola oil and 1 tsp. vanilla. Beat into dry ingredients just until moistened. Fold in ½ cup chopped walnuts. Bake in greased 8x4 pan at 350° for 50-55 minutes.

BEST EVER BANANA BREAD

Whenever I pass a display of bananas in the grocery store, I can almost smell the wonderful aroma of this bread. It really is good!

—Gert Kaiser, Kenosha, WI

PREP: 15 MIN. • **BAKE:** 1¼ HOURS + COOLING
MAKES: 1 LOAF (16 PIECES)

- 1¾ cups all-purpose flour
- 1½ cups sugar
- 1 tsp. baking soda
- ½ tsp. salt
- 2 large eggs, room temperature
- 2 medium ripe bananas, mashed (1 cup)
- ½ cup canola oil
- ¼ cup plus 1 Tbsp. buttermilk
- 1 tsp. vanilla extract
- 1 cup chopped walnuts

1. Preheat oven to 350°. In a large bowl, stir together flour, sugar, baking soda and salt. In another bowl, combine eggs, bananas, oil, buttermilk and vanilla; add to flour mixture, stirring just until combined. Fold in nuts.
2. Pour into a greased or parchment-lined 9x5-in. loaf pan. Sprinkle with additional walnuts if desired. Bake until a toothpick comes out clean, 1¼-1½ hours. Cool in pan 15 minutes before removing to a wire rack.
1 piece: 255 cal., 12g fat (1g sat. fat), 27mg chol., 166mg sod., 34g carb. (21g sugars, 1g fiber), 4g pro.

TEST KITCHEN TIP

If your recipe calls for nuts, chocolate chips or fruits (or if you're adding them to a recipe), toss them in a tablespoon or two of flour before adding them to the batter. This will prevent them from sinking to the bottom of the pan.

BAKING 101

BANANA NUT BREAD

BANANA NUT BREAD

This quick bread is a family favorite, so I always try to have ripe bananas on hand especially for this recipe. I'm sure your family will love this tasty, nutty bread as much as mine does.

—Susan Jones, La Grange Park, IL

PREP: 10 MIN. • **BAKE:** 50 MIN. + COOLING
MAKES: 1 LOAF (16 PIECES)

- ¼ cup butter, softened
- ¾ cup sugar
- 2 large eggs, room temperature
- ¾ cup mashed ripe banana (about 1 large)
- ½ cup sour cream
- 2¼ cups all-purpose flour
- 1 tsp. ground cinnamon
- ¾ tsp. baking soda
- ½ tsp. salt
- ½ cup chopped walnuts

Optional: Additional walnuts, semisweet chocolate chips or coarse sugar

1. Preheat oven to 350°. Beat butter and sugar until blended. Add eggs, 1 at a time, beating well after each addition. Stir in banana and sour cream. Whisk together flour, cinnamon, baking soda and salt. Add to butter mixture, stirring just until moistened. Fold in ½ cup walnuts.
2. Transfer batter to a greased 9x5-in. loaf pan. If desired, sprinkle with additional walnuts.
3. Bake until a toothpick inserted in center comes out clean, 50-60 minutes. Cool in pan 10 minutes before removing to a wire rack to cool.
1 piece: 244 cal., 10g fat (4g sat. fat), 52mg chol., 220mg sod., 35g carb. (15g sugars, 1g fiber), 5g pro.

CONTEST-WINNING
CHOCOLATE CHIP
PUMPKIN BREAD

BAKING 101

ENGLISH MARMALADE PECAN BREAD

My dad was Canadian, but had a very British upbringing. And, boy, did he love his marmalade! I know it's an acquired taste for some, but when I baked the jam into this nutty bread, everyone loved it— even my kids.
—Nancy Heishman, Las Vegas, NV

PREP: 20 MIN. • **BAKE:** 50 MIN. + COOLING
MAKES: 1 LOAF (16 PIECES)

- ½ cup butter, softened
- ½ cup packed brown sugar
- 2 large eggs, room temperature
- 1 jar (10 oz.) orange marmalade spreadable fruit
- 2⅔ cups all-purpose flour
- 3 tsp. baking powder
- 2 tsp. ground cinnamon
- 1 tsp. salt
- ⅓ cup orange juice
- ½ cup chopped pecans

1. Preheat oven to 350°. Grease and flour a 9x5-in. loaf pan. In a large bowl, beat the butter and brown sugar until blended. Add eggs, 1 at a time, beating well after each addition. Gradually beat in marmalade. In another bowl, whisk flour, baking powder, cinnamon and salt; add to butter mixture alternately with orange juice, beating well after each addition. Fold in pecans.
2. Transfer to prepared pan. Bake for 50-60 minutes or until a toothpick inserted in center comes out clean. Cool in pan 10 minutes before removing to a wire rack to cool.

1 piece: 226 cal., 9g fat (4g sat. fat), 39mg chol., 132mg sod., 33g carb. (15g sugars, 1g fiber), 3g pro.

CONTEST-WINNING CHOCOLATE CHIP PUMPKIN BREAD

A touch of cinnamon helps blend the flavors in this tender pumpkin chocolate chip bread. Since the recipe makes two loaves, you can send one to a bake sale and keep one at home for your family to enjoy.
—Lora Stanley, Bennington, KS

PREP: 15 MIN. • **BAKE:** 1 HOUR + COOLING
MAKES: 2 LOAVES (16 PIECES EACH)

- 3 cups all-purpose flour
- 2 tsp. ground cinnamon
- 1 tsp. salt
- 1 tsp. baking soda
- 4 large eggs, room temperature
- 2 cups sugar
- 2 cups canned pumpkin
- 1½ cups canola oil
- 1½ cups semisweet chocolate chips

1. Preheat oven to 350°. In a large bowl, combine the flour, cinnamon, salt and baking soda. In another bowl, beat the eggs, sugar, pumpkin and oil. Stir into the dry ingredients just until moistened. Fold in chocolate chips.
2. Pour batter into 2 greased 8x4-in. loaf pans. Bake for 60-70 minutes or until a toothpick inserted in the center comes out clean. Cool for 10 minutes before removing from pans to wire racks.
1 piece: 234 cal., 13g fat (3g sat. fat), 27mg chol., 123mg sod., 28g carb. (17g sugars, 1g fiber), 3g pro.

CELERY-ONION POPOVERS

I found this handwritten recipe in a cookbook I received from my mom. With onion and celery, these pleasing popovers taste a little like stuffing.
—Barbara Carlucci, Orange Park, FL

PREP: 15 MIN. • **BAKE:** 40 MIN.
MAKES: 9 POPOVERS

- 2 cups all-purpose flour
- 1 tsp. onion salt
- 1/8 tsp. celery salt
- 4 large eggs, room temperature
- 2 cups 2% milk
- 1/4 cup grated onion
- 1/4 cup grated celery
- 3 Tbsp. butter, melted

1. Preheat oven to 450°. In a large bowl, combine flour, onion salt and celery salt. Combine eggs, milk, onion, celery and butter; whisk into the dry ingredients just until blended. Grease and flour the bottom and sides of 9 popover cups; fill two-thirds full with batter.

2. Bake for 15 minutes. Reduce heat to 350° (do not open oven door). Bake 25 minutes longer or until deep golden brown (do not underbake). Immediately cut a slit in the top of each popover to allow steam to escape.
1 popover: 202 cal., 8g fat (4g sat. fat), 98mg chol., 306mg sod., 25g carb. (3g sugars, 1g fiber), 7g pro.

MOROCCAN SPICED FRUIT & NUT BREAD

Red pepper flakes combined with the cinnamon and allspice give each slice of this bread a subtle hint of warmth.
—Donna-Marie Ryan, Topsfield, MA

PREP: 30 MIN. • **BAKE:** 50 MIN. + COOLING
MAKES: 1 LOAF (16 PIECES), 1/2 CUP BUTTER

- 1/2 cup chopped dried apricots
- 1/2 cup chopped dates
- 1/4 cup orange juice
- 2 cups all-purpose flour
- 1/2 cup sugar
- 1/4 cup packed brown sugar
- 2 tsp. baking powder
- 3/4 tsp. salt
- 1/2 tsp. ground cinnamon
- 1/4 tsp. ground allspice
- 1/4 tsp. crushed red pepper flakes
- 2 large eggs, room temperature
- 3/4 cup 2% milk
- 1/4 cup unsalted butter, melted
- 1 Tbsp. grated orange zest
- 1/3 cup sweetened shredded coconut
- 1/4 cup chopped pecans

ORANGE BUTTER
- 1/2 cup unsalted butter, softened
- 4 tsp. confectioners' sugar
- 2 tsp. grated orange zest
- 4 tsp. orange juice

1. Preheat oven to 350°. In a small saucepan, combine apricots, dates and orange juice; bring to a boil. Cook, uncovered, 1 minute. Remove from heat; let stand, covered, 10 minutes.
2. In a large bowl, whisk flour, sugars, baking powder, salt and spices. In a another bowl, whisk eggs, milk, melted butter and orange zest until blended. Add to the flour mixture; stir just until moistened. Fold in coconut, pecans and apricot mixture.
3. Transfer to a greased 9x5-in. loaf pan. Bake 50-55 minutes or until a toothpick inserted in center comes out clean. Cool in pan 10 minutes before removing to a wire rack to cool.
4. In a small bowl, beat the remaining ingredients until blended. Serve bread with orange butter.
1 piece with 1½ tsp. butter: 238 cal., 12g fat (6g sat. fat), 50mg chol., 186mg sod., 32g carb. (18g sugars, 2g fiber), 3g pro.

PARMESAN-SAGE BEER BREAD

I'm asked to bring this savory loaf to nearly every function I attend. It's great as a side dish, but if you're in the mood for an extraordinary sandwich, start with two slices of beer bread.
—Elizabeth King, Duluth, MN

PREP: 10 MIN. • **BAKE:** 45 MIN.
MAKES: 1 LOAF (12 PIECES)

2½ cups all-purpose flour
1 cup grated Parmesan cheese
2 Tbsp. sugar
3 tsp. baking powder
1 Tbsp. chopped fresh sage
1 tsp. salt
1½ cups beer
¼ cup melted butter, divided

1. Preheat oven to 375°. In a small bowl, whisk flour, Parmesan cheese, sugar, baking powder, chopped sage and salt. Add beer and 3 Tbsp. melted butter; stir just until moistened.
2. Transfer to a greased 8x4-in. loaf pan. Drizzle with the remaining butter. Bake for 45-50 minutes or until a toothpick inserted in center comes out clean. Cool in pan 5 minutes before removing to a wire rack to cool.
1 piece: 177 cal., 6g fat (4g sat. fat), 16mg chol., 469mg sod., 24g carb. (3g sugars, 1g fiber), 5g pro.

. . . .
TEST KITCHEN TIP
When the recipe just calls for "beer," as this one does, don't choose one that you wouldn't want to drink—choose a flavor you actually like! A pale, amber or light brown ale is a safe choice, but avoid IPAs, as their bitterness will show up in the finished bread.

PARMESAN-SAGE
BEER BREAD
. . . .

LEMON-THYME BREAD

Lemon and thyme go together like milk and cookies. Fresh thyme is best, but if you only have dried available, reduce the amount to 1 tablespoon and crush it between your fingers before adding it to the batter.
—Cathy Tang, Redmond, WA

PREP: 25 MIN. • **BAKE:** 40 MIN. + COOLING
MAKES: 1 LOAF (12 PIECES)

- ½ cup butter, softened
- ¾ cup sugar
- 1 large egg, room temperature
- ½ cup buttermilk
- ½ cup sour cream
- 1¾ cups all-purpose flour
- 2 Tbsp. minced fresh thyme
- 1 Tbsp. grated lemon zest
- ½ tsp. baking soda
- ¼ tsp. salt
  Confectioners' sugar

1. Preheat oven to 350°. In a large bowl, cream butter and sugar until light and fluffy, 5-7 minutes. Beat in the egg. Combine buttermilk and sour cream. Combine the flour, thyme, lemon zest, baking soda and salt; add to the creamed mixture alternately with buttermilk mixture, beating well after each addition.
2. Transfer batter to a greased 8x4-in. loaf pan. Bake 40-50 minutes or until a toothpick inserted in the center comes out clean. Cool for 10 minutes before removing from pan to a wire rack. Cool completely; sprinkle with confectioners' sugar. Or, if desired, drizzle the bread with Lemon-Thyme Icing or serve with Lemony Cream Cheese.
1 piece: 212 cal., 10g fat (6g sat. fat), 45mg chol., 176mg sod., 27g carb. (14g sugars, 1g fiber), 3g pro.

LEMON-THYME MINI LOAVES: Use 3 greased 5¾x3x2-in. loaf pans. Bake at 350° until a toothpick comes out clean, 25-30 minutes.
LEMON-THYME MUFFINS: Make batter as directed; fill 12 greased or paper-lined muffin cups two-thirds full. Bake at 400° for 16-20 minutes or until a toothpick comes out clean. Yield: 1 dozen muffins.
LEMON-THYME MINIATURE MUFFINS: Make batter as directed; fill greased or paper-lined muffin cups two-thirds full. Bake at 400° until a toothpick comes out clean, 10-12 minutes. Yield: 4 dozen miniature muffins.
LEMON-THYME ICING: In a small bowl, combine ½ cup confectioners' sugar, ½ tsp. minced fresh thyme and 3 to 4 tsp. lemon juice, as needed to reach a drizzling consistency. Yield: 2 Tbsp.
LEMONY CREAM CHEESE: Beat 8 oz. softened cream cheese until fluffy. Add ⅓ cup confectioners' sugar, 4 tsp. lemon juice and 1 tsp. grated lemon zest; beat until smooth. Yield: 1 cup.

YORKSHIRE PUDDING WITH BACON & SAGE

DUTCH APPLE LOAF

Being of Dutch descent, I knew I had to try this recipe for a moist, fruity quick bread. It freezes well, so I often have a loaf on hand for church bazaars.
—Gladys Meyer, Ottumwa, IA

PREP: 15 MIN. • **BAKE:** 55 MIN. + COOLING
MAKES: 1 LOAF (16 PIECES)

- ½ cup butter, softened
- 1 cup sugar
- 2 large eggs, room temperature
- ¼ cup buttermilk
- 1 tsp. vanilla extract
- 2 cups all-purpose flour
- 1½ tsp. baking powder
- ½ tsp. salt
- ¼ tsp. baking soda
- 2 cups diced peeled tart apples
- ½ cup chopped walnuts

TOPPING

- ¼ cup sugar
- ¼ cup all-purpose flour
- 2 tsp. ground cinnamon
- ¼ cup cold butter, cubed

1. Preheat oven to 350°. In a large bowl, cream butter and sugar until light and fluffy, 5-7 minutes. Add eggs, 1 at a time, beating well after each addition. Beat in buttermilk and vanilla. Combine flour, baking powder, salt and baking soda; gradually add to the creamed mixture. Fold in apples and walnuts. Pour into a greased 9x5-in. loaf pan.
2. For topping, combine the sugar, flour and cinnamon. Cut in butter until mixture resembles coarse crumbs. Sprinkle over batter.
3. Bake for 55-60 minutes or until a toothpick inserted in the center comes out clean. Cool for 10 minutes before removing from pan to a wire rack.
1 piece: 243 cal., 12g fat (6g sat. fat), 50mg chol., 252mg sod., 32g carb. (17g sugars, 1g fiber), 4g pro.

YORKSHIRE PUDDING WITH BACON & SAGE

These are a nice change from traditional dinner rolls. The savory popovers are tastefully topped with crumbled bacon and fresh sage.
—Melissa Jelinek, Apple Valley, MN

PREP: 15 MIN. • **BAKE:** 20 MIN.
MAKES: 1 DOZEN

- 5 bacon strips, chopped
- 2 Tbsp. butter, melted
- 1½ cups all-purpose flour
- 3 Tbsp. minced fresh sage, divided
- ½ tsp. salt
- 1½ cups 2% milk
- 3 large eggs, room temperature

1. Preheat oven to 450°. In a large skillet, cook bacon over medium heat until crisp. Remove to paper towels with a slotted spoon; drain, reserving the drippings.
2. Transfer drippings to a measuring cup; add enough melted butter to measure ¼ cup. Pour into 12 ungreased muffin cups. Place in oven until hot.
3. Meanwhile, in a small bowl, combine the flour, 2 Tbsp. sage and salt; beat in milk and eggs until smooth. Fold in two-thirds of the bacon. Divide batter among prepared muffin cups.
4. Bake at 450° for 10 minutes. Reduce heat to 350° (do not open oven door). Bake 10-12 minutes longer or until puffed and golden brown. Sprinkle with the remaining bacon and sage.
1 popover: 150 cal., 8g fat (3g sat. fat), 67mg chol., 224mg sod., 14g carb. (2g sugars, 0 fiber), 5g pro.

DUTCH APPLE LOAF

A BIT NUTTY BOSTON BROWN BREAD

Hearty and dense, my homemade Boston brown bread features hazelnuts for a delightfully nutty taste. Thick slices pair well with just about anything, from soups and stews to roasts and casseroles.
—LORRAINE CALAND, SHUNIAH, ON

PREP: 30 MIN. • **BAKE:** 45 MIN. + COOLING
MAKES: 2 LOAVES (12 PIECES EACH)

  3 cups whole wheat flour
  1 cup all-purpose flour
2½ tsp. baking soda
  1 tsp. salt
2½ cups buttermilk
  1 cup molasses
  1 cup golden raisins
  ¾ cup chopped hazelnuts

1. In a large bowl, combine the flours, baking soda and salt. In a small bowl, whisk buttermilk and molasses. Stir into the dry ingredients just until moistened. Fold in raisins and nuts. Transfer to 2 greased 8x4-in. loaf pans.
2. Bake at 350° for 45-50 minutes or until a toothpick inserted in the center comes out clean. Cool the loaves for 10 minutes before removing from pans to wire racks.

1 slice: 159 cal., 3g fat (0 sat. fat), 1mg chol., 263mg sod., 31g carb. (13g sugars, 3g fiber), 4g pro.

CARROT BREAD

This lovely, moist quick bread is flecked with crunchy walnuts and colorful shredded carrot. I sometimes substitute a cup of shredded raw zucchini for the carrot or add a half cup of drained crushed pineapple.
—Connie Simon, Jensen Beach, FL

PREP: 15 MIN. • **BAKE:** 50 MIN. + COOLING
MAKES: 1 LOAF (12 PIECES)

  1 cup sugar
  1 cup all-purpose flour
  ½ cup whole wheat flour
  1 tsp. baking powder
  1 tsp. baking soda
  1 tsp. salt
  1 tsp. ground cinnamon
  2 large eggs, room temperature
  ¾ cup unsweetened applesauce
  1 tsp. vanilla extract
  1 cup shredded carrot
  ¼ cup chopped walnuts

1. Preheat oven to 350°. Grease and flour an 8x4-in. loaf pan; set aside. In a bowl, combine sugar, flours, baking powder, baking soda, salt and cinnamon. In another bowl, combine eggs, applesauce and vanilla; stir into dry ingredients until just moistened. Fold in carrots and walnuts. Pour into prepared pan.
2. Bake until a toothpick comes out clean, 50-55 minutes. Cool the loaf for 10 minutes before removing from pan to a wire rack.
1 piece: 160 cal., 3g fat (0 sat. fat), 31mg chol., 361mg sod., 32g carb. (19g sugars, 2g fiber), 3g pro.

NO-FUSS ROLLS

These four-ingredient rolls are ready in no time. And they're fantastic with herb butter or jam.
—Glenda Trail, Manchester, TN

TAKES: 25 MIN. • **MAKES:** 6 ROLLS

  1 cup self-rising flour
  ½ cup 2% milk
  2 Tbsp. mayonnaise
  ½ tsp. sugar

Preheat oven to 450°. In a small bowl, combine all of the ingredients. Spoon into 6 muffin cups coated with cooking spray. Bake until a toothpick comes out clean, 12-14 minutes. Cool for 5 minutes before removing from pan to a wire rack. Serve warm.
1 roll: 111 cal., 4g fat (1g sat. fat), 3mg chol., 275mg sod., 16g carb. (1g sugars, 0 fiber), 3g pro. **Diabetic exchanges:** 1 starch, 1 fat.

BAKING 101

COUNTRY CINNAMON SWIRL BREAD

With three active sons, I'm always busy, so this rich quick bread is a favorite. I like to wrap these loaves to give as gifts.
—Sharon Walker, Huntington Station, NY

PREP: 15 MIN. • **BAKE:** 45 MIN. + COOLING
MAKES: 1 LOAF (12 PIECES)

- ¼ cup butter, softened
- 1⅓ cups sugar, divided
- 1 large egg, room temperature
- 2 cups all-purpose flour
- 1 tsp. baking powder
- ½ tsp. baking soda
- ½ tsp. salt
- 1 cup buttermilk
- 1 Tbsp. ground cinnamon

1. Preheat oven to 350°. In a large bowl, beat the butter, 1 cup sugar and the egg until blended. Combine the flour, baking powder, baking soda and salt; add to the egg mixture alternately with buttermilk. In a small bowl, combine the cinnamon and the remaining ⅓ cup sugar.
2. Pour a third of the batter into a greased 8x4-in. loaf pan; sprinkle with a third of the cinnamon sugar. Repeat layers twice. Bake for 45-50 minutes or until a toothpick inserted in the center comes out clean. Cool for 10 minutes before removing from pan to a wire rack to cool completely.

1 piece: 212 cal., 5g fat (3g sat. fat), 26mg chol., 267mg sod., 40g carb. (23g sugars, 1g fiber), 3g pro.

. . . .
TEST KITCHEN TIP

If you'd like, you can add a honey glaze to this bread. Mix together ¾ cup confectioners' sugar, 1 Tbsp. honey and 2 to 4 tsp. milk to reach drizzling consistency.

CARAWAY CHEESE BREAD

BAKING 101

CARAWAY CHEESE BREAD

We enjoy cheese in a variety of ways. In this savory bread, cheddar cheese blends beautifully with just the right amount of caraway.
—Homer Wooten, Ridgetown, ON

PREP: 10 MIN. • **BAKE:** 30 MIN. + COOLING
MAKES: 1 LOAF (16 PIECES)

- 2½ cups all-purpose flour
- 2 cups shredded cheddar cheese
- 1½ to 2 tsp. caraway seeds
- ¾ tsp. salt
- ½ tsp. baking powder
- ½ tsp. baking soda
- 2 large eggs, room temperature
- 1 cup plain yogurt
- ½ cup butter, melted
- 1 Tbsp. Dijon mustard

1. Preheat oven to 375°. In a large bowl, combine the first 6 ingredients. In another bowl, combine remaining ingredients. Stir into dry ingredients just until moistened.
2. Pour into a greased 9x5-in. loaf pan. Bake until a toothpick comes out clean, 30-35 minutes. Cool 10 minutes before removing from pan to a wire rack. Serve warm. Refrigerate leftovers.

1 piece: 199 cal., 12g fat (7g sat. fat), 55mg chol., 338mg sod., 16g carb. (1g sugars, 1g fiber), 7g pro.

FETA & CHIVE
MUFFINS

MUFFINS

FETA & CHIVE MUFFINS

This is a spring variation on a savory muffin my husband has made for years. It has a light texture almost like a popover and tastes best eaten hot right from the oven.
—Angela Buchanan, Boulder, CO

PREP: 15 MIN. • **BAKE:** 20 MIN.
MAKES: 1 DOZEN

- 1½ cups all-purpose flour
- 3 tsp. baking powder
- ¼ tsp. salt
- 2 large eggs, room temperature
- 1 cup fat-free milk
- 2 Tbsp. butter, melted
- ½ cup crumbled feta cheese
- 3 Tbsp. minced chives

1. Preheat oven to 400°. In a large bowl, combine the flour, baking powder and salt. In another bowl, combine the eggs, milk and butter; stir into dry ingredients just until moistened. Fold in the feta cheese and chives.

2. Fill 12 greased or paper-lined muffin cups two-thirds full. Bake for 18-22 minutes or until a toothpick inserted in the center comes out clean. Cool for 5 minutes before removing from pan to a wire rack. Serve warm. Refrigerate leftovers.

1 muffin: 105 cal., 4g fat (2g sat. fat), 43mg chol., 235mg sod., 13g carb. (1g sugars, 1g fiber), 4g pro. **Diabetic exchanges:** 1 starch, ½ fat.

APPLE STREUSEL MUFFINS

APPLE STREUSEL MUFFINS

These muffins remind us of coffee cake, and my husband and kids love them as a quick breakfast or snack on the run. The drizzle of glaze makes them pretty enough for company.
—Dulcy Grace, Roaring Spring, PA

PREP: 20 MIN. • **BAKE:** 15 MIN.
MAKES: 1 DOZEN

- 2 cups all-purpose flour
- 1 cup sugar
- 1 tsp. baking powder
- ½ tsp. baking soda
- ½ tsp. salt
- 2 large eggs, room temperature
- ½ cup butter, melted
- 1¼ tsp. vanilla extract
- 1½ cups peeled chopped tart apples

STREUSEL TOPPING
- ⅓ cup packed brown sugar
- 1 Tbsp. all-purpose flour
- ⅛ tsp. ground cinnamon
- 1 Tbsp. cold butter

GLAZE
- ¾ cup confectioners' sugar
- 2 to 3 tsp. 2% milk
- 1 tsp. butter, melted
- ⅛ tsp. vanilla extract
  Dash salt

1. Preheat oven to 375°. Whisk together the first 5 ingredients. In another bowl, whisk together eggs, melted butter and vanilla; add to the flour mixture, stirring just until moistened (batter will be stiff). Fold in apples.

2. Fill 12 greased or paper-lined muffin cups three-fourths full. For the topping, mix brown sugar, flour and cinnamon; cut in butter until crumbly. Sprinkle over the batter.

3. Bake until a toothpick inserted in center comes out clean, 15-20 minutes. Cool 5 minutes before removing from pan to a wire rack to cool. Mix glaze ingredients; drizzle over tops.

1 muffin: 295 cal., 10g fat (6g sat. fat), 55mg chol., 398mg sod., 49g carb. (32g sugars, 1g fiber), 3g pro.

LEMON MERINGUE MUFFINS

CREAM CHEESE PUMPKIN MUFFINS

I first made this recipe back in 1987 and have since made it many times over the years—it's my children's very favorite muffin recipe.

—Wendy Stenman, Germantown, WI

PREP: 20 MIN. • **BAKE:** 20 MIN.
MAKES: 2 DOZEN

   1 pkg. (8 oz.) cream cheese, softened
   1 large egg
   1 Tbsp. sugar
MUFFIN
 2¼ cups all-purpose flour
   3 tsp. pumpkin pie spice
   1 tsp. baking soda
  ½ tsp. salt
   2 large eggs, room temperature, lightly beaten
   2 cups sugar
   1 cup canned pumpkin
  ½ cup canola oil
 24 pecan halves, optional

1. Preheat oven to 350°. For the filling, in a small bowl, beat the cream cheese, egg and sugar until smooth; set aside.
2. In a large bowl, combine the flour, pumpkin pie spice, baking soda and salt. Beat the eggs, sugar, pumpkin and oil; stir into dry ingredients just until moistened.
3. Divide half of the batter among 24 greased or paper-lined muffin cups. Drop filling by teaspoonfuls over the batter. Top with the remaining batter. Place a pecan half on top of each muffin if desired.
4. Bake for 20-22 minutes or until a toothpick comes out clean. Cool for 5 minutes before removing from pans to wire racks.
1 muffin: 207 cal., 10g fat (3g sat. fat), 37mg chol., 138mg sod., 28g carb. (17g sugars, 1g fiber), 3g pro.

LEMON MERINGUE MUFFINS

These muffins taste like a favorite pie of mine, and the meringue makes them unlike any muffin out there!

—Nancy Kearney, Massillon, OH

PREP: 25 MIN. • **BAKE:** 25 MIN.
MAKES: 1 DOZEN

   6 Tbsp. butter, softened
   1 cup sugar, divided
   2 large eggs, room temperature
  ½ cup plain yogurt
   2 Tbsp. lemon juice
   1 Tbsp. grated lemon zest
  ¼ tsp. lemon extract
 1⅓ cups all-purpose flour
  ½ tsp. baking powder
  ½ tsp. baking soda
   2 large egg whites

1. Preheat oven to 350°. In a large bowl, cream butter and ⅔ cup sugar until light and fluffy, 5-7 minutes. Add eggs, 1 at a time, beating well after each addition. Beat in next 4 ingredients.
2. In another bowl, whisk flour, baking powder and baking soda. Add to the creamed mixture; stir just until moistened. Fill greased or paper-lined muffin cups three-fourths full. Bake for 17-19 minutes or until a toothpick inserted in center comes out clean. Remove from the oven. Increase oven setting to 400°.
3. Meanwhile, in a small bowl, beat egg whites on medium speed until soft peaks form. Gradually add remaining ⅓ cup sugar, 1 Tbsp. at a time, beating on high after each addition until sugar is dissolved. Continue beating until stiff glossy peaks form.
4. Spread or pipe meringue onto muffins. Bake 6-8 minutes longer or until meringue is golden brown.
5. Cool for 5 minutes before removing from pan to a wire rack. Serve warm. Refrigerate leftovers.
1 muffin: 188 cal., 7g fat (4g sat. fat), 52mg chol., 135mg sod., 28g carb. (18g sugars, 0 fiber), 4g pro. **Diabetic exchanges:** 2 starch, 1 fat.

CREAM CHEESE
PUMPKIN MUFFINS

LEMON-FILLED GINGERBREAD MUFFINS

These seemingly plain gingerbread muffins hide a delicious surprise—a sweet lemon filling! You can add frosting or glaze if you'd like, but the simple appearance makes the surprise all the sweeter.

—Suzette Jury, Keene, CA

PREP: 25 MIN. • **BAKE:** 15 MIN.
MAKES: 1½ DOZEN

- ½ cup butter, softened
- ⅔ cup sugar
- 2 large eggs, room temperature
- ½ cup molasses
- 2 cups all-purpose flour
- 1½ tsp. ground ginger
- 1 tsp. baking soda
- ½ tsp. salt
- ½ tsp. ground allspice
- 1 cup water

FILLING
- 4 oz. cream cheese, softened
- ¼ cup confectioners' sugar
- 1 Tbsp. lemon juice
- 2 tsp. grated lemon zest

1. Preheat oven to 375°. In a large bowl, cream butter and sugar until light and fluffy, 5-7 minutes. Add eggs, 1 at a time, beating well after each addition. Beat in molasses. In another bowl, whisk flour, ginger, baking soda, salt and allspice; add to creamed mixture alternately with water, beating after each addition just until combined. (Batter may appear curdled.)

2. Fill paper-lined muffin cups one-fourth full. In a small bowl, beat the filling ingredients until blended. Drop filling by rounded teaspoonfuls into the center of each muffin; cover with the remaining batter.

3. Bake until a toothpick inserted in the muffin portion comes out clean, 14-18 minutes. Cool 5 minutes before removing from pans to wire racks. Serve warm.

1 muffin: 188 cal., 8g fat (5g sat. fat), 41mg chol., 207mg sod., 27g carb. (16g sugars, 0 fiber), 3g pro.

PINEAPPLE UPSIDE-DOWN MUFFINS

For a modern version of upside-down cake, we use pineapple and a sweet batter to make fun muffins with a cherry on top.

—Suzeanne Longwill, Ortonville, MI

PREP: 25 MIN. • **BAKE:** 10 MIN.
MAKES: ABOUT 3 DOZEN MINI MUFFINS OR 10 REGULAR MUFFINS

- 1 can (8 oz.) crushed pineapple
- 1½ cups all-purpose flour
- ¾ cup sugar
- 2 tsp. baking powder
- ¼ tsp. salt
- 2 large eggs, room temperature
- ½ cup vanilla yogurt
- ¼ cup canola oil
- 5 tsp. brown sugar
- 18 to 20 maraschino cherries, halved

1. Preheat oven to 400°. Drain the pineapple, reserving 1 Tbsp. juice. Set pineapple aside.

2. In a large bowl, whisk flour, sugar, baking powder and salt. In another bowl, whisk eggs, yogurt, oil and reserved pineapple juice. Add to the flour mixture; stir just until moistened. Fold in reserved pineapple.

3. Fill greased mini-muffin cups two-thirds full. Sprinkle tops with brown sugar; top with halved cherries.

4. Bake 9-12 minutes or until a toothpick inserted in center comes out clean. Cool 5 minutes before removing from pans to wire racks. Serve warm.

1 mini muffin: 68 cal., 2g fat (0 sat. fat), 11mg chol., 50mg sod., 12g carb. (8g sugars, 0 fiber), 1g pro.

GRANDMA'S HONEY MUFFINS

I can remember my Grandma Wheeler making these delicious muffins—we'd eat them nice and warm, fresh from the oven! She was a "pinch of this" and "handful of that" kind of cook, so getting the ingredient amounts correct for the recipe was a challenge. Now it's a family treasure!
—Darlis Wilfer, West Bend, WI

TAKES: 30 MIN. • **MAKES:** 1 DOZEN

- 2 cups all-purpose flour
- ½ cup sugar
- 3 tsp. baking powder
- ½ tsp. salt
- 1 large egg, room temperature
- 1 cup 2% milk
- ¼ cup butter, melted
- ¼ cup honey

1. Preheat oven to 400°. In a large bowl, combine flour, sugar, baking powder and salt. In a small bowl, combine egg, milk, butter and honey. Stir into the dry ingredients just until moistened.
2. Fill greased or paper-lined muffin cups three-fourths full. Bake until a toothpick inserted in center comes out clean, 15-18 minutes. Cool 5 minutes before removing from pan to a wire rack. Serve warm.

Freeze option: Freeze cooled muffins in freezer containers. To use, thaw at room temperature or, if desired, microwave each muffin on high until heated through, 20-30 seconds.

1 muffin: 179 cal., 5g fat (3g sat. fat), 29mg chol., 242mg sod., 31g carb. (15g sugars, 1g fiber), 3g pro.

WILD BLUEBERRY MUFFINS

BAKING 101

WILD BLUEBERRY MUFFINS

Nothing is better than a warm blueberry muffin in the morning. These muffins are the best I have ever made. The wild blueberries make them extra special.
—Dewey Grindle, Blue Hill, ME

PREP: 15 MIN. • **BAKE:** 20 MIN.
MAKES: 1 DOZEN

- ¼ cup butter, softened
- ⅓ cup sugar
- 1 large egg, room temperature
- 2⅓ cups all-purpose flour
- 4 tsp. baking powder
- ½ tsp. salt
- 1 cup 2% milk
- 1 tsp. vanilla extract
- 1½ cups fresh or frozen wild blueberries or 1 can (15 oz.) water-packed wild blueberries, well drained

STREUSEL TOPPING
- ½ cup sugar
- ⅓ cup all-purpose flour
- ½ tsp. ground cinnamon
- ¼ cup cold butter, cubed

1. In a bowl, cream butter and sugar. Add egg; mix well. Combine the dry ingredients; add to the creamed mixture alternately with milk. Stir in vanilla. Gently fold in blueberries. Fill greased or paper-lined muffin cups two-thirds full.
2. In a small bowl, combine the sugar, flour and cinnamon; cut in the butter until crumbly. Sprinkle over muffins. Bake at 375° for 20-25 minutes.

1 muffin: 252 cal., 9g fat (5g sat. fat), 41mg chol., 325mg sod., 39g carb. (17g sugars, 1g fiber), 4g pro.

BAKING 101

SWEET CORN MUFFINS

I love to make cornbread and corn muffins, but often the results are not moist or sweet enough for my taste. So I experimented until I came up with these light, pleasantly sweet muffins. They ended up winning a blue ribbon at our county fair.

—Patty Bourne, Owings, MD

PREP: 10 MIN. • **BAKE:** 25 MIN.
MAKES: 1 DOZEN

- 1½ cups all-purpose flour
- 1 cup sugar
- ¾ cup cornmeal
- 1 Tbsp. baking powder
- ½ tsp. salt
- 2 large eggs, room temperature
- ½ cup shortening
- 1 cup 2% milk, divided

1. Preheat oven to 350°. Combine the dry ingredients. Add eggs, shortening and ½ cup of milk; beat 1 minute. Add remaining milk; beat just until blended.
2. Fill 12 paper-lined muffin cups three-fourths full. Bake until muffins test done, 25-30 minutes.
1 muffin: 254 cal., 10g fat (3g sat. fat), 33mg chol., 241mg sod., 38g carb. (18g sugars, 1g fiber), 4g pro.

MORNING GLORY MUFFINS

Once I took these muffins to a brunch. Three other women had brought muffins, too, but mine disappeared first, and everyone wanted the recipe! Even my husband, who doesn't normally like muffins, just can't seem to get enough of these!

—Paddy Webber, Exeter, ON

TAKES: 30 MIN. • **MAKES:** ABOUT 1½ DOZEN

- 2 cups all-purpose flour
- 1¼ cups sugar
- 2 tsp. baking soda
- 2 tsp. ground cinnamon
- ½ tsp. salt
- 3 large eggs, room temperature
- 1 cup canola oil
- 1 medium apple, shredded
- 2 tsp. vanilla extract
- 2 cups grated carrot
- ½ cup raisins
- ½ cup sweetened shredded coconut
- ½ cup chopped pecans

1. Preheat oven to 350°. In large bowl, combine the flour, sugar, baking soda, cinnamon and salt. In another bowl, combine the eggs, oil, apple and vanilla. Stir into the dry ingredients just until combined. Fold in the carrot, raisins, coconut and pecans.
2. Fill greased or paper-lined muffin cups three-fourths full. Bake for 15-18 minutes or until a toothpick inserted in the center comes out clean. Cool for 5 minutes before removing from pans to wire racks. Serve warm.
1 muffin: 283 cal., 16g fat (3g sat. fat), 35mg chol., 228mg sod., 32g carb. (19g sugars, 2g fiber), 3g pro.

PUMPKIN BANANA MUFFINS

PUMPKIN BANANA MUFFINS

These pumpkin banana muffins are the perfect bite-sized snack for fall.
—Desiree Rasch, Blue Springs, MO

PREP: 20 MIN. • **BAKE:** 15 MIN.
MAKES: 15 MUFFINS

- 1 cup all-purpose flour
- 1 cup whole wheat flour
- ⅔ cup packed brown sugar
- 1 tsp. baking soda
- 1 tsp. salt
- 1 tsp. ground cinnamon
- ½ tsp. ground ginger
- ½ tsp. ground allspice
- ¼ tsp. ground nutmeg
- 2 large eggs, room temperature
- 1 cup canned pumpkin
- ½ cup mashed ripe bananas (about 2 small)
- ⅓ cup buttermilk
- ¼ cup canola oil
- 2 tsp. vanilla extract

1. Preheat oven to 400°. In a large bowl, combine the first 9 ingredients. In another bowl, combine the eggs, pumpkin, bananas, buttermilk, oil and vanilla. Stir into dry ingredients just until moistened.
2. Coat muffin cups with cooking spray; fill three-fourths full with batter. Bake for 15-18 minutes or until a toothpick inserted in muffin comes out clean. Cool for 5 minutes before removing from pans to wire racks. Serve warm.
1 muffin: 153 cal., 5g fat (1g sat. fat), 28mg chol., 262mg sod., 25g carb. (11g sugars, 2g fiber), 3g pro. **Diabetic exchanges:** 1½ starch, ½ fat.

BROWN SUGAR OAT MUFFINS

JAVA MUFFINS

I look to these muffins to get me going in the morning. They're especially satisfying with a cup of coffee.

—Zainab Ahmed, Mountlake Terrace, WA

TAKES: 30 MIN. • **MAKES:** 1 DOZEN

- ¼ cup butter, softened
- 1 cup packed brown sugar
- 2 large eggs, room temperature
- ¼ cup unsweetened applesauce
- ½ cup buttermilk
- ½ cup strong brewed coffee
- 1 Tbsp. instant coffee granules
- ½ tsp. vanilla extract
- 1 cup all-purpose flour
- ¾ cup whole wheat flour
- 1½ tsp. baking powder
- ½ tsp. baking soda
- ½ tsp. ground cinnamon
- ¼ tsp. salt
- ½ cup finely chopped pecans, divided

1. Preheat oven to 375°. In a large bowl, beat the butter and brown sugar until crumbly, about 2 minutes. Add eggs; mix well. Beat in applesauce. In a small bowl, whisk buttermilk, coffee, coffee granules and vanilla until granules are dissolved; gradually add to the butter mixture.
2. In another bowl, whisk flours, baking powder, baking soda, cinnamon and salt. Add to the butter mixture; stir just until moistened. Fold in ¼ cup pecans.
3. Coat 12 muffin cups with cooking spray or use paper liners; fill three-fourths full. Sprinkle with remaining pecans. Bake 15-20 minutes or until a toothpick inserted in center comes out clean. Cool 5 minutes before removing from pan to a wire rack. Serve warm.
1 muffin: 220 cal., 9g fat (3g sat. fat), 46mg chol., 209mg sod., 33g carb. (19g sugars, 2g fiber), 4g pro. **Diabetic exchanges:** 2 starch, 1½ fat.

BROWN SUGAR OAT MUFFINS

With Kansas being one of the top wheat-producing states, it seems only fitting to share a recipe containing whole wheat flour. These are great muffins to have for breakfast or a late night snack with a cup of hot cocoa.

—Regina Stock, Topeka, KS

TAKES: 35 MIN. • **MAKES:** 1 DOZEN

- 1 cup old-fashioned oats
- 1 cup whole wheat flour
- ¾ cup packed brown sugar
- ½ cup all-purpose flour
- 2 tsp. baking powder
- ½ tsp. salt
- 2 large eggs, room temperature
- ¾ cup 2% milk
- ¼ cup canola oil
- 1 tsp. vanilla extract
  Peanut butter and honey, optional

1. Preheat oven to 400°. Mix the first 6 ingredients. In another bowl, whisk together eggs, milk, oil and vanilla. Add to oat mixture; stir just until moistened.
2. Fill greased or paper-lined muffin cups two-thirds full. Bake until a toothpick inserted in center comes out clean, 15-17 minutes. Cool 5 minutes before removing muffins to a wire rack. Serve warm. If desired, spread with peanut butter and honey.
1 muffin: 192 cal., 7g fat (1g sat. fat), 32mg chol., 202mg sod., 30g carb. (14g sugars, 2g fiber), 4g pro. **Diabetic exchanges:** 2 starch, 1½ fat.

1. Preheat oven to 350°. In a bowl, combine the first 6 ingredients. Combine egg and oil; stir into dry ingredients just until moistened. Fold in the zucchini, walnuts and currants.
2. Fill greased or paper-lined muffin cups three-fourths full with batter. Bake until a toothpick in center comes out clean, 22-25 minutes. Cool for 5 minutes before removing from pan to a wire rack.

1 muffin: 318 cal., 16g fat (1g sat. fat), 35mg chol., 180mg sod., 40g carb. (25g sugars, 2g fiber), 6g pro.

LEMON POUND CAKE MUFFINS

I make these lemony muffins for all kinds of occasions. My family is always asking for them. They have a rich cakelike taste and a sweet, tangy flavor. All I can say is: They're so unbelievably good!
—Lola Baxter, Winnebago, MN

PREP: 15 MIN. • **BAKE:** 20 MIN.
MAKES: 1 DOZEN

- ½ cup butter, softened
- 1 cup sugar
- 2 large eggs, room temperature
- ½ cup sour cream
- 1 tsp. vanilla extract
- ½ tsp. lemon extract
- 1¾ cups all-purpose flour
- ½ tsp. salt
- ¼ tsp. baking soda
- GLAZE
- 2 cups confectioners' sugar
- 3 Tbsp. lemon juice

1. Preheat oven to 400°. In a large bowl, cream the butter and sugar until light and fluffy, 5-7 minutes. Add eggs, 1 at a time; beat well after each addition. Beat in sour cream and extracts. Combine the flour, salt and baking soda; add to creamed mixture just until moistened.
2. Fill 12 greased or paper-lined muffin cups three-fourths full. Bake until a toothpick inserted in the center comes out clean, 18-20 minutes. Cool for 5 minutes before removing from pan to a wire rack.
3. Combine the glaze ingredients; drizzle over muffins. Serve warm.

1 muffin: 311 cal., 10g fat (6g sat. fat), 63mg chol., 218mg sod., 51g carb. (36g sugars, 1g fiber), 3g pro.

ZUCCHINI MUFFINS

These yummy zucchini, currant and walnut muffins are an excellent way to use up your garden surplus of zucchini.
—Peg Gausz, Watchung, NJ

PREP: 20 MIN. • **BAKE:** 25 MIN.
MAKES: 6 MUFFINS

- ¾ cup all-purpose flour
- ½ cup sugar
- ¼ tsp. baking powder
- ¼ tsp. baking soda
- ¼ tsp. salt
- ¼ tsp. ground cinnamon
- 1 large egg, room temperature
- ¼ cup canola oil
- 1 cup finely shredded unpeeled zucchini
- ½ cup chopped walnuts
- ¼ cup dried currants or chopped raisins

CLASSIC IRISH
SODA BREAD

SODA BREAD & SCONES

CLASSIC IRISH SODA BREAD

This traditional Irish soda bread can be made with an assortment of mix-ins such as dried fruit and nuts, but I like it with a handful of raisins. It's the perfect change-of-pace item to bring to a get-together.
—Gloria Warczak, Cedarburg, WI

PREP: 15 MIN. • **BAKE:** 30 MIN.
MAKES: 1 LOAF (8 PIECES)

- 2 cups all-purpose flour
- 2 Tbsp. brown sugar
- 1 tsp. baking powder
- 1 tsp. baking soda
- ½ tsp. salt
- 3 Tbsp. cold butter, cubed
- 2 large eggs, room temperature, divided use
- ¾ cup buttermilk
- ⅓ cup raisins

1. Preheat oven to 375°. Whisk together first 5 ingredients. Cut in butter until mixture resembles coarse crumbs. In another bowl, whisk together 1 egg and buttermilk. Add to flour mixture; stir just until moistened. Stir in raisins.
2. Turn onto a lightly floured surface; knead gently 6-8 times. Shape into a 6½-in. round loaf; place on a greased baking sheet. Using a sharp knife, make a shallow cross in top of loaf. Whisk remaining egg; brush over top.
3. Bake until crust is golden brown, 30-35 minutes. Remove from pan to a wire rack. Serve warm.
1 piece: 210 cal., 6g fat (3g sat. fat), 59mg chol., 463mg sod., 33g carb. (8g sugars, 1g fiber), 6g pro.

TRADITIONAL SCONES

Making scones is very simple—I learned how when my wife and I hosted an English tea. These are light and very tasty.
—Chuck Hinz, Parma, OH

PREP: 20 MIN. • **BAKE:** 25 MIN.
MAKES: 1 DOZEN

- 2 cups all-purpose flour
- 2 Tbsp. sugar
- 3 tsp. baking powder
- ⅛ tsp. baking soda
- 6 Tbsp. cold butter, cubed
- 1 large egg, room temperature
- ½ cup buttermilk
  Jam of your choice, optional

1. Preheat oven to 350°. In a large bowl, combine the flour, sugar, baking powder and baking soda. Cut in butter until the mixture resembles coarse crumbs. In a small bowl, whisk egg and buttermilk until blended; add to crumb mixture just until moistened.
2. Turn onto a lightly floured surface; gently knead 10 times. Divide dough in half; pat each portion into a 5-in. circle. Cut each circle into 6 wedges.
3. Separate wedges and place 1 in. apart on an ungreased baking sheet. Bake 25-30 minutes or until golden brown. Serve warm, with jam if desired.
1 scone: 144 cal., 6g fat (4g sat. fat), 33mg chol., 170mg sod., 19g carb. (3g sugars, 1g fiber), 3g pro.

GINGERBREAD SCONES

These moist scones' gingerbread flavor make them just right for serving around Christmastime — especially with hot tea.
—David Bostedt, Zephyrhills, FL

PREP: 20 MIN. • **BAKE:** 15 MIN.
MAKES: 1 DOZEN

- 2 cups all-purpose flour
- 3 Tbsp. brown sugar
- 2 tsp. baking powder
- 1 tsp. ground ginger
- ½ tsp. salt
- ½ tsp. baking soda
- ½ tsp. ground cinnamon
- ¼ cup cold butter, cubed
- ⅓ cup molasses
- ¼ cup 2% milk
- 1 large egg, separated, room temperature
  Coarse sugar

1. Preheat oven to 400°. In a large bowl, whisk the first 7 ingredients. Cut in the butter until mixture resembles coarse crumbs. In another bowl, whisk the molasses, milk and egg yolk until blended; stir into the crumb mixture just until moistened.

2. Turn onto a lightly floured surface; knead gently 6-8 times. Pat into an 8-in. circle. Cut into 12 wedges. Place wedges 1 in. apart on a greased baking sheet.
3. In a small bowl, beat egg white until frothy; brush over scones. Sprinkle with sugar. Bake until golden brown, 12-15 minutes. Serve warm.
1 scone: 157 cal., 5g fat (3g sat. fat), 29mg chol., 269mg sod., 26g carb. (9g sugars, 1g fiber), 3g pro.

LEMON BLUEBERRY DROP SCONES

I enjoy serving these fruity scones for baby and bridal showers. They're a bit lower in fat than most other scone recipes, so you can indulge with little guilt.
—Jacqueline Hendershot, Orange, CA

TAKES: 30 MIN. • **MAKES:** 14 SCONES

- 2 cups all-purpose flour
- ⅓ cup sugar
- 2 tsp. baking powder
- 1 tsp. grated lemon zest
- ½ tsp. baking soda
- ¼ tsp. salt
- 1 cup lemon yogurt
- 1 large egg, room temperature
- ¼ cup butter, melted
- 1 cup fresh or frozen blueberries

GLAZE
- ½ cup confectioners' sugar
- 1 Tbsp. lemon juice
- ½ tsp. grated lemon zest

1. Preheat oven to 400°. In a large bowl, combine the first 6 ingredients. In another bowl, combine the yogurt, egg and butter. Stir into dry ingredients just until moistened. Fold in blueberries.
2. Drop by heaping tablespoonfuls 2 in. apart onto a greased baking sheet. Bake for 15-18 minutes or until lightly browned. Combine glaze ingredients; drizzle over warm scones.

1 scone: 158 cal., 4g fat (2g sat. fat), 25mg chol., 192mg sod., 28g carb. (13g sugars, 1g fiber), 3g pro.

HAZELNUT CHOCOLATE CHIP SCONES

With chocolate, hazelnuts and the tangy taste of buttermilk, these delicious scones are easy to make, come together fast and taste so good with your morning coffee.
—Trisha Kruse, Eagle, ID

PREP: 20 MIN. • **BAKE:** 15 MIN.
MAKES: 8 SCONES

- 2 cups all-purpose flour
- ¼ cup packed brown sugar
- 1½ tsp. baking powder
- ½ tsp. baking soda
- ½ tsp. salt
- ½ cup cold butter, cubed
- 1 large egg, room temperature
- ½ cup buttermilk
- 1½ tsp. vanilla extract
- 1 cup semisweet chocolate chips
- 1 cup hazelnuts, coarsely chopped

1. Preheat oven to 400°. Whisk together first 5 ingredients; cut in butter until mixture resembles coarse crumbs. In another bowl, whisk together egg, buttermilk and vanilla; stir into the crumb mixture just until moistened. Stir in chocolate chips and hazelnuts.
2. Turn onto a lightly floured surface; knead gently 8 times. Pat dough into a 6-in. circle. Cut circle into 8 wedges; place on a greased baking sheet. Bake until golden brown, 15-20 minutes. Serve warm.
1 scone: 409 cal., 23g fat (10g sat. fat), 76mg chol., 327mg sod., 47g carb. (20g sugars, 3g fiber), 8g pro.

HAZELNUT
CHOCOLATE CHIP
SCONES

MOIST PUMPKIN SCONES

3. Bake at 400° for 12-15 minutes or until golden brown. Remove to wire racks; cool for 10 minutes.

4. Combine the glaze ingredients; drizzle over scones. Serve warm.

1 scone: 338 cal., 13g fat (8g sat. fat), 59mg chol., 348mg sod., 51g carb. (23g sugars, 2g fiber), 5g pro.

FEATHERLIGHT SCONES

Scones fit into just about every meal. This dough bakes up beautifully into fully golden wedges. We love the tender triangles with butter and cinnamon-sugar.
—Stephanie Moon, Boise, ID

TAKES: 30 MIN. • **MAKES:** 8 SERVINGS

- 3 cups all-purpose flour
- 3 tsp. baking powder
- ½ tsp. baking soda
- ½ tsp. salt
- 1 cup cold butter, cubed
- 1 large egg, room temperature
- 1 cup vanilla yogurt
- ½ tsp. vanilla extract
- 2 tsp. milk
  Sugar

1. Preheat oven to 425°. In a large bowl, combine flour, baking powder, baking soda and salt; cut in butter until mixture resembles coarse crumbs. Stir in egg, yogurt and vanilla just until combined.

2. Turn onto a floured surface; knead 6-8 times. Roll into a 9-in. circle; cut into 8 wedges. Place wedges on an ungreased baking sheet. Brush tops with milk; sprinkle with sugar.

3. Bake 12-15 minutes or until golden brown. Serve warm.

1 scone: 413 cal., 25g fat (15g sat. fat), 91mg chol., 637mg sod., 40g carb. (5g sugars, 1g fiber), 7g pro.

MOIST PUMPKIN SCONES

After trying a pumpkin scone at a coffeehouse, I was inspired to look for a recipe to try at home. The glaze nicely complements the pumpkin flavor.
—Amy McCavour, Gresham, OR

PREP: 15 MIN. • **BAKE:** 15 MIN. + COOLING
MAKES: 16 SCONES

- 4½ cups all-purpose flour
- ½ cup packed brown sugar
- 4 tsp. baking powder
- 3 tsp. pumpkin pie spice
- 1 tsp. ground cinnamon
- ½ tsp. baking soda
- ½ tsp. salt
- 1 cup cold butter
- 2 large eggs, room temperature
- 1¼ cups canned pumpkin
- ¾ cup 2% milk, divided

GLAZE
- 2 cups confectioners' sugar
- 3 Tbsp. 2% milk
- ¼ tsp. pumpkin pie spice

1. In a large bowl, combine the first 7 ingredients. Cut in butter until mixture resembles coarse crumbs. In another bowl, whisk the eggs, pumpkin and ½ cup milk. Stir into dry ingredients just until moistened.

2. Turn onto a floured surface; knead 10 times. Divide dough in half. Pat each portion into an 8-in. circle; cut each into 8 wedges. Separate wedges and place 1 in. apart on ungreased baking sheets. Brush with the remaining ¼ cup milk.

ONION & GARLIC SODA BREAD

This is one of my favorite recipes for soda bread. It's versatile—you can do endless sweet or savory variations. I serve it sliced alongside assorted spreads and cheeses.
—Theresa Vujosevic, Hamburg, NJ

PREP: 20 MIN. • **BAKE:** 35 MIN. + COOLING
MAKES: 1 LOAF (12 PIECES)

- 1   Tbsp. olive oil
- 1   medium onion, chopped
- 5   garlic cloves, minced
- 4   cups all-purpose flour
- 1   tsp. salt
- 1   tsp. baking soda
- ¼   cup cold butter, cubed
- 1   large egg, room temperature
- 1½ cups buttermilk

1. Preheat oven to 425°. In a small skillet, heat oil over medium-high heat. Add onion; cook and stir until light golden brown, 3-5 minutes. Add garlic; cook and stir 30 seconds longer. Cool.

2. Whisk flour, salt and baking soda. Cut in butter until mixture resembles coarse crumbs. Stir in cooled onion mixture; make a well in center. In a small bowl, whisk egg and buttermilk; pour into well. Using a wooden spoon, mix dough until too stiff to stir. Turn dough onto a lightly floured surface; knead gently 10 times.

3. Shape into a round loaf. Transfer to a large greased cast-iron skillet or baking sheet. Using a sharp knife, cut a shallow "X" on the top of loaf. Bake until golden brown, 35-40 minutes.

4. Remove loaf from pan to a wire rack; serve warm.

1 piece: 219 cal., 6g fat (3g sat. fat), 27mg chol., 398mg sod., 35g carb. (2g sugars, 1g fiber), 6g pro.

Savory Irish bread: Omit sugar and raisin and replace with 1 cup cooked spicy sausage.

Cheesy Irish Bread: Omit ¼ cup buttermilk, raisins and sugar and add 1½ cups shredded cheese.

Maple Irish Bread: Omit ¼ cup buttermilk and replace with ¼ cup of quality maple syrup and additional nuts of your choice.

CARAMEL APPLE SCONES

A drizzle of caramel complements the apple and whole wheat flavors of these rustic scones.
—Arlene Cook, Bainbridge, GA

PREP: 20 MIN. • **BAKE:** 15 MIN. + COOLING
MAKES: 4 SCONES

- ½   cup whole wheat flour
- ½   cup all-purpose flour
- 2   Tbsp. brown sugar
- 1½ tsp. baking powder
- ¼   tsp. salt
- 3   Tbsp. cold butter
- ¼   cup plus 2 Tbsp. half-and-half cream
- 1   large egg yolk, room temperature
- 1½ tsp. vanilla extract
- ⅔   cup shredded peeled apple
- 1   Tbsp. caramel ice cream topping

1. Preheat oven to 400°. In a small bowl, combine the flours, brown sugar, baking powder and salt. Cut in the butter until mixture resembles coarse crumbs. In a small bowl, whisk the cream, egg yolk and vanilla; add to dry ingredients just until moistened. Stir in apple. Turn onto a floured surface; knead 10 times.

2. Pat into a 5-in. circle. Cut into 4 wedges. Separate wedges and place on an ungreased baking sheet. Bake for 15-20 minutes or until golden brown. Cool for 10 minutes. Drizzle with the caramel topping.

1 scone: 278 cal., 12g fat (7g sat. fat), 85mg chol., 393mg sod., 36g carb. (10g sugars, 3g fiber), 5g pro.

DOUBLE CHOCOLATE SCONES

Chocolate lovers will adore these moist, decadent scones that won me a blue ribbon in a baking competition. They're perfect for a tea or brunch, and they're sweet enough for dessert.
—Stephanie Sorbie, Peoria, AZ

PREP: 15 MIN. • **BAKE:** 20 MIN.
MAKES: 8 SCONES

- 1¾ cups all-purpose flour
- ½ cup baking cocoa
- ⅓ cup sugar
- 1½ tsp. baking powder
- ½ tsp. salt
- 4 oz. cream cheese, cubed
- ¼ cup cold butter, cubed
- 2 large eggs, room temperature, divided use
- ¾ cup heavy whipping cream
- 2 tsp. vanilla extract
- ⅔ cup semisweet chocolate chips

1. Preheat oven to 375°. In a large bowl, whisk the first 5 ingredients. Cut in cream cheese and butter until mixture resembles coarse crumbs. In another bowl, whisk 1 egg, cream and vanilla; stir into the crumb mixture just until moistened. Stir in chocolate chips.

2. Turn dough onto a floured surface; knead gently 10 times. Pat dough into a 6-in. circle. Cut into 8 wedges. Place wedges on a greased baking sheet. In a small bowl, whisk the remaining egg; brush over scones. Bake 18-20 minutes or until a toothpick inserted in center comes out clean. Serve warm.

1 scone: 412 cal., 25g fat (15g sat. fat), 114mg chol., 334mg sod., 42g carb. (17g sugars, 3g fiber), 8g pro.

SAVORY COCKTAIL SCONES

Scones are comfort food to me, and I wanted to make a savory version with roasted garlic butter. The addition of bacon seemed natural. Their cocktail size makes them fun; they also work for a brunch buffet.
—Donna-Marie Ryan, Topsfield, MA

PREP: 55 MIN. • **BAKE:** 15 MIN.
MAKES: 16 SCONES (ABOUT ⅔ CUP BUTTER)

- 1 whole garlic bulb
- 2 tsp. olive oil
- ½ cup butter, softened

SCONES

- 2 bacon strips, chopped
- ⅓ cup chopped onion
- 2 cups all-purpose flour
- 3 tsp. baking powder
- ½ tsp. baking soda
- ½ tsp. salt
- ½ cup cold butter
- 1 large egg, room temperature
- ½ cup sherry
- ⅓ cup heavy whipping cream
- ¼ cup 2% milk

1. Preheat oven to 400°. Remove papery outer skin from garlic (do not peel or separate cloves). Cut top off of garlic bulb. Brush with oil. Wrap the bulb in heavy-duty foil. Bake 40-45 minutes or until softened. Cool for 10-15 minutes. Squeeze softened garlic into a small bowl; mash with fork. Stir in butter; set aside.

2. Meanwhile, in a small skillet, cook bacon over medium heat until crisp. Remove bacon to paper towels with a slotted spoon; drain, reserving 1 Tbsp. drippings. In the same skillet, cook and stir onion in the drippings until softened. Reduce the heat to medium-low; cook, stirring occasionally, until deep golden brown, about 30 minutes. Set aside.

3. In a large bowl, combine the flour, baking powder, baking soda and salt. Cut in butter until the mixture resembles coarse crumbs. Whisk the egg, sherry and cream; stir into the crumb mixture just until moistened. Fold in onion and bacon.

4. Turn dough onto a floured surface; knead 10 times. Pat into a 10x5-in. rectangle. Using a floured knife, cut into eight 2½-in. squares; cut each square diagonally in half.

5. Place on a parchment-lined baking sheet; brush with milk. Bake at 400° for 12-15 minutes or until golden brown. Serve warm, with garlic butter.

1 scone with about 2 tsp. butter: 204 cal., 15g fat (9g sat. fat), 52mg chol., 297mg sod., 13g carb. (1g sugars, 1g fiber), 3g pro.

STRAWBERRIES & CREAM SCONES

When it comes to a special treat from the oven, these scones are hard to beat. I can never eat just one!
—Agnes Ward, Stratford, ON

TAKES: 30 MIN. • **MAKES:** 8 SCONES

- 2 cups all-purpose flour
- ⅓ cup plus 2 tsp. sugar, divided
- 2¼ tsp. baking powder
- 1 tsp. grated lemon zest
- ¾ tsp. salt
- ¼ tsp. ground cinnamon
- ¼ cup cold butter, cubed
- ⅔ cup half-and-half cream
- ½ cup coarsely chopped fresh strawberries
- 1 large egg, lightly beaten

1. Preheat oven to 425°. In a large bowl, combine the flour, ⅓ cup sugar, baking powder, lemon zest, salt and cinnamon. Cut in butter until mixture resembles coarse crumbs. Stir in cream just until moistened.
2. Turn onto a lightly floured surface; knead 5 times. Gently knead in the strawberries, about 5 times. Pat into an 8-in. circle; brush with egg and sprinkle with remaining sugar. Cut into 8 wedges.
3. Separate the wedges and place 2 in. apart on a greased baking sheet. Bake for 9-12 minutes or until golden brown. Serve warm.
Freeze option: Wrap scones in foil; transfer to a freezer container. May be frozen for up to 3 months. To use frozen scones, remove the foil; thaw at room temperature. Warm if desired.
1 scone: 233 cal., 8g fat (5g sat. fat), 33mg chol., 387mg sod., 35g carb. (11g sugars, 1g fiber), 4g pro.

IRISH SODA BREAD MUFFINS

IRISH SODA BREAD MUFFINS

Irish soda bread is traditionally prepared in a loaf shape, but these muffins have the same terrific flavor.
—Lorraine Ballsieper, Deep River, CT

TAKES: 30 MIN. • **MAKES:** 1 DOZEN

- 2¼ cups all-purpose flour
- ½ cup plus 1 Tbsp. sugar, divided
- 2 tsp. baking powder
- ½ tsp. salt
- ¼ tsp. baking soda
- 1 tsp. caraway seeds
- 1 large egg, room temperature
- 1 cup buttermilk
- ¼ cup butter, melted
- ¼ cup canola oil
- ¾ cup dried currants or raisins

1. Preheat oven to 400°. In a large bowl, combine the flour, ½ cup sugar, the baking powder, salt, baking soda and caraway seeds. In another bowl, beat the egg, buttermilk, butter and oil. Stir into the dry ingredients just until moistened. Fold in currants.
2. Fill greased muffin cups three-fourths full. Sprinkle with the remaining 1 Tbsp. sugar. Bake for 15 minutes or until a toothpick inserted in the center comes out clean. Cool for 5 minutes before removing from pan to wire rack. Serve warm.
1 muffin: 235 cal., 9g fat (3g sat. fat), 28mg chol., 247mg sod., 35g carb. (17g sugars, 1g fiber), 4g pro.

BISCUITS & CORNBREAD

CHEDDAR CORN BISCUITS

*Everyone asks for my biscuits with cheddar
and corn, especially when I serve soup. If
you're lucky enough to have leftovers,
rewarm and pass the butter and jam.*
—Susan Braun, Swift Current, SK

PREP: 20 MIN. • **BAKE:** 20 MIN.
MAKES: 16 BISCUITS

4¼ cups all-purpose flour
2 Tbsp. baking powder
1 tsp. ground mustard
¾ tsp. salt
¾ cup cold butter, cubed
1 can (14¾ oz.) cream-style corn
1½ cups shredded cheddar cheese
2 large eggs, room temperature,
   lightly beaten
2 Tbsp. 2% milk

1. Preheat oven to 425°. In a large bowl,
whisk flour, baking powder, mustard
and salt. Cut in the butter until the
mixture resembles coarse crumbs.
Add corn, cheese and eggs; stir just
until moistened.
2. Turn the dough onto a lightly floured
surface; knead gently 8-10 times. Pat or
roll dough to 1-in. thickness; cut with a
floured 2½-in. biscuit cutter. Place 2 in.
apart on ungreased baking sheets;
brush with milk. Bake 18-22 minutes
or until golden brown. Serve warm.
1 biscuit: 270 cal., 13g fat (8g sat. fat),
57mg chol., 476mg sod., 30g carb.
(1g sugars, 1g fiber), 7g pro.

BUTTERMILK ANGEL BISCUITS

*While this isn't technically considered a
quick bread (this recipe uses yeast), it
doesn't have a long rising time and the
tender, slightly sweet biscuits will never
disappoint!*
—Carol Holladay, Danville, AL

PREP: 30 MIN. + STANDING • **BAKE:** 10 MIN.
MAKES: 2 DOZEN

2 pkg. (¼ oz. each) active dry yeast
¼ cup warm water (105° to 115°)
5¼ to 5½ cups self-rising flour
⅓ cup sugar
1 tsp. baking soda
1 cup shortening
1¾ cups buttermilk

1. In a small bowl, dissolve yeast in
warm water. In a large bowl, whisk
5¼ cups flour, the sugar and baking
soda. Cut in shortening until mixture
resembles coarse crumbs. Stir in the
buttermilk and yeast mixture to form
a soft dough (dough will be sticky).
2. Turn dough onto a floured surface;
knead gently 8-10 times, adding flour if
needed. Roll dough to ¾-in. thickness;
cut with a floured 2½-in. biscuit cutter.
Place 2 in. apart on greased baking
sheets. Let stand at room temperature
20 minutes.
3. Bake at 450° for 8-12 minutes or until
golden brown. Serve warm.
1 biscuit: 180 cal., 8g fat (2g sat. fat), 1mg
chol., 386mg sod., 23g carb. (4g sugars,
1g fiber), 3g pro.

BUTTERMILK
ANGEL BISCUITS

TUSCAN CORNBREAD
WITH ASIAGO BUTTER

TUSCAN CORNBREAD WITH ASIAGO BUTTER

I had some fresh basil on hand and needed to find a use for it. Peering into my pantry, I saw a bag of cornmeal and figured that cornbread with a Tuscan twist would be delicious. During peak tomato season, I substitute the canned tomatoes with fresh—just remove the skins, seed and finely dice.

—Michelle Anderson, Eagle, ID

PREP: 25 MIN. • **BAKE:** 20 MIN.
MAKES: 8 SERVINGS (1¼ CUPS BUTTER)

- 2 oz. sliced pancetta or bacon strips, finely chopped
- 1 to 2 Tbsp. olive oil, as needed
- 1½ cups white cornmeal
- ½ cup all-purpose flour
- 2 tsp. baking powder
- ½ tsp. salt
- 2 large eggs, room temperature
- 1 cup buttermilk
- ¼ cup minced fresh basil
- 1 garlic clove, minced
- 1 can (14½ oz.) diced tomatoes, drained
- 1 can (2¼ oz.) sliced ripe olives, drained

BUTTER
- 1 cup butter, softened
- 2 Tbsp. olive oil
- ⅓ cup shredded Asiago cheese
- 2 Tbsp. thinly sliced green onion
- 1½ tsp. minced fresh basil
- ½ tsp. minced fresh oregano
- 1 garlic clove, minced, optional

1. Preheat oven to 400°. In a 10-in. cast-iron or other ovenproof skillet, cook pancetta over medium heat until crisp, stirring occasionally. Remove with a slotted spoon; drain on paper towels. Reserve drippings in skillet. If necessary, add enough oil to measure 2 Tbsp. drippings.

2. In a large bowl, whisk the cornmeal, flour, baking powder and salt. In another bowl, whisk eggs, buttermilk, basil and garlic until blended; stir in tomatoes. Add to the flour mixture; stir just until moistened. Fold in olives and pancetta.
3. Place skillet with drippings in oven; heat for 2 minutes. Tilt pan to coat the bottom and sides with drippings. Add batter to the hot pan. Bake until a toothpick inserted in center comes out clean, 20-25 minutes. Cool in pan on a wire rack.
4. Meanwhile, in a small bowl, beat butter until light and fluffy. Beat in oil until blended; stir in cheese, green onion, basil, oregano and, if desired, garlic. Serve ½ cup butter mixture with warm cornbread (save remaining butter for another use).

1 wedge with 1 Tbsp. butter: 329 cal., 18g fat (8g sat. fat), 79mg chol., 695mg sod., 34g carb. (4g sugars, 2g fiber), 8g pro.

FLUFFY BISCUITS

If you're looking for a basic flaky biscuit, this recipe is the best. These golden brown rolls bake up tall, light and tender. Their mild flavor is even better when the warm biscuits are spread with butter or jam.

—Nancy Horsburgh, Everett, ON

TAKES: 30 MIN. • **MAKES:** ABOUT 8 BISCUITS

- 2 cups all-purpose flour
- 4 tsp. baking powder
- 1 Tbsp. sugar
- ½ tsp. salt
- ½ cup shortening
- 1 large egg, room temperature
- ⅔ cup 2% milk

1. Preheat oven to 400°. In a bowl, whisk together the first 4 ingredients. Cut in shortening until the mixture resembles coarse crumbs. Whisk together egg and milk. Add to dry ingredients; stir just until moistened.

BAKING 101

2. On a well-floured surface, knead dough gently 8-10 times. Roll to ½-in. thickness; cut with a floured 2½-in. biscuit cutter. Place on a lightly greased baking sheet. Bake until golden brown, 10-12 minutes. Serve warm.
1 biscuit: 249 cal., 13g fat (4g sat. fat), 25mg chol., 407mg sod., 26g carb. (3g sugars, 1g fiber), 5g pro.
Italian Biscuits: Add 1 tsp. Italian seasoning to the flour mixture.

TEST KITCHEN TIP
Using a biscuit cutter gives biscuits the clean edge they need to be able to rise properly; a dull edge will compress the dough and impede the rise. If you don't have a cutter, or if your cutter is dull, use a bench scraper or a sharp knife and press straight down to cut the dough.

BAKING POWDER DROP BISCUITS

One day I had company coming and realized I had run out of biscuit mix. I'd never made biscuits from scratch before, but I decided to give this recipe a try. Now this is the only way I make them!
—Sharon Evans, Clear Lake, IA

TAKES: 20 MIN. • **MAKES:** 1 DOZEN

2	cups all-purpose flour
2	Tbsp. sugar
4	tsp. baking powder
½	tsp. cream of tartar
½	tsp. salt
½	cup shortening
⅔	cup 2% milk
1	large egg

1. Preheat oven to 450°. In a large bowl, combine the first 5 ingredients. Cut in shortening until the mixture resembles coarse crumbs. In a small bowl, whisk milk and egg. Stir into crumb mixture just until moistened.

2. Drop by ¼ cupfuls 2 in. apart onto an ungreased baking sheet. Bake until golden brown, 10-12 minutes. Serve biscuits warm.

1 biscuit: 170 cal., 9g fat (2g sat. fat), 17mg chol., 271mg sod., 19g carb. (3g sugars, 1g fiber), 3g pro.

BAKING 101

BAKING POWDER
DROP BISCUITS

FLAKY BISCUITS WITH HERB BUTTER

Nothing says spring like fresh herbs, and these flaky, flavorful biscuits are the ideal way to showcase tarragon and chives. They can be on the table in 30 minutes, which makes them an ideal choice for last-minute entertaining.
—Theresa Stanek, Evans City, PA

TAKES: 30 MIN.
MAKES: 1 DOZEN (½ CUP BUTTER)

- 2 cups all-purpose flour
- 3 tsp. baking powder
- 1 Tbsp. sugar
- 1½ tsp. minced fresh chives
- 1½ tsp. minced fresh tarragon
- 1 tsp. salt
- ½ tsp. garlic powder
- ½ cup shortening
- ¾ cup 2% milk

HERB BUTTER
- ½ cup butter, softened
- 1½ tsp. minced fresh chives
- 1½ tsp. minced fresh tarragon
- ½ tsp. garlic powder

1. Preheat oven to 425°. In a small bowl, combine the first 7 ingredients. Cut in shortening until mixture resembles coarse crumbs. Stir in milk just until moistened. Turn onto a lightly floured surface; knead 8-10 times.
2. Pat or roll out to ½-in. thickness; cut with a floured 2½-in. biscuit cutter. Place 2 in. apart on an ungreased baking sheet. Bake for 8-12 minutes or until golden brown.
3. Meanwhile, in a small bowl, beat the butter ingredients until blended; serve with warm biscuits.
1 biscuit with 2 tsp. butter: 229 cal., 16g fat (7g sat. fat), 21mg chol., 359mg sod., 18g carb. (2g sugars, 1g fiber), 3g pro.

BAKING 101

QUICK BUTTERMILK CORNBREAD

The tattered recipe card for this cornbread proves it's been a family favorite for years. It's my daughter's top request.
—Judy Sellgren, Grand Rapids, MI

TAKES: 30 MIN. • **MAKES:** 9 SERVINGS

- 1¼ cups cornmeal
- 1 cup all-purpose flour
- ⅔ cup packed brown sugar
- ⅓ cup sugar
- 1 tsp. baking soda
- ½ tsp. salt
- 1 large egg, room temperature
- 1 cup buttermilk
- ¾ cup canola oil

1. Preheat oven to 425°. In a large bowl, combine cornmeal, flour, sugars, baking soda and salt. In another bowl, whisk the egg, buttermilk and oil; stir into dry ingredients just until moistened. Pour into a greased 9-in. round or square baking pan (pan will be full).
2. Bake until a toothpick inserted in the center comes out clean, 20-25 minutes. Cool on a wire rack for 5 minutes. Serve cornbread warm.
1 piece: 390 cal., 19g fat (3g sat. fat), 25mg chol., 314mg sod., 50g carb. (25g sugars, 2g fiber), 5g pro.

SPICED APPLE CORNBREAD

2. Transfer to a greased 10-in. cast-iron skillet (pan will be very full). Bake on a lower oven rack until a toothpick inserted in center comes out clean, 40-50 minutes. Serve warm.

1 piece: 371 cal., 10g fat (5g sat. fat), 82mg chol., 404mg sod., 64g carb. (27g sugars, 2g fiber), 6g pro.

CHIVE & LEMON BISCUITS

An unexpected pairing of flavors makes these biscuits delightfully different. They're wonderful fresh from the oven and spread with a light butter.
—Jim Gales, Milwaukee, WI

TAKES: 30 MIN. • **MAKES:** 9 BISCUITS

- 2   cups all-purpose flour
- 3   tsp. baking powder
- 1   tsp. sugar
- 1   tsp. salt
- ½   cup cold butter
- ¾   cup half-and-half cream
- ½   cup minced chives
- 1½ tsp. grated lemon zest
- 1   large egg
- 1   Tbsp. water

1. Preheat oven to 400°. In a large bowl, combine flour, baking powder, sugar and salt. Cut in the cold butter until the mixture resembles coarse crumbs. Stir in the cream just until moistened. Stir in chives and lemon zest.
2. Turn dough onto a lightly floured surface; knead 8-10 times. Pat or roll out to ¾-in. thickness; cut with a floured 2½-in. biscuit cutter.
3. Place 2 in. apart on a greased baking sheet. In a small bowl, whisk egg and water; brush over the biscuits. Bake until golden brown, 15-20 minutes. Serve warm.

1 biscuit: 222 cal., 13g fat (8g sat. fat), 43mg chol., 480mg sod., 23g carb. (2g sugars, 1g fiber), 4g pro.

SPICED APPLE CORNBREAD

There's just nothing better than a big piece of cornbread to go with a supper of fried chicken, chops or baked ham! I've sweetened the pot with a little apple and spice, and everyone raves over this tender, moist and delicious cornbread!
—Kelly Williams, Forked River, NJ

PREP: 15 MIN. • **BAKE:** 40 MIN.
MAKES: 12 SERVINGS

- 2   cups all-purpose flour
- 2   cups yellow cornmeal
- 1   Tbsp. baking powder
- 1   tsp. salt
- ½   tsp. ground cinnamon
- ½   tsp. pumpkin pie spice
- ½   cup butter, softened
- 1½ cups sugar
- ½   tsp. vanilla extract
- 4   large eggs, room temperature
- 2   cups water
- 1   cup shredded peeled apple

1. Preheat oven to 400°. Whisk together the first 6 ingredients. In a large bowl, beat butter and sugar until blended. Add the vanilla and eggs, 1 at a time, beating well after each. Stir in the flour mixture alternately with water, adding water slowly (mixture may appear slightly curdled). Stir in apple.

ROLLED BUTTERMILK BISCUITS

I scribbled down this recipe when our family visited The Farmers' Museum in Cooperstown, New York, more than 25 years ago. I must have gotten it right, because these biscuits turn out great every time.
—Patricia Kile, Elizabethtown, PA

PREP: 20 MIN. • **BAKE:** 15 MIN.
MAKES: 8 BISCUITS

- 2 cups all-purpose flour
- 3 tsp. baking powder
- ½ tsp. baking soda
- ¼ tsp. salt
- 3 Tbsp. cold butter
- ¾ to 1 cup buttermilk
- 1 Tbsp. fat-free milk

1. Preheat oven to 450°. In a large bowl, combine the flour, baking powder, baking soda and salt; cut in butter until mixture resembles coarse crumbs. Stir in enough buttermilk just to moisten the dough.

2. Turn dough onto a lightly floured surface; knead 3-4 times. Pat or roll to ¾-in. thickness. Cut dough with a floured 2½-in. biscuit cutter. Place in a large ungreased cast-iron or other ovenproof skillet.

3. Brush with milk. Bake until golden brown, 12-15 minutes.

1 biscuit: 162 cal., 5g fat (3g sat. fat), 12mg chol., 412mg sod., 25g carb. (1g sugars, 1g fiber), 4g pro. **Diabetic exchanges:** 1½ starch, 1 fat.

JALAPENO CORNBREAD FILLED WITH BLUEBERRY QUICK JAM

Fresh jalapenos and blueberry quick jam make the perfect blend of sweet and spicy in this special cornbread. Once you eat one piece, you won't be able to resist going back for another.
—Colleen Delawder, Herndon, VA

PREP: 20 MIN. + CHILLING
BAKE: 30 MIN. + COOLING
MAKES: 12 SERVINGS

- 2 cups fresh blueberries
- 1 cup sugar
- 1 Tbsp. cider vinegar
- ¼ tsp. kosher salt

CORNBREAD

- ½ cup 2% milk
- 1 Tbsp. lemon juice
- 1½ cups all-purpose flour
- ½ cup yellow cornmeal
- ½ cup sugar
- 3 tsp. baking powder
- ½ tsp. kosher salt
- 2 Tbsp. unsalted butter
- 1 Tbsp. honey
- 2 large eggs, room temperature
- ⅓ cup canola oil
- 2 jalapeno peppers, seeded and minced

1. In a large heavy saucepan, combine blueberries, sugar, vinegar and kosher salt. Bring to a boil over high heat. Cook, stirring constantly, 5 minutes. Cool mixture completely. Refrigerate, covered, overnight.

2. For cornbread, preheat oven to 350°. Combine the milk and lemon juice; let stand briefly. In another bowl, whisk the next 5 ingredients. In a small bowl, microwave butter and honey on high for 30 seconds; cool slightly. Whisk eggs and oil into milk mixture (mixture may appear curdled). Add butter mixture; whisk until well combined. Add flour mixture; whisk just until combined. Fold in jalapenos.

3. Pour 2 cups batter into a well-buttered 10-in. fluted tube pan. Spoon half to three-fourths of the blueberry quick jam over the batter. Cover with the remaining batter. Bake until a toothpick inserted in center comes out clean, 30-35 minutes. Cool 10 minutes; invert onto a cake plate or serving platter. Drizzle with remaining quick jam.

1 piece: 289 cal., 10g fat (2g sat. fat), 37mg chol., 258mg sod., 48g carb. (30g sugars, 1g fiber), 4g pro.

CRANBERRY CORNBREAD

During the holidays, I make several pans of this sweet cakelike cornbread for family and friends. Try using whole blueberries—coated in flour—instead of cranberries.
—Sylvia Gidwani, Milford, NJ

PREP: 15 MIN. • **BAKE:** 40 MIN.
MAKES: 9 SERVINGS

- ½   cup butter, softened
- 1   cup sugar
- 2   large eggs, room temperature
- 1½ cups all-purpose flour
- 1   cup cornmeal
- 2   tsp. baking powder
- ½   tsp. salt
- 1½ cups buttermilk
- 1   cup cranberries, halved

1. Preheat oven to 375°. In a bowl, cream butter and sugar until light and fluffy, 5-7 minutes. Add eggs; mix well. Combine the flour, cornmeal, baking powder and salt. Add to the creamed mixture alternately with buttermilk. Fold in cranberries.
2. Transfer to a greased 9-in. square baking pan. Bake until a toothpick inserted in the center comes out clean, 40-45 minutes. Serve warm.
1 piece: 350 cal., 12g fat (7g sat. fat), 70mg chol., 414mg sod., 54g carb. (25g sugars, 1g fiber), 6g pro.

CHEESE & PESTO BISCUITS

Biscuits always liven up a meal, especially when they're golden brown and filled with pesto, garlic and cheese for extra zip.
—Liz Bellville, Tonasket, WA

TAKES: 25 MIN. • **MAKES:** 1 DOZEN

- 2   cups all-purpose flour
- 2   tsp. baking powder
- ½   tsp. salt
- ¼   tsp. baking soda
- ⅓   cup cold butter, cubed
- 1   cup shredded Italian cheese blend
- 1¼ cups buttermilk
- 1   Tbsp. prepared pesto
- 1   Tbsp. butter, melted
- 1   garlic clove, minced

1. Preheat oven to 450°. In a large bowl, whisk flour, baking powder, salt and baking soda. Cut in the butter until the mixture resembles coarse crumbs. Stir in cheese. In a small bowl, whisk buttermilk and pesto until blended; stir into flour mixture just until moistened.
2. Drop dough by ¼ cupfuls 2 in. apart onto an ungreased baking sheet. Bake 10-12 minutes or until golden brown.
3. Mix melted butter and garlic; brush over biscuits. Serve warm.
1 biscuit: 175 cal., 9g fat (5g sat. fat), 24mg chol., 357mg sod., 18g carb. (1g sugars, 1g fiber), 5g pro.

CREOLE CORNBREAD

Cornbread is a staple of Cajun and Creole cuisine. This version is an old favorite, and it really tastes wonderful. I found the recipe in the bottom of my recipe drawer.
—Enid Hebert, Lafayette, LA

PREP: 15 MIN. • **BAKE:** 45 MIN.
MAKES: 12 SERVINGS

- 2   cups cooked rice
- 1   cup yellow cornmeal
- ½   cup chopped onion
- 1   to 2 Tbsp. seeded chopped jalapeno peppers
- 1   tsp. salt
- ½   tsp. baking soda
- 2   large eggs, room temperature
- 1   cup 2% milk
- ¼   cup canola oil
- 1   can (16½ oz.) cream-style corn
- 3   cups shredded cheddar cheese
     Additional cornmeal

1. Preheat oven to 350°. In a large bowl, combine rice, cornmeal, onion, peppers, salt and baking soda. In another bowl, beat eggs, milk and oil. Add corn; mix well. Stir into rice mixture until blended. Fold in cheese.
2. Sprinkle a well-greased 10-in. ovenproof skillet with cornmeal. Pour batter into skillet.
3. Bake for 45-50 minutes or until the bread tests done. Cut into wedges and serve warm.
1 piece: 272 cal., 14g fat (7g sat. fat), 68mg chol., 551mg sod., 26g carb. (3g sugars, 2g fiber), 10g pro.

FAVORITE MEXICAN CORNBREAD

I love to cook and my supportive and encouraging mom finally convinced me to submit this recipe. I often serve this cornbread with chili.
—Donna Hypes, Ramona, CA

BAKING 101

PREP: 10 MIN. • **BAKE:** 35 MIN.
MAKES: 9 SERVINGS

- 1 cup yellow cornmeal
- 1 cup all-purpose flour
- 3 tsp. baking powder
- 1 tsp. salt
- 2 Tbsp. sugar
- 1 cup buttermilk
- 1 large egg, room temperature, beaten
- 1 can (8¼ oz.) cream-style corn
  Dash hot pepper sauce
- ¼ cup bacon drippings, melted
- ¼ cup chopped green onions
- ½ cup shredded cheddar cheese
  Honey, optional

1. Preheat oven to 400°. Combine the first 5 ingredients in a large bowl; set aside. In another bowl, combine buttermilk and egg; add corn and remaining ingredients. Add to the dry ingredients; stir just until combined. Pour batter into a greased 8-in. square baking pan.
2. Bake for 35 minutes or until a toothpick comes out clean. Cool for 5 minutes before cutting into squares. Serve warm. Drizzle with honey if desired.
1 piece: 235 cal., 9g fat (5g sat. fat), 38mg chol., 583mg sod., 32g carb. (5g sugars, 2g fiber), 6g pro.

GRANDMA'S SWEET POTATO BISCUITS

GRANDMA'S SWEET POTATO BISCUITS

The recipe for these mild-tasting biscuits was my grandmother's. They're a family favorite that we always serve at holidays.
—Nancy Daugherty, Cortland, OH

TAKES: 30 MIN. • **MAKES:** 1½ DOZEN

- 2½ cups all-purpose flour
- 1 Tbsp. baking powder
- 1 tsp. salt
- ⅓ cup shortening
- 1 can (15¾ oz.) sweet potatoes, drained
- ¾ cup 2% milk

1. Preheat oven to 425°. In a large bowl, combine the flour, baking powder and salt. Cut in shortening until mixture resembles coarse crumbs. In another bowl, mash the sweet potatoes and milk. Add to the crumb mixture just until combined.
2. Turn onto a floured surface; knead 8-10 times. Roll to ½-in. thickness; cut with a 2½-in. biscuit cutter. Place on ungreased baking sheets.
3. Bake until tops are golden brown, 8-10 minutes. Remove to wire racks. Serve warm.
1 biscuit: 124 cal., 4g fat (1g sat. fat), 1mg chol., 214mg sod., 19g carb. (4g sugars, 1g fiber), 2g pro.

COOKIES

From after-school snacks to additions to goodie bags
to elaborately decked-out holiday displays, cookies
are a cornerstone of our baking obsession!

. . . .

COOKIES 101

- Use the fat the recipe calls for. Different fats melt at different temperatures—and spreading is a risk if the fat melts more quickly than the recipe accounts for.

- If a recipe calls for softened butter, let it stand at room temperature until pliable, no more than 30 minutes. If the butter is too soft, the cookies will be flat.

- Avoid overmixing the dough or the cookies will be tough.

- Use heavy-gauge dull aluminum baking sheets with one or two low sides. Dark finishes may cause overbrowning.

- When a recipe calls for a greased baking sheet, grease it lightly with shortening or cooking spray.

- For even baking, make cookies the same size and thickness. Unless the recipe states otherwise, place cookie dough 2-3 inches apart on a cool baking sheet.

- Leave at least 2 inches of space between the baking sheet and the oven walls to allow for good heat circulation. Arrange oven rack so the cookies will bake in the center of the oven.

- If using two racks, stagger pans rather than placing one directly over the other. Switch positions of the baking sheets halfway through the baking time.

- Check for doneness at the minimum recommended baking time, then every 1-2 minutes. Refer to the recipe for doneness descriptions.

- Unless otherwise directed, let cookies cool for 1 minute on the baking sheet before removing to a wire rack. Let them cool completely before storing.

- Let baking sheets cool completely between each batch—residual heat will soften the dough and make it spread.

- If the cookies crumble when removed from the baking sheet, let them cool for 1-2 minutes longer. However, if they remain on the pan too long, they will harden and may break when removed. If this occurs, return the baking sheet to the oven to warm the cookies slightly.

COMMON COOKIE TYPES

DROP COOKIES

Drop cookies are among the easiest to make; the batter is simply dropped from a spoon onto a baking sheet. For even baking, the cookies should be the same size. Measure out the dough using a teaspoon or tablespoon from your flatware or use a small ice cream scoop. Drop cookies generally soften and spread on their own during baking. However, a recipe may instruct you to flatten the dough with a fork or the bottom of a glass.

Drop cookie dough is usually quite firm and some can even strain your mixer. If your mixer shows signs of stress—a high-pitched noise, slowing of the beaters, or the motor heating up—use a wooden spoon to stir in the last few ingredients, or even mix them in with your hands.

SHAPED COOKIES

Shaped cookies include those formed by hand as well as those, like spritz, that are created using a press. Some traditional shaped cookies have their own special molds.

The dough is easier to handle, and creates more distinct shapes, when chilled. Dust your hands lightly with flour to keep the dough from sticking to them when shaping it.

Many shaped cookies require you to roll the dough into a ball. A 1-in. ball requires about a teaspoon of cookie dough.

SLICED COOKIES

These cookies—also called icebox, refrigerator or slice-and-bake cookies—are among the most convenient. The dough is shaped into logs and then refrigerated until firm enough to slice. It can be refrigerated for up to a week or frozen for up to 3 months—perfect for providing a fresh-baked treat in a few minutes if unexpected company drops in.

Keep the dough chilled until you're ready to slice it. To keep a nice round shape, place each roll of dough inside a tall glass and place the glass on its side in the refrigerator. To slice the cookies, use a thin, sharp knife and rotate the roll after each slice to avoid having one flat side. If your recipe calls for nuts or fruits, make sure they're finely chopped; if they're too large, the dough can be difficult to slice.

CUTOUT COOKIES

Cutout cookies are cut into shapes or patterns from a sheet of rolled-out dough. Cookie cutters come in all shapes and sizes; you can also cut out simple diamond or square shapes with a knife.

To make the dough easier to handle, chill it before rolling it out and cutting it. To prevent dough from sticking to cookie cutters, dip the cutters in flour or spritz them with cooking spray. Save the scraps and reroll them just once.

To keep cutout cookies intact before and after baking, transfer them to and from the baking sheet with a large spatula that supports the entire shape.

PLAY WITH INGREDIENTS
CHOCOLATE CHIP COOKIES

If you're looking to adapt a cookie recipe to get a different effect, use these guidelines for your experiments.

EXTRA FLOUR
Adding extra flour keeps the cookies from spreading as they bake, so you get a thicker cookie with a gooey center.

BAKING POWDER ONLY
If you use only baking powder, the cookies will have a cakelike texture.

BAKING SODA ONLY
If you like your cookies a bit denser and lighter in color. Omit baking powder and increase baking soda.

REFRIGERATED DOUGH
Refrigerating the dough for 24 hours before baking means your cookies will be chewier, with a more obvious butterscotch flavor. Place portioned dough into an airtight container, separating layers with waxed paper.

ALL GRANULATED SUGAR
Using 100% granulated sugar will result in a cookie that is pale, chewy and slightly crunchy.

MELTED BUTTER
Melting, then cooling your butter before mixing it with the sugar will result in cookies that are flatter and have a shiny, crinkly top with crispy edges.

ALL BROWN SUGAR
Using all brown sugar instead of all or part granulated sugar, makes soft, golden brown butterscotch-flavored cookies.

TWO LEAVENERS
When you use both baking soda and baking powder, the cookies will be golden brown with a soft, chewy center and crisp edges.

TROUBLESHOOTING COOKIES

COOKIES ARE SPREADING TOO MUCH:
• Make sure baking sheets are cool.

• Chill the dough before baking.

• Oven may be too hot, melting the fat too quickly; check with an oven thermometer.

COOKIES ARE NOT SPREADING ENOUGH:
• Add 1-2 tablespoons of liquid, such as milk or water, to the remaining dough.

• Let the dough stand at room temperature before baking.

COOKIES ARE TOUGH:
• Too much flour was worked into the dough. Add 1-2 tablespoons of shortening, butter or sugar to the remaining dough.

COOKIES ARE TOO BROWN
• Oven temperature is too high. Check with an oven thermometer.

COOKIES ARE TOO PALE
• Oven temperature is too low. Check with an oven thermometer.

• If you are using a gas oven that does not have a heating element at the top of the oven, your cookies may not brown on top. Try moving your baking sheet to the top rack to capture the reflected heat.

WHY YOU NEED TO CHILL YOUR COOKIE DOUGH

Chilling your cookie dough for 30 minutes before baking is almost always recommended. First of all, chilling prevents cookies from spreading out too quickly in the oven. If you use a higher-fat butter (like a European style butter), chilling your dough is essential. When the fats are cool, the cookies will expand more slowly, holding on to their texture.

Cookies made from chilled dough are also more flavorful. The dough becomes hydrated as the dry ingredients soak up moisture from the wet ingredients. This makes the dough less wet, concentrating the flavors. The result is cookies with a nice even bake and lovely golden-brown color. While this hydration is taking place, the flour also breaks down into sugar, making the dough taste sweeter.

HOW TO ROLL OUT COOKIE DOUGH

Give yourself plenty of elbow room and have your materials ready: a good rolling pin, waxed paper, and a small bowl of flour for dusting the work surface.

Separate your dough into portions so you can keep some in the fridge while you're working. After rolling out the dough, put the cutout shapes in the fridge to chill for at least 15 minutes. Chilled dough will give you cleaner edges once the cookies are baked.

Go easy on the flour. A lightly floured surface means just that—lightly. For the tenderest cookies, roll out the dough between two sheets of very lightly floured waxed paper. Then chill the whole assembly—dough and paper—for 15 minutes to make it easy to remove.

Roll from center to edge, maintaining a uniform thickness. If you do vary the thickness of your cookies, bake thicker and thinner cookies separately, as they will require different baking times.

Keep your cutouts as close to each other as possible without overlapping. Use different sized cookie cutters to maximize all the dough you've rolled out. The ideal is to reroll the scraps just once; any more than that, and the cookies will get tough. You can bake the scraps, too—baked and crushed, they make a good foundation for a cookie-crumb crust (see p. 361).

FREEZING COOKIE DOUGH

Most cookie doughs are extremely freezer-friendly. (Cookies with a thinner batter are the exception—those should be baked right away.) Depending on the type of dough, it can be frozen in a variety of ways.

For chunky cookies (like chocolate chip or oatmeal raisin), line a baking sheet with parchment. Drop heaping tablespoons of dough onto the baking sheet as if you were going to bake them. Place the baking sheet in the freezer for about an hour, until the dough is frozen. Place the individual dough balls into a freezer container. To use, simply place the balls of dough on a baking sheet. Either let them thaw for about 15 minutes before baking, then bake according to the recipe, or bake them frozen and simply increase the baking time as needed until done.

To freeze dough for sliced cookies, roll it into a tube shape, then wrap it in waxed paper and place it in a freezer container. To use, let the dough defrost on your kitchen counter for about 30 minutes or in the refrigerator for about an hour. It should still be cold when you slice it so the slices hold their shape. Bake as directed.

To freeze sugar cookie dough, make sure the dough is fully chilled. Once it is, press it into a disk and wrap it tightly in waxed paper. Place the wrapped disk into a freezer container. To use, let the disk defrost on your kitchen counter or in the refrigerator for a few hours. This dough should still be cold when you roll it out. Bake as directed in the recipe instructions.

When freezing cookie dough, label your containers with the date, as well as any baking instructions you'll want to remember. Frozen dough will keep for about 3 months.

HOW TO FREEZE COOKIES

Cookies freeze well once they're baked, as well as in dough form. This makes them a convenient snack to always have on hand, and also is a timesaver when it comes to baking for the holidays or for other special occasions and get-togethers.

Theoretically, you can put any type of cookies in the freezer, but some varieties definitely hold up better than others. Avoid freezing any overly delicate treats, such as meringues. The best cookies to freeze are sturdy and simple—drop cookies, undecorated cutout cookies, or cookie-type bars.

As for decorated cookies, whether it's a cutout cookie decorated with royal icing or a cookie with frosting or glaze, always freeze the cookies bare, and decorate them when you're ready to use them. Make sure the cookies are thawed before decorating them, as they will release moisture as they thaw.

Once your baked cookies are completely cool, arrange them in a single layer on a baking sheet. Place the sheet in the freezer for 30 minutes or until the cookies are frozen solid. Then, layer frozen cookies in airtight containers, with parchment separating each layer. This will help prevent the cookies from sticking to each other.

Repeat until all of the cookies are packed, then freeze the containers for up to 3 months. Let them thaw at room temperature or heat in the microwave for a few seconds before serving.

DROP

DAD'S CHOCOLATE CHIP COOKIES

Back when I was in college, I'd get care packages from home with cookies baked by my dad instead of my mom! These classics have long been a favorite in our family.
—Art Winter, Trumbull, CT

PREP: 15 MIN. • **BAKE:** 10 MIN./BATCH
MAKES: ABOUT 6 DOZEN

- ⅔ **cup butter, softened**
- ⅔ **cup shortening**
- 1 **cup sugar**
- 1 **cup packed brown sugar**
- 2 **large eggs, room temperature**
- 2 **tsp. vanilla extract**
- 3½ **cups all-purpose flour**
- 1 **tsp. salt**
- 1 **tsp. baking soda**
- 2 **cups semisweet chocolate chips**
- 1 **cup chopped walnuts**

1. Preheat oven to 350°. In a large bowl, cream butter, shortening and sugars until light and fluffy, 5-7 minutes. Beat in eggs and vanilla. Combine flour, salt and baking soda; gradually add to the creamed mixture and mix well. Stir in chocolate chips and nuts.
2. Form dough into 1½-in. balls and place on ungreased baking sheets. Bake until golden brown, 10-13 minutes. Remove from pans to wire racks to cool.
1 cookie: 134 cal., 7g fat (3g sat. fat), 12mg chol., 81mg sod., 16g carb. (10g sugars, 1g fiber), 2g pro.

FROSTED PEANUT COOKIES

FROSTED PEANUT COOKIES

Oats, chopped peanuts and peanut butter frosting make this a nice change of pace from a traditional peanut butter cookie. After folks sample these, compliments and recipe requests always follow.
—Alicia Surma, Tacoma, WA

PREP: 20 MIN.
BAKE: 10 MIN./BATCH + COOLING
MAKES: 5 DOZEN

- 1 cup butter, softened
- 1½ cups packed brown sugar
- 2 large eggs, room temperature
- 1 tsp. vanilla extract
- 2 cups all-purpose flour
- 2 tsp. baking powder
- 1 cup quick-cooking oats
- 1 cup chopped salted peanuts

FROSTING
- ½ cup peanut butter
- 3 cups confectioners' sugar
- ⅓ to ½ cup 2% milk

1. Preheat oven to 350°. In a large bowl, cream butter and brown sugar until light and fluffy, 5-7 minutes. Beat in eggs and vanilla. Combine flour and baking powder; gradually add to the creamed mixture and mix well. Stir in oats and peanuts.
2. Drop by rounded teaspoonfuls 2 in. apart onto ungreased baking sheets. Bake for 10-12 minutes or until golden brown. Remove to wire racks to cool.
3. For frosting, in a bowl, beat peanut butter, confectioners' sugar and ⅓ cup milk; add additional milk if necessary. Frost cookies.

1 cookie: 122 cal., 6g fat (2g sat. fat), 14mg chol., 64mg sod., 17g carb. (12g sugars, 1g fiber), 2g pro.

GRANDMA BRUBAKER'S
ORANGE COOKIES

CHEWY GOOD OATMEAL COOKIES

Here's a classic oatmeal cookie with all my favorite extras: dried cherries, white chocolate chips and macadamia nuts.
—Sandy Harz, Spring Lake, MI

PREP: 20 MIN. • **BAKE:** 10 MIN./BATCH
MAKES: 3½ DOZEN

- 1 **cup butter, softened**
- 1 **cup packed brown sugar**
- ½ **cup sugar**
- 2 **large eggs, room temperature**
- 1 **Tbsp. honey**
- 2 **tsp. vanilla extract**
- 2½ **cups quick-cooking oats**
- 1½ **cups all-purpose flour**
- 1 **tsp. baking soda**
- ½ **tsp. salt**
- ½ **tsp. ground cinnamon**
- 1⅓ **cups dried cherries**
- 1 **cup white baking chips**
- 1 **cup chopped macadamia nuts**

1. Preheat oven to 350°. In a large bowl, cream butter and sugars until light and fluffy, 5-7 minutes. Beat in the eggs, honey and vanilla. In another bowl, mix the oats, flour, baking soda, salt and cinnamon; gradually beat into the creamed mixture. Stir in the remaining ingredients.
2. Drop by rounded tablespoonfuls 2 in. apart onto greased baking sheets. Bake 10-12 minutes or until golden brown. Cool on pan for 2 minutes; remove to wire racks to cool.
1 cookie: 161 cal., 8g fat (4g sat. fat), 22mg chol., 105mg sod., 20g carb. (13g sugars, 1g fiber), 2g pro.

GRANDMA BRUBAKER'S ORANGE COOKIES

At least two generations of my family have enjoyed the recipe for these light, delicate orange-flavored cookies.
—Sheri DeBolt, Huntington, IN

PREP: 20 MIN.
BAKE: 10 MIN./BATCH + COOLING
MAKES: ABOUT 6 DOZEN

- 1 **cup shortening**
- 2 **cups sugar**
- 2 **large eggs, separated, room temperature**
- 1 **cup buttermilk**
- 5 **cups all-purpose flour**
- 2 **tsp. baking powder**
- 2 **tsp. baking soda**
  Pinch salt
  Juice and grated zest of
  2 **medium navel oranges**

ICING

- 2 **cups confectioners' sugar**
- ¼ **cup orange juice**
- 1 **Tbsp. butter**
- 1 **Tbsp. grated orange zest**

1. Preheat the oven to 325°. In a bowl, cream shortening and sugar. Beat in egg yolks and buttermilk. Sift together flour, baking powder, soda and salt; add to the creamed mixture alternately with orange juice and zest. Add egg whites and beat until smooth.
2. Drop by rounded teaspoonfuls onto greased cookie sheets. Bake until set, about 10 minutes. Remove to wire racks to cool completely.
3. For icing, combine all ingredients and beat until smooth. Frost cooled cookies.
1 cookie: 97 cal., 3g fat (1g sat. fat), 6mg chol., 58mg sod., 16g carb. (9g sugars, 0 fiber), 1g pro.

BROWNED BUTTER SPICE COOKIES

If you like spice cake, you'll love this recipe! Browned butter, dark chocolate and a splash of rum produce an unconventional spice cookie that's guaranteed to please.
—Kristin Kenney, Newport Beach, CA

PREP: 20 MIN. + CHILLING
BAKE: 10 MIN./BATCH
MAKES: ABOUT 2 DOZEN

- ½ cup unsalted butter, cubed
- 1 cup packed brown sugar
- 1 large egg, room temperature
- 1 Tbsp. spiced rum
- 1¼ cups all-purpose flour
- 1½ tsp. ground cinnamon
- ½ tsp. baking soda
- ¼ tsp. salt
- ¼ tsp. ground ginger
- ¼ tsp. ground nutmeg
- ½ cup dark chocolate chips

1. Place the butter in a small heavy saucepan. Cook over medium heat until golden brown, 5-7 minutes; cool slightly.
2. Beat brown sugar and browned butter in a large bowl until blended. Beat in egg, then rum. Combine the flour, cinnamon, baking soda, salt, ginger and nutmeg; gradually add to the brown sugar mixture and mix well. Stir in the chocolate chips. Cover and refrigerate for at least 30 minutes.
3. Drop by rounded tablespoonfuls 2 in. apart onto greased baking sheets. Bake at 350° until bottoms are lightly browned, 10-12 minutes. Remove to wire racks to cool.

1 cookie: 111 cal., 5g fat (3g sat. fat), 17mg chol., 54mg sod., 16g carb. (11g sugars, 1g fiber), 1g pro.

COCONUT CLOUDS

The big dollop of buttercream and a sprinkle of roasty-toasty coconut make these soft cookies the first to disappear from Christmas cookie trays. Take care to toast the coconut for absolutely heavenly flavor.
—Donna Scofield, Yakima, WA

PREP: 45 MIN.
BAKE: 10 MIN./BATCH + COOLING
MAKES: ABOUT 5½ DOZEN

- ¼ cup butter, softened
- ¼ cup shortening
- 1 cup sugar
- ½ cup packed brown sugar
- 2 large eggs, room temperature
- 1 tsp. coconut extract
- 1 tsp. vanilla extract
- 1 cup sour cream
- 2¾ cups all-purpose flour
- 1 tsp. salt
- ½ tsp. baking soda
- 1 cup sweetened shredded coconut, toasted

BROWNED BUTTER FROSTING
- ⅓ cup butter, cubed
- 3 cups confectioners' sugar
- 3 Tbsp. evaporated milk
- 1 tsp. coconut extract
- 1 tsp. vanilla extract
- 2 cups sweetened shredded coconut, toasted

1. Preheat oven to 375°. Cream butter, shortening and sugars until light and fluffy, 5-7 minutes; beat in eggs and extracts. Stir in sour cream. In another bowl, whisk together flour, salt and baking soda; gradually beat into the creamed mixture. Stir in coconut.
2. Drop the dough by tablespoonfuls 2 in. apart onto lightly greased baking sheets. Bake until set, 8-10 minutes. Remove the cookies to wire racks to cool completely.
3. For the frosting, in a small heavy saucepan, heat butter over medium heat until golden brown, 5-7 minutes, stirring constantly. Transfer to a small bowl; gradually beat in confectioners' sugar, milk and extracts. Spread over cookies. Dip in coconut; let stand until set. Store in an airtight container.

1 cookie: 110 cal., 5g fat (3g sat. fat), 13mg chol., 72mg sod., 16g carb. (11g sugars, 0 fiber), 1g pro.

RANGER COOKIES

These golden brown cookies are crispy on the outside and cakelike on the inside. Their tasty blend of oats, rice cereal, coconut and brown sugar have made them a favorite with our family. You won't be able to eat just one.
—Mary Lou Boyce, Wilmington, DE

PREP: 25 MIN. • **BAKE:** 10 MIN./BATCH
MAKES: 7½ DOZEN

- 1   cup shortening
- 1   cup sugar
- 1   cup packed brown sugar
- 2   large eggs, room temperature
- 1   tsp. vanilla extract
- 2   cups all-purpose flour
- 1   tsp. baking soda
- ½   tsp. baking powder
- ½   tsp. salt
- 2   cups quick-cooking oats
- 2   cups crisp rice cereal
- 1   cup sweetened shredded coconut

1. Preheat oven to 350°. In a large bowl, cream shortening and sugars until light and fluffy, 5-7 minutes. Beat in eggs and vanilla. Combine the flour, baking soda, baking powder and salt; gradually add to the creamed mixture and mix well. Stir in oats, cereal and coconut.
2. Drop by rounded tablespoonfuls 2 in. apart onto ungreased baking sheets. Bake until golden brown, 7-9 minutes. Remove from pans to wire racks to cool.
1 cookie: 63 cal., 3g fat (1g sat. fat), 5mg chol., 40mg sod., 9g carb. (5g sugars, 0 fiber), 1g pro.
Peanut Butter Ranger Cookies: Before creaming the shortening and sugars, add 1 cup peanut butter.

HOMEMADE COCONUT MACAROONS

Chewy, simple and so good, these bite-sized cookies are perfect for bake sales—that is, if your family doesn't devour them first!
—Sabrina Shafer, Minooka, IL

BAKING 101

TAKES: 25 MIN. • **MAKES:** 1½ DOZEN

- 2½   cups sweetened shredded coconut
- ⅓   cup all-purpose flour
- ⅛   tsp. salt
- ⅔   cup sweetened condensed milk
- 1   tsp. vanilla extract

1. Preheat oven to 350°. In a small bowl, combine the coconut, flour and salt. Add milk and vanilla; mix well (batter will be stiff).
2. Drop by tablespoonfuls 1 in. apart onto a greased baking sheet. Bake 15-20 minutes or until golden brown. Remove to wire racks.
1 cookie: 110 cal., 6g fat (5g sat. fat), 4mg chol., 65mg sod., 14g carb. (11g sugars, 1g fiber), 2g pro.

FROSTED RED VELVET COOKIES

My student job in college was in the bakery. These dreamy morsels take me back to that special place and time. Red velvet cake lovers will appreciate this fun riff.
—Christina Petri, Alexandria, MN

PREP: 20 MIN.
BAKE: 10 MIN./BATCH + COOLING
MAKES: 5 DOZEN

- 2 oz. unsweetened chocolate, chopped
- ½ cup butter, softened
- ⅔ cup packed brown sugar
- ⅓ cup sugar
- 1 large egg, room temperature
- 1 Tbsp. red food coloring
- 1 tsp. vanilla extract
- 2 cups all-purpose flour
- ½ tsp. baking soda
- ½ tsp. salt
- 1 cup sour cream
- 1 cup semisweet chocolate chips
- 1 can (16 oz.) cream cheese frosting
  Sprinkles, optional

1. In a microwave, melt unsweetened chocolate; stir until smooth. Cool.
2. Preheat oven to 375°. In a large bowl, cream the butter and sugars until light and fluffy, 5-7 minutes. Beat in the egg, food coloring and vanilla. Add cooled chocolate; beat until blended. In another bowl, mix flour, baking soda and salt; add to the creamed mixture alternately with sour cream, beating well after each addition. Stir in chocolate chips.
3. Drop by tablespoonfuls 2 in. apart onto parchment-lined baking sheets. Bake for 6-9 minutes or until set. Remove cookies to wire racks to cool completely. Spread with frosting. If desired, decorate with sprinkles.
1 cookie: 103 cal., 5g fat (3g sat. fat), 8mg chol., 62mg sod., 14g carb. (10g sugars, 0 fiber), 1g pro.

FROSTED RED VELVET
COOKIES

GINGERBREAD
AMARETTI COOKIES

GINGERBREAD AMARETTI COOKIES

These are classic Italian cookies with a new gingerbread twist! Don't overbake—they should be slightly chewy.

—Tina Zaccardi, Eastchester, NY

PREP: 20 MIN. • **BAKE:** 10 MIN./BATCH
MAKES: 2 DOZEN

1   can (8 oz.) almond paste
¾ cup sugar
1   Tbsp. baking cocoa
1   tsp. ground ginger
½ tsp. ground cinnamon
    Dash ground cloves
2   large egg whites, room temperature
2   Tbsp. molasses
1   cup pearl or coarse sugar

1. Preheat oven to 375°. Crumble the almond paste into a food processor; add sugar, baking cocoa and spices. Pulse until combined. Add egg whites and molasses; process until smooth.
2. Drop by tablespoonfuls into pearl sugar; roll to coat. Place 2 in. apart on parchment-lined baking sheets. Bake until set, 10-12 minutes. Cool on pans for 1 minute before removing to wire racks to cool. Store the cookies in an airtight container.
1 cookie: 107 cal., 3g fat (0 sat. fat), 0 chol., 6mg sod., 21g carb. (19g sugars, 1g fiber), 1g pro.

SOUR CREAM CHOCOLATE COOKIES

You can easily alter these soft, chocolaty cookies to make different varieties—I've added everything from macadamia nuts to mints to them.

—Tina Sawchuk, Ardmore, AB

PREP: 15 MIN.
BAKE: 15 MIN./BATCH + COOLING
MAKES: ABOUT 3 DOZEN

½ cup butter, softened
¾ cup sugar
½ cup packed brown sugar
1   large egg, room temperature
½ cup sour cream
1   tsp. vanilla extract
1¾ cups all-purpose flour
½ cup baking cocoa
1   tsp. baking powder
½ tsp. baking soda
¼ tsp. salt
1   cup semisweet chocolate chips
½ cup vanilla or white chips

1. Preheat oven to 350°. Cream the butter and sugars until light and fluffy, 5-7 minutes. Beat in egg, sour cream and vanilla. Combine dry ingredients; gradually add to the creamed mixture. Stir in chips.
2. Drop by rounded tablespoonfuls 2 in. apart onto greased baking sheets. Bake 12-15 minutes or until set. Cool for 2 minutes on pan; remove to wire racks.
2 cookies: 239 cal., 11g fat (7g sat. fat), 31mg chol., 156mg sod., 34g carb. (20g sugars, 1g fiber), 3g pro.

AMISH SUGAR COOKIES

I've passed this recipe around to many friends. The cookies are so easy to make and simply melt in your mouth. My sister entered them in a local fair and won the best of show prize!

—Sylvia Ford, Kennett, MO

PREP: 10 MIN. • **BAKE:** 10 MIN./BATCH
MAKES: ABOUT 5 DOZEN

1   cup butter, softened
1   cup vegetable oil
1   cup sugar
1   cup confectioners' sugar
2   large eggs, room temperature
1   tsp. vanilla extract
4½ cups all-purpose flour
1   tsp. baking soda
1   tsp. cream of tartar

BAKING 101

1. Preheat oven to 375°. In a large bowl, beat the butter, oil and sugars. Beat in eggs until well blended. Beat in vanilla. Combine the flour, baking soda and cream of tartar; gradually add to the creamed mixture.
2. Drop by small teaspoonfuls onto ungreased baking sheets. Bake until lightly browned, 8-10 minutes. Remove to wire racks to cool.
1 cookie: 117 cal., 7g fat (2g sat. fat), 14mg chol., 48mg sod., 13g carb. (5g sugars, 0 fiber), 1g pro.

. . . .
TEST KITCHEN TIP
Salted butter and a splash of extract (try almond!) make these cookies extra flavorful. If you like your treats on the sweeter side, add a pinch of coarse sugar to the tops of these light and airy cookies.

1. Preheat oven to 375°. In a large bowl, beat butter and sugars until crumbly, about 2 minutes. Beat in egg and vanilla. Combine the flour, salt and baking soda; gradually add to butter mixture and mix well. Stir in cranberries and chips.
2. Drop by tablespoonfuls 2 in. apart onto baking sheets coated with cooking spray. Bake until the cookies are lightly browned, 8-10 minutes. Cool 1 minute before removing to wire racks.

1 cookie: 78 cal., 3g fat (2g sat. fat), 10mg chol., 69mg sod., 13g carb. (9g sugars, 0 fiber), 1g pro

PUMPKIN COOKIES WITH BROWNED BUTTER FROSTING

The recipe for these pleasantly spiced pumpkin cookies won a champion ribbon at our local county fair. These are a family favorite, and everyone enjoys the soft cakelike texture.
—Robin Nagel, Whitehall, MT

PREP: 25 MIN.
BAKE: 10 MIN./BATCH + COOLING
MAKES: ABOUT 9 DOZEN

- 1½ cups butter, softened
-   2 cups packed brown sugar
-   1 cup canned pumpkin
-   2 large eggs, room temperature
-   ½ cup crystallized ginger, finely chopped
-   5 cups all-purpose flour
-   2 tsp. baking soda
-   2 tsp. ground cinnamon
-   2 tsp. ground ginger
-   ½ tsp. salt

FROSTING
-   ⅔ cup butter, cubed
-   4 cups confectioners' sugar
-   1 tsp. vanilla extract
-   4 to 5 Tbsp. 2% milk

1. Preheat oven to 375°. In a large bowl, cream butter and brown sugar until light and fluffy, 5-7 minutes. Beat in pumpkin, eggs and crystallized ginger. In another bowl, whisk flour, baking soda, cinnamon, ginger and salt; gradually beat into creamed mixture.
2. Drop dough by tablespoonfuls 2 in. apart onto ungreased baking sheets. Bake 6-8 minutes or until golden brown. Remove to wire racks to cool completely.
3. For the frosting, in a small heavy saucepan, melt butter over medium heat. Heat 5-7 minutes or until golden brown, stirring constantly. Transfer to a large bowl. Gradually beat in confectioners' sugar, vanilla and enough milk to reach spreading consistency. Spread over cookies.

1 cookie: 93 cal., 4g fat (2g sat. fat), 14mg chol., 64mg sod., 14g carb. (9g sugars, 0 fiber), 1g pro.

WHITE CHOCOLATE CRANBERRY COOKIES

These sweet cookies feature white chocolate and cranberries for a delightful taste. The red and white coloring adds a great holiday feel to any cookie tray.
—Donna Beck, Scottdale, PA

PREP: 20 MIN. • **BAKE:** 10 MIN./BATCH
MAKES: 3 DOZEN

- ⅓ cup butter, softened
- ½ cup packed brown sugar
- ⅓ cup sugar
-   1 large egg, room temperature
-   1 tsp. vanilla extract
- 1½ cups all-purpose flour
- ½ tsp. salt
- ½ tsp. baking soda
- ¾ cup dried cranberries
- ½ cup white baking chips

ALMOND TOFFEE SANDIES

I knew after sampling these cookies from a friend that I had to add them to my bulging recipe files!
—Vicki Crowley, Monticello, IA

PREP: 15 MIN. • **BAKE:** 10 MIN./BATCH
MAKES: 9 DOZEN

1	cup butter, softened
1	cup sugar
1	cup confectioners' sugar
2	large eggs, room temperature
1	cup canola oil
1	tsp. almond extract
4½	cups all-purpose flour
1	tsp. baking soda
1	tsp. cream of tartar
1	tsp. salt
2	cups sliced almonds
1	pkg. (8 oz.) toffee bits

1. Preheat oven to 350°. In a large bowl, cream butter and sugars until blended. Add eggs, 1 at a time, beating well after each addition. Gradually beat in oil and extract. Combine the flour, baking soda, cream of tartar and salt; gradually add to the creamed mixture and mix well. Stir in almonds and toffee bits.
2. Drop by teaspoonfuls 2 in. apart onto ungreased baking sheets. Bake until golden brown, 10-12 minutes. Remove to wire racks to cool.
2 cookies: 178 cal., 11g fat (4g sat. fat), 19mg chol., 134mg sod., 18g carb. (9g sugars, 1g fiber), 2g pro.
Toffee Pecan Sandies: Substitute 2 cups of coarsely chopped pecans for the almonds.

BAKING 101

CHERRY CHOCOLATE CHUNK COOKIES

CHERRY CHOCOLATE CHUNK COOKIES

These rich, fudgy cookies are chewy and studded with tangy dried cherries. It's a good thing the recipe makes only a small batch, because we eat them all in one night!
—Trisha Kruse, Eagle, ID

PREP: 15 MIN. • **BAKE:** 15 MIN./BATCH
MAKES: ABOUT 1½ DOZEN

½	cup butter, softened
¾	cup sugar
1	large egg, room temperature
2	Tbsp. 2% milk
½	tsp. vanilla extract
1	cup all-purpose flour
6	Tbsp. baking cocoa
¼	tsp. baking soda
¼	tsp. salt
1	cup semisweet chocolate chunks
½	cup dried cherries

1. Preheat oven to 350°. Cream the butter and sugar until light and fluffy, 5-7 minutes. Beat in egg, milk and vanilla. In a separate bowl, whisk flour, cocoa, baking soda and salt; gradually beat into creamed mixture. Stir in the chocolate and cherries.
2. Drop by rounded tablespoonfuls 2 in. apart onto baking sheets lightly coated with cooking spray. Bake until firm, 12-14 minutes. Cool for 1 minute before removing to a wire rack.
1 cookie: 159 cal., 8g fat (5g sat. fat), 22mg chol., 88mg sod., 22g carb. (15g sugars, 1g fiber), 2g pro.

PEANUT BUTTER BLOSSOM COOKIES

These classic cookies prove peanut butter and chocolate just belong together. They're an easy family favorite that never fail to make my children smile.

—Tammie Merrill, Wake Forest, NC

PREP: 15 MIN.
BAKE: 10 MIN./BATCH + COOLING
MAKES: 3 DOZEN

- ½ cup butter, softened
- ½ cup creamy peanut butter
- ½ cup sugar
- ½ cup packed brown sugar
- 1 large egg, room temperature
- 1¼ cups all-purpose flour
- ¾ tsp. baking soda
- ½ tsp. baking powder
- ¼ tsp. salt
- 36 milk chocolate kisses

1. Preheat oven to 350°. Cream butter, peanut butter and sugars until light and fluffy, 5-7 minutes. Beat in the egg. In another bowl, sift together flour, baking soda, baking powder and salt; beat into peanut butter mixture.

2. Drop by level tablespoonfuls 2 in. apart onto ungreased baking sheets. Bake until light brown, 10-12 minutes. Remove from oven; immediately push a chocolate kiss into the top of each cookie. Cool on pans 2 minutes; remove the cookies from pans to wire racks to cool completely.

1 cookie: 106 cal., 6g fat (3g sat. fat), 13mg chol., 92mg sod., 13g carb. (9g sugars, 0 fiber), 2g pro.

TEST KITCHEN TIP

If you prefer more texture, you can use chunky peanut butter instead; the measurements will be the same.

PEANUT BUTTER BLOSSOM COOKIES

VERMONT
MAPLE COOKIES

VERMONT MAPLE COOKIES

I created this recipe after tasting maple cookies with a maple glaze at a bakery in Stowe, Vermont, some years ago. I get many requests to bring them for bake sales, parties and ski trips.
—Delores Day, Wolcott, VT

PREP: 20 MIN.
BAKE: 10 MIN./BATCH + COOLING
MAKES: 5 DOZEN

- 1 cup butter, softened
- ¾ cup sugar
- ¾ cup packed brown sugar
- 2 large eggs, room temperature
- 1 tsp. maple flavoring
- 2½ cups all-purpose flour
- 1 tsp. baking soda
- 1 tsp. salt
- 2 cups white baking chips
- 1 cup chopped pecans

MAPLE GLAZE

- ⅓ cup butter, cubed
- 1¾ cups confectioners' sugar
- ⅓ cup maple syrup
- ¼ tsp. maple flavoring

1. Preheat oven to 350°. In a large bowl, cream butter and sugars until light and fluffy, 5-7 minutes. Beat in the eggs and maple flavoring. In another bowl, whisk flour, baking soda and salt; gradually beat into the creamed mixture. Stir in baking chips and pecans.
2. Drop by rounded tablespoonfuls 2 in. apart onto ungreased baking sheets. Bake for 10-12 minutes or until golden brown. Cool on pans for 2 minutes, then remove to wire racks to cool completely.
3. For glaze, in a saucepan, melt butter over medium heat. Remove from heat. Gradually beat in confectioners' sugar, syrup and maple flavoring until smooth.
4. Drizzle glaze over cookies; let dry completely. Store between pieces of waxed paper in airtight containers.
1 cookie: 139 cal., 7g fat (4g sat. fat), 18mg chol., 101mg sod., 18g carb. (13g sugars, 0 fiber), 1g pro.

MEXICAN TEA
COOKIES

CUTOUT

MEXICAN TEA COOKIES

Mexican tea cookies are a holiday favorite in our family. I updated the recipe by frosting them with a buttercream made with dulce de leche. They are a tender, crumbly cookie that everyone enjoys.
—David Ross, Spokane Valley, WA

PREP: 45 MIN. + CHILLING
BAKE: 10 MIN./BATCH + COOLING
MAKES: 3 DOZEN

- 1 cup butter, softened
- ½ cup confectioners' sugar
- ½ cup sugar
- 1 large egg, room temperature
- 1 tsp. vanilla extract
- 3¼ cups all-purpose flour
- ¾ cup finely chopped pecans
- 1 tsp. baking powder
- ¼ tsp. salt
- ¼ tsp. ground cinnamon

BUTTERCREAM
- ½ cup butter, softened
- 1 Tbsp. heavy whipping cream
- 1 tsp. vanilla extract
- 2 cups confectioners' sugar
- ½ cup dulce de leche
- 2 Tbsp. ground pecans

1. In a large bowl, cream butter and sugars until light and fluffy, 5-7 minutes. Beat in egg and vanilla. In another bowl, whisk flour, pecans, baking powder, salt and cinnamon; gradually beat into the creamed mixture; dough will be soft. Form into a disk; wrap and refrigerate 1 hour or until chilled.

2. Preheat oven to 350°. On a floured surface, roll dough to ¼-in. thickness. Cut with a floured 2-in. round cookie cutter; re-roll dough scraps as needed. Place 2 in. apart on parchment-lined baking sheets. Bake until until edges begin to lightly brown, 10-12 minutes. Remove from pans to wire racks to cool completely.

3. For buttercream, in a large bowl, beat butter, cream and vanilla until creamy. Beat in confectioners' sugar alternately with dulce de leche until smooth. Sprinkle the cookies with additional confectioners' sugar. Pipe buttercream onto cookies; sprinkle with pecans. Store, covered, in refrigerator.

1 cookie: 188 cal., 10g fat (5g sat. fat), 27mg chol., 101mg sod., 23g carb. (13g sugars, 1g fiber), 2g pro.

CHOCOLATE WALNUT CRESCENTS

Use a round cookie cutter to form the crescent shapes for these nutty favorites. They're so pretty sprinkled with sugar and drizzled with chocolate.

—TerryAnn Moore, Vineland, NJ

PREP: 40 MIN. + CHILLING
BAKE: 10 MIN./BATCH + COOLING
MAKES: ABOUT 10½ DOZEN

- 1 cup butter, softened
- ½ cup sugar
- 1 tsp. vanilla extract
- 2 cups all-purpose flour
- 2 cups ground walnuts
- 3 Tbsp. baking cocoa
- 2 to 3 Tbsp. confectioners' sugar
- 2 cups semisweet chocolate chips
- 2 tsp. shortening

1. In a large bowl, cream the butter and sugar until light and fluffy, 5-7 minutes. Beat in the vanilla. Combine the flour, walnuts and cocoa; gradually add to the creamed mixture and mix well. Cover and refrigerate for 1 hour or until easy to handle.

2. Preheat oven to 350°. On a lightly floured surface, roll out dough to ¼-in. thickness. Using a floured plain or finely scalloped 2-in. round cookie cutter, cut a semicircle off 1 corner of the dough, forming the inside of a crescent shape. Reposition cutter 1¼ in. from inside of crescent; cut cookie, forming a crescent 1¼ in. wide at its widest point. Repeat. Chill and reroll scraps if desired.

3. Place 1 in. apart on ungreased baking sheets. Bake 9-11 minutes or until set. Cool for 1 minute before removing to wire racks to cool completely.

4. Sprinkle cookies with confectioners' sugar. In a microwave, melt chocolate chips and shortening; stir until smooth. Drizzle over cookies; let stand until set. Store in an airtight container.

1 cookie: 46 cal., 3g fat (2g sat. fat), 4mg chol., 12mg sod., 4g carb. (2g sugars, 0 fiber), 1g pro.

LINZER COOKIES

These cookies have an old-world elegance and a special flavor that delights. The bright red spark of raspberry jam and the wreath shape make them a perfect addition to any holiday cookie platter.

—Jane Pearcy, Verona, WI

PREP: 30 MIN. + CHILLING
BAKE: 10 MIN./BATCH + COOLING
MAKES: 3 DOZEN

- 1¼ cups butter, softened
- 1 cup sugar
- 2 large eggs, room temperature
- 3 cups all-purpose flour
- 1 Tbsp. baking cocoa
- ½ tsp. salt
- ¼ tsp. ground cinnamon
- ¼ tsp. ground nutmeg
- ⅛ tsp. ground cloves
- 2 cups ground almonds
- 6 Tbsp. seedless raspberry jam
- 3 Tbsp. confectioners' sugar

1. In a large bowl, cream the butter and sugar until light and fluffy, 5-7 minutes. Add eggs, 1 at a time, beating well after each addition. Combine flour, cocoa, salt and spices; gradually add to the creamed mixture and mix well. Stir in almonds. Refrigerate for 1 hour or until easy to handle.

2. Preheat oven to 350°. On a lightly floured surface, roll out dough to ⅛-in. thickness. Cut with a floured 2½-in. round or cookie cutter. From the center of half the cookies, cut out a 1½-in. shape.

3. Place on ungreased baking sheets. Bake 10-12 minutes or until the edges are golden brown. Remove to wire racks to cool completely.

4. Spread the bottom of each solid cookie with ½ tsp. jam. Sprinkle cutout cookies with confectioners' sugar; carefully place over jam.

1 cookie: 161 cal., 9g fat (4g sat. fat), 28mg chol., 82mg sod., 17g carb. (9g sugars, 1g fiber), 3g pro. **Diabetic exchanges:** 1½ fat, 1 starch.

GRANDMA'S SCOTTISH SHORTBREAD

BAKING 101

Traditional shortbread can be shaped several ways—rolled out and cut into wedges, pressed into molds or cut into bars after baking.
—Jane Kelly, Wayland, MA

PREP: 15 MIN. • **BAKE:** 45 MIN. + COOLING
MAKES: 4 DOZEN

- 1 lb. butter, softened
- 8 oz. superfine sugar (about 1¼ cups)
- 1 lb. all-purpose flour (3⅔ cups)
- 8 oz. white rice flour (1⅓ cups)

1. Preheat oven to 300°. Cream the butter and sugar until light and fluffy, 5-7 minutes. Combine flours; gradually beat into the creamed mixture. Press the dough into an ungreased 13x9-in. baking pan. Prick with a fork.
2. Bake until light brown, 45-50 minutes. Cut into 48 bars or triangles while still warm. Cool completely on a wire rack.
1 bar: 139 cal., 8g fat (5g sat. fat), 20mg chol., 61mg sod., 16g carb. (5g sugars, 0 fiber), 1g pro.

LAVENDER & LEMON BISCOCHITOS

Biscochitos are the state cookie for our home state of New Mexico. I substituted lavender and lemon for the traditional anise flavor. The result is intriguing and delicious! I have also made these with lemon and dried thyme and they were scrumptious.
—Marla Clark, Albuquerque, NM

PREP: 30 MIN. + CHILLING
BAKE: 10 MIN./BATCH • **MAKES:** 6 DOZEN

- ½ cup unsalted butter, softened
- ⅔ cup sugar

LAVENDER & LEMON BISCOCHITOS

- 1 large egg, room temperature
- 1 Tbsp. dried lavender flowers
- 1 Tbsp. grated lemon zest
- 1½ cups all-purpose flour
- 1 tsp. baking powder
- ¼ tsp. salt
  Additional sugar

1. In a large bowl, cream butter and sugar until light and fluffy, 5-7 minutes. Beat in egg, lavender and lemon zest. In another bowl, whisk flour, baking powder and salt; gradually beat into the creamed mixture. Divide dough in half. Shape each half into a disk; cover and refrigerate 30 minutes or until firm enough to roll.
2. Preheat oven to 350°. On a lightly floured surface, roll out each portion of dough to ¼-in. thickness. Cut with a floured 1-in. round cookie cutter. Place

1 in. apart on parchment-lined baking sheets. Sprinkle with additional sugar.
3. Bake until bottoms are light brown, 9-11 minutes. Remove from pans to wire racks to cool. Store the cookies in airtight containers.
1 cookie: 29 cal., 1g fat (1g sat. fat), 6mg chol., 16mg sod., 4g carb. (2g sugars, 0 fiber), 0 pro.

TEST KITCHEN TIP

If adding fresh lavender or other fresh herbs to the top of the cookies (as shown in some of the cookies above), brush unbaked cutouts with some lightly beaten egg white before gently pressing on the herbs. Bake as directed.

HIDDEN MINT MORSELS

Is it a cookie or a candy? No matter which answer folks choose, they find these minty morsels yummy. The recipe makes so much that you can whip up dozens at once.
—Adina Skilbred, Prairie du Sac, WI

PREP: 30 MIN. + CHILLING
BAKE: 10 MIN./BATCH + CHILLING
MAKES: ABOUT 10 DOZEN

- ⅓ cup shortening
- ⅓ cup butter, softened
- ¾ cup sugar
- 1 large egg, room temperature
- 1 Tbsp. 2% milk
- 1 tsp. vanilla extract
- 1¾ cups all-purpose flour
- ⅓ cup baking cocoa
- 1½ tsp. baking powder
- ¼ tsp. salt
- ⅛ tsp. ground cinnamon

PEPPERMINT LAYER
- 4 cups confectioners' sugar
- 6 Tbsp. light corn syrup
- 6 Tbsp. butter, melted
- 2 to 3 tsp. peppermint extract

CHOCOLATE COATING
- 2 pkg. (11½ oz. each) milk chocolate chips
- ¼ cup shortening

1. In a large bowl, cream the shortening, butter and sugar until light and fluffy, 5-7 minutes. Beat in the egg, milk and vanilla. Combine the flour, cocoa, baking powder, salt and cinnamon; gradually add to the creamed mixture. Cover tightly and refrigerate for 8 hours or overnight.
2. Preheat oven to 375°. On a lightly floured surface, roll out dough to ⅛-in. thickness. Cut with a lightly floured 1½-in. round cookie cutter; place on ungreased baking sheets.
3. Bake until set, 6-8 minutes. Cool for 2 minutes before removing to wire racks to cool completely.
4. In a large bowl, combine all the peppermint layer ingredients. Knead for 1 minute or until smooth. Shape into 120 balls, ½ in. each. Place a ball on each cookie; flatten ball to cover cookie. Place on waxed paper-lined baking sheets; refrigerate for 30 minutes.
5. In a microwave, melt the chocolate chips and shortening; stir until smooth. Spread about 1 tsp. chocolate over each cookie. Chill until firm.

2 cookies: 127 cal., 6g fat (3g sat. fat), 11mg chol., 50mg sod., 18g carb. (14g sugars, 0 fiber), 1g pro.

VANILLA-BUTTER SUGAR COOKIES

These are one of my favorite cookies to bake for Christmas. The dough recipe is versatile and you can use it for other holidays, too. Children like to help with decorating.
—Cynthia Ettel, Glencoe, MN

PREP: 35 MIN. + CHILLING
BAKE: 10 MIN./BATCH + COOLING
MAKES: ABOUT 7 DOZEN

- 1½ cups butter, softened
- 1½ cups sugar
- 2 large eggs, room temperature
- 2 Tbsp. vanilla extract
- 4 cups all-purpose flour
- 1 tsp. salt
- 1 tsp. baking soda
- 1 tsp. cream of tartar

FROSTING
- 1½ cups confectioners' sugar
- 3 Tbsp. butter, softened
- 1 Tbsp. vanilla extract
- 1 to 2 Tbsp. whole milk
  Food coloring, optional
  Colored sugar

1. Cream butter and sugar until light and fluffy, 5-7 minutes. Beat in eggs and vanilla. In another bowl, whisk flour, salt, baking soda and cream of tartar. Gradually beat into creamed mixture. Refrigerate, covered, for 30 minutes.
2. Preheat oven to 350°. On a lightly floured surface, roll dough to ¼-in. thickness. Cut with floured 2½-in. cookie cutters. Place 1 in. apart on ungreased baking sheets. Bake for 10-12 minutes. Cool on wire racks.
3. For frosting, beat confectioners' sugar, butter, vanilla and enough milk to reach desired consistency. If desired, add a few drops of food coloring. Fit a pastry bag with a fine, round tip or cut a small hole in the tip of a food-safe plastic bag; transfer frosting to bag. Pipe decorations and sprinkle with colored sugar.

1 cookie: 80 cal., 4g fat (2g sat. fat), 14mg chol., 74mg sod., 10g carb. (6g sugars, 0 fiber), 1g pro.

VANILLA-BUTTER
SUGAR COOKIES

PEANUT BUTTER CINNAMON SNAP COOKIES

This recipe makes a lot of cookies, which makes it perfect for bake sales, potlucks, or holiday gift baskets. Use fun cookie cutters for any occasion you are celebrating. Peanut butter, molasses, orange and cinnamon flavors combine so nicely. The cookie glaze dries shiny, so they look quite professional.
—Kallee Krong-McCreery, Escondido, CA

PREP: 30 MIN. + CHILLING
BAKE: 10 MIN./BATCH + COOLING
MAKES: 5 DOZEN

- ½ cup butter, softened
- ½ cup creamy peanut butter
- ½ cup sugar
- 1 large egg, room temperature
- ½ cup molasses
- 2 Tbsp. thawed orange juice concentrate
- 3½ cups all-purpose flour
- 2 tsp. ground cinnamon
- ½ tsp. baking soda
- GLAZE
- 2½ cups confectioners' sugar
- 2 to 4 Tbsp. water
- 1 Tbsp. butter, softened
- 1 Tbsp. light corn syrup
- ½ tsp. vanilla or orange extract

1. Cream the butter, peanut butter and sugar until light and fluffy, 5-7 minutes. Beat in egg, molasses and orange juice concentrate. In another bowl, whisk the flour, cinnamon and baking soda; gradually beat into creamed mixture.
2. Divide dough into 3 portions. Shape each portion into a disk; wrap tightly. Refrigerate 30 minutes or until firm enough to roll.
3. Preheat oven to 350°. On a lightly floured surface, roll each portion of dough to ⅛-in. thickness. Cut with a floured 3-in. star-shaped cookie cutter. Place 2 in. apart on parchment-lined baking sheets. Bake until edges are firm and begin to brown, 8-10 minutes. Remove from pans to wire racks to cool completely.
4. Combine glaze ingredients; drizzle over cookies. Let stand until set. Store between pieces of waxed paper in airtight containers.
1 cookie: 86 cal., 3g fat (1g sat. fat), 7mg chol., 34mg sod., 14g carb. (9g sugars, 0 fiber), 1g pro.

. . . .
DID YOU KNOW?

You can use natural peanut butter instead of processed in recipes, but there are some differences. Processed butters contain sugar, more salt (depending on the brand) and oils to help maintain creaminess. Stir natural peanut butter well to reincorporate any the natural oils that have separated before adding it to your recipe.

GREAT-GRANDMA'S OATMEAL COOKIES

This recipe—a favorite of my husband's—goes back to my great-grandmother. We make them year-round, but at Christmastime, we use colored sugar to add a festive touch.
—Mary Ann Konechne, Kimball, SD

PREP: 35 MIN.
BAKE: 15 MIN./BATCH
MAKES: ABOUT 12 DOZEN

- 1½ cups shortening
- 2 cups sugar
- 4 large eggs, room temperature
- 4 tsp. water
- 4 cups all-purpose flour
- 2 tsp. baking soda
- 2 tsp. ground cinnamon
- ½ tsp. salt
- 4 cups quick-cooking oats
- 2 cups chopped raisins
- 1 cup chopped walnuts
  Additional sugar or colored sugar

1. Preheat oven to 350°. Cream the shortening and sugar until light and fluffy, 5-7 minutes. Add eggs, 1 at a time, beating well after each addition. Beat in water. In another bowl, whisk together flour, baking soda, cinnamon and salt; add to the creamed mixture and mix well. Stir in the oats, raisins and walnuts.
2. On a surface sprinkled with additional sugar, roll out dough to ¼-in. thickness. Cut with a floured 2½-in. cookie cutter in desired shapes. Place 2 in. apart on greased baking sheets. Bake until set, 12-15 minutes. Remove to wire racks to cool.

1 cookie: 63 cal., 3g fat (1g sat. fat), 5mg chol., 28mg sod., 9g carb. (4g sugars, 0 fiber), 1g pro.

GINGERBREAD CUTOUT COOKIES

The smell of these cookies always makes me think of going to Grandma's house. My boys like to linger around the kitchen when I make them.
—Christy Thelen, Kellogg, IA

PREP: 30 MIN. + CHILLING
BAKE: 10 MIN./BATCH + COOLING
MAKES: 5 DOZEN

- ¾ cup butter, softened
- 1 cup packed brown sugar
- 1 large egg, room temperature
- ¾ cup molasses
- 4 cups all-purpose flour
- 2 tsp. ground ginger
- 1½ tsp. baking soda
- 1½ tsp. ground cinnamon
- ¾ tsp. ground cloves
- ¼ tsp. salt
  Vanilla frosting of your choice
  Red and green paste food coloring

1. In a large bowl, cream the butter and brown sugar until light and fluffy, 5-7 minutes. Add egg and molasses. Combine the flour, ginger, baking soda, cinnamon, cloves and salt; gradually add to the creamed mixture and mix well. Cover and refrigerate until easy to handle, about 4 hours or overnight.
2. Preheat oven to 350°. On a lightly floured surface, roll dough to ⅛-in. thickness. Cut with floured 2½-in. cookie cutters. Place 1 in. apart on ungreased baking sheets.
3. Bake until the edges are firm, 8-10 minutes. Remove to wire racks to cool completely. Tint some of the frosting red and some green; leave remaining frosting plain. Decorate cookies as desired.

1 cookie: 77 cal., 2g fat (1g sat. fat), 10mg chol., 69mg sod., 13g carb. (6g sugars, 0 fiber), 1g pro.

GINGERBREAD
CUTOUT COOKIES

GINGER BUDDIES

A gingerbread man cookie cutter doesn't have to make cookie-cutter cookies! With some imagination, you can make your cookies into anything—even a yeti! See p. 430 for tips on working with royal icing.

1 sandwich cookie: 314 cal., 19g fat (9g sat. fat), 34mg chol., 131mg sod., 33g carb. (17g sugars, 2g fiber), 5g pro.

LEMON POPPY SEED CUTOUTS

I love to package up these tart, tender cookies to share with friends! You could spread buttercream or cream cheese frosting on them to make lemony sandwich cookies. And they'd be delicious dipped in white chocolate.

—Ilana Pulda, Bellevue, WA

PREP: 30 MIN. + CHILLING
BAKE: 10 MIN./BATCH
MAKES: ABOUT 3 DOZEN

- 1 cup unsalted butter, softened
- ½ cup confectioners' sugar
- 1 Tbsp. sugar
- 1 Tbsp. grated lemon zest
- 4 tsp. lemon juice
- ½ tsp. vanilla extract
- 2 cups all-purpose flour
- 1 Tbsp. poppy seeds
- ¼ tsp. salt

1. Cream butter and sugars until light and fluffy, 5-7 minutes. Beat in lemon zest, juice and vanilla. In another bowl, whisk the flour, poppy seeds and salt; gradually beat into creamed mixture. Shape dough into a disk; cover tightly. Refrigerate for 4 hours or until firm enough to roll.
2. Preheat oven to 350°. Roll dough between 2 sheets of waxed paper to ¼-in. thickness. Cut with a floured 1½-in. cookie cutter; reroll scraps. Place 1 in. apart on parchment-lined baking sheets. Bake until edges begin to brown, 10-12 minutes. Remove from pans to wire racks to cool.
1 cookie: 80 cal., 5g fat (3g sat. fat), 14mg chol., 17mg sod., 7g carb. (2g sugars, 0 fiber), 1g pro.

PISTACHIO SHORTBREAD SANDWICHES

PISTACHIO SHORTBREAD SANDWICHES

We tasted these melt-in-your-mouth morsels at a Christmas party several years ago. We tweaked the recipe to include pistachios. The cookies disappear so quickly at parties, you just might have to watch the plate—and check the kids' pockets!

—Lorraine Caland, Shuniah, ON

PREP: 20 MIN.
BAKE: 20 MIN./BATCH + COOLING
MAKES: ABOUT 1½ DOZEN

- 1¼ cups unsalted butter, softened
- 1 cup sugar
- 1 tsp. vanilla extract
- 2 cups all-purpose flour
- ½ tsp. salt
- 2 cups ground pistachios
  Confectioners' sugar
- ⅔ cup apricot preserves

GLAZE (OPTIONAL)
- 1½ cups confectioners' sugar
- 4 tsp. lemon juice

1. Cream butter and sugar until light and fluffy, 5-7 minutes. Beat in vanilla. In another bowl, whisk flour and salt; gradually beat into creamed mixture. Stir in pistachios.
2. Preheat oven to 300°. On a surface sprinkled with confectioners' sugar, roll dough to ¼-in. thickness. Cut with a 2½-in. fluted round cookie cutter dusted with confectioners' sugar. Place cookies 1 in. apart on ungreased baking sheets. Bake until edges begin to brown, 18-20 minutes. Cool cookies on pans for 5 minutes, then remove to wire racks to cool completely.
3. Spread preserves on bottoms of half of the cookies; cover with the remaining cookies. If desired, combine confectioners' sugar and lemon juice until smooth. Drizzle over cookies.

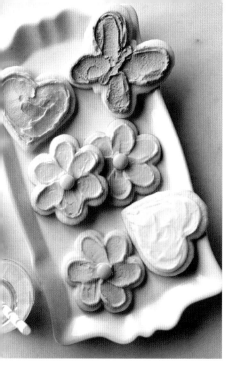

WHITE VELVET CUTOUTS

We make these cutouts every year and give lots of them as gifts. Last year, we baked a batch a week all through December to be sure we'd have plenty for ourselves, too. These rich cookies melt in your mouth!
—Kim Hinkle, Wauseon, OH

PREP: 25 MIN. + CHILLING
BAKE: 10 MIN./BATCH + COOLING
MAKES: ABOUT 5½ DOZEN

- 2 cups butter, softened
- 1 pkg. (8 oz.) cream cheese, softened
- 2 cups sugar
- 2 large egg yolks, room temperature
- 1 tsp. vanilla extract
- 4½ cups all-purpose flour
  FROSTING
- 3 Tbsp. butter, softened
- 1 Tbsp. shortening
- ½ tsp. vanilla extract
- 3½ cups confectioners' sugar
- 4 to 5 Tbsp. 2% milk
  Food coloring, optional

1. In a large bowl, cream butter, cream cheese and sugar until light and fluffy, 5-7 minutes. Beat in egg yolks and vanilla. Gradually beat in flour. Divide dough in half. Shape each into a disk; wrap and refrigerate until firm enough to roll, about 2 hours.
2. Preheat oven to 350°. On a lightly floured surface, roll each portion of dough to ¼-in. thickness. Cut with floured 3-in. cookie cutters. Place 1 in. apart on greased baking sheets. Bake until set (do not brown), 10-12 minutes. Cool on pans 5 minutes. Remove to wire racks to cool completely.
3. For frosting, beat butter, shortening and vanilla until blended. Beat in the confectioners' sugar and enough milk to reach spreading consistency; beat until light and fluffy, about 3 minutes. If desired, beat in food coloring. Frost cookies. (While you're working, keep frosting covered with a damp towel to prevent it from drying out.)
1 cookie: 149 cal., 8g fat (5g sat. fat), 26mg chol., 62mg sod., 19g carb. (13g sugars, 0 fiber), 1g pro.

FRENCH BUTTER COOKIES

The Brittany region of France is known for its use of butter. These French butter cookies, also known as sable Breton, shine the spotlight on the famous ingredient. This recipe is mildly sweet, rich, crisp and has a hint of salt. You won't be able to resist having a second—or third.
—*Taste of Home* Test Kitchen

PREP: 15 MIN. + CHILLING
BAKE: 15 MIN./BATCH + COOLING
MAKES: 2 DOZEN

- ⅔ cup European-style salted butter, softened
- ½ cup sugar
- 3 large egg yolks, room temperature, divided use,
- 1 tsp. vanilla extract
- 2 cups all-purpose flour
- ¼ tsp. salt
- 2 Tbsp. water

1. Cream butter and sugar until light and fluffy, 5-7 minutes. Beat in 2 egg yolks and vanilla. Gradually beat in the flour and salt. Divide the dough in half; shape each portion into a disk. Cover; refrigerate until firm enough to roll, about 30 minutes.
2. Preheat oven to 350°. Working with 1 portion of dough at a time, roll to ¼-in. thickness between parchment. Cut with floured 2-in. round cookie cutter. Place 1 in. apart on ungreased baking sheets. Whisk the remaining egg yolk and the water; brush over cookies. Drag the tines of a fork across each cookie to create a cross-hatch design.
3. Bake until edges are light golden, 12-15 minutes. Cool on pans 5 minutes. Remove to wire racks to cool completely.
1 cookie: 107 cal., 6g fat (3g sat. fat), 37mg chol., 42mg sod., 12g carb. (4g sugars, 0 fiber), 1g pro.

SLICED

CHOCOLATE MINT CREAMS

This recipe came from an old family friend and is always high on everyone's cookie request list. I make at least six batches for Noel nibbling and give some away as gifts.
—Beverly Fehner, Gladstone, MO

PREP: 20 MIN. + CHILLING
BAKE: 10 MIN./BATCH + COOLING
MAKES: ABOUT 6 DOZEN

- 1 cup butter, softened
- 1½ cups confectioners' sugar
- 2 oz. unsweetened chocolate, melted and cooled
- 1 large egg, room temperature
- 1 tsp. vanilla extract
- 2½ cups all-purpose flour
- 1 tsp. baking soda
- 1 tsp. cream of tartar
- ¼ tsp. salt

FROSTING
- ¼ cup butter, softened
- 2 cups confectioners' sugar
- 2 Tbsp. 2% milk
- ½ tsp. peppermint extract
  Green food coloring, optional

1. Cream the butter and confectioners' sugar until light and fluffy, 5-7 minutes. Add chocolate, egg and vanilla; mix well. In another bowl, whisk together flour, baking soda, cream of tartar and salt; gradually add to the creamed mixture, beating well. Divide dough in half; shape each half into a 2-in.-diameter roll. Wrap in waxed paper; refrigerate until firm, about 1 hour.
2. Preheat oven to 400°. Unwrap dough and cut crosswise into ⅛-in. slices. Place 2 in. apart on ungreased baking sheets. Bake until the edges are firm, 7-8 minutes. Remove from pans to wire racks to cool completely.
3. For frosting, combine all ingredients; beat until smooth. Spread over the cookies; let dry completely. Store in airtight containers.
1 cookie: 73 cal., 4g fat (2g sat. fat), 11mg chol., 53mg sod., 9g carb. (6g sugars, 0 fiber), 1g pro.

MANGO FUDGE REFRIGERATOR RIBBON COOKIES

A ribbon cookie is especially nice because although it's a single snack, it really tastes like two different cookies because of its lovely layers. These refrigerated cookies have a rich chocolate layer balanced by a bright orange-mango layer—a truly special combination.
—Jeanne Holt, Saint Paul, MN

PREP: 30 MIN. + CHILLING
BAKE: 10 MIN./BATCH
MAKES: 4 DOZEN

- 1 cup butter, softened
- 1 cup sugar
- 1 large egg, room temperature
- 2 Tbsp. 2% milk
- 1½ tsp. vanilla extract
- 3 cups all-purpose flour
- 1½ tsp. baking powder
- ½ tsp. salt
- ½ cup 60% cacao bittersweet chocolate baking chips, melted and cooled
- ⅓ cup miniature semisweet chocolate chips
- ½ cup finely chopped dried mango
- ⅓ cup finely chopped pistachios
- 2 tsp. grated orange zest

1. Cream the butter and sugar until light and fluffy, 5-7 minutes. Beat in the egg, milk and vanilla. In another bowl, whisk together flour, baking powder and salt; gradually add to the creamed mixture.
2. Divide dough in half. Mix the melted chocolate into 1 half; stir in miniature chips. Mix the mango, pistachios and orange zest into the remaining half of the dough.
3. Line an 8x4-in. loaf pan with plastic wrap, letting ends extend over sides. Press half the chocolate dough onto the bottom of the pan; top with half the mango dough. Repeat layers.
4. Lifting with plastic, remove dough from pan; fold plastic over the dough to wrap completely. Refrigerate dough in pan until firm, 2 hours or overnight.
5. Preheat oven to 375°. Unwrap dough and cut loaf crosswise into ½-in.-thick slices; cut each slice crosswise into thirds. Place 2 in. apart on ungreased baking sheets.
6. Bake until edges are lightly browned, 10-12 minutes. Remove from pans to wire racks to cool.
1 cookie: 104 cal., 5g fat (3g sat. fat), 14mg chol., 58mg sod., 13g carb. (7g sugars, 1g fiber), 1g pro.

MANGO FUDGE
REFRIGERATOR
RIBBON COOKIES

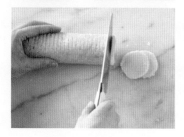

SMART SLICES

To perfect your roll of dough, lay it on a sheet of parchment; fold the paper over the dough with the edges facing you. Hold a ruler on top of the parchment, at the base of the dough. Gently and firmly pull on one end of the paper, tightening it to form a log.

When you're ready to bake, use the ruler and a pencil or food-safe marker to mark every ¼ in. along the parchment. Use a sharp knife to cut through the paper and lightly score the dough at each mark. Unwrap the log, and slice along the cut marks.

OAT & COCONUT
ICEBOX COOKIES

OAT & COCONUT ICEBOX COOKIES

This recipe was passed down through my family from Grandma Irene and is a favorite of my dad and my cousin Dennis. It's a true cookie lover's cookie: crispy on the outside, chewy on the inside and perfectly dunkable.
—Lori Rowe, Tigerton, WI

PREP: 20 MIN. + CHILLING
BAKE: 10 MIN./BATCH
MAKES: ABOUT 3½ DOZEN

- ½ cup butter, softened
- ½ cup shortening
- 1 cup sugar
- 1 cup packed brown sugar
- 2 large eggs, room temperature
- 1 tsp. vanilla extract
- 1½ cups all-purpose flour
- 1 tsp. baking soda
- 1 tsp. salt
- 3 cups old-fashioned oats
- ½ cup sweetened shredded coconut
- ½ cup chopped walnuts

1. Cream butter, shortening and sugars until light and fluffy, 5-7 minutes. Beat in the eggs and vanilla. In another bowl, whisk the flour, baking soda and salt; gradually beat into creamed mixture. Stir in oats, coconut and walnuts.
2. Divide dough in half. Shape each into a 10-in.-long roll. Wrap each roll tightly; refrigerate overnight.
3. Preheat oven to 375°. Unwrap dough and cut crosswise into ½-in. slices. Place 2 in. apart on ungreased baking sheets. Bake until edges begin to brown, 8-10 minutes. Cool 2 minutes before removing from pans to wire racks.
1 cookie: 142 cal., 7g fat (3g sat. fat), 15mg chol., 117mg sod., 19g carb. (11g sugars, 1g fiber), 2g pro.

FINNISH CHRISTMAS COOKIES

My friend bakes these cookies at Christmas. They're popular at cookie exchanges, but my friend's husband urges her not to trade any of them!
—Judith Outlaw, Portland, OR

PREP: 20 MIN. + CHILLING
BAKE: 10 MIN./BATCH
MAKES: ABOUT 6 DOZEN

- 2 cups butter, softened
- 1 cup sugar
- 4 cups all-purpose flour
- 1 large egg, lightly beaten
- ⅔ cup finely chopped almonds
  Colored sugar, optional

1. In a large bowl, cream the butter and sugar until light and fluffy, 5-7 minutes. Gradually beat in flour and mix well. Cover and refrigerate for 1 hour.
2. Preheat oven to 350°. Roll dough onto a well-floured surface to ¼-in. thickness. Brush lightly with egg. Sprinkle with almonds and sugar if desired. Using a fluted pastry cutter or knife, cut into 2x1-in. strips.
3. Place 1 in. apart on ungreased baking sheets. Bake 10-12 minutes or until lightly browned. Cool on wire racks.
1 cookie: 89 cal., 6g fat (3g sat. fat), 16mg chol., 42mg sod., 8g carb. (3g sugars, 0 fiber), 1g pro.

RASPBERRY NUT
PINWHEELS

JEWELED COOKIE SLICES

I often mark my recipes with "G" for good or "VG" for very good. This seasonal favorite is marked "VVG!" I usually double the recipe.
—Rosella Peters, Gull Lake, , SK

PREP: 20 MIN. + CHILLING
BAKE: 10 MIN./BATCH
MAKES: ABOUT 2½ DOZEN

- ⅓ cup butter, melted
- ⅓ cup sugar
- ¼ cup packed brown sugar
- 1 large egg, room temperature
- ½ tsp. vanilla extract
- 1½ cups all-purpose flour
- 1 tsp. baking powder
- ⅛ tsp. baking soda
- ⅛ tsp. ground nutmeg
- ½ cup red and green candied cherries or chopped candied pineapple
- 2 Tbsp. chopped blanched almonds

1. Line an 8x4-in. loaf pan with plastic wrap. In a large bowl, beat the melted butter and sugars until blended. Beat in egg and vanilla. In a small bowl, whisk flour, baking powder, baking soda and nutmeg; gradually beat into the butter mixture. Stir in cherries and almonds. Transfer to prepared pan. Refrigerate, covered, at least 2 hours or until firm.
2. Preheat oven to 350°. Invert dough onto a cutting board; remove plastic wrap. Cut dough crosswise into ¼-in. slices. Place 2 in. apart on greased baking sheets. Bake 10-12 minutes or until light brown. Remove from pans to wire racks to cool.

1 cookie: 138 cal., 5g fat (3g sat. fat), 25mg chol., 87mg sod., 21g carb. (11g sugars, 1g fiber), 2g pro.

RASPBERRY NUT PINWHEELS

I won first prize in a recipe contest with these yummy swirl cookies. The taste of raspberry and walnuts really comes through and they're so much fun to make!
—Pat Habiger, Spearville, KS

PREP: 20 MIN. + CHILLING
BAKE: 10 MIN./BATCH
MAKES: ABOUT 3½ DOZEN

- ½ cup butter, softened
- 1 cup sugar
- 1 large egg, room temperature
- 1 tsp. vanilla extract
- 2 cups all-purpose flour
- 1 tsp. baking powder
- ¼ cup seedless raspberry jam
- ¾ cup finely chopped walnuts

1. In a large bowl, cream butter and sugar until light and fluffy, 5-7 minutes. Beat in egg and vanilla. In another bowl, whisk the flour and baking powder; gradually beat into creamed mixture.
2. Roll out dough between 2 sheets of waxed paper into a 12-in. square. Remove waxed paper. Spread dough with jam; sprinkle with nuts. Roll up tightly, jelly-roll style; cover. Refrigerate until firm, about 2 hours.
3. Preheat oven to 375°. Uncover dough and cut crosswise into ¼-in. slices. Place 2 in. apart on ungreased baking sheets. Bake until the edges are light brown, 9-12 minutes. Remove from pans to wire racks to cool.

1 cookie: 79 cal., 4g fat (1g sat. fat), 11mg chol., 27mg sod., 11g carb. (6g sugars, 0 fiber), 1g pro.

NEAPOLITAN COOKIES

My sister shared the recipe for these tricolor treats several years ago. The crisp cookies are fun to eat one section at a time or with all three in one bite.

—Jan Mallo, White Pigeon, MI

PREP: 20 MIN. + CHILLING
BAKE: 10 MIN./BATCH
MAKES: ABOUT 11 DOZEN

- 1 cup butter, softened
- 1½ cups sugar
- 1 large egg, room temperature
- 1 tsp. vanilla extract
- 2½ cups all-purpose flour
- 1½ tsp. baking powder
- ½ tsp. salt
- ½ tsp. almond extract
- 6 drops red food coloring
- ½ cup chopped walnuts
- 1 oz. unsweetened chocolate, melted

1. Line a 9x5-in. loaf pan with waxed paper, letting ends extend up the sides of the pan. Cream the butter and sugar until light and fluffy, 5-7 minutes. Beat in the egg and vanilla. In another bowl, whisk the flour, baking powder and salt; gradually beat into creamed mixture.
2. Divide the dough into 3 portions. Mix almond extract and food coloring into 1 portion; spread evenly into prepared pan. Mix walnuts into another portion; spread evenly over the first layer. Mix melted chocolate into the remaining portion; spread over top. Refrigerate, covered, overnight.
3. Preheat oven to 350°. Lifting with waxed paper, remove dough from pan. Cut lengthwise in half; cut each half crosswise into ⅛-in. slices.
4. Place 1 in. apart on ungreased baking sheets. Bake until edges are firm, 10-12 minutes. Remove from pans to wire racks to cool.

1 cookie: 35 cal., 2g fat (1g sat. fat), 5mg chol., 25mg sod., 4g carb. (2g sugars, 0 fiber), 0 pro.

SNICKERDOODLE CRISPS

This classic cookie from New England can be made two ways: soft or crunchy. My happy version with cinnamon, ginger and nutmeg is crispy to perfection.

—Jenni Sharp, Milwaukee, WI

BAKING 101

PREP: 20 MIN. + CHILLING
BAKE: 10 MIN./BATCH
MAKES: ABOUT 5 DOZEN

- 1 cup butter, softened
- 2 cups sugar
- 2 large eggs, room temperature
- 2 tsp. vanilla extract
- 3 cups all-purpose flour
- 4 tsp. ground cinnamon
- 2 tsp. ground ginger
- ¾ tsp. ground nutmeg
- ½ tsp. ground allspice
- 2 tsp. cream of tartar
- 1 tsp. baking soda
- ½ tsp. salt

SPICED SUGAR
- ⅓ cup sugar
- 1 tsp. ground cinnamon
- ¾ tsp. ground ginger
- ¼ tsp. ground nutmeg
- ¼ tsp. ground allspice

1. In a large bowl, cream the butter and sugar until light and fluffy, 5-7 minutes. Beat in the eggs and vanilla. In another bowl, whisk the flour, spices, cream of tartar, baking soda and salt; gradually beat into the creamed mixture.
2. Divide dough in half; shape each into an 8-in.-long roll. Wrap and refrigerate 2 hours or until firm.
3. Preheat oven to 350°. In a small bowl, mix spiced sugar ingredients. Unwrap the dough and cut crosswise into ¼-in. slices; press the cookies into the sugar mixture to coat both sides or sprinkle sugar mixture over cookies. Place 2 in. apart on greased baking sheets. Bake 7-9 minutes or until the edges are light brown. Cool on pans 2 minutes. Remove to wire racks to cool.

1 cookie: 84 cal., 3g fat (2g sat. fat), 14mg chol., 68mg sod., 13g carb. (8g sugars, 0 fiber), 1g pro.

ORANGE PISTACHIO COOKIES

I had never tried pistachios until I visited a friend who served me these cookies. I was in love! I made the recipe my own, and now my family can't get enough of them!
—Lorraine Caland, Shuniah, ON

PREP: 20 MIN. + CHILLING
BAKE: 10 MIN./BATCH + COOLING
MAKES: ABOUT 4½ DOZEN

- ¾   cup butter, softened
- 1   cup sugar
- 1   large egg, room temperature
- 1   Tbsp. grated orange zest
- 1   tsp. vanilla extract
- 2   cups all-purpose flour
- ¼   cup cornstarch
- ½   cup pistachios, toasted and finely chopped

ICING
- 2¼ cups confectioners' sugar
- ¼   cup orange juice
- 1   Tbsp. butter, melted
       Additional pistachios, toasted and finely chopped, optional

1. In a large bowl, cream the butter and sugar until light and fluffy, 5-7 minutes. Beat in egg, orange zest and vanilla. In another bowl, whisk the flour and cornstarch; gradually beat into the creamed mixture.

2. Divide dough in half. Roughly shape each portion into a 7-in. roll along the long end of a 14x8-in. sheet of waxed paper. Tightly roll waxed paper over the dough, using the paper to mold the dough into a smooth roll. Place the waxed paper-covered roll in an airtight container; freeze 30 minutes or until firm, or refrigerate overnight.

3. Preheat oven to 350°. Sprinkle the pistachios on a rimmed baking sheet. Unwrap each roll of dough and roll it in the pistachios. Cut dough crosswise into ¼-in. slices. Place slices ½ in. apart on parchment-lined baking sheets. Bake 6-8 minutes or until bottoms are light brown. Cool slightly on pan. Remove from pans to wire racks to cool completely.

4. For icing, in a small bowl, combine the confectioners' sugar, orange juice and butter until smooth. Spread over the cookies. If desired, sprinkle with additional pistachios. Let stand until set.

1 cookie: 83 cal., 3g fat (2g sat. fat), 10mg chol., 27mg sod., 13g carb. (9g sugars, 0 fiber), 1g pro.

. . . .
TEST KITCHEN TIP
Unsalted nuts are best for baking, but unsalted pistachios can be difficult to find. Check ethnic stores or online sources if your local market doesn't carry them. If all else fails, rinse salted pistachios well, then let them dry before toasting and chopping them.

SINTERKLAAS
COOKIES

SINTERKLAAS COOKIES

After opening our gifts on Christmas Eve as a child, we would make these cookies for Santa Claus to snack on with his glass of milk. These crisp spice cookies are delicious dipped in milk—or in coffee on Christmas morning.
—Charli Fontana, Pella, IA

PREP: 20 MIN. + CHILLING
BAKE: 10 MIN./ BATCH
MAKES: ABOUT 5 DOZEN

2½ cups butter, softened
 2 cups sugar
 2 cups packed brown sugar
 2 large eggs, room temperature
 6 cups all-purpose flour
 1 Tbsp. ground cinnamon
1½ tsp. baking soda
 1 tsp. ground cloves
 1 tsp. ground nutmeg

1. Cream butter and sugars until light and fluffy, 5-7 minutes. Beat in eggs. In another bowl, whisk the remaining ingredients; gradually beat into the creamed mixture. Divide dough into quarters; shape each portion of dough into a 12-in.-long roll. Wrap tightly in waxed paper; refrigerate overnight.
2. Preheat oven to 375°. Unwrap each roll and cut dough crosswise into ¾-in. slices. Place slices 2 in. apart on ungreased baking sheets. Bake until set, 10-12 minutes. Remove from pans to wire racks to cool.
1 cookie: 160 cal., 7g fat (5g sat. fat), 25mg chol., 91mg sod., 22g carb. (13g sugars, 0 fiber), 2g pro.

BAKING
101

BAKING
101

LEMON THYME
ICEBOX COOKIES

I found this recipe at my grandmother's house, and I made it as soon as I got home. The lovely melt-in-your-mouth butter cookie is very unique. It's almost savory because of the thyme, which pairs well with the lemon.

—Catherine Adams, Westwego, LA

PREP: 15 MIN. + CHILLING
BAKE: 15 MIN./BATCH + COOLING
MAKES: ABOUT 2 DOZEN

½   cup butter, softened
5   Tbsp. sugar
1   Tbsp. minced fresh thyme
1   to 2 tsp. grated lemon zest
1   large egg yolk, room temperature
1   cup all-purpose flour
¼   tsp. baking powder
¼   tsp. salt

1. Cream the butter, sugar, thyme and lemon zest until light and fluffy, 5-7 minutes. Beat in the egg yolk. In another bowl, whisk the flour, baking powder and salt; gradually beat into the creamed mixture.
2. Roughly shape dough into a 12-in. roll along the edge of a 12x12-in. sheet of waxed paper. Tightly roll waxed paper over dough, using the paper to mold the dough into a smooth roll. Place in an airtight container; refrigerate 1 hour or overnight.
3. Preheat oven to 350°. Unwrap dough and cut crosswise into ½-in. slices. Place 2 in. apart on ungreased baking sheets. Bake until edges begin to brown, 12-15 minutes. Cool in pans 5 minutes. Remove to wire racks to finish cooling.
1 cookie: 65 cal., 4g fat (3g sat. fat), 18mg chol., 61mg sod., 7g carb. (3g sugars, 0 fiber), 1g pro.

BEST COCONUT PECAN
COOKIES

Baking big batches of cookies is easy when you've got a great recipe like this one. I love to give cookies to friends, and these are always a favorite.

—Betty Matthews, South Haven, MI

PREP: 30 MIN. + CHILLING
BAKE: 20 MIN./BATCH + COOLING
MAKES: 4½ DOZEN

1   cup butter, softened
1   cup sugar
1   large egg, room temperature
2¼   cups all-purpose flour
½   tsp. baking soda
½   tsp. salt
3   cups sweetened shredded
     coconut, divided
     Pecan halves

1. In a large bowl, cream butter and sugar until light and fluffy, 5-7 minutes. Beat in egg. Combine the flour, baking soda and salt; add to creamed mixture and mix well. Stir in 2 cups coconut.
2. Divide dough in half; shape each into a 7-in. long roll. Roll in remaining 1 cup coconut. Wrap tightly in waxed paper; refrigerate 1 hour or until firm.
3. Unwrap dough; cut into ¼-in. slices. Place 3 in. apart on ungreased baking sheets. Place a pecan half in the center of each. Bake at 325° for 20-25 minutes or until lightly browned. Cool cookies for 2-3 minutes before removing to wire racks to cool completely.
1 cookie: 100 cal., 6g fat (4g sat. fat), 13mg chol., 83mg sod., 10g carb. (6g sugars, 1g fiber), 1g pro.

GINGERBREAD PEPPERMINT PINWHEELS

Two holiday flavors—gingerbread and peppermint—come together in these impressive pinwheel cookies. I created the recipe especially for my husband, who loves the combination.

—Joanna Quelch, Burlington, VT

PREP: 1 HOUR + CHILLING
BAKE: 10 MIN./BATCH
MAKES: ABOUT 6 DOZEN

GINGERBREAD DOUGH
- ½ cup butter, softened
- ½ cup packed brown sugar
- 1 large egg, room temperature
- ¼ cup molasses
- 2¼ cups all-purpose flour
- 1 tsp. ground ginger
- ½ tsp. ground cinnamon
- ¼ tsp. baking soda
- ¼ tsp. ground cloves

PEPPERMINT DOUGH
- ⅓ cup butter, softened
- 3 oz. cream cheese, softened
- 1 cup sugar
- 1 large egg, room temperature
- ½ tsp. vanilla extract
- ⅛ tsp. peppermint extract
- 2¼ cups all-purpose flour
- ½ tsp. baking powder
- 2 Tbsp. crushed peppermint candies

GINGERBREAD PEPPERMINT PINWHEELS

1. For the gingerbread dough, in a large bowl, cream butter and brown sugar until light and fluffy, 5-7 minutes. Beat in egg and molasses. In another bowl, whisk flour, ginger, cinnamon, baking soda and cloves; gradually beat into the creamed mixture. Divide dough in half; shape each portion into a disk. Wrap and refrigerate 1 hour or until firm enough to roll.

2. For the peppermint dough, in a large bowl, cream butter, cream cheese and sugar until light and fluffy, 5-7 minutes. Beat in egg and extracts. In another bowl, whisk flour and baking powder; gradually beat into creamed mixture. Stir in the peppermint candies. Divide dough in half; shape each portion into a disk. Wrap and refrigerate 1 hour or until firm enough to roll.

3. On a baking sheet, roll 1 portion of gingerbread dough between 2 sheets of waxed paper into a 10x8-in. rectangle. Roll 1 portion of the peppermint dough between 2 sheets of waxed paper into a 10x8-in. rectangle. Remove top sheet of waxed paper; invert over gingerbread dough. Refrigerate 30 minutes. Remove waxed paper. Roll up tightly jelly-roll style, starting with a long side. Wrap in waxed paper. Repeat with the remaining dough. Refrigerate 2 hours or until firm.

4. Preheat oven to 375°. Unwrap dough and cut crosswise into ¼-in. slices. Place 2 in. apart on greased baking sheets. Bake 10-12 minutes or until set. Remove from pans to wire racks to cool.

1 cookie: 74 cal., 3g fat (2g sat. fat), 12mg chol., 31mg sod., 11g carb. (5g sugars, 0 fiber), 1g pro.

SHAPED

. . . .

BENNE SEED WAFERS

Crisp, chewy, nutty and caramelized benne cookies, also known as sesame cookies or benne wafers, are perfect for your holiday or Kwanzaa celebrations. For a more traditional cookie, leave them plain. If you feel like dressing them up, drizzle them with melted chocolate. Both ways are equally delicious.
—April Wright, Elkridge, MD

PREP: 30 MIN.
BAKE: 20 MIN./BATCH + COOLING
MAKES: 8 DOZEN

  1   cup sesame seeds
1¼   cups packed light brown sugar
  ½   cup unsalted butter, softened
  1   large egg, room temperature
  1   tsp. vanilla extract
  ¾   cup all-purpose flour
  ¼   tsp. salt
  ⅛   tsp. baking powder
CHOCOLATE DRIZZLE (OPTIONAL)
1¼   to 2½ cups 60% cacao bittersweet
      chocolate baking chips
  2   tsp. shortening or coconut oil

1. Preheat oven to 350°. Place sesame seeds on an ungreased baking sheet. Bake until fragrant and lightly browned, 10-15 minutes; cool.
2. Reduce oven temperature to 300°. In a large bowl, beat brown sugar and butter until crumbly. Beat in egg and vanilla extract. In a small bowl, whisk together flour, salt and baking powder. Gradually beat into sugar mixture. Add cooled sesame seeds and stir to combine.
3. Roll level teaspoons of dough into balls. Place 2 in. apart on parchment-lined baking sheets. Reduce oven temperature to 275°; bake until set but still soft, 18-20 minutes. Cool on pan 5 minutes before removing to a wire rack to cool completely.
4. For chocolate drizzle, if desired, in a large microwave-safe bowl, melt chocolate, uncovered, at 50% power until melted, stirring every 30 seconds, 1-1½ minutes. Add shortening and stir until melted. Drizzle over cookies; let stand until set.
1 wafer: 32 cal., 2g fat (1g sat. fat), 4mg chol., 9mg sod., 4g carb. (3g sugars, 0 fiber), 0 pro.

. . . .
TEST KITCHEN TIP
Store plain cookies in an airtight container up to 4 days at room temperature. Refrigerate chocolate-drizzled cookies in an airtight container up to 4 days.

BENNE SEED WAFERS

CHOCOLATE MACADAMIA
MELTAWAYS

SUGAR COOKIES

This is truly an oldie, dating back to a Swedish woman born in 1877! Her daughter shared the recipe with me and came up with all the exact measurements, since the original cookies were mixed by feel and taste.
—Helen Wallis, Vancouver, WA

PREP: 30 MIN. • **BAKE:** 10 MIN./BATCH
MAKES: 5 DOZEN

- ½ cup butter, softened
- ½ cup shortening
- 1 cup sugar
- 1 large egg, room temperature
- 1 tsp. vanilla extract
- 2¼ cups all-purpose flour
- ½ tsp. baking powder
- ½ tsp. baking soda
  Additional sugar

1. Preheat oven to 350°. Cream butter, shortening and sugar until light and fluffy, 5-7 minutes. Beat in egg and vanilla. In another bowl, whisk flour, baking powder and baking soda; gradually beat into creamed mixture.
2. Shape into 1-in. balls. Roll the balls in additional sugar. Place on greased baking sheets; flatten with a glass. Bake until set, 10-12 minutes. Remove to wire racks to cool.
1 cookie: 60 cal., 3g fat (1g sat. fat), 7mg chol., 28mg sod., 7g carb. (3g sugars, 0 fiber), 1g pro.

CHOCOLATE MACADAMIA MELTAWAYS

I came up with this recipe by accident one day when I wanted to make some cookies. I decided to use some ingredients already in my cupboard, and these were the delicious result.
—Barbara Sepcich, Galt, CA

PREP: 20 MIN. + CHILLING • **BAKE:** 15 MIN.
MAKES: 2½ DOZEN

- ½ cup butter, softened
- ¼ cup confectioners' sugar
- ½ tsp. vanilla extract
- 1¼ cups all-purpose flour
- 1 jar (3½ oz.) macadamia nuts, finely chopped
- 1 cup semisweet chocolate chips
- ½ cup coarsely chopped macadamia nuts
  Additional confectioners' sugar

1. In a small bowl, cream butter and sugar until light and fluffy, 5-7 minutes. Beat in vanilla. Gradually add flour and mix well. Stir in nuts (dough will be stiff); set aside.
2. For the filling, in a microwave-safe bowl, melt chocolate chips; stir until smooth. Stir in the nuts; cool slightly. Drop by ½ teaspoons onto a waxed paper-lined baking sheet; cover and refrigerate for 30 minutes.
3. Shape 1 teaspoon of dough around each piece of the chocolate-nut mixture so it is completely covered. Place 2 in. apart on ungreased baking sheets.
4. Bake at 375° until lightly browned, 12-14 minutes. Roll the warm cookies in confectioners' sugar; cool cookies on wire racks.
1 piece: 117 cal., 9g fat (4g sat. fat), 8mg chol., 45mg sod., 9g carb. (4g sugars, 1g fiber), 1g pro.

BAKING 101

ITALIAN CHOCOLATE SPICE COOKIES

I recently found this old family recipe in my mom's kitchen. I made a few adjustments to streamline the process, and the cookies turned out wonderfully.
—Shawn Barto, Palmetto, FL

PREP: 30 MIN. • **BAKE:** 10 MIN. + COOLING
MAKES: 5 DOZEN

- ¾ cup shortening
- 1 cup sugar
- 4 large eggs, room temperature
- ½ cup 2% milk
- 1 tsp. vanilla extract
- 4 cups all-purpose flour
- ½ cup baking cocoa
- 2 tsp. ground cinnamon
- 2 tsp. baking soda
- 1 tsp. baking powder
- 1 tsp. ground cloves
- ½ cup chopped walnuts

GLAZE
- 2¼ cups confectioners' sugar
- 2 tsp. light corn syrup
- 3 to 4 Tbsp. 2% milk
  Sprinkles, optional

1. Preheat oven to 350°. In a large bowl, cream shortening and sugar until light and fluffy, 5-7 minutes. Beat in the eggs, milk and vanilla. In another bowl, whisk the flour, cocoa, cinnamon, baking soda, baking powder and cloves; gradually beat into the creamed mixture. Stir in the walnuts.
2. Shape level tablespoons of dough into balls; place balls 1 in. apart on ungreased baking sheets. Bake until bottoms are light brown, 10-12 minutes. Remove from pans to wire racks to cool completely.
3. For glaze, in a large bowl, mix the confectioners' sugar, corn syrup and enough milk to reach the desired consistency. Dip tops of the cookies into glaze; if desired, decorate with sprinkles. Let stand until set. Store between pieces of waxed paper in airtight containers.

1 cookie: 99 cal., 4g fat (1g sat. fat), 13mg chol., 57mg sod., 15g carb. (8g sugars, 0 fiber), 2g pro.

VANILLA MERINGUE COOKIES

These sweet little swirls are airy and light as can be. They're all you need after a big special dinner.
—Jenni Sharp, Milwaukee, WI

PREP: 20 MIN. • **BAKE:** 40 MIN. + STANDING
MAKES: ABOUT 5 DOZEN

- 3 large egg whites
- 1½ tsp. clear or regular vanilla extract
- ¼ tsp. cream of tartar
  Dash salt
- ⅔ cup sugar

1. Place egg whites in a small bowl; let stand at room temperature 30 minutes.
2. Preheat oven to 250°. Add vanilla, cream of tartar and salt to egg whites; beat on medium speed until foamy. Gradually add sugar, 1 Tbsp. at a time, beating on high after each addition, until the sugar is dissolved. Continue beating until stiff glossy peaks form, about 7 minutes.
3. Cut a small hole in the tip of a pastry bag or in a corner of a food-safe plastic bag; insert a #32 star tip. Transfer the meringue to bag. Pipe 1¼-in.-diameter cookies 2 in. apart onto parchment-lined baking sheets.
4. Bake until cookies are firm to the touch, 40-45 minutes. Turn off oven; leave meringues in oven 1 hour (leave oven door closed). Remove from the oven; cool completely on baking sheets. Remove meringues from paper; store the cookies in an airtight container at room temperature.

1 cookie: 10 cal., 0 fat (0 sat. fat), 0 chol., 5mg sod., 2g carb. (2g sugars, 0 fiber), 0 pro. **Diabetic exchanges:** 1 free food.

BUTTERY SPRITZ COOKIES

BAKING 101

This tender spritz cookie recipe is very eye-catching on my Christmas cookie tray. The dough is easy to work with, so it's fun to make these into a variety of festive shapes.
—Beverly Launius, Sandwich, IL

PREP: 20 MIN.
BAKE: 10 MIN./BATCH + COOLING
MAKES: ABOUT 7½ DOZEN

- 1   cup butter, softened
- 2¼ cups confectioners' sugar, divided
- ½   tsp. salt
- 1   large egg, room temperature
- 1   tsp. vanilla extract
- ½   tsp. almond extract
- 2½ cups all-purpose flour
      Melted semisweet chocolate, optional
- 2   to 3 Tbsp. water
      Colored sugar and sprinkles

1. Preheat oven to 375°. In a large bowl, cream butter, 1¼ cups confectioners' sugar and salt until light and fluffy, 5-7 minutes. Beat in the egg and extracts. Gradually beat flour into the creamed mixture.
2. Using a cookie press fitted with a disk of your choice, press dough 2 in. apart onto ungreased baking sheets. Bake until set, 6-8 minutes (do not brown). Remove to wire racks to cool completely.
3. If desired, dip in melted chocolate and let stand until set or, in a small bowl, mix the remaining 1 cup confectioners' sugar and enough water to reach desired consistency. Dip cookies in glaze; decorate with colored sugar or sprinkles. Let stand until set.
1 cookie: 43 cal., 2g fat (1g sat. fat), 7mg chol., 30mg sod., 6g carb. (3g sugars, 0 fiber), 0 pro.

HOW TO MAKE SPRITZ COOKIES

Spritz cookies in all flavors are holiday classics. If you've never used a cookie press, they can look intimidating. But it's really very easy!

STEP 1
Cream butter and sugar until fluffy. Creaming incorporates air into the batter, giving cookies a lighter texture. Butter and cream cheese blend best when they're softened but not warm.

STEP 2
Beat in the flour gradually (instead of adding it all at once). This ensures the flour is thoroughly mixed in. It also helps eliminate mess (the flour won't splatter), which saves time

STEP 3
Fit a cookie press with the disk of your choice. Roll the dough into a cylinder to make it easier to insert into the press. The dough should be cool, but not too stiff.

STEP 4
Hold the press against the cookie sheet—not above it—when releasing the dough. Use cool, ungreased baking sheets so the dough will stick. Never press dough onto a warm sheet.

CARDAMOM SPRITZ

CARDAMOM SPRITZ

I have always loved cardamom. My grandmother often added the spice to her baked goods. I usually make these cookies with a spritz press—and camel-shaped disk—that I found at a thrift shop. It reminds me of a time when I rode a camel in the desert while deployed with the Navy. Of course, any design will do!
—Crystal Schlueter, Northglenn, CO

PREP: 20 MIN. • **BAKE:** 10 MIN./BATCH
MAKES: ABOUT 6 DOZEN

  1 **cup butter, softened**
  1 **cup plus 2 Tbsp. sugar, divided**
  1 **large egg, room temperature**
1½ **tsp. vanilla extract**
  1 **tsp. lemon extract**
2½ **cups all-purpose flour**
  2 **tsp. ground cardamom, divided**
  ¼ **tsp. salt**

1. Preheat oven to 350°. Cream butter and 1 cup sugar until light and fluffy, 5-7 minutes. Beat in egg and extracts. In another bowl, whisk the flour, ½ tsp. cardamom and salt; gradually beat into the creamed mixture.
2. Using a cookie press fitted with a disk of your choice, press dough 1 in. apart onto ungreased baking sheets. Mix the remaining 2 Tbsp. sugar and remaining 1½ tsp. cardamom; sprinkle over the cookies. Bake until set, 8-10 minutes (do not brown). Remove from pans to wire racks to cool.
1 cookie: 52 cal., 3g fat (2g sat. fat), 9mg chol., 30mg sod., 7g carb. (3g sugars, 0 fiber), 1g pro.

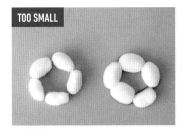

SPRITZ SIZING

Use the above images to get yours just right.

TOO SMALL
When too little dough is pressed out, the design will not meet at all the indentations. The cookie will be too small and break easily

TOO BIG
When too much dough is pressed out, the design will lose its form.

JUST RIGHT
When just the right amount of dough is pressed out, the baked cookie will have a uniform design and crisp indentations.

WHITE CHOCOLATE RASPBERRY THUMBPRINTS

3. Using the end of a wooden spoon handle, make an indentation in the center of each cookie. Place 1 in. apart on greased baking sheets. Bake until set, 8-10 minutes. Remove to wire racks to cool completely.

4. In a microwave, melt white chocolate and butter; stir until smooth. Spoon about ½ tsp. into each cookie. Top each cookie with about ¼ tsp. jam. Store in an airtight container.

1 cookie: 120 cal., 8g fat (4g sat. fat), 22mg chol., 43mg sod., 11g carb. (7g sugars, 1g fiber), 2g pro.

ANISE & WINE COOKIES

My grandmother did not speak English well, but she knew the language of great food. These cookies are crisp and best eaten after being dunked in wine.
—Julia Meyers, Scottsdale, AZ

PREP: 30 MIN. + STANDING
BAKE: 20 MIN./BATCH • **MAKES:** 4½ DOZEN

- 1¼ cups sugar, divided
- 1 cup canola oil
- 1 cup white wine or dry red wine
- 2 tsp. aniseed, crushed
  Dash salt
- 4 to 4½ cups all-purpose flour

1. In a large bowl, whisk 1 cup sugar, oil, wine, aniseed and salt until blended. Gradually stir in enough flour to form a soft dough. Cover; let rest 1 hour.
2. To shape each cookie, roll a level tablespoon of dough into a 6-in. rope and then form it a ring, pinching ends together to seal. Dip tops of cookies into remaining ¼ cup sugar. Place 1 in. apart on greased baking sheets.
3. Bake at 350° until golden brown, 20-25 minutes. Remove from pans to wire racks to cool.

1 cookie: 92 cal., 4g fat (0 sat. fat), 0 chol., 3mg sod., 12g carb. (5g sugars, 0 fiber), 1g pro.

WHITE CHOCOLATE RASPBERRY THUMBPRINTS

When I pass around the cookie tray, all eyes land on these fancy thumbprints. The white chocolate filling and dab of jewel-toned jam will satisfy the most discriminating sweet tooth.
—Agnes Ward, Stratford, ON

PREP: 25 MIN. + CHILLING
BAKE: 10 MIN./BATCH + COOLING
MAKES: ABOUT 3 DOZEN

- ¾ cup butter, softened
- ½ cup packed brown sugar
- 2 large eggs, separated, room temperature
- 1¼ cups all-purpose flour
- ¼ cup baking cocoa
- 1¼ cups finely chopped pecans or walnuts

FILLING
- 4 oz. white baking chocolate, coarsely chopped
- 2 Tbsp. butter
- ¼ cup seedless raspberry jam

1. In a large bowl, cream the butter and brown sugar until light and fluffy, 5-7 minutes. Beat in egg yolks. Combine flour and cocoa; gradually add to the creamed mixture and mix well. Cover and refrigerate for 1-2 hours or until easy to handle.
2. Preheat oven to 350°. In a shallow bowl, whisk the egg whites until foamy. Place nuts in a second shallow bowl. Shape dough into 1-in. balls. Dip into egg whites, then roll in nuts.

MEXICAN WEDDING CAKES

As part of a Mexican tradition, I tucked these sugar-dusted cookies into small gift boxes for the guests at my sister's wedding. Most folks said the cookies never made it home!
—Sarita Johnston, San Antonio, TX

PREP: 30 MIN. • **BAKE:** 15 MIN.
MAKES: ABOUT 6 DOZEN

- 2 cups butter, softened
- 1 cup confectioners' sugar
- 1 tsp. vanilla extract
- 4 cups all-purpose flour
- 1 cup finely chopped pecans
  Additional confectioners' sugar

1. Preheat oven to 350°. Cream butter and 1 cup confectioners' sugar until light and fluffy, 5-7 minutes; beat in vanilla. Gradually beat in flour. Stir in pecans.
2. Shape tablespoons of dough into 2-in. crescents. Place 2 in. apart on ungreased baking sheets.

3. Bake until light brown, 12-15 minutes. Roll cookies in additional confectioners' sugar while warm; cool on wire racks.
1 cookie: 88 cal., 6g fat (3g sat. fat), 14mg chol., 41mg sod., 7g carb. (2g sugars, 0 fiber), 1g pro.

PINEAPPLE STAR COOKIES

With their pretty shape, tangy pineapple filling and sweet frosting, these treats are worth the little bit of extra effort.
—Sarah Lukaszewicz, Batavia, NY

PREP: 25 MIN. + CHILLING
BAKE: 10 MIN./BATCH + COOLING
MAKES: 2 DOZEN

- 1 cup butter, softened
- 1 pkg. (8 oz.) cream cheese, softened
- 2 cups all-purpose flour

FILLING
- 1/3 cup sugar
- 2 1/4 tsp. all-purpose flour
- 1/2 cup unsweetened crushed pineapple

FROSTING
- 1 cup confectioners' sugar
- 2 Tbsp. butter, melted
- 2 Tbsp. whole milk
- 1/2 tsp. vanilla extract
- 1/2 cup chopped walnuts

1. In a large bowl, cream the butter and cream cheese until light and fluffy, 5-7 minutes. Add the flour and mix well. Cover and refrigerate until easy to handle, about 2 hours.
2. Meanwhile, in a saucepan, combine sugar and flour; add the pineapple and stir until blended. Cook over low heat until the mixture comes to a boil and is thickened. Cover and refrigerate.
3. Preheat oven to 375°. Divide dough in half. On a lightly floured surface, roll out each portion to 1/8-in. thickness. Cut into 3-in. squares. Place squares 1 in. apart on ungreased baking sheets.

4. To form stars, make a 1 1/4-in. cut from each corner toward center (do not cut through the center). Place 1/2 tsp. of pineapple filling in the center of each square. Fold every other point toward the center, overlapping the tips; press lightly to seal.
5. Bake until set, 8-10 minutes. Remove to wire racks to cool.
6. For frosting, in a bowl, combine the confectioners' sugar, butter, milk and vanilla until smooth. Drizzle frosting over the cooled cookies; sprinkle with chopped walnuts.
1 cookie: 199 cal., 14g fat (8g sat. fat), 33mg chol., 99mg sod., 18g carb. (9g sugars, 0 fiber), 2g pro.

RUGELACH

The crisp texture of these crescent-shaped cookies makes them a terrific treat to serve alongside a steaming mug of hot chocolate or coffee.

—Becky Phillips, Chippewa Falls, WI

PREP: 40 MIN. + CHILLING
BAKE: 25 MIN./BATCH • **MAKES:** 4 DOZEN

- 1 cup butter, softened
- 1 pkg. (8 oz.) cream cheese, softened
- 2 cups all-purpose flour
- ½ tsp. salt

FILLING
- 1 cup sugar
- 2 Tbsp. ground cinnamon
- ½ cup butter, melted, divided
- ½ cup finely chopped pecans

1. In a large bowl, beat the butter and cream cheese until smooth. Combine the flour and salt; gradually add to the cream cheese mixture and mix well. Divide dough into fourths. Wrap each portion in waxed paper; refrigerate for 1 hour or until easy to handle.

2. Roll out each dough portion between 2 sheets of waxed paper into a 12-in. circle. Remove the top sheet of waxed paper. Combine sugar and cinnamon. Brush each circle with 1 Tbsp. melted butter. Sprinkle each with 3 Tbsp. cinnamon-sugar and 2 Tbsp. pecans. Cut each into 12 wedges.

3. Roll up each wedge from the wide end; place pointed side down 2 in. apart on ungreased baking sheets. Curve ends to form a crescent shape.

4. Bake at 350° for 24-26 minutes or until golden brown. Remove to wire racks. Brush warm cookies with remaining butter; sprinkle with remaining cinnamon-sugar.

1 pastry: 111 cal., 8g fat (5g sat. fat), 20mg chol., 85mg sod., 9g carb. (4g sugars, 0 fiber), 1g pro.

RUGELACH

ORANGE-CRANBERRY NUT TARTS

My friend gave me a recipe for orange cookies. I just had to embellish it. Now my friends and family crave these tarts.
—Nancy Bruce, Big Timber, MT

PREP: 50 MIN. + CHILLING
BAKE: 10 MIN./BATCH + COOLING
MAKES: 4 DOZEN

- ½ cup butter, softened
- 1 cup sugar
- 1 large egg, room temperature
- 4 tsp. grated orange zest
- ¼ cup orange juice
- 2 Tbsp. evaporated milk or 2% milk
- 3 cups all-purpose flour
- 3 tsp. baking powder
- ¼ tsp. salt

FILLING
- 1 can (14 oz.) whole-berry cranberry sauce
- ½ cup sugar
- 2 Tbsp. orange juice
- 1 cup chopped walnuts
- 4 oz. white baking chocolate, melted

1. In a large bowl, cream the butter and sugar until light and fluffy, 5-7 minutes. Beat in egg until blended. Beat in orange zest, orange juice and milk. In another bowl, whisk the flour, baking powder and salt; gradually beat into the creamed mixture.
2. Divide dough into 3 portions. On a lightly floured surface, shape each into a 10-in.-long roll. Wrap securely; refrigerate overnight or until firm.
3. For filling, in a small saucepan, combine cranberry sauce, sugar and orange juice. Bring to a boil, stirring constantly; cook and stir 2 minutes. Remove from heat; cool completely. Stir in walnuts.
4. Preheat oven to 375°. Unwrap each portion of dough and cut crosswise into 16 slices. Press onto bottoms and up the sides of greased mini-muffin cups. Fill each with 2 tsp. cranberry mixture.
5. Bake 8-10 minutes or until edges are light golden. Cool in pans 10 minutes, then remove to wire racks to cool completely. Drizzle with melted white chocolate; let stand until set.

1 tart: 113 cal., 4g fat (2g sat. fat), 9mg chol., 60mg sod., 18g carb. (10g sugars, 1g fiber), 2g pro.

TENDER PECAN LOGS

Folks always expect to find these tender, nutty logs on the cookie gift trays I give at Christmas. Not overly sweet, they're just right with a hot cup of coffee or tea.
—Joyce Beck, Gadsden, AL

PREP: 15 MIN. + CHILLING
BAKE: 15 MIN./BATCH • **MAKES:** 2½ DOZEN

- 1 cup butter, softened
- 5 Tbsp. confectioners' sugar
- 2 tsp. vanilla extract
- 2 cups all-purpose flour
- 1 cup finely chopped pecans
  Confectioners' sugar

1. In a small bowl, cream butter and sugar until light and fluffy, 5-7 minutes. Beat in vanilla. Add the flour, beating on low speed just until combined. Stir in pecans. Cover and refrigerate for 30 minutes or until easy to handle.
2. Preheat oven to 350°. Shape ½ cups of dough into ½-in.-thick logs. Cut logs into 2-in. pieces. Place 2 in. apart on greased baking sheets. Bake until lightly browned, 15-18 minutes. Roll warm cookies in confectioners' sugar; cool on wire racks.

1 cookie: 117 cal., 9g fat (4g sat. fat), 16mg chol., 62mg sod., 8g carb. (1g sugars, 1g fiber), 1g pro.

BAKING 101

CHOCOLATE GINGERSNAPS

When my daughter Jennifer was 15 years old, she created this recipe as a way to combine two of her favorite flavors. These cookies are perfect with a glass of milk.
—Paula Zsiray, Logan, UT

PREP: 45 MIN. + CHILLING
BAKE: 10 MIN./BATCH
MAKES: ABOUT 3½ DOZEN

- ½ cup butter, softened
- ½ cup packed light brown sugar
- ¼ cup molasses
- 1 Tbsp. water
- 2 tsp. minced fresh gingerroot
- 1½ cups all-purpose flour
- 1 Tbsp. baking cocoa
- 1¼ tsp. ground ginger
- 1 tsp. baking soda
- 1 tsp. ground cinnamon
- ¼ tsp. ground nutmeg
- ¼ tsp. ground cloves
- 7 oz. semisweet chocolate, finely chopped
- ¼ cup coarse sugar

1. In a large bowl, cream butter and brown sugar until light and fluffy, 5-7 minutes. Beat in molasses, water and gingerroot. Combine flour, cocoa, ginger, baking soda, cinnamon, nutmeg and cloves; gradually add to creamed mixture and mix well. Stir in chocolate. Cover and refrigerate until easy to handle, about 2 hours.
2. Preheat oven to 350°. Shape dough into 1-in. balls; roll in sugar. Place 2 in. apart on greased baking sheets.
3. Bake until tops begin to crack, 10-12 minutes. Cool for 2 minutes before removing to wire racks.
1 cookie: 80 cal., 4g fat (2g sat. fat), 6mg chol., 47mg sod., 9g carb. (6g sugars, 0 fiber), 1g pro.

HONEY WALNUT DELIGHTS

HONEY WALNUT DELIGHTS

Even after being frozen, these no-fail cookies stay moist and taste freshly baked. They are among my best holiday giveaway treats and are so easy to make. If you prefer, you can use other nut varieties, such as pecans or almonds.
—Jessica Clemens, Wimbledon, ND

PREP: 30 MIN. • **BAKE:** 10 MIN./BATCH
MAKES: ABOUT 8 DOZEN

- 1 cup butter, softened
- 2¼ cups sugar, divided
- 2 large eggs, room temperature
- ½ cup honey
- 2 Tbsp. lemon juice
- 4 cups all-purpose flour
- 2½ tsp. baking soda
- 1 tsp. ground cinnamon
- ½ tsp. salt
- ½ tsp. ground ginger
- 1 cup finely chopped walnuts, toasted

1. Preheat oven to 350°. In a large bowl, cream butter and 1½ cups sugar until light and fluffy, 5-7 minutes. Beat in the eggs, honey and lemon juice. In another bowl, whisk the flour, baking soda, cinnamon, salt and ginger; gradually beat into the creamed mixture. Stir in walnuts.
2. Shape dough into 1-in. balls; roll in the remaining ¾ cup sugar. Place 2 in. apart on ungreased baking sheets. Bake until golden brown, 7-9 minutes. Cool on pans 1 minute. Remove the cookies to wire racks to cool. Store in an airtight container.
1 cookie: 66 cal., 3g fat (1g sat. fat), 9mg chol., 60mg sod., 10g carb. (6g sugars, 0 fiber), 1g pro.

FRENCH MACARONS

Even decorated simply—a sprinkle of sugar, a drizzle of icing—these stylish beauties will be the showstoppers on any cookie tray.
—Josh Rink, Milwaukee, WI

PREP: 1 HOUR + STANDING
BAKE: 15 MIN./BATCH + COOLING
MAKES: 26 MACARONS

MACARON SHELL

- 1⅓ **cups almond flour**
- 2¼ **cups confectioners' sugar, divided**
- 3 **extra large egg whites, room temperature**
- 2 **Tbsp. superfine sugar**
- ⅛ **tsp. salt**

BUTTERCREAM FILLING

- ¼ **cup unsalted butter, softened**
- 1 **cup confectioners' sugar**
- 2 **Tbsp. heavy whipping cream**
- ½ **tsp. vanilla extract**
- ⅛ **tsp. salt**

1. Place the almond flour and 1½ cups plus 3 Tbsp. confectioners' sugar in a food processor; pulse until thoroughly mixed to ensure almond flour is very fine. Pass almond flour mixture through a fine-mesh sieve; discard any large pieces that remain.

2. Place egg whites in a very clean bowl of a stand mixer fitted with the whisk attachment; whisk on medium-low speed until frothy. Slowly add superfine sugar; whisk until dissolved, 1-2 minutes. Slowly add the remaining confectioners' sugar; increase speed to high and whip until meringue is glossy and stiff peaks form, 2-3 minutes.

3. Gently fold one-third of the almond flour mixture into meringue; gently fold in the remaining almond flour mixture in 2 additions. Using side of spatula, smooth batter up sides of bowl several times to remove air bubbles and ensure there are no lumps; do not overmix. Run spatula down the center of the bowl; the line in the batter should remain visible for a moment before mixture runs back into itself.

4. Position rack in upper third of oven; preheat oven to 300°. Transfer batter into a pastry bag fitted with a #7 or #10 round tip. Line baking trays with parchment; pipe 1⅜-in. rounds onto the parchment about 1 in. apart. (Drawing guides on the parchment, as shown at right, will help you keep your macarons even.)

5. Tap the baking tray against counter 2-3 times to remove excess air bubbles. Let macarons rest until no longer wet or sticky to the touch, 30-60 minutes.

6. Bake, 1 tray at a time, 14-16 minutes or until cookies rise about ⅛ in. to form feet, rotating the tray halfway through baking. Remove tray and let macarons cool completely; repeat with remaining trays. Once macarons have cooled completely, remove from parchment.

7. To make filling, cream the butter in a stand mixer fitted with whisk attachment; slowly add powdered sugar until incorporated. Add heavy cream, vanilla and salt; mix until smooth. Pour frosting into a pastry bag fitted with a small round tip; pipe buttercream onto half the macarons. Top with remaining macaron shells. Refrigerate, covered, until ready to serve.

1 macaron: 253 cal., 11g fat (3g sat. fat), 13mg chol., 69mg sod., 37g carb. (34g sugars, 1g fiber), 4g pro.

TACKLING MACARONS

Not to be confused with a macaroon (a dense, moist cookie made with shredded coconut), a French macaron is a delicate meringue-based sandwich cookie made with almond flour. The perfect macaron has a smooth, eggshell-like exterior that, when broken open, reveals a light, fluffy interior. They're challenging to make, but with precision and a light touch, so rewarding!

ALMOND FLOUR
If you can't find almond flour, grind raw blanched almonds in your food processor; gradually add the sugar and pulse as you go. Grind too quickly, you may get almond butter!

ARE THEY READY TO PIPE?
To tell if your batter is mixed and ready to pipe, lift your spatula and drizzle a small amount of batter back into the bowl. The drizzled batter should make a ribbon-like line that's visible for a moment, then disappears.

ARE THEY READY TO BAKE?
After you've piped the batter and tapped the baking tray (air bubbles in the mix will cause pitting and burst seams), let them rest before baking. When the surface is no longer sticky or wet, and you're able to run your finger lightly over the thin skin on top, they're ready to bake.

ARE THEY READY TO EAT?
Finished macarons still aren't quite ready to eat—the flavors develop over time, so it's best to refrigerate them for 24 hours before serving.

BIG & BUTTERY CHOCOLATE CHIP COOKIES

BIG & BUTTERY CHOCOLATE CHIP COOKIES
Our version of the classic cookie is based on a recipe from a bakery in California called Hungry Bear. It's big, thick and chewy-perfect for dunking.
—Irene Yeh, Mequon, WI

PREP: 35 MIN. + CHILLING
BAKE: 10 MIN./BATCH
MAKES: ABOUT 2 DOZEN

- 1   cup butter, softened
- 1   cup packed brown sugar
- ¾   cup sugar
- 2   large eggs, room temperature
- 1½ tsp. vanilla extract
- 2⅔ cups all-purpose flour
- 1¼ tsp. baking soda
- 1   tsp. salt
- 1   pkg. (12 oz.) semisweet chocolate chips
- 2   cups coarsely chopped walnuts, toasted

1. In a large bowl, beat the butter and sugars until blended. Beat in eggs and vanilla. In a small bowl, whisk the flour, baking soda and salt; gradually beat into the butter mixture. Stir in chocolate chips and walnuts.

2. Shape ¼ cupfuls of dough into balls. Flatten each ball to ¾-in. thickness (2½-in. diameter), smoothing edges as necessary. Place balls in an airtight container, separating the layers with waxed paper or parchment; refrigerate, covered, overnight.

3. To bake, place the dough portions 2 in. apart on parchment-lined baking sheets; let stand at room temperature 30 minutes before baking. Preheat oven to 400°.

4. Bake until edges are golden brown (centers will be light), 10-12 minutes. Cool on pans 2 minutes. Remove to wire racks to cool.

1 cookie: 311 cal., 19g fat (8g sat. fat), 38mg chol., 229mg sod., 35g carb. (23g sugars, 2g fiber), 4g pro.

BISCOTTI

DRIZZLED GINGERBREAD BISCOTTI

After stumbling across a community recipe for gingerbread biscotti, I made several batches and tweaked it to our tastes. These became an instant obsession at our house.
—Susan Board, Palmer, AK

PREP: 35 MIN. **BAKE:** 35 MIN. + COOLING
MAKES: 3½ DOZEN

7 Tbsp. butter, softened
1 cup sugar
3 large eggs, room temperature
⅓ cup molasses
2 tsp. vanilla extract
2½ cups all-purpose flour
1 cup whole wheat flour
5 tsp. ground ginger
2 tsp. ground cinnamon
1½ tsp. ground cloves
½ tsp. coarsely ground pepper
¼ tsp. ground nutmeg
1 Tbsp. baking powder
½ tsp. salt
½ cup finely chopped crystallized ginger
1¼ cups white baking chips
1½ tsp. shortening
   Red Hots

1. Preheat oven to 375°. In a large bowl, cream butter and sugar until light and fluffy, 5-7 minutes. Beat in the eggs, molasses and vanilla. In another bowl, whisk flours, spices, baking powder and salt; gradually beat into the creamed mixture. Stir in crystallized ginger.
2. Divide dough in half. On an ungreased baking sheet, shape each half into a 14x2-in. rectangle. Bake 20-25 minutes or until firm to the touch.
3. Cool on pans on wire racks until cool enough to handle. Transfer baked rectangles to a cutting board. Using a serrated knife, cut diagonally into ½-in. slices. Place upright 1 in. apart on ungreased baking sheets. Bake for 12-14 minutes or until golden brown. Remove from pans to wire racks to cool completely.
4. In a microwave, melt baking chips and shortening; stir until smooth. Drizzle over biscotti. Decorate with Red Hots.
1 cookie: 124 cal., 4g fat (2g sat. fat), 19mg chol., 90mg sod., 20g carb. (11g sugars, 1g fiber), 2g pro.

CRANBERRY SWIRL BISCOTTI

Crunchy glazed biscotti are ideal for dunking into a hot cup of coffee, cocoa or tea.
—Lisa Kilcup, Gig Harbor, WA

PREP: 20 MIN. • **BAKE:** 40 MIN. + COOLING
MAKES: ABOUT 2½ DOZEN

⅔ cup dried cranberries
½ cup cherry preserves
½ tsp. ground cinnamon
½ cup butter, softened
⅔ cup sugar
2 large eggs, room temperature
1 tsp. vanilla extract
2¼ cups all-purpose flour
¾ tsp. baking powder
¼ tsp. salt
GLAZE
¾ cup confectioners' sugar
1 Tbsp. 2% milk
2 tsp. butter, melted
1 tsp. almond extract

1. Preheat oven to 325°. Place the dried cranberries, preserves and cinnamon in a food processor; process until smooth.
2. Cream the butter and sugar until light and fluffy, 5-7 minutes. Beat in the eggs and vanilla. In a second bowl, whisk the flour, baking powder and salt; gradually beat into the creamed mixture.
3. Divide dough in half. On a lightly floured surface, roll each portion of dough into a 12x8-in. rectangle. Spread each with half of the cranberry mixture; roll up jelly-roll style, starting with a short side.
4. Place the rolls 4 in. apart on a lightly greased baking sheet, seam side down. Bake the rolls for 25-30 minutes or until lightly browned.
5. Carefully transfer rolls to a cutting board; cool 5 minutes. Using a serrated knife, cut crosswise into ½-in. slices. Place slices upright on lightly greased baking sheets.
6. Bake 15-20 minutes longer or until centers are firm and dry. Remove from pans to wire racks.
7. In a small bowl, mix glaze ingredients. Drizzle over the warm cookies; let cool completely. Store in an airtight container.
1 cookie: 120 cal., 4g fat (2g sat. fat), 23mg chol., 58mg sod., 20g carb. (12g sugars, 0 fiber), 1g pro.

CRANBERRY
SWIRL BISCOTTI

CHOCOLATE CHIP MANDELBROT COOKIES

"Mandelbrot" in Yiddish literally means almond bread. The twice-baked cookie made with oil and almonds dates back to 19th-century Eastern Europe. There are many variations made of different dried fruits and nuts. My chocolate chip version is more modern-American.

—Kimberly Scott, Kosciusko, MS

PREP: 25 MIN. + CHILLING
BAKE: 35 MIN./BATCH + COOLING
MAKES: ABOUT 4 DOZEN

- 3 large eggs, room temperature
- 1¼ cups sugar, divided
- ¾ cup canola oil
- 2 to 3 Tbsp. grated orange zest
- 2 tsp. almond extract
- 3 cups all-purpose flour
- 4 tsp. ground cinnamon, divided
- 1 tsp. baking powder
- ½ tsp. salt
- 1 cup unblanched almonds, coarsely chopped
- 1 cup dark chocolate chips

1. Whisk eggs and 1 cup sugar until well blended. Add oil, orange zest and extract; whisk until smooth. In another bowl, whisk the flour, 1 tsp. cinnamon, baking powder and salt; gradually beat into the orange mixture. Stir in almonds and chocolate chips. Refrigerate dough, covered, for 3 hours.

2. Preheat oven to 350°. Using lightly oiled hands, divide the dough into 4 even portions. On a parchment-lined baking sheet, shape 2 portions into 7x4-in. rectangles. Repeat with the remaining dough. Bake until tops are golden brown, 25-30 minutes.

3. Cool on pans on wire racks until cool enough to handle. Transfer the baked rectangles to a cutting board. Using a serrated knife, cut diagonally into 1-in. slices. Place cut side down on baking sheets. Combine remaining ¼ cup sugar and remaining 3 tsp. cinnamon; sprinkle over the slices. Bake until golden brown, 10-12 minutes. Remove to wire racks to cool. Store in an airtight container.

1 cookie: 127 cal., 7g fat (1g sat. fat), 12mg chol., 42mg sod., 15g carb. (8g sugars, 1g fiber), 2g pro.

EGGNOG BISCOTTI

You may substitute additional eggnog if rum isn't your thing. For a variation, try using one of the flavored eggnogs available around the holidays.

—Shannon Dobos, Calgary, AB

PREP: 25 MIN. • **BAKE:** 40 MIN. + COOLING
MAKES: ABOUT 3 DOZEN

- ½ cup butter, softened
- 1 cup sugar
- 2 large eggs, room temperature
- ¼ cup eggnog
- ½ tsp. vanilla extract
- 2⅓ cups all-purpose flour
- 2 tsp. baking powder
- ½ tsp. ground nutmeg
  Dash salt

GLAZE
- ¾ cup confectioners' sugar
- 3 to 5 tsp. eggnog
- 1 tsp. dark rum, optional

1. Preheat oven to 375°. Beat the butter and sugar until blended. Beat in eggs, 1 at a time. Beat in eggnog and vanilla. In another bowl, whisk together the flour, baking powder, nutmeg and salt; gradually beat into the butter mixture (dough will be sticky).

2. Divide dough in half. On a greased baking sheet, shape each portion into a 12x3-in. rectangle. Bake until a toothpick inserted in center comes out clean, 16-19 minutes. Reduce oven setting to 300°. Remove rectangles from pans to wire racks; cool for 10 minutes.

3. Place rectangles on a cutting board. Using a serrated knife, trim ends of rectangles and cut diagonally into ½-in. slices. Return to baking sheets, cut side down. Bake until firm, about 10 minutes per side. Remove from pans to wire racks; cool completely.

4. Mix glaze ingredients. Drizzle over biscotti with a spoon.

1 cookie: 90 cal., 3g fat (2g sat. fat), 18mg chol., 56mg sod., 15g carb. (8g sugars, 0 fiber), 1g pro.

. . . .

TEST KITCHEN TIP

Since the dough for these biscotti is on the sticky side, use a gentle touch or lightly floured hands, if necessary, when shaping.

ALMOND BISCOTTI

I've learned to bake a double batch of these crisp dunking cookies, because one batch goes too fast!
—H. Michaelsen, St. Charles, IL

PREP: 15 MIN. • **BAKE:** 35 MIN. + COOLING
MAKES: 3 DOZEN

- ½ cup butter, softened
- 1¼ cups sugar, divided
- 3 large eggs, room temperature
- 1 tsp. anise extract
- 2 cups all-purpose flour
- 2 tsp. baking powder
  Dash salt
- ½ cup chopped almonds
- 2 tsp. 2% milk

1. In a large bowl, cream the butter and 1 cup sugar until light and fluffy, 5-7 minutes. Add eggs, 1 at a time, beating well after each addition. Beat in extract. Combine dry ingredients; gradually add to the creamed mixture and mix well. Stir in almonds.

2. Line a baking sheet with foil and grease the foil. Divide dough in half; on the foil, shape each portion into a 12x3-in. rectangle. Brush with milk; sprinkle with remaining ¼ cup sugar.

3. Bake at 375° until golden brown and firm to the touch, 15-20 minutes. Lift foil with rectangles onto a wire rack; cool for 15 minutes. Reduce heat to 300°.

4. Transfer rectangles to a cutting board; cut diagonally with a serrated knife into ½-in. slices. Place cut side down on ungreased baking sheets.

5. Bake for 10 minutes. Turn and bake until firm, 10 minutes longer. Remove cookies to wire racks to cool. Store in an airtight container.

1 cookie: 207 cal., 9g fat (4g sat. fat), 50mg chol., 129mg sod., 29g carb. (16g sugars, 1g fiber), 4g pro.

CHOCOLATE PISTACHIO BISCOTTI

Chocolate, pistachios and cranberries are great together. Adding the cranberries to this recipe made it not only sweeter, but healthier, too.
—Gilda Lester, Millsboro, DE

PREP: 30 MIN. • **BAKE:** 30 MIN. + COOLING
MAKES: 40 COOKIES

- ⅓ cup butter, softened
- 1 cup plus 1 Tbsp. sugar, divided
- 3 large eggs, room temperature
- 2 tsp. vanilla extract
- 2¾ cups all-purpose flour
- ⅓ cup baking cocoa
- 2½ tsp. baking powder
- ½ tsp. ground cinnamon
- 1 cup semisweet chocolate chips
- ½ cup pistachios
- ½ cup dried cranberries

1. Preheat oven to 350°. In a large bowl, cream butter and 1 cup sugar until light and fluffy, 5-7 minutes. Add eggs, 1 at a time, beating well after each addition. Beat in vanilla. Mix flour, cocoa, baking powder and cinnamon; add to creamed mixture and mix well (the dough will be sticky). Stir in the chocolate chips, pistachios and cranberries.

2. Divide the dough into 4 portions. On ungreased baking sheets, shape into 10x2½-in. rectangles. Sprinkle with remaining 1 Tbsp. sugar. Bake until set, 20-25 minutes. Carefully remove to wire racks; cool 5 minutes.

3. Transfer to a cutting board; cut each rectangle into 10 slices. Place cut side down on ungreased baking sheets. Bake 5-8 minutes on each side or until lightly browned. Remove to wire racks to cool. Store in an airtight container.

1 serving: 107 cal., 4g fat (2g sat. fat), 20mg chol., 48mg sod., 17g carb. (9g sugars, 1g fiber), 2g pro. **Diabetic exchanges:** 1 starch, 1 fat.

BROWNIES
& BARS

A cross between a cookie and a cake, a delicious homemade
bar hits all the right notes for pure indulgence. A favorite at
bake sales, potlucks and late-night snack sessions,
these might just be the perfect treat.

. . . .

BARS & BROWNIES

Bar cookies (including brownies) can be made from pourable batter, spreadable dough, or a crumb crust that needs to be patted into the pan. The one thing all bars have in common is that they're baked in a pan rather than on a baking sheet.

QUICK TIPS FOR SUCCESSFUL BARS & BROWNIES

- Use butter, stick margarine (with at least 80% fat) or shortening. Tub, reduced-fat, whipped, soft or liquid products contain air and water and will produce flat, tough bars.

- Make sure your eggs are room temperature. Adding cold eggs to the batter will make the other ingredients firm up. If your recipe calls for combining eggs with melted chocolate, add the warm chocolate to the eggs a little at a time—otherwise, it could cook the eggs.

- Avoid overmixing. If the batter is handled too much, the gluten in the flour will develop, and the bars or brownies will be tough. You may want to just mix by hand; use a whisk to combine the wet ingredients, then fold in the dry ingredients, mixing just until the flour disappears.

- If the recipe doesn't call for a specific type of pan, use a dull aluminum baking pan. Dark-colored pans may cause overbrowning, and thick glass dishes may keep the treats from baking evenly. If you have only dark metal pans, reduce the oven temperature by 25°; if you only have glass or Pyrex dishes, extend the baking time and regularly test for doneness.

- Choose the right size of baking ban. If you choose to use a pan size other than the one the recipe calls for, you may need to adjust the baking time.

- Use shortening or nonstick cooking spray to grease pans.

- Spread the batter evenly in the pan. If one corner is thinner than another, it will bake faster and be overbaked when the rest of the pan is baked to the appropriate texture.

- Center the pan on a rack placed in the middle of the oven.

- Don't overbake. Brownies will keep cooking after you take them out of the oven, so trust your toothpick test. Fudgy brownies should show streaks of batter and a few moist crumbs on the toothpick; cakelike brownies will show a few moist crumbs.

- Generally, brownies and bars should cool completely in the pan on a wire rack before being cut. However, crisp bars should be cut while still slightly warm. They can be cut into rectangular bars, squares, fingers, triangles or diamonds.

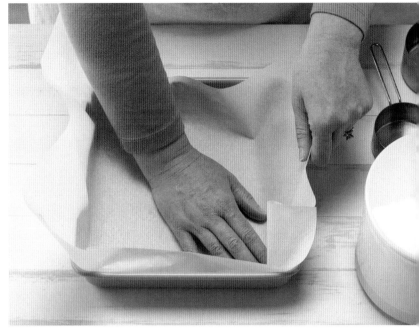

EASILY LIFT BROWNIES & BARS

Line your pan with aluminum foil or parchment, making sure it extends up and above the sides of the pan. Grease with shortening, or coat with cooking spray.

After the bars cool, use the foil or parchment to lift them out of the pan. Move them to a cutting board to cut them—not having to work within the sides of the pan will make this an easy task.

CUTTING BROWNIES & BARS

In *Taste of Home* Test Kitchen, we use a bench scraper rather than a knife to cut brownies and dessert bars, as it gives more control over the cuts. Made of thin metal, a bench scraper can be used to divide doughs, chop vegetables, cut pasta and scrape bits and pieces off your counters and pans.

Cut by pressing the scraper straight down and pulling it straight out, rather using a sawing motion. This will keep your cuts straight and even, and the edges won't be full of crumbs and loose chunks. A pizza wheel is also a good way to cut many bars, including crispy ones—the thin rotating blade lets you make long cuts in one go.

If your bars or brownies are extremely dense and moist, you may have an issue with them sticking to your blade, no matter what kind of blade you're using. If you're having sticking issues, warm your blade in hot water, then dry it and make a cut. Clean and rewarm the blade after each cut.

WHICH CHOCOLATE?

Selecting the right chocolate for your recipe is key to experiencing everything this dreamy indulgence has to offer.

Unsweetened Chocolate
Also known as baking or bitter chocolate, unsweetened chocolate has no sugars or added flavors.

Bittersweet and Semisweet Chocolate
The FDA mandates that bittersweet and semisweet chocolate contain at least 35% pure chocolate (cocoa), but doesn't specify what those percentages must be. In general, the higher the percentage, the less sweet. Bittersweet is generally 60-72% cocoa; semisweet is generally 35-55%. Both are tasty in baked goods, and can be used more or less interchangeably; bittersweet chocolate will produce a more dominant chocolate flavor.

Bars vs. Chips
Most solid chocolates are available as bars and chips. Bars usually melt quickly and smoothly; chips have less cocoa butter and contain stabilizers to help them keep their shape. This makes a difference in candies and sauces, but there won't be a significant difference in the texture of a brownie.

Natural Unsweetened Cocoa Powder
Remove most of the cocoa butter from unsweetened chocolate and you get natural unsweetened cocoa powder.

Dutch-Processed Cocoa Powder
Also known as alkalized cocoa powder, this type has been treated to reduce its acidity, giving it a smooth flavor and reddish color. It's best to stick to the cocoa the recipe calls for; the two cocoa powders do behave differently. If you do want to substitute Dutch cocoa for natural, pay attention to the leavener— if the recipe calls for baking soda, replace it with twice that amount of baking powder.

CAKEY VS. FUDGY?

The great debate over whether brownies should be cakey or fudgy will continue as long as brownies are being made, with the verdict being a purely personal preference. When choosing a recipe, take a look at the amount of fat (butter or oil) and the flour to determine whether the recipe will make a cakelike brownie or a dense, fudgelike brownie. Fudgy brownies will have a higher fat-to-flour ratio; a cakey brownie will have more flour and a leavener—usually baking powder.

STORING BARS

To store, cover a pan of uncut brownies or bars with foil or place the whole pan in a large resealable plastic bag. Once the bars are cut, store them in an airtight container. Whether cut or uncut, all treats made with perishable ingredients, such as cream cheese, should be covered and refrigerated.

For longer-term storage, freezing a whole pan of bars before cutting is the best way to protect them from freezer burn. Wrap the whole sheet of bars or brownies in plastic wrap, then in foil.

Freezing treats after they've been cut makes it easy to thaw just one or two when you want them. Place cut treats in layers in an airtight glass or plastic container, covering each layer (including the top layer) with waxed paper or parchment and pressing lightly to create a seal. To serve, let them come to room temperature, or heat individual treats in the microwave in 15-second increments.

Some bars and brownies freeze better than others. If a recipe calls for a cream cheese swirl or jam filling, those dairy and liquid-based ingredients may sweat moisture as they come to room temperature. This won't change the flavor, but it will affect the appearance. Leave any frosted recipes unfrosted for freezing; add the frosting after they're thawed.

STABLE MIXING

Brownies and bars are more likely to be mixed by hand or with hand mixer than other kinds of baked goods. Need an extra hand while mixing batter? Professional chefs often place a damp dish towel or paper towel under their mixing bowl. This keeps the bowl from sliding away or tipping over while you are mixing. It also lets you have a free hand so you can easily add other ingredients. Place a damp towel under a cutting board for the same stability when cutting or chopping.

BROWNIES

PEANUT CARAMEL BROWNIE BITES

With their three irresistible layers, these brownies are my family's absolute favorite.
—Ella Agans, Birch Tree, MO

PREP: 1 HOUR + CHILLING
BAKE: 20 MIN. + COOLING
MAKES: 4 DOZEN

- ¾ cup butter, cubed and softened
- ⅔ cup sugar
- 2 Tbsp. water
- 1 cup semisweet chocolate chips
- 2 large eggs, room temperature
- 1 tsp. vanilla extract
- 1 cup all-purpose flour
- ½ tsp. baking powder

CANDY BAR TOPPING
- 1 cup sugar
- ¼ cup butter, cubed
- ¼ cup 2% milk
- 1 cup marshmallow creme
- ½ cup creamy peanut butter, divided
- ½ tsp. vanilla extract
- 2½ cups dry roasted peanuts, divided
- 40 caramels
- 2 Tbsp. water
- 1¼ cups semisweet chocolate chips

1. Preheat oven to 350°. Line a 13x9-in. baking pan with foil, letting ends extend up sides; coat foil with cooking spray.
2. Microwave butter, sugar and water on high just until mixture comes to a boil, 3-4 minutes; stir until blended. Stir in chocolate chips until melted. Whisk in eggs, 1 at a time, stirring well after each addition. Whisk in vanilla. Stir in flour and baking powder.
3. Spread into prepared pan. Bake until a toothpick inserted in center comes out clean, 18-20 minutes. Cool 30 minutes.
4. For topping, combine sugar, butter and milk in a large saucepan; bring to a boil, stirring constantly, over medium heat. Boil 5 minutes, stirring frequently. Stir in the marshmallow creme, ¼ cup peanut butter and the vanilla; pour over brownies. Sprinkle with 2 cups peanuts.
5. In a small saucepan, combine the caramels and water; cook, stirring, over medium-high heat until blended. Pour over peanuts.
6. Microwave chocolate chips on high until softened, about 1 minute. Stir in remaining ¼ cup peanut butter until smooth; pour over caramel layer. Chop remaining ½ cup peanuts; sprinkle on top. Refrigerate at least 1 hour.
7. Lifting with foil, remove brownies from pan. Cut into bars. Store in an airtight container in the refrigerator.

1 brownie bite: 212 cal., 12g fat (5g sat. fat), 19mg chol., 135mg sod., 24g carb. (19g sugars, 1g fiber), 4g pro.

. . . .
TEST KITCHEN TIP
These bars are spectacularly rich, so cut them small. Chilling the brownies in the pan makes them easier to lift out and cut, so don't skip that step.

PEANUT CARAMEL
BROWNIE BITES

FAVORITE FROSTED BROWNIES

I used candy sprinkles to dress up my tried-and-true brownies for Valentine's Day. Everyone always agrees that they are absolutely yummy!
—Barbara Birk, St. George, UT

PREP: 15 MIN. • **BAKE:** 25 MIN. + COOLING
MAKES: 15 SERVINGS

- 1 **cup butter, softened**
- 2 **cups sugar**
- 4 **large eggs, room temperature**
- 2 **tsp. vanilla extract**
- 1¾ **cups all-purpose flour**
- 6 **Tbsp. baking cocoa**
- 1 **tsp. baking powder**
- ¼ **tsp. salt**

FROSTING
- ½ **cup butter, softened**
- ¼ **cup evaporated milk**
- 1 **tsp. vanilla extract**
- 2 **Tbsp. baking cocoa**
- 3 **cups confectioners' sugar**
   Decorating sprinkles, optional

1. Preheat oven to 350°. In a large bowl, cream butter and sugar. Add eggs, 1 at a time, beating well after each addition. Beat in vanilla. Combine the flour, cocoa, baking powder and salt; gradually add to creamed mixture and mix well.

2. Spread into a greased 13x9-in. baking pan. Bake for 25-30 minutes or until a toothpick inserted in the center comes out clean. Cool on a wire rack.

3. For frosting, in a bowl, beat the butter, milk and vanilla; add cocoa. Gradually beat in the confectioners' sugar until smooth. Spread over cooled brownies. Decorate with sprinkles if desired.

1 brownie: 445 cal., 20g fat (12g sat. fat), 107mg chol., 273mg sod., 64g carb. (49g sugars, 1g fiber), 4g pro.

ULTIMATE FUDGY BROWNIES

Coffee granules enhance the chocolate flavor in these amazingly fudgy brownies. Add chocolate chips to the batter and you've got some seriously irresistible treats.
—Sarah Farmer, Waukesha, WI

PREP: 20 MIN. • **BAKE:** 40 MIN. + COOLING
MAKES: 16 SERVINGS

- 1 **cup sugar**
- ½ **cup packed brown sugar**
- ⅔ **cup butter, cubed**
- ¼ **cup water**
- 2 **tsp. instant coffee granules, optional**
- 2¾ **cups bittersweet chocolate chips, divided**
- 4 **large eggs, room temperature**
- 2 **tsp. vanilla extract**
- 1½ **cups all-purpose flour**
- ½ **tsp. baking soda**
- ½ **tsp. salt**

1. Preheat oven to 325°. Line a 9-in. square baking pan with parchment, letting ends extend up sides. In a large heavy saucepan, combine sugars, butter, water and, if desired, coffee granules; bring to a boil, stirring constantly. Remove from heat; add 1¾ cups chocolate chips and stir until melted. Cool slightly.

2. In a large bowl, whisk eggs until foamy, about 3 minutes. Add vanilla; gradually whisk in chocolate mixture. In another bowl, whisk flour, baking soda and salt; stir into the chocolate mixture. Fold in remaining 1 cup chocolate chips.

3. Pour batter into prepared pan. Bake on a lower oven rack for 40-50 minutes or until a toothpick inserted in center comes out with moist crumbs (do not overbake). Cool completely in pan on a wire rack.

4. Lifting with parchment, remove brownies from pan. Cut into squares.

1 brownie: 344 cal., 18g fat (10g sat. fat), 67mg chol., 197mg sod., 47g carb. (35g sugars, 2g fiber), 4g pro.

BAKING
101

FUDGY LAYERED IRISH MOCHA BROWNIES

My husband and I are big fans of Irish cream, so I wanted to incorporate it into a brownie. I started with my mom's brownie recipe, then added frosting and ganache. This decadent recipe is the result, and we are really enjoying them!
—Sue Gronholz, Beaver Dam, WI

PREP: 35 MIN. • **BAKE:** 25 MIN. + CHILLING
MAKES: 16 SERVINGS

- ⅔ cup all-purpose flour
- ½ tsp. baking powder
- ¼ tsp. salt
- ⅓ cup butter
- 6 Tbsp. baking cocoa
- 2 Tbsp. canola oil
- ½ tsp. instant coffee granules
- 1 cup sugar
- 2 large eggs, room temperature, beaten
- 1 tsp. vanilla extract

FROSTING
- 2 cups confectioners' sugar
- ¼ cup butter, softened
- 3 Tbsp. Irish cream liqueur

GANACHE TOPPING
- 1 cup semisweet chocolate chips
- 3 Tbsp. Irish cream liqueur
- 2 Tbsp. heavy whipping cream
- ½ tsp. instant coffee granules

1. Preheat oven to 350°. Sift together flour, baking powder and salt; set aside. In a small saucepan over low heat, melt butter. Remove from heat; stir in cocoa, oil and instant coffee granules. Cool slightly; stir in sugar and beaten eggs. Gradually add flour mixture and vanilla; mix well. Spread batter into a greased 8-in. square pan; bake until the center is set (do not overbake), about 25 minutes. Cool in pan on wire rack.

2. For frosting, whisk together the confectioners' sugar and butter (mixture will be lumpy). Gradually whisk in Irish cream liqueur; beat until smooth. Spread over slightly warm brownies. Refrigerate until frosting is set, about 1 hour.

3. Meanwhile, prepare the ganache: Combine all ingredients and microwave on high for 1 minute; stir. Microwave 30 seconds longer; stir until smooth. Cool slightly until ganache reaches a spreading consistency. Spread over frosting. Refrigerate until ganache is set, 45-60 minutes.

1 brownie: 295 cal., 14g fat (7g sat. fat), 43mg chol., 116mg sod., 41g carb. (34g sugars, 1g fiber), 2g pro.

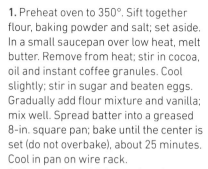

. . . .

DID YOU KNOW?

The ingredients for true, classic ganache are simply cream and chocolate, in different proportions for a pourable glaze (soft ganache) or a firmer mixture that will hold its shape for fillings or truffles (hard ganache). Various flavorings can be added as desired—in this case, Irish cream and coffee. Ganache will naturally turn matte and lose its shine when refrigerated. Some cooks add a bit of corn syrup to keep it glossy.

FUDGY LAYERED IRISH MOCHA BROWNIES

CAPPUCCINO BROWNIES

There's something magical in coffee that intensifies the flavor of chocolate. These three-layer wonders freeze well, but somehow most of them disappear before they reach the freezer.
—Susie Jones, Buhl, ID

PREP: 30 MIN. + CHILLING
BAKE: 25 MIN. + COOLING • **MAKES:** 2 DOZEN

- 8   oz. bittersweet chocolate, chopped
- ¾   cup butter, cut up
- 2   Tbsp. instant coffee granules
- 1   Tbsp. hot water
- 4   large eggs, room temperature
- 1½ cups sugar
- 2   tsp. vanilla extract
- 1   cup all-purpose flour
- ½   tsp. salt
- 1   cup chopped walnuts

TOPPING
- 1   pkg. (8 oz.) cream cheese, softened
- 6   Tbsp. butter, softened
- 1½ cups confectioners' sugar
- 1   tsp. ground cinnamon
- 1   tsp. vanilla extract

GLAZE
- 4   tsp. instant coffee granules
- 1   Tbsp. hot water
- 5   oz. bittersweet chocolate, chopped
- 2   Tbsp. butter
- ½   cup heavy whipping cream

1. Preheat oven to 350°. In a microwave, melt chocolate and butter; stir until smooth. Cool slightly. In a separate small bowl, dissolve the coffee granules in hot water.
2. In a large bowl, beat eggs and sugar. Stir in vanilla, the chocolate mixture and the coffee mixture. Combine flour and salt; gradually add to the chocolate mixture until blended. Fold in walnuts.

3. Transfer batter to a greased and floured 13x9-in. baking pan. Bake until a toothpick inserted in center comes out clean, 25-30 minutes. Cool completely on a wire rack.
4. For topping, in a large bowl, beat cream cheese and butter until blended. Add confectioners' sugar, cinnamon and vanilla extract; beat on low speed until combined. Spread over bars. Refrigerate until firm, about 1 hour.
5. For glaze, dissolve coffee granules in hot water. In a microwave, melt chocolate and butter; cool slightly. Stir in cream and the coffee mixture. Spread over cream cheese layer. Let stand until set. Cut into bars. Refrigerate leftovers.

1 brownie: 353 cal., 25g fat (13g sat. fat), 78mg chol., 158mg sod., 33g carb. (25g sugars, 2g fiber), 4g pro.

CINNAMON BROWNIES

For Christmas one year, a friend gave us a pan of these delicious brownies. Before I figured out their secret was cinnamon, half the pan was already gone!
—Gail Mehle, Rock Springs, WY

PREP: 20 MIN. • **BAKE:** 40 MIN. + COOLING
MAKES: 3 DOZEN

- ¾   cup baking cocoa
- ½   tsp. baking soda
- ⅔   cup butter, melted, divided
- ½   cup boiling water
- 2   cups sugar
- 2   large eggs, room temperature, beaten
- 1   tsp. vanilla extract
- 1⅓ cups all-purpose flour
- 1½ to 2 tsp. ground cinnamon
- ¼   tsp. salt
- 1   cup semisweet chocolate chips

FROSTING
- 6   Tbsp. butter, softened
- ½   cup baking cocoa

- 2⅔ cups confectioners' sugar
- 1   to 1½ tsp. ground cinnamon
- ⅓   cup evaporated milk
- 1   tsp. vanilla extract

1. Preheat oven to 350°. Combine baking cocoa and baking soda; blend in ⅓ cup of the melted butter. Add boiling water, stirring until thickened. Stir in sugar, eggs, vanilla and the remaining ⅓ cup melted butter. Add flour, cinnamon and salt. Fold in chocolate chips.
2. Pour batter into a greased 13x9-in. baking pan. Bake until a toothpick inserted in center comes out with moist crumbs, about 40 minutes. Cool.
3. For frosting, cream butter in a bowl. Combine cocoa, confectioners' sugar and cinnamon; add alternately with the milk. Beat to a spreading consistency; add vanilla. Add more milk if necessary. Spread over the brownies.

1 brownie: 137 cal., 7g fat (4g sat. fat), 27mg chol., 94mg sod., 17g carb. (11g sugars, 1g fiber), 2g pro.

CHEWY CREAM CHEESE BROWNIES

Brownies are a common dessert in our household—they're just about the only form of chocolate my husband will eat! I love this version, which makes a big batch and has a rich cream cheese layer in the center.
—Barbara Nitcznski, Denver, CO

PREP: 20 MIN.
BAKE: 45 MIN. + CHILLING
MAKES: 4 DOZEN

    4   oz. unsweetened chocolate,
        chopped
    ½   cup butter, cubed
    4   large eggs, room temperature
    2   cups sugar
    2   tsp. vanilla extract
  1½   cups all-purpose flour
    1   cup chopped nuts, optional
FILLING
    2   pkg. (8 oz. each) cream cheese,
        softened
    ½   cup sugar
    1   large egg
    2   tsp. vanilla extract

1. Preheat oven to 350°. In a microwave, melt chocolate and butter; stir until smooth. Cool slightly. In a large bowl, beat eggs and sugar. Stir in vanilla and the chocolate mixture. Gradually add flour to chocolate mixture (batter will be thick). Stir in nuts if desired. Spread half of the batter evenly into a greased 13x9-in. baking pan; set aside.
2. In a small bowl, beat the filling ingredients until blended. Gently spread over the batter in pan. Spoon remaining batter over filling; spread to cover.
3. Bake for 45-50 minutes or until the filling is set. Cool on a wire rack 1 hour. Refrigerate at least 2 hours. Cut into bars. Refrigerate leftovers.
1 brownie: 124 cal., 7g fat (4g sat. fat), 37mg chol., 49mg sod., 14g carb. (11g sugars, 0 fiber), 2g pro.

BANANA SPLIT BROWNIES

How's this for a dish—all the joy of a banana split without the mess. Everything in my recipe fits into one pan of delectable brownie bars.
—Constance Sheckler, Chestertown, MD

PREP: 45 MIN. • **BAKE:** 40 MIN. + COOLING
MAKES: 2 DOZEN

    8   oz. unsweetened chocolate,
        chopped
    ¾   cup butter, cubed
    3   large eggs, room temperature
    2   cups sugar
    1   tsp. vanilla extract
    1   cup plus 2 Tbsp. all-purpose flour
    1   cup maraschino cherries, chopped
TOPPING
    1   pkg. (8 oz.) cream cheese,
        softened
    ½   cup mashed ripe banana
        (about 1 medium)
    ⅓   cup strawberry preserves
    1   large egg, room temperature,
        lightly beaten
    ¼   cup chopped salted peanuts

Optional: Sliced bananas and additional chopped maraschino cherries

1. Preheat oven to 350°. In a microwave oven, melt chocolate and butter; stir until smooth.
2. In a large bowl, beat eggs and sugar on high speed 10 minutes. Stir in vanilla and the chocolate mixture. Gradually stir in flour. Fold in cherries. Spread into a greased 13x9-in. baking pan.
3. For topping, in a small bowl, beat cream cheese until smooth. Beat in mashed banana and preserves. Add egg; beat on low speed just until blended. Spread over brownie batter in pan; sprinkle with peanuts.
4. Bake until the topping is set and a toothpick inserted in brownie portion comes out mostly clean, 40-45 minutes. Cool completely on a wire rack.
5. Cut into bars. If desired, serve the bars topped with banana slices and additional cherries. Store in an airtight container in the refrigerator.
1 brownie: 262 cal., 16g fat (9g sat. fat), 57mg chol., 101mg sod., 31g carb. (23g sugars, 2g fiber), 4g pro.

ZUCCHINI BROWNIES

A fast peanut butter and chocolate frosting tops these cakelike brownies. What a sweet way to use up your garden bounty!
—Allyson Wilkins, Amherst, NH

PREP: 20 MIN. • **BAKE:** 35 MIN.
MAKES: 1½ DOZEN

- 1   cup butter, softened
- 1½ cups sugar
- 2   large eggs, room temperature
- ½   cup plain yogurt
- 1   tsp. vanilla extract
- 2½ cups all-purpose flour
- ¼   cup baking cocoa
- 1   tsp. baking soda
- ½   tsp. salt
- 2   cups shredded zucchini

FROSTING

- ⅔   cup semisweet chocolate chips
- ½   cup creamy peanut butter

1. Preheat oven to 350°. In a large bowl, cream butter and sugar until light and fluffy, 5-7 minutes. Add eggs, 1 at a time, beating well after each addition. Beat in yogurt and vanilla.
2. In another bowl, combine flour, cocoa, baking soda and salt; gradually add to creamed mixture. Stir in zucchini.
3. Pour batter into a greased 13x9-in. baking pan. Bake until a toothpick inserted in the center comes out clean, 35-40 minutes.
4. For frosting, in a small saucepan, combine chocolate chips and peanut butter. Cook and stir over low heat until smooth. Spread over warm brownies. Cool on a wire rack. Cut into bars.
1 brownie: 307 cal., 17g fat (8g sat. fat), 52mg chol., 283mg sod., 37g carb. (21g sugars, 2g fiber), 5g pro.

SKILLET STOUT BROWNIES

SKILLET STOUT BROWNIES

These stout brownies are so rich and fudgy. This quick but decadent dessert is perfect for a busy weeknight or a weekend party.
—Mandy Naglich, New York, NY

PREP: 30 MIN.
BAKE: 25 MIN. + COOLING
MAKES: 12 SERVINGS

- 8   oz. semisweet chocolate, chopped
- 1   cup butter, cubed
- 1   cup milk stout beer
- 1   large egg, room temperature
- 2   large egg yolks, room temperature
- ¾   cup sugar
- ¼   cup packed brown sugar
- ¾   cup all-purpose flour
- ⅓   cup baking cocoa
- ½   tsp. salt
     Vanilla ice cream, optional

1. Preheat oven to 350°. Place chocolate in a large bowl. In a 10-in. cast-iron or other ovenproof skillet, combine butter and stout. Bring to a boil; reduce heat. Simmer 10 minutes, stirring constantly. Pour over chocolate; stir with a whisk until smooth. Cool slightly.
2. In another large bowl, beat egg, egg yolks and sugars until blended. Stir in the chocolate mixture. In another bowl, mix flour, baking cocoa and salt; gradually add to the chocolate mixture, mixing well.
3. Spread batter into skillet. Bake until set, 25-30 minutes. Cool completely in skillet on a wire rack. If desired, serve with vanilla ice cream.
1 brownie: 363 cal., 24g fat (14g sat. fat), 87mg chol., 229mg sod., 29g carb. (21g sugars, 1g fiber), 4g pro.

PEPPERMINT
BROWNIES

PEPPERMINT BROWNIES

My grandmother encouraged me to enter these mint brownies in the county fair some years ago, and they earned top honors! They're a delicious treat to serve during the holidays.
—Marcy Greenblatt, Redding, CA

PREP: 15 MIN. • **BAKE:** 35 MIN. + COOLING.
MAKES: 2 DOZEN

- 1⅓ cups all-purpose flour
- 1 cup baking cocoa
- 1 tsp. salt
- 1 tsp. baking powder
- ¾ cup canola oil
- 2 cups sugar
- 4 large eggs, room temperature
- 2 tsp. vanilla extract
- ⅔ cup crushed peppermint candies
GLAZE
- 1 cup semisweet chocolate chips
- 1 Tbsp. shortening
- 2 Tbsp. crushed peppermint candies

1. Preheat oven to 350°. Line a 13x9-in. baking pan with foil and grease the foil; set pan aside.
2. In a bowl, whisk together the first 4 ingredients. In a large bowl, beat oil and sugar until blended. Add eggs, 1 at a time, beating well after each addition. Beat in vanilla. Gradually add the flour mixture; stir in the peppermint candies. Spread into prepared pan.
3. Bake until a toothpick inserted in center comes out clean, 35-40 minutes. Cool in pan on a wire rack.
4. For glaze, in a microwave, melt the chocolate chips and shortening; stir until smooth. Spread over brownies; sprinkle with candies. Cut into bars.
1 brownie: 222 cal., 11g fat (3g sat. fat), 35mg chol., 128mg sod., 31g carb. (22g sugars, 1g fiber), 3g pro.

S'MORES BROWNIES

My family simply adores our daughter's fudgy s'mores brownies. The cinnamon graham cracker crust and dark chocolate brownies bring our passion for s'mores to a whole new level!
—Jennifer Gilbert, Brighton, MI

PREP: 20 MIN. • **BAKE:** 30 MIN.
MAKES: 2 DOZEN

- 1½ cups graham cracker crumbs (about 10 whole crackers)
- ¼ cup sugar
- 1 tsp. ground cinnamon
- ½ cup butter, melted
BROWNIES
- 1 oz. unsweetened baking chocolate
- ½ cup butter, softened
- 1¼ cups sugar
- 3 large eggs, room temperature
- 1 tsp. vanilla extract
- 1¼ cups all-purpose flour
- ⅓ cup dark baking cocoa
- ½ tsp. baking powder
- ¼ tsp. salt
- 1 cup miniature marshmallows
TOPPING
- 1 cup miniature marshmallows
- 5 whole graham crackers, broken into bite-sized pieces

1. Preheat oven to 350°. Combine cracker crumbs, sugar and cinnamon. Stir in melted butter. Press onto bottom of an ungreased 13x9-in. baking pan. Bake until lightly browned, 7-9 minutes. Cool on a wire rack.
2. Melt unsweetened chocolate on high in a microwave, stirring every 30 seconds. Cool slightly. Cream butter and sugar on medium speed until light and fluffy, 5-7 minutes. Add eggs, 1 at a time, beating well after each addition. Beat in melted chocolate and vanilla. In another bowl, whisk flour, cocoa, baking powder and salt; stir into creamed mixture. Fold in 1 cup marshmallows.

3. Spread batter over graham cracker crust. Top with 1 cup marshmallows and broken graham crackers. Bake until the center is set, 18-22 minutes (do not overbake).
1 brownie: 215 cal., 10g fat (6g sat. fat), 44mg chol., 157mg sod., 30g carb. (17g sugars, 1g fiber), 3g pro.

. . . .
TEST KITCHEN TIP
While you don't want to overcook your brownies, you don't want to undercook your crust, either. Underbaking results in a soggy bottom and a less-than-perfect brownie. Make sure your crust is lightly browned and crisp before you take it out of the oven and let it cool.

BAKING 101

GOOEY BUTTER CAKE

BARS

GOOEY BUTTER CAKE

It's called a cake, but this bake produces servings that are more like sweet and gooey dessert bars—delicious served warm or cool. A friend gave me a recipe using cake mix, but I prefer baking from scratch so I made my own version. It's normal for the middle to sink a little.

—Cheri Foster, Vail, AZ

PREP: 20 MIN. • **BAKE:** 40 MIN. + COOLING
MAKES: 16 SERVINGS

2½ cups all-purpose flour
1¾ cups sugar
2½ tsp. baking powder
½ tsp. salt
1 cup butter, melted
1 large egg, room temperature
1½ tsp. vanilla extract
TOPPING
1 pkg. (8 oz.) cream cheese, softened
2 large eggs, beaten, room temperature
2 cups confectioners' sugar

1. Preheat oven to 325°. In a large bowl, combine flour, sugar, baking powder and salt. In another bowl, whisk melted butter, egg and vanilla extract; add to flour mixture and stir to combine. Press onto the bottom of a greased 13x9-in. baking dish.

2. For topping, in a large bowl, beat the cream cheese and eggs until smooth. Add the confectioners' sugar; stir to combine. Pour over the crust. Bake until the center is almost set and the edges just start to brown, 40-45 minutes. Cool for 1 hour on a wire rack. Sprinkle with additional confectioners' sugar if desired.

1 bar: 381 cal., 17g fat (10g sat. fat), 80mg chol., 299mg sod., 53g carb. (37g sugars, 1g fiber), 4g pro.

CARDAMOM CHEESECAKE BARS

Fans of cheesecake will love these bite-sized desserts. Crunchy and smooth, they make the perfect treat any time of day.
—Judi Oudekerk, Buffalo, MN

PREP: 35 MIN. • **BAKE:** 35 MIN. + CHILLING
MAKES: 16 SERVINGS

- ¾ cup graham cracker crumbs
- 2 Tbsp. butter, melted
- 2 pkg. (8 oz. each) cream cheese, softened
- ½ cup sugar
- 2 tsp. ground cardamom, divided
- 1 tsp. vanilla extract
- 2 large eggs, room temperature, lightly beaten
- ⅓ cup all-purpose flour
- ⅓ cup quick-cooking oats
- ⅓ cup packed brown sugar
- ¼ cup cold butter
- ⅓ cup sliced almonds

1. Preheat oven to 350°. In a small bowl, combine graham cracker crumbs and melted butter. Press onto the bottom of a greased 9-in. square baking pan.

Beat the cream cheese, sugar, 1 tsp. cardamom and the vanilla until smooth. Add eggs; beat on low speed just until combined. Pour over crust.
2. In a small bowl, combine flour, oats, brown sugar and the remaining 1 tsp. cardamom. Cut in the cold butter until mixture is crumbly. Stir in almonds. Sprinkle over top.
3. Bake 35-40 minutes or until center is almost set and topping is golden brown. Cool on a wire rack for 1 hour. Cover and refrigerate at least 2 hours before serving. Cut into 16 bars.
1 bar: 232 cal., 16g fat (9g sat. fat), 69mg chol., 149mg sod., 18g carb. (12g sugars, 1g fiber), 4g pro.

. . . .

DID YOU KNOW?

Cardamom is a member of the same family as ginger, and comes in green or black pods. Most ground cardamom in markets is from green pods; smoky black cardamom is usually used whole.

CLASSIC
LEMON BARS

CLASSIC LEMON BARS

These bars are simple enough for no-fuss dinners yet elegant enough for special celebrations. Regardless of when you serve them, I'm sure they'll be a hit at your home.
—Melissa Mosness, Loveland, CO

PREP: 15 MIN. • **BAKE:** 25 MIN. + COOLING
MAKES: 9 SERVINGS

- ½ cup butter, softened
- ¼ cup sugar
- 1 cup all-purpose flour

FILLING

- ¾ cup sugar
- 2 large eggs
- 3 Tbsp. lemon juice
- 2 Tbsp. all-purpose flour
- 1 tsp. grated lemon zest
- ¼ tsp. baking powder
  Confectioners' sugar

1. Preheat oven to 350°. In a small bowl, cream butter and sugar until light and fluffy, 5-7 minutes; gradually beat in flour until blended. Press into an ungreased 8-in. square baking dish. Bake for 15-20 minutes or until edges are lightly browned.
2. For filling, in a small bowl, beat the sugar, eggs, lemon juice, flour, lemon zest and baking powder until frothy. Pour over the crust.
3. Bake 10-15 minutes longer or until set and lightly browned. Cool on a wire rack. Sprinkle with confectioners' sugar. Cut into squares.
1 bar: 250 cal., 11g fat (7g sat. fat), 74mg chol., 99mg sod., 35g carb. (23g sugars, 0 fiber), 3g pro.

BAKING
101

BLUEBERRY LATTICE BARS

Since our area has an annual blueberry festival, my daughters and I are always looking for great new berry recipes to enter in the cooking contest. These lovely, yummy bars won a blue ribbon one year.
—Debbie Ayers, Baileyville, ME

PREP: 25 MIN. + CHILLING • **BAKE:** 30 MIN.
MAKES: 2 DOZEN

- 1⅓ cups butter, softened
- ⅔ cup sugar
- ¼ tsp. salt
- 1 large egg, room temperature
- ½ tsp. vanilla extract
- 3¾ cups all-purpose flour
- FILLING
- 3 cups fresh or frozen blueberries
- 1 cup sugar
- 3 Tbsp. cornstarch

1. Cream butter, sugar and salt until light and fluffy, 5-7 minutes; beat in egg and vanilla. Gradually beat in flour. Divide dough in half; shape each into a 1-in.-thick rectangle. Wrap and refrigerate for 2 hours or overnight.
2. Preheat oven to 375°. Place the blueberries, sugar and cornstarch in a small saucepan. Bring to a boil over medium heat, stirring frequently; cook and stir until thickened, about 2 minutes. Cool slightly.
3. Roll each portion of dough between 2 sheets of waxed paper into a 14x10-in. rectangle. Place each rectangle on a separate baking sheet; freeze until firm, 5-10 minutes. Place 1 rectangle in a greased 13x9-in. baking pan, pressing the dough onto bottom and about ½ in. up the sides. Add filling.
4. Cut the remaining rectangle into ½-in. strips; freeze 5-10 minutes. Arrange strips over filling in crisscross fashion. If desired, press edges with a fork to seal strips. Bake until top crust is golden brown, 30-35 minutes. Cool on a wire rack. Cut into bars.
1 bar: 233 cal., 11g fat (7g sat. fat), 35mg chol., 109mg sod., 32g carb. (16g sugars, 1g fiber), 3g pro.

FROSTED BANANA BARS

These bars are always a hit at potlucks in the small rural farming community where my husband and I live. I also like to provide them for coffee hour after church. They're so moist and delicious that wherever I take them, they don't last long.
—Karen Dryak, Niobrara, NE

PREP: 15 MIN. • **BAKE:** 20 MIN. + COOLING
MAKES: 3 DOZEN

- ½ cup butter, softened
- 2 cups sugar
- 3 large eggs, room temperature
- 1½ cups mashed ripe bananas (about 3 medium)
- 1 tsp. vanilla extract
- 2 cups all-purpose flour
- 1 tsp. baking soda
- Dash salt
- FROSTING
- 1 pkg. (8 oz.) cream cheese, softened
- ½ cup butter, softened
- 4 cups confectioners' sugar
- 2 tsp. vanilla extract

1. Preheat oven to 350°. In a large bowl, cream butter and sugar until light and fluffy, 5-7 minutes. Beat in the eggs, bananas and vanilla. Combine the flour, baking soda and salt; stir into creamed mixture just until blended.
2. Transfer to a greased 15x10x1-in. baking pan. Bake 20-25 minutes or until a toothpick inserted in the center comes out clean. Cool in pan on a wire rack.
3. For frosting, in a small bowl, beat cream cheese and butter until fluffy. Add confectioners' sugar and vanilla; beat until smooth. Frost bars.
1 bar: 202 cal., 8g fat (5g sat. fat), 38mg chol., 100mg sod., 32g carb. (25g sugars, 0 fiber), 2g pro.

TOPPING OPTIONS

If you're not partial to cream cheese frosting, there are other great toppings for these bars. A creamy caramel frosting would go very well with the banana flavor.

If you're feeling a bit more adventurous, go Elvis-inspired—spread the bars with a chocolate peanut butter frosting, then sprinkle with chopped peanuts or crumbled cooked bacon!

For a simple and elegant solution, try a classic homemade chocolate ganache. Cool and spread over the top, then decorate with dried banana chips or chopped pecans.

Or, for the simplest topping of all, just lightly dust the bars with confectioners' sugar.

GIMLET BARS

I love a tangy gimlet when the weather turns steamy—but these bars are just the thing when the craving hits and summer seems too far away. Add more lime zest if you want these a bit tangier.
—Trisha Kruse, Eagle, ID

PREP: 20 MIN. + STANDING
BAKE: 35 MIN. + COOLING • **MAKES:** 4 DOZEN

- 2 cups all-purpose flour
- ½ cup confectioners' sugar
- ½ tsp. salt
- 1 cup butter

FILLING
- 4 large eggs
- 2 cups sugar
- ⅓ cup all-purpose flour
- ¼ cup lime juice
- ¼ cup gin
- 1 Tbsp. grated lime zest
- ½ tsp. baking powder

GLAZE
- 1½ cups confectioners' sugar
- 2 Tbsp. lime juice
- 2 Tbsp. gin
- 1 tsp. grated lime zest

1. Preheat oven to 350°. Whisk flour, confectioners' sugar and salt; cut in butter until crumbly. Press onto bottom of a greased 15x10x1-in. baking pan. Bake until golden brown, about 10 minutes. Cool on a wire rack.
2. For filling, whisk the 7 ingredients; spread over crust. Bake until filling is set, about 25 minutes. Cool completely in pan on a wire rack.
3. For glaze, whisk all ingredients until smooth; spread evenly over cooled bars. Let glaze set before serving.
1 bar: 117 cal., 4g fat (3g sat. fat), 26mg chol., 66mg sod., 18g carb. (13g sugars, 0 fiber), 1g pro.

RAISIN PUMPKIN BARS

RAISIN PUMPKIN BARS

These moist bars will keep well—if your family doesn't eat them all right away! They're nice to take to a potluck supper or as a snack or dessert anytime.
—J.B. Hendrix, Ganado, TX

PREP: 20 MIN. • **BAKE:** 25 MIN. + COOLING
MAKES: 2 DOZEN

- 2 cups sugar
- 1 can (15 oz.) pumpkin
- 1 cup canola oil
- 4 large eggs, room temperature
- 2 cups all-purpose flour
- 2 tsp. baking powder
- 1 tsp. baking soda
- 1 tsp. ground cinnamon
- 1 tsp. ground nutmeg
- ½ tsp. salt
- ⅛ tsp. ground cloves
- ½ cup raisins
- ⅓ cup chopped pecans or walnuts

FROSTING
- ⅓ cup butter, softened
- 3 oz. cream cheese, softened
- 1 Tbsp. 2% milk
- 1 tsp. vanilla extract
- 2 cups confectioners' sugar

1. Preheat oven to 350°. In a large bowl, beat the sugar, pumpkin, oil and eggs. Combine the flour, baking powder, baking soda, cinnamon, nutmeg, salt and cloves; gradually add to pumpkin mixture and mix well. Stir in raisins and nuts.
2. Pour batter into a greased 15x10x1-in. baking pan. Bake 25-30 minutes or until a toothpick is inserted in the center comes out clean. Cool on a wire rack.
3. For frosting, combine butter, cream cheese, milk and vanilla in a bowl; beat until smooth. Gradually beat in the confectioners' sugar. Spread over top; cut into bars. Store in the refrigerator.
1 bar: 297 cal., 15g fat (4g sat. fat), 46mg chol., 184mg sod., 39g carb. (28g sugars, 1g fiber), 3g pro.

SNICKERDOODLE BLONDIE BARS

When asked to bring a dessert for my boys' football team to share, I whipped up these unique blondies and was instantly named the greatest mom by all.
—Valonda Seward, Coarsegold, CA

PREP: 15 MIN. • **BAKE:** 35 MIN. + COOLING
MAKES: 20 BARS

1	cup butter, softened
2	cups packed brown sugar
3	tsp. vanilla extract
2	large eggs, room temperature
2⅔	cups all-purpose flour
2	tsp. baking powder
1	tsp. ground cinnamon
¼	tsp. ground nutmeg
½	tsp. salt

TOPPING
1½	tsp. sugar
½	tsp. ground cinnamon

1. Preheat oven to 350°. Cream butter and brown sugar until light and fluffy, 5-7 minutes. Beat in the vanilla. Beat in eggs, 1 at a time, beating well after each addition. In another bowl, whisk flour, baking powder, spices and salt; gradually beat into creamed mixture. Spread in a greased 9-in. square pan.
2. Mix the topping ingredients; sprinkle over top. Bake until set and golden brown, 35-40 minutes. Cool completely in pan on a wire rack. Cut into bars.
1 bar: 235 cal., 10g fat (6g sat. fat), 45mg chol., 180mg sod., 35g carb. (22g sugars, 1g fiber), 2g pro.

. . . .

TEST KITCHEN TIP

For thinner bars, prepare recipe as directed, using a greased 13x9-in. pan and decreasing bake time to 25-30 minutes.

SNICKERDOODLE
BLONDIE BARS

BAKING
101

CARAMEL HEAVENLIES

Before I cut these bars into triangles, I usually trim the edges so all the cookies look the same. My husband and daughter love that part because they get to eat all the scraps!
—Dawn Burns, Lake St. Louis, MO

PREP: 20 MIN. • **BAKE:** 15 MIN. + COOLING
MAKES: ABOUT 3 DOZEN

- 12 whole graham crackers
- 2 cups miniature marshmallows
- ¾ cup butter, cubed
- ¾ cup packed brown sugar
- 1 tsp. ground cinnamon
- 1 tsp. vanilla extract
- 1 cup sliced almonds
- 1 cup sweetened shredded coconut

1. Preheat the oven to 350°. Line a 15x10x1-in. baking pan with foil, letting foil extend over sides by 1 in.; lightly coat foil with cooking spray. Arrange graham crackers in prepared pan; sprinkle with marshmallows.
2. In a small saucepan, combine butter, brown sugar and cinnamon; cook and stir over medium heat until butter is melted and sugar is dissolved. Remove from heat; stir in vanilla.
3. Spoon the butter mixture over the marshmallows. Sprinkle with sliced almonds and shredded coconut. Bake until browned, 14-16 minutes. Cool completely in pan on a wire rack.
4. Using foil, lift bars out of the pan. Cut into triangles; discard foil.
1 bar: 110 cal., 7g fat (3g sat. fat), 10mg chol., 68mg sod., 13g carb. (8g sugars, 1g fiber), 1g pro.

BAKING 101

PEANUT BUTTER CAKE BARS

These cakelike bars are packed with peanut butter and chocolate chips, and they are perfect for any occasion. Kids and adults alike are in for a treat with these gems.
—Charlotte Ennis, Lake Arthur, NM

PREP: 15 MIN. • **BAKE:** 45 MIN. + COOLING
MAKES: 2 DOZEN

- ⅔ cup butter, softened
- ⅔ cup peanut butter
- 1 cup sugar
- 1 cup packed brown sugar
- 4 large eggs, room temperature
- 2 tsp. vanilla extract
- 2 cups all-purpose flour
- 2 tsp. baking powder
- ½ tsp. salt
- 1 pkg. (11½ oz.) milk chocolate chips

1. Preheat oven to 350°. In a large bowl, cream the butter, peanut butter, sugar and brown sugar. Add the eggs, 1 at a time, beating well after each addition. Beat in vanilla extract. Combine the flour, baking powder and salt; gradually add to the creamed mixture. Stir in chocolate chips.
2. Spread batter into a greased 13x9-in. baking pan. Bake until a toothpick inserted in the center comes out clean, 45-50 minutes. Cool on a wire rack. Cut into bars.
1 bar: 277 cal., 14g fat (6g sat. fat), 52mg chol., 178mg sod., 35g carb. (25g sugars, 1g fiber), 5g pro.

GLAZED APPLE-MAPLE BLONDIES

3. Bake until top is golden brown and a toothpick inserted in center comes out with moist crumbs, 25-30 minutes.
4. Meanwhile, in a small saucepan, melt butter over medium-low heat; stir in syrup and brown sugar. Bring to a boil over medium heat; cook and stir until slightly thickened, 2-3 minutes. Remove from heat; cool slightly.
5. Pour glaze over warm blondies. Let cool completely in pan on a wire rack. Cut into bars.

1 blondie: 192 cal., 6g fat (4g sat. fat), 31mg chol., 149mg sod., 33g carb. (25g sugars, 0 fiber), 2g pro.

EASY LAYER BARS

These rich bar cookies will melt in your mouth! They're ideal to have on hand for a snack.
—Pauline Schrag, Theresa, NY

BAKING 101

PREP: 15 MIN.
BAKE: 30 MIN. + COOLING
MAKES: 16 BARS

- ½ cup butter, cubed
- 1 cup graham cracker crumbs
- 1 cup sweetened shredded coconut
- 1 cup semisweet chocolate chips
- 1 cup chopped nuts
- 1 can (14 oz.) sweetened condensed milk

Preheat oven to 350°. Melt butter in a 9-in. square baking pan. On top of melted butter, sprinkle crumbs, then coconut, then chocolate chips, then nuts. Pour milk over all. Do not stir. Bake until a toothpick inserted in center comes out clean, about 30 minutes. Cool several hours before cutting.

1 bar: 279 cal., 18g fat (9g sat. fat), 24mg chol., 138mg sod., 28g carb. (22g sugars, 1g fiber), 5g pro.

GLAZED APPLE-MAPLE BLONDIES

My 6-year-old son and I conjured up this recipe to use up the last of the apples we picked from the local apple orchard. Serve with a dollop of sweetened whipped cream.
—Heather Bates, Athens, ME

PREP: 25 MIN. • **BAKE:** 25 MIN. + COOLING
MAKES: 2 DOZEN

- 1⅓ cups packed brown sugar
- ½ cup butter, melted and cooled
- ½ cup maple syrup
- 2 tsp. vanilla extract
- 2 large eggs, room temperature
- 2 cups all-purpose flour
- ¾ tsp. salt
- ¼ tsp. baking soda
- 3 cups chopped peeled apples (about 3 medium)

GLAZE
- ¼ cup butter, cubed
- ½ cup maple syrup
- ¼ cup packed brown sugar

1. Preheat oven to 350°. Line a 13x9-in. baking pan with parchment, letting ends extend up sides; set aside.
2. In a large bowl, beat brown sugar, melted butter, syrup and vanilla until blended. Beat in eggs, 1 at a time, beating well after each addition. In another bowl, whisk flour, salt and baking soda; gradually beat into brown sugar mixture. Stir in apples (batter will be thick). Transfer to prepared pan.

CHOCOLATE SALTED CARAMEL BARS

I enjoy experimenting with different recipes and combining classic and new flavors. I adore salted caramel and dark chocolate, so I layered these two flavors with my favorite shortbread crust. It's melt-in-your-mouth good, and it is quickly becoming a favorite with my family, friends and customers! For even more gooey goodness, drizzle bottled caramel sauce over the top.
—Lisa Glenn, Sarasota, FL

PREP: 20 MIN. • **BAKE:** 50 MIN. + COOLING
MAKES: 2½ DOZEN

- 2 cups butter, softened
- 1½ cups confectioners' sugar
- 1 cup sugar
- 6 tsp. vanilla extract
- 4 cups all-purpose flour
- 1 pkg. (14 oz.) caramels
- ⅓ cup heavy whipping cream
- 1 tsp. kosher salt
- 1 pkg. (12 oz.) dark chocolate chips

1. Preheat oven to 325°. Beat butter, sugars and vanilla until light and fluffy, 5-7 minutes. Gradually beat in flour, mixing well. Press 3 cups of dough onto bottom of a greased 13x9-in. pan. Bake until set, 20-22 minutes. Cool 10 minutes on a wire rack.
2. Meanwhile, in a small saucepan, melt caramels with the cream over low heat until smooth. Pour over crust. Sprinkle with salt, then chocolate chips. Drop remaining dough by teaspoonfuls over top.
3. Bake until light golden brown, 30-35 minutes. Cool on a wire rack.
1 bar: 334 cal., 18g fat (11g sat. fat), 37mg chol., 199mg sod., 43g carb. (28g sugars, 1g fiber), 3g pro.

CHERRY CHEWBILEES

This is a good dish to carry to potlucks and parties. It's a hit at home, too—my husband rates it as one of his favorite desserts.
—Debbi Smith, Crossett, AR

PREP: 25 MIN. • **BAKE:** 30 MIN. + CHILLING
MAKES: 20 SERVINGS

- 1¼ cups all-purpose flour
- ½ cup packed brown sugar
- ½ cup butter-flavored shortening
- 1 cup chopped walnuts, divided
- ½ cup sweetened shredded coconut

FILLING
- 2 pkg. (8 oz. each) cream cheese, softened
- ⅔ cup sugar
- 2 large eggs, room temperature
- 2 tsp. vanilla extract
- 2 cans (21 oz. each) cherry pie filling

1. Preheat oven to 350°. Line a 13x9-in. baking pan with foil, letting ends extend up sides; grease foil.
2. Combine flour and brown sugar; cut in shortening until fine crumbs form. Stir in ½ cup nuts and the coconut. Set aside ½ cup crumb mixture for topping. Press the remaining mixture into the prepared pan. Bake until top is lightly browned, 12-15 minutes.
3. Meanwhile, for filling, beat cream cheese, sugar, eggs and vanilla until smooth. Spread over hot crust. Bake 15 minutes.
4. Spread pie filling on top. Combine remaining ½ cup nuts and the reserved crumb mixture; sprinkle over cherries. Bake 15 minutes more.
5. Cool completely on a wire rack. Refrigerate until chilled. Lifting with foil, remove mixture from pan. Cut into bars. Refrigerate leftovers.
1 bar: 251 cal., 14g fat (5g sat. fat), 34mg chol., 54mg sod., 29g carb. (20g sugars, 1g fiber), 4g pro.

TOFFEE PECAN BARS

Curl up with a hot cup of coffee and one of these oh-so-sweet treats. The golden topping and flaky crust give way to the heartwarming taste of old-fashioned pecan pie.
—Dianna Croskey, Gibsonia, PA

PREP: 15 MIN. • **BAKE:** 40 MIN. + CHILLING
MAKES: 3 DOZEN

- 2 cups all-purpose flour
- ½ cup confectioners' sugar
- 1 cup cold butter, cubed
- 1 large egg, room temperature
- 1 can (14 oz.) sweetened condensed milk
- 1 tsp. vanilla extract
- 1 pkg. English toffee bits (10 oz.) or almond brickle chips (7½ oz.)
- 1 cup chopped pecans

1. Preheat oven to 350°. In a large bowl, mix flour and confectioners' sugar; cut in butter until mixture is crumbly. Press into a greased 13x9-in. baking pan. Bake 15 minutes.
2. Meanwhile, in a small bowl, mix egg, milk and vanilla. Fold in toffee bits and pecans. Spoon over crust. Bake until top is golden brown, 24-26 minutes. Refrigerate until firm. Cut into bars.
1 bar: 179 cal., 11g fat (5g sat. fat), 26mg chol., 112mg sod., 18g carb. (13g sugars, 1g fiber), 2g pro.

PIES

The most beloved treat of family kitchens and holiday spreads,
state fairs and summer road trips, pies make everyone happy!
From classic down-home apple pie to stunning galettes,
pies offer a limitless range of sweet options.

THE PERFECT PIE CRUST

When it comes to baking pies, the most daunting part of the process is the crust. Once you master making pie crust, you can easily whip up flaky homemade crusts anytime.

There are many crust variations, and we've shared a few in this chapter. Many find it a personal preference whether to make their crust with shortening, lard or butter—or a combination. This Classic Butter Pie Pastry (recipe on p. 210) is the default crust in the Taste of Home Test Kitchen.

1. Cut in the fat:
Whisk the salt and flour in a large mixing bowl, then use a pastry blender to cut in the cold butter until the bits are pea-sized. Avoid using your fingers to mix—your hands are warm and will melt the butter.

2. Add water: Start by adding just 2-3 tablespoons cold water; add more as needed. Use a fork to toss (don't press) the water into the flour just until everything is mixed and coated. The dough is the right consistency when it holds together when pressed.

3. Chill the dough: Form the dough into a disk and cover it tightly with plastic wrap or waxed paper. Chill in the fridge for at least an hour to help firm up the butter. You can keep it in the fridge for a few days or even freeze it for several weeks. To freeze the dough, wrap it tightly in waxed paper and freeze it in an airtight container. When you're ready to use it, let it thaw in the refrigerator overnight.

4. Roll out the dough: Lightly dust your work surface and rolling pin with flour. Roll from the center outward to the edges. To help ensure an even shape, give the dough a quarter turn after each roll. Roll until you reach the desired size and thickness. Add an extra sprinkling of flour as needed to prevent sticking.

If the dough rips as it's rolled out, dip a finger into cold water and patch with a bit of extra dough.

You can also roll out the dough between layers of waxed paper to prevent sticking and make it easy to turn and move.

5. Move crust to pan: Drape the crust over your rolling pin and move it to the pan. Lay it in place and allow it to ease into the plate; let the crust settle before you manipulate it. Avoid stretching the crust as much as possible; stretching will cause it to shrink back during baking. Trim the edge; leave some excess to crimp.

CRUMB CRUSTS

For information on making your own crumb crusts, see p. 361.

PIE PASTRY POINTERS

- Combine the flour and salt before cutting in the fat; this ensures the ingredients are evenly distributed.

- Add 1-2 ice cubes to a ½ cup of water and let stand for a few minutes to get cold; add a small bit at a time to your other ingredients.

- Add water just until the mixture "grabs" and you can form it into a ball. Avoid overmixing—that will toughen the crust.

- For crisp crusts, choose dull-finished aluminum or glass pie plates.

- Because of pastry's high fat content, don't grease the pie plate unless the recipe directs.

- Bake pies in the center of a preheated oven. Cover edge with foil if it begins to brown too quickly.

BLIND BAKING

To "blind bake" a crust is to partially or fully bake it before adding the filling. Any pie filling that requires a shorter bake time than its pastry needs a blind-baked crust. Full blind baking is reserved for pies that won't be put back in the oven after their filling is added. Blind baking the crust about halfway (also called parbaking) is useful for pies with fillings that give up liquid that might make the bottom crust soggy. The technique is common with custard pies, fruit pies, quiches and cream pies.

After placing the crust in the pie plate and fluting the edge, line the shell with a double thickness of foil or parchment.

Fill with dried beans, uncooked rice or pie weights. This will keep the crust from puffing up, shrinking and slipping down the pie plate during baking.

Bake at 450° for 8 minutes. Carefully remove the foil or parchment and weights. At this stage, some bakers dock the crust (poke holes in it with the tines of a fork) to further prevent air pockets from forming. Depending on the pie, however, the filling could seep into these holes. Try both methods to see what works for you.

Bake 5-6 minutes longer or until light golden brown. Cool on a wire rack. Let the pie weights cool, then store. Beans and rice may be reused as pie weights but cannot be cooked and used in recipes.

Parbaking doesn't work for double-crust pies, as you want both crusts to be the same level of doneness. Instead, brush the bottom crust with beaten egg white and then add the filling just before baking to prevent the bottom crust from getting soggy.

FINISHING TOUCHES

To add color and sheen to double-crust pies, use a pastry brush to gently apply a wash before baking, avoiding the edge of the pie. For a sparkle effect, sprinkle the crust with granulated sugar or decorator's sugar after brushing on the wash.

You can also add shine to a baked crust by brushing it with 1 Tbsp. warmed corn syrup.

EFFECT	WASH
Shine, light browning	1 egg white lightly beaten with 1 tsp. water
Glossy, golden	1 egg yolk beaten with 1 tsp. water
Subtle sheen	Half-and-half or heavy whipping cream
Crisp, brown	Water

HOT WATER PIE CRUST?

The rules for successful pie crust emphasize the cold—cold fat, cold water. However, many home bakers have memories of their grandmothers making hot-water crusts—another way that Grandma broke the rules! For a simple version:

1. Pour 3 Tbsp. hot water over ⅓ cup shortening and beat until combined.

2. Add 1 cup all-purpose flour and ¼ tsp. salt; beat until crumbly.

3. Shape dough into a ball, and then roll out to fit a 9-in. pie plate.

4. Parbake the crust (see instructions at left) by baking at 450° for 8 minutes, then removing the foil and baking 5 minutes longer.

ROLLED EDGE

FLUTED EDGE

ROPED EDGE

SUNFLOWER EDGE

LEAF TRIM

SIMPLE DECORATIVE EDGES

Turn overhanging crust under to form a **Rolled Edge**. This is the start of the other decorative edges shown here.

For a **Leaf Trim,** make pastry for a double-crust pie. Roll out half for the bottom crust. Roll out remaining dough; cut out shapes with small cutters, or by hand. Dip your finger in water and wet the back of the shape; press gently to seal to the edge of the bottom crust.

MAKING A BRAIDED EDGE

1. Make enough pastry for a double-crust pie. Line your pie plate with the bottom crust and trim so it's even with the edge. Roll out the remaining dough into a 10x8-in. rectangle. With a sharp knife or a pizza cutter, cut twelve ¼-in. strips.

2. Carefully braid 3 of the strips.

3. Brush the edge of the crust with water; place braid on the edge and press lightly to secure.

4. Repeat with the remaining strips, attaching braids until the entire edge is covered.

DECORATIVE TOPS FOR DOUBLE-CRUST PIES

The top crust of a double-crust pie needs to have vents to let steam escape, so why not make them pretty? Use stars, hearts or other simple cookie cutters to create openings in the crust. Working quickly, place top crust over filling as soon as you've removed the cutouts. Affix cutouts to the top crust, if desired, by brushing them with water and gently pressing them into place before baking.

MAKING A LATTICE CRUST

This is a classic finish for summer fruit pies. You can make a lattice open or tight.

1. Make pastry for a double-crust pie; chill. Roll out bottom crust from the larger piece of dough and use it to line a 9-in. pie plate; trim to ½ in. beyond the edge. Add pie filling.

Roll out the smaller ball of dough to a 12-in. circle. With a fluted pastry wheel, pizza cutter or sharp knife, cut dough into strips that are ½ to 1 in. wide.

2. Lay the longest strip across the center of the pie; lay remaining strips ½ to ¾ in. apart. Fold back every other strip. Starting in the center, add strips at right angles to weave the strips together, lifting every other strip as the cross strips are placed back down.

3. Continue to add strips, lifting and weaving until the lattice top is complete.

4. Trim the strips even with the bottom crust edge. Fold bottom crust up and over the ends of the top strips and press to seal.

PIE DONENESS TESTS & STORAGE

PIE TYPE	DONENESS TEST	STORAGE
BAKED SHELL	Pastry is light golden brown.	N/A
FRUIT PIE	Filling is clear and bubbles. Crust is light golden brown.	1 day at room temperature, 5 days in refrigerator
MERINGUE PIE	Top is set and meringue peaks are brown.	3 days in refrigerator
CUSTARD PIE	Knife inserted in center comes out clean. A small area in center of pie will jiggle.	3 days in refrigerator

PIE CRUSTS

CLASSIC BUTTER PIE PASTRY

This all-butter pastry makes a flavorful, flaky pie crust that's easy to handle and bakes up golden brown and beautiful. It's just like Mom's—only better!
—*Taste of Home* Test Kitchen

PREP: 10 MIN. + CHILLING
MAKES: PASTRY FOR ONE 9-IN. PIE

FOR SINGLE-CRUST PIE
1¼ cups all-purpose flour
¼ tsp. salt
½ cup cold butter, cubed
3 to 4 Tbsp. ice water

FOR DOUBLE-CRUST PIE
2½ cups all-purpose flour
½ tsp. salt
1 cup cold butter, cubed
⅓ to ⅔ cup ice water

Combine flour and salt; cut in butter until crumbly. Gradually add ice water, tossing with a fork until dough holds together when pressed.

For a single-crust pie: Shape the dough into a disk; wrap and refrigerate 1 hour or overnight. On a lightly floured surface, roll out the dough to a ⅛-in.-thick circle; transfer to a 9-in. pie plate. Trim crust to ½ in. beyond rim of plate; flute edge. Fill or bake according to recipe directions.

For a double-crust pie: Divide dough and shape into 2 disks, 1 slightly larger than the other; wrap and refrigerate for 1 hour or overnight. On a lightly floured surface, roll the larger portion to a ⅛-in.-thick circle; transfer to a 9-in. pie plate. Add filling. Roll the remaining dough to a ⅛-in.-thick circle. Place over filling. Trim, seal and flute edge. Cut slits in top. Bake according to recipe directions.

1 piece (⅛ recipe) single-crust pastry: 173 cal., 12g fat (7g sat. fat), 31mg chol., 165mg sod., 15g carb. (0 sugars, 1g fiber), 2g pro.

ALI'S GLUTEN-FREE PIE PASTRY

Who needs gluten? This recipe produces a tender, nutty crust that's as tasty as any traditional pastry. It's the perfect base for all your pie favorites.
—Harriet Stichter, Milford, IN

PREP: 15 MIN. + CHILLING
MAKES: PASTRY FOR ONE 9-IN. PIE

FOR SINGLE-CRUST PIE
1 cup gluten-free all-purpose baking flour
⅓ cup ground almonds
3 Tbsp. sugar
¼ tsp. salt
¼ tsp. xanthan gum
6 Tbsp. cold butter or margarine, cubed
2 Tbsp. beaten egg
1 to 2 Tbsp. ice water

FOR DOUBLE-CRUST PIE
2 cups gluten-free all-purpose baking flour
⅔ cup ground almonds
⅓ cup sugar
½ tsp. salt
½ tsp. xanthan gum
¾ cup cold butter or margarine, cubed
1 large egg, beaten
3 to 4 Tbsp. ice water

In a large bowl, combine the flour, almonds, sugar, salt and xanthan gum. Cut in the butter until crumbly. Stir in egg. Gradually add water, tossing with a fork just until dough holds together when pressed.

For a single-crust pie: Shape dough into a disk; wrap and refrigerate 1 hour or until easy to handle. Roll out dough to fit a 9-in. pie plate. Transfer crust to pie plate. Trim crust to ½ in. beyond edge of plate; flute edge. Fill or bake shell according to recipe directions.

For a double-crust pie: Divide dough in half so that 1 portion is slightly larger than the other; form into disks. Wrap disks and refrigerate for 1 hour or until easy to handle. Roll out larger portion of dough to fit a 9-in. pie plate. Transfer crust to pie plate. Trim the crust even with edge of plate. Add filling. Roll out remaining dough to fit top of pie; place over filling. Trim, seal and flute edge. Cut slits in top. Bake pie according to recipe instructions.

Note: Cover edge with foil. Remove foil during the last 15-20 minutes of baking.

1 piece: 172 cal., 11g fat (6g sat. fat), 39mg chol., 141mg sod., 17g carb. (5g sugars, 2g fiber), 3g pro.

EGG YOLK PASTRY

Egg yolk lends an attractive golden color to this pie pastry. The recipe makes enough pastry for one double-crust pie or two single-crust pies.

—Dolores Skrout, Summerhill, PA

PREP: 20 MIN. + CHILLING
MAKES: PASTRY FOR ONE 9-IN. DOUBLE-CRUST PIE

2½ cups all-purpose flour
2 tsp. sugar
¼ tsp. baking powder
¼ tsp. salt
¾ cup shortening
1 large egg yolk, lightly beaten
5 to 6 Tbsp. cold water

1. In a small bowl, combine the flour, sugar, baking powder and salt; cut in shortening until mixture is crumbly. Combine the egg yolk and water; gradually add to flour mixture, tossing with a fork until a ball forms. Cover and refrigerate for 30 minutes or until easy to handle.
2. Divide dough roughly in half so that 1 ball is slightly larger than the other. Roll out larger ball to fit a 9-in. pie plate. Transfer crust to pie plate. Trim crust even with edge of plate. Add filling.
3. Roll out the remaining dough to fit the top of the pie; place over the filling. Trim, seal and flute edge. Cut slits in top. Bake according to recipe directions.
Note: For 2 single-crust pies, divide the dough in half. Roll out each portion to fit a 9-in. pie plate, then transfer the crust to the pie plate. Trim to ½ in. beyond edge of plate; flute edge. Fill or bake shell according to recipe directions.
1 piece: 212 cal., 13g fat (3g sat. fat), 18mg chol., 59mg sod., 21g carb. (1g sugars, 1g fiber), 3g pro.

EASY NO-ROLL PIE PASTRY

Beginning pie bakers can expect success with this simple pat-in crust. Made with oil, it has a wonderful texture and homemade goodness that's sure to impress.

—Cindy Curtis, Southington, CT

TAKES: 15 MIN. • **MAKES:** 1 PIE CRUST (9 IN.)

2 cups all-purpose flour
1 Tbsp. sugar
1 tsp. salt
⅔ cup canola oil
¼ cup cold 2% milk

1. In a small bowl, combine the flour, sugar and salt; stir in the oil and milk. Set aside ⅓ cup for topping. Press the remaining mixture onto the bottom and up the sides of a greased 9-in. pie plate. Add filling. Sprinkle with the reserved crumb mixture.
2. Bake at 375° for 60-70 minutes or until crust is golden and filling is bubbly. Cool on a wire rack.
1 piece: 289 cal., 19g fat (2g sat. fat), 1mg chol., 299mg sod., 26g carb. (2g sugars, 1g fiber), 3g pro.

MOM'S LARD PIE CRUST

Mom always knew the best pie crusts are made with lard. This recipe creates one of the flakiest crusts I have ever had. It is so easy too!

—Virginia Jung, Janesville, WI

PREP: 15 MIN. + CHILLING
MAKES: ONE 10-IN. CRUST

1½ cups all-purpose flour
    Pinch salt
½ cup lard
3 to 4 Tbsp. cold water

1. In a bowl, combine flour and salt. Cut in lard until mixture resembles coarse crumbs. Sprinkle in water, a tablespoon at a time, until the dough holds together. Shape into a ball; chill for 30 minutes.
2. On a lightly floured surface, roll the dough to ⅛-in. thickness. Transfer to a 10-in. pie plate. Flute edge; fill and bake as pie recipe directs.
1 piece: 201 cal., 13g fat (5g sat. fat), 12mg chol., 19mg sod., 18g carb. (0 sugars, 1g fiber), 2g pro.

PASTRY FOR SINGLE-CRUST PIE

This single-crust pie pastry uses all shortening—it's easy to work with and turns out flaky and delicious every time. The process is much like the classic butter crust, but the ingredient proportions are slightly different.

—*Taste of Home* Test Kitchen

TAKES: 10 MIN.
MAKES: 1 PASTRY SHELL (8 SERVINGS)

1¼ cups all-purpose flour
½ tsp. salt
⅓ cup shortening
4 to 5 Tbsp. cold water

1. In a large bowl, combine the flour and salt; cut in the shortening until crumbly. Gradually add water, tossing with a fork until a ball forms. Roll out dough to fit a 9-in. or 10-in. pie plate.
2. Transfer crust to pie plate. Trim crust to ½ in. beyond edge of pie plate; flute edge. Fill or bake the shell according to recipe directions.
1 piece: 144 cal., 8g fat (2g sat. fat), 0 chol., 148mg sod., 15g carb. (0 sugars, 1g fiber), 2g pro.

CITRUS
CRANBERRY PIE

FRUIT PIES

CITRUS CRANBERRY PIE

To showcase bright red cranberries, we came up with this lattice-topped pie. A dollop of orange cream complements the slightly tart flavor.
—*Taste of Home* Test Kitchen

PREP: 30 MIN. • **BAKE:** 50 MIN. + COOLING
MAKES: 8 SERVINGS

3½ cups fresh or frozen cranberries
1 cup sugar
2 tsp. grated lemon zest
1 tsp. grated orange zest
1 small navel orange, peeled, sectioned and chopped
2 Tbsp. butter, melted
2 Tbsp. all-purpose flour
¼ tsp. salt
 Pastry for double-crust pie
1 large egg, lightly beaten
 Additional sugar
ORANGE CREAM
1 cup heavy whipping cream
1 Tbsp. sugar
2 tsp. grated orange zest
½ tsp. orange extract, optional

1. Preheat oven to 450°. Toss together the first 8 ingredients.
2. On a lightly floured surface, roll half of dough to a ⅛-in.-thick circle; transfer to a 9-in. pie plate. Trim crust even with rim. Add filling.
3. Roll remaining dough to a ⅛-in.-thick circle; cut into strips. Arrange over the filling in a lattice pattern (p. 209). Trim and seal strips to edge of bottom crust; flute the edge. Brush lattice with egg; sprinkle with additional sugar.

4. Bake 10 minutes. Reduce oven setting to 350°; bake for 40-45 minutes or until golden brown, covering edge with foil if the crust is getting too dark. Cool pie completely on a wire rack; refrigerate until serving.
5. Beat whipping cream until it begins to thicken. Add the remaining ingredients; beat until soft peaks form. Refrigerate until serving. Serve with pie.
1 piece: 515 cal., 29g fat (15g sat. fat), 85mg chol., 323mg sod., 62g carb. (33g sugars, 2g fiber), 4g pro.

RHUBARB STRAWBERRY PIE

This strawberry rhubarb pie with frozen fruit has become a favorite with us. My husband never liked rhubarb until he tasted this pie. Now he asks me to make it often.
—Sandy Brown, Lake Worth, FL

PREP: 15 MIN. + STANDING
BAKE: 40 MIN. + COOLING
MAKES: 8 SERVINGS

¾ cup sugar
¼ cup quick-cooking tapioca
3 cups sliced fresh or frozen rhubarb (¼-in. pieces)
3 cups sliced fresh or frozen strawberries, thawed
⅓ cup orange juice
4½ tsp. orange marmalade, optional
¼ tsp. grated orange zest
 Pastry for double-crust pie

1. Preheat oven to 400°. In a large bowl, combine the sugar and tapioca. Add the fruit; toss to coat. Gently stir in the juice, marmalade if desired and orange zest. Let stand for 15 minutes.
2. On a lightly floured surface, roll half of dough to a ⅛-in.-thick circle; transfer to 9-in. deep-dish pie plate. Trim even with rim. Fill with fruit filling. Roll out remaining dough; make a lattice crust (p. 209). Trim, seal and flute crust edge. Cover edge with foil. Bake until filling

BAKING 101

is bubbly and the rhubarb is tender, 40-50 minutes. Remove foil. Cool on a wire rack. Store in the refrigerator.
1 piece: 470 cal., 23g fat (14g sat. fat), 60mg chol., 312mg sod., 62g carb. (24g sugars, 3g fiber), 5g pro.
Rhubarb-Cherry Pie: Omit the strawberries, orange juice and zest, and marmalade. Increase sugar to 1¼ cups. Add 1 can (14½ oz.) pitted tart red cherries (drained). Use a standard 9-in. pie plate.
Rhubarb-Raspberry Pie: Omit the strawberries, orange juice and zest, and marmalade. Increase sugar to 1⅓ cups. Add 1 cup fresh or frozen raspberries (thawed) and ¼ tsp. ground cinnamon. Use a standard 9-in. pie plate; decrease bake time to 35-40 minutes.

TEST KITCHEN TIP

See pp. 210-211 for pastry recipes for single- and double-crust pies. You can use your preferred homemade crust for any recipe that calls for refrigerated pie crust.

GREEN
TOMATO PIE

GREEN TOMATO PIE

When frost nips our garden, I quickly gather all the green tomatoes still on the vine and make this old family favorite.
—Violet Thompson, Port Ludlow, WA

PREP: 15 MIN. • **BAKE:** 1 HOUR + COOLING
MAKES: 8 SERVINGS

1½   **cups sugar**
  5   **Tbsp. all-purpose flour**
  1   **tsp. ground cinnamon**
      Pinch salt
  3   **cups thinly sliced green tomatoes
      (4 to 5 medium)**
  1   **Tbsp. cider vinegar**
      Pastry for double-crust pie
  1   **Tbsp. butter**

1. Preheat oven to 350°. In a bowl, combine the sugar, flour, cinnamon and salt. Add tomatoes and vinegar; toss to coat.

2. On a lightly floured surface, roll half of the dough into a ⅛-in.-thick circle; transfer to a 9-in. pie plate. Trim to ½ in. beyond rim of plate. Add the filling; dot with butter.

3. Roll out the remaining dough; make a lattice crust (p. 209). Trim, seal and flute the edge. Bake for 1 hour or until the tomatoes are tender. Cool on a wire rack to room temperature. Store pie in the refrigerator.

1 piece: 433 cal., 16g fat (7g sat. fat), 14mg chol., 242mg sod., 71g carb. (40g sugars, 1g fiber), 3g pro.

THICKENERS FOR FRUIT PIES

You'll often see all-purpose flour, cornstarch or quick-cooking tapioca called for among the ingredients in the filling for fruit pies. These act as thickeners, keeping the filling from being too runny.

APPEARANCE

Flour gives the filling an opaque appearance, cornstarch gives a clear appearance, and tapioca gives a clear to almost gel-like appearance.

SUBSTITUTES

You can substitute one thickener for another, but the thickening power of each is different and you may need to make adjustments to your measurements, your method, or both.

Quick-cooking tapioca and cornstarch can be substituted for each other in equal amounts. When replacing flour, use half the amount of cornstarch or use 1½ to 2 tsp. of quick-cooking tapioca for every 2 Tbsp. of flour. (Use the high end of that range if you prefer a very set filling.)

USING TAPIOCA

When using quick-cooking tapioca, mix it with the other filling ingredients and allow the mixture to stand for 15 minutes before proceeding with the recipe.

MINCE PIES

Most people use canned mincemeat, but this is the old-fashioned way to make a mince pie. It is a sweet holiday dish that will satisfy you and your loved ones.
—Diane Selich, Vassar, MI

PREP: 20 MIN. + CHILLING
BAKE: 25 MIN./BATCH
MAKES: 20 MINI PIES

- 4 cups all-purpose flour
- 2 tsp. salt
- 1⅓ cups shortening
- ½ cup plus 2 Tbsp. ice water
FILLING
- ¼ lb. ground beef
- 3 medium apples, peeled and chopped
- 1 medium apricot, peeled and chopped
- ¾ cup packed light brown sugar
- ½ cup golden raisins
- ½ cup unsweetened apple juice
- 1 Tbsp. cider vinegar
- 1½ tsp. grated orange zest
- 1½ tsp. ground cinnamon
- ½ tsp. salt
- ½ tsp. ground cloves
- ¼ cup rum
- 1 large egg, beaten
- 1 to 2 Tbsp. coarse sugar

1. In a large bowl, mix flour and salt; cut in shortening until crumbly. Gradually add ice water, tossing with a fork until dough forms a ball. Divide dough in half. Shape each portion into a disk; wrap and refrigerate 1 hour or overnight.
2. For the filling, in a large skillet or Dutch oven, cook beef over medium heat until no longer pink, 3-5 minutes, breaking into crumbles; drain. Add the apples, apricot, brown sugar, raisins, apple juice, vinegar, orange zest and seasonings. Bring to a boil; reduce heat. Simmer 15-17 minutes or until apples are tender. Stir in rum. Remove from heat; cool slightly.
3. Preheat oven to 375°. On a lightly floured surface, roll half of dough to ⅛-in. thickness. Cut 20 circles with a floured 2¾-in. round biscuit cutter. Top half the circles with 1 Tbsp. filling each. Top with the remaining circles; press edges with a fork to seal. Cut slits in top. Brush tops with egg; sprinkle with coarse sugar. Repeat with remaining dough and filling.
4. Bake until crust is golden brown and filling is bubbly, 20-25 minutes. Cool on a wire rack.
1 mini pie: 280 cal., 14g fat (4g sat. fat), 4mg chol., 302mg sod., 34g carb. (14g sugars, 1g fiber), 4g pro.

FRESH BLACKBERRY PIE

I grew up on a farm. We always picked blackberries in early summer and used them to make pies, like this stunner.
—Gladys Gibbs, Brush Creek, TN

PREP: 20 MIN. + STANDING
BAKE: 35 MIN. + COOLING
MAKES: 8 SERVINGS

- 1 cup sugar
- ⅓ cup quick-cooking tapioca
- ¼ tsp. salt
- 4 cups fresh blackberries, divided
  Pastry for double-crust pie
- 2 Tbsp. butter

1. In a large saucepan, combine the sugar, tapioca and salt. Add 1 cup blackberries; toss to coat. Let stand for 15 minutes. Cook and stir over medium heat until berries burst and mixture comes to a gentle boil. Remove from heat; gently stir in remaining berries.
2. Preheat oven to 400°. On a lightly floured surface, roll half of dough to a ⅛-in.-thick circle; transfer to a 9-in. pie plate. Trim even with rim. Add filling; dot with butter. Roll remaining dough to a ⅛-in.-thick circle. Place over filling. Trim, seal and flute edge. Cut slits in top.
3. Bake until crust is golden brown and filling is bubbly, 35-40 minutes. Cool on a wire rack.
1 piece: 524 cal., 26g fat (16g sat. fat), 68mg chol., 407mg sod., 69g carb. (29g sugars, 5g fiber), 5g pro.

AUTUMN SURPRISE PIE

What better way to welcome fall than with a homemade pie? This one calls for apples, pears and raisins flavored with rum extract.
—Karen Gauvreau, Portage, MI

PREP: 40 MIN. + CHILLING • **BAKE:** 45 MIN.
MAKES: 8 SERVINGS

- 1½ cups all-purpose flour
- 3 Tbsp. sugar
- ¼ tsp. plus ⅛ tsp. salt
- ¼ tsp. plus ⅛ tsp. baking powder
- 6 Tbsp. cold butter, cubed
- ⅓ cup fat-free milk
- 1½ tsp. cider vinegar

FILLING
- ½ cup sugar
- ¼ cup all-purpose flour
- 1 tsp. ground cinnamon
- ¼ tsp. ground nutmeg
- ¼ tsp. ground cloves
- 5 cups sliced peeled apples
- 2 cups sliced peeled ripe pears
- ⅓ cup raisins
- ¾ tsp. rum extract

TOPPING
- 1 large egg, lightly beaten
- 1 tsp. coarse sugar

1. Mix the first 4 ingredients; cut in butter until crumbly. Mix milk and vinegar; add gradually to the crumb mixture, tossing with a fork until the dough holds together when pressed. Divide dough into 2 portions, 1 slightly larger than the other. Shape each into a disk; cover and refrigerate 1 hour or overnight.

2. Preheat oven to 425°. On a lightly floured surface, roll larger portion of dough to a ⅛-in.-thick circle; transfer to a greased 9-in. pie plate. Trim crust even with rim. Refrigerate crust while preparing filling.

3. Mix the first 5 filling ingredients. Place apples, pears and raisins in a large bowl. Add sugar mixture and extract; toss to combine. Spoon the filling into crust.

4. Roll out the remaining dough to a ⅛-in.-thick circle; cut into ¾-in.-wide strips. Arrange over filling in a lattice pattern (p. 209). Trim and seal strips to edge of bottom crust; flute edge. Brush lattice with beaten egg. Sprinkle with coarse sugar.

5. Bake pie on a lower oven rack for 15 minutes. Reduce oven setting to 350°. Bake until crust is golden brown and filling is bubbly, 30-35 minutes. Cool on a wire rack.

1 piece: 331 cal., 10g fat (6g sat. fat), 46mg chol., 217mg sod., 59g carb. (32g sugars, 3g fiber), 5g pro.

· · · · · · · · · · · · · · · · · · · ·

TEST KITCHEN TIP

To prevent your pies from bubbling over during baking, use less filling and be sure to cut vents in the top crust (in the case of double-crust pies). If you do love overstuffed pies—as many do!—simply accept spills as a fact of life and place a baking sheet on the oven rack below your pie to catch them.

WASHINGTON STATE
APPLE PIE

WASHINGTON STATE APPLE PIE

This pie won Grand Champion in the Apple Pie category at the 1992 Okanogan County Fair. It may look traditional, but making your own filling gives it a different flair and great taste.

—Dolores Scholz, Tonasket, WA

PREP: 25 MIN. • **BAKE:** 45 MIN. + COOLING
MAKES: 8 SERVINGS

- 6 cups sliced peeled tart apples (about 5 to 6 medium)
- 2 Tbsp. water
- 1 Tbsp. lemon juice
- ½ cup sugar
- ½ cup packed brown sugar
- 3 Tbsp. all-purpose flour
- 1 tsp. ground cinnamon
- ¼ tsp. ground nutmeg
- ⅛ tsp. ground ginger
- ⅛ tsp. salt
  Pastry for double-crust pie

1. In a large saucepan, combine the apples, water and lemon juice; cook over medium-low heat just until apples are tender. Remove from the heat and cool (do not drain).

2. Preheat the oven to 450°. In a large bowl, combine sugars, flour, cinnamon, nutmeg, ginger and salt; add apples and toss to coat. On a lightly floured surface, roll half of dough to a ⅛-in.-thick circle; transfer to a 9-in. pie plate. Trim even with rim. Add the apple mixture. Roll remaining dough to a ⅛-in.-thick circle. Place over filling. Trim, seal and flute edge. Cut slits in top.

3. Bake for 10 minutes. Reduce oven setting to 350°; bake pie until golden brown, 35-45 minutes longer. Cool on a wire rack.

1 piece: 496 cal., 23g fat (14g sat. fat), 60mg chol., 351mg sod., 69g carb. (35g sugars, 2g fiber), 5g pro.

BAKING 101

GOLDEN PEACH PIE

Years ago, I entered this pie in the Park County Fair in Livingston. It won a first-place blue ribbon plus a purple ribbon for best all around! Family and friends agree with the judges—it's a perfectly peachy pie.
—Shirley Olson, Polson, MT

PREP: 20 MIN. • **BAKE:** 50 MIN. + COOLING
MAKES: 8 SERVINGS

- 2 sheets refrigerated pie crust
- 5 cups sliced peeled fresh peaches (about 5 medium)
- 2 tsp. lemon juice
- ½ tsp. grated orange zest
- ⅛ tsp. almond extract
- 1 cup sugar
- ¼ cup cornstarch
- ¼ tsp. ground nutmeg
- ⅛ tsp. salt
- 2 Tbsp. butter

1. Preheat oven to 400°. Line a 9-in. pie plate with 1 crust; trim, leaving a 1-in. overhang around rim. Set aside. In a large bowl, combine the peaches, lemon juice, orange zest and extract. Combine the sugar, cornstarch, nutmeg and salt. Add to the peach mixture; toss gently to coat. Pour into the crust; dot with butter.

2. Roll out the remaining crust to a ⅛-in.-thick circle; cut into strips. Arrange over filling in a lattice pattern (p. 209). Trim and seal strips to bottom crust; fold overhang over. Lightly press or flute edge. Cover the edge loosely with foil.

3. Bake for 40 minutes. Remove foil; bake until the crust is golden brown and filling is bubbly, 10-15 minutes longer. Cool on a wire rack. Store in the refrigerator.

1 piece: 425 cal., 17g fat (8g sat. fat), 18mg chol., 267mg sod., 67g carb. (36g sugars, 2g fiber), 3g pro.

GOLDEN PEACH PIE

BAKING 101

PEAR GRUYERE PIE

I love cheese and fruit, so this pie is a natural pairing for me. Sweet and spicy wine-poached pears and a flaky, buttery cheese crust make for a winning dessert you'll want to make again and again.
—Alexandra Penfold, Brooklyn, NY

PREP: 30 MIN+ CHILLING
BAKE: 40 MIN. + COOLING
MAKES: 8 SERVINGS

- 2½ cups all-purpose flour
- 3 oz. Gruyere cheese, finely grated
- 1 Tbsp. sugar
- 1 tsp. salt
- 1 cup cold unsalted butter, cubed
- 6 to 8 Tbsp. ice water

FILLING

- 1½ cups water
- ¾ cup port wine
- ¼ cup sugar
- 1 cinnamon stick (3 in.)
- 2 tsp. vanilla extract
- ½ tsp. ground ginger
- ¼ tsp. ground nutmeg
- ¼ tsp. ground cloves
- 6 medium pears (about 3 lbs.) peeled and thinly sliced
- 2 tsp. cornstarch
- 1 Tbsp. water
- 1 large egg, lightly beaten
  Vanilla ice cream, optional

1. Place flour, cheese, sugar and salt in a food processor; pulse until blended. Add butter; pulse until butter is the size of peas. While pulsing, add just enough ice water to form moist crumbs. Divide dough in half. Shape each half into a disk; wrap and refrigerate for 1 hour or overnight.

2. In a large saucepan, combine water, wine, sugar, cinnamon stick, vanilla and spices; bring to a boil. Add pears to poaching liquid. Cook, uncovered, 10-15 minutes or until tender.

3. Using a slotted spoon, remove the pears and cool slightly. Refrigerate until cooled; discard cinnamon stick. Meanwhile, return poaching liquid to a boil. Cook 12-15 minutes or until liquid is reduced to ¾ cup. In a small bowl, mix cornstarch and water until smooth; stir into the reduced liquid. Return to a boil, stirring constantly; cook and stir 1-2 minutes or until thickened. Pour into a 1-cup measuring cup. Cool slightly; refrigerate until chilled.

4. Preheat oven to 400°. On a well-floured surface, roll 1 dough portion to a ⅛-in.-thick circle; transfer to a 9-in. pie plate. Trim crust to ½ in. beyond rim of plate; flute edge. Add the pear filling; pour syrup over the pears. Roll remaining dough to a ⅛-in.-thick circle. Cut decorative cutouts from remaining crust and arrange over filling; re-roll scraps as needed. Brush crust with egg. Place pie on a baking sheet.

5. Bake 30-40 minutes or until crust is golden brown and filling is bubbly. Cover edge with foil during the last 15 minutes to prevent overbrowning if necessary. Cool on a wire rack. If desired, serve with ice cream.

1 piece: 557 cal., 28g fat (17g sat. fat), 96mg chol., 388mg sod., 65g carb. (25g sugars, 6g fiber), 9g pro.

HUCKLEBERRY CHEESE PIE

To us Idahoans, huckleberries are a real treasure. My family enjoys this recipe a lot, and I serve it as a special treat when we have guests.
—Pat Kuper, McCall, ID

PREP: 30 MIN. • **BAKE:** 20 MIN. + CHILLING
MAKES: 10 SERVINGS

BUTTER CRUNCH CRUST
  1   cup all-purpose flour
  ¼   cup packed brown sugar
  ½   cup finely chopped nuts
  ½   cup cold butter
CHEESE FILLING
  1   pkg. (8 oz.) cream cheese, softened
  ¾   cup confectioners' sugar
  1   tsp. vanilla extract
  1   cup whipped cream or 1 cup whipped topping
FRUIT TOPPING
  ½   cup sugar
  4½ tsp. cornstarch
      Dash salt
  ½   cup water
  2   cups fresh huckleberries or blueberries, divided
  1½ tsp. butter
      Additional whipped cream, optional

1. Preheat oven to 400°. Combine the flour, brown sugar and nuts. Cut in butter until mixture resembles coarse crumbs. Spread on baking sheet; bake for 20 minutes, stirring occasionally.
2. Remove from oven. While mixture is still hot, press into a 9-in. pie plate, forming a pie shell. Cool completely.
3. For cheese filling, beat cream cheese, sugar and vanilla until smooth; gently fold in whipped cream. Pour or spoon filling into cooled crust; refrigerate.
4. For topping, combine the sugar, cornstarch and salt in saucepan. Stir in water until smooth; add 1 cup berries. Bring to a boil. Cook and stir until thickened, 1-2 minutes. Add butter and the remaining berries. Cool; pour over cheese filling. Top with additional whipped cream if desired.
1 piece: 379 cal., 23g fat (12g sat. fat), 56mg chol., 192mg sod., 41g carb. (28g sugars, 1g fiber), 5g pro.

SPECIAL RAISIN PIE

When I first made this pie, I thought it was great. Then I entered it at the county fair and I guess the judges thought it was great, too, since it won first place.
—Laura Fall-Sutton, Buhl, ID

PREP: 40 MIN. • **BAKE:** 35 MIN. + COOLING
MAKES: 8 SERVINGS

  2½ cups raisins
  2   cups water
  ⅓   cup packed brown sugar
  ⅓   cup sugar
  ⅛   tsp. salt
  2   Tbsp. plus 1½ tsp. cornstarch
  ¼   cup cold water
  2   Tbsp. lemon juice
  1   Tbsp. orange juice
  2   tsp. grated orange zest
  1   tsp. grated lemon zest
  ½   tsp. rum extract
      Pastry for double-crust pie
  2   Tbsp. butter

1. In a small saucepan, combine the raisins and water. Bring to a boil; cook 2 minutes. Add sugars and salt; cook until sugars are dissolved. Combine the cornstarch and cold water until smooth; gradually stir into the pan. Cook and stir for 2 minutes or until thickened and bubbly. Remove from the heat; stir in the juices, zests and extract.
2. Roll out half of the pie dough to fit a 9-in. pie plate; transfer to pie plate. Fill with raisin mixture. Dot with butter.
3. Roll out the remaining dough; make a lattice crust (p. 209). Trim, seal and flute edge. Bake at 375° for 35-40 minutes or until crust is golden brown and filling is bubbly, covering edge with foil during the last 10 minutes. Cool on a wire rack. Refrigerate leftovers.
Note: To achieve this special tightly woven lattice crust, use an additional batch of pastry for a single-crust pie.
1 piece: 481 cal., 17g fat (8g sat. fat), 18mg chol., 266mg sod., 82g carb. (46g sugars, 2g fiber), 3g pro.

HAND-HELD APPLE PIES

When I was in high school, my best friend's mother baked mini apple pies every year. I was thrilled when she shared the recipe with me—it made me feel like I was finally an adult!

—Katie Ferrier, Houston, TX

PREP: 1 HOUR + CHILLING • **BAKE:** 15 MIN.
MAKES: 2 DOZEN

1 pkg. (8 oz.) cream cheese, softened
1 cup unsalted butter, softened
2 cups all-purpose flour
¼ tsp. salt
FILLING
¼ cup sugar
¼ tsp. ground cinnamon
⅛ tsp. ground allspice
2 cups finely chopped peeled tart apples
2 Tbsp. cold unsalted butter

FINISHING
1 large egg yolk
2 Tbsp. water
Coarse sugar and cinnamon-sugar

1. In a large bowl, beat cream cheese and butter until smooth. Combine flour and salt; gradually add to butter mixture until well blended. Divide dough in half. Shape each into a ball, then flatten into a disk. Wrap in plastic and refrigerate for 1 hour.
2. Combine the sugar, cinnamon and allspice; set aside. Divide each portion of dough into 12 balls. On a lightly floured surface, roll each ball into a 4-in. circle. Place a tablespoonful of chopped apples on one side. Sprinkle with ½ tsp. sugar mixture; dot with ¼ tsp. butter.
3. In a small bowl, whisk egg yolk and water. Brush edges of pastry with egg wash; fold pastry over filling and seal edges well with a fork. Place 2 in. apart on ungreased baking sheets. Brush remaining egg wash over tops. Cut slits in pastry. Sprinkle with coarse sugar and cinnamon-sugar.
4. Bake at 425° for 11-14 minutes or until golden brown. Remove to wire racks to cool.
1 pie: 162 cal., 12g fat (7g sat. fat), 40mg chol., 56mg sod., 12g carb. (3g sugars, 0 fiber), 2g pro.
Make ahead: Pastry can be prepared and rolled out a day in advance. Stack pastry rounds between floured sheets of waxed paper.

WHICH APPLES?

Sometimes, the best apples for eating aren't necessarily the best for baking. So which should you choose when it's time to make a perfect pie or cobbler?

Choose a firm apple that will hold up to heat without becoming mushy—and with a tartness that will offset sugary baked goods. Cortland, Braeburn, Granny Smith, Gravenstein, Rome Beauty and Northern Spy apples—known as "cooking apples"—are particularly good for baking.

Other popular apples that hold their form fairly well are Cameo, Empire, Fuji, Golden Delicious, Honeycrisp, Jazz and Pink Lady.

You may even want to try a mix of apples in your baking, balancing sweet Honeycrisp with tart, firm Northern Spy to find a magic balance.

CUSTARD & MERINGUE PIES

GRANDMA PRUIT'S
VINEGAR PIE

3. Roll the remaining two-thirds of pie dough to a ⅛-in.-thick circle. Place over the filling, pressing against sides of skillet or casserole. Cut a slit in top. Add vinegar to hot water; slowly pour vinegar mixture through slit in dough. Liquid may bubble up through crust; this is normal.

4. Line an oven rack with foil; set pie on a rack above and bake until the crust is golden brown, about 1 hour. Cover edge with foil during the last 15-20 minutes if needed to prevent overbrowning. Remove foil. Cool on a wire rack.

1 piece: 545 cal., 25g fat (13g sat. fat), 41mg chol., 316mg sod., 78g carb. (50g sugars, 0 fiber), 2g pro.

GRANDMA PRUIT'S VINEGAR PIE

This historic pie has been in our family for many generations and is always served at our family get-togethers.
—Suzette Pruit, Houston, TX

PREP: 40 MIN. • **BAKE:** 1 HOUR + COOLING
MAKES: 8 SERVINGS

- 2 cups sugar
- 3 Tbsp. all-purpose flour
- ¼ to ½ tsp. ground nutmeg
  Pastry for double-crust pie
- ½ cup butter, cubed
- ⅔ cup white vinegar
- 1 qt. hot water

1. Preheat oven to 450°. Whisk together sugar, flour and nutmeg; set aside. On a lightly floured surface, roll one-third of pie dough to a ⅛-in.-thick circle; cut into 2x1-in. strips.

2. Layer a deep 12-in. enamel-coated cast-iron skillet or ovenproof casserole with half the strips; sprinkle with half the sugar mixture. Dot with half the butter. Repeat sugar and butter layers.

OLD-FASHIONED CUSTARD PIE

This recipe came from the best cook in West Virginia—my mother! I just added a little to her ingredients. I make my custard pie mostly for church and club functions. It's wonderfully different from all the other ones in my collection.
—Maxine Linkenauger, Montverde, FL

PREP: 20 MIN. + CHILLING
BAKE: 25 MIN. + CHILLING
MAKES: 8 SERVINGS

 1 sheet refrigerated pie crust
 4 large eggs
2½ cups whole milk
 ½ cup sugar
 1 tsp. ground nutmeg
 1 tsp. vanilla extract
 1 tsp. almond extract
 ½ tsp. salt

1. Unroll crust into a 9-in. pie plate; flute edge. Refrigerate 30 minutes. Preheat oven to 400°.
2. Line unpricked crust with a double thickness of foil. Fill with pie weights, dried beans or uncooked rice. Bake on a lower oven rack until edges are golden brown, 10-15 minutes. Remove foil and weights; bake until bottom is golden brown, 3-6 minutes longer. Cool on a wire rack.
3. In a large bowl, whisk eggs. Whisk in remaining ingredients until blended. Pour into crust. Cover edges with foil. Bake until a knife inserted in the center comes out clean, 25-30 minutes. Cool on a wire rack for 1 hour. Refrigerate for at least 3 hours before serving. Refrigerate leftovers.
1 piece: 258 cal., 12g fat (5g sat. fat), 122mg chol., 317mg sod., 30g carb. (17g sugars, 0 fiber), 7g pro.

GRANDMA'S SOUR CREAM RAISIN PIE

The aroma of this pie baking in my farm kitchen oven reminds me of my dear grandma who made this pretty pie for special occasions.
—Beverly Medalen, Willow City, ND

PREP: 30 MIN. • **BAKE:** 10 MIN. + CHILLING
MAKES: 8 SERVINGS

 1 cup raisins
 ⅔ cup sugar
 3 Tbsp. cornstarch
 ⅛ tsp. salt
 ⅛ tsp. ground cloves
 ½ tsp. ground cinnamon
 1 cup sour cream
 ½ cup 2% milk
 3 large egg yolks, room temperature
 ½ cup chopped nuts, optional
 1 pie shell (9 in.), baked
MERINGUE
 3 large egg whites, room temperature
 ¼ tsp. salt
 6 Tbsp. sugar

1. In a small saucepan, place raisins and enough water to cover; bring to a boil. Remove from the heat; set aside.
2. In a large saucepan, combine the sugar, cornstarch, salt, cloves and cinnamon. Stir in the sour cream and milk until smooth. Cook and stir over medium-high heat until thickened and bubbly. Reduce heat to low; cook and stir for 2 minutes longer. Remove from the heat. Stir a small amount of hot filling into the egg yolks; return all to the pan, stirring constantly. Bring to a gentle boil; cook and stir for 2 minutes. Remove from the heat.
3. Drain raisins, reserving ½ cup liquid. Gently stir liquid into filling. Add raisins, and nuts if desired. Pour into pie shell.
4. For meringue, in a small bowl, beat egg whites and salt on medium speed until soft peaks form. Gradually beat in the sugar, 1 Tbsp. at a time, on high until stiff peaks form. Spread over hot filling, sealing edge to crust.
5. Bake at 350° for 15 minutes or until golden brown. Cool on a wire rack for 1 hour; refrigerate for 1-2 hours before serving. Refrigerate leftovers.
1 piece: 381 cal., 15g fat (7g sat. fat), 82mg chol., 253mg sod., 58g carb. (40g sugars, 1g fiber), 5g pro.

BAKING
101

AUTUMN HARVEST
PUMPKIN PIE

AUTUMN HARVEST PUMPKIN PIE

This is the best holiday pie I've ever tasted. I will use fresh pumpkin if I have a little extra time, but canned works just as well.
—Stan Strom, Gilbert, AZ

PREP: 30 MIN. + CHILLING
BAKE: 55 MIN. + COOLING
MAKES: 8 SERVINGS

- 2 cups all-purpose flour
- 1 cup cake flour
- 2 Tbsp. sugar
- ½ tsp. salt
- ½ cup cold unsalted butter, cubed
- ½ cup butter-flavored shortening
- 1 large egg
- ⅓ cup cold water
- 1 Tbsp. cider vinegar

FILLING
- 2½ cups canned pumpkin (about 19 oz.)
- 1¼ cups packed light brown sugar
- ¾ cup half-and-half cream
- 2 large eggs
- ¼ cup apple butter
- 2 Tbsp. orange juice
- 2 Tbsp. maple syrup
- 2 tsp. ground cinnamon
- 2 tsp. pumpkin pie spice
- ¼ tsp. salt

1. In a large bowl, mix the first 4 ingredients; cut in the butter and shortening until crumbly. Whisk together the egg, water and vinegar; gradually add to flour mixture, tossing with a fork until dough holds together when pressed. Divide dough in half so that 1 portion is slightly larger than the other; shape each into a disk. Wrap; refrigerate 1 hour or overnight.
2. Preheat oven to 425°. On a lightly floured surface, roll larger portion of dough to a ⅛-in.-thick circle; transfer to a 9-in. deep-dish pie plate. Trim the crust to ½ in. beyond rim of pie plate. Refrigerate until ready to fill.

3. Roll smaller portion of dough to ⅛-in. thickness. Cut with a floured pumpkin-shaped cookie cutter; place some cutouts 1 in. apart on a baking sheet, reserving unbaked cutouts for decorative edge if desired. Bake until golden brown, 8-10 minutes.
4. Meanwhile, beat together the filling ingredients until blended; transfer to crust. Flute or decorate the edge with the unbaked cutouts, brushing off any remaining flour before pressing lightly onto edge. Bake on a lower oven rack 10 minutes. Cover edge loosely with foil. Reduce oven setting to 350°. Bake until a knife inserted near the center comes out clean, 45-50 minutes.
5. Cool the pie on a wire rack; serve or refrigerate within 2 hours. Top with baked pumpkin cutouts before serving.
1 piece: 647 cal., 28g fat (12g sat. fat), 112mg chol., 277mg sod., 89g carb. (47g sugars, 4g fiber), 9g pro.

MAKE YOUR OWN PUMPKIN PIE SPICE

Mix 4 tsp. ground cinnamon, 2 tsp. ground ginger, 1 tsp. ground cloves and ½ tsp. ground nutmeg. Store in an airtight container in a cool, dry place for up to 6 months.

CAN'T-MISS COCONUT CUSTARD PIE

BAKING 101

This soft custard pie has a mild coconut flavor. Who wouldn't love a hearty slice topped with a dollop of whipped cream?
—Betty Swain, Bear, DE

PREP: 20 MIN. • **BAKE:** 45 MIN. + COOLING
MAKES: 8 SERVINGS

- Pastry for single-crust pie
- 1 cup sweetened shredded coconut, chopped
- 3 large eggs, beaten
- 2½ cups 2% milk
- ⅔ cup sugar
- 3 Tbsp. all-purpose flour
- 1 tsp. vanilla extract
- ½ tsp. salt
- ¼ tsp. ground nutmeg
- Toasted sweetened shredded coconut, optional

1. Preheat oven to 450°. On a lightly floured surface, roll the dough to a ⅛-in.-thick circle; transfer to a 9-in. deep-dish pie plate. Trim and flute edge. Line unpricked crust with a double thickness of heavy-duty foil. Bake for 10 minutes. Remove foil; bake 5 minutes longer. Sprinkle coconut over crust; set aside. Reduce oven setting to 350°.
2. In a large bowl, combine the eggs, milk, sugar, flour, vanilla and salt. Pour over coconut; sprinkle with nutmeg.
3. Bake, uncovered, 45-50 minutes or until a knife inserted in the center comes out clean. Cool on a wire rack for 1 hour. If desired, top with toasted coconut to serve. Refrigerate leftovers.
1 piece: 322 cal., 15g fat (8g sat. fat), 90mg chol., 345mg sod., 42g carb. (26g sugars, 1g fiber), 7g pro.

CONTEST-WINNING GERMAN CHOCOLATE CREAM PIE

I've won quite a few awards in recipe contests over the years, and I was truly delighted when this luscious pie sent me to the Great American Pie Show finals in Branson, Missouri.

—Marie Rizzio, Interlochen, MI

PREP: 20 MIN. • **BAKE:** 45 MIN. + COOLING
MAKES: 8 SERVINGS

      Pastry for single-crust pie
   4 oz. German sweet chocolate, chopped
  ¼ cup butter, cubed
   1 can (12 oz.) evaporated milk
  1½ cups sugar
   3 Tbsp. cornstarch
      Dash salt
   2 large eggs
   1 tsp. vanilla extract
  1⅓ cups sweetened shredded coconut
  ½ cup chopped pecans
TOPPING
   2 cups heavy whipping cream
   2 Tbsp. confectioners' sugar
   1 tsp. vanilla extract

1. Preheat oven to 375°. On a lightly floured surface, roll the dough to a ⅛-in.-thick circle; transfer to a 9-in. pie plate. Trim crust to ½ in. beyond rim of plate; flute edge. Refrigerate crust while preparing filling.
2. Place chocolate and butter in a small saucepan. Cook and stir over low heat until smooth. Remove from the heat; stir in milk. In a large bowl, combine sugar, cornstarch and salt. Add eggs, vanilla and chocolate mixture; mix well. Pour filling into crust. Sprinkle with coconut and pecans.
3. Bake until a knife inserted in the center comes out clean, 45-50 minutes. Cool completely on a wire rack.
4. For topping, in a large bowl, beat cream until it begins to thicken. Add confectioners' sugar and vanilla; beat until stiff peaks form. Spread over pie; sprinkle with additional coconut and pecans. Refrigerate until serving.
1 piece: 808 cal., 53g fat (30g sat. fat), 168mg chol., 280mg sod., 78g carb. (58g sugars, 3g fiber), 9g pro.

BANANA CREAM PIE

Made from our farm-fresh dairy products, this pie was a sensational creamy treat any time Mom served it. Her recipe is a real treasure, and I've never found one that tastes better!

—Bernice Morris, Marshfield, MO

PREP: 35 MIN. + CHILLING
COOK: 10 MIN. + COOLING
MAKES: 8 SERVINGS

      Pastry for single-crust pie
  ¾ cup sugar
  ⅓ cup all-purpose flour
  ¼ tsp. salt
   2 cups whole milk
   3 large egg yolks, room temperature, lightly beaten
   2 Tbsp. butter
   1 tsp. vanilla extract
   3 medium, firm bananas
      Whipped cream, optional

1. On a lightly floured surface, roll out dough to a ⅛-in.-thick circle; transfer to a 9-in. pie plate. Trim to ½ in. beyond rim of plate; flute edge. Refrigerate 30 minutes. Preheat oven to 425°.
2. Line crust with a double thickness of foil. Fill with pie weights, dried beans or uncooked rice. Bake on a lower oven rack 20-25 minutes or until the edge is golden brown. Remove foil and weights; bake until the bottom is golden brown, 3-6 minutes longer. Cool on a wire rack.
3. Meanwhile, in a saucepan, combine sugar, flour and salt; stir in milk and mix well. Cook over medium-high heat until mixture is thickened and bubbly. Cook and stir for 2 minutes longer. Remove from the heat. Stir a small amount into egg yolks; return all to saucepan. Bring to a gentle boil. Cook and stir 2 minutes; remove from the heat. Add butter and vanilla; cool slightly.
4. Slice bananas into crust; pour filling over top. Cool on wire rack for 1 hour. Store in the refrigerator. If desired, garnish with whipped cream and additional sliced bananas.
1 piece: 338 cal., 14g fat (7g sat. fat), 101mg chol., 236mg sod., 49g carb. (30g sugars, 1g fiber), 5g pro.

SUGAR CREAM PIE

I absolutely love creamy sugar pie, especially the one that my grandma made for me. Here in Indiana, we serve it warm or chilled.
—Laura Kipper, Westfield, IN

PREP: 40 MIN. + COOLING
BAKE: 15 MIN. + CHILLING
MAKES: 8 SERVINGS

    Pastry for single-crust pie
1 **cup sugar**
¼ **cup cornstarch**
2 **cups 2% milk**
½ **cup butter, cubed**
1 **tsp. vanilla extract**
¼ **tsp. ground cinnamon**

1. Preheat oven to 450°. On a lightly floured surface, roll the dough to a ⅛-in.-thick circle; transfer to a 9-in. pie plate. Trim crust to ½ in. beyond the rim of plate; flute edge. Refrigerate for 30 minutes.
2. Line unpricked crust with a double thickness of foil. Fill with pie weights, dried beans or uncooked rice. Bake on a lower oven rack until edge is light golden brown, 15-20 minutes. Remove foil and weights; bake until bottom is golden brown, 3-6 minutes longer. Cool on a wire rack. Reduce oven setting to 375°.
3. Meanwhile, in a large saucepan, combine sugar and cornstarch; stir in milk until smooth. Bring to a boil. Reduce heat; cook and stir 2 minutes or until thickened and bubbly. Remove from heat; stir in butter and vanilla. Transfer to the crust; sprinkle with cinnamon. Bake until golden brown, 15-20 minutes. Cool on a wire rack; refrigerate until chilled.
1 piece: 418 cal., 24g fat (15g sat. fat), 66mg chol., 275mg sod., 47g carb. (28g sugars, 1g fiber), 4g pro.

CHOCOLATE CHESS PIE

CHOCOLATE CHESS PIE

This is one of my mother's go-to recipes. It's a yummy spin on classic chocolate chess pie.
—Ann Dickens, Nixa, MO

PREP: 30 MIN. • **COOK:** 40 MIN. + CHILLING
MAKES: 8 SERVINGS

1¼ **cups all-purpose flour**
¼ **tsp. salt**
¼ **cup cold butter, cubed**
¼ **cup shortening**
3 **to 4 Tbsp. ice water**
FILLING
2 **large eggs, room temperature**
1 **cup packed brown sugar**
½ **cup sugar**
1½ **oz. unsweetened chocolate, melted and cooled**
2 **Tbsp. 2% milk**
1 **Tbsp. all-purpose flour**
1 **tsp. vanilla extract**
½ **cup butter, melted**

1. Combine flour and salt; cut in butter and shortening until crumbly. Gradually add ice water, tossing with a fork until dough holds together when pressed. Shape dough into a disk. Wrap and refrigerate 1 hour or overnight.
2. On a floured surface, roll dough to fit a 9-in. pie plate. Trim and flute edge. Refrigerate 30 minutes. Preheat oven to 425°. Line unpricked crust with a double thickness of foil. Fill with pie weights. Bake on a lower oven rack until light golden brown, 15-20 minutes. Remove foil and weights; bake until bottom is golden brown, 3-6 minutes. Cool on a wire rack. Reduce oven setting to 325°.
3. In a large bowl, whisk eggs, sugars, melted chocolate, milk, flour and vanilla. Gradually whisk in butter. Pour into crust. Cover edge with foil to prevent overbrowning.
4. Bake at 325° 35-40 minutes or until a knife inserted in the center comes out clean. Remove foil. Cool on a wire rack. Refrigerate the pie, covered, for 3 hours or until chilled.
1 piece: 436 cal., 22g fat (13g sat. fat), 93mg chol., 240mg sod., 57g carb. (40g sugars, 1g fiber), 5g pro.

CLASSIC LEMON
MERINGUE PIE

CLASSIC LEMON MERINGUE PIE

Love lemon meringue pie? This is the only recipe you'll ever need. The flaky, tender, made-from-scratch crust is worth the effort.
—Lee Bremson, Kansas City, MO

PREP: 30 MIN. • **BAKE:** 25 MIN. + CHILLING
MAKES: 8 SERVINGS

1⅓ cups all-purpose flour
½ tsp. salt
½ cup shortening
1 to 3 Tbsp. cold water
FILLING
1¼ cups sugar
¼ cup cornstarch
3 Tbsp. all-purpose flour
¼ tsp. salt
1½ cups water
3 large egg yolks, lightly beaten
2 Tbsp. butter
1½ tsp. grated lemon zest
⅓ cup lemon juice
MERINGUE
½ cup sugar, divided
1 Tbsp. cornstarch
½ cup cold water
4 large egg whites
¾ tsp. vanilla extract

1. In a small bowl, combine flour and salt; cut in shortening until crumbly. Gradually add 3 Tbsp. cold water, tossing with a fork until the dough forms a ball.

2. Roll out dough to fit a 9-in. pie plate. Transfer the crust to pie plate. Trim to ½ in. beyond edge of plate; flute edge. Bake at 425° for 12-15 minutes or until lightly browned. Reduce oven setting to 350°.

3. Place egg whites in a large bowl; let stand at room temperature for 30 minutes. Meanwhile, in a large saucepan, combine sugar, cornstarch, flour and salt. Gradually stir in the cold water until smooth. Cook and stir over medium-high heat until thickened and bubbly. Reduce the heat; cook and stir 2 minutes longer.

4. Remove from the heat. Stir a small amount of hot filling into egg yolks; return all to pan, stirring constantly. Bring to a gentle boil; cook and stir 2 minutes longer.

5. Remove from the heat. Gently stir in butter and lemon zest. Gradually stir in lemon juice just until combined. Pour into the crust.

6. For the meringue, in a saucepan, combine 2 Tbsp. sugar and cornstarch. Gradually stir in cold water. Cook and stir over medium heat until mixture is clear. Transfer to a bowl; cool.

7. Beat the egg whites and vanilla until soft peaks form. Gradually beat in the remaining sugar, 1 Tbsp. at a time. Beat in the cornstarch mixture on high until stiff glossy peaks form and the sugar is dissolved. Spread evenly over hot filling, sealing edge to crust.

8. Bake at 350° for 25 minutes or until the meringue is golden brown. Cool on a wire rack for 1 hour. Refrigerate for at least 3 hours before serving. Refrigerate leftovers.

1 piece: 444 cal., 17g fat (5g sat. fat), 87mg chol., 282mg sod., 68g carb. (43g sugars, 1g fiber), 5g pro.

THE BEST SWEET POTATO PIE

I love this recipe's rich, sweet potato flavor and irresistibly buttery crust. Sour cream makes the filling super smooth, and the brown sugar and spices make it extra cozy. There's no doubt that this is the best sweet potato pie!
—Shannon Norris, Cudahy, WI

PREP: 1½ HOURS + CHILLING
BAKE: 35 MIN. + COOLING
MAKES: 8 SERVINGS

CRUST:
- 1 large egg yolk
- ¼ to ½ cup ice water, divided
- 2½ cups all-purpose flour
- 3 Tbsp. sugar
- ½ tsp. salt
- ½ cup cold shortening, cubed
- ½ cup cold butter, cubed

FILLING:
- 2½ lbs. sweet potatoes
- ⅔ cup packed brown sugar
- ½ cup sour cream
- 3 large eggs, lightly beaten
- ⅓ cup butter, melted
- 1 Tbsp. bourbon
- 2 tsp. vanilla extract
- 1½ tsp. ground cinnamon
- ½ tsp. ground nutmeg
- ½ tsp. salt
  Optional: Whipped cream and sugared cranberries (see p. 305)

1. In a small bowl, mix egg yolk with ¼ cup ice water; set aside. Place the flour, sugar and salt in a food processor; pulse until blended. Add shortening and butter; pulse until shortening and butter are the size of peas. While pulsing, add egg yolk mixture. Add just enough of the remaining ice water to form moist crumbs. Divide dough in half. Shape each into a disk; wrap and refrigerate 1 hour or overnight.

2. Preheat oven to 400°. Scrub sweet potatoes; place in a 13x9-in. baking pan with 1½ cups water. Bake until tender, 45-50 minutes.

3. Meanwhile, on a lightly floured surface, roll 1 disk of dough to a ⅛-in.-thick circle; transfer to a 9-in. deep-dish pie plate. Trim crust to ½ in. beyond rim of plate; flute edge. Roll remaining disk to ⅛-in. thickness; cut into desired shapes with floured 1-in. cookie cutters. Place on a parchment-lined baking sheet. Refrigerate crust and cutouts for at least 30 minutes.

4. Peel the potatoes when they are cool enough to handle; place in a food processor. Pulse to coarsely mash. Add brown sugar and the next 8 ingredients; blend until smooth. Pour the filling into chilled crust. Bake on lowest oven rack 15 minutes. Reduce the oven setting to 350°; bake until the center is just set, 20-25 minutes. Bake crust cutouts on an upper oven rack until golden brown, 10-12 minutes. Cool on a wire rack; decorate pie with cutouts and toppings as desired.

1 piece: 726 cal., 37g fat (18g sat. fat), 147mg chol., 500mg sod., 88g carb. (38g sugars, 6g fiber), 10g pro.

TARTS & GALETTES

CHAI TRUFFLE TART

As winter descends on us, I long for a decadent dessert to whip up. This chai-flavored tart with a salty caramel sauce delights the palate.
—Chantal Bourbon, Montreal, QC

PREP: 55 MIN. + CHILLING
MAKES: 16 SERVINGS

- 2 cups crushed pretzels
- ¼ cup packed brown sugar
- ¾ cup butter, melted
- ½ cup hot caramel ice cream topping
- 16 oz. 70% cacao dark baking chocolate, chopped
- 1 cup heavy whipping cream
- 2 Tbsp. butter
- 4 chai tea bags
- 2 Tbsp. baking cocoa
- 3 oz. milk chocolate, melted
- 2 Tbsp. finely chopped crystallized ginger

1. Preheat oven to 350°. In a large bowl, mix pretzels and brown sugar; stir in melted butter. Press the crumbs onto bottom and up sides of greased 9-in. fluted tart pan with removable bottom. Bake 12-15 minutes or until golden brown. Drizzle caramel topping over crust; cool on a wire rack.

2. Place dark chocolate in a large bowl; set aside. In a small saucepan, bring cream and butter just to a boil; remove from heat. Add the tea bags; let stand 10 minutes.

3. Discard the tea bags. Reheat cream mixture just to a boil. Pour over dark chocolate; let stand 5 minutes. Stir with a whisk until smooth. Pour 1½ cups of the ganache into prepared crust. Refrigerate, covered, 1 hour or until firm. Press plastic wrap onto surface of remaining ganache. Refrigerate until firm enough to shape, 35-40 minutes.

4. Shape reserved ganache into sixteen 1-in. balls; roll in cocoa. Drizzle the milk chocolate over tart; sprinkle with ginger. Arrange truffles around edge or over tart. Refrigerate until serving.

1 piece: 392 cal., 28g fat (17g sat. fat), 46mg chol., 286mg sod., 40g carb. (26g sugars, 3g fiber), 4g pro.

PEACH-BLUEBERRY CRUMBLE TART

This easy-to-prepare tart is a family favorite, whether fresh out of the oven or at room temperature with a scoop of vanilla ice cream.
—James Schend, Pleasant Prairie, WI

PREP: 30 MIN. • **BAKE:** 35 MIN. + COOLING
MAKES: 12 SERVINGS

- 1⅓ cups all-purpose flour
- ¼ cup sugar
- ¼ tsp. ground cinnamon
- ½ cup butter, melted
- 2 cups frozen unsweetened blueberries, thawed
- 2 cups frozen unsweetened sliced peaches, thawed
- 1 Tbsp. honey

CRUMB TOPPING
- ¼ cup all-purpose flour
- ¼ cup packed brown sugar
- ¼ cup old-fashioned oats
- ¼ cup chopped pecans
- ⅛ tsp. ground cloves
- 2 Tbsp. butter, melted

1. Preheat oven to 350°. In a small bowl, mix flour, sugar and cinnamon; stir in butter just until blended. Press into a 9-in. fluted tart pan with removable bottom. Bake 15-20 minutes or until lightly browned. Cool on a wire rack.

2. Meanwhile, in a large bowl, combine blueberries, peaches and honey; toss to coat. In a small bowl, combine first 5 topping ingredients; stir in butter.

3. Spoon fruit mixture into crust; sprinkle with topping. Bake at 350° for 35-40 minutes or until the topping is golden brown and the filling is bubbly. Cool on a wire rack at least 15 minutes before serving.

1 slice: 229 cal., 12g fat (6g sat. fat), 25mg chol., 70mg sod., 30g carb. (15g sugars, 2g fiber), 3g pro.

RUSTIC ORANGE-RHUBARB TART

This rustic rhubarb and orange tart is the perfect light dessert. We love it with fresh rhubarb in the spring, but it also tastes fantastic made with frozen fruit.
—*Taste of Home* Test Kitchen

PREP: 20 MIN. + STANDING • **BAKE:** 30 MIN.
MAKES: 6 SERVINGS

- 1   sheet refrigerated pie crust
- 2   Tbsp. apricot preserves
- 1   cup sliced fresh or frozen rhubarb, thawed
- 1   can (15 oz.) mandarin oranges, drained
- ½   cup plus 2 Tbsp. sugar, divided
- 3   Tbsp. quick-cooking tapioca
- ½   tsp. ground cinnamon
- ¼   cup slivered almonds
- 1   large egg white, room temperature
- 1   Tbsp. water
- ½   cup white baking chips
- 1   Tbsp. shortening

1. On a lightly floured surface, roll out crust into a 14-in. circle. Spread preserves to within 2 in. of edges. Transfer to a parchment-lined baking sheet; set aside.
2. In a large bowl, combine the rhubarb, oranges, ½ cup sugar, tapioca and cinnamon; let stand for 15 minutes. Preheat oven to 375°.
3. Spoon filling over crust to within 2 in. of edges; sprinkle with almonds. Fold edges of crust over filling, leaving center uncovered.
4. Beat egg white and water; brush over folded pastry. Sprinkle with the remaining 2 Tbsp. sugar. Bake for 30-35 minutes or until crust is golden and filling is bubbly. Using parchment, slide tart onto a wire rack to cool.
5. In a microwave, melt white chips and shortening; stir until smooth. Drizzle over tart.
1 piece: 432 cal., 18g fat (7g sat. fat), 10mg chol., 163mg sod., 65g carb. (40g sugars, 2g fiber), 4g pro.

HEAVENLY BLUEBERRY TART

Mmm—this tart is bursting with the fresh flavor of blueberries! Not only do I bake berries with the crust, but I also top the tart with more just-picked fruit after I take it out of the oven.
—Lyin Schramm, Berwick, ME

PREP: 20 MIN. • **BAKE:** 40 MIN. + COOLING
MAKES: 6 SERVINGS

- 1   cup all-purpose flour
- 2   Tbsp. sugar
- ⅛   tsp. salt
- ½   cup cold butter
- 1   Tbsp. vinegar
- FILLING
- 4   cups fresh blueberries, divided
- ⅔   cup sugar
- 2   Tbsp. all-purpose flour
- ½   tsp. ground cinnamon
- ⅛   tsp. ground nutmeg

1. Preheat oven to 400°. In a small bowl, combine the flour, sugar and salt; cut in butter until crumbly. Add the vinegar, tossing with a fork to moisten. Press onto the bottom and up the sides of a lightly greased 9-in. tart pan with removable bottom.
2. Lightly smash 2 cups of blueberries in a bowl. Combine the sugar, flour, cinnamon and nutmeg; stir into the smashed blueberries. Spread mixture evenly into crust; sprinkle with 1 cup of the remaining whole blueberries. Place tart pan on a baking sheet.
3. Bake for 40-45 minutes or until crust is browned and filling is bubbly. Remove from the oven; arrange remaining 1 cup berries over top. Cool on a wire rack. Store in the refrigerator.
1 piece: 380 cal., 16g fat (10g sat. fat), 41mg chol., 173mg sod., 59g carb. (36g sugars, 3g fiber), 3g pro.

BAKING 101

BOURBON PUMPKIN TART WITH WALNUT STREUSEL

Because my husband loves pumpkin pie, I've looked high and low for that perfect recipe. But as soon as he tasted this tart, he told me to stop searching, declaring this the best he's ever tried!

—Brenda Ryan, Marshall, MO

PREP: 45 MIN. + CHILLING
BAKE: 45 MIN. + COOLING
MAKES: 14 SERVINGS

- 2   cups all-purpose flour
- ⅓   cup sugar
- 1   tsp. grated orange zest
- ½   tsp. salt
- ⅔   cup cold butter, cubed
- 1   large egg, lightly beaten
- ¼   cup heavy whipping cream

FILLING

- 3   large eggs
- 1   can (15 oz.) pumpkin
- ½   cup sugar
- ½   cup heavy whipping cream
- ¼   cup packed brown sugar
- ¼   cup bourbon
- 2   Tbsp. all-purpose flour
- 1   tsp. ground cinnamon
- 1   tsp. ground ginger
- ¼   tsp. salt
- ¼   tsp. ground cloves

TOPPING

- ¾   cup all-purpose flour
- ⅓   cup sugar
- ⅓   cup packed brown sugar
- ½   tsp. salt
- ½   tsp. ground cinnamon
- ½   cup cold butter, cubed
- ¾   cup coarsely chopped walnuts, toasted
- ¼   cup chopped crystallized ginger

1. Combine the flour, sugar, orange zest and salt. Cut in butter until crumbly. Add egg. Gradually add cream, tossing with a fork until a ball forms. Refrigerate, covered, until easy to handle, at least 30 minutes.

2. Preheat oven to 350°. On a lightly floured surface, roll out dough into a 13-in. circle. Press onto bottom and up sides of an ungreased 11-in. fluted tart pan with removable bottom.

3. Combine all the filling ingredients; pour into crust.

4. For topping, whisk flour, sugar, brown sugar, salt and cinnamon. Cut in butter until crumbly. Stir in walnuts and ginger. Sprinkle over filling.

5. Bake until a knife inserted in center comes out clean, 45-55 minutes. Cool on a wire rack. Refrigerate leftovers.

1 piece: 463 cal., 26g fat (14g sat. fat), 108mg chol., 364mg sod., 53g carb. (29g sugars, 2g fiber), 6g pro.

DID YOU KNOW?

Unlike pie plates, tart pans have a vertical edge and no rim. That edge lets you trim the dough to fit exactly. Tart pans with removable bottoms allow you to unmold the tart before serving.

To unmold the tart, let it cool. Then place it on a freestanding object with a diameter smaller than the hole in the bottom of the pan (an inverted pickle jar or something similar works well) and slide the rim down and off. You can leave the tart on the remaining metal circle, or gently slide it off onto a serving plate.

BOURBON PUMPKIN TART WITH WALNUT STREUSEL

PEAR TART

This pretty pastry looks like it came from a fancy bakery. My sister-in-law brought this fruity dessert to dinner one night, and we all went back for seconds. It is truly scrumptious.
—Kathryn Rogers, Suisun City, CA

PREP: 15 MIN. • **BAKE:** 25 MIN. + CHILLING
MAKES: 12 SERVINGS

- 3 Tbsp. butter, softened
- ½ cup sugar
- ¾ tsp. ground cinnamon
- ¾ cup all-purpose flour
- ⅓ cup finely chopped walnuts

FILLING

- 1 pkg. (8 oz.) reduced-fat cream cheese
- ¼ cup plus 1 Tbsp. sugar, divided
- 1 large egg, room temperature
- 1 tsp. vanilla extract
- 1 can (15 oz.) reduced-sugar sliced pears, drained well and thinly sliced
- ¼ tsp. ground cinnamon

1. Preheat oven to 425°. Beat the butter, sugar and cinnamon until crumbly. Beat in flour and walnuts. Press onto bottom and up sides of a 9-in. fluted tart pan with a removable bottom coated with cooking spray.
2. For filling, beat cream cheese and ¼ cup sugar until smooth. Beat in egg and vanilla. Spread into crust. Arrange pears over top. Mix the cinnamon and remaining sugar; sprinkle over pears.
3. Bake for 10 minutes. Reduce oven setting to 350°; bake until the filling is set, 15-20 minutes. Cool 1 hour on a wire rack. Refrigerate at least 2 hours before serving.
1 piece: 199 cal., 9g fat (5g sat. fat), 36mg chol., 112mg sod., 25g carb. (18g sugars, 1g fiber), 4g pro. **Diabetic exchanges:** 2 fat, 1½ starch.

RUSTIC CARAMEL APPLE TART

Like an apple pie without the pan, this most scrumptious tart has a crispy crust that cuts nicely and a yummy caramel topping.
—Betty Fulks, Onia, AR

PREP: 20 MIN. + CHILLING • **BAKE:** 25 MIN.
MAKES: 4 SERVINGS

- ⅔ cup all-purpose flour
- 1 Tbsp. sugar
- ⅛ tsp. salt
- ¼ cup cold butter, cubed
- 6½ tsp. cold water
- ⅛ tsp. vanilla extract

FILLING
- 1½ cups chopped peeled tart apples
- 3 Tbsp. sugar
- 1 Tbsp. all-purpose flour

TOPPING
- 1 tsp. sugar
- ¼ tsp. ground cinnamon
- 1 large egg
- 1 Tbsp. water
- 2 Tbsp. caramel ice cream topping, warmed

1. In a large bowl, combine flour, sugar and salt; cut in the butter until crumbly. Gradually add water and vanilla, tossing with a fork until the dough forms a ball. Cover and refrigerate until the dough is easy to handle, about 30 minutes.

2. Preheat the oven to 400°. On a lightly floured surface, roll dough into a 10-in. circle. Transfer to a parchment-lined baking sheet. Combine the filling ingredients; spoon over crust to within 2 in. of edges. Fold up edges of crust over filling, leaving center uncovered. Combine sugar and cinnamon; sprinkle over filling. Whisk egg and water; brush over crust.

3. Bake until crust is golden and the filling is bubbly, 25-30 minutes. Using parchment, slide the tart onto a wire rack. Drizzle with caramel topping. Serve warm.

1 slice: 298 cal., 13g fat (8g sat. fat), 77mg chol., 218mg sod., 42g carb. (24g sugars, 1g fiber), 4g pro.

FUDGE PECAN BROWNIE TART

I love inventing my own recipes and entering contests—I won a blue ribbon at the Iowa State Fair for this one!
—Gloria Kratz, Des Moines, IA

PREP: 30 MIN. • **BAKE:** 30 MIN. + COOLING
MAKES: 12 SERVINGS

- 1 cup all-purpose flour
- ¼ cup packed light brown sugar
- ¼ cup finely chopped pecans
- ½ cup cold butter
- 2 Tbsp. 2% milk
- 1 tsp. vanilla extract

BROWNIE FILLING
- 3 oz. unsweetened chocolate
- ½ cup chocolate chips
- ½ cup butter, cut into pieces
- 1½ cups sugar
- 3 large eggs, room temperature
- 2 tsp. vanilla extract
- ¾ cup all-purpose flour
- 1 cup chopped pecans

FUDGE FROSTING
- 1½ oz. unsweetened chocolate
- ⅔ cup sweetened condensed milk
- ¼ cup butter
- 1 large egg yolk, beaten
- ½ tsp. vanilla extract
  Optional: Whipped cream and whole pecans for garnish

1. Preheat oven to 350°. Combine flour, brown sugar and ¼ cup pecans in a large bowl; cut in butter until mixture resembles coarse meal. Mix in the milk and vanilla with a fork just until blended. Pat onto bottom and up the sides of an 11-in. tart pan; set aside.

2. For the filling, melt chocolate and chips in the top of a double boiler over hot water. Remove from heat and stir in butter. Transfer to a large bowl and combine with sugar. Add the eggs and vanilla; blend well. Gradually add flour, blending well after each addition. Add 1 cup pecans. Pour over crust.

3. Bake for 30-35 minutes or until the center is just set and toothpick comes out clean. Cool on wire rack.

4. Meanwhile, for the frosting, melt the chocolate in a small saucepan over low heat. Add condensed milk, butter, yolk and vanilla. Heat, stirring vigorously, until smooth and thick, about 5 minutes. Spread over tart. Garnish with whipped cream and whole pecans if desired.

1 slice: 580 cal., 37g fat (17g sat. fat), 128mg chol., 236mg sod., 61g carb. (43g sugars, 3g fiber), 7g pro.

FUDGE PECAN
BROWNIE TART

BRANDIED APRICOT TART

Canned apricots make this golden, buttery tart a wonderful option any time of year. I brush it with preserves and brandy, then sprinkle with almonds.
—Johnna Johnson, Scottsdale, AZ

PREP: 25 MIN. • **BAKE:** 20 MIN.
MAKES: 8 SERVINGS

- 1⅓ cups all-purpose flour
- 2 Tbsp. sugar
- ½ cup cold butter
- 1 large egg yolk
- 2 to 3 Tbsp. 2% milk

FILLING
- ¾ cup apricot preserves
- 2 Tbsp. apricot brandy
- 4 cans (15¼ oz. each) apricot halves, drained and halved
- 2 Tbsp. slivered almonds, toasted

1. Preheat oven to 450°. In a large bowl, combine flour and sugar. Cut in butter until crumbly. Add egg yolk. Gradually add the milk, tossing with a fork until a ball forms. Press onto the bottom and up the sides of an ungreased 11-in. fluted tart pan with removable bottom. Bake for 8-10 minutes or until lightly browned. Cool on a wire rack. Reduce heat to 350°.

2. In a small saucepan, combine the preserves and brandy; cook and stir over low heat until melted. Brush 2 Tbsp. over crust. Arrange apricots over crust and brush with remaining preserve mixture.

3. Bake 18-22 minutes longer or until crust is golden brown. Cool on a wire rack. Sprinkle with almonds.
1 piece: 468 cal., 13g fat (8g sat. fat), 54mg chol., 115mg sod., 85g carb. (59g sugars, 4g fiber), 4g pro.

CAST-IRON PEACH CROSTATA

While the crostata, an open-faced fruit tart, is actually Italian, my version's peach filling is American all the way.
—Lauren McAnelly, Des Moines, IA

PREP: 45 MIN. + CHILLING • **BAKE:** 45 MIN.
MAKES: 10 SERVINGS

- 1½ cups all-purpose flour
- 2 Tbsp. plus ¾ cup packed brown sugar, divided
- 1¼ tsp. salt, divided
- ½ cup cold unsalted butter, cubed
- 2 Tbsp. shortening
- 3 to 5 Tbsp. ice water
- 8 cups sliced peaches (about 7-8 medium)
- 1 Tbsp. lemon juice
- 3 Tbsp. cornstarch
- ½ tsp. ground cinnamon
- ¼ tsp. ground nutmeg
- 1 large egg, beaten
- 2 Tbsp. sliced almonds
- 1 Tbsp. coarse sugar
- ⅓ cup water
- 1 cup fresh raspberries, optional

1. Mix flour, 2 Tbsp. brown sugar and 1 tsp. salt; cut in butter and shortening until crumbly. Gradually add ice water, tossing with a fork until dough holds together when pressed. Shape into a disk. Cover dough and refrigerate for 1 hour or overnight.

2. Combine peaches and lemon juice. Add the remaining ¾ cup brown sugar, cornstarch, spices and remaining ¼ tsp. salt; toss gently. Let stand 30 minutes.
3. Preheat oven to 400°. On a lightly floured surface, roll dough into a 13-in. circle; transfer to a 10-in. cast-iron skillet, letting excess hang over edge. Using a slotted spoon, transfer peaches into crust, reserving liquid. Fold crust edge over filling, pleating as you go, leaving center uncovered. Brush folded crust with beaten egg; sprinkle with almonds and coarse sugar. Bake until crust is dark golden and the filling is bubbly, 45-55 minutes.
4. In a small saucepan, combine reserved liquid and water; bring to a boil. Simmer until thickened, 1-2 minutes; serve warm with pie. If desired, top with fresh raspberries.
1 slice: 322 cal., 13g fat (7g sat. fat), 43mg chol., 381mg sod., 49g carb. (30g sugars, 3g fiber), 4g pro.

STREUSEL-TOPPED CHERRY ALMOND GALETTE

Inspired by favorite French desserts, this ruby red galette is a rustic yet elegant tart everyone will love. The edges of the pastry are folded over the cherry filling before baking.
—Lisa Speer, Palm Beach, FL

PREP: 15 MIN. • **BAKE:** 30 MIN. + COOLING
MAKES: 8 SERVINGS

- 1 sheet refrigerated pie crust
- 1 pkg. (7 oz.) almond paste
- 1 can (21 oz.) cherry pie filling
- ¼ cup chopped pecans
- ¼ cup packed light brown sugar
- 2 Tbsp. all-purpose flour
- 1 Tbsp. unsalted butter, melted
- 1 large egg
- 1 Tbsp. water
- ½ tsp. sugar
- 1 tsp. confectioners' sugar

1. Preheat oven to 375°. On a lightly floured surface, roll crust into a 12-in. circle. Transfer to a parchment-lined baking sheet.
2. Shape almond paste into a ball, then flatten into a disk. Roll out between 2 sheets of waxed paper into a 10-in. circle. Center on pastry. Spoon cherry pie filling over almond paste.
3. In a small bowl, combine the pecans, brown sugar, flour and butter; sprinkle over pie filling. Fold up edges of pastry over filling, leaving center uncovered. Combine egg and water; brush over folded pastry and sprinkle with sugar.
4. Bake for 30-35 minutes or until crust is golden and filling is bubbly. Using the parchment, slide the galette onto a wire rack to cool completely. Sprinkle with confectioners' sugar.

1 piece: 390 cal., 18g fat (5g sat. fat), 32mg chol., 128mg sod., 53g carb. (32g sugars, 2g fiber), 5g pro.

BAKING 101

BLUEBERRY, BASIL & GOAT CHEESE PIE

BLUEBERRY, BASIL & GOAT CHEESE PIE

To send off a friend who was moving, I made a galette of blueberries, creamy goat cheese and fresh basil. Bake one, share it and start a precious memory.
—Ashley Lecker, Green Bay, WI

PREP: 15 MIN. • **BAKE:** 40 MIN.
MAKES: 6 SERVINGS

- Pastry for single-crust pie
- 2 cups fresh blueberries
- 2 Tbsp. plus 2 tsp. sugar, divided
- 1 Tbsp. cornstarch
- 1 Tbsp. minced fresh basil
- 1 large egg
- 1 tsp. water
- ¼ cup crumbled goat cheese
- Fresh basil leaves, torn

1. Preheat oven to 375°. On a floured sheet of parchment, roll dough into a 10-in. circle. Leave on parchment and transfer to a baking sheet.
2. Mix blueberries, 2 Tbsp. sugar, the cornstarch and basil. Spoon blueberry mixture over crust to within 2 in. of the edge. Fold crust edge over the filling, pleating as you go and leaving the center uncovered.
3. Whisk egg and water; brush over crust. Sprinkle with remaining 2 tsp. sugar. Bake for 30 minutes. Sprinkle with goat cheese; bake until the crust is golden and filling is bubbly, about 10 minutes longer. Transfer to a wire rack to cool. Top with torn basil leaves before serving.

1 piece: 308 cal., 18g fat (11g sat. fat), 77mg chol., 241mg sod., 34g carb. (11g sugars, 2g fiber), 5g pro.

CINNAMON APPLE TART

I got the idea for this delicious fall dessert from a lovely Italian woman who's also a fabulous cook. It's so simple to make—and cleanup is just as easy! I often make two and freeze one.
—Stacie Blemings, Heath, TX

PREP: 20 MIN. • **BAKE:** 20 MIN.
MAKES: 6 SERVINGS

- 1   large apple, peeled and chopped
- 1   tsp. lemon juice
- 1   sheet refrigerated pie crust
- 2   Tbsp. apple jelly
- 2   Tbsp. sugar
- ¼   cup cinnamon baking chips
- ⅓   cup sliced almonds
- 1   tsp. 2% milk

ICING
- 1   cup confectioners' sugar
- ¼   tsp. almond extract
- 1   to 2 Tbsp. 2% milk

1. Preheat oven to 400°. Toss apple with lemon juice.

2. On a large sheet of parchment, roll crust into a 14-in. circle; transfer to a baking sheet. Spread jelly onto crust to within 2 in. of edges. Sprinkle with apple, sugar, baking chips and almonds. Fold up edges of crust over the filling, leaving opening in center. Brush folded crust with milk.

3. Bake 20-25 minutes or until golden brown. Transfer to a wire rack to cool.

4. Mix icing ingredients, using enough milk to reach desired consistency. Drizzle over tart.

1 piece: 370 cal., 15g fat (6g sat. fat), 7mg chol., 159mg sod., 57g carb. (39g sugars, 1g fiber), 3g pro.

BLOOD ORANGE
& GOAT CHEESE
GALETTE

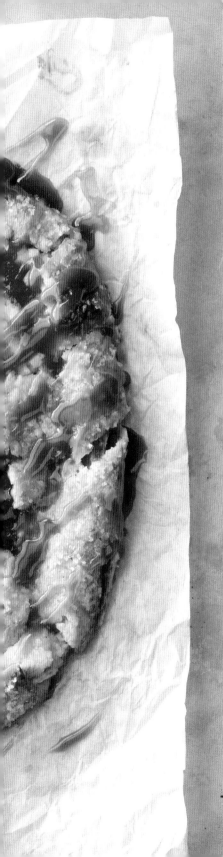

BLOOD ORANGE & GOAT CHEESE GALETTE

I made this galette for my mother-in-law's birthday, and it was a sensational hit. The gorgeous hue of the oranges transforms a rustic pie into an elegant dessert.
—Tia Laws, Enterprise, OR

PREP: 1 HOUR + FREEZING
BAKE: 1 HOUR + COOLING
MAKES: 8 SERVINGS (⅔ CUP SAUCE)

- 1   cup all-purpose flour
- 2   Tbsp. sugar
- ½   tsp. salt
- ⅓   cup cold butter, cubed
- ¼   cup quick-cooking oats
- 4   to 6 Tbsp. ice water

FILLING
- 10   medium blood oranges
- ¾   cup crumbled goat cheese
- 3   oz. cream cheese, softened
- ⅓   cup sour cream
- ¼   cup honey
- 2   large egg yolks, divided use
- ¼   tsp. salt
- 3   Tbsp. coarse sugar, divided
- 1   Tbsp. butter
- 1   Tbsp. water

SAUCE
- ¼   cup butter, cubed
- ½   cup packed brown sugar
- 2   Tbsp. half-and-half cream
- 2   Tbsp. honey
- ½   tsp. ground cinnamon

1. In a large bowl, mix flour, sugar and salt; cut in butter until crumbly. Stir in oats. Gradually add ice water, tossing with a fork until dough holds together when pressed. Shape into a disk; cover and refrigerate for 1 hour or overnight.

2. On a lightly floured surface, roll dough to a 13-in. circle. Transfer to a parchment-lined 14-in. pizza pan or large baking sheet. Refrigerate, covered, while preparing filling.

3. For filling, cut a thin slice from the top and bottom of oranges; stand oranges upright on a cutting board. With a knife, cut the peel and outer membrane from oranges. Cut along the membrane of each segment to remove fruit from 8 oranges. Thinly slice the remaining 2 oranges; remove seeds. Place orange segments and slices between layers of paper towels to remove excess moisture; let stand while preparing filling.

4. In a small bowl, beat goat cheese, cream cheese, sour cream, honey, 1 egg yolk and salt until smooth. Spread over the crust to within 2 in. of edge. Arrange orange segments over cheese mixture. Sprinkle with 2 Tbsp. coarse sugar; dot with butter.

5. Fold crust edge over filling, pleating as you go and leaving an opening in the center. Whisk the remaining egg yolk and 1 Tbsp. water; brush over folded crust. Arrange orange slices over crust to within 1 in. of edge. Sprinkle with the remaining 1 Tbsp. coarse sugar. Freeze, covered, overnight.

6. Preheat the oven to 375°. Bake until the crust is golden and filling is bubbly, 60-70 minutes. Transfer to a wire rack to cool.

7. For sauce, in a small saucepan, melt butter over medium heat. Add brown sugar, cream, honey and cinnamon; bring to a boil. Boil 1 minute, stirring constantly to dissolve sugar. Serve with galette.

1 piece: 488 cal., 25g fat (15g sat. fat), 79mg chol., 434mg sod., 63g carb. (46g sugars, 4g fiber), 6g pro.

NUTS & MORE

BAKING 101

YUMMY TEXAS PECAN PIE

This ooey-gooey pie's luscious and creamy filling offers that good old familiar flavor so many of us love!
—Laurel Leslie, Sonora, CA

PREP: 20 MIN. • **BAKE:** 70 MIN. + COOLING
MAKES: 8 SERVINGS

- 1 sheet refrigerated pie crust
- ½ cup sugar
- 3 Tbsp. all-purpose flour
- 1 cup light corn syrup
- 1 cup dark corn syrup
- 3 large eggs, room temperature
- 1 tsp. white vinegar
- ½ tsp. vanilla extract
- 1 cup chopped pecans

1. Preheat oven to 350°. Unroll crust into a 9-in. pie plate; flute edge. In a large bowl, whisk sugar, flour, corn syrups, eggs, vinegar and vanilla until smooth. Stir in pecans. Pour filling into crust. Cover edge with foil.
2. Bake for 35 minutes. Remove foil; bake until puffed and golden (center will not be set), 35-45 minutes. Cool on a wire rack. Refrigerate leftovers.
1 piece: 543 cal., 20g fat (5g sat. fat), 84mg chol., 215mg sod., 93g carb. (36g sugars, 2g fiber), 5g pro.
Mixed Nuts Pie: Reduce pecans to ½ cup. Add ½ cup cashew halves and ½ cup chopped hazelnuts

MACADAMIA NUT PIE

When I was young, friends of our family traveled to Hawaii and brought back macadamia nuts. My mom used them in this recipe. It's a tasty twist on traditional pecan pie.
—Brenda Hildebrandt, Moosomin, , SK

PREP: 25 MIN. • **BAKE:** 50 MIN. + COOLING
MAKES: 10 SERVINGS

- 1 sheet refrigerated pie crust
- 3 large eggs
- 1 cup dark corn syrup
- ⅔ cup sugar
- 2 Tbsp. butter, melted
- 2 tsp. vanilla extract
- 2 cups chopped macadamia nuts

Preheat oven to 325°. Unroll crust and place in a 9-in. pie plate; flute edge and set aside. In a small bowl, beat the eggs, corn syrup, sugar, butter and vanilla until combined. Stir in the nuts. Pour into the crust. Bake 50-55 minutes or until the center is set and top is golden brown. Cool on a wire rack. Refrigerate leftovers.
1 piece: 476 cal., 30g fat (8g sat. fat), 66mg chol., 264mg sod., 52g carb. (40g sugars, 2g fiber), 5g pro.

MOM-MOM BESSIE'S COCONUT MOLASSES PIE

I have my husband's grandmother's handwritten recipe book. Mom-Mom Bessie was one of the best cooks I knew, and we think of her every time we make this pie. The flavor combination of coconut and molasses is a family favorite.
—Susan Bickta, Kutztown, PA

PREP: 10 MIN. • **BAKE:** 45 MIN. + COOLING
MAKES: 8 SERVINGS

- 1 cup packed light brown sugar
- 1 cup sour cream
- ½ cup dark corn syrup
- ½ cup dark molasses
- 2 large eggs, room temperature, lightly beaten
- ¼ cup 2% milk
- 2 Tbsp. all-purpose flour
- ¼ tsp. baking soda
- 1½ cups sweetened shredded coconut
- 1 frozen deep-dish pie crust (9 in.)
  Whipped cream, optional

Preheat oven to 350°. In a large bowl, combine the first 8 ingredients. Stir in coconut. Pour into crust; cover edge loosely with foil. Bake until center is set, 45-55 minutes. Remove foil; cool on a wire rack. If desired, serve with whipped cream.
1 piece: 486 cal., 19g fat (10g sat. fat), 54mg chol., 243mg sod., 80g carb. (66g sugars, 1g fiber), 5g pro.

TEST KITCHEN TIP

For less molasses flavor, use ½ cup additional dark Karo syrup in place of the molasses.

MOM-MOM
BESSIE'S COCONUT
MOLASSES PIE

BAKING
101

CRANBERRY CHOCOLATE
WALNUT PIE

MAMA ARNOLD'S
HONEY PIE
....

CRANBERRY CHOCOLATE WALNUT PIE

For a showstopping holiday pie, I mix some cranberries, chocolate and walnuts. A little touch of rum makes it even happier.
—Lorrie Melerine, Houston, TX

PREP: 30 MIN. + CHILLING
BAKE: 30 MIN. + COOLING
MAKES: 8 SERVINGS

      Pastry for single-crust pie
3   large eggs
¾   cup sugar
½   cup butter, melted
3   Tbsp. all-purpose flour
1   cup chopped walnuts
1   cup fresh or frozen cranberries
1   cup semisweet chocolate chips
2   Tbsp. dark rum

1. On a lightly floured surface, roll the dough to a ⅛-in.-thick circle; transfer to a 9-in. pie plate. Trim the crust to ½ in. beyond rim of plate; flute edge. Refrigerate 30 minutes. Preheat oven to 450°.

2. Line unpricked crust with a double thickness of foil. Fill with pie weights, dried beans or uncooked rice. Bake on a lower oven rack 15-20 minutes or until edges are light golden brown. Remove the foil and weights; bake 3-6 minutes longer or until bottom is golden brown. Cool on a wire rack. Reduce the oven setting to 350°.

3. In a large bowl, beat eggs, sugar and melted butter until well blended. Gradually add flour until blended. Stir in remaining ingredients; pour into crust.

4. Bake 30-35 minutes or until top is bubbly and crust is golden brown. Cool on a wire rack. Refrigerate leftovers.

1 piece: 594 cal., 41g fat (20g sat. fat), 130mg chol., 276mg sod., 53g carb. (32g sugars, 3g fiber), 8g pro.

MAMA ARNOLD'S HONEY PIE

This sweet, custardy pie could not be simpler to make, but will have your guests asking for more. The boiled honey gives it a caramel-like flavor that's divine.
—Ruth Arnold, Pearsall, TX

PREP: 15 MIN. • **BAKE:** 25 MIN.
MAKES: 8 SERVINGS

- 1 **cup honey**
- 3 **large eggs, lightly beaten**
- 3 **Tbsp. butter**
- 1 **tsp. vanilla extract**
- 1 **cup chopped pecans**
  Dash nutmeg
- 1 **pie shell (9 in.), unbaked**

1. Preheat the oven to 325°. In a large saucepan, bring honey to a boil. Remove from heat. Stir a small amount of the hot honey into the eggs; return all to the pan, stirring constantly. Bring to a gentle boil; gently stir in the butter, vanilla, pecans and nutmeg.
2. Pour filling into the crust and bake for 25 minutes or until filling is set.
1 piece: 418 cal., 24g fat (7g sat. fat), 96mg chol., 169mg sod., 50g carb. (35g sugars, 2g fiber), 5g pro.

· · · · · · · · · · · · · · · · ·
DID YOU KNOW?
Honey takes on different flavors depending on the flowers the bees sourced it from. Most honeys in the U.S. are sourced from clover, alfafa, orange blossom or sage. Have fun experimenting with local honeys to see the results of using different flavors.

BAKING 101

MAPLE SYRUP PIE

Everyone in New Hampshire loves maple syrup almost as much as we do in Vermont. When my husband and I took a road trip through New Hampshire we discovered this pie at a number of diners and restaurants. We loved it so much we created our own version when we got home.
—Laurie Herr, Westford, VT

PREP: 30 MIN. • **BAKE:** 45 MIN. + COOLING
MAKES: 8 SERVINGS

- 3 Tbsp. cornstarch
- ⅔ cup water
- 1½ cups real maple syrup
- 2 Tbsp. butter
  Pastry for double-crust pie

1. In a large saucepan, whisk cornstarch and water until smooth; whisk in maple syrup. Bring to boil; cook and stir until thickened, about 4 minutes. Remove from heat; stir in butter until melted. Set aside to cool.
2. On a lightly floured surface, roll the dough for bottom crust to a ⅛-in.-thick circle; transfer to a 9-in. pie plate. Trim crust to ½ in. beyond rim of plate; flute edge. Chill 30 minutes. Meanwhile, roll remaining dough to ¼-in.-thickness; cut out maple leaves with 1½- to 2½-in. cookie cutters. Place the cutouts on a baking sheet; chill.
3. Transfer filling to crust. Bake on a lower oven rack at 400° for 10 minutes; reduce oven setting to 350° and bake until crust is golden and filling is bubbly, 35-40 minutes longer. Cool completely on a wire rack.
4. Bake leaf cutouts until golden brown, 8-10 minutes, and arrange on top of pie.
1 piece: 536 cal., 26g fat (16g sat. fat), 68mg chol., 340mg sod., 73g carb. (37g sugars, 1g fiber), 4g pro.

SHOOFLY PIE

My grandmother made the best shoofly pie in the tradition of the Pennsylvania Dutch. Shoofly pie is to the Amish as pecan pie is to a Southerner.
—Mark Morgan, Waterford, WI

PREP: 20 MIN. + CHILLING
BAKE: 65 MIN. + COOLING
MAKES: 8 SERVINGS

- Pastry for single-crust pie
- ½ cup packed brown sugar
- ½ cup molasses
- 1 large egg, room temperature
- 1½ tsp. all-purpose flour
- ½ tsp. baking soda
- 1 cup boiling water
- 1 large egg yolk, room temperature, lightly beaten

TOPPING
- 1½ cups all-purpose flour
- ¾ cup packed brown sugar
- ¾ tsp. baking soda
  Dash salt
- 6 Tbsp. cold butter, cubed

1. On a floured surface, roll the dough to fit a 9-in. deep-dish pie plate. Trim and flute edge. Refrigerate for at least 30 minutes.
2. Meanwhile, preheat oven to 425°. For filling, mix brown sugar, molasses, egg, flour and baking soda. Gradually stir in boiling water; cool completely.
3. Line unpricked crust with a double thickness of foil. Fill with pie weights, dried beans or uncooked rice. Bake on a lower oven rack 15 minutes. Remove foil and pie weights; brush crust with egg yolk. Bake 5 minutes. Cool on a wire rack. Reduce oven setting to 350°.
4. In another bowl, whisk together the first 4 topping ingredients. Cut in the butter until crumbly. Add filling to crust; sprinkle with topping. Cover edge of pie with foil.
5. Bake until filling is set and golden brown, 45-50 minutes. Cool on a wire rack. Store in the refrigerator.
1 piece: 540 cal., 22g fat (13g sat. fat), 99mg chol., 630mg sod., 82g carb. (49g sugars, 1g fiber), 6g pro.

OLD-FASHIONED PEANUT BUTTER PIE

BAKING 101

My mother made a chewy, gooey peanut butter pie I loved as a child. Now I continue the tradition for our generation of peanut butter lovers.
—Brianna DeBlake, Fremont, MI

PREP: 20 MIN. • **BAKE:** 1 HOUR
MAKES: 8 SERVINGS

      Pastry for single-crust pie
1½ cups light corn syrup
 ½ cup sugar
 ½ cup creamy peanut butter
 ¼ tsp. salt
  4 large eggs
 ½ tsp. vanilla extract
      Optional toppings: Chopped peanuts, broken Nutter Butter cookies and whipped topping

1. Preheat oven to 350°. On a lightly floured surface, roll the dough to a ⅛-in.-thick circle; transfer to a 9-in. pie plate. Trim to ½ in. beyond rim of plate; flute edge.
2. In a large bowl, beat corn syrup, sugar, peanut butter and salt until blended. Beat in eggs and vanilla until smooth. Pour into crust. Bake 60-70 minutes or until top is puffed and center is almost set; cover the top loosely with foil during the last 30 minutes to prevent overbrowning.
3. Remove foil. Cool on a wire rack. (Top may sink and crack slightly upon cooling.) Serve or refrigerate within 2 hours. Top as desired.
1 piece: 538 cal., 22g fat (10g sat. fat), 123mg chol., 379mg sod., 82g carb. (65g sugars, 1g fiber), 9g pro.

WALNUT MINCEMEAT PIE

WALNUT MINCEMEAT PIE

Mincemeat pie is a tradition for many families at Thanksgiving and Christmas. It's so simple to make. For a tasty finishing touch, top with a dollop of whipped cream or scoop of vanilla ice cream!
—Laverne Kamp, Kutztown, PA

PREP: 15 MIN. • **BAKE:** 50 MIN. + COOLING
MAKES: 8 SERVINGS

      Pastry for single-crust pie
  2 large eggs, room temperature
  1 cup sugar
  2 Tbsp. all-purpose flour
 ⅛ tsp. salt
  2 cups prepared mincemeat
 ½ cup chopped walnuts
 ¼ cup butter, melted

1. Preheat oven to 400°. On a lightly floured surface, roll the dough to a ⅛-in.-thick circle. Line a 9-in. pie plate with crust; trim and flute edge. In a large bowl, lightly beat eggs. Combine the sugar, flour and salt; gradually add to eggs. Stir in mincemeat, walnuts and butter; pour into crust.
2. Bake for 15 minutes. Reduce heat to 325°; bake until a knife inserted in the center comes out clean, 35-40 minutes. Let the pie cool completely; store in the refrigerator.
1 piece: 440 cal., 18g fat (7g sat. fat), 73mg chol., 231mg sod., 65g carb. (45g sugars, 2g fiber), 5g pro.

VERMONT MAPLE OATMEAL PIE

This yummy pie has an old-fashioned feeling, but is so easy to prepare. Serve it with ice cream drizzled with maple syrup or top it with maple- or cinnamon-flavored whipped cream.

—Barbara J. Miller, Oakdale, MN

PREP: 20 MIN. • **BAKE:** 50 MIN. + COOLING
MAKES: 8 SERVINGS

	Pastry for single-crust pie
4	large eggs, room temperature
1	cup sugar
3	Tbsp. all-purpose flour
1	tsp. ground cinnamon
½	tsp. salt
1	cup quick-cooking oats
¾	cup corn syrup
½	cup maple syrup
¼	cup butter, melted
3	tsp. vanilla extract
1	cup sweetened shredded coconut
	Vanilla ice cream, optional

1. Preheat oven to 350°. On a lightly floured surface, roll the dough to a ⅛-in.-thick circle; transfer to a 9-in. pie plate. Trim crust to ½ in. beyond rim of plate; flute edge.

2. In a large bowl, combine eggs, sugar, flour, cinnamon and salt. Stir in the oats, syrups, butter and vanilla; pour into the crust. Sprinkle with coconut.

3. Bake until set, 50-60 minutes. Cover edge with foil during the last 15 minutes to prevent overbrowning if necessary. Cool on a wire rack. If desired, serve with ice cream. Refrigerate leftovers.

1 piece: 612 cal., 25g fat (15g sat. fat), 138mg chol., 438mg sod., 94g carb. (68g sugars, 2g fiber), 7g pro.

VERMONT MAPLE
OATMEAL PIE

BAKING
101

COCONUT
PECAN PIE

COCONUT PECAN PIE

We top this sweet pie with sliced bananas, whipped cream and more sliced bananas. It's based on a recipe my mom got from a potholder she bought at the Patti's 1880s Settlement in Grand Rivers, Kentucky.
—Jennifer Choisser, Paducah, KY

PREP: 15 MIN. • **BAKE:** 25 MIN. + COOLING
MAKES: 8 SERVINGS

   Pastry for single-crust pie
7 large egg whites
1½ cups sugar
1½ cups sweetened shredded coconut
1½ cups graham cracker crumbs
1½ cups chopped pecans
   Whipped cream, optional

1. On a lightly floured surface, roll the dough to a ⅛-in.-thick circle; transfer to a 9-in. pie plate. Trim crust to ½ in. beyond rim of plate; flute edge.
2. Combine egg whites, sugar, coconut, cracker crumbs and pecans. Pour into crust. Bake at 325° for 25-30 minutes or until set. Cool on a wire rack. Serve with whipped cream if desired.
1 piece: 642 cal., 34g fat (14g sat. fat), 30mg chol., 335mg sod., 79g carb. (51g sugars, 4g fiber), 9g pro.

BUTTERMILK PECAN PIE

This is the treasured golden oldie that my grandmother made so often whenever we'd come to visit. Grandma grew her own pecans—we never tired of cracking them and picking out the meat when we knew we'd be treated to her special pie!
—Mildred Sherrer, Fort Worth, TX

PREP: 15 MIN. • **BAKE:** 55 MIN. + COOLING
MAKES: 8 SERVINGS

- ½ cup butter, softened
- 2 cups sugar
- 5 large eggs, room temperature
- 2 Tbsp. all-purpose flour
- 2 Tbsp. lemon juice
- 1 tsp. vanilla extract
- 1 cup buttermilk
- 1 cup chopped pecans
  Pastry for single-crust pie

1. Preheat the oven to 325°. In a bowl, cream the butter and sugar until light and fluffy, 5-7 minutes. Add eggs, 1 at a time, beating well after each addition. Blend in flour, lemon juice and vanilla. Stir in buttermilk and pecans.

2. On a lightly floured surface, roll the dough to a ⅛-in.-thick circle; transfer to a 9-in. deep-dish pie plate. Trim crust to ½ in. beyond rim of plate; flute edge.
3. Add the filling to crust. Bake until set, 55-60 minutes. Cool pie on a wire rack. Store in the refrigerator.
1 piece: 691 cal., 41g fat (20g sat. fat), 191mg chol., 401mg sod., 75g carb. (53g sugars, 2g fiber), 9g pro.

DOUBLE PEANUT PIE

I created this recipe for a national pie contest and won second place for my state. Many peanuts are grown here, and I always look for ways to use local products.
—Vivian Cleeton, Richmond, VA

BAKING 101

PREP: 10 MIN. • **BAKE:** 30 MIN. + COOLING
MAKES: 8 SERVINGS

- 2 large eggs, room temperature
- ⅓ cup creamy peanut butter
- ⅓ cup sugar
- ⅓ cup light corn syrup
- ⅓ cup dark corn syrup
- ⅓ cup butter, melted
- 1 tsp. vanilla extract
- 1 cup salted peanuts
- 1 pie shell (9 in.), unbaked
  Optional: Whipped cream or ice cream

1. In a large bowl, lightly beat the eggs. Gradually add the peanut butter, sugar, corn syrups, butter and vanilla until well blended. Fold in peanuts.
2. Pour filling into the crust. Bake at 375° for 30-35 minutes or until set. Cool. Serve with whipped cream or ice cream if desired.
1 piece: 484 cal., 30g fat (10g sat. fat), 79mg chol., 358mg sod., 48g carb. (23g sugars, 2g fiber), 10g pro.

KENTUCKY DERBY PIE

This rich, dense pie is traditionally served at parties everywhere on Derby day. It features a delicious dark chocolate filling topped with plenty of toasted pecans.
—Emily Baldwin, Fort Collins, CO

PREP: 10 MIN. • **BAKE:** 40 MIN. + COOLING
MAKES: 8 SERVINGS

- 3 large eggs, lightly beaten
- 1 cup light corn syrup
- ½ cup packed brown sugar
- 2 Tbsp. all-purpose flour
- ½ tsp. vanilla extract
- ¼ tsp. salt
- 1 cup chopped pecans
- 1 cup semisweet chocolate chips
- 2 Tbsp. butter, melted
- 1 pie shell (9 in.), unbaked

1. Preheat oven to 350°. Whisk the eggs, corn syrup, brown sugar, flour, vanilla and salt. Stir in pecans, chocolate chips and butter. Pour into crust. Cover edge loosely with foil.
2. Bake for 25 minutes. Remove foil; bake 15-20 minutes longer or until a knife inserted in the center comes out clean. Cool on a wire rack. Refrigerate any leftovers.
1 piece: 552 cal., 29g fat (10g sat. fat), 92mg chol., 253mg sod., 75g carb. (38g sugars, 3g fiber), 6g pro.

TEST KITCHEN TIP

Kentucky Derby Pie should be refrigerated after 2 hours at room temperature. You can then cover and store it in the fridge for up to 4 days. You can also freeze your pie for up to 2 months.

KENTUCKY DERBY PIE

BAKING
101

COBBLERS, CRISPS, CRUMBLES & MORE

Fruit steps to the forefront with these incredibly delicious desserts. Whether it's the fresh taste of summer berries in a strawberry shortcake or the richly spiced flavors of harvest fruits in a brown betty, these treats are quick to pull together and sure to please.

. . . .

WHICH DESSERT IS WHICH?

Everyone knows a bubbly-fruit-plus-carb combo is sweet bliss, but it can be hard to distinguish pandowdies from buckles from crisps. Here's how to tell them apart.

Crumbles & Crisps: The lines between crumbles and crisps have become irrevocably blurred. The rule used to be that only one of them contained oats, but now there's no agreement as to which one does and which doesn't. Both are made with fruit on the bottom and are topped with a streusel-like mixture of flour, sugar, butter....and maybe oats and/or nuts, maybe not.

The essential difference is right there in the name. The topping for a crumble is crumbly and softer, while a crisp tends to have a crunchier topping.

Cobbler: To make a cobbler, the fruit mixture is placed in a deep casserole dish and topped with a biscuit mixture—either dropped by the spoonful or cut out and laid on top. Some cobblers are made with something more resembling a cake batter, which is poured over top of the fruit—this style of cobbler is like a buckle in reverse.

Grunt: Closely related to cobblers, grunts are made in a skillet. Some grunts are made entirely on the stovetop, others are finished in the oven.

Buckle: Buckles start with a cake batter with the fruit sprinkled on top. While the dish bakes, the fruit sinks into the batter, so it's dotted throughout the finished dessert.

Betty: Made by layering bread or bread crumbs with fresh fruit, and then baking, a betty is kind of a cross between a bread pudding and a pie. Apples are the classic choice for a betty, but we suggest experimenting with other fruits, too, such as fresh rhubarb, berries or pears. This dessert is best made with day-old bread with a firm texture.

Pandowdy: For a pandowdy, the fruit filing is covered with a full layer of pastry crust, much like a double-crust pie. However, a pandowdy's filling is more liquid, and is expected to stay that way; after baking, the crust is broken up into bite-sized pieces to soak up the fruit juices. You can also make a pandowdy using scraps of leftover pie crust dough—no post-bake breaking up required.

Shortcake: The cake—whether a biscuit, a kind of quick bread or a cake—is baked first, and then topped with fresh fruit. The fruit is usually tossed with a little bit of sugar to create its own natural syrup. Shortcake is what you make when you have strawberries (most famously) in the perfect state of ripeness. If your fruit isn't perfectly in-season, sweet and scrumptious enough to eat on its own, make something else!

CRUMBLE

CRISP

COBBLER

GRUNT

BUCKLE

BETTY

PANDOWDY

SHORTCAKE

HOW TO MAKE A COBBLER WITH ANY FRUIT

Follow this easy formula to craft your own bubbly beauty any time!

1. MIX THE FRUIT

Use about 6 cups of fruit for a greased 2-quart baking dish, preferably glass or ceramic. Mix and match your favorite flavors, such as apples and cranberries, strawberries and rhubarb, or cherries and pears.

2. ADD 3 KEY INGREDIENTS

Besides fruit, a cobbler's filling needs three things: a thickener, a sweetener and at least one flavoring. Toss everything together in the dish so the fruit is evenly coated.

Cornstarch is the go-to thickener for fruits, although you can use an equal amount of quick-cooking tapioca. Use about 1 to 2 tablespoons of cornstarch or tapioca for a 2-quart cobbler. (Flour is also a traditional thickener, but you may need a little bit more of it.)

Depending on the type and ripeness of the fruit you're using, add ¾ to 1 cup of sugar. It's best to err on the side of less sugar; you can easily adjust after baking by adding a sprinkling of coarse sugar or a drizzle of honey.

Add your preferred spices—cinnamon, ginger, nutmeg and cloves are all good choices to add depth to the fruit flavors. A little bit of vanilla or almond extract adds brightness.

3. ADD THE TOPPING

Cobblers are traditionally made with biscuit dough. You can go with a favorite homemade biscuit recipe (p. 110) or take a shortcut by using a biscuit mix or premade refrigerated biscuit dough.

You can also experiment with refrigerated cinnamon roll dough. If your topping isn't particularly sweet, sprinkle the biscuit dough with coarse sugar before baking.

4. BAKE

Bake at 375° for 25-40 minutes. The cobbler is done when the fruit juices are bubbly and the topping is golden brown. If the biscuits brown too quickly, loosely cover the dish with foil.

5. SET & SERVE

A cobbler is best served warm, but not right out of the oven. Let it cool in the dish on a cooling rack for 15-20 minutes to allow the juices to thicken slightly. Serve warm all by itself, or with a scoop of ice cream, sweetened whipped cream or a drizzle of half-and-half or full cream.

COBBLERS, CRISPS, CRUMBLES & MORE

BLUEBERRY CORNMEAL COBBLER

Cornbread, blueberries and maple syrup butter give this special dessert a taste that's different from any cobbler you've had before. I came across the recipe many years ago.
—Judy Watson, Tipton, IN

PREP: 20 MIN. + STANDING • **BAKE:** 35 MIN.
MAKES: 12 SERVINGS

4 cups fresh blueberries
1 cup plus 2 Tbsp. sugar
1 Tbsp. quick-cooking tapioca
2 tsp. grated lemon zest
1 tsp. ground cinnamon
¼ to ½ tsp. ground nutmeg
TOPPING
½ cup butter, softened, divided
1 cup confectioners' sugar
1 large egg, room temperature
1 cup all-purpose flour
½ cup cornmeal
2 tsp. baking powder
½ tsp. baking soda
½ tsp. salt
¾ cup buttermilk
2 Tbsp. maple syrup

1. Preheat oven to 375°. In a large bowl, combine the blueberries, sugar, tapioca, lemon zest, cinnamon and nutmeg. Let stand for 15 minutes. Pour into a greased 11x7-in. baking dish.
2. In a small bowl, beat ¼ cup butter and confectioners' sugar. Add egg; beat well. Combine the flour, cornmeal, baking powder, baking soda and salt; add to the creamed mixture alternately with buttermilk, beating just until combined. Pour over the berry mixture.
3. Bake until a toothpick inserted in the center comes out clean, 35-40 minutes.
4. In a small saucepan, melt remaining ¼ cup butter over low heat. Remove from heat; stir in the syrup. Brush over cornbread. Broil 4-6 in. from the heat until bubbly, 1-2 minutes. Serve warm.
1 piece: 290 cal., 9g fat (5g sat. fat), 39mg chol., 317mg sod., 52g carb. (35g sugars, 2g fiber), 3g pro.

CHERRY PUDDING CAKE

A cross between a cake and a cobbler, this cherry dessert is awesome. Add it to your list of trusty potluck recipes, because this one is sure to go fast.
—Brenda Parker, Kalamazoo, MI

BAKING 101

PREP: 10 MIN. • **BAKE:** 40 MIN.
MAKES: 12 SERVINGS

2 cups all-purpose flour
2½ cups sugar, divided
4 tsp. baking powder
1 cup 2% milk
2 Tbsp. canola oil
2 cans (14½ oz. each) water-packed pitted tart red cherries, well drained
⅛ tsp. almond extract
Optional: Whipped cream or ice cream

1. Preheat oven to 375°. Combine flour, 1 cup sugar, baking powder, milk and oil; pour into a greased shallow 3-qt. baking dish. In a bowl, combine the cherries, extract and the remaining 1½ cup sugar; spoon over batter.
2. Bake for 40-45 minutes or until a toothpick inserted in the cake portion comes out clean. Serve warm, with whipped cream or ice cream if desired.
1 serving: 296 cal., 3g fat (1g sat. fat), 3mg chol., 147mg sod., 65g carb. (48g sugars, 1g fiber), 3g pro.

APPLE BROWN BETTY

BAKING 101

This classic treat can whipped up in hardly any time. It's light on the wallet but big on flavor.

—Florence Palmer, Marshall, IL

PREP: 15 MIN. • **BAKE:** 1 HOUR
MAKES: 4 SERVINGS

- 4 slices white bread, toasted
- 3 cups sliced peeled tart apples
- ½ cup sugar
- ½ cup packed brown sugar
- 1 tsp. ground cinnamon
- ¼ cup butter, melted
- ½ cup half-and-half cream

1. Preheat oven to 350°. Tear toast into bite-sized pieces; place in a greased 1½-qt. casserole. Top with apples. Combine sugars and cinnamon; sprinkle over apples. Drizzle with butter.
2. Cover and bake for 1 hour, stirring after 30 minutes. Serve warm and drizzled with cream.

1 serving: 456 cal., 16g fat (9g sat. fat), 46mg chol., 276mg sod., 78g carb. (63g sugars, 2g fiber), 3g pro.

PEACH SUGAR COOKIE CRUMBLE

This is like peach crisp with a sugar cookie topping. Since it uses canned peaches, you don't have to save this recipe just for peach season. It's delicious with ice cream.

—Teri Rasey, Cadillac, MI

PREP: 30 MIN.
BAKE: 35 MIN. + COOLING
MAKES: 12 SERVINGS

- 2 Tbsp. butter
- 4 cans (15¼ oz. each) sliced peaches, drained
- 1¾ cups sugar, divided
- 3 tsp. vanilla extract, divided
- 1 tsp. crystallized ginger, finely chopped
- ½ tsp. ground cinnamon
- 1 cup shortening
- ¼ cup packed brown sugar
- 1 large egg, room temperature
- 1 tsp. almond extract
- 2½ cups all-purpose flour
- 1 Tbsp. cornstarch
- 1 tsp. baking soda
- ½ tsp. baking powder
  Optional: Chopped pecans, coarse sugar and vanilla ice cream

1. Preheat oven to 350°. Melt butter in a 12-in. cast-iron or other ovenproof skillet over medium heat. Add peaches, ¾ cup sugar, 2 tsp. vanilla, ginger and cinnamon. Cook and stir until peaches soften and begin to break down, about 10 minutes. Remove from the heat.
2. In a large bowl, cream shortening, brown sugar and remaining 1 cup sugar until light and fluffy, 5-7 minutes. Beat in egg, almond extract and remaining 1 tsp. vanilla. In another bowl, whisk flour, cornstarch, baking soda and baking powder; gradually beat into creamed mixture. Crumble dough over the peach mixture. If desired, sprinkle with pecans and coarse sugar.
3. Bake until a toothpick inserted in center comes out clean, 35-40 minutes. Cool on a wire rack. If desired, serve with vanilla ice cream.

1 serving: 480 cal., 19g fat (5g sat. fat), 21mg chol., 156mg sod., 73g carb. (52g sugars, 2g fiber), 3g pro.

PEACH SUGAR COOKIE CRUMBLE

TROPICAL CRISP

One bite of this sweet, juicy, crunchy crisp, and you just might hear the crash of the ocean and feel warm sand under your toes!
—*Taste of Home* Test Kitchen

PREP: 20 MIN. • **BAKE:** 30 MIN.
MAKES: 9 SERVINGS

- 1 fresh pineapple, peeled and cubed
- 4 medium bananas, sliced
- ¼ cup packed brown sugar
- 2 Tbsp. all-purpose flour

TOPPING
- ⅓ cup old-fashioned oats
- ¼ cup all-purpose flour
- 2 Tbsp. sweetened shredded coconut, toasted
- 2 Tbsp. brown sugar
- ¼ tsp. ground nutmeg
- ¼ cup cold butter, cubed

1. Preheat oven to 350°. In a large bowl, combine the pineapple and bananas. Sprinkle with brown sugar and flour; toss to coat. Transfer to an 11x7-in. baking dish coated with cooking spray.
2. In a small bowl, mix the first 5 topping ingredients; cut in butter until crumbly. Sprinkle over the pineapple mixture.
3. Bake 30-35 minutes or until filling is bubbly and topping is golden brown. Serve warm or at room temperature.
1 serving: 188 cal., 6g fat (4g sat. fat), 13mg chol., 44mg sod., 34g carb. (21g sugars, 3g fiber), 2g pro. **Diabetic exchanges:** 1 starch, 1 fruit, 1 fat.

GRANDMA'S OLD-FASHIONED STRAWBERRY SHORTCAKE

GRANDMA'S OLD-FASHIONED STRAWBERRY SHORTCAKE

When my grandma served this shortcake, she usually topped it with homemade vanilla ice cream.
—Angela Lively, Conroe, TX

PREP: 30 MIN. + STANDING • **BAKE:** 20 MIN.
MAKES: 8 SERVINGS

- 6 cups sliced fresh strawberries
- ½ cup sugar
- 1 tsp. vanilla extract

SHORTCAKE
- 3 cups all-purpose flour
- 5 Tbsp. sugar, divided
- 3 tsp. baking powder
- 1 tsp. baking soda
- ½ tsp. salt
- ¾ cup cold butter, cubed
- 1¼ cups buttermilk
- 2 Tbsp. heavy whipping cream

TOPPING
- 1½ cups heavy whipping cream
- 2 Tbsp. sugar
- ½ tsp. vanilla extract

1. Combine strawberries with sugar and vanilla; mash slightly. Let stand at least 30 minutes, tossing occasionally.
2. Preheat oven to 400°. For shortcakes, whisk together flour, 4 Tbsp. sugar, the baking powder, baking soda and salt. Cut in cold butter until crumbly. Add buttermilk; stir just until combined (do not overmix).
3. Drop batter by ⅓ cupfuls 2 in. apart onto an ungreased baking sheet. Brush with 2 Tbsp. heavy cream; sprinkle with remaining 1 Tbsp. sugar. Bake until golden, 18-20 minutes. Remove to wire racks to cool completely.
4. For topping, beat heavy whipping cream until it begins to thicken. Add sugar and vanilla; beat until soft peaks form. To serve, cut shortcakes in half; top each shortcake with strawberries and whipped cream.
1 shortcake with ½ cup strawberries and ⅓ cup whipped cream: 638 cal., 36g fat (22g sat. fat), 102mg chol., 710mg sod., 72g carb. (33g sugars, 4g fiber), 9g pro.

SECRETS TO TENDER SHORTCAKE

KEEP IT COLD
Make sure the butter is cold and cut it into the dry ingredients until it's about pea size; as it melts during baking, small air pockets are created, giving the biscuits their flakiness.

GOLDEN BROWN GOODNESS
Brushing the biscuit tops with cream helps the sugar stay in place. It also gives the biscuit crust a rich, golden brown color when they're baked.

BUMP UP THE BISCUIT
If you like, stir a little grated lemon zest, grated orange zest or a bit of ground cardamom into the biscuit mixture. Add a pinch of cinnamon and nutmeg to the sugar on top.

WHIP SMART
It's important the heavy cream is cold when you mix it—you'll get more volume. Start out on low speed and be patient. You can make the whipped cream up to 2 hours ahead, then gently stir to reincorporate when you're ready to serve.

TENNESSEE PEACH PUDDING

DATE PUDDING COBBLER

There were eight children in my family when I was a girl, and all of us enjoyed this cobbler. I now serve it for everyday and special occasions alike.
—Carolyn Miller, Guys Mills, PA

PREP: 15 MIN. • **BAKE:** 25 MIN.
MAKES: 8 SERVINGS

- 1 cup all-purpose flour
- 1½ cups packed brown sugar, divided
- 2 tsp. baking powder
- 1 Tbsp. cold butter
- ½ cup 2% milk
- ¾ cup chopped dates
- ¾ cup chopped walnuts
- 1 cup water
  Optional: Whipped cream and ground cinnamon

1. Preheat oven to 350°. In a large bowl, combine the flour, ½ cup brown sugar and the baking powder. Cut in butter until crumbly. Gradually add milk, dates and walnuts.
2. In a large saucepan, combine water and the remaining 1 cup brown sugar; bring to a boil. Remove from the heat; add the date mixture and mix well.
3. Transfer to a greased 10-in. cast-iron skillet or 8-in. square baking pan. Bake for 25-30 minutes or until the top is golden brown and the fruit is tender. Serve warm, with whipped cream and cinnamon if desired.
1 serving: 347 cal., 9g fat (2g sat. fat), 5mg chol., 150mg sod., 65g carb. (50g sugars, 2g fiber), 4g pro.

TENNESSEE PEACH PUDDING

This out-of-this-world dish is one of our favorite, easy peach recipes. I was raised in Oklahoma, and we used Elberta peaches right off our trees when we made this outstanding cobbler.
—Virginia Crowell, Lyons, OR

PREP: 20 MIN. • **BAKE:** 40 MIN.
MAKES: 8 SERVINGS

- 1 cup all-purpose flour
- ½ cup sugar
- 2 tsp. baking powder
- ½ tsp. salt
- ½ tsp. ground cinnamon, optional
- ½ cup 2% milk
- 3 cups sliced peeled fresh or frozen peaches

TOPPING
- 1½ cups water
- ½ cup sugar
- ½ cup packed brown sugar
- 1 Tbsp. butter
- ¼ tsp. ground nutmeg
  Vanilla ice cream, optional

1. Preheat oven to 400°. Combine the flour, sugar, baking powder, salt and, if desired, cinnamon. Stir in milk just until combined; fold in peaches. Spread into a greased 8-in. square baking dish.
2. For topping, combine water, sugars, butter and nutmeg in a large saucepan. Bring to a boil, stirring until sugars are dissolved. Pour over peach mixture.
3. Bake until the filling is bubbly and a toothpick inserted in topping comes out clean, 40-50 minutes. Serve warm or cold with ice cream, if desired.
1 serving: 253 cal., 2g fat (1g sat. fat), 5mg chol., 269mg sod., 57g carb. (44g sugars, 1g fiber), 3g pro.
Plum Cobbler: Substitute sliced plums for the peaches.

BERRY BLISS COBBLER

A little bit sweet, a little bit tart and topped off with golden sugar-kissed biscuits, this cobbler is summer perfection.
—*Taste of Home* Test Kitchen

PREP: 10 MIN. + STANDING • **BAKE:** 20 MIN.
MAKES: 6 SERVINGS

  3   cups fresh strawberries, halved
1½   cups fresh raspberries
1½   cups fresh blueberries
⅔   cup plus 1 Tbsp. sugar, divided
  3   Tbsp. quick-cooking tapioca
  1   cup all-purpose flour
  2   tsp. baking powder
¼   tsp. salt
¼   cup cold butter, cubed
  1   large egg, room temperature
¼   cup plus 2 Tbsp. 2% milk
      Coarse sugar

1. Preheat oven to 400°. Toss the strawberries, raspberries and blueberries with ⅔ cup sugar and the tapioca. Transfer to a greased 10-in. cast-iron or other ovenproof skillet; let stand for 20 minutes.
2. Meanwhile, whisk flour, the remaining 1 Tbsp. sugar, baking powder and salt.

Cut in butter until mixture resembles coarse crumbs. In another bowl, whisk together egg and milk; stir into the crumb mixture just until moistened. Drop by tablespoonfuls onto fruit. Sprinkle with coarse sugar.
3. Bake, uncovered, until the filling is bubbly and the topping is golden brown, 20-25 minutes. Serve warm.
1 serving: 335 cal., 9g fat (5g sat. fat), 52mg chol., 298mg sod., 60g carb. (34g sugars, 5g fiber), 5g pro.

CRAN-APPLE CRUMBLE

A toasted almond streusel topping makes this fruity dessert extra delicious. We think it's wonderful for the holidays.
—Billie Moss, Walnut Creek, CA

PREP: 40 MIN. + STANDING • **BAKE:** 15 MIN.
MAKES: 15 SERVINGS

  1   cup orange juice
  1   cup sugar, divided
  4   tsp. grated orange zest
  1   pkg. (12 oz.) fresh or frozen cranberries, thawed
  2   Tbsp. butter
  2   Tbsp. maple syrup
  2   Tbsp. honey
  5   medium tart apples, peeled and cut into ½-in. slices
  2   Tbsp. quick-cooking tapioca
TOPPING
1½   cups all-purpose flour
¾   cup packed brown sugar
1½   tsp. ground cinnamon
½   tsp. ground nutmeg
½   cup cold butter, cubed
  3   Tbsp. almond paste
  1   cup slivered almonds, toasted

1. Preheat oven to 400°. In a saucepan, combine orange juice, ¾ cup sugar and the orange zest; mix well. Bring to a boil. Reduce heat; simmer, uncovered, for 5 minutes, stirring occasionally. Add cranberries; simmer, uncovered, for 8-10 minutes or until the berries begin to pop. Remove from heat.
2. Melt butter in a large saucepan. Stir in syrup, honey and the remaining ¼ cup sugar. Add apples; cook over medium heat for 5 minutes. Remove from heat; stir in cranberry mixture. Sprinkle with tapioca; mix gently. Let stand 15 minutes. Transfer to a greased 13x9-in. baking dish.
3. For topping, combine the flour, brown sugar, cinnamon and nutmeg in a bowl; cut in butter and almond paste until mixture resembles coarse crumbs. Sprinkle crumb mixture and almonds over cranberry mixture (dish will be full). Bake for 15-20 minutes or until bubbly around the edges.
1 serving: 322 cal., 12g fat (5g sat. fat), 20mg chol., 83mg sod., 52g carb. (36g sugars, 3g fiber), 3g pro.

APPLE DUMPLINGS
WITH SAUCE

These warm and comforting apple dumplings are incredible by themselves or served with ice cream. You can decorate each dumpling by cutting out 1-inch leaves and a ½-inch stem from the leftover dough.
—Robin Lendon, Cincinnati, OH

PREP: 1 HOUR + CHILLING • **BAKE:** 50 MIN.
MAKES: 8 SERVINGS

- 3   cups all-purpose flour
- 1   tsp. salt
- 1   cup shortening
- ⅓   cup cold water
- 8   medium tart apples, peeled and cored
- 8   tsp. butter
- 9   tsp. cinnamon sugar, divided

SAUCE
- 1½   cups packed brown sugar
- 1   cup water
- ½   cup butter, cubed

1. In a large bowl, combine flour and salt; cut in shortening until crumbly. Gradually add water, tossing with a fork until dough forms a ball. Divide into 8 portions. Cover and refrigerate at least 30 minutes or until easy to handle.
2. Preheat oven to 350°. Roll each portion of dough between 2 lightly floured sheets of waxed paper into a 7-in. square. Place an apple on each square of dough. Place 1 tsp. butter and 1 tsp. cinnamon sugar in the center of each apple.
3. Gently bring up corners of pastry to each center, trimming any excess; pinch edges to seal. If desired, cut out apple leaves and stems from dough scraps; attach to dumplings with water. Place in a greased 13x9-in. baking dish. Sprinkle with the remaining cinnamon sugar.
4. In a large saucepan, combine sauce ingredients. Bring just to a boil, stirring until blended. Pour over apples.
5. Bake until apples are tender and pastry is golden brown, 50-55 minutes, basting occasionally with the sauce. Serve warm.

1 dumpling: 764 cal., 40g fat (16g sat. fat), 41mg chol., 429mg sod., 97g carb. (59g sugars, 3g fiber), 5g pro.

. . . .
DID YOU KNOW?
Apple dumplings have been traced back to 18th century England and Bavaria. These days, they're most associated with areas with strong Amish influence, especially Pennsylvania, where apple dumplings can be served as a breakfast dish or a dessert.

CLASSIC BLUEBERRY
BUCKLE

CLASSIC BLUEBERRY BUCKLE

This blueberry buckle recipe came from my grandmother. As children, my sister and I remember going to Pennsylvania for blueberry picking. Mother taught us to pick only perfect berries, and those gems went into this wonderful recipe.
—Carol Dolan, Mount Laurel, NJ

PREP: 20 MIN. • **BAKE:** 30 MIN. + COOLING
MAKES: 9 SERVINGS

- ¼ cup butter, softened
- ¾ cup sugar
- 1 large egg, room temperature
- 2 cups all-purpose flour
- 2 tsp. baking powder
- ¼ tsp. salt
- ½ cup 2% milk
- 2 cups fresh blueberries

TOPPING

- ⅔ cup sugar
- ½ cup all-purpose flour
- ½ tsp. ground cinnamon
- ⅓ cup cold butter, cubed
   Whipped cream, optional

1. Preheat oven to 375°. In a small bowl, cream butter and sugar until light and fluffy, 5-7 minutes. Add egg; beat well. In another bowl, combine flour, baking powder and salt; add to the creamed mixture alternately with milk, beating well after each addition. Fold in the blueberries. Spread into a greased 9-in. square baking pan.
2. For topping, in a small bowl, combine the sugar, flour and cinnamon; cut in butter until crumbly. Sprinkle over the blueberry mixture.
3. Bake until a toothpick inserted in the center comes out clean, 40-45 minutes. Cool on a wire rack. If desired, serve with whipped cream and additional blueberries.
1 piece: 390 cal., 13g fat (8g sat. fat), 54mg chol., 282mg sod., 64g carb. (36g sugars, 2g fiber), 5g pro.

CINNAMON-SUGAR PEACH KUCHEN

My comforting cinnamon peach kuchen showcases fresh summer fruit. You can use other stone fruits, too, such as plums or nectarines. This is one of those homey desserts that is perfect with a scoop of ice cream on top!
—Mary Bilyeu, Ann Arbor, MI

PREP: 25 MIN. • **BAKE:** 40 MIN. + COOLING
MAKES: 15 SERVINGS

- 1   cup butter, softened
- 1   cup plus 3 Tbsp. sugar, divided
- 4   large eggs, room temperature
- 2   tsp. vanilla extract
- ½   tsp. almond extract
- 2   cups all-purpose flour
- 2   tsp. baking powder
- 1   tsp. salt
- ¼   cup chopped crystallized ginger
- 4   to 5 medium peaches, sliced
- ½   tsp. ground cinnamon

1. Preheat oven to 350°. In a large mixing bowl, cream butter and 1 cup sugar until light and fluffy, 5-7 minutes. Add eggs, 1 at a time, beating well after each addition. Stir in extracts. Combine the flour, baking powder and salt; gradually add to the creamed mixture. Fold in ginger.
2. Transfer to a greased 13x9-in. baking dish. Arrange peaches over batter. Combine cinnamon and the remaining 3 Tbsp. sugar; sprinkle over top.
3. Bake for 40-45 minutes or until a toothpick inserted near the center comes out clean. Cool on a wire rack for 10 minutes before cutting. Serve warm.
1 piece: 273 cal., 14g fat (8g sat. fat), 89mg chol., 318mg sod., 35g carb. (20g sugars, 1g fiber), 4g pro.

SKILLET CARAMEL APRICOT GRUNT

Here's an old-fashioned pantry dessert made with items you can easily keep on hand. Mix up a second batch of the dry ingredients for the dumplings to save a few minutes the next time you prepare it.
—Shannon Norris, Cudahy, WI

PREP: 20 MIN. + STANDING • **BAKE:** 20 MIN.
MAKES: 8 SERVINGS

- 2   cans (15¼ oz. each) apricot halves, undrained
- 2   tsp. quick-cooking tapioca
- ⅓   cup packed brown sugar
- 1   Tbsp. butter
- 1   Tbsp. lemon juice
- DUMPLINGS
- 1½ cups all-purpose flour
- ½   cup sugar
- 2   tsp. baking powder
- 2   Tbsp. cold butter
- ½   cup 2% milk
- TOPPING
- ¼   cup packed brown sugar
- 1   Tbsp. water
     Half-and-half cream, optional

1. Preheat oven to 425°. In a large saucepan, combine the apricots and tapioca; let stand for 15 minutes. Add the brown sugar, butter and lemon juice. Cook and stir until the mixture comes to a full boil. Reduce heat to low; keep warm.
2. For dumplings, in a large bowl, combine the flour, sugar and baking powder; cut in butter until crumbly. Add milk; mix just until combined. Pour warm fruit mixture into an ungreased 9- or 10-in. cast-iron skillet. Drop the batter in 6 mounds onto fruit mixture.
3. Bake, uncovered, until a toothpick inserted into a dumpling comes out clean, about 15 minutes.
4. For topping, stir together brown sugar and water; microwave until the sugar is dissolved, stirring frequently, about 30 seconds. Spoon topping over dumplings; bake 5 minutes longer. Serve with cream if desired.
1 serving: 336 cal., 5g fat (3g sat. fat), 13mg chol., 170mg sod., 71g carb. (51g sugars, 2g fiber), 4g pro.

PECAN PIE COBBLER

I couldn't find a recipe, so I took it upon myself to devise this amazing dessert that combines the ease of a cobbler and the rich taste of pecan pie. It tastes even better with ice cream or whipped topping.
—Willa Kelley, Edmond, OK

PREP: 20 MIN • **BAKE:** 30 MIN. + COOLING
MAKES: 12 SERVINGS

- ½ cup butter, cubed
- 1 cup plus 2 Tbsp. all-purpose flour
- ¾ cup sugar
- 3 tsp. baking powder
- ¼ tsp. salt
- ⅔ cup 2% milk
- 1 tsp. vanilla extract
- 1½ cups coarsely chopped pecans
- 1 cup packed brown sugar
- ¾ cup brickle toffee bits
- 1½ cups boiling water
  Vanilla ice cream, optional

1. Preheat oven to 350°. Place butter in a 13x9-in. baking pan; heat pan in oven 3-5 minutes or until butter is melted. Meanwhile, combine the flour, sugar, baking powder and salt. Stir in milk and vanilla until combined.
2. Remove pan from oven; add batter. Sprinkle with pecans, brown sugar and toffee bits. Slowly pour boiling water over top (do not stir). Bake, uncovered, until golden brown, 30-35 minutes. Cool on wire rack for 30 minutes (cobbler will thicken upon cooling). Serve warm, with ice cream if desired.
1 serving: 411 cal., 23g fat (8g sat. fat), 26mg chol., 327mg sod., 51g carb. (41g sugars, 2g fiber), 3g pro.

PLUM GOOD CRISP

PLUM GOOD CRISP

This is a great crisp that goes well with any meal, but you can also serve it as a breakfast treat or snack. When it's warm, it can't be beat!
—Peter Halferty, Corpus Christi, TX

PREP: 20 MIN. • **BAKE:** 30 MIN. + STANDING
MAKES: 8 SERVINGS

- 4 cups sliced fresh plums (about 1½ lbs.)
- 3 medium nectarines, sliced
- 1½ cups fresh blueberries
- 3 Tbsp. brown sugar
- 2 Tbsp. cornstarch
- ¼ tsp. ground ginger
- ⅛ tsp. ground nutmeg
- ¼ cup maple syrup
- 2 Tbsp. lemon juice

TOPPING
- ½ cup old-fashioned oats
- ½ cup all-purpose flour
- ¼ cup packed brown sugar
- ¼ tsp. salt
- 4 tsp. unsweetened apple juice
- 4 tsp. canola oil
- 1½ tsp. butter, melted

1. Preheat oven to 400°. Place fruit in a large bowl. Mix brown sugar, cornstarch, spices, syrup and lemon juice; toss with fruit. Transfer fruit mixture to an 11x7-in. baking dish coated with cooking spray.
2. For topping, mix oats, flour, brown sugar and salt; stir in the remaining ingredients until crumbly. Sprinkle over the fruit.
3. Bake, uncovered, until the filling is bubbly and topping is golden brown, about 30 minutes. Let stand 15 minutes before serving.
¾ cup: 233 cal., 4g fat (1g sat. fat), 2mg chol., 85mg sod., 49g carb. (33g sugars, 3g fiber), 3g pro.

MAMA'S BLACKBERRY COBBLER

Alabama has some tasty fresh blackberries. Fifty years ago my mama was going to pick blackberries to make a cobbler, but she went to the hospital to have me instead! This is her mama's recipe.

—Lisa Allen, Joppa, AL

PREP: 15 MIN. • **BAKE:** 45 MIN
MAKES: 6 SERVINGS

- ½ cup plus 2 Tbsp. melted butter, divided
- 1 cup self-rising flour
- 1½ cups sugar, divided
- 1 cup 2% milk
- ½ tsp. vanilla extract
- 3 cups fresh blackberries or frozen unsweetened blackberries

1. Preheat oven to 350°. Pour ½ cup melted butter into an 8-in. square baking dish. In a small bowl, combine flour, 1 cup sugar, milk and vanilla until blended; pour into prepared dish.
2. In another bowl, combine the blackberries, remaining ½ cup sugar and remaining 2 Tbsp. melted butter; toss until combined. Spoon over batter.
3. Bake until topping is golden brown and fruit is tender, 45-50 minutes. Serve warm.

¾ cup: 491 cal., 21g fat (13g sat. fat), 54mg chol., 421mg sod., 75g carb. (56g sugars, 4g fiber), 5g pro.

NOTE: Be sure to disperse the berry mixture evenly and all the way to the edges of the dish.

MAMA'S
BLACKBERRY
COBBLER

APPLE ROLY-POLY

This apple dessert isn't very fancy, but it's genuine regional fare. It came from my grandmother. With 13 children plus the men at Grandpa's sawmill, she had to do lots of cooking each day!
—Megan Newcombe, Cookstown, ON

PREP: 25 MIN. • **BAKE:** 30 MIN.
MAKES: 12 SERVINGS

1¾ cups all-purpose flour
¼ cup sugar
4 tsp. baking powder
½ tsp. salt
¼ cup shortening
¼ cup cold butter
⅔ cup sour cream
FILLING
¼ cup butter, softened
1 cup packed brown sugar
2 tsp. ground cinnamon
6 medium Granny Smith apples, peeled and coarsely shredded (about 5 cups)
TOPPING
2½ cups water
2 Tbsp. brown sugar
1 tsp. ground cinnamon
½ cup half-and-half cream

1. Preheat oven to 350°. In a bowl, combine flour, sugar, baking powder and salt. Cut in shortening and butter until crumbly. Add sour cream and blend until a ball forms.
2. Roll out on a floured surface into a 15x10-in. rectangle. Spread dough with softened butter; sprinkle with remaining filling ingredients.
3. Roll up rectangle, jelly-roll style, starting with a long side. Cut into 12 slices. Place slices, cut side down, in a 13x9-in. baking pan.
4. For topping, combine water, brown sugar and cinnamon in a saucepan. Bring to a boil; remove from the heat. Stir in the cream.

5. Carefully pour the hot topping over the dumplings. Bake, uncovered, for 35 minutes or until bubbly. (Center will jiggle when dumplings are hot out of the oven but will set as dumplings stand for a few minutes.) Serve warm.
1 serving: 336 cal., 15g fat (8g sat. fat), 34mg chol., 329mg sod., 48g carb. (32g sugars, 2g fiber), 3g pro.

TEST KITCHEN TIP

This recipe may seem to have a lot of liquid when it goes in the oven, but don't worry—as it bakes, the dumplings will puff up and the liquid will thicken. It's like an apple dumpling that creates its own sauce during baking!

BAKING 101

RHUBARB CRISP

I found this recipe on a box of Quaker Oats about 20 years ago. It's quicker and easier to make than pie. It's versatile, too, because you can add strawberries in spring or apples in fall. I usually pop it into the oven shortly before we sit down to eat so we can enjoy it warm for dessert!
—C.E. Adams, Charlestown, NH

PREP: 15 MIN. • **BAKE:** 45 MIN.
MAKES: 8 SERVINGS

- ¾ cup sugar
- 3 Tbsp. cornstarch
- 3 cups sliced fresh rhubarb or frozen rhubarb, thawed
- 2 cups sliced peeled apples or sliced strawberries
- 1 cup quick-cooking or old-fashioned oats
- ½ cup packed brown sugar
- ½ cup butter, melted
- ⅓ cup all-purpose flour
- 1 tsp. ground cinnamon
  Vanilla ice cream, optional

1. Preheat oven to 350°. In a large bowl, combine sugar and cornstarch. Add rhubarb and apples or strawberries; toss to coat. Spoon into an 8-in. cast-iron or other ovenproof skillet.
2. In a small bowl, combine the oats, brown sugar, butter, flour and cinnamon until the mixture resembles coarse crumbs. Sprinkle over fruit. Bake until crisp is bubbly and fruit is tender, about 45 minutes. If desired, serve warm with ice cream.

1 cup: 320 cal., 12g fat (7g sat. fat), 31mg chol., 124mg sod., 52g carb. (36g sugars, 3g fiber), 3g pro.

LEMON RASPBERRY BUCKLE

I've given a fresh summery twist to the classic blueberry buckle everyone loves by swapping out the blueberries for raspberries (my favorite) and adding sweet and tart lemon curd. This berry buckle cake recipe tastes great with vanilla ice cream!
—Jenna Fleming, Lowville, NY

PREP: 30 MIN. • **BAKE:** 45 MIN.
MAKES: 15 SERVINGS

- ½ cup butter, softened
- 1 cup sugar
- 2 large eggs plus 1 large egg yolk, room temperature
- 1 tsp. vanilla extract
- 1½ cups all-purpose flour
- 1½ tsp. baking powder
- ¼ tsp. salt
- ⅔ cup buttermilk
- 4 cups fresh raspberries
- ¼ cup sugar
- 1 jar (10 oz.) lemon curd

TOPPING

- ½ cup sugar
- ½ cup all-purpose flour
- ¼ cup butter, melted
- ½ tsp. ground cinnamon
  Whipped cream, optional

1. Preheat oven to 350°. In a large bowl, cream butter and sugar until light and fluffy, 5-7 minutes. Add eggs and egg yolk, 1 at a time, beating well after each addition. Beat in vanilla. In another bowl, whisk flour, baking powder and salt; add to creamed mixture alternately with buttermilk, beating well after each addition. Transfer to greased 13x9-in. baking dish.
2. Combine raspberries and sugar; sprinkle over batter. Drop lemon curd by tablespoonfuls over raspberries.
3. Combine topping ingredients; sprinkle over batter. Bake until fruit is bubbly and a toothpick inserted into the cake comes out clean, 45-50 minutes. Let stand 20 minutes before serving. If desired, serve with whipped cream and more fresh raspberries.

1 piece: 335 cal., 12g fat (7g sat. fat), 76mg chol., 206mg sod., 54g carb. (38g sugars, 3g fiber), 4g pro.

BAKING 101

DUTCH OVEN APPLE COBBLER

BLACKBERRY-MANGO CRUMBLE

My husband loves fresh blackberries at the height of summer, and mango is a favorite combination with the berries in this crumble. A little lime adds just enough zing to balance the sweetness of the filling.
—Patricia Quinn, Omaha, NE

PREP: 20 MIN. • **BAKE:** 35 MIN.
MAKES: 8 SERVINGS

- 4 cups cubed peeled mangoes (about 4 medium)
- 4 cups fresh blackberries
- 1 Tbsp. lime juice
- ½ cup sugar
- ¼ cup cornstarch
- ¼ tsp. salt

TOPPING
- ½ cup quick-cooking oats
- ¼ cup macadamia nuts, chopped
- ¼ cup packed brown sugar
- 2 Tbsp. sweetened shredded coconut
- 2 Tbsp. all-purpose flour
- 1 Tbsp. grated lime zest
   Dash salt
- ¼ cup cold butter, cubed

1. Preheat oven to 375°. In a large bowl, toss mangoes and blackberries with lime juice. In a small bowl, mix sugar, cornstarch and salt; add to fruit and toss to coat. Transfer to a greased 11x7-in. baking dish.
2. In a small bowl, mix the first 7 topping ingredients; cut in butter until crumbly. Sprinkle over fruit. Bake until filling is bubbly and topping is golden brown, 35-40 minutes. Serve warm.
1 serving: 285 cal., 10g fat (5g sat. fat), 15mg chol., 161mg sod., 49g carb. (35g sugars, 6g fiber), 3g pro

DUTCH OVEN APPLE COBBLER

This homey dessert is always a big hit with my family. We like to serve it with ice cream or whipped cream.
—Cindy Jajuga, Weed, CA

PREP: 20 MIN. • **BAKE:** 45 MIN.
MAKES: 8 SERVINGS

- 8 large tart apples, peeled and sliced
- 1 cup sugar, divided
- ¾ tsp. ground cinnamon, divided
- 2 cups all-purpose flour
- ¾ cup packed brown sugar
- 1 tsp. baking powder
- ½ tsp. salt
- 2 large eggs, room temperature, lightly beaten
- ⅔ cup butter, melted
   Vanilla ice cream, optional

1. Preheat oven to 350°. In a 6-qt. Dutch oven, combine apples, ¾ cup sugar and ½ tsp. cinnamon.
2. In a bowl, whisk flour, brown sugar, remaining ¼ cup sugar, baking powder, salt and remaining ¼ tsp. cinnamon; stir in eggs (mixture will be lumpy). Spoon over apples. Drizzle butter over batter (do not stir).
3. Cover and bake until lightly browned and apples are tender, 45-50 minutes. Serve warm with ice cream, if desired.
1 serving: 531 cal., 17g fat (10g sat. fat), 87mg chol., 354mg sod., 93g carb. (64g sugars, 3g fiber), 5g pro.

CAKES

Nothing turns an ordinary day into a special occasion—
or a special celebration into an unforgettable event—like cake.
For after-school snacking and late-night indulgences,
potlucks and office parties, birthdays and holidays,
there's a cake that's perfect for the moment.

· ·

TYPES OF CAKE

There are seemingly endless variations on cake, but most cake recipes fall into one of two major categories: shortened and foam. Most shortened cakes begin by creaming butter or shortening with sugar to make a smooth batter. This traps air, which then expands during baking and helps the cake to rise. Some shortened cakes use oil and have no creaming step, resulting in a cake that is more moist and dense.

Foam cakes (such as angel food or chiffon cakes) contain a higher proportion of eggs or egg whites to flour, and have a light, fluffy texture thanks to beaten eggs.

TIPS FOR SHORTENED CAKES

- Arrange oven racks so the cake will bake in the center of the oven.

- Bring all fat and dairy, including butter and eggs, to room temperature before you mix them for batter. If an ingredient is too cold, the batter may curdle as the butter seizes. To fix curdled batter, add 1-2 tablespoons of flour and stir in just until the batter is emulsified again.

- When creaming, use a mixer to beat softened butter or shortening together with the sugar until it's a light and fluffy consistency, about 5-7 minutes.

- Mix dry ingredients together with a whisk or sift them together to evenly distribute the leavener throughout the flour.

- Scrape the batter down the sides of the bowl occasionally (after first turning off the mixer!).

- Use the pan size recommended in the recipe. If substituting, be sure you use a mathematical equivalent (see p. 439)

- Fill pans halfway to three-quarters full. Thinner batters rise higher than thicker ones and should only fill the pan halfway.

- Pour thinner batters into pans, then tap pans on the counter to remove air bubbles. Spoon firmer batters into pans and spread gently with a spatula to even them out.

- Leave at least 1 inch of space between each pan and the sides of the oven to allow good heat circulation. If using two oven racks, stagger pans rather than placing one directly above another. Switch pan positions and rotate pans from front to back halfway through baking.

- Unless the recipe directs otherwise, cool cakes in pans on wire racks for at least 10 minutes before removing them from the pan, and let the cake cool completely before filling or frosting.

- If a cake sticks to the pan and will not come out when the pan is inverted, return it to a heated oven for 1 minute longer and try again.

TIPS FOR FOAM CAKES

- Set the oven rack in the lowest position in the oven; preheat for 10-15 minutes.

- Eggs are easier to separate when they are cold, but egg whites obtain a better volume when they are at room temperature. After separating eggs, let the egg whites stand at room temperature for 30 minutes before beating.

- Specks of egg yolk, oil or grease will interfere with the whites reaching their maximum volume. Beaters and metal or glass bowls should be clean and dry. Plastic bowls, even freshly washed, may have an oily film that will prevent stiff peaks from forming.

- Do not grease or flour tube pans for foam cakes.

- To avoid large air pockets in the cake, cut through the batter with a knife after pouring batter in the pan.

- Do not cover the hole in the center of a tube cake pan; the hot air must circulate through the center for the cake to bake evenly.

- Foam cakes in tube pans need to cool upside down or they will collapse. If using a pan with legs, invert the pan onto the legs. If the pan does not have legs, invert the pan and place the neck over a funnel or narrow bottle.

- Cool tube cakes completely, for about an hour, before removing from the pan.

ABOUT COFFEE CAKES

Cakelike coffee cakes can be made in anything from a tube pan to a skillet. Coffee cakes also can stray outside the realm of cake, and be made with yeast or as quick breads. See p. 408 for a variety of coffee cake recipes.

HOW TO TEST DONENESS

Different kinds of cake require different methods of testing for doneness. These tips will ensure your treats turn out perfect every time.

The toothpick test is the go-to method for testing doneness in most shortened cakes, from layer cakes to cupcakes. A toothpick or wooden skewer works well; special metal testers are also available. In a pinch, you can use a strand of uncooked spaghetti.

Insert a toothpick near the center of the cake. If the tester comes out with crumbs or wet batter, the cake needs more time to bake. If the tester comes out clean, your cake is ready to pull from the oven. If in doubt, check the cake's edges. The batter will begin to pull away from the pan as it finishes baking. The cake will continue to bake for a short time after it is removed from the oven.

To test a foam cake (chiffon or angel food), press gently on the top of the cake with your finger. When the cake springs back, it's done. If the indentation remains, give the cake a few more minutes of baking time. The top of the cake should feel dry to the touch, especially around any cracked areas.

TOOTHPICK TEST

TOUCH TEST

A SIMPLE (SYRUP) TRICK TO MOIST CAKES

Gently brushing simple syrup over your cake layers with a pastry brush adds the perfect amount of extra moisture and gives a touch of added sweetness. It's also a helpful remedy if you overbaked your cake, because the simple syrup puts moisture back in.

Some bakers brush flavored syrups on their cakes. For example, you could brush cherry simple syrup on a chocolate cake for a subtle burst of flavor.

Use only a few tablespoons of liquid per layer—don't go too heavy or your cake will get soggy. Allow the liquid to soak in, and then add your frosting.

To make a basic, plain simple syrup, stir together equal parts water and sugar in a small saucepan, then bring to a boil over medium heat. Reduce the heat and let the mixture simmer, stirring occasionally, until the sugar is completely dissolved and the syrup is clear. This will take about 5 minutes. Turn off the heat, cover the pan and allow the syrup to cool.

To store simple syrup, pour it into a lidded glass container and keep it in the refrigerator. Basic unflavored simple syrup will last about 3-4 weeks.

GREASING CAKE PANS

Unless instructed otherwise (or if you're making a foam cake), you should grease and flour your cake pan. Prepare the pans before you mix your ingredients so the batter doesn't sit before baking. If the batter sits for long, it will lose air.

Use butter, shortening or a cooking spray. If you're using butter or shortening, use a piece of parchment or paper towel to spread the grease generously over the entire inside of the pan.

Add a spoonful of flour. Working over your sink, tilt the pan back and forth to distribute the flour over the greased areas of the pan. Turn the pan upside down and gently tap the bottom to shake out any excess.

If you're making a chocolate cake, you can use cocoa powder to dust your pan—it adds even more chocolate to your cake, and matches the color nicely.

Lining your greased and floured pan with parchment ensures your cake will never stick. If you don't have precut rounds, make your own. Cut a piece of parchment longer than the pan is wide. Fold it in half, then in half again. Fold into a triangle, keeping the folded sides together. Fold into another triangle, again with the folded sides together. Set the point at the center of your pan; make a crease where it reaches the edge. Trim at the crease, and when you unfold the paper, the circle will be the size of the pan. (Be sure to grease and flour the parchment as well after adding it to the pan.)

For fluted tube pans, use shortening; milk solids in butter can cling to the nooks and crannies of the pan, making it harder for the cake to come out. After adding the flour, take a close look—if you see any bare spots where the pan is showing, add more shortening to those spots, and then add more flour. You can also use a cooking spray formulated with flour.

Do not grease or flour tube pans for foam cakes. To rise properly, the light batter for a chiffon or angel food cake needs to cling to the sides of the pan.

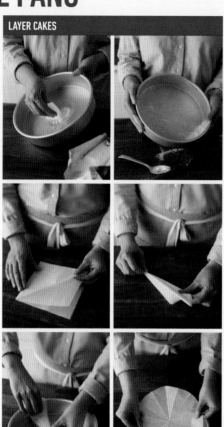

LAYER CAKES

TUBE CAKES

FROSTINGS

Most cake recipes come with a recommended frosting as part of the instructions. However, you can mix and match as you please if you prefer different flavors or kinds of frostings. See p. 426 for recipes and frosting techniques.

• •

TIPS FOR CUTTING CAKE

Use a serrated knife: It seems like a straight blade would be cleaner, but a serrated blade cuts through cake more easily. A thin blade, like a tomato knife, is best, but a serrated bread knife also works. Use a gentle sawing motion to cut.

Chill the cake for 10-15 minutes: Cooling the cake and frosting makes both sturdier and less likely to squish, tear or crumble.

Use a hot, clean knife for every slice: Before your first cut, run the knife under hot water and dry it thoroughly. After every slice, wipe the knife clean, and then run it under hot water and dry it again. It takes a little extra time, but a warm knife will cut more cleanly.

Mark the center: If you're cutting a round cake, it's easy to end up with uneven slices. Before you cut, take a piece of fishing line or plain dental floss and mark a line down the middle the cake. Rotate 90° and mark the midway line again. The "X" marks the center of the cake—the tip of each slice should end at this spot. The lines also lay out a template of four quarters, which makes it easy to calculate how large to cut slices to serve your guests. In general, slices should be about 1 or 1½ in. wide.

HOW MANY PIECES OF CAKE?

PAN SHAPE	PAN SIZE	SERVINGS
ROUND	8 in.	12
ROUND	9 in	12-16
ROUND	10 in	24
SQUARE	8- or 9-in.	9
SHEET	9x13-in.	15
SHEET	10x15-in.	24

STORING CAKES

Cakes are best eaten within a week and stored in a cake keeper or cake dome. If the frosting is heat-sensitive (think cream cheese frosting or whipped cream), keep the cake in the fridge.

You can freeze cakes as well, although it's safest to freeze them before they're frosted, as some frostings freeze better than others.

To freeze unfrosted cakes, place individual layers on a baking sheet and place in the freezer. Once they're frozen, wrap them tightly in plastic wrap or seal them in an airtight bag or container. Freeze unfrosted shortened cakes for up to 4 months. If you're freezing a frosted cake, consider cutting it into slices and freezing them individually; frosted shortened cakes can be frozen for up to 2 months. Freeze foam cakes in their pan or in plastic bags for up to 2 months. Thaw all types of cakes in the refrigerator.

BAKING CAKES AT HIGH ALTITUDE

Conditions at high altitudes (over 3,000 feet) affect baked goods. The lower air pressure allows the gases created by leavening agents to expand more quickly and causes liquids to evaporate and boil at lower temperatures. The drier air dries out the flour.

For cakes, this means that there might be excessive rising, which could result in a coarse texture or cause the cake to fall before its structure is set by baking. Faster evaporation of the liquid (due to a lower boiling point) could reduce the amount of liquid and increase the concentration of sugar—which also may weaken the structure of the cake.

To compensate, increase the oven temperature by 15-25° to allow the cake to set faster and prevent falling. Fill pans halfway, not two-thirds full, since the cakes will rise higher. And reduce the leavener and sugar and increase the liquid. Here are some general guidelines for adjusting ingredients for shortened cakes.

ADJUSTMENT	3,000 FT.	5,000 FT.	7,000 FT.
FOR EACH TEASPOON OF BAKING POWDER, REDUCE BY:	⅛ tsp.	⅛ to ¼ tsp.	¼ tsp.
FOR EACH CUP OF SUGAR, REDUCE BY:	0 to 1 Tbsp.	0 to 2 Tbsp.	1 to 3 Tbsp.
FOR EACH CUP OF LIQUID, INCREASE BY:	1 to 2 Tbsp.	2 to 4 Tbsp.	3 to 4 Tbsp.

For foam cakes, beat the egg whites only until soft peaks form (see p. 14). To strengthen the cake's structure, decrease the sugar by 1-2 tablespoons and increase the flour or egg component a little. Increasing the oven temperature by 15-25° will also help set the cake structure sooner.

FLOUR FACTS

All-purpose flour is most commonly used in cake recipes, but there are other options. Cake flour is made with a softer, lower-gluten wheat, and it lends a more tender, delicate crumb to cakes. Self-rising flour is all-purpose flour with baking powder and salt added. It's helpful in eliminating some measuring.

LAYER CAKES

HUMMINGBIRD CAKE

This cake is my dad's favorite, so I always make it for his birthday. The beautiful, old-fashioned layered delight makes a memorable celebration dessert.
—Nancy Zimmerman, Cape May Court House, NJ

PREP: 40 MIN. • **BAKE:** 25 MIN. + COOLING
MAKES: 14 SERVINGS

- 2 cups mashed ripe bananas
- 1½ cups canola oil
- 3 large eggs, room temperature
- 1 can (8 oz.) unsweetened crushed pineapple, undrained
- 1½ tsp. vanilla extract
- 3 cups all-purpose flour
- 2 cups sugar
- 1 tsp. salt
- 1 tsp. baking soda
- 1 tsp. ground cinnamon
- 1 cup chopped walnuts

PINEAPPLE FROSTING
- ¼ cup shortening
- 2 Tbsp. butter, softened
- 1 tsp. grated lemon zest
- ¼ tsp. salt
- 6 cups confectioners' sugar
- ½ cup unsweetened pineapple juice
- 2 tsp. half-and-half cream
  Chopped walnuts, optional

1. In a large bowl, beat bananas, oil, eggs, pineapple and vanilla until well blended. In another bowl, combine the flour, sugar, salt, baking soda and cinnamon; gradually beat into banana mixture until blended. Stir in walnuts.
2. Pour into 3 greased and floured 9-in. round baking pans. Bake at 350° until a toothpick inserted in the center comes out clean, 25-30 minutes. Cool for 10 minutes before removing from pans to wire racks to cool completely.
3. For frosting, in a large bowl, beat the shortening, butter, lemon zest and salt until fluffy. Add confectioners' sugar alternately with pineapple juice. Beat in cream. Spread between layers and over top and sides of cake. Sprinkle with chopped walnuts if desired.
1 piece: 777 cal., 35g fat (6g sat. fat), 50mg chol., 333mg sod., 113g carb. (85g sugars, 2g fiber), 7g pro.

SPECIAL-OCCASION CHOCOLATE CAKE

This recipe won grand champion at the Alaska State Fair—and with one bite, you will see why! My decadent chocolate cake boasts a luscious ganache filling and fudge buttercream frosting.
—Cindi DeClue, Anchorage, AK

PREP: 40 MIN. + CHILLING
BAKE: 25 MIN. + COOLING
MAKES: 16 SERVINGS

- 1 cup baking cocoa
- 2 cups boiling water
- 1 cup butter, softened
- 2¼ cups sugar
- 4 large eggs, room temperature
- 1½ tsp. vanilla extract
- 2¾ cups all-purpose flour
- 2 tsp. baking soda
- ½ tsp. baking powder
- ½ tsp. salt

GANACHE
- 10 oz. semisweet chocolate, chopped
- 1 cup heavy whipping cream
- 2 Tbsp. sugar

FROSTING
- 1 cup butter, softened
- 4 cups confectioners' sugar
- ½ cup baking cocoa
- ¼ cup 2% milk
- 2 tsp. vanilla extract

GARNISH
- ¾ cup sliced almonds, toasted

1. Preheat oven to 350°. In a small bowl, combine cocoa and water; set aside to cool completely. In a large bowl, cream butter and sugar until light and fluffy, 5-7 minutes. Add eggs, 1 at a time, beating well after each addition. Beat in vanilla. Whisk together the flour, baking soda, baking powder and salt; add to the creamed mixture alternately with the cocoa mixture, beating well after each addition.
2. Pour batter into three greased and floured 9-in. round baking pans. Bake until a toothpick inserted in the center comes out clean, 25-30 minutes. Cool for 10 minutes before removing from pans to wire racks to cool completely.
3. For ganache, place chocolate in a bowl. In a small heavy saucepan over low heat, bring cream and sugar just to a boil. Pour over chocolate; whisk gently until smooth. Allow mixture to cool until it reaches a spreadable consistency, stirring occasionally.
4. For frosting, in a large bowl, beat butter until fluffy. Add the confectioners' sugar, cocoa, milk and vanilla extract; beat until smooth.
5. Place 1 cake layer on a serving plate; spread with 1 cup frosting. Top with the second cake layer and 1 cup of ganache; sprinkle with ½ cup almonds. Top with the third cake layer; frost top and sides of cake. Warm ganache until pourable; pour over the cake, allowing some to drape down the sides. Sprinkle with the remaining sliced almonds. Refrigerate until serving.
1 piece: 736 cal., 39g fat (22g sat. fat), 125mg chol., 454mg sod., 86g carb. (63g sugars, 3g fiber), 8g pro.

SPECIAL-OCCASION
CHOCOLATE CAKE

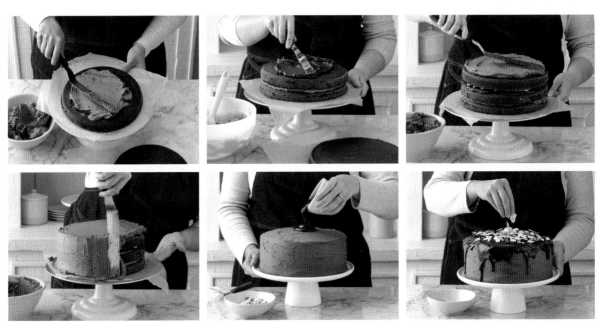

GRANDMA'S RED VELVET CAKE

No one believes it's Christmas at our house until this jolly cake appears. It's different from other red velvets I've tasted; the icing is as light as snow.

—Kathryn Davison, Charlotte, NC

PREP: 30 MIN. • **BAKE:** 20 MIN. + COOLING
MAKES: 14 SERVINGS

- ½ cup butter, softened
- 1½ cups sugar
- 2 large eggs, room temperature
- 2 bottles (1 oz. each) red food coloring
- 1 Tbsp. white vinegar
- 1 tsp. vanilla extract
- 2¼ cups cake flour
- 2 Tbsp. baking cocoa
- 1 tsp. baking soda
- 1 tsp. salt
- 1 cup buttermilk

FROSTING
- ½ cup cold water
- 1 Tbsp. cornstarch
- 2 cups butter, softened
- 2 tsp. vanilla extract
- 3½ cups confectioners' sugar

1. Preheat oven to 350°. Cream the butter and sugar until light and fluffy, 5-7 minutes. Add the eggs, 1 at a time, beating well after each addition. Beat in food coloring, vinegar and vanilla. In another bowl, whisk together the flour, cocoa, baking soda and salt; add to the creamed mixture alternately with buttermilk, beating well after each addition.

2. Pour into 2 greased and floured 9-in. round baking pans. Bake until a toothpick inserted in the center comes out clean, 20-25 minutes. Cool layers 10 minutes before removing from pans to wire racks to cool completely.

3. For frosting, combine water and cornstarch in a small saucepan over medium heat. Stir until thickened and opaque, 2-3 minutes. Cool to room temperature. Beat butter and vanilla until light and fluffy. Beat in cornstarch mixture. Gradually add confectioners' sugar; beat until light and fluffy. Spread frosting between layers and over top and sides of cake.

1 piece: 595 cal., 34g fat (21g sat. fat), 115mg chol., 564mg sod., 71g carb. (52g sugars, 1g fiber), 4g pro.

CRANBERRY CAKE WITH TANGERINE FROSTING

Sugary cranberries and candied citrus dress up to this smartly elegant cake. It's my favorite Christmas dessert for its sheer wow factor.

—Sandy Gaulitz, Spring, TX

PREP: 30 MIN. • **BAKE:** 35 MIN. + COOLING
MAKES: 16 SERVINGS

- ¼ cup butter, softened
- 2 cups sugar
- 2 tsp. vanilla extract
- 4 cups plus 2 Tbsp. cake flour, divided
- 2 Tbsp. baking powder
- 1 tsp. salt
- 2 cups 2% milk
- 4 cups fresh or frozen cranberries

FROSTING
- 2 pkg. (8 oz. each) cream cheese, softened
- ¾ cup butter, softened
- 4 cups confectioners' sugar
- 2 Tbsp. tangerine or orange juice
- ½ tsp. grated tangerine or orange zest
  Optional: Sugared cranberries, candied tangerine or orange slices and red sprinkles

1. Preheat oven to 400°. Line the bottoms of 2 greased 8-in. square or 9-in. round baking pans with parchment; grease paper. In a large bowl, beat butter and sugar until crumbly, about 2 minutes. Beat in vanilla.

2. In another bowl, mix 4 cups flour, the baking powder and salt; add to butter mixture alternately with milk, beating well after each addition. In a large bowl, toss cranberries with the remaining 2 Tbsp. flour; fold into batter.

3. Transfer to prepared pans. Bake for 35-40 minutes or until a toothpick inserted in center comes out clean. Cool for 10 minutes before removing from pans to wire racks; remove parchment. Cool completely.

4. For frosting, in a large bowl, beat cream cheese and butter until smooth. Gradually beat in the confectioners' sugar, tangerine juice and zest. Spread between cake layers and over the top and sides of cake. Refrigerate, covered, until serving. If desired, top with sugared cranberries, candied tangerines and sprinkles.

1 piece: 572 cal., 22g fat (13g sat. fat), 62mg chol., 524mg sod., 89g carb. (58g sugars, 2g fiber), 6g pro.

CHOCOLATE GINGERBREAD TOFFEE CAKE WITH GINGER WHIPPED CREAM

This cake literally stands above the rest—exactly what you want in a special-occasion dessert. With notes of ginger coming though in both the frosting and cake, it is absolutely delicious and worth the extra steps involved.
—Marie Rizzio, Interlochen, MI

PREP: 45 MIN. + CHILLING
BAKE: 30 MIN. + COOLING
MAKES: 16 SERVINGS

2   cups heavy whipping cream
5   slices fresh gingerroot
    (⅛ in. thick)
CAKE
1½ cups dark chocolate chips
½   cup butter, softened
1½ cups packed brown sugar
3   large eggs, room temperature
2   tsp. vanilla extract
2¾ cups all-purpose flour
1   tsp. baking soda
¾   tsp. ground ginger
¾   tsp. ground cinnamon
½   tsp. salt
¼   tsp. ground allspice
¼   tsp. ground nutmeg
1   cup sour cream
1   cup hot water
½   cup molasses
GANACHE
1   pkg. (10 oz.) dark chocolate chips
¼   tsp. salt
1   can (14 oz.) sweetened
    condensed milk
2   Tbsp. butter
1   tsp. vanilla extract
2   Tbsp. heavy whipping cream
6   Tbsp. confectioners' sugar
ASSEMBLY
1   cup brickle toffee bits

1. In a small heavy saucepan, heat cream and ginger until bubbles form around sides of pan. Remove from the heat; let cool slightly. Cover and refrigerate for 8 hours or overnight.
2. Preheat oven to 350°. In a microwave, melt chocolate; stir until smooth. Set aside. In a large bowl, cream butter and brown sugar until blended. Add eggs, 1 at a time, beating well after each addition. Beat in melted chocolate and the vanilla. Combine the flour, baking soda, ginger, cinnamon, salt, allspice and nutmeg; add to the creamed mixture alternately with sour cream, beating well after each addition.
3. In a small bowl, combine the hot water and molasses; beat into batter. Transfer to 3 greased and floured 8-in. round baking pans.
4. Bake until a toothpick inserted in the center comes out clean, 30-35 minutes. Cool for 10 minutes before removing cakes from pans to wire racks to cool completely.
5. Meanwhile, for ganache, place the chocolate and salt in a double boiler or metal bowl over simmering water; cook and stir until melted, 2-3 minutes.

CHOCOLATE GINGERBREAD TOFFEE CAKE WITH GINGER WHIPPED CREAM

Stir in the condensed milk until smooth. Remove from the heat; stir in butter and vanilla until butter is melted.
6. Cool, stirring occasionally, to room temperature or until the mixture reaches spreading consistency, about 45 minutes. Add cream; beat until smooth, 2-3 minutes.
7. Strain the ginger-cream mixture into a large bowl, discarding ginger slices. Beat until the cream begins to thicken. Add the 6 Tbsp. confectioners' sugar; beat until stiff peaks form.
8. To assemble, place 1 cake layer on a serving plate; spread with half the ganache. Sprinkle with half the toffee bits. Repeat layers once. Top with the remaining cake layer; spread ginger whipped cream over top and sides of cake. Refrigerate at least 2 hours. Store leftovers in the refrigerator.
1 piece: 765 cal., 42g fat (25g sat. fat), 107mg chol., 409mg sod., 96g carb. (76g sugars, 3g fiber), 9g pro.

COASTAL COCONUT CREAM CAKE

This is my son's county fair cake. He was awarded a top-10 prize and auctioned off his coconut cream creation for big bucks!
—Amy Freeze, Avon Park, FL

PREP: 45 MIN. + CHILLING
BAKE: 35 MIN. + COOLING
MAKES: 16 SERVINGS

- 1   cup butter, softened
- 2   cups sugar
- 4   large eggs, room temperature
- 1½ tsp. coconut extract
- 3   cups all-purpose flour
- 1½ tsp. baking soda
- 1½ tsp. baking powder
- 1   tsp. salt
- 1   cup canned coconut milk
- ½   cup cream of coconut
- ¼   cup sweetened shredded coconut

FILLING
- 1   cup sugar
- 6   Tbsp. cornstarch
- 1   can (20 oz.) unsweetened crushed pineapple, undrained
- 2   Tbsp. butter

FROSTING
- 3¾ cups confectioners' sugar
- 1   cup shortening
- ½   cup butter, softened
- 1½ tsp. meringue powder
- ¾   tsp. coconut extract
- ¼   tsp. salt
- 2   to 3 Tbsp. canned coconut milk
- 2   cups sweetened shredded coconut, toasted

1. Preheat oven to 350°. Line bottoms of 2 greased 9-in. round baking pans with parchment; grease paper.

2. In a large bowl, cream butter and sugar until light and fluffy, 5-7 minutes. Add eggs, 1 at a time, beating well after each addition. Beat in coconut extract. In another bowl, whisk the flour, baking soda, baking powder and salt; add to the creamed mixture alternately with coconut milk, beating well after each addition. Fold in cream of coconut and shredded coconut.

3. Transfer to prepared pans. Bake until a toothpick inserted in center comes out clean, 35-40 minutes. Cool in pans 10 minutes before removing to wire racks; remove paper. Cool completely.

4. For filling, in a large saucepan, mix sugar and cornstarch. Whisk in pineapple and butter. Cook and stir over medium heat until thickened and bubbly. Reduce heat to low; cook and stir 2 minutes longer. Remove from heat; cool completely.

5. For frosting, in a large bowl, beat confectioners' sugar, shortening, butter, meringue powder, coconut extract, salt and enough coconut milk to reach desired consistency.

6. To assemble cake, using a long serrated knife, cut each cake in half horizontally. Place 1 cake layer on a serving plate; spread with a third of the filling. Repeat twice. Top with the remaining cake layer. Frost top and sides of cake with frosting. Gently press toasted coconut into frosting on sides of cake. Refrigerate at least 4 hours before serving.

1 piece: 788 cal., 41g fat (23g sat. fat), 96mg chol., 560mg sod., 103g carb. (81g sugars, 2g fiber), 5g pro.

COASTAL COCONUT CREAM CAKE

MOCHA HAZELNUT TORTE

I make this pretty cake on birthdays and other special occasions because it looks and tastes amazing. The mild hazelnut and coffee flavors are impossible to resist.
—Christina Pope, Speedway, IN

PREP: 35 MIN. • **BAKE:** 25 MIN. + COOLING
MAKES: 16 SERVINGS

- ¾ cup butter, softened
- 1¼ cups packed brown sugar
- 1 cup sugar
- 3 large eggs, room temperature
- 3 oz. unsweetened chocolate, melted and cooled slightly
- 2 tsp. vanilla extract
- 2¼ cups all-purpose flour
- 1 Tbsp. instant espresso powder
- 1 tsp. baking soda
- ½ tsp. baking powder
- ¼ tsp. salt
- 1½ cups 2% milk

FROSTING
- 1 cup butter, softened
- 1 cup Nutella
- 4 cups confectioners' sugar
- 1 tsp. vanilla extract
- 3 to 4 Tbsp. 2% milk
- ½ cup chopped hazelnuts, toasted

1. Preheat oven to 350°. Line bottoms of 2 greased 9-in. round baking pans with parchment; grease parchment.
2. Cream butter and sugars until light and fluffy, 5-7 minutes. Add eggs, 1 at a time, beating well after each addition. Beat in melted chocolate and vanilla. In another bowl, whisk flour, espresso powder, baking soda, baking powder and salt; add to the creamed mixture alternately with milk, beating well after each addition.
3. Transfer batter to prepared pans. Bake 25-30 minutes or until a toothpick inserted in center comes out clean. Cool in pans 10 minutes before removing to wire racks; remove parchment. Cool cakes completely.
4. For frosting, in a large bowl, beat butter and Nutella until blended. Gradually beat in confectioners' sugar, vanilla and enough milk to reach desired consistency.
5. Place 1 cake layer on a serving plate; spread with 1 cup frosting. Sprinkle with ¼ cup hazelnuts. Top with the remaining cake layer. Frost top and sides with remaining frosting. Sprinkle with the remaining hazelnuts.
1 piece: 639 cal., 32g fat (16g sat. fat), 94mg chol., 311mg sod., 88g carb. (69g sugars, 2g fiber), 6g pro.

TRICKS FOR LEVELING A CAKE

If your cake has only a slight dome, lay a clean kitchen towel over it and press down gently to smooth the top. This works when the cake is hot out of the oven and you don't need to press too hard.

Alternatively, wait until the the cake is completely cool and then slice off the dome. There are special tools for leveling cakes, but all you really need is a standard serrated bread knife. Start with the knife just at the edge of the dome, not down the side of the cake, wasting as little cake as possible.

Hold the blade parallel to the countertop and cut about 2 in. inches into the dome. Turn the cake a quarter turn and make another cut. Repeat until you have sliced all the way around the cake. Once you've made a preliminary slice around the edge of the dome, slice all the way through.

SPICED POMEGRANATE-PEAR CAKE

SPICED POMEGRANATE-PEAR CAKE

Featuring the tart flavor and rich color of pomegranate juice, this three-layer cake is a delicious combination of tender and buttery cake, sweet buttercream and tangy fruit. It will be the star attraction of your meal and stay moist for days.
—Kelly Koutahi, Moore, OK

PREP: 1 HOUR + CHILLING
BAKE: 20 MIN. + COOLING
MAKES: 16 SERVINGS

1½	cups pomegranate juice
3	Tbsp. brown sugar
1	tsp. ground ginger
1	tsp. vanilla extract
1	can (29 oz.) pear halves in juice, drained and cut into ⅛-in. slices

CAKE

¾	cup 2% milk
1	tsp. white vinegar
10	Tbsp. butter, softened
1¼	cups sugar
4	large eggs, room temperature
2	tsp. vanilla extract
2	cups cake flour
2	tsp. baking powder
¼	tsp. salt

BUTTERCREAM FROSTING

1½	cups butter, softened
2	tsp. vanilla extract
2	to 3 drops red food coloring, optional
7½	cups confectioners' sugar
4	to 5 Tbsp. 2% milk
	Pomegranate seeds

1. In a small saucepan, combine juice, brown sugar and ground ginger. Cook and stir over medium heat until sugar is dissolved; remove from heat. Stir in vanilla. Place pears in a bowl or shallow dish; pour juice mixture over pears and turn to coat. Cover and refrigerate at least 4 hours.

2. Meanwhile, preheat oven to 350°. Line bottoms of 3 greased 8-in. round baking pans with parchment; grease paper. In a small bowl, combine milk and vinegar; let stand 5 minutes until curdled. In a large bowl, cream butter and sugar until light and fluffy, 5-7 minutes. Add eggs, 1 at a time, beating well after each addition. Beat in vanilla. In another bowl, whisk flour, baking powder and salt; add to creamed mixture alternately with milk mixture, beating well after each addition.

3. Transfer to prepared pans. Bake until a toothpick inserted in center comes out clean, 18-20 minutes. Cool in pans 10 minutes before removing to wire racks; remove paper. Cool completely.

4. Drain pears, reserving marinade; pat dry. For frosting, in a large bowl, beat butter, 2 Tbsp. reserved marinade, vanilla and, if desired, food coloring until blended. Beat in confectioners' sugar alternately with enough milk to reach spreading consistency.

5. To assemble, using a long serrated knife, cut each cake in half horizontally. Place 1 cake layer on a serving plate; brush with ¼ cup reserved marinade. Top with ⅔ cup pears. Top with another cake layer; spread with ½ cup frosting. Repeat layers, ending with remaining cake layer. Frost the top and sides of cake with remaining frosting. Sprinkle pomegranate seeds over top of cake. Refrigerate cake for at least 2 hours before serving.

1 piece: 614 cal., 26g fat (16g sat. fat), 113mg chol., 321mg sod., 93g carb. (75g sugars, 1g fiber), 4g pro.

ITALIAN CREAM CHEESE CAKE

Creamy buttermilk makes every bite of this awesome Italian cream cheese cake moist and flavorful.
—Joyce Lutz, Centerview, MO

PREP: 40 MIN. • **BAKE:** 20 MIN. + COOLING
MAKES: 16 SERVINGS

- ½ cup butter, softened
- ½ cup shortening
- 2 cups sugar
- 5 large eggs, separated, room temperature
- 1 tsp. vanilla extract
- 2 cups all-purpose flour
- 1 tsp. baking soda
- 1 cup buttermilk
- 1½ cups sweetened shredded coconut
- 1 cup chopped pecans

CREAM CHEESE FROSTING
- 11 oz. cream cheese, softened
- ¾ cup butter, softened
- 6 cups confectioners' sugar
- 1½ tsp. vanilla extract
- ¾ cup chopped pecans

1. Preheat oven to 350°. Grease and flour three 9-in. round baking pans. Cream butter, shortening and sugar until light and fluffy, 5-7 minutes. Beat in egg yolks and vanilla. Combine flour and baking soda; add to the creamed mixture alternately with buttermilk. Beat until just combined. Stir in coconut and pecans.

2. In another bowl, beat egg whites with clean beaters until stiff but not dry. Fold one-fourth of the egg whites into batter, then fold in the remaining whites. Pour into prepared pans.

3. Bake until a toothpick inserted in center comes out clean, 20-25 minutes. Cool 10 minutes before removing from pans to wire racks to cool completely.

4. For frosting, beat cream cheese and butter until smooth. Beat in the confectioners' sugar and vanilla until fluffy. Stir in pecans. Spread frosting between layers and over top and sides of cake. Refrigerate.

1 piece: 736 cal., 41g fat (19g sat. fat), 117mg chol., 330mg sod., 90g carb. (75g sugars, 2g fiber), 7g pro.

APPLE SPICE CAKE WITH BROWN SUGAR FROSTING

I am a healthy eater most of the time...but this apple spice cake is worth the splurge! Every year, I treasure the opportunity to make my own birthday cake, and I choose this. You can add a cup of raisins to the batter before baking if you'd like.
—Jennifer Owen, Louisville, KY

PREP: 30 MIN. • **BAKE:** 35 MIN. + COOLING
MAKES: 16 SERVINGS

- 4 medium Honeycrisp apples, peeled and cut into 1-in. pieces (about 1½ lbs.)
- 2 cups sugar
- ½ cup canola oil
- 2 large eggs, room temperature
- 2 tsp. vanilla extract
- 2 cups all-purpose flour
- 1 Tbsp. pumpkin pie spice
- 2 tsp. baking powder
- 1 tsp. salt
- ½ cup buttermilk
- 1½ cups chopped walnuts, toasted

FROSTING
- 1 pkg. (8 oz.) cream cheese, softened
- ½ cup butter, softened
- 1 cup confectioners' sugar
- 1 cup packed brown sugar
- 1½ tsp. vanilla extract
- 1 tsp. pumpkin pie spice
- 1½ cups chopped walnuts, toasted

1. Preheat oven to 350°. Line bottoms of 2 greased 9-in. round baking pans with parchment; grease parchment.

2. Place apples in a food processor; pulse until finely chopped. In a large bowl, beat sugar, oil, eggs and vanilla until well blended. In another bowl, whisk flour, pie spice, baking powder and salt; gradually beat into sugar mixture alternately with buttermilk. Stir in apples and walnuts.

3. Transfer to prepared pans. Bake until a toothpick inserted in center comes out clean, 35-40 minutes. Cool in pans for 10 minutes before removing to wire racks; remove paper. Cool completely.

4. In a large bowl, beat cream cheese, butter, sugars, vanilla and pie spice until smooth. Spread frosting between layers and over top and sides of cake. Gently press walnuts into frosting on top of cake. Refrigerate leftovers.

1 piece: 574 cal., 33g fat (9g sat. fat), 53mg chol., 326mg sod., 67g carb. (51g sugars, 2g fiber), 7g pro.

BAKING 101

BEST VANILLA CAKE

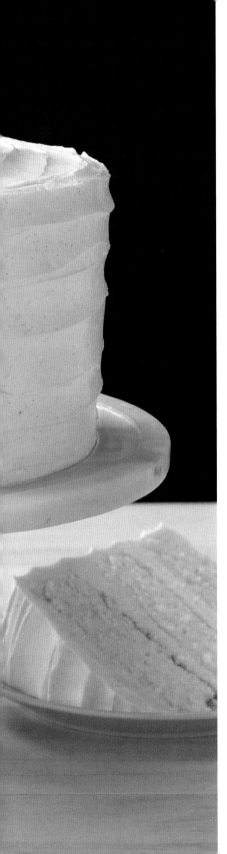

BEST VANILLA CAKE

There's a reason this vanilla cake recipe is the best. Adding creamy vanilla bean paste into the moist, rich batter creates a power-packed vanilla flavor that can't be bought in stores. This cake makes a great base for any flavor frosting you like, but try Best Vanilla Buttercream frosting (p. 431) for a perfect vanilla combination.

—Margaret Knoebel, Milwaukee, WI

PREP: 20 MIN. + STANDING
BAKE: 30 MIN. + COOLING
MAKES: 16 SERVINGS

- 1½ cups sour cream
- 1 Tbsp. vanilla bean paste
- 1 Tbsp. vanilla extract
- 4 cups cake flour
- 2½ cups sugar
- 4½ tsp. baking powder
- 2 tsp. salt
- 1 cup unsalted butter, softened
- ¼ cup canola oil
- 6 large egg whites, room temperature
- 2 large eggs, room temperature

1. Preheat oven to 350°. In a small bowl, mix sour cream, vanilla paste and vanilla extract until combined. Let stand 10 minutes. Line bottoms of 3 greased 9-in. round baking pans with parchment; grease paper.
2. Sift cake flour, sugar, baking powder and salt together twice into a large bowl. Add butter and canola oil; beat until mixture is crumbly. Add egg whites, 1 at a time, beating well after each addition. Add eggs, 1 at a time, beating well after each addition. Beat in sour cream mixture just until combined.
3. Transfer batter to prepared pans. Bake until a toothpick inserted in center comes out clean, 30-35 minutes. Cool in pans 10 minutes before removing to wire racks; remove paper. Cool completely. Frost cake as desired.

1 piece: 399 cal., 16g fat (8g sat. fat), 54mg chol., 462mg sod., 59g carb. (32g sugars, 1g fiber), 5g pro.

. . . .

WHAT IS A CRUMB COAT?

A crumb coat is simply a thin layer of icing applied to seal the cake layers and trap errant crumbs. This first coat of icing prevents crumbs from coming loose and spreading throughout your final icing, ensuring a smooth surface. Once you've applied a thin layer, place the cake in the refrigerator or freezer for 10-15 minutes to set the icing. This will give you a firm foundation to work with when applying thicker, more decorative layers of icing.

. . . .

CARROT CAKE WITH PECAN FROSTING

This impressive cake is one of my husband's favorites. It's homey and old-fashioned, so it's perfect for special holidays or Sunday family dinners.

—Adrian Badon, Denham Springs, LA

PREP: 35 MIN. • **BAKE:** 40 MIN. + COOLING
MAKES: 16 SERVINGS

- 1 cup shortening
- 2 cups sugar
- 4 large eggs, room temperature
- 1 can (8 oz.) unsweetened crushed pineapple, undrained
- 2½ cups all-purpose flour
- 2 tsp. ground cinnamon
- 1 tsp. baking powder
- 1 tsp. baking soda
- ¾ tsp. salt
- 3 cups shredded carrots (about 6 medium carrots)

FROSTING
- 1 pkg. (8 oz.) reduced-fat cream cheese
- ½ cup butter, softened
- 1 tsp. vanilla extract
- 3¾ cups confectioners' sugar
- 1 cup chopped pecans

1. Preheat oven to 325°. Line bottoms of 2 greased 9-in. round baking pans with parchment; grease paper.

2. In a large bowl, cream shortening and sugar until fluffy. Add eggs, 1 at a time, beating well after each addition. Beat in pineapple. In another bowl, whisk flour, cinnamon, baking powder, baking soda and salt; gradually add to the creamed mixture. Stir in carrots.

3. Transfer the batter to prepared pans. Bake until a toothpick inserted in center comes out clean, 40-45 minutes. Cool in pans 10 minutes before removing to wire racks; remove parchment. Cool cakes completely.

4. In a large bowl, beat cream cheese, butter and vanilla extract until blended. Gradually beat in confectioners' sugar until smooth. Stir in pecans.

5. Spread frosting between layers and over top and sides of cake. Refrigerate until serving.

1 piece: 557 cal., 27g fat (10g sat. fat), 72mg chol., 358mg sod., 74g carb. (57g sugars, 2g fiber), 6g pro.

PINA COLADA CAKE

I'm an avid baker and wanted to create something original that was from my heart. My goal was to make a cake that tastes like the perfect pina colada drink, and I think I accomplished it with this recipe.

—Stephanie McShan, Apopka, FL

PREP: 35 MIN. • **BAKE:** 20 MIN. + COOLING
MAKES: 12 SERVINGS

- 1 cup butter, softened
- 2 cups sugar
- 6 large eggs, room temperature
- 1 tsp. coconut extract
- 3 cups all-purpose flour
- 1 tsp. baking powder
- ½ tsp. baking soda
- 1 cup sour cream
- 1 can (8 oz.) crushed pineapple, undrained

FROSTING
- 1 cup butter, softened
- 4 cups confectioners' sugar
- 2 tsp. coconut extract
- 3 to 4 Tbsp. water

FILLING
- 1 jar (18 oz.) pineapple preserves
  Optional: Dried pineapple slices and toasted sweetened shredded coconut

1. Preheat oven to 350°. In a large bowl, cream butter and sugar until light and fluffy, 5-7 minutes. Add eggs, 1 at a time, beating well after each addition. Beat in extract. Combine flour, baking powder and baking soda; add to the creamed mixture alternately with sour cream, beating well after each addition.

2. In a food processor, cover and pulse pineapple until almost smooth. Stir into batter. Transfer to 3 greased, floured 9-in. round baking pans. Bake until a toothpick inserted in center comes out clean, 20-25 minutes.

3. Cool in pans for 10 minutes before removing from pans to wire racks to cool completely.

4. For frosting, in a large bowl, beat the butter until fluffy. Beat in the confectioners' sugar, extract and enough water to achieve a spreading consistency.

5. To assemble, place 1 cake layer on a serving plate; spread with half the preserves. Repeat layers. Top with the remaining cake layer. Frost top and sides. Garnish with pineapple slices and coconut if desired.

1 piece: 868 cal., 36g fat (22g sat. fat), 199mg chol., 344mg sod., 129g carb. (101g sugars, 1g fiber), 7g pro.

MALTED CHOCOLATE & STOUT LAYER CAKE

If you want a dessert that will take the cake at your St. Patrick's Day celebration, look no further! The rich chocolate cake is incredibly moist and has a nice malt flavor that's perfectly complemented by the Irish cream frosting.

—Jennifer Wayland, Morris Plains, NJ

PREP: 45 MIN. + CHILLING
BAKE: 35 MIN. + COOLING
MAKES: 16 SERVINGS

- 2 cups stout beer
- 1¾ cups butter, cubed
- 3 oz. bittersweet chocolate, chopped
- 1 cup malted milk powder
- 1 cup baking cocoa
- 1½ cups sour cream
- 4 large eggs, room temperature
- 3½ cups sugar
- 3½ cups cake flour
- 2½ tsp. baking soda
- 1 tsp. salt

FROSTING
- 1 cup sugar
- ½ cup Irish cream liqueur
- 6 large egg yolks, beaten
- 1½ tsp. vanilla extract
- 1½ cups butter, softened
- ½ cup malted milk powder
  Chopped malted milk balls, optional

MALTED CHOCOLATE
& STOUT LAYER CAKE

1. Preheat oven to 350°. Grease and flour three 9-in. round baking pans; set aside. In a large saucepan, combine beer, butter and chocolate. Cook and stir over medium-low heat until butter and chocolate are melted. Remove from heat; whisk in milk powder and cocoa. Transfer to a large bowl. Let stand for 15 minutes.
2. Add sour cream and eggs to the chocolate mixture; beat until well blended. Combine sugar, flour, baking soda and salt; gradually beat into the chocolate mixture until blended. Pour batter into prepared pans.
3. Bake until a toothpick inserted in the center comes out clean, 32-36 minutes. Cool 10 minutes before removing from pans to wire racks to cool completely.
4. For the frosting, in a large heavy saucepan, bring sugar and liqueur to a gentle boil over medium heat; cook until sugar is dissolved. Remove from heat. Add a small amount of the hot mixture to egg yolks; return all to pan, stirring constantly. Cook until mixture thickens, about 2 minutes longer, stirring constantly. Remove from heat; stir in vanilla. Cool to room temperature.
5. Using a mixer with a whisk attachment, cream butter until fluffy, about 5 minutes. Gradually beat in the sugar mixture. Add malted milk powder; beat until fluffy, about 5 minutes. If necessary, refrigerate until frosting reaches spreading consistency.
6. Place bottom cake layer on a serving plate; spread with ⅔ cup of frosting. Repeat layers. Top with remaining cake layer. Spread remaining frosting over top and sides of cake. Refrigerate at least 1 hour before serving. If desired, top with chopped malted milk balls.

1 piece: 821 cal., 48g fat (29g sat. fat), 220mg chol., 760mg sod., 90g carb. (64g sugars, 2g fiber), 7g pro.

YELLOW LAYER CAKE
WITH CHOCOLATE
BUTTERCREAM

YELLOW LAYER CAKE WITH CHOCOLATE BUTTERCREAM

This will become your go-to recipe for celebrating birthdays. The tender yellow cake with flavorful chocolate buttercream is perfect for any occasion, though.
—*Taste of Home* Test Kitchen

PREP: 15 MIN. • **BAKE:** 25 MIN. + COOLING
MAKES: 16 SERVINGS

- ⅔ cup butter, softened
- 1¾ cups sugar
- 2 large eggs, room temperature
- 1½ tsp. vanilla extract
- 2½ cups all-purpose flour
- 2½ tsp. baking powder
- ½ tsp. salt
- 1¼ cups 2% milk

CHOCOLATE BUTTERCREAM

- 2 cups butter, softened
- 4 cups confectioners' sugar, sifted
- ½ cup Dutch-processed cocoa, sifted
- 1½ tsp. vanilla extract
- ⅛ tsp. salt
- ⅓ cup 2% milk

1. Preheat oven to 350°. Grease and flour two 9-in. round baking pans. In a large bowl, cream butter and sugar until light and fluffy, 5-7 minutes. Add eggs, 1 at a time, beating well after each addition. Beat in vanilla extract. In another bowl, whisk flour, baking powder and salt; add to the creamed mixture alternately with milk, beating well after each addition.

2. Transfer to prepared pans. Bake until a toothpick inserted in the center comes out clean, 25-30 minutes. Cool in pans 10 minutes before removing to wire racks to cool completely.

3. For buttercream, in a large bowl, beat butter until creamy. Gradually beat in confectioners' sugar and cocoa until smooth. Add vanilla extract and salt. Add milk; beat until light and fluffy, about 5 minutes.

4. Spread buttercream between layers and over top and sides of cake.

1 piece: 593 cal., 33g fat (21g sat. fat), 107mg chol., 432mg sod., 72g carb. (53g sugars, 4g fiber), 5g pro.

LEMON RICOTTA CAKE

This recipe is a family gem that was passed down from my grandmother and mother. Garnished with shaved lemon peel, this moist four-layer cake is the perfect dessert when you want to impress.

—Nanette Slaughter, Sammamish, WA

PREP: 1 HOUR + CHILLING
BAKE: 30 MIN. + COOLING
MAKES: 16 SERVINGS

    3 large eggs, room temperature
    2 large egg yolks, room
       temperature
  ⅔   cup sugar
  ⅓   cup lemon juice
  ⅓   cup butter, cubed
CAKE BATTER
    1 cup butter, softened
    2 cups sugar
    3 large eggs, room temperature
    1 cup ricotta cheese
    1 cup buttermilk
    1 Tbsp. grated lemon zest
  1½ tsp. vanilla extract
    1 tsp. lemon juice
    3 cups all-purpose flour
  ½   tsp. baking powder
  ½   tsp. baking soda
  ½   tsp. salt

SUGARED LEMON ZEST
    6 medium lemons
  ¼   cup sugar
FROSTING
  ⅔   cup butter, softened
  5½ cups confectioners' sugar
  ⅓   cup 2% milk
  1½ tsp. grated lemon zest
  1½ tsp. vanilla extract
  ⅛   tsp. salt
       Colored sugar, optional

1. For lemon curd, in a small bowl, combine eggs and egg yolks. In a heavy saucepan, cook and stir the sugar, lemon juice and butter over medium heat until smooth. Stir a small amount of the hot mixture into eggs; return all to the pan, stirring constantly. Bring to a gentle boil; cook and stir until thickened, about 2 minutes. Cool slightly. Cover; chill until thickened, about 1½ hours or overnight.

2. Preheat oven to 350°. In a large bowl, cream butter and sugar until light and fluffy, 5-7 minutes. Add eggs, 1 at a time, beating well after each addition. In another bowl, combine the ricotta cheese, buttermilk, lemon zest, vanilla extract and lemon juice. In a third bowl, combine flour, baking powder, baking soda and salt; add to the creamed mixture alternately with the buttermilk mixture. Beat well after each addition.

3. Pour into 2 greased and floured 9-in. round baking pans. Bake until a toothpick inserted in the center comes out clean, 30-35 minutes. Cool for 10 minutes before removing from pans to wire racks to cool completely.

4. Using a citrus zester, remove zest from lemons in long narrow strips; toss with sugar. Let stand for 30 minutes. (Save fruit for another use.)

5. Meanwhile, in a large bowl, cream butter until light and fluffy. Add the confectioners' sugar, milk, grated lemon zest, vanilla and salt; beat until smooth.

6. Cut each cake in half horizontally. Place 1 cake layer on a serving plate. Pipe a circle of frosting around the edge of cake. Spread a third of the lemon curd inside frosting. Repeat layers twice. Top with remaining cake layer. Frost top and sides. If desired, pipe a decorative border of frosting using a star tip, and decorate sides of cake with colored sugar. Garnish with lemon zest strips. Store in the refrigerator.

1 piece: 657 cal., 27g fat (16g sat. fat), 172mg chol., 370mg sod., 98g carb. (77g sugars, 1g fiber), 8g pro.

· ·

KEEP YOUR CAKE IN PLACE

When it comes time to frost your cake, start by piping a dab of frosting in the center of your plate before setting down the bottom layer. It'll help keep your cake from sliding while you're adding the rest of the frosting.

· ·

CUPCAKES

. . . .

CREME DE MENTHE CUPCAKES

We use creme de menthe liqueur (the term means "mint cream" in French) to add a cool touch to these impressive mascarpone-frosted cupcakes.
—Keri Whitney, Castro Valley, CA

PREP: 30 MIN. • **BAKE:** 15 MIN. + COOLING
MAKES: 1 DOZEN

- ¾ cup butter, softened
- 1 cup sugar
- 2 large eggs, room temperature
- ½ tsp. mint extract
- 1½ cups cake flour
- 1½ tsp. baking powder
- ¼ tsp. salt
- ⅔ cup 2% milk
- 2 Tbsp. white (clear) creme de menthe
  Green paste food coloring

FROSTING
- 1 carton (8 oz.) mascarpone cheese
- ⅓ cup heavy whipping cream
- ¼ cup confectioners' sugar
- 4 tsp. white (clear) creme de menthe
  Green paste food coloring

1. Preheat oven to 350°. Cream the butter and sugar until light and fluffy, 5-7 minutes. Add the eggs, 1 at a time, beating well after each addition. Add mint extract. In another bowl, whisk flour, baking powder and salt; add to creamed mixture alternately with milk and creme de menthe, beating well after each addition. Transfer 2 cups of batter to a separate bowl. Mix food coloring paste into the remaining batter.

2. Cut a small hole in the tip of a pastry bag; insert a #12 round tip. Spoon the batters alternately into the bag. Pipe the batter into 12 paper-lined muffin cups until three-fourths full. Bake until a toothpick comes out clean, 15-20 minutes. Cool 10 minutes; remove from pan to a wire rack to cool completely.

3. For frosting, stir the mascarpone and cream together until smooth. Add the confectioners' sugar and creme de menthe; stir until blended. Transfer half the frosting to a separate bowl; mix food coloring paste into the remaining frosting. Stir each portion vigorously until stiff peaks form (do not overmix).

4. Cut a small hole in the tip of a pastry bag; insert a #12 round tip. Spoon the frostings alternately into the bag. Pipe frosting onto cupcakes. Refrigerate any leftovers.

Note: For extra-thick frosting like that in the photo, double all the frosting ingredients.

1 cupcake: 372 cal., 24g fat (14g sat. fat), 95mg chol., 222mg sod., 35g carb. (21g sugars, 0 fiber), 5g pro.

CREME DE MENTHE
CUPCAKES

SO-SIMPLE
SWIRLED FROSTING

To achieve this pretty cupcake look, place a pastry bag in a tumbler for easy filling. Spoon a different color of frosting into each half of the bag.

CHAI CUPCAKES

BAKING 101

CHAI CUPCAKES

You'll get a double dose of the spicy blend that's frequently used to flavor tea in these tender cakes. Both the cupcake and frosting use the sweet blend of spices.
—*Taste of Home* Test Kitchen

PREP: 25 MIN. • **BAKE:** 25 MIN. + COOLING
MAKES: 1 DOZEN

½ tsp. each ground ginger, cinnamon, cardamom and cloves
⅛ tsp. pepper
½ cup butter, softened
1 cup sugar
1 large egg, room temperature
½ tsp. vanilla extract
1½ cups cake flour
1½ tsp. baking powder
¼ tsp. salt
⅔ cup 2% milk
FROSTING
6 Tbsp. butter, softened
3 cups confectioners' sugar
¾ tsp. vanilla extract
3 to 4 Tbsp. 2% milk

1. Preheat oven to 350°. In a small bowl, combine the ground ginger, cinnamon, cardamom, cloves and pepper; set aside.
2. In a large bowl, cream butter and sugar until light and fluffy, 5-7 minutes. Beat in egg and vanilla. Combine the flour, baking powder, salt and 1½ tsp. spice mixture. Gradually add to the creamed mixture alternately with milk, beating well after each addition.
3. Fill 12 paper-lined muffin cups two-thirds full. Bake until a toothpick inserted in the center comes out clean, 24-28 minutes. Cool for 10 minutes before removing from pans to wire racks to cool completely.
4. In a large bowl, beat butter until fluffy; beat in the confectioners' sugar, vanilla and remaining spice mixture until smooth. Add enough milk to reach desired consistency. Pipe the frosting over cupcakes.
1 cupcake: 377 cal., 14g fat (9g sat. fat), 54mg chol., 209mg sod., 61g carb. (46g sugars, 0 fiber), 3g pro.

AMARETTO DREAM CUPCAKES

Treat yourself to these indulgent little cupcakes laced with the irresistible flavor of amaretto and slivered almonds.
—Anette Stevens, Olds, AB

PREP: 20 MIN. • **BAKE:** 15 MIN. + COOLING
MAKES: 2 DOZEN

¾ cup butter, softened
1½ cups packed brown sugar
2 large eggs, room temperature
2 cups all-purpose flour
1½ tsp. baking powder
½ tsp. baking soda
¼ tsp. salt
½ cup buttermilk
¼ cup amaretto
⅓ cup slivered almonds
AMARETTO BUTTER FROSTING
3 cups confectioners' sugar
¼ cup butter, melted
3 to 4 Tbsp. heavy whipping cream
2 to 3 Tbsp. amaretto

1. Preheat oven to 375°. In a large bowl, cream butter and brown sugar until light and fluffy, 5-7 minutes. Add eggs, 1 at a time, beating well after each.
2. Combine the flour, baking powder, baking soda and salt. Add to the creamed mixture alternately with buttermilk and amaretto, beating well after each addition. Stir in almonds.
3. Fill paper-lined muffin cups two-thirds full. Bake until a toothpick comes out clean, 14-16 minutes. Cool for 5 minutes; remove to wire racks to cool completely.
4. In a small bowl, beat confectioners' sugar and butter. Add 3 Tbsp. cream and 2 Tbsp. amaretto; beat until smooth. Add cream and amaretto if needed for spreading consistency. Frost cupcakes.
1 cupcake: 253 cal., 10g fat (6g sat. fat), 38mg chol., 163mg sod., 39g carb. (30g sugars, 0 fiber), 2g pro.

PINEAPPLE UPSIDE-DOWN CUPCAKES

I have baked cupcakes for years since I served as a room mother at my children's school. These easy-to-make jumbo treats make an attractive dessert for special occasions or everyday.
—Barbara Hahn, Park Hills, MO

PREP: 30 MIN. • **BAKE:** 30 MIN. + COOLING
MAKES: 1 DOZEN JUMBO CUPCAKES

- 6 Tbsp. butter, cubed
- 1 cup packed light brown sugar
- 2 Tbsp. light corn syrup
- 12 slices pineapple, drained
- 12 maraschino cherries, well drained
- 3 large eggs, room temperature
- 2 cups sugar
- 1 cup canola oil
- 1 cup sour cream
- 2 tsp. vanilla extract
- 2½ cups all-purpose flour
- ½ tsp. baking powder
- ½ tsp. baking soda
- ½ tsp. salt
  Whipped topping, optional

1. Line the bottom of 12 greased jumbo muffin cups with waxed paper; grease the paper and set aside.

2. In a small saucepan, melt butter over low heat; stir in brown sugar and corn syrup. Cook and stir over medium heat until sugar is dissolved. Remove from the heat. Spoon 1 Tbsp. into each muffin cup; top each with a pineapple slice and a cherry.

3. In a large bowl, beat eggs and sugar until thickened and lemon-colored. Beat in the oil, sour cream and vanilla until smooth. Combine the flour, baking powder, baking soda and salt. Add to egg mixture and mix well.

4. Fill muffin cups two-thirds full. Bake at 350° until a toothpick inserted in the center comes out clean, 28-32 minutes. Cool for 5 minutes before inverting onto wire racks to cool completely. Garnish with whipped topping if desired.

1 cupcake: 602 cal., 29g fat (9g sat. fat), 82mg chol., 264mg sod., 82g carb. (61g sugars, 1g fiber), 5g pro.

HUMMINGBIRD CUPCAKES

Turn the traditional hummingbird cake—flavored with pineapple, bananas and walnuts—into a bite-sized treat with these moist cupcakes.
—Jessie Oleson, Santa Fe, NM

PREP: 40 MIN. • **BAKE:** 20 MIN. + COOLING
MAKES: 2 DOZEN

- 1 cup butter, softened
- 2 cups sugar
- 3 large eggs, room temperature
- 2 tsp. vanilla extract
- 2 cups mashed ripe bananas
- ½ cup drained canned crushed pineapple
- 3 cups all-purpose flour
- 1 tsp. baking soda
- 1 tsp. ground cinnamon
- ½ tsp. salt
- 1 cup sweetened shredded coconut
- 1 cup chopped walnuts

CREAM CHEESE FROSTING
- 1 pkg. (8 oz.) cream cheese, softened
- ½ cup butter, softened
- 3¾ cups confectioners' sugar
- 1 tsp. vanilla extract

1. Preheat oven to 350°. In a large bowl, cream butter and sugar until light and fluffy, 5-7 minutes. Add the eggs, 1 at a time, beating well after each addition. Beat in vanilla. In a small bowl, combine bananas and pineapple.

2. Combine the flour, baking soda, cinnamon and salt; add to the creamed mixture alternately with the banana mixture, beating well after each addition. Fold in coconut and walnuts.

3. Fill 24 paper-lined muffin cups about two-thirds full. Bake until a toothpick inserted in the center comes out clean, 20-25 minutes. Cool the cupcakes for 10 minutes before removing from pans to wire racks to cool completely.

4. In a small bowl, beat softened cream cheese and butter until fluffy. Add the confectioners' sugar and vanilla; beat until smooth. Frost cupcakes.

1 cupcake: 410 cal., 20g fat (11g sat. fat), 67mg chol., 230mg sod., 56g carb. (39g sugars, 2g fiber), 4g pro.

EASY CUPCAKE DECORATING IDEAS

BUTTERCREAM ROSE

FROSTING POMPOM

MINI FLORAL CUPCAKE

WATERCOLOR INSPIRED

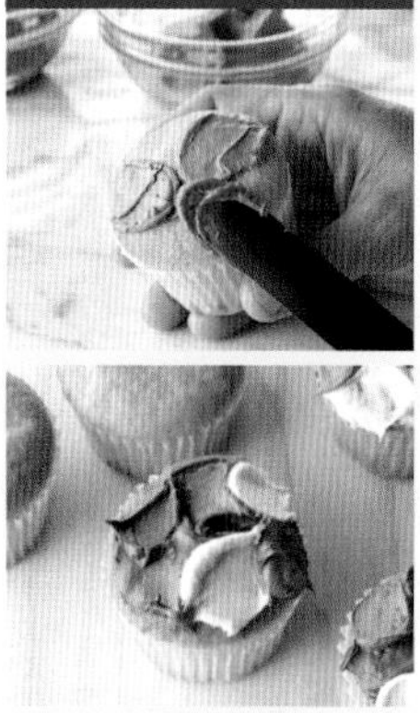

SIMPLE TOPPERS

SPRINKLE DIPPED

OMBRE EFFECT

CONFETTI TRIM

CHOCOLATE DECORATIONS

Buttercream rose: Using a pastry bag and a closed star tip, make a spiral, moving from the inside of the cupcake to the outer perimeter. (Practice on a scrap of waxed paper first!)

Frosting pompom: Use a pastry bag fitted with a round tip to pipe dots around the cupcake. Make these frosting dots the same or random sizes. Dust the cupcakes with decorative sugar or sprinkles.

Mini floral cupcake: Use a pastry bag fitted with a small star tip to pipe small florets, being sure to fill the top of cake completely. For variation, use two similar hues when frosting.

Watercolor inspired: Separate the frosting into portions; dye each a different color. Use an offset spatula to spread daubs of frosting across the cupcake until it's covered. Stop there or use your spatula to blend the edges.

Simple toppers: A simple basic buttercream base makes pretty cupcake toppers stand out. You can top with just about anything: birthday candles, sugar decorations or edible flowers.

Sprinkle dipped: Frost a cupcake with your favorite frosting, then roll the top in the sprinkles of your choosing.

Ombre effect: Divide the frosting into four portions, dying each a deeper shade of your chosen color and leaving one plain white. Use a round pastry tip to pipe concentric circles onto your cupcake—stacked high or flat and low.

Confetti trim: After frosting the cupcake, roll the outer edge in sprinkles.

Chocolate decorations: Draw a simple shape onto waxed or parchment paper, then trace it using a piping bag filled with melted chocolate—bittersweet, semisweet or white. Place in the fridge until they're completely cool and solid. Set a chocolate piece into the frosting on top of each cupcake for an edible garnish.

BROWNIE KISS CUPCAKES

It's fun to prepare individual brownie cupcakes with a chocolaty surprise inside. My goddaughter, Cara, asks me to make them for her birthday to share at school. This year, she requested 32. I later found out she only needed 27 for her class... wonder where the other five went!

—Pamela Lute, Mercersburg, PA

TAKES: 30 MIN.
MAKES: 9 SERVINGS

BAKING 101

- ⅓ cup butter, softened
- 1 cup sugar
- 2 large eggs, room temperature
- 1 tsp. vanilla extract
- ¾ cup all-purpose flour
- ½ cup baking cocoa
- ¼ tsp. baking powder
- ¼ tsp. salt
- 9 milk chocolate kisses

1. Preheat oven to 350°. In a large bowl, cream butter and sugar until light and fluffy, 5-7 minutes. Beat in eggs and vanilla. Combine the flour, cocoa, baking powder and salt; gradually add to the creamed mixture and mix well.
2. Fill paper- or foil-lined muffin cups two-thirds full. Place a chocolate kiss, tip end down, in the center of each.
3. Bake until the top of the brownie springs back when lightly touched, 20-25 minutes.
1 cupcake: 239 cal., 10g fat (5g sat. fat), 66mg chol., 163mg sod., 36g carb. (24g sugars, 1g fiber), 4g pro.

OREO CUPCAKES WITH
COOKIES & CREAM FROSTING

BAKING 101

OREO CUPCAKES WITH COOKIES & CREAM FROSTING

Kids and adults alike find these Oreo cupcakes irresistible. If you want to pipe the frosting, be sure to thoroughly crush the Oreos.

—*Taste of Home* Test Kitchen

PREP: 20 MIN. • **BAKE:** 20 MIN. + COOLING
MAKES: 2 DOZEN

- ⅔ cup butter, softened
- 1¾ cups sugar
- 2 large eggs, room temperature
- 1½ tsp. vanilla extract
- 2½ cups all-purpose flour
- 2½ tsp. baking powder
- ½ tsp. salt
- 1¼ cups 2% milk
- 2 cups coarsely crushed Oreo cookies

FROSTING
- 1 cup butter, softened
- 3 cups confectioners' sugar
- 2 Tbsp. 2% milk
- 1 tsp. vanilla extract
- 1½ cups finely crushed Oreo cookie crumbs

Optional: Additional Oreo cookie crumbs and mini Oreo cookies

1. Preheat oven to 350°. Line 24 muffin cups with paper liners.
2. In a large bowl, cream butter and sugar until light and fluffy, 5-7 minutes. Add eggs, 1 at a time, beating well after each addition. Beat in vanilla. In another bowl, whisk flour, baking powder and salt; add to creamed mixture alternately with the milk, beating well after each addition. Fold in the crushed cookies.
3. Fill prepared cups three-fourths full. Bake 20-22 minutes or until a toothpick inserted in center comes out clean. Cool in pans 10 minutes before removing to wire racks to cool completely.
4. In a large bowl, combine the butter, confectioners' sugar, milk and vanilla; beat until smooth. Fold in the cookie crumbs. Pipe or spread frosting over cupcakes. If desired, sprinkle with additional cookie crumbs and garnish with mini Oreo cookies.
1 cupcake: 411 cal., 19g fat (10g sat. fat), 51mg chol., 346mg sod., 58g carb. (40g sugars, 2g fiber), 4g pro.

BOSTON CREAM CUPCAKES

Boston cream bismarcks have been my favorite bakery treat since I was a child, so I put together this easy-to-make cupcake version.
—Jeanne Holt, St. Paul, MN

PREP: 25 MIN. • **BAKE:** 15 MIN. + COOLING
MAKES: ½ DOZEN

- 3 Tbsp. shortening
- ⅓ cup sugar
- 1 large egg, room temperature
- ½ tsp. vanilla extract
- ½ cup all-purpose flour
- ½ tsp. baking powder
- ¼ tsp. salt
- 3 Tbsp. 2% milk
- ⅔ cup prepared vanilla pudding
- ½ cup semisweet chocolate chips
- ¼ cup heavy whipping cream

1. Preheat oven to 350°. In a small bowl, cream shortening and sugar until light and fluffy, 5-7 minutes. Beat in egg and vanilla. Combine the flour, baking powder and salt; add to the creamed mixture alternately with milk, beating well after each addition.
2. Fill paper-lined muffin cups half full. Bake until a toothpick inserted in the center comes out clean, 15-20 minutes. Cool 10 minutes in pan before removing to a wire rack to cool completely.
3. Cut a small hole in the corner of a pastry bag; insert a small tip. Fill bag with pudding. Push the tip through the top to fill each cupcake.
4. Place the chocolate chips in a small bowl. In a small saucepan, bring cream just to a boil. Pour over chocolate; whisk until smooth. Cool, stirring occasionally, to room temperature or until ganache thickens slightly, about 10 minutes. Spoon over cupcakes. Let stand until set. Store in an airtight container in the refrigerator.

1 cupcake: 283 cal., 15g fat (7g sat. fat), 45mg chol., 204mg sod., 34g carb. (20g sugars, 1g fiber), 4g pro.

BOSTON CREAM CUPCAKES

S'MORES CUPCAKES

Marshmallow frosting puts these cupcakes over the top. Chocolate bar pieces and graham cracker crumbs on top make them extra indulgent and even more like the real thing—but better!
—Erin Rachwal, Hartland, WI

PREP: 30 MIN. • **BAKE:** 20 MIN. + COOLING
MAKES: 2 DOZEN

- ¾ cup water
- ¾ cup buttermilk
- 2 large eggs, room temperature
- 3 Tbsp. canola oil
- 1 tsp. vanilla extract
- 1½ cups all-purpose flour
- 1½ cups sugar
- ¾ cup baking cocoa
- 1½ tsp. baking soda
- ¾ tsp. salt
- ¾ tsp. baking powder
- FROSTING
- 1½ cups butter, softened
- 2 cups confectioners' sugar
- ½ tsp. vanilla extract
- 2 jars (7 oz. each) marshmallow creme
- 2 Tbsp. graham cracker crumbs
- 2 milk chocolate candy bars (1.55 oz. each)
   Optional: Toasted marshmallows and graham cracker pieces

1. Preheat oven to 350°. In a large bowl, beat water, buttermilk, eggs, oil and vanilla until well blended. Combine flour, sugar, cocoa, baking soda, salt and baking powder; gradually beat into water mixture until blended.
2. Fill paper-lined muffin cups half full. Bake until a toothpick comes out clean, 16-20 minutes. Cool in pans 10 minutes before removing from the pans to wire racks to cool completely.
3. For frosting, in a large bowl, beat butter until fluffy; beat in confectioners' sugar and vanilla until smooth. Add marshmallow creme; beat until light and fluffy. Spread or pipe frosting over cupcakes. Sprinkle with cracker crumbs. Break each candy bar into 12 pieces; garnish cupcakes. If desired, top with toasted marshmallows and graham cracker pieces.
1 cupcake: 330 cal., 15g fat (8g sat. fat), 47mg chol., 298mg sod., 43g carb. (35g sugars, 1g fiber), 3g pro.

LEMON CREAM CUPCAKES

Delicate cupcakes like these are sure to disappear at your next potluck or bake sale!
—Ruth Ann Stelfox, Raymond, AB

PREP: 20 MIN. • **BAKE:** 25 MIN. + COOLING
MAKES: ABOUT 2½ DOZEN

- 1 cup butter, softened
- 2 cups sugar
- 3 large eggs, room temperature
- 2 tsp. grated lemon zest
- 1 tsp. vanilla extract
- 3½ cups all-purpose flour
- 1 tsp. baking soda
- ½ tsp. baking powder
- ½ tsp. salt
- 2 cups sour cream
- FROSTING
- 3 Tbsp. butter, softened
- 2¼ cups confectioners' sugar
- 2 Tbsp. lemon juice
- ¾ tsp. vanilla extract
- ¼ tsp. grated lemon zest
- 1 to 2 Tbsp. 2% milk
   Additional lemon zest, optional

1. Preheat oven to 350°. In a large bowl, cream butter and sugar until light and fluffy, 5-7 minutes. Add eggs, 1 at a time, beating well after each addition. Beat in lemon zest and vanilla. Combine flour, baking soda, baking powder and salt; add to creamed mixture alternately with sour cream, beating well after each addition (batter will be thick).
2. Fill greased or paper-lined muffin cups with ¼ cup of batter. Bake for 25-30 minutes or until a toothpick inserted in the center comes out clean. Cool in pans for 10 minutes before removing from pans to wire racks to cool completely.
3. For frosting, cream butter and confectioners' sugar in a small bowl until light and fluffy, 5-7 minutes. Add the lemon juice, vanilla, lemon zest and milk; beat until smooth. Frost cupcakes. If desired, sprinkle tops with additional lemon zest.
1 cupcake: 244 cal., 11g fat (6g sat. fat), 48mg chol., 178mg sod., 34g carb. (22g sugars, 0 fiber), 3g pro.

VANILLA BEAN CUPCAKES

APPLESAUCE SPICE CUPCAKES

These moist cupcakes have been a favorite for my whole life. I began making them in grade school and I still bake them today.
—Edna Hoffman, Hebron, IN

PREP: 15 MIN. • **BAKE:** 25 MIN. + COOLING
MAKES: 1 DOZEN

- ⅓ cup butter, softened
- ¾ cup sugar
- 2 large eggs. room temperature
- 1 tsp. vanilla extract
- 1⅓ cups all-purpose flour
- 1 tsp. baking powder
- ½ tsp. baking soda
- ½ tsp. salt
- 1 tsp. ground cinnamon
- ½ tsp. ground nutmeg
- ⅛ tsp. ground cloves
- ¾ cup applesauce
- 1 cup prepared cream cheese frosting

1. In a large bowl, cream butter and sugar. Add eggs, 1 at a time, beating well after each addition. Beat in vanilla extract. Combine dry ingredients; add to creamed mixture alternately with the applesauce.

2. Fill greased or paper-lined muffin cups two-thirds full. Bake at 350° for 25 minutes or until a toothpick inserted in the center comes out clean. Cool for 10 minutes before removing to a wire rack. Frost cooled cupcakes.

1 cupcake: 258 cal., 9g fat (5g sat. fat), 45mg chol., 291mg sod., 41g carb. (27g sugars, 1g fiber), 3g pro.

VANILLA BEAN CUPCAKES

My 3-year-old son loves these! Vanilla bean flecks give the moist, tender cupcakes special-occasion status.
—Alysha Braun, St. Catharines, ON

PREP: 30 MIN. • **BAKE:** 20 MIN. + COOLING
MAKES: 1½ DOZEN

- ¾ cup unsalted butter, softened
- 1¼ cups sugar
- 2 large eggs, room temperature
- 2 vanilla beans
- 2 cups cake flour
- 2 tsp. baking powder
- ½ tsp. salt
- ⅔ cup 2% milk

FROSTING
- 1 pkg. (8 oz.) cream cheese, softened
- 6 Tbsp. unsalted butter, softened
- 1½ tsp. vanilla extract
- 3 cups confectioners' sugar
  Assorted sprinkles and coarse sugar

1. Preheat oven to 375°. Line 18 muffin cups with paper liners.

2. In a large bowl, cream butter and sugar until light and fluffy, 5-7 minutes. Add eggs, 1 at a time, beating well after each addition. Split the vanilla beans lengthwise; using the tip of a sharp knife, scrape seeds from the center of the bean into creamed mixture. In another bowl, whisk flour, baking powder and salt; add to the creamed mixture alternately with milk, beating well after each addition.

3. Fill prepared cups half full. Bake until a toothpick inserted in center comes out clean, 18-20 minutes. Cool in pans 10 minutes before removing to wire racks to cool completely.

4. In a large bowl, beat cream cheese, butter and vanilla extract until blended. Gradually beat in confectioners' sugar until smooth. Frost cupcakes. Decorate with sprinkles and coarse sugar as desired. Refrigerate leftovers.

1 cupcake: 266 cal., 13g fat (8g sat. fat), 56mg chol., 143mg sod., 36g carb. (24g sugars, 0 fiber), 3g pro.

BAKING 101

MAPLE CARROT CUPCAKES

I come from a line of family cooks and have liked to cook and bake since I was young. Mother and Grandmom were always in the kitchen cooking up something delicious. These carrot cupcakes were Grandmom's specialty, and we always have them at family gatherings.

—Lisa Ann Panzino DiNunzio, Vineland, NJ

PREP: 15 MIN. • **BAKE:** 20 MIN. + COOLING
MAKES: 1½ DOZEN

- 2 cups all-purpose flour
- 1 cup sugar
- 1 tsp. baking powder
- 1 tsp. baking soda
- 1 tsp. ground cinnamon
- ½ tsp. salt
- 4 large eggs, room temperature
- 1 cup canola oil
- ½ cup maple syrup
- 3 cups grated carrots
  (about 6 medium)

FROSTING
- 1 pkg. (8 oz.) cream cheese, softened
- ¼ cup butter, softened
- ¼ cup maple syrup
- 1 tsp. vanilla extract
  Walnuts, optional

1. Preheat oven to 350°. In a large bowl, combine the first 6 ingredients. In another bowl, beat eggs, oil and syrup. Stir into the dry ingredients just until moistened. Fold in carrots.
2. Fill 18 greased or paper-lined muffin cups two-thirds full. Bake for 20-25 minutes or until a toothpick inserted in the center comes out clean. Cool for 5 minutes before removing from pans to wire racks.
3. For frosting, combine the cream cheese, butter, syrup and vanilla in a bowl; beat until smooth. Frost cooled cupcakes. Add nuts if desired. Store in the refrigerator.

1 cupcake: 327 cal., 20g fat (6g sat. fat), 68mg chol., 243mg sod., 33g carb. (21g sugars, 1g fiber), 4g pro.

PINK VELVET CUPCAKES

My daughter loves all things pink, so this recipe was just right for her birthday. Even my teenage son (not a fan of pink) ate his share.

—Paulette Smith, Winston-Salem, NC

PREP: 30 MIN. + CHILLING
BAKE: 25 MIN. + COOLING
MAKES: 2 DOZEN

- 1 cup butter, softened
- 1¼ cups sugar
- ⅛ tsp. pink paste food coloring
- 3 large eggs, room temperature
- 1 tsp. vanilla extract
- 2½ cups all-purpose flour
- 1½ tsp. baking powder
- ¼ tsp. baking soda
- ¼ tsp. salt
- 1 cup buttermilk

WHITE CHOCOLATE GANACHE
- 2 cups white baking chips
- ½ cup heavy whipping cream
- 1 Tbsp. butter
  Pink coarse sugar and
  sugar pearls

1. Preheat oven to 350°. In a large bowl, cream butter, sugar and food coloring until light and fluffy, 5-7 minutes. Add eggs, 1 at a time, beating well after each addition. Beat in vanilla. Combine the flour, baking powder, baking soda and salt; add to creamed mixture alternately with the buttermilk, beating well after each addition.
2. Fill 24 paper-lined muffin cups two-thirds full. Bake for 23-27 minutes or until a toothpick inserted in center comes out clean. Cool for 10 minutes before removing from pans to wire racks to cool completely.
3. Meanwhile, place white chips in a small bowl. In a small saucepan, bring cream just to a boil. Pour over chips; whisk until smooth. Stir in the butter. Transfer to a large bowl. Chill for 30 minutes, stirring once.
4. Beat on high speed for 2-3 minutes or until soft peaks form and frosting is light and fluffy. Frost cupcakes. Top cupcakes with coarse sugar and sugar pearls. Store in the refrigerator.

1 cupcake: 266 cal., 15g fat (9g sat. fat), 57mg chol., 154mg sod., 29g carb. (20g sugars, 0 fiber), 3g pro.

NANA'S CHOCOLATE CUPCAKES WITH MINT FROSTING

Nana used to make these cupcakes at Christmas every year. Even though she is no longer with us, the cakes have special meaning and it brings me so much joy to bake them. For a more indulgent version, double the frosting and pile it high on top of each cupcake.
—Chekota Hunter, Cassville, MO

PREP: 25 MIN. • **BAKE:** 15 MIN. + COOLING
MAKES: 1 DOZEN

- ½   cup baking cocoa
- 1   cup boiling water
- ¼   cup butter, softened
- 1   cup sugar
- 2   large eggs, room temperature
- 1⅓ cups all-purpose flour
- 2   tsp. baking powder
- ¼   tsp. salt
- ¼   cup unsweetened applesauce

FROSTING
- 1   cup confectioners' sugar
- 3   Tbsp. butter, softened
- 4   tsp. heavy whipping cream
     Dash peppermint extract
- 1   drop green food coloring, optional
- 2   Tbsp. miniature semisweet chocolate chips
     Mint Andes candies, optional

NANA'S CHOCOLATE CUPCAKES
WITH MINT FROSTING

1. Preheat oven to 375°. Line 12 muffin cups with paper or foil liners. Mix baking cocoa and boiling water until smooth; cool completely.

2. Beat butter and sugar until blended. Beat in eggs, 1 at a time. In another bowl, whisk together flour, baking powder and salt; add to butter mixture alternately with applesauce, beating well after each addition. Beat in the cocoa mixture.

3. Fill prepared muffin cups three-fourths full. Bake until a toothpick inserted in center comes out clean, 15-18 minutes. Cool for 10 minutes before removing from pan to a wire rack to cool completely.

4. Beat confectioners' sugar, butter, cream and extract until smooth. If desired, tint frosting green with food coloring. Stir in miniature chocolate chips. Spread over cupcakes. If desired, top with candies.

1 cupcake: 253 cal., 9g fat (5g sat. fat), 51mg chol., 196mg sod., 41g carb. (28g sugars, 1g fiber), 3g pro.

HOW BIG?

Standard cupcake pans typically have wells that are 2½ in. in diameter. Each well can hold a bit more than 1 oz. of batter. Jumbo cupcake pans have 3½-in. wells that hold around 4 oz. of batter.

BUNDT CAKES & POUND CAKES

LEMON LOVER'S POUND CAKE

Everyone raves about this pretty dessert, and it sure doesn't last long in my family. It also freezes beautifully, so why not make two and pop one into the freezer for another day?

—Annettia Mounger, Kansas City, MO

PREP: 20 MIN. • **BAKE:** 55 MIN. + COOLING
MAKES: 12 SERVINGS

- 1 cup butter, softened
- 3 cups sugar
- 6 large eggs, room temperature
- 5 Tbsp. lemon juice
- 1 Tbsp. grated lemon zest
- 1 tsp. lemon extract
- 3 cups all-purpose flour
- ½ tsp. baking soda
- ¼ tsp. salt
- 1¼ cups sour cream

ICING

- ¼ cup sour cream, room temperature
- 2 Tbsp. butter, softened
- 2½ cups confectioners' sugar
- 2 to 3 Tbsp. lemon juice
- 2 tsp. grated lemon zest

BAKING 101

LEMON LOVER'S POUND CAKE

1. Preheat oven to 350°. In a large bowl, cream butter and sugar until light and fluffy, 5-7 minutes. Add eggs, 1 at a time, beating well after each addition. Stir in lemon juice, zest and extract. Combine the flour, baking soda and salt; add to the creamed mixture alternately with sour cream. Beat just until combined.
2. Pour into a greased and floured 10-in. fluted tube pan. Bake until a toothpick inserted near the center comes out clean, 55-60 minutes. Cool in pan for 10 minutes before removing to a wire rack to cool completely.
3. For icing, in a small bowl, beat the sour cream and butter until smooth. Gradually add confectioners' sugar. Beat in lemon juice and zest. Drizzle over the cake. If desired, top with additional grated lemon zest. Store in the refrigerator.
1 piece: 658 cal., 26g fat (15g sat. fat), 146mg chol., 286mg sod., 101g carb. (76g sugars, 1g fiber), 8g pro.

BROWN SUGAR PECAN CAKE

My great-aunt from Kentucky was famous in our family for her cooking. She made a cake like this one many times during my childhood. I found a similar recipe years later, changing it a bit to use what I had on hand. The added crunch of the pecans gives it a southern flair she would have loved.
—Lisa Varner, El Paso, TX

PREP: 20 MIN. • **BAKE:** 70 MIN. + COOLING
MAKES: 16 SERVINGS

1½ cups butter, softened
2   cups packed brown sugar
½   cup sugar
6   large eggs, room temperature
2   tsp. vanilla extract
3   cups all-purpose flour
½   tsp. baking powder
1   cup sour cream
1½ cups chopped pecans
    Confectioners' sugar
    Optional: Vanilla ice
    cream and butterscotch
    ice cream topping

BAKING 101

1. Preheat oven to 350°. Grease and flour a 10-in. fluted tube pan.
2. In a large bowl, cream butter, brown sugar and sugar until light and fluffy, 5-7 minutes. Add eggs, 1 at a time, beating well after each addition. Beat in vanilla. In another bowl, whisk flour and baking powder; add to the creamed mixture alternately with sour cream, beating well after each addition. Fold in pecans.
3. Transfer the batter to prepared pan. Bake until a toothpick inserted in center comes out clean, 70-80 minutes. Cool in pan for 30 minutes before removing to a wire rack to cool completely. Dust with confectioners' sugar. If desired, serve with ice cream and drizzle with topping.
1 piece: 496 cal., 30g fat (14g sat. fat), 119mg chol., 192mg sod., 53g carb. (34g sugars, 2g fiber), 6g pro.

7UP POUND CAKE

BASIC CHOCOLATE POUND CAKE

This chocolate pound cake is one of my favorite cakes to bake. A friend of mine gave me this recipe years ago. Somehow it just gets better each time you bake it!
—Doris Fletcher, Hendersonville, NC

PREP: 15 MIN.
BAKE: 1 HOUR 10 MIN. + COOLING
MAKES: 16 SERVINGS

1 cup butter, softened
½ cup shortening
3 cups sugar
6 large eggs, room temperature
3 cups all-purpose flour
½ tsp. baking powder
¼ cup baking cocoa
1 cup 2% milk
1 Tbsp. vanilla extract
  Confectioners' sugar, optional

1. Preheat oven to 350°. In a large bowl, cream butter, shortening and sugar until light and fluffy, 5-7 minutes. Add eggs, 1 at a time, beating well after each addition. Combine the flour, baking powder and cocoa. Combine the milk and vanilla. Add dry ingredients to creamed mixture alternately with the milk mixture. Mix well.
2. Pour into greased 10-in. tube pan. Bake until a toothpick inserted in the center comes out clean, 70-80 minutes. Cool the cake for 15 minutes before removing from pan to a wire rack to cool completely. If desired, sprinkle with confectioners' sugar.
1 piece: 429 cal., 20g fat (10g sat. fat), 112mg chol., 160mg sod., 57g carb. (38g sugars, 1g fiber), 6g pro.

7UP POUND CAKE

My grandmother gave me my first cake recipe—a pound cake using 7UP—and her grandmother had given it to her. On top of being delicious, this cake represents family tradition, connection and love.
—Marsha Davis, Desert Hot Springs, CA

PREP: 25 MIN. • **BAKE:** 65 MIN. + COOLING
MAKES: 16 SERVINGS

1½ cups butter, softened
3 cups sugar
5 large eggs, room temperature
2 Tbsp. lemon juice
1 tsp. vanilla extract
3 cups all-purpose flour
¾ cup 7UP soda
GLAZE
1½ cups confectioners' sugar
1 Tbsp. lemon or lime juice
1 to 2 Tbsp. 7UP soda
½ tsp. grated lemon or lime zest, optional

1. Preheat oven to 350°. Grease and flour a 10-in. fluted or plain tube pan.
2. In a large bowl, cream butter and sugar until light and fluffy, 5-7 minutes. Add eggs, 1 at a time, beating well after each addition. Beat in lemon juice and vanilla. Add flour alternately with 7UP, beating well after each addition.
3. Transfer batter to prepared pan. Bake until a toothpick inserted in the center comes out clean, 65-75 minutes. Cool in pan 20 minutes before removing to a wire rack to cool completely.
4. For the glaze, in a small bowl, mix the confectioners' sugar, lemon juice and enough 7UP to reach desired consistency. If desired, stir in zest. Drizzle over cake.
1 piece: 457 cal., 19g fat (11g sat. fat), 104mg chol., 177mg sod., 69g carb. (50g sugars, 1g fiber), 5g pro.

SPARKLING CIDER POUND CAKE

Sparkling apple cider in the batter and the glaze gives this incredible pound cake a delicious and distinctive flavor. It reminds me of fall with every bite. I love everything about it!
—Nikki Barton, Providence, UT

PREP: 20 MIN. • **BAKE:** 40 MIN. + COOLING
MAKES: 12 SERVINGS

- ¾ cup butter, softened
- 1½ cups sugar
- 3 large eggs, room temperature
- 1½ cups all-purpose flour
- ¼ tsp. baking powder
- ¼ tsp. salt
- ½ cup sparkling apple cider

GLAZE
- ¾ cup confectioners' sugar
- 3 to 4 tsp. sparkling apple cider

1. Preheat oven to 350°. Line the bottom of a greased 9x5-in. loaf pan with parchment; grease parchment.
2. In a large bowl, cream butter and sugar until light and fluffy, 5-7 minutes.

Add eggs, 1 at a time, beating well after each addition. In another bowl, whisk flour, baking powder and salt; add to creamed mixture alternately with cider, beating well after each addition.
3. Transfer to prepared pan. Bake until a toothpick inserted in center comes out clean, 40-50 minutes. Cool in pan 10 minutes before removing to a wire rack to cool completely.
4. In a small bowl, mix glaze ingredients until smooth; spoon over top of cake, allowing it to flow over sides.
1 piece: 308 cal., 13g fat (8g sat. fat), 77mg chol., 169mg sod., 46g carb. (34g sugars, 0 fiber), 3g pro.

PEANUT BUTTER BUNDT CAKE

This peanut butter cake with frosting is heavenly to me. I use smooth peanut butter, but crunchy would work just fine, too.
—Karen Holt, Rock Hill, SC

BAKING 101

PREP: 15 MIN. • **BAKE:** 75 MIN. + COOLING
MAKES: 16 SERVINGS

- 1 cup butter, softened
- ½ cup creamy peanut butter
- 1 cup sugar
- 1 cup packed brown sugar
- 5 large eggs, room temperature
- 3 tsp. vanilla extract
- 3 cups all-purpose flour
- ½ tsp. salt
- ½ tsp. baking powder
- ¼ tsp. baking soda
- 1 cup 2% milk

FROSTING
- ¼ cup butter, softened
- 2 Tbsp. creamy peanut butter
- 2 cups confectioners' sugar
- 1 to 3 Tbsp. 2% milk

1. Preheat oven to 325°. Grease and flour a 10-in. fluted tube pan.
2. In a large bowl, cream butter, peanut butter and sugars until light and fluffy, 5-7 minutes. Add eggs, 1 at a time, beating well after each addition. Beat in vanilla. In another bowl, whisk flour, salt, baking powder and baking soda; add to creamed mixture alternately with milk, beating after each addition just until combined. Transfer to the prepared pan.
3. Bake until a toothpick inserted in center comes out clean, 65-75 minutes. Cool in pan 5 minutes before removing to a wire rack to cool completely.
4. For frosting, in a large bowl, beat butter, peanut butter and sugar. Beat in enough milk to achieve desired consistency. Spread over top of cake.
1 piece: 465 cal., 22g fat (11g sat. fat), 98mg chol., 300mg sod., 62g carb. (43g sugars, 1g fiber), 7g pro.

BUTTERMILK POUND CAKE

Once people taste this cake, they won't go back to their other pound cake recipes. It is a truly southern recipe, and one I think can't be topped—it's the cake I make most often.
—Gracie Hanchey, DeRidder, LA

PREP: 10 MIN. • **BAKE:** 70 MIN. + COOLING
MAKES: 20 SERVINGS

BAKING 101

- 1 cup butter, softened
- 2½ cups sugar
- 4 large eggs, room temperature
- 1 tsp. vanilla extract
- 3 cups all-purpose flour
- ¼ tsp. baking soda
- 1 cup buttermilk
   Confectioners' sugar, optional

1. Preheat oven to 325°. In a large bowl, cream butter and sugar until light and fluffy, 5-7 minutes. Add eggs, 1 at a time, beating well after each addition. Beat in vanilla. Combine the flour and baking soda; add alternately with the buttermilk and beat well.
2. Pour into a greased and floured 10-in. fluted tube pan. Bake until a toothpick inserted in the center comes out clean, about 70 minutes. Cool in pan for 15 minutes before removing to a wire rack to cool completely. Dust with confectioners' sugar if desired.
1 piece: 285 cal., 10g fat (6g sat. fat), 68mg chol., 134mg sod., 45g carb. (30g sugars, 1g fiber), 4g pro.

TEST KITCHEN TIP
What does buttermilk do to cake? Its acidic nature tenderizes the gluten in flour, yielding a moist and tender crumb.

FESTIVE CRANBERRY CAKE

FESTIVE CRANBERRY CAKE

This cake, a favorite in my family, makes good use of our area's cranberry harvest. What's more, since you can prepare it the night before, the recipe is a real time-saver.
—Gladys Wilson, Anchorage, AK

PREP: 10 MIN. • **BAKE:** 1 HOUR + CHILLING
MAKES: 16 SERVINGS

- ¾ cup butter, softened
- 1 cup sugar
- 2 large eggs, room temperature
- 2¼ cups all-purpose flour
- 1 tsp. baking powder
- 1 tsp. baking soda
- 1 cup buttermilk
- 1 cup fresh or frozen cranberries
- 1 cup chopped dates
- 1 cup chopped pecans

GLAZE
- ½ cup orange juice
- ¼ cup sugar
- Optional: Sugared cranberries and rosemary sprigs

1. Preheat oven to 350°. In a bowl, cream butter and sugar. Add eggs; beat well. Combine the dry ingredients; add to the creamed mixture alternately with buttermilk. Stir in cranberries, dates and pecans.
2. Spread into a greased and floured 10-in. tube pan. Bake for 60-70 minutes or until a toothpick inserted in the center comes out clean. Cool in pan for 10 minutes.
3. Meanwhile, for glaze, heat orange juice and sugar in a small saucepan until sugar dissolves.
4. Invert cake onto a serving plate. With a toothpick, punch holes in cake. Spoon glaze over cake. Cover and refrigerate for at least 8 hours. If desired, top with sugared cranberries and rosemary.
1 piece: 304 cal., 15g fat (6g sat. fat), 50mg chol., 215mg sod., 41g carb. (25g sugars, 2g fiber), 4g pro.

MAKING THE GARNISH

You'll need:

Toss 12 oz. fresh or frozen cranberries in a large mixing bowl with 2 Tbsp. water and 1 Tbsp. pasteurized egg whites until coated. Spread on a baking sheet and sprinkle with ½ cup coarse and ½ cup superfine sugar until coated.

Move to a wire rack and let berries dry; they should be completely set within 2 hours.

Repeat to toss 5-6 sprigs of fresh rosemary in the egg-white mixture; coat with the sugar mixture and dry on a wire rack.

GLAZED SPICED RUM POUND CAKES

My recipe makes two loaf-size treats, perfect for sharing. The spiced rum flavor in the cake and glaze really comes through.
—Christine Russell, Littleton, NH

PREP: 30 MIN. • **BAKE:** 45 MIN. + COOLING
MAKES: 2 LOAVES (16 PIECES EACH)

- 1 cup butter, softened
- 2 cups packed brown sugar
- 5 large eggs, room temperature
- ⅓ cup spiced rum
- 2 tsp. vanilla extract
- 3½ cups all-purpose flour
- 2 tsp. baking powder
- ½ tsp. baking soda
- ½ tsp. salt
- ½ cup 2% milk

GLAZE
- ½ cup sugar
- ¼ cup butter, cubed
- 2 tsp. water
- 2 tsp. spiced rum
- ½ cup chopped pecans, toasted

1. Preheat oven to 350°. Grease and flour two 9x5-in. loaf pans. In a large bowl, cream butter and brown sugar until light and fluffy, 5-7 minutes. Add eggs, 1 at a time, beating well after each addition. Beat in rum and vanilla. In another bowl, whisk the flour, baking powder, baking soda and salt; add to creamed mixture alternately with milk, beating well after each addition.

2. Spoon the batter into prepared pans. Bake until a toothpick inserted in center comes out clean, 45-50 minutes. Cool in pans for 10 minutes before removing to wire racks to cool.

3. Meanwhile, in a small saucepan, combine sugar, butter, water and rum. Bring to a boil. Remove from the heat; drizzle over warm cakes. Sprinkle with pecans. Cool completely on wire racks.

1 piece: 209 cal., 9g fat (5g sat. fat), 48mg chol., 161mg sod., 28g carb. (17g sugars, 1g fiber), 3g pro.

AUNT LOU'S FRESH APPLE CAKE

My Great-Aunt Lou made a luscious apple cake that became a family tradition. My mom makes it for our annual beach trip to the Outer Banks.
—Cristy King, Scott Depot, WV

PREP: 15 MIN. • **BAKE:** 50 MIN. + COOLING
MAKES: 12 SERVINGS

- 2 cups sugar
- 1 cup canola oil
- 3 large eggs, room temperature
- 2 tsp. vanilla extract
- 3 cups all-purpose flour
- 1 tsp. salt
- 1 tsp. baking powder
- 3 cups chopped peeled apples (about 3 medium)
  Confectioners' sugar

1. Preheat oven to 350°. Grease and flour a 10-in. fluted tube pan.

2. In a large bowl, beat sugar, oil, eggs and vanilla until well blended. In another bowl, whisk flour, salt and baking powder; gradually beat into oil mixture. Stir in apples. Transfer batter to prepared pan.

3. Bake until a toothpick inserted in center comes out clean, 50-60 minutes. Cool in pan 10 minutes. Run a knife around sides and center tube of pan, then remove the cake to a wire rack to cool completely. Dust cooled cake with confectioners' sugar.

1 piece: 445 cal., 20g fat (2g sat. fat), 47mg chol., 249mg sod., 62g carb. (37g sugars, 2g fiber), 5g pro.

BAKING 101

RASPBERRY
MOSCOW MULE CAKE

RASPBERRY MOSCOW MULE CAKE

This Moscow mule cake is the best cake I've ever made from scratch. It's so moist and flavorful and reminds me of my favorite cocktail.
—Becky Hardin, St. Peters, MO

PREP: 25 MIN. • **BAKE:** 70 MIN. + COOLING
MAKES: 16 SERVINGS

- 1½ cups unsalted butter, softened
- 2¾ cups sugar
- 5 large eggs, room temperature
- 1 Tbsp. vanilla extract
- 3 cups cake flour
- ½ tsp. salt
- 1 cup alcoholic raspberry ginger beer or nonalcoholic plain ginger beer
- 2 cups fresh raspberries

SYRUP
- ½ cup alcoholic raspberry ginger beer or nonalcoholic plain ginger beer
- ½ cup sugar
- ¼ cup lime juice

GLAZE
- 1½ cups confectioners' sugar
- 2 to 3 Tbsp. lime juice

1. Preheat oven to 325°. Grease and flour a 10-in. fluted tube pan.
2. In a large bowl, cream butter and sugar until light and fluffy, 5-7 minutes. Add eggs, 1 at a time, beating well after each addition. Beat in vanilla. In another bowl, whisk cake flour and salt; add to the creamed mixture alternately with the ginger beer, beating well after each addition (the mixture may appear curdled).
3. Gently fold raspberries into batter; pour into the prepared pan. Bake until a toothpick inserted near the center comes out clean, 70-80 minutes.
4. Meanwhile, for the syrup, in a small saucepan, bring ginger beer, sugar and lime juice to a boil. Reduce heat; simmer 10 minutes. Cool slightly.
5. Poke holes in warm cake using a fork or wooden skewer. Slowly spoon syrup over cake. Cool for 15 minutes before removing from pan to a wire rack to cool completely.
6. In a small bowl, mix confectioners' sugar and enough lime juice to reach desired consistency; pour over cooled cake. Let stand until set. If desired, top with additional fresh raspberries.
1 piece: 488 cal., 19g fat (11g sat. fat), 104mg chol., 100mg sod., 75g carb. (53g sugars, 1g fiber), 5g pro.

GINGERBREAD WITH FIG-WALNUT SAUCE

I experimented with aniseed this past holiday season and fell in love with the flavor. It really enhances the gingerbread spices and fig sauce in this extraordinary fluted tube cake.

—Shelly Bevington, Hermiston, OR

PREP: 30 MIN. • **BAKE:** 40 MIN. + COOLING
MAKES: 12 SERVINGS

- 1 cup unsalted butter, softened
- 1 cup packed brown sugar
- 3 large eggs, room temperature
- 1 cup molasses
- 2½ cups all-purpose flour
- 2 tsp. baking soda
- 2 tsp. ground ginger
- 1½ tsp. aniseed, crushed
- 1 tsp. salt
- 1 tsp. ground cinnamon
- ½ tsp. ground allspice
- ¼ tsp. ground cloves
- 1 cup buttermilk
- 1 Tbsp. lemon juice
  Confectioners' sugar, optional

SAUCE

- 12 oz. Calimyrna dried figs, cut into eighths
- 1 cup finely chopped walnuts
- 2 Tbsp. walnut or canola oil
- 1 Tbsp. aniseed, crushed
- 1 tsp. ground cinnamon
- ½ tsp. ground cloves
- 1¾ cups water
- 1 cup sugar
- 2 Tbsp. lemon juice
- ¼ tsp. salt

1. In a large bowl, cream butter and brown sugar until light and fluffy, 5-7 minutes. Add eggs, 1 at a time, beating well after each addition. Beat in molasses (mixture will appear curdled).

2. In a small bowl, combine the flour, baking soda, ginger, aniseed, salt, cinnamon, allspice and cloves. Add to the creamed mixture alternately with buttermilk and lemon juice, beating well after each addition.

3. Pour batter into a greased and floured 10-in. fluted tube pan. Bake at 350° until a toothpick inserted in the center comes out clean, 40-50 minutes.

4. Cool for 10 minutes in pan before removing from pan to a wire rack to cool completely. Dust cake with confectioners' sugar if desired.

5. For sauce, in a large skillet, cook figs and walnuts in oil over medium heat for 4 minutes. Stir in the spices; cook until aromatic, 1-2 minutes longer.

6. Stir in water, sugar, lemon juice and salt. Bring to a boil. Reduce heat; simmer, uncovered, until thickened, 8-12 minutes, stirring occasionally. Let cool to room temperature. Serve with gingerbread.

1 piece with ⅓ cup sauce: 629 cal., 26g fat (11g sat. fat), 88mg chol., 534mg sod., 97g carb. (70g sugars, 5g fiber), 8g pro.

. . . .
DID YOU KNOW?

Be sure to use Calimyrna figs instead of Mission figs for this recipe; they're larger, with a more delicate flavor and a yellowish skin when dried. You can also use Smyrna figs (also called Turkish figs). They're the same variety—the name "Calimyrna" is a marketing term to identify smyrna figs grown in California.

GINGERBREAD WITH FIG-WALNUT SAUCE

BLUEBERRY SOUR CREAM POUND CAKE

Original recipes for pound cake called for a pound each of butter, sugar, eggs and flour! Through the years, recipes have been adjusted to be a little lighter yet still have outstanding results.
—Juanita Miller, Arnett, OK

PREP: 20 MIN. • **BAKE:** 1 HOUR
MAKES: 20 SERVINGS

BAKING 101

- 6 large eggs, separated, room temperature
- 1 cup butter, softened
- 3 cups sugar
- 1 tsp. almonds extract
- 1 tsp. vanilla extract
- 1 tsp. butter flavoring
- 3 cups all-purpose flour
- ¼ tsp. baking soda
- 1 cup sour cream
- 1½ cups fresh or frozen blueberries

1. Preheat oven to 350°. Grease and flour a 10-in. tube pan. In a large bowl, cream the butter and sugar until light and fluffy, 5-7 minutes. Add egg yolks, 1 at a time, beating well after each addition. Add the extracts and butter flavoring. Combine flour and baking soda; add to the creamed mixture alternately with sour cream, beating well after each addition.
2. In another bowl and with clean beaters, beat egg whites on high speed until stiff peaks form. Fold into batter. Fold in blueberries.
3. Spoon into the prepared pan. Bake until a toothpick inserted in the center comes out clean, 60-70 minutes. Cool cake for 10 minutes in pan before removing from pan to a wire rack to cool completely.
1 piece: 320 cal., 13g fat (8g sat. fat), 96mg chol., 134mg sod., 46g carb. (31g sugars, 1g fiber), 4g pro.

PEPPERMINT CREAM POUND CAKE

I came up with this recipe because I was looking for a new twist on a tried-and-true pound cake, and I really like the look and flavor of peppermint, especially around Christmas. Everyone at work loved the results, and my family did, too.

—Carolyn Webster, Winston-Salem, NC

PREP: 35 MIN. • **BAKE:** 1 HOUR + COOLING
MAKES: 12 SERVINGS

- 1 cup unsalted butter, softened
- ½ cup butter-flavored shortening
- 2 cups sugar
- 6 large eggs, room temperature
- 1 tsp. vanilla extract
- ½ tsp. peppermint extract
- 3 cups all-purpose flour
- 1 tsp. baking powder
- 1 cup heavy whipping cream
- ½ cup finely crushed peppermint candies

GLAZE
- 1½ cups confectioners' sugar
- 1 tsp. unsalted butter, melted
- ¼ tsp. vanilla extract
- ⅛ tsp. salt
- 4 to 5 Tbsp. heavy whipping cream
  Additional crushed peppermint candies

1. Preheat oven to 325°. In a large bowl, cream the butter, shortening and sugar until light and fluffy, 5-7 minutes. Add eggs, 1 at a time, beating well after each addition. Beat in extracts. Combine flour and baking powder; add to the creamed mixture alternately with the whipping cream. Fold in candies.
2. Transfer to a well-greased and floured 10-in. fluted tube pan. Bake until a toothpick inserted in the center comes out clean, 1-1¼ hours. Cool for 10 minutes before removing from pan to a wire rack to cool completely.
3. For the glaze, in a small bowl, combine confectioners' sugar, butter, vanilla and salt. Stir in enough cream to achieve a drizzling consistency. Drizzle over the cake. Sprinkle with additional crushed peppermint candies. Refrigerate any leftovers.
1 piece: 649 cal., 35g fat (18g sat. fat), 181mg chol., 107mg sod., 77g carb. (50g sugars, 1g fiber), 7g pro.

GRANDMA'S CARROT CAKE

My grandma was very special to me. She had a big country kitchen that was full of wonderful aromas any time we visited. This was one of her prized cake recipes, and it continues to be a favorite from generation to generation.

—Denise Strasz, Detroit, MI

PREP: 30 MIN. • **BAKE:** 50 MIN. + COOLING
MAKES: 16 SERVINGS

- 2 cups sugar
- 1½ cups canola oil
- 4 large eggs, room temperature
- 2 tsp. vanilla extract
- 2½ cups all-purpose flour
- 1½ tsp. baking soda
- ½ tsp. salt
- 1 tsp. ground cinnamon
- 3 cups shredded carrots (about 6 medium)
- 1 cup chopped walnuts

FROSTING
- 1 pkg. (8 oz.) cream cheese, softened
- ¼ cup butter, softened
- 3 cups confectioners' sugar

1. Preheat oven to 350°. Grease and flour a 10-in. fluted tube pan.
2. Beat the first 4 ingredients until well blended. Whisk together flour, baking soda, salt and cinnamon; gradually beat into the sugar mixture. Stir in carrots and walnuts.
3. Transfer to prepared pan. Bake until a toothpick inserted in the center comes out clean, 50-60 minutes. Cool in pan 10 minutes before removing to a wire rack to cool completely.
4. For frosting, beat cream cheese and butter until smooth. Gradually beat in confectioners' sugar. Spread over cake.
1 piece: 593 cal., 35g fat (7g sat. fat), 68mg chol., 292mg sod., 67g carb. (49g sugars, 2g fiber), 6g pro.

BAKING 101

GINGER-GLAZED LEMON BUNDT

Tangy ginger, tart lemon and puckery cranberries make this melt-in-your-mouth cake as crisp—and gorgeous—as autumn.
—*Taste of Home* Test Kitchen

PREP: 20 MIN. • **BAKE:** 1 HOUR + COOLING
MAKES: 12 SERVINGS

SUGARED CRANBERRIES
- 3 Tbsp. light corn syrup
- 1 cup fresh or frozen, thawed cranberries
- ⅓ cup sugar

CAKE
- 1 cup butter, softened
- 2 cups sugar
- 4 large eggs, room temperature
- 2 Tbsp. grated lemon zest
- 1 tsp. lemon extract
- 2½ cups all-purpose flour
- 2 tsp. baking powder
- ½ tsp. salt
- 1 cup fat-free vanilla Greek yogurt

GLAZE
- ⅔ cup confectioners' sugar
- 2 Tbsp. butter, melted
- 1 to 3 tsp. lemon juice
- ½ tsp. ground ginger

1. For sugared cranberries, heat corn syrup in a microwave until warm; gently toss cranberries in syrup, allowing excess to drip off. Toss in sugar to coat. Place on waxed paper; let stand until set, about 1 hour.

2. Preheat oven to 325°. Grease and flour a 10-in. fluted tube pan. In a large bowl, cream butter and sugar until light and fluffy, 5-7 minutes. Add eggs, 1 at a time, beating well after each addition. Beat in lemon zest and extract.

3. In another bowl, whisk the flour, baking powder and salt; add to the creamed mixture alternately with yogurt, beating well after each addition.

GINGER-GLAZED LEMON BUNDT

4. Transfer to prepared pan. Bake until a toothpick inserted in center comes out clean, 60-70 minutes. Cool in pan for 10 minutes before removing to a wire rack to cool completely.

5. For glaze, mix confectioners' sugar, butter, lemon juice and ginger until smooth. Drizzle over the cake. Top with sugared cranberries.

1 piece: 468 cal., 19g fat (12g sat. fat), 108mg chol., 350mg sod., 69g carb. (48g sugars, 1g fiber), 7g pro.

TEST KITCHEN TIP

Want your cranberries to really sparkle? Mix half sanding sugar with regular sugar to use when coating them. See p. 305 for an alternative method for making this decorative garnish.

FOAM CAKES

STRAWBERRY MASCARPONE CAKE

Don't let the number of steps in this recipe fool you—it's easy to assemble. The cake bakes up high and fluffy, and the berries add fresh, fruity flavor. Cream cheese is a good substitute in case you don't have mascarpone cheese handy.
—Carol Witczak, Tinley Park, IL

PREP: 1 HOUR + CHILLING
BAKE: 30 MIN. + COOLING
MAKES: 12 SERVINGS

- 6 cups fresh strawberries, halved (2 lbs.)
- 2 Tbsp. sugar
- 1 tsp. grated orange zest
- 1 Tbsp. orange juice
- ½ tsp. almond extract

CAKE
- 6 large eggs, separated
- 2 cups cake flour
- 2 tsp. baking powder
- ¼ tsp. salt
- 1½ cups sugar, divided
- ½ cup canola oil
- ¼ cup water
- 1 Tbsp. grated orange zest
- ½ tsp. almond extract

WHIPPED CREAM
- 2 cups heavy whipping cream
- ⅓ cup confectioners' sugar
- 2 tsp. vanilla extract

FILLING
- 1 cup mascarpone cheese
- ½ cup heavy whipping cream

1. In a large bowl, combine the first 5 ingredients. Refrigerate, covered, at least 30 minutes. Place egg whites in a large bowl; let stand at room temperature 30 minutes.
2. Preheat oven to 350°. Grease bottoms (not the sides) of two 8-in. round baking pans; line with parchment. Sift flour, baking powder and salt together twice; place in another large bowl.
3. In a small bowl, whisk the egg yolks, 1¼ cups sugar, oil, water, orange zest and almond extract until blended. Add to flour mixture; beat until well blended.
4. With clean beaters, beat the egg whites on medium until soft peaks form. Gradually add remaining ¼ cup sugar, 1 Tbsp. at a time, beating on high after each addition until the sugar is dissolved. Continue beating until soft glossy peaks form. Fold a fourth of the egg whites into the batter, then fold in the remaining whites.

5. Gently transfer batter to prepared pans. Bake on lowest oven rack for 30-35 minutes or until top springs back when lightly touched. Cool in pans 10 minutes before removing to wire racks; remove paper. Cool completely.
6. Meanwhile, for whipped cream, in a large bowl, beat cream until it begins to thicken. Add confectioners' sugar and vanilla; beat until soft peaks form. Refrigerate, covered, at least 1 hour.
7. For filling, in a small bowl, beat mascarpone cheese and cream until stiff peaks form. Refrigerate until assembling.
8. Drain strawberries, reserving the juice mixture. Using a serrated knife, trim tops of cakes if domed. Place 1 cake layer on a serving plate. Brush with half of reserved juice mixture; spread with ¾ cup filling. Arrange strawberries over top, creating an even layer; spread with the remaining filling. Brush the remaining cake layer with remaining juice mixture; place layer over filling, brushed side down.
9. Gently stir whipped cream; spread over the top and sides of cake. Just before serving, arrange strawberries over cake.

1 piece: 677 cal., 48g fat (22g sat. fat), 196mg chol., 200mg sod., 56g carb. (36g sugars, 2g fiber), 10g pro.

CHOCOLATE CHIFFON CAKE

CHOCOLATE CHIFFON CAKE

If you want to offer family and friends a dessert that really stands out from the rest, this is the cake to make. The beautiful high, rich sponge cake is drizzled with a succulent chocolate glaze.

—Erma Fox, Memphis, MO

PREP: 25 MIN. + COOLING
BAKE: 1 HOUR + COOLING
MAKES: 20 SERVINGS

- 7 large eggs, separated
- ½ cup baking cocoa
- ¾ cup boiling water
- 1¾ cups cake flour
- 1¾ cups sugar
- 1½ tsp. baking soda
- 1 tsp. salt
- ½ cup canola oil
- 2 tsp. vanilla extract
- ¼ tsp. cream of tartar

ICING
- ⅓ cup butter
- 2 cups confectioners' sugar
- 2 oz. unsweetened chocolate, melted and cooled
- 1½ tsp. vanilla extract
- 3 to 4 Tbsp. hot water
  Chopped nuts, optional

1. Let eggs stand at room temperature for 30 minutes. Combine cocoa and water until smooth; cool for 20 minutes.
2. In a large bowl, combine flour, sugar, baking soda and salt. In another bowl, whisk the egg yolks, oil and vanilla; add to the dry ingredients along with the cocoa mixture. Beat until well blended.
3. In another large bowl and with clean beaters, beat egg whites and cream of tartar on high speed until stiff peaks form. Gradually fold into the egg yolk mixture.
4. Gently spoon the batter into an ungreased 10-in. tube pan. Cut through the batter with a knife to remove any air pockets. Bake on lowest rack at 325° for 60-65 minutes or until top springs back when lightly touched. Immediately invert pan; cool completely. Run a knife around sides and center tube of pan. Invert cake onto a serving plate.
5. For icing, melt butter in a saucepan. Remove from heat; stir in confectioners' sugar, chocolate, vanilla and water. Drizzle over cake. Sprinkle with nuts if desired.
1 piece: 268 cal., 11g fat (3g sat. fat), 73mg chol., 262mg sod., 40g carb. (30g sugars, 1g fiber), 4g pro.

MINT ANGEL CAKE

MINT ANGEL CAKE

One look at this lovely cake will have guests saving room for dessert! For an easy garnish, sprinkle the bright white frosting with crushed mint candies.
—Agnes Ward, Stratford, ON

PREP: 20 MIN. • **BAKE:** 40 MIN. + COOLING
MAKES: 16 SERVINGS

- 12 large egg whites
- 1 cup cake flour
- 1 tsp. cream of tartar
- 1 tsp. almond extract
- ¼ tsp. salt
- 1¼ cups sugar
- ¼ cup plus 3 Tbsp. crushed peppermint candies, divided
- ¼ cup water
- 1¾ cups heavy whipping cream

1. Let egg whites stand at room temperature 30 minutes. Sift flour twice; set aside.
2. Preheat oven to 350°. Add cream of tartar, almond extract and salt to egg whites; beat on medium speed until soft peaks form. Gradually add sugar, about 2 Tbsp. at a time, beating on high until stiff peaks form. Gradually fold in flour, about ½ cup at a time.
3. Gently spoon into an ungreased 10-in. tube pan. Cut through batter with a knife to remove air pockets. Bake on lowest oven rack until lightly browned and entire top appears dry, 40-50 minutes. Immediately invert pan; cool completely, about 1 hour.
4. In a small saucepan, combine ¼ cup crushed candies and water. Cook and stir over medium heat until candies are melted and syrupy. In a large bowl, beat cream until stiff peaks form.
5. Run a knife around side and center tube of pan. Remove cake to a serving plate; cut horizontally into 3 layers. Place bottom layer on a serving plate; brush with 2 Tbsp. mint syrup. Spread with ½ cup whipped cream; sprinkle with 1 Tbsp. crushed mint candies. Repeat layers.
6. Top with third cake layer. Frost top and sides of cake with the remaining whipped cream. Top with remaining candies. Store in refrigerator.
1 piece: 213 cal., 10g fat (6g sat. fat), 36mg chol., 90mg sod., 27g carb. (19g sugars, 0 fiber), 4g pro.

LEMON-THYME ANGEL FOOD CAKE

Thyme adds a new twist to the classic angel food cake. The flavors pair well together. We enjoy this alongside strawberry ice cream.
—Janie Colle, Hutchinson, KS

PREP: 40 MIN. • **BAKE:** 30 MIN. + COOLING
MAKES: 12 SERVINGS

- 1¼ cups egg whites (about 9 large)
- 1 cup cake flour
- ½ cup confectioners' sugar
- 3 Tbsp. lemon juice
- 1 tsp. cream of tartar
- ½ tsp. salt
- 1 cup sugar
- 2 Tbsp. minced fresh thyme
- 2 Tbsp. lemon zest

1. Place egg whites in a large bowl; let stand at room temperature 30 minutes.
2. Preheat oven to 350°. Sift flour and confectioners' sugar together twice.
3. Add lemon juice, cream of tartar and salt to egg whites; beat on medium speed until soft peaks form. Gradually add sugar, 1 Tbsp. at a time, beating on high after each addition until sugar is dissolved. Continue beating until soft glossy peaks form. Beat in thyme and lemon zest. Gradually fold in the flour mixture, about ½ cup at a time.
4. Gently transfer to an ungreased 10-in. tube pan. Cut through batter with a knife to remove air pockets. Bake on lowest oven rack for 30-35 minutes or until top crust is golden brown and cracks feel dry. Immediately invert pan; cool completely in pan, about 1½ hours.
5. Run a knife around the sides and center tube of pan. Remove cake to a serving plate.
1 piece: 141 cal., 0 fat (0 sat. fat), 0 chol., 141mg sod., 32g carb. (22g sugars, 0 fiber), 4g pro.

TROUBLESHOOTING FOAM CAKES

CAKE IS HEAVY AND DENSE
- Oven temperature was too low. Check temperature with an oven thermometer.

  - Ingredients were folded in too vigorously.

  - Eggs were underbeaten.

  - There was egg yolk in the egg whites before beating.

  - Egg whites were beaten in a bowl that wasn't clean.

CAKE TOP HAS SUNK
- Oven temperature was too high. Check temperature with an oven thermometer.

  - Cake was underbaked.

LAYERED ORANGE SPONGE CAKE

This recipe's been handed down in my family for 40 years, from a relative who was a French baker. It's light, delicate and delicious, just like a great cake should be.
—Joyce Speerbrecher, Grafton, WI

PREP: 30 MIN. • **BAKE:** 45 MIN. + COOLING
MAKES: 12 SERVINGS

- 8 large eggs, separated
- 1 cup plus 2 Tbsp. all-purpose flour
- ⅔ cup plus ⅔ cup sugar, divided
- ½ cup orange juice
- 3 Tbsp. grated orange zest
- ½ tsp. salt
- ¼ tsp. cream of tartar
- FROSTING
- 1½ cups sugar
- 6 Tbsp. all-purpose flour
- ⅔ cup orange juice
- 3 Tbsp. grated orange zest
- 2 large eggs
- 2 cups heavy whipping cream
- 1 cup chopped pecans

1. Place egg whites in a large bowl; let stand at room temperature 30 minutes. Meanwhile, preheat oven to 325°. Sift flour twice.

2. In a large bowl, beat egg yolks until slightly thickened. Gradually add ⅔ cup sugar, beating on high speed until thick and lemon-colored. Beat in orange juice and orange zest. Fold in flour.

3. Add salt and cream of tartar to the egg whites; with clean beaters, beat on medium until soft peaks form. Gradually add remaining ⅔ cup sugar, 1 Tbsp. at a time, beating on high after each addition until sugar is dissolved. Continue beating until soft glossy peaks form. Fold a fourth of the egg whites into batter, then fold in the remaining whites.

4. Gently transfer to an ungreased 10-in. tube pan. Bake on lowest oven rack for 45-55 minutes or until the top springs back when lightly touched. Immediately invert pan; cool cake in pan, about 1½ hours.

5. In a large heavy saucepan, mix sugar and flour. Whisk in the orange juice and orange zest. Cook and stir over medium heat until thickened and bubbly. Reduce heat to low; cook and stir 2 minutes longer. Remove from heat.

6. In a small bowl, whisk a small amount of the hot mixture into eggs; return all to pan, whisking constantly. Bring to a gentle boil; cook and stir 2 minutes. Immediately transfer to a clean bowl. Cool for 30 minutes. Press plastic wrap onto the surface of the orange mixture; refrigerate until cold.

7. In a large bowl, beat cream until soft peaks form; fold into orange mixture. Run a knife around sides and center tube of pan. Remove cake to a serving plate. Using a long serrated knife, cut cake horizontally into 3 layers. Spread frosting between layers and over top and sides of cake. Sprinkle with pecans. Refrigerate until serving.

1 piece: 518 cal., 26g fat (11g sat. fat), 231mg chol., 172mg sod., 65g carb. (50g sugars, 2g fiber), 9g pro.

COOLING FOAM CAKES

If your tube pan has legs, invert the pan until the cake is completely cool. If your pan does not have legs, place it over a funnel or the neck of a narrow bottle until the cake is completely cool.

Unless instructed otherwise, always invert foam cakes while cooling; otherwise, gravity will make the cake sink into the pan.

RICH RUM CAKE

We enjoy a touch of rum for the holidays, and this orangy rum cake is decadent alone or with swoops of whipped cream. You can add a bit of rum to the whipped cream, too.
—Nancy Heishman, Las Vegas, NV

PREP: 35 MIN. • **BAKE:** 25 MIN. + COOLING
MAKES: 12 SERVINGS

    4   large eggs, separated
 2½   cups confectioners' sugar
    ¾   cup orange juice
    ¼   cup butter, cubed
    ¾   cup rum
    1   cup all-purpose flour
    1   tsp. baking powder
    ½   tsp. ground cinnamon
    ¼   tsp. salt
    ¼   tsp. ground nutmeg
    ½   cup packed brown sugar, divided
    1   tsp. vanilla extract
    ¾   cup butter, melted
        Optional: Whipped cream and
        finely chopped glazed pecans

1. Place egg whites in a large bowl; let stand at room temperature 30 minutes. For sauce, in a saucepan, combine confectioners' sugar, juice and cubed butter; cook and stir over medium-low heat until sugar is dissolved. Remove from heat; stir in rum. Reserve ¾ cup sauce for serving.

2. Preheat oven to 375°. Grease and flour a 10-in. tube pan. Sift flour, baking powder, cinnamon, salt and nutmeg together twice; set aside.

3. In a bowl, beat egg whites on medium until soft peaks form. Gradually add ¼ cup brown sugar, 1 Tbsp. at a time, beating on high after each addition until sugar is dissolved. Continue beating until stiff peaks form.

4. In another bowl, beat egg yolks until slightly thickened. Gradually add the remaining ¼ cup brown sugar and the vanilla, beating on high speed until thick. Fold a fourth of the egg whites into batter. Alternately fold in flour mixture and the remaining whites. Fold in melted butter.

5. Transfer to prepared pan. Bake on lowest oven rack 25-30 minutes or until top springs back when lightly touched. Immediately poke holes in cake with a fork; slowly pour the remaining sauce over cake, allowing sauce to absorb into cake. Cool completely in pan on a wire rack, then invert onto a serving plate. Serve with the reserved sauce and, if desired, whipped cream and glazed pecans.

1 piece: 371 cal., 17g fat (10g sat. fat), 103mg chol., 233mg sod., 44g carb. (35g sugars, 0 fiber), 3g pro.

MOCHA-HAZELNUT GLAZED ANGEL FOOD CAKE

I love this recipe because it combines three of my favorite flavors: coffee, hazelnuts and cherries.
—Joan Pecsek, Chesapeake, VA

PREP: 25 MIN. • **BAKE:** 30 MIN. + COOLING
MAKES: 16 SERVINGS

  12   large egg whites (about 1⅔ cups)
    1   cup cake flour
    ¼   tsp. instant coffee granules
    1   tsp. cream of tartar
    1   tsp. almond extract
    ½   tsp. salt
 1¼   cups sugar
GLAZE
    1   cup Nutella
    ½   cup confectioners' sugar
    ⅓   cup brewed coffee
    ¼   cup chopped hazelnuts
  16   maraschino cherries with stems

1. Place egg whites in a large bowl; let stand at room temperature 30 minutes.

2. Preheat oven to 350°. In a small bowl, mix flour and coffee granules until blended.

3. Add cream of tartar, extract and salt to egg whites; beat on medium speed until soft peaks form. Gradually add sugar, 1 Tbsp. at a time, beating on high after each addition until sugar is dissolved. Continue beating until soft glossy peaks form. Gradually fold in flour mixture, about ½ cup at a time.

4. Gently transfer to an ungreased 10-in. tube pan. Cut through the batter with a knife to remove air pockets. Bake on lowest oven rack 30-40 minutes or until top springs back when lightly touched. Immediately invert pan; cool cake in pan, about 1½ hours.

5. Run a knife around sides and center tube of pan. Remove cake to a serving plate. In a small bowl, whisk Nutella, confectioners' sugar and coffee until smooth. Drizzle over cake; sprinkle with hazelnuts. Serve with cherries.

1 piece: 234 cal., 7g fat (1g sat. fat), 0 chol., 123mg sod., 41g carb. (33g sugars, 1g fiber), 5g pro.

CLASSIC TRES
LECHES CAKE

CLASSIC TRES LECHES CAKE

This cake has been a classic in Mexican kitchens for generations. The name refers to the three types of milk—evaporated, sweetened condensed and heavy whipping cream—used to create a super moist and tender texture.

—*Taste of Home* Test Kitchen

PREP: 45 MIN. • **BAKE:** 20 MIN. + CHILLING
MAKES: 10 SERVINGS

- 4 **large eggs, separated, room temperature**
- ⅔ **cup sugar, divided**
- ⅔ **cup cake flour**
  Dash salt
- ¾ **cup heavy whipping cream**
- ¾ **cup evaporated milk**
- ¾ **cup sweetened condensed milk**
- 2 **tsp. vanilla extract**
- ¼ **tsp. rum extract**

TOPPING

- 1¼ **cups heavy whipping cream**
- 3 **Tbsp. sugar**
  Optional: Dulce de leche or sliced fresh strawberries

1. Place egg whites in a large bowl. Line the bottom of a 9-in. springform pan with parchment; grease the paper.
2. Meanwhile, preheat oven to 350°. In another large bowl, beat egg yolks until slightly thickened. Gradually add ⅓ cup sugar, beating on high speed until thick and lemon-colored. Fold in flour, a third at a time.
3. Add salt to the egg whites; with clean beaters, beat on medium until soft peaks form. Gradually add remaining ⅓ cup sugar, 1 Tbsp. at a time, beating on high after each addition until sugar is dissolved. Continue beating until soft glossy peaks form. Fold a third of the whites into batter, then fold in the remaining whites. Gently spread batter into the prepared pan.
4. Bake until top springs back when lightly touched, 20-25 minutes. Cool 10 minutes before removing from pan to a wire rack to cool completely.
5. Place cake on a rimmed serving plate. Poke holes in top with a skewer. In a small bowl, mix cream, evaporated milk, sweetened condensed milk and the extracts; brush slowly over cake. Refrigerate, covered, 2 hours.
6. For topping, beat heavy whipping cream until it begins to thicken. Add sugar; beat until peaks form. Spread over top of cake. If desired, top cake with dulce de leche or strawberries just before serving.

1 piece: 392 cal., 23g fat (14g sat. fat), 142mg chol., 104mg sod., 40g carb. (33g sugars, 0 fiber), 8g pro.

SOFT PEAKS

STIFF PEAKS

WHIPPING EGG WHITES: SOFT VS. STIFF PEAKS

To create soft or stiff peaks, beat egg whites with an electric mixer on medium speed until they are thick and white.

To test for **soft peaks,** lift the beaters from the whites—the egg white peaks should curl down from the beaters as shown in the top photo.

For **stiff peaks,** continue beating the egg whites after they have reached the soft-peak stage until the volume increases and thickens.

To test for stiff peaks, lift the beaters from the whites—the egg white peaks should stand straight out from beaters as shown in the bottom photo. If you tilt the bowl, the whites should not slide around.

TOFFEE ANGEL FOOD CAKE

Toffee bits and whipped cream make angel food cake even more indulgent. For best results, refrigerate the cake for at least an hour before serving.
—Collette Gaugler, Fogelsville, PA

PREP: 45 MIN. • **BAKE:** 50 MIN. + COOLING
MAKES: 16 SERVINGS

- 11 **large egg whites**
- 1 **cup confectioners' sugar**
- 1 **cup cake flour**
- 1 **tsp. cream of tartar**
- 1 **tsp. vanilla extract**
  Pinch salt
- 1¼ **cups superfine sugar**

WHIPPED CREAM
- 2 **cups heavy whipping cream**
- ½ **cup hot caramel ice cream topping, room temperature**
- 1 **tsp. vanilla extract**
- 4 **Heath candy bars (1½ oz. each), chopped**
  Chocolate curls, optional

1. Place egg whites in a large bowl; let stand at room temperature 30 minutes.
2. Place oven rack in lowest position; remove upper rack if needed. Preheat oven to 325°. Sift confectioners' sugar and cake flour together twice.
3. Add cream of tartar, vanilla and salt to egg whites; beat on medium speed until soft peaks form. Gradually add superfine sugar, 1 Tbsp. at a time, beating on high after each addition until sugar is dissolved. Continue beating until soft glossy peaks form. Gradually fold in the flour mixture, about ½ cup at a time.
4. Gently transfer to an ungreased 10-in. tube pan. Cut through batter with a knife to remove air pockets. Bake on lowest rack until top crust is golden brown and cracks feel dry, 50-60 minutes. Immediately invert pan; cool completely in pan, about 1½ hours.

5. Run a knife around sides and center tube of pan. Remove cake to a serving plate. Using a long serrated knife, cut cake horizontally into 3 layers. In a large bowl, beat cream until it begins to thicken. Gradually add caramel topping and vanilla; beat until soft peaks form.
6. Place 1 cake layer on a serving plate; spread with 1 cup of the whipped cream mixture. Sprinkle with a third of the chopped candies. Repeat layers. Top with the remaining cake layer. Frost top and sides of cake with remaining whipped cream mixture; sprinkle with remaining candy. If desired, sprinkle chocolate curls over top and around bottom of cake.

1 piece: 315 cal., 14g fat (9g sat. fat), 36mg chol., 117mg sod., 44g carb. (36g sugars, 0 fiber), 5g pro.

SHEET CAKES & CAKE ROLLS

2½ cups all-purpose flour
2 tsp. baking powder
2 tsp. ground cinnamon
1 tsp. salt
½ tsp. ground allspice
4 large pears (about 2 lbs.), peeled and cut into ½-in. cubes
1 cup chopped walnuts
1 cup golden raisins

GLAZE
1 cup confectioners' sugar
2 Tbsp. rum

1. Preheat oven to 350°. In a small heavy saucepan, heat rum over medium heat. Bring to a boil; cook until liquid is reduced by half, 8-10 minutes. Remove from heat; cool.
2. Beat sugar, eggs, oil, vanilla and cooled rum until slightly thickened, about 5 minutes. Sift together the next 5 ingredients; gradually beat into rum mixture. Stir in pears, walnuts and raisins. Transfer to a greased and floured 13x9-in. baking pan.
3. Bake until a toothpick inserted in center comes out clean, 45-50 minutes. Cool cake in pan on rack.
4. For glaze, mix confectioners' sugar and rum; spread over cake.
1 piece: 337 cal., 13g fat (1g sat. fat), 28mg chol., 179mg sod., 52g carb. (35g sugars, 3g fiber), 4g pro.

SPICED RUM & PEAR CAKE

The flavors in this cake make it stand out as a special-occasion dessert. With raisins, fresh chunks of sweet pear, rich spices, crunchy walnuts and rum, it's a great choice for your holiday spread. If you don't cook with alcohol, try substituting apple juice for the rum—it'll still be delicious!
—Julie Peterson, Crofton, MD

PREP: 25 MIN. • **BAKE:** 45 MIN+ COOLING
MAKES: 20 SERVINGS

½ cup spiced rum
2 cups sugar
3 large eggs, room temperature
¾ cup canola oil
2 tsp. vanilla extract

TEST KITCHEN TIP
Change up the flavor by switching out the rum. The cake is exceptional with dark rum or coconut rum. It would also be great made with bourbon!

SOUR CREAM
SUGAR COOKIE CAKE

SOUR CREAM SUGAR COOKIE CAKE

My husband requested a giant sugar cookie for his birthday. I wanted to do something a bit more exciting than birthday cookies, so I came up with this sugar cookie cake. The secret to a dense yet cakelike texture is to make sure you don't overbake the cake.
—Carmell Childs, Orangeville, UT

PREP: 20 MIN. • **BAKE:** 20 MIN. + COOLING
MAKES: 20 SERVINGS

½ cup butter, softened
1½ cups sugar
2 large eggs, room temperature
1 tsp. vanilla extract
3 cups all-purpose flour
¾ tsp. salt
½ tsp. baking powder
½ tsp. baking soda
1 cup sour cream
1 can (16 oz.) vanilla frosting
Optional: Coarse sugar, sprinkles and additional frosting

1. Preheat oven to 350°. In a large bowl, cream butter and sugar until light and fluffy, 5-7 minutes. Beat in eggs and vanilla. In another bowl, whisk flour, salt, baking powder and baking soda; add to creamed mixture alternately with sour cream, beating after each addition just until combined. Spread into a greased 13x9-in. baking pan.
2. Bake until a toothpick inserted in center comes out clean, 20-25 minutes. Cool completely on a wire rack. Spread frosting over top. Decorate with optional toppings as desired.
Note: Instead of canned frosting, choose your own from the recipes in Chapter 10 (p. 426).
1 piece: 295 cal., 11g fat (6g sat. fat), 34mg chol., 228mg sod., 46g carb. (29g sugars, 1g fiber), 3g pro.

BAKING 101

CINNAMON TWIRL
ROLY-POLY

CINNAMON TWIRL ROLY-POLY

My whole house smells incredible when this cake is in the oven. Change it up by using other extracts—maple is heavenly.
—Holly Balzer-Harz, Malone, NY

PREP: 40 MIN. + CHILLING
BAKE: 10 MIN. + COOLING
MAKES: 12 SERVINGS

- 3 large eggs, room temperature
- ¾ cup sugar
- ⅓ cup water
- 1 tsp. vanilla extract
- 1 cup all-purpose flour
- 1½ tsp. baking powder
  Dash salt
- 6 Tbsp. butter, softened
- ½ cup packed brown sugar
- 2 tsp. ground cinnamon

FILLING
- 4 oz. cream cheese, softened
- ¼ cup butter, softened
- 1 cup confectioners' sugar
- ½ tsp. ground cinnamon
- 1 to 2 tsp. half-and-half cream or 2% milk
- ¼ cup finely chopped walnuts, optional

GLAZE
- ¼ cup butter
- 1½ cups confectioners' sugar
- 1 tsp. vanilla extract
- 2 to 3 Tbsp. half-and-half cream or 2% milk
- ¼ cup chopped walnuts, optional

1. Preheat oven to 375°. Line bottom and sides of a greased 15x10x1-in. baking pan with parchment; grease the parchment.

2. Beat eggs on high speed until thick and pale, about 5 minutes. Gradually beat in sugar until well mixed. Reduce speed to low; beat in water and vanilla. In another bowl, whisk together flour, baking powder and salt; add to the egg mixture, mixing just until combined.

3. Transfer batter to prepared pan. Bake until cake springs back when lightly touched, 10-12 minutes. Cool 5 minutes. Invert onto a kitchen towel dusted with confectioners' sugar. Gently peel off parchment. Roll up cake in the towel jelly-roll style, starting with a short side. Cool completely on a wire rack.

4. Meanwhile, beat butter, brown sugar and cinnamon until creamy. Unroll cake; spread brown sugar mixture over cake to within ½ in. of edges.

5. Beat cream cheese and butter until creamy. Beat in confectioners' sugar and cinnamon; gradually add cream until mixture reaches a spreadable consistency. Spread over brown sugar mixture. If desired, sprinkle with walnuts. Roll up cake again, without towel; trim ends if needed. Place on a platter, seam side down.

6. For glaze, heat butter in a small saucepan over medium-low heat until foamy and golden, 6-8 minutes. Remove from heat. Stir in confectioners' sugar and vanilla, then add cream 1 Tbsp. at a time, stirring well, until mixture reaches a pourable consistency.

7. Slowly pour glaze over top of cake, allowing some to flow over sides. If desired, top with walnuts. Refrigerate, covered, at least 2 hours before serving.

1 piece: 396 cal., 18g fat (11g sat. fat), 93mg chol., 341mg sod., 56g carb. (47g sugars, 1g fiber), 4g pro.

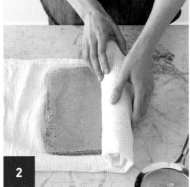

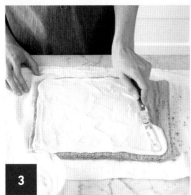

HOW TO MAKE A PERFECT CAKE ROLL

1. BAKE IT
Grease a 15x10x1-in. baking pan and line it with greased and floured parchment. Spread the batter evenly into the pan.

2. ROLL IT UP
As soon as the cake is done baking, turn it out onto a tea towel lightly dusted with powdered sugar. Peel off the parchment.

Starting at one of the short ends, roll up the cake in the towel; allow it to cool completely. This will "train" the cake to hold the rolled shape.

3. FILL IT
Once the cake has cooled completely, gently unroll it. Spread filling across the cake, leaving about ½ in. around the edge unfrosted. Add any other fillings, such as chopped nuts.

4. ROLL IT UP (AGAIN)
Roll your cake again. Use the towel to help the process, but don't roll it up with the cake.

To maintain the perfect spiral—and to prevent filling from oozing out when you cut it—chill the cake until you're ready to serve.

CARDAMOM CRUMB CAKE

This cake has a thick cardamom-scented crumb topping, and it brings the family to the table fast when the aroma of the cardamom drifts out from the oven to the rest of the house.
—Lily Julow, Lawrenceville, GA

PREP: 25 MIN. • **BAKE:** 30 MIN. + COOLING
MAKES: 15 SERVINGS

- 1 cup butter, melted
- ½ cup sugar
- ½ cup packed brown sugar
- ½ tsp. ground cardamom
- ¼ tsp. salt
- 2½ cups all-purpose flour

CAKE

- 3 cups all-purpose flour
- 1¼ cups sugar
- 1½ tsp. baking powder
- 1 tsp. salt
- ½ tsp. grated orange zest
- ¼ tsp. ground cardamom
- 2 large eggs
- 1 cup 2% milk
- ¾ cup butter, melted

1. Preheat oven to 350°. Grease a 13x9-in. pan. Mix the first 5 ingredients until blended; stir in flour until crumbly.
2. In a large bowl, whisk together the first 6 cake ingredients. In another bowl, whisk together eggs, milk and melted butter; add to the dry ingredients, stirring just until moistened.
3. Transfer batter to prepared pan. Top with crumb mixture. Bake until a toothpick inserted in center comes out clean, 30-35 minutes. Cool in pan on a wire rack.
1 piece: 494 cal., 23g fat (14g sat. fat), 83mg chol., 435mg sod., 67g carb. (32g sugars, 1g fiber), 6g pro.

CHOCOLATE BEET CAKE

The first time I baked this cake, my son loved its moistness, and he couldn't even taste the beets.
—Peggy Van Arsdale, Crosswicks, NJ

PREP: 20 MIN. • **BAKE:** 35 MIN. + COOLING
MAKES: 15 SERVINGS

- 1 cup grated peeled uncooked beets (about 2 medium)
- 2 tsp. lemon juice
- 4 large eggs, room temperature
- 1¼ cups butter, melted
- ½ cup 2% milk
- 2 Tbsp. honey
- 2 tsp. vanilla extract
- 2½ cups all-purpose flour
- 2 cups sugar
- ½ cup baking cocoa
- 2 tsp. baking soda
- 1 tsp. salt

FROSTING

- 3 oz. cream cheese, softened
- ¼ cup heavy whipping cream
- 1 tsp. vanilla extract
- 3¾ cups confectioners' sugar
  Dash salt
  Chopped walnuts, optional

1. Toss beets with lemon juice; set aside. In a bowl, beat eggs, butter, milk, honey and vanilla. Combine the flour, sugar, cocoa, baking soda and salt; add to the egg mixture and beat just until blended. Stir in the beet mixture.
2. Pour into a greased 13x9-in. baking dish. Bake at 350° for 35-40 minutes or until a toothpick inserted in the center comes out clean. Cool on a wire rack.
3. For frosting, in a bowl, beat the cream cheese, cream and vanilla until smooth. Beat in confectioners' sugar and salt. Spread over cooled cake. If desired, sprinkle with nuts.
1 piece: 509 cal., 21g fat (12g sat. fat), 110mg chol., 534mg sod., 78g carb. (58g sugars, 1g fiber), 5g pro.

CRANBERRY CAKE ROLL

Here's a low-fat angel food cake roll that's a guilt-free indulgence—much appreciated during the Christmas season!
—Paige Kowolewski, Topton, PA

PREP: 45 MIN. + CHILLING
BAKE: 20 MIN. + COOLING
MAKES: 12 SERVINGS

- 9 large egg whites
- 1½ tsp. vanilla extract
- ¾ tsp. cream of tartar
- ¼ tsp. salt
- 1 cup plus 2 Tbsp. sugar
- ¾ cup cake flour
  Confectioners' sugar

FILLING

- 2⅓ cups fresh or frozen cranberries
- 1 cup sugar
- 6 Tbsp. water, divided
- ⅓ cup chopped candied orange peel, optional
- 1 Tbsp. orange liqueur, optional
- 1 tsp. grated orange zest, optional
- 2 Tbsp. cornstarch
  Optional: Additional confectioners' sugar, candied orange peel and sugared cranberries

1. Place egg whites in a large bowl; let stand at room temperature 30 minutes. Meanwhile, line a greased 15x10x1-in. baking pan with waxed paper; grease the paper and set aside.
2. Add vanilla, cream of tartar and salt to the egg whites; beat on medium speed until soft peaks form. Gradually beat in sugar, 2 Tbsp. at a time, on high until stiff glossy peaks form and sugar is dissolved. Fold in flour, about ¼ cup at a time.
3. Carefully spread batter into the prepared pan. Bake at 350° until the cake springs back when lightly touched, 15-20 minutes. Cool in pan 5 minutes. Turn onto a kitchen towel dusted with confectioners' sugar. Gently peel off waxed paper. Roll up cake in the towel jelly-roll style, starting with a short side. Cool completely on a wire rack.
4. For filling, in a large saucepan, combine cranberries, sugar and 4 Tbsp. water. Bring to a boil. Reduce heat; simmer, uncovered, for 5-6 minutes or until berries pop. Mash the berries; strain, reserving juice and discarding pulp. Return juice to the pan; if desired, add chopped candied orange peel, orange liqueur and orange zest. Combine cornstarch and remaining 2 Tbsp. water until smooth; gradually add to the cranberry juice mixture. Bring to a boil; cook and stir until thickened, about 2 minutes. Chill.
5. Unroll cake and spread the filling to within ½ in. of edges. Roll up again. Cover and refrigerate for 1 hour before serving. If desired, top with confectioners' sugar and garnish with candied orange peel and sugared cranberries. Refrigerate leftovers.
Note: See p. 305 for instructions for making sugared cranberries.
1 piece: 196 cal., 0 fat (0 sat. fat), 0 chol., 91mg sod., 46g carb. (36g sugars, 1g fiber), 3g pro.

CRANBERRY
CAKE ROLL

CLASSIC CHOCOLATE CAKE

CARROT SHEET CAKE

We sold pieces of this to-die-for carrot cake at an art show and before long, we had sold every last piece of the 10 whole cakes we'd made!

—Dottie Cosgrove, South El Monte, CA

PREP: 20 MIN. • **BAKE:** 35 MIN. + COOLING
MAKES: 30 SERVINGS

    4   large eggs, room temperature
    1   cup canola oil
    2   cups sugar
    2   cups all-purpose flour
    2   tsp. baking soda
    ¼   tsp. baking powder
    2   tsp. ground cinnamon
    ½   tsp. salt
    3   cups shredded carrots
    ⅔   cup chopped walnuts
FROSTING
    1   pkg. (8 oz.) cream cheese,
        softened
    ½   cup butter, softened
    1   tsp. vanilla extract
    4   cups confectioners' sugar
    ⅔   cup chopped walnuts

1. Preheat oven to 350°. In a bowl, beat eggs, canola oil and sugar until smooth. Combine flour, baking soda, baking powder, cinnamon and salt; add to egg mixture and beat well. Stir in carrots and walnuts. Pour the batter into a greased 15x10x1-in. baking pan. Bake until a toothpick inserted in the center comes out clean, about 35 minutes. Cool on a wire rack.
2. For frosting, beat cream cheese, butter and vanilla in a bowl until smooth; beat in sugar. Spread over cake. Sprinkle with nuts. Decorate as desired.
1 piece: 311 cal., 17g fat (5g sat. fat), 45mg chol., 193mg sod., 38g carb. (29g sugars, 1g fiber), 4g pro.

CLASSIC CHOCOLATE CAKE

This recipe appeared on a can of Hershey's cocoa way back in 1943. I tried it, my boys liked it, and I've been making it ever since. I make all my cakes from scratch, and this is one of the best!

—Betty Follas, Morgan Hill, CA

PREP: 15 MIN. • **BAKE:** 35 MIN.
MAKES: 15 SERVINGS

    ⅔   cup butter, softened
    1⅔ cups sugar
    3   large eggs, room temperature
    2   cups all-purpose flour
    ⅔   cup baking cocoa
    1¼ tsp. baking soda
    1   tsp. salt
    1⅓ cups whole milk
        Confectioners' sugar or favorite
        frosting

1. Peheat oven to 350°. In a bowl, cream butter and sugar until light and fluffy, 5-7 minutes. Add eggs, 1 at a time, beating well after each addition. Combine flour, cocoa, baking soda and salt; add to the creamed mixture alternately with milk, beating until smooth after each addition. Pour batter into a greased and floured 13x9-in. baking pan.
2. Bake until a toothpick inserted in center comes out clean, 35-40 minutes. Cool on a wire rack. When cake is cool, dust with confectioners' sugar or top with your favorite frosting.
1 piece: 257 cal., 10g fat (6g sat. fat), 67mg chol., 368mg sod., 38g carb. (23g sugars, 1g fiber), 4g pro.

LUSCIOUS LEMON CAKE ROLL

A co-worker shared the recipe for this elegant cake roll. It's perfect for rounding out a special meal.

—Darlene Brenden, Salem, OR

PREP: 1 HOUR • **BAKE:** 10 MIN. + CHILLING
MAKES: 10 SERVINGS

- 4 large eggs, separated, room temperature
- ¾ cup sugar, divided
- 1 Tbsp. canola oil
- 1 tsp. lemon extract
- ⅔ cup cake flour
- 1 tsp. baking powder
- ¼ tsp. salt
  Confectioners' sugar

CREAMY LEMON FILLING
- 1 can (14 oz.) sweetened condensed milk
- ⅓ cup lemon juice
- 2 tsp. grated lemon zest
- 7 drops yellow liquid food coloring, divided
- 1½ cups whipped topping
- ½ tsp. water
- ½ cup sweetened shredded coconut

1. Preheat oven to 375°. Line a greased 15x10x1-in. baking pan with waxed paper and grease the paper; set aside. In a large bowl, beat egg yolks until lemon-colored. Gradually beat in ¼ cup sugar. Stir in oil and lemon extract.
2. In another large bowl, beat egg whites on medium speed until soft peaks form. Gradually add the remaining sugar, 2 Tbsp. at a time, beating until stiff glossy peaks form and sugar is dissolved. Fold into egg yolk mixture. Combine the flour, baking powder and salt; fold into egg mixture.
3. Transfer to prepared pan. Bake for 10-12 minutes or until cake springs back when lightly touched. Cool for 5 minutes. Turn cake onto a kitchen towel dusted with confectioners' sugar.

Gently peel off waxed paper. Roll up cake in towel, starting with a short side. Cool completely on a wire rack.
4. For filling, in a small bowl, combine the milk, lemon juice, lemon zest and 5 drops of food coloring. Fold in the whipped topping. Unroll cake; spread half the filling over cake to within 1 in. of edges. Roll up again. Place seam side down on a platter. Spread remaining filling over cake.
5. In a small bowl, combine water and remaining food coloring; add coconut. Stir until the coconut is evenly tinted. Sprinkle coconut over cake. Refrigerate roll for at least 2 hours before serving. Refrigerate leftovers.

1 piece: 318 cal., 10g fat (6g sat. fat), 98mg chol., 187mg sod., 49g carb. (40g sugars, 0 fiber), 7g pro.

GRANNY'S GINGERBREAD CAKE WITH CARAMEL SAUCE

A buttery caramel sauce complements the rich molasses and autumn spices in this old-time dessert.

—Joy Sparks, Muskegon, MI

PREP: 25 MIN. • **BAKE:** 35 MIN.
MAKES: 9 SERVINGS

- 9 Tbsp. butter, softened
- ⅓ cup sugar
- 1 cup molasses
- 1 large egg, room temperature
- 2¼ cups all-purpose flour
- 1 tsp. baking soda
- 1 tsp. ground ginger
- 1 tsp. ground cinnamon
- ¼ tsp. salt
- ¾ cup water

CARAMEL SAUCE
- 1 cup packed brown sugar
- 1 Tbsp. cornstarch
- 1 cup cold water
- ¼ cup butter, cubed
- 1 tsp. vanilla extract
  Whipped cream, optional

1. Preheat oven to 325°. In a large bowl, cream butter and sugar until light and fluffy, 5-7 minutes. Beat in molasses and egg until well blended. In another bowl, whisk together the flour, baking soda, ginger, cinnamon and salt; add to the creamed mixture alternately with water.
2. Transfer to a greased 9-in. square baking pan. Bake 35-40 minutes or until a toothpick inserted in the center comes out clean. Place on a wire rack.
3. For the caramel sauce, in a small saucepan, combine brown sugar and cornstarch. Stir in water until smooth. Bring to a boil; cook and stir 2 minutes or until thickened. Remove from heat; stir in butter and vanilla until smooth. Serve with warm cake. If desired, top with whipped cream.

1 piece: 497 cal., 17g fat (11g sat. fat), 67mg chol., 353mg sod., 83g carb. (51g sugars, 1g fiber), 4g pro.

CRANBERRY CAKE WITH ALMOND-BUTTER SAUCE

Make room for this recipe in your collection. Tart cranberries and sweet almond glaze turn this potluck cake into something truly special.
—Elizabeth King, Duluth, MN

PREP: 20 MIN. • **BAKE:** 35 MIN. + COOLING
MAKES: 9 SERVINGS (1¼ CUPS SAUCE)

- 3 Tbsp. butter, softened
- 1 cup sugar
- 1 cup 2% milk
- 2 cups all-purpose flour
- 2 tsp. baking powder
- 1 tsp. salt
- 2 cups fresh or frozen cranberries

SAUCE
- ½ cup butter, cubed
- 1 cup sugar
- ½ cup half-and-half cream
- 1 tsp. almond extract

1. Preheat oven to 350°. Grease an 8-in. square baking pan. Beat butter and sugar until crumbly. Beat in milk. Whisk together flour, baking powder and salt; stir into the butter mixture. Stir in the cranberries. Transfer batter to the prepared pan.

2. Bake until a toothpick inserted in center comes out clean, 35-40 minutes. Cool in pan on a wire rack.

3. For sauce, in a saucepan, melt butter over medium heat. Add the sugar and cream; cook and stir until sugar is dissolved, about 5 minutes. Remove from heat; stir in extract. Serve warm with cake.

1 piece with about 2 Tbsp. sauce: 442 cal., 16g fat (10g sat. fat), 46mg chol., 501mg sod., 70g carb. (47g sugars, 2g fiber), 4g pro.

DEVIL'S FOOD SNACK CAKE

My husband and his friends request this devil's food cake for camping trips because it's easy to transport. That makes it great for taking to potlucks and other events, too, and you don't have to worry about frosting. You can add that, of course, but it's fine without!
—Julie Danler, Bel Aire, KS

PREP: 30 MIN. • **BAKE:** 35 MIN. + COOLING
MAKES: 24 SERVINGS

- 1 cup quick-cooking oats
- 1¾ cups boiling water
- ¼ cup butter, softened
- ½ cup sugar
- ½ cup packed brown sugar
- 2 large eggs, room temperature
- ⅓ cup buttermilk
- 3 Tbsp. canola oil
- 1 tsp. vanilla extract
- ¾ cup all-purpose flour
- ¾ cup whole wheat flour
- 2 Tbsp. dark baking cocoa
- 1 Tbsp. instant coffee granules
- 1 tsp. baking soda
- ⅛ tsp. salt
- 1 cup miniature semisweet chocolate chips, divided
- ¾ cup chopped pecans, divided

1. Preheat oven to 350°. Place oats in a large bowl. Cover with boiling water; let stand for 10 minutes.

2. Meanwhile, in a large bowl, beat butter and sugars until crumbly, about 2 minutes. Add eggs, 1 egg at a time, beating well after each addition. Beat in buttermilk, oil and vanilla. Combine flours, cocoa, coffee granules, baking soda and salt. Gradually add to creamed mixture. Stir in the oat mixture, ½ cup chocolate chips and ⅓ cup pecans.

3. Pour into a greased 13x9-in. baking pan. Sprinkle with remaining chips and pecans. Bake until a toothpick inserted in the center comes out clean, 35-40 minutes. Cool on a wire rack before cutting.

1 piece: 174 cal., 9g fat (3g sat. fat), 23mg chol., 91mg sod., 22g carb. (13g sugars, 2g fiber), 3g pro. **Diabetic exchanges:** 2 fat, 1½ starch.

FAVORITE PUMPKIN CAKE ROLL

Keep this cake roll in the freezer for a quick dessert for family or unexpected guests, to take to a gathering, or to give away as a yummy gift.

—Erica Berchtold, Freeport, IL

PREP: 30 MIN. • **BAKE:** 15 MIN. + FREEZING
MAKES: 10 SERVINGS

- 3 large eggs, separated, room temperature
- 1 cup sugar, divided
- ⅔ cup canned pumpkin
- ¾ cup all-purpose flour
- 1 tsp. baking soda
- ½ tsp. ground cinnamon
- ⅛ tsp. salt

FILLING
- 8 oz. cream cheese, softened
- 2 Tbsp. butter, softened
- 1 cup confectioners' sugar
- ¾ tsp. vanilla extract
  Additional confectioners' sugar

1. Peheat oven to 375°. Line a 15x10x1-in. baking pan with waxed paper; grease the paper and set aside. In a large bowl, beat egg yolks on high speed until thick and lemon-colored. Gradually add ½ cup sugar and pumpkin, beating on high until sugar is almost dissolved.
2. In a small bowl, beat egg whites until soft peaks form. Gradually add remaining ½ cup sugar, beating until stiff peaks form. Fold into egg yolk mixture. Combine flour, baking soda, cinnamon and salt; fold into pumpkin mixture. Spread into the prepared pan.
3. Bake until cake springs back when lightly touched, 12-15 minutes. Cool for 5 minutes. Turn cake onto a kitchen towel dusted with confectioners' sugar. Gently peel off waxed paper. Roll up cake in the towel jelly-roll style, starting with a short side. Cool completely on a wire rack.

4. Beat the cream cheese, butter, confectioners' sugar and vanilla until smooth. Unroll cake; spread filling to within ½ in. of edges. Roll up again, without towel. Cover and freeze until firm. Dust with confectioners' sugar.
1 piece: 285 cal., 12g fat (7g sat. fat), 94mg chol., 261mg sod., 41g carb. (32g sugars, 1g fiber), 5g pro.

FAVORITE PUMPKIN CAKE ROLL

TEST KITCHEN TIP
Add extra flavor to the already delicious filling by swirling in apricot preserves, blackberry jam or even apple butter.

PUMPKIN SNACK CAKE

The crunchy, sweet topping makes this simple pumpkin snack cake taste extra special. If you prefer a sweeter cake, omit the topping and spread with your favorite frosting instead.
—Steven Schend, Grand Rapids, MI

PREP: 15 MIN. • **BAKE:** 25 MIN. + COOLING
MAKES: 16 SERVINGS

- ¼ cup butter, softened
- ¾ cup sugar
- 1 large egg, room temperature
- 1 cup all-purpose flour
- 1 Tbsp. baking cocoa
- ½ tsp. baking soda
- ½ tsp. ground cinnamon
- 1 cup canned pumpkin

TOPPING

- ½ cup semisweet chocolate chips
- ½ cup salted pumpkin seeds or pepitas
- 1 Tbsp. sugar

1. Preheat oven to 350°. In a large bowl, cream butter and sugar. Beat in egg. Combine flour, cocoa, baking soda and cinnamon; gradually add to creamed mixture and mix well. Stir in pumpkin. Pour into a greased 8-in. square baking pan. Combine the topping ingredients; sprinkle over batter.

2. Bake until a toothpick inserted in the center comes out clean, about 25 minutes. Cool cake in pan on a wire rack.

1 piece: 151 cal., 7g fat (3g sat. fat), 19mg chol., 78mg sod., 22g carb. (14g sugars, 1g fiber), 3g pro. **Diabetic exchanges:** 1½ starch, 1½ fat.

BAKING 101

PUMPKIN SNACK CAKE

ORANGE RICOTTA CAKE ROLL

I come from a big Italian family. When I was growing up, my mom cooked and baked many delicious meals and desserts from scratch. Now I do the same for my family. This cake is my finale whenever we have a special-occasion dinner.
—Cathy Banks, Encinitas, CA

PREP: 45 MIN. • **BAKE:** 10 MIN. + CHILLING
MAKES: 12 SERVINGS

- 4   large eggs, separated, room temperature
- ¼   cup baking cocoa
- 2   Tbsp. all-purpose flour
- ⅛   tsp. salt
- ⅔   cup confectioners' sugar, sifted, divided
- 1   tsp. vanilla extract
- ½   tsp. cream of tartar

FILLING
- 1   container (15 oz.) ricotta cheese
- 3   Tbsp. mascarpone cheese
- ⅓   cup sugar
- 1   Tbsp. Kahlua (coffee liqueur)
- 1   Tbsp. grated orange zest
- ½   tsp. vanilla extract
     Additional confectioners' sugar

1. Place egg whites in a bowl. Preheat oven to 325°. Line bottom of a greased 15x10x1-in. baking pan with parchment; grease paper. Sift cocoa, flour and salt together twice.
2. In a large bowl, beat egg yolks until slightly thickened. Gradually add ⅓ cup confectioners' sugar, beating on high speed until thick and lemon-colored. Beat in vanilla. Fold in cocoa mixture (batter will be very thick).
3. Add cream of tartar to egg whites; with clean beaters, beat on medium until soft peaks form. Gradually add remaining ⅓ cup confectioners' sugar, 1 Tbsp. at a time, beating on high after each addition until sugar is dissolved. Continue beating until soft glossy peaks form. Fold a fourth of the whites into batter, then fold in the remaining whites. Transfer batter to prepared pan, spreading evenly.
4. Bake until top of cake springs back when lightly touched, 9-11 minutes. Cover cake with waxed paper; cool completely on a wire rack.
5. Remove waxed paper; invert cake onto an 18-in.-long sheet of waxed paper dusted with confectioners' sugar. Gently peel off parchment.
6. In a small bowl, beat ricotta cheese, mascarpone and sugar until blended. Stir in Kahlua, orange zest and vanilla. Spread filling over cake to within ½ in. of edges. Roll up jelly-roll style, starting with a short side. Trim ends; place on a platter, seam side down.
7. Refrigerate, covered, for at least 1 hour before serving. To serve, dust with confectioners' sugar.
1 piece: 169 cal., 9g fat (5g sat. fat), 94mg chol., 95mg sod., 17g carb. (14g sugars, 0 fiber), 7g pro. **Diabetic exchanges:** 2 fat, 1 starch.

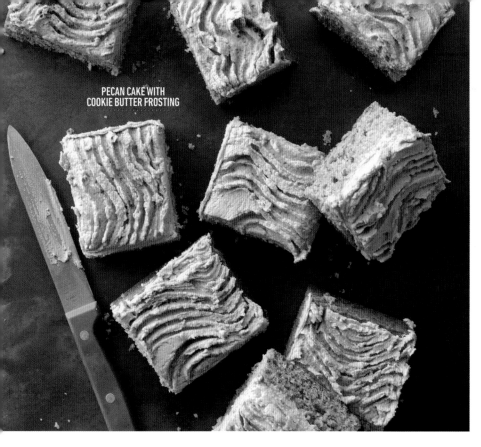

PECAN CAKE WITH COOKIE BUTTER FROSTING

PECAN CAKE WITH COOKIE BUTTER FROSTING

My mom and I bought a jar of cookie butter to try it out, and we fell in love with it. I knew the flavor would go well with maple syrup and pecans, so I came up with this cake. If you like, make a pretty design on top of the cake with pecan halves.
—Natalie Larsen, Grand Prairie, TX

PREP: 20 MIN. • **BAKE:** 25 MIN. + COOLING
MAKES: 20 SERVINGS

- ½ cup pecan halves
- ½ cup sugar
- ½ cup packed brown sugar
- 1 cup butter, softened
- 4 large eggs, room temperature
- ¼ cup maple syrup
- 2 Tbsp. 2% milk
- 1⅔ cups all-purpose flour
- 3 tsp. baking powder
- ½ tsp. salt

FROSTING
- ½ cup butter, softened
- 2 cups confectioners' sugar
- 1 cup Biscoff creamy cookie spread
- ¼ cup 2% milk

1. Preheat oven to 350°. Grease a 13x9-in. baking pan.
2. Place pecans and sugars in a food processor; process until ground. In a large bowl, cream butter and pecan mixture until blended. Add eggs, 1 at a time, beating well after each addition. Beat in syrup and milk. In another bowl, whisk flour, baking powder and salt; gradually add to the creamed mixture, beating well.
3. Transfer batter to prepared pan. Bake until a toothpick inserted in center comes out clean, 25-30 minutes. Cool completely in pan on a wire rack.
4. In a large bowl, combine all frosting ingredients; beat until smooth. Spread over cake. Refrigerate leftovers.
1 piece: 363 cal., 21g fat (10g sat. fat), 74mg chol., 259mg sod., 41g carb. (29g sugars, 1g fiber), 3g pro.

PINEAPPLE SHEET CAKE

This sheet cake is perfect for serving to a crowd. It keeps so well that you can easily prepare it a day ahead and it will stay moist. I often bring it to church potlucks, and I have yet to take much of it home.
—Kim Miller Spiek, Sarasota, FL

PREP: 15 MIN. • **BAKE:** 35 MIN. + COOLING
MAKES: ABOUT 24 SERVINGS

BAKING 101

CAKE
- 2 cups all-purpose flour
- 2 cups sugar
- 2 large eggs, room temperature
- 1 cup chopped nuts
- 2 tsp. baking soda
- ½ tsp. salt
- 1 tsp. vanilla extract
- 1 can (20 oz.) crushed pineapple, undrained

CREAM CHEESE ICING
- 1 pkg. (8 oz.) cream cheese, softened
- ½ cup butter, softened
- 3¾ cups confectioners' sugar
- 1 tsp. vanilla extract
- ½ cup chopped nuts

1. Preheat oven to 350°. In a large bowl, combine cake ingredients; beat until smooth. Pour into a greased 15x10x1-in. baking pan. Bake for 35 minutes. Cool.
2. For icing, in a small bowl, combine the cream cheese, butter, confectioners' sugar and vanilla until smooth. Spread over cake and sprinkle with nuts.
1 piece: 315 cal., 12g fat (5g sat. fat), 38mg chol., 227mg sod., 49g carb. (39g sugars, 1g fiber), 4g pro.

PEANUT BUTTER SHEET CAKE

I received the recipe for this cake from a minister's wife, and my family loves it.
—Brenda Jackson, Garden City, KS

PREP: 15 MIN. • **BAKE:** 20 MIN.
MAKES: 24 SERVINGS

- 2 cups all-purpose flour
- 2 cups sugar
- 1 tsp. baking soda
- ½ tsp. salt
- 1 cup water
- ¾ cup butter, cubed
- ½ cup chunky peanut butter
- ¼ cup canola oil
- 2 large eggs, room temperature
- ½ cup buttermilk
- 1 tsp. vanilla extract

GLAZE
- ⅔ cup sugar
- ⅓ cup evaporated milk
- 1 Tbsp. butter
- ⅓ cup chunky peanut butter
- ⅓ cup miniature marshmallows
- ½ tsp. vanilla extract

1. Preheat oven to 350°. Grease a 15x10x1-in. baking pan. In a large bowl, whisk flour, sugar, baking soda and salt. In a small saucepan, combine water and butter; bring just to a boil. Stir in peanut butter and oil until blended. Stir into the flour mixture. In a small bowl, whisk the eggs, buttermilk and vanilla until blended; add to the flour mixture, whisking constantly.

2. Transfer the batter to prepared pan. Bake until a toothpick inserted in center comes out clean, 20-25 minutes.

3. Meanwhile, for glaze, combine sugar, milk and butter in a saucepan. Bring to a boil, stirring constantly; cook and stir 2 minutes. Remove from heat; stir in the peanut butter, marshmallows and vanilla until blended. Spoon over warm cake, spreading evenly to cover. Cool on a wire rack.

1 piece: 266 cal., 14g fat (5g sat. fat), 36mg chol., 222mg sod., 33g carb. (23g sugars, 1g fiber), 4g pro.

CITRUS POKE CAKE

My old-fashioned citrus snack cake tastes even better the day after it is made. It is perfect for picnics or gatherings because it transports easily and is so good chilled.
—Judi Stowell, West Kelowna, BC

PREP: 25 MIN. • **BAKE:** 20 MIN. + COOLING
MAKES: 15 SERVINGS

- 1 cup 2% milk
- 2 Tbsp. white vinegar
- ½ cup butter, softened
- 1⅔ cups sugar, divided
- 1 large egg, room temperature
- 2 cups all-purpose flour
- 2 tsp. baking powder
- 1 tsp. baking soda
- ⅛ tsp. salt
- ⅔ cup raisins
- ⅔ cup sweetened shredded coconut or chopped walnuts
- 1 Tbsp. grated orange zest
- 2 tsp. grated lemon zest
- ½ cup orange juice
- 3 Tbsp. lemon juice

1. Preheat oven to 350°. Grease and flour a 13x9-in. baking pan. In a small bowl, mix milk and vinegar; let stand for 5 minutes.

2. In a large bowl, cream the butter and 1 cup sugar until light and fluffy, 5-7 minutes. Beat in milk mixture and egg. In another bowl, whisk flour, baking powder, baking soda and salt; gradually add to creamed mixture. Stir in raisins, coconut and orange and lemon zests. Pour batter into prepared pan. Bake for 20-25 minutes or until a toothpick inserted in center comes out clean.

3. In a small saucepan, bring juices and remaining ⅔ cup sugar to a boil. Reduce heat; cook and stir until sugar is dissolved. Remove cake from oven; place on a wire rack. Poke holes in warm cake with a skewer or chopstick. Pour sugar mixture evenly over cake.

1 piece: 259 cal., 8g fat (6g sat. fat), 30mg chol., 241mg sod., 44g carb. (30g sugars, 1g fiber), 3g pro.

RUSTIC HONEY CAKE

SKILLET CAKES & UPSIDE-DOWN CAKES

RUSTIC HONEY CAKE

When my boys were young, they couldn't drink milk but they could have yogurt. This was a cake they could eat. And it's a dessert that doesn't taste overly sweet, which is always a nice change of pace.
—Linda Leuer, Hamel, MN

PREP: 15 MIN. • **BAKE:** 30 MIN. + COOLING
MAKES: 12 SERVINGS

½ cup butter, softened
1 cup honey
2 large eggs, room temperature
½ cup plain yogurt
1 tsp. vanilla extract
2 cups all-purpose flour
2 tsp. baking powder
½ tsp. salt
    Assorted fresh fruit and additional honey
    Chopped pistachios, optional

1. Preheat oven to 350°. Grease a 9-in. cast-iron skillet.
2. In a large bowl, beat butter and honey until blended. Add eggs, 1 at a time, beating well after each addition. Beat in yogurt and vanilla. In another bowl, whisk flour, baking powder and salt; add to butter mixture. Transfer batter to prepared skillet.
3. Bake until a toothpick inserted in center comes out clean, 30-35 minutes. Cool completely in pan on a wire rack. Serve with fruit, additional honey and, if desired, chopped pistachios.
1 piece: 248 cal., 9g fat (5g sat. fat), 53mg chol., 257mg sod., 40g carb. (24g sugars, 1g fiber), 4g pro.

UPSIDE-DOWN PEAR GINGERBREAD CAKE

The aroma of baking gingerbread stirs up such warm memories. This cake looks festive and is even on the lighter side.
—Nancy Beckman, Helena, MT

PREP: 25 MIN. • **BAKE:** 25 MIN. + COOLING
MAKES: 8 SERVINGS

3 Tbsp. butter
⅓ cup packed dark brown sugar
2 medium Bosc pears, peeled and thinly sliced
CAKE
½ cup 2% milk
1 Tbsp. cider vinegar
1 large egg, room temperature
½ cup packed dark brown sugar
⅓ cup molasses
¼ cup butter, melted
1¼ cups all-purpose flour
2 tsp. ground cinnamon
1 tsp. baking soda
1 tsp. ground ginger
¼ tsp. salt
¼ tsp. ground cloves
    Whipped cream, optional

1. Preheat oven to 350°. In a small saucepan, melt butter over medium heat; stir in brown sugar. Spread over bottom of a greased 9-in. round baking pan. Arrange pears over top.
2. For cake, mix milk and vinegar; let stand 5 minutes. In a large bowl, beat egg, brown sugar, molasses, melted butter and the milk mixture until well blended. In another bowl, whisk flour, cinnamon, baking soda, ginger, salt and cloves; gradually beat into molasses mixture. Spoon carefully over pears.
3. Bake until a toothpick inserted in the center comes out clean, 25-30 minutes. Cool for 10 minutes before inverting onto a serving plate. Serve warm or at room temperature with whipped cream, if desired.
1 piece: 331 cal., 11g fat (7g sat. fat), 51mg chol., 348mg sod., 56g carb. (37g sugars, 2g fiber), 4g pro.

CAST IRON: THE BENEFITS OF PREHEATING

Baking in cast iron has some incredible benefits—a cast-iron skillet holds heat better than other materials and is incredibly versatile. However, cast iron does not heat up evenly—or quickly—so preheating is a must to help your food cook faster and more evenly. Preheating also keeps dough from sticking and helps to caramelize the bottom of a skillet cake.

The easiest way to preheat your skillet is to simply put it in the oven while it preheats. You can also heat it on the stovetop: Heat the pan gradually, over about 10 minutes, rotating it every few minutes so heat is evenly applied and you don't get a hot spot. If you forget to rotate the pan, let it cool down and start again.

APPLE GINGERBREAD SKILLET CAKE

This gingerbread recipe came from my grandmother, and we always ate it with warm applesauce. I adapted it to make a one-pan dessert by layering the apples around the bottom of a cast-iron skillet and topping them with the gingerbread batter. The skillet creates a wonderfully thick crust on the gingerbread.

—Mary Leverette, Columbia, SC

PREP: 30 MIN. • **BAKE:** 35 MIN. + COOLING
MAKES: 16 SERVINGS

- ¼ cup butter, cubed
- ½ cup chopped pecans
- ¼ cup packed brown sugar
- ¼ cup molasses
- 2 medium tart apples, peeled and thinly sliced

GINGERBREAD

- ½ cup butter, softened
- ½ cup sugar
- 1 large egg, room temperature
- 1 cup molasses
- 2½ cups all-purpose flour
- 1½ tsp. baking soda
- 1 tsp. ground ginger
- ½ tsp. salt
- ½ tsp. ground cloves
- 1 cup hot water
  Warmed applesauce, optional

1. Preheat oven to 350°. Place ¼ cup butter in a 12-in. cast-iron or other ovenproof skillet. Place in oven until butter is melted, 4-5 minutes; carefully swirl to coat evenly. Sprinkle with pecans and brown sugar; drizzle with molasses. Arrange apple slices in a single layer over the sugar mixture, cut side down.

2. In a large bowl, cream butter and sugar until light and fluffy, 5-7 minutes. Beat in egg, then molasses. In another bowl, whisk flour, baking soda, ginger, salt and cloves; gradually add to the creamed mixture. Stir in hot water.

3. Pour batter over apples. Bake until a toothpick inserted in center comes out clean, 35-40 minutes. Cool 10 minutes before inverting onto a serving plate. If desired, serve warm with applesauce.

1 piece: 294 cal., 12g fat (6g sat. fat), 35mg chol., 276mg sod., 46g carb. (30g sugars, 1g fiber), 3g pro.

STRAWBERRY-RHUBARB FLIP CAKE

My friend Dave always brought two strawberry rhubarb cakes to work to celebrate his birthday. He'd use up the rhubarb growing in his yard and treat his co-workers!

—Charlene Schwartz, Maple Plain, MN

PREP: 20 MIN. • **BAKE:** 40 MIN. + COOLING
MAKES: 12 SERVINGS

- 1 cup packed brown sugar
- 3 Tbsp. quick-cooking tapioca
- 6 cups sliced fresh or frozen rhubarb, thawed
- 3 cups sliced fresh or frozen strawberries, thawed
- ½ cup butter, softened
- 1 cup sugar
- 2 large eggs, room temperature
- 1 tsp. vanilla extract
- 2 cups all-purpose flour
- 2½ tsp. baking powder
- ¼ tsp. salt
- 1 cup 2% milk
  Optional: Sweetened whipped cream or vanilla ice cream

1. Preheat oven to 350°. In a large bowl, mix brown sugar and tapioca. Add the rhubarb and strawberries; toss to coat. Let stand 15 minutes.

2. Meanwhile, in a large bowl, cream butter and sugar until light and fluffy, 5-7 minutes. Add eggs, 1 at a time, beating well after each addition. Beat in vanilla. In another bowl, whisk the flour, baking powder and salt; add to the creamed mixture alternately with milk, beating well after each addition.

3. Transfer the rhubarb mixture to a greased 13x9-in. baking dish; pour batter over top. Bake for 40-45 minutes or until a toothpick inserted in center comes out clean. Cool completely in pan on a wire rack. Invert each piece onto a serving plate. If desired, serve with whipped cream or ice cream.

1 piece: 338 cal., 9g fat (5g sat. fat), 53mg chol., 223mg sod., 60g carb. (38g sugars, 2g fiber), 5g pro.

BAKING 101

BLUEBERRY UPSIDE-DOWN SKILLET CAKE

Living in Maine, I am lucky to have an endless amount of wild blueberries. This recipe is similar to a pineapple upside-down cake. It's easy, light and also great made with cranberries.

—Nettie Moore, Belfast, ME

PREP: 25 MIN. • **BAKE:** 20 MIN.
MAKES: 8 SERVINGS

- ¼ cup butter, cubed
- 1 cup packed brown sugar
- ¼ cup orange juice
- 1 cup fresh or frozen blueberries
- 1½ cups all-purpose flour
- ½ cup sugar
- 2 tsp. baking powder
- ½ tsp. salt
- 1 large egg, room temperature
- ½ cup 2% milk
- ½ cup butter, melted
- ½ tsp. almond extract
  Optional toppings: Vanilla ice cream, whipped cream and toasted almonds

1. Preheat oven to 400°. In a 10-in. cast-iron or other ovenproof skillet, melt cubed butter over medium-low heat; stir in brown sugar until dissolved. Remove from heat. Stir in orange juice; sprinkle with blueberries.
2. In a large bowl, whisk flour, sugar, baking powder and salt. In another bowl, whisk egg, milk, melted butter and extract until blended. Add to the flour mixture; stir just until moistened. Pour over blueberries.
3. Bake until a toothpick inserted in center comes out clean, 18-22 minutes. Cool 10 minutes before inverting onto a serving plate. Top as desired.
1 piece: 454 cal., 21g fat (11g sat. fat), 73mg chol., 396mg sod., 63g carb. (43g sugars, 2g fiber), 5g pro.

APRICOT
UPSIDE-DOWN
CAKE

APRICOT UPSIDE-DOWN CAKE

My Aunt Anne, who is a great cook, gave me a taste of this golden cake and I couldn't believe how delicious it was. Apricots give it a distinctive and attractive twist.

—Ruth Ann Stelfox, Raymond, AB

PREP: 30 MIN. • **BAKE:** 35 MIN. + COOLING
MAKES: 9 SERVINGS

- 2 large eggs, separated
- 2 cans (15 oz. each) apricot halves
- ¼ cup butter, cubed
- ½ cup packed brown sugar
- ⅔ cup cake flour
- ¾ tsp. baking powder
- ¼ tsp. salt
- ⅔ cup sugar

1. Place egg whites in a small bowl; let stand at room temperature 30 minutes. Preheat oven to 350°. Drain apricots, reserving 3 Tbsp. syrup (discard the remaining syrup); set aside.
2. Place butter in a 9-in. square baking dish. Place in oven 3-4 minutes or until butter is melted; swirl carefully to coat dish evenly. Sprinkle with brown sugar. Carefully arrange apricot halves in a single layer over the brown sugar, cut side up.
3. In a small bowl, whisk flour, baking powder and salt. In a large bowl, beat the egg yolks until slightly thickened. Gradually add sugar, beating on high speed until thick and lemon-colored. Beat in the reserved apricot syrup. Fold in the flour mixture.
4. With clean beaters, beat egg whites on medium speed until stiff peaks form. Fold into batter. Spoon over apricots. Bake 35-40 minutes or until a toothpick inserted in center comes out clean. Cool for 10 minutes before inverting onto a serving plate. Serve warm.
1 piece: 272 cal., 6g fat (4g sat. fat), 55mg chol., 162mg sod., 53g carb. (44g sugars, 1g fiber), 3g pro.

BANANA UPSIDE-DOWN CAKE

For a fun and different way to use bananas, try this distinctive spin on upside-down cake. Every time I serve this treat, someone requests the recipe.

—Ruth Andrewson, Leavenworth, WA

PREP: 30 MIN. • **BAKE:** 35 MIN. + COOLING
MAKES: 8 SERVINGS

- ½ cup packed brown sugar
- 2 Tbsp. lemon juice, divided
- 1 Tbsp. butter
- ½ cup pecan halves
- 2 medium firm bananas, sliced

CAKE
- 1½ cups all-purpose flour
- ½ cup sugar
- 1 tsp. baking soda
- 1 tsp. baking powder
- ¼ tsp. salt
- ¼ cup cold butter, cubed
- 1 cup plain yogurt
- 2 large eggs, room temperature, lightly beaten
- 2 tsp. grated lemon zest
- 1 tsp. vanilla extract
   Whipped cream, optional

1. Preheat oven to 375°. In a small saucepan, combine the brown sugar, 1 Tbsp. lemon juice and butter; bring to a boil. Reduce heat to medium; cook without stirring until sugar is dissolved.
2. Pour into a greased 9-in. springform pan. Sprinkle with pecans. Pour the remaining 1 Tbsp. lemon juice into a small bowl; add bananas and stir carefully. Drain. Arrange bananas in a circular pattern over the pecans; set aside.
3. In a large bowl, combine the flour, sugar, baking soda, baking powder and salt. Cut in butter until mixture resembles coarse crumbs. In a small bowl, combine the yogurt, eggs, lemon zest and vanilla extract; stir into the dry ingredients just until moistened. Spoon over bananas.
4. Bake until a toothpick inserted in the center comes out clean, 35-40 minutes. Cool 10 minutes. Run a knife around edge of pan; invert cake onto a serving plate. Serve with whipped cream if desired.
1 piece: 362 cal., 15g fat (6g sat. fat), 76mg chol., 390mg sod., 54g carb. (33g sugars, 2g fiber), 6g pro.

· · · · · · · · · · · · · · · · ·
DID YOU KNOW?
When using yogurt for baking, use full-fat yogurt unless the recipe specifically calls for low-fat or fat-free. Reduced-fat yogurts (both regular or Greek) often contain stabilizers, which can affect the end result.

TILLIE'S GINGER
CRUMB CAKE

BAKING 101

TILLIE'S GINGER CRUMB CAKE

This recipe goes back at least as far as my grandmother, who was born in the early 1900s. Our sons and I enjoy eating it in a bowl with milk poured on it—much to the dismay of my husband, who prefers it plain!
—Kathy Nienow Clark, Byron, MI

PREP: 20 MIN. • **BAKE:** 35 MIN.
MAKES: 16 SERVINGS

- 4 cups all-purpose flour
- 2 cups sugar
- 1 cup cold butter
- ½ tsp. ground ginger
- ¼ tsp. ground cloves
- ½ tsp. ground cinnamon
- ½ tsp. ground nutmeg
- 1 cup plus 2 Tbsp. buttermilk
- 1¼ tsp. baking soda
- 2 large eggs, room temperature
  Confectioners' sugar, optional

1. Preheat oven to 350°. In a large bowl, combine the flour and sugar; cut in butter until crumbly. Set aside 2 cups. Combine the remaining crumb mixture with the remaining ingredients.
2. Sprinkle 1 cup of reserved crumbs into a greased 12-in. cast-iron skillet or 13x9-in. baking dish. Pour batter over crumbs; sprinkle with the remaining 1 cup of crumbs.
3. Bake until a toothpick inserted in the center comes out clean, about 35 minutes. If desired, sprinkle with confectioners' sugar before serving.
1 piece: 330 cal., 13g fat (8g sat. fat), 54mg chol., 232mg sod., 50g carb. (26g sugars, 1g fiber), 5g pro.

HOMEMADE RHUBARB UPSIDE-DOWN CAKE

This light and airy yellow cake is moist but not too sweet, and the caramelized rhubarb topping adds tangy flavor and visual appeal. We like it served with strawberry ice cream.

—Joyce Rowe, Stratham, NH

PREP: 30 MIN. • **BAKE:** 40 MIN. + COOLING
MAKES: 12 SERVINGS

- ⅔ cup packed brown sugar
- 3 Tbsp. butter, melted
- 2¼ cups diced fresh or frozen rhubarb
- 4½ tsp. sugar

BATTER
- 6 Tbsp. butter, softened
- ¾ cup sugar
- 2 large eggs, separated, room temperature
- 1 tsp. vanilla extract
- 1 cup plus 2 Tbsp. all-purpose flour
- 1½ tsp. baking powder
- ½ tsp. salt
- ¼ cup milk
- ¼ tsp. cream of tartar
  Optional: Whipped cream or vanilla ice cream

1. Preheat oven to 325°. In a small bowl, combine the brown sugar and butter. Spread into a greased 10-in cast-iron or other ovenproof skillet. Layer with rhubarb; sprinkle with sugar. Set aside.
2. In a large bowl, cream the butter and sugar until light and fluffy, 5-7 minutes. Beat in egg yolks and vanilla. Combine the flour, baking powder and salt; add to the creamed mixture alternately with milk, beating well after each addition.
3. In a small bowl with clean beaters, beat the egg whites and cream of tartar on medium speed until stiff peaks form. Gradually fold into the creamed mixture, about ½ cup at a time. Gently spoon over rhubarb.
4. Bake until cake springs back when lightly touched, 40-50 minutes. Cool for 10 minutes before inverting onto a serving plate. Serve warm with whipped cream or ice cream as desired.

1 piece: 240 cal., 10g fat (6g sat. fat), 59mg chol., 254mg sod., 36g carb. (27g sugars, 1g fiber), 3g pro.

HOMEMADE RHUBARB
UPSIDE-DOWN CAKE

STRAWBERRY BUTTERMILK SKILLET SHORTCAKE

This scratch-made buttermilk shortcake recipe is a family favorite. It's over 100 years old. My grandmother used to make it, and we carry on the tradition every summer.
—Claudia Lamascolo, Melbourne, FL

PREP: 25 MIN. • **BAKE:** 50 MIN.
MAKES: 10 SERVINGS

- 10 Tbsp. shortening
- ¼ cup butter, softened
- 1 cup sugar
- 2 large eggs, room temperature
- 2½ cups all-purpose flour
- 3 tsp. baking powder
- ½ tsp. salt
- ⅔ cup buttermilk

STREUSEL TOPPING
- ⅔ cup all-purpose flour
- ½ cup sugar
- 1 tsp. ground cinnamon
- ¼ tsp. ground allspice
- ½ cup butter, softened
- 2 cups sliced fresh strawberries
  Whipped cream

1. Preheat oven to 350°. In a large bowl, cream shortening, butter and sugar until light and fluffy, 5-7 minutes. Add eggs, 1 at a time, beating well after each addition. In another bowl, whisk flour, baking powder and salt; add to creamed mixture alternately with the buttermilk, beating well after each addition. Transfer to a 12-in. cast-iron or other ovenproof skillet.
2. For streusel topping, in a small bowl, mix flour, sugar, cinnamon and allspice; cut in butter until crumbly. Sprinkle over batter. Top with strawberries. Bake until center is puffed and edges are golden brown, 50-60 minutes. Serve warm with whipped cream.

1 piece: 526 cal., 27g fat (12g sat. fat), 74mg chol., 418mg sod., 64g carb. (33g sugars, 2g fiber), 6g pro.

SWEET CHERRY UPSIDE-DOWN CAKE

This cake is a summer staple in our house and is always welcomed at neighborhood and family barbecues. Served warm with some vanilla ice cream and/or whipped cream, it really puts the cherry on top of a good meal.
—Nicole Nutter, Prosser, WA

PREP: 25 MIN. • **BAKE:** 35 MIN. + COOLING
MAKES: 20 SERVINGS

- ⅓ cup butter, cubed
- 2¼ cups sugar, divided
- 1 lb. fresh dark sweet cherries, pitted and halved (about 2 cups)
- ¾ cup shortening
- 2 large eggs, room temperature
- 1 Tbsp. vanilla extract
- 2¼ cups all-purpose flour
- 2 tsp. baking powder
- 1 tsp. salt
- 1½ cups 2% milk

1. Preheat oven to 350°. Place butter in a 13x9-in. baking pan; heat in oven until butter is melted, 2-3 minutes. Remove pan from oven; tilt carefully to coat bottom and sides with butter. Immediately sprinkle with ¾ cup sugar. Arrange cherries in a single layer over sugar, cut side down.
2. In a large bowl, cream shortening and remaining 1½ cups sugar until crumbly. Add eggs, 1 at a time, beating well after each addition. Beat in vanilla. In another bowl, whisk flour, baking powder and salt; add to creamed mixture alternately with milk, beating well after each addition. (Batter may appear curdled.) Spoon over cherries.
3. Bake until a toothpick inserted in center comes out clean, 35-40 minutes. Cool 10 minutes before inverting onto a serving plate. Serve warm.

1 piece: 266 cal., 11g fat (4g sat. fat), 28mg chol., 207mg sod., 39g carb. (26g sugars, 1g fiber), 3g pro.

UPSIDE-DOWN APPLE CAKE WITH BUTTERSCOTCH TOPPING

This cake is a favorite of mine. I love the smell of the apples and butterscotch as it is baking. It fills the house with a perfect autumn aroma.

—Sabrina Haught, Spencer, WV

PREP: 25 MIN. • **BAKE:** 20 MIN.
MAKES: 6 SERVINGS

- ¼ cup butter, softened
- ⅓ cup sugar
- 1 large egg, room temperature
- ¾ tsp. vanilla extract
- ¾ cup all-purpose flour
- ¾ tsp. baking powder
- ¼ tsp. salt
- ¼ cup sour cream
- ⅔ cup finely chopped peeled tart apple

BUTTERSCOTCH APPLE TOPPING
- 2 Tbsp. butter
- 2 Tbsp. butterscotch chips
- 2 Tbsp. brown sugar
- ¾ cup thinly sliced peeled tart apple

1. Preheat oven to 375°. In a small bowl, cream butter and sugar until light and fluffy, 5-7 minutes. Beat in egg. Beat in vanilla extract. Combine flour, baking powder and salt; add to the creamed mixture alternately with sour cream, beating well after each addition. Fold in chopped apple; set aside.

2. In a 7-in. cast-iron or other ovenproof skillet, melt butter and chips with brown sugar over medium heat. Stir in sliced apple. Spoon and spread batter over apple mixture.

3. Bake until a toothpick inserted in the center comes out clean, 20-25 minutes. Cool for 5 minutes before inverting onto a serving plate. Serve warm.

1 piece: 290 cal., 15g fat (10g sat. fat), 72mg chol., 249mg sod., 35g carb. (19g sugars, 1g fiber), 4g pro.

SKILLET PINEAPPLE UPSIDE-DOWN CAKE

This old-fashioned recipe is a true timeless classic. But if you want a change of pace, you can substitute fresh or frozen peach slices for the pineapple.

—Bernardine Melton, Paola, KS

PREP: 20 MIN. • **BAKE:** 30 MIN. + COOLING
MAKES: 8 SERVINGS

- ½ cup butter
- 1 cup packed brown sugar
- 1 can (20 oz.) sliced pineapple
- ½ cup chopped pecans
- 3 large eggs, separated, room temperature
- 1 cup sugar
- 1 tsp. vanilla extract
- 1 cup all-purpose flour
- 1 tsp. baking powder
- ¼ tsp. salt
  Maraschino cherries

1. Preheat oven to 375°. Melt butter in a 9- or 10-in. ovenproof skillet. Add brown sugar; mix well until sugar is melted. Drain pineapple, reserving ⅓ cup juice. Arrange about 8 pineapple slices in a single layer over the sugar (refrigerate remaining pineapple slices for another use). Sprinkle pecans over pineapple; set aside.

2. In a large bowl, beat egg yolks until thick and lemon-colored. Gradually add sugar, beating well. Blend in vanilla and reserved pineapple juice. Combine flour, baking powder and salt; gradually add to batter and mix well.

3. In a small bowl with clean beaters, beat egg whites on high speed until stiff peaks form; fold into batter. Spoon into skillet.

4. Bake until a toothpick inserted in the center comes out clean, 30-35 minutes (cover loosely with foil if cake browns too quickly). Let stand 10 minutes, then invert onto a serving plate. Place the cherries in center of pineapple slices.

1 piece: 380 cal., 15g fat (7g sat. fat), 88mg chol., 224mg sod., 59g carb. (48g sugars, 1g fiber), 4g pro.

UPSIDE-DOWN PLUM CAKE

This cake is different with the addition of plums. It is fancy enough to serve to guests.
—Robert Fallon, Sayville, NY

PREP: 20 MIN. • **BAKE:** 30 MIN.
MAKES: 6-8 SERVINGS

- 7 Tbsp. butter, softened and divided
- ¾ cup sugar, divided
- 3 to 4 plums, pitted and thinly sliced
- 1 large egg
- 1 cup all-purpose flour
- ¼ tsp. salt
- 1 tsp. baking powder
- ⅓ cup whole milk
- 1 tsp. vanilla extract

1. Preheat oven to 350°. Place 1 Tbsp. butter in a 9-in. round baking pan. Put pan in hot oven to melt. Remove from oven and sprinkle with ⅓ cup sugar. Arrange plum slices in a circular pattern over sugar; bake for 10 minutes.
2. Cream the remaining 6 Tbsp. butter with remaining sugar; beat in the egg. Combine flour, salt and baking powder. Add to creamed mixture alternately with the milk and vanilla, beating until smooth.
3. Spread evenly over plums; bake for 30 minutes or until cake tests done. Remove from the oven and invert onto a large serving platter. Serve warm.
1 piece: 248 cal., 11g fat (7g sat. fat), 55mg chol., 238mg sod., 34g carb. (21g sugars, 1g fiber), 3g pro.

SOUTHERN PEACH UPSIDE-DOWN CAKE

A dear friend from the South gave me the idea for this peachy cake. I add bourbon and top each slice with vanilla or cinnamon ice cream.
—Trista Jefferson, Batavia, OH

PREP: 25 MIN. • **BAKE:** 40 MIN.
MAKES: 10 SERVINGS

SOUTHERN PEACH UPSIDE-DOWN CAKE

- 2 cups sliced peeled peaches or frozen unsweetened sliced peaches, thawed
- 2 Tbsp. bourbon, optional
- ¼ cup butter
- ½ cup packed brown sugar
BATTER
- ½ cup butter, softened
- ¾ cup sugar
- 1 large egg, room temperature
- 1 tsp. vanilla extract
- 1¼ cups all-purpose flour
- 1¼ tsp. baking powder
- ¼ tsp. salt
- ½ cup 2% milk

1. Preheat oven to 350°. If desired, combine peaches and bourbon; let stand 10 minutes.
2. Meanwhile, place ¼ cup butter in a 10-in. cast-iron or other ovenproof skillet; heat in oven until butter melts, 5-7 minutes. Sprinkle the brown sugar evenly over butter. Arrange peach slices over brown sugar.
3. For batter, in a large bowl, cream the butter and sugar until light and fluffy, 5-7 minutes. Beat in egg and vanilla. In another bowl, whisk flour, baking powder and salt; add to creamed mixture alternately with milk, beating after each addition just until combined. Spread batter evenly over peaches.
4. Bake until a toothpick inserted in center comes out clean, 40-45 minutes. Cool for 5 minutes before inverting onto a serving plate. Serve warm.
1 piece: 306 cal., 15g fat (9g sat. fat), 56mg chol., 235mg sod., 41g carb. (29g sugars, 1g fiber), 3g pro.

ASSORTED CAKES & TORTES

OMA'S APFELKUCHEN (GRANDMA'S APPLE CAKE)

For more than 150 years, members of my husband's German family have made this scrumptious apple cake recipe. Try it with any apples you have on hand. I like to use Granny Smith.
—Amy Kirchen, Loveland, OH

PREP: 20 MIN. • **BAKE:** 45 MIN. + COOLING
MAKES: 10 SERVINGS

- 5   large egg yolks
- 2   medium tart apples, peeled, cored and halved
- 1   cup plus 2 Tbsp. unsalted butter, softened
- 1¼ cups sugar
- 2   cups all-purpose flour
- 2   Tbsp. cornstarch
- 2   tsp. cream of tartar
- 1   tsp. baking powder
- ½   tsp. salt
- ¼   cup 2% milk
     Confectioners' sugar

1. Preheat oven to 350°. Let the egg yolks stand at room temperature for 30 minutes. Starting ½ in. from 1 end, cut apple halves lengthwise into ¼-in. slices, leaving them attached at the top so they fan out slightly. Set aside.
2. Cream butter and sugar until light and fluffy, 5-7 minutes. Add egg yolks, 1 at a time, beating well after each addition. In another bowl, sift flour, cornstarch, cream of tartar, baking powder and salt twice. Gradually beat into the creamed mixture. Add milk; mix well (batter will be thick).
3. Spread batter into a greased 9-in. springform pan wrapped in a sheet of heavy-duty foil. Gently press apples, round side up, into batter. Bake until a toothpick inserted in the center comes out with moist crumbs, 45-55 minutes.
4. Cool in pan on a wire rack 10 minutes. Loosen sides from the pan with a knife; remove foil. Cool 1 hour longer. Remove rim from pan. Dust the cake with confectioners' sugar.
1 piece: 422 cal., 23g fat (14g sat. fat), 148mg chol., 177mg sod., 50g carb. (28g sugars, 1g fiber), 4g pro.

OMA'S APFELKUCHEN
(GRANDMA'S APPLE CAKE)

CHOCOLATE GUINNESS CAKE

4. In a large bowl, beat cream cheese until fluffy. Add confectioners' sugar and cream; beat until smooth (do not overbeat). Frost top of cake; leave sides bare. Refrigerate any leftovers.
1 piece: 494 cal., 22g fat (13g sat. fat), 99mg chol., 288mg sod., 69g carb. (49g sugars, 2g fiber), 6g pro.

HOLIDAY WHITE FRUITCAKE
Years ago, when I attended the Koloa Missionary Church in Hawaii, a friend gave me this recipe. Now I whip up at least 60 loaves for the holidays!
—Eileen Flatt, Chandler, AZ

BAKING 101

PREP: 20 MIN.
BAKE: 50 MIN. + COOLING
MAKES: 4 LOAVES
(16 PIECES EACH)

    1   pkg. (8 oz.) chopped mixed
        candied fruit
 1¼   cups golden raisins
    1   cup chopped walnuts, toasted
    3   cups all-purpose flour, divided
    2   cups butter, softened
    2   cups sugar
    6   large eggs, room temperature

1. Preheat oven to 275°. Line bottoms of four greased 9x5-in. loaf pans with parchment; grease parchment.
2. In a small bowl, toss candied fruit, raisins and walnuts with ½ cup flour. In a large bowl, cream butter and sugar until light and fluffy, 5-7 minutes. Add eggs, 1 at a time, beating well after each addition. Gradually beat in the remaining flour. Fold in fruit mixture.
3. Transfer batter to the prepared pans. Bake until a toothpick inserted in center comes out clean, 50-60 minutes. Cool in pans 10 minutes before removing to wire racks to cool.
1 piece: 133 cal., 7g fat (4g sat. fat), 33mg chol., 61mg sod., 16g carb. (10g sugars, 1g fiber), 2g pro.

CHOCOLATE GUINNESS CAKE
One bite and everyone will propose a toast to this silky-smooth chocolate cake. The cream cheese frosting reminds us of the foamy head on a perfectly poured pint.
—Marjorie Hennig, Seymour, IN

PREP: 25 MINUTES
BAKE: 45 MIN. + COOLING
MAKES: 12 SERVINGS

    1   cup Guinness (dark beer)
   ½   cup butter, cubed
    2   cups sugar
   ¾   cup baking cocoa
    2   large eggs, beaten,
        room temperature
  ⅔   cup sour cream
    3   tsp. vanilla extract
    2   cups all-purpose flour
 1½   tsp. baking soda

TOPPING
    1   pkg. (8 oz.) cream cheese,
        softened
 1½   cups confectioners' sugar
   ½   cup heavy whipping cream

1. Preheat oven to 350°. Grease a 9-in. springform pan and line the bottom with parchment; set aside.
2. In a small saucepan, heat beer and butter until butter is melted. Remove from the heat; whisk in sugar and cocoa until blended. Combine the eggs, sour cream and vanilla; whisk into the beer mixture. Combine flour and baking soda; whisk into beer mixture until smooth. Pour batter into prepared pan.
3. Bake until a toothpick inserted in the center comes out clean, 45-50 minutes. Cool completely in pan on a wire rack. Remove cake from the pan and place on a platter or cake stand.

SPICED CHOCOLATE MOLTEN CAKES

Take some time to linger over this decadent dessert. There is nothing better than a chocolate cake with a warm melted center.
—Deb Carpenter, Hastings, MI

TAKES: 30 MIN. • **MAKES:** 2 SERVINGS

- ¼ cup butter, cubed
- 2 oz. semisweet chocolate, chopped
- 1½ tsp. dry red wine
- ½ tsp. vanilla extract
- 1 large egg, room temperature
- 2 tsp. egg yolk, room temperature
- ½ cup confectioners' sugar
- 3 Tbsp. all-purpose flour
- ⅛ tsp. ground ginger
- ⅛ tsp. ground cinnamon
  Additional confectioners' sugar

1. Preheat oven to 425°. In a microwave, melt butter and chocolate; stir until smooth. Stir in wine and vanilla.

2. In a small bowl, beat the egg, egg yolk and confectioners' sugar until thick and lemon-colored. Beat in flour, ginger and cinnamon until well blended. Gradually beat in the butter mixture.

3. Transfer to 2 greased 6-oz. ramekins or custard cups. Place ramekins on a baking sheet. Bake until a thermometer inserted in the center reads 160° and sides of cakes are set, 10-12 minutes.

4. Remove from the oven and let stand for 1 minute. Run a knife around edges of ramekins; invert onto dessert plates. Dust with additional confectioners' sugar. Serve immediately.

1 cake: 560 cal., 36g fat (21g sat. fat), 234mg chol., 200mg sod., 56g carb. (43g sugars, 2g fiber), 8g pro.

TUSCAN SUN ORANGE CRANBERRY CAKE

Growing up, my family used farina flour in desserts, and I thought it would lend a nice texture to this cake. It's an Old World Italian-style cake, delicious but not too sweet. The orange-cranberry combination is perfect!
—Ninette Holbrook, Orlando, FL

PREP: 25 MIN. • **BAKE:** 20 MIN. + COOLING
MAKES: 8 SERVINGS

- ⅓ cup sugar
- ⅓ cup canola oil
- 2 large eggs, room temperature
- 1 Tbsp. grated orange zest
- 1 Tbsp. orange juice
- ⅓ cup all-purpose flour
- ⅓ cup cream of wheat or farina flour
- ½ tsp. salt
- ¼ tsp. baking powder
- ⅓ cup dried cranberries, chopped
- ¼ cup sliced almonds

ORANGE GLAZE
- ¾ cup confectioners' sugar
- 1 Tbsp. orange juice
- 2 tsp. 2% milk
  Grated orange zest, optional

1. Preheat oven to 350°. Grease an 8-in. round baking pan; set aside.

2. In a large bowl, beat sugar, oil, eggs, orange zest and juice until well blended. In another bowl, whisk flour, cream of wheat, salt and baking powder; gradually beat into oil mixture. Stir in the cranberries.

3. Transfer batter to prepared pan; sprinkle with almonds. Bake until a toothpick inserted in center comes out clean, 20-25 minutes.

4. Combine glaze ingredients; pour over the warm cake. Cool 10 minutes before serving. If desired, sprinkle cake with orange zest.

1 piece: 263 cal., 12g fat (1g sat. fat), 47mg chol., 182mg sod., 36g carb. (25g sugars, 1g fiber), 4g pro.

CRANBERRY ZUCCHINI WEDGES

I try to slip zucchini into as many dishes as possible. These cake wedges have wonderful flavor and a tender texture. They are pretty, too, with bits of pineapple, cranberries and zucchini. And they're perfect for brunch.

—Redawna Kalynchuk, Rochester, AB

PREP: 15 MIN. • **BAKE:** 30 MIN. + COOLING
MAKES: 2 CAKES (8 PIECES EACH)

- 1 can (20 oz.) pineapple chunks
- 3 cups all-purpose flour
- 1¾ cups sugar
- 1 tsp. baking powder
- 1 tsp. baking soda
- 1 tsp. salt
- 3 large eggs, room temperature
- 1 cup canola oil
- 2 tsp. vanilla extract
- 1 cup tightly packed shredded zucchini
- 1 cup fresh or frozen cranberries, halved
- ½ cup chopped walnuts
  Confectioners' sugar
  Sugared cranberries, optional

1. Drain pineapple, reserving ⅓ cup juice (save remaining juice for another use). Place the pineapple and reserved juice in a blender; cover and process until smooth. Set aside.

2. In a large bowl, combine the flour, sugar, baking powder, baking soda and salt. In a small bowl, whisk the eggs, oil, vanilla and pineapple mixture; stir into the dry ingredients until blended. Fold in the zucchini, cranberries and nuts.

3. Pour into 2 greased and floured 9-in. round baking pans. Bake at 350° for 30-35 minutes or until a toothpick inserted in the center comes out clean.

4. Cool for 10 minutes before removing from the pans to wire racks to cool completely. Just before serving, dust with confectioners' sugar. If desired, top with sugared cranberries.

1 piece: 354 cal., 17g fat (2g sat. fat), 40mg chol., 264mg sod., 47g carb. (27g sugars, 1g fiber), 5g pro.

ROSEMARY & THYME LEMON PUDDING CAKES

These simple little cakes are absolutely divine and are perfect with hot tea. Think English tea party! Your guests will love them.

—Crystal Jo Bruns, Iliff, CO

PREP: 30 MIN. + STANDING • **BAKE:** 20 MIN.
MAKES: 6 SERVINGS

- 3 large eggs, separated
- 2 Tbsp. butter, melted, divided
- 7 Tbsp. sugar, divided
- 1 cup unsweetened vanilla almond milk
- 2 tsp. dried rosemary, crushed
- 2 tsp. dried thyme
- ¼ cup all-purpose flour
- 3 tsp. grated lemon zest
- ¼ cup lemon juice
- 1 Tbsp. coarse sugar

1. Let egg yolks and whites stand at room temperature 30 minutes. Lightly brush the inside of six 6-oz. ramekins or custard cups with 1 Tbsp. melted butter. Dust each with ½ tsp. sugar.

2. Preheat oven to 350°. In a small saucepan, combine milk and herbs; bring just to a boil. Immediately remove from heat; let stand 10 minutes. Strain milk through a fine-mesh strainer; discard herbs.

3. Place flour and 2 Tbsp. sugar in a large bowl; whisk in yolks, lemon zest, lemon juice, remaining 1 Tbsp. melted butter and strained milk. In a separate bowl, beat egg whites on medium speed until foamy. Gradually add remaining 4 Tbsp. sugar, 1 Tbsp. at a time, beating on high after each addition until sugar is dissolved. Continue beating until stiff glossy peaks form; fold gently into flour mixture. Divide among ramekins.

4. Bake until tops spring back when lightly touched, 17-20 minutes. (Cakes will fall slightly.) Sprinkle with coarse sugar; cool 5 minutes on a wire rack. Serve warm.

1 cake: 165 cal., 7g fat (3g sat. fat), 103mg chol., 97mg sod., 23g carb. (17g sugars, 1g fiber), 4g pro. **Diabetic exchanges:** 1½ starch, 1½ fat.

CHUNKY FRESH MANGO CAKE

This delicious cake, a family favorite, originated years ago with a great-aunt who lived in Florida and had her own mango tree. It's a sweet, moist cake, with slightly crisp edges.

—Allene Bary-Cooper, Wichita Falls, TX

PREP: 20 MIN. • **BAKE:** 30 MIN. + COOLING
MAKES: 4 SERVINGS

PENNSYLVANIA DUTCH FUNNY CAKE

½ cup sugar
⅓ cup canola oil
1 large egg, room temperature
½ cup plus 2 Tbsp. all-purpose flour
¾ tsp. baking powder
¼ tsp. salt
¼ tsp. ground cinnamon
⅛ tsp. ground nutmeg
¾ cup chopped peeled mango
¼ cup chopped pecans
Optional: Confectioners' sugar and whipped topping

BAKING 101

1. Preheat oven to 375°. In a small bowl, beat the sugar, oil and egg until well blended. In another bowl, combine the flour, baking powder, salt, cinnamon and nutmeg; gradually beat into sugar mixture and mix well. Fold in mango and pecans.
2. Transfer to a greased 6-in. round baking pan. Bake for 25-30 minutes or until a toothpick inserted in the center comes out clean. Cool for 10 minutes before removing from pan to a wire rack to cool completely.
3. Garnish with confectioners' sugar and whipped topping if desired.
1 piece: 423 cal., 26g fat (2g sat. fat), 53mg chol., 241mg sod., 46g carb. (30g sugars, 2g fiber), 4g pro.

PENNSYLVANIA DUTCH FUNNY CAKE

Every time I bake this unusual cake (that looks like a pie!), it takes me back to special days at Grandma's. I can still see her serving this delicious cake on the big wooden table in her farm kitchen.

—Diane Ganssle, Bethlehem, PA

PREP: 20 MIN. • **BAKE:** 40 MIN.
MAKES: 16 SERVINGS

2 cups sugar, divided
½ cup baking cocoa
1½ cups milk, divided
2 unbaked pastry shells (9 in.)
2 cups all-purpose flour
2 tsp. baking powder
¼ tsp. salt
1 large egg, room temperature
2 Tbsp. shortening
1 tsp. vanilla extract
Whipped cream, optional

1. Preheat oven to 350°. In a small saucepan, combine 1 cup of sugar and cocoa. Blend in ½ cup milk. Cook and stir over medium heat until mixture comes to a boil. Cook and stir until thickened, about 2 minutes. Pour into unbaked pastry shells, tipping to coat the pastry halfway up the sides; set shells aside.
2. Combine flour, baking powder, salt and remaining 1 cup sugar. Add egg, shortening, vanilla and remaining 1 cup milk; beat until smooth. Starting at the edge, spoon the batter into the pastry shells, completely covering the chocolate.
3. Bake for 40 minutes or until a toothpick inserted in the center comes out clean. Serve warm or chilled, with whipped cream if desired.
1 piece: 314 cal., 10g fat (4g sat. fat), 21mg chol., 203mg sod., 53g carb. (27g sugars, 1g fiber), 4g pro.

CARDAMOM PUMPKIN PUDDING CAKE

This no-egg cake is quick, easy and bursting with flavor. I like to serve it with ice cream or whipped cream.

—J. Fleming, Almonte, ON

PREP: 20 MIN. • **BAKE:** 25 MIN. + COOLING
MAKES: 9 SERVINGS

- 1¼ cups all-purpose flour
- ¾ cup sugar
- 2 tsp. baking soda
- 1¼ tsp. ground cinnamon
- 1 tsp. ground cardamom
- ¼ tsp. salt
- ½ cup evaporated milk
- ½ cup canned pumpkin
- ¼ cup butter, melted
- 1 tsp. vanilla extract
- ½ cup chopped pecans

TOPPING
- 1 cup packed brown sugar
- ½ tsp. ground cinnamon
- 1½ cups boiling water
   Optional: Vanilla ice cream or sweetened whipped cream

1. Preheat oven to 350°. In a large bowl, combine first 6 ingredients. Add milk, pumpkin, butter and vanilla; mix until blended. Stir in pecans. Transfer to a greased 9-in. square baking pan.
2. For topping, combine brown sugar and cinnamon; sprinkle over batter. Pour water over top (do not stir).
3. Bake until a toothpick inserted in the center comes out clean and liquid is bubbling around the edges, 25-30 minutes. Cool completely in pan on a wire rack. Serve with ice cream or whipped cream if desired.
1 piece: 334 cal., 11g fat (4g sat. fat), 18mg chol., 407mg sod., 58g carb. (43g sugars, 2g fiber), 4g pro.

MINI CHOCOLATE CAKES WITH CARAMELIZED BANANAS

This was one of my first times spreading my wings with a recipe and trying to go a little bit fancy. It's a breeze to make and such a delight to serve. The recipe may look intimidating but after you try it once, you'll have it down pat.

—Lorraine Caland, Shuniah, ON

PREP: 50 MIN. • **BAKE:** 15 MIN. + COOLING
MAKES: 8 SERVINGS

- 5 oz. bittersweet chocolate, chopped
- ½ cup unsalted butter
- 4 large eggs, room temperature
- ⅓ cup sugar
- 1 tsp. vanilla extract
- ⅛ tsp. salt
- ¼ cup all-purpose flour
   Baking cocoa

CARAMELIZED BANANAS
- 2 Tbsp. unsalted butter
- 2 medium bananas, cut into 1-in. slices
- 2 Tbsp. sugar

SAUCE
- 1 cup white wine or unsweetened apple juice
- ½ cup sugar
- 2 oz. bittersweet chocolate, chopped

1. Preheat oven to 400°. In a microwave, melt chocolate and butter; stir until smooth. Cool. Beat the eggs, sugar, vanilla and salt on high speed until thick and pale, about 5 minutes. Sift in flour; mix just until combined. Fold in the chocolate mixture.
2. Spoon batter into 8 buttered 4-oz. ramekins dusted with cocoa. Place ramekins on a baking sheet. Bake until a toothpick inserted in centers comes out clean, 12-15 minutes. Run a small knife around sides of ramekins. Invert onto cooling rack; let stand 5 minutes. Remove ramekins; place cakes on individual plates.
3. For bananas, melt butter in a large skillet over medium heat. Toss banana slices with sugar until well coated; arrange in a single layer in skillet. Do not stir bananas until the bottoms are golden brown, 4-5 minutes. Turn; cook until second side is golden brown, 4-5 minutes longer. Remove from heat. Place bananas on plates with cakes.
4. For sauce, heat wine and sugar in a small saucepan over medium heat. Bring to a boil. Reduce the heat; simmer until slightly thickened, about 10 minutes. Remove from heat; cool slightly. Whisk in chocolate. Pour sauce over cakes.
1 serving: 458 cal., 26g fat (15g sat. fat), 131mg chol., 76mg sod., 38g carb. (30g sugars, 2g fiber), 6g pro.

. . . .

TEST KITCHEN TIP
You can make these in muffin cups if you don't have ramekins but you'll need to turn them over immediately after they come out of the oven so they don't stick.

FLOURLESS
CHOCOLATE TORTE

BAKING 101

DUSTED DESIGN

You don't need piping bags to create a pretty finish on an otherwise plain cake. Lay a paper doily on top of the cake, press down gently, and dust with powdered sugar. Carefully remove the doily to reveal a gorgeous finish.

You can use the same technique with a stencil from a craft store, or create your own by drawing or tracing a design onto card stock and then cutting it out.

FLOURLESS CHOCOLATE TORTE

Here's the perfect dessert for chocoholics like me! I bake this melt-in-your-mouth torte all the time for special occasions. For an elegant finish, just dust it with confectioners' sugar.
—Kayla Albrecht, Freeport, IL

PREP: 20 MIN. • **BAKE:** 40 MIN. + COOLING
MAKES: 12 SERVINGS

- 5 large eggs, separated
- 12 oz. semisweet chocolate, chopped
- ¾ cup butter, cubed
- ¼ tsp. cream of tartar
- ½ cup sugar
  Confectioners' sugar, optional

1. Place egg whites in a large bowl; let stand at room temperature 30 minutes. Preheat oven to 350°. In top of a double boiler or a metal bowl over barely simmering water, melt chocolate and butter; stir until smooth. Remove from heat; cool slightly.

2. In another large bowl, beat egg yolks until thick and lemon-colored. Beat in chocolate mixture. With clean beaters, beat egg whites and cream of tartar on medium speed until foamy.

3. Gradually add sugar, 1 Tbsp. at a time, beating on high after each addition until sugar is dissolved. Continue beating until stiff glossy peaks form. Fold a fourth of the egg whites into the chocolate mixture, then fold in the remaining whites.

4. Transfer batter to a greased 9-in. springform pan. Bake until a toothpick inserted in the center comes out with moist crumbs, 40-45 minutes (do not overbake). Set pan on a wire rack to cool completely.

5. Loosen sides from pan with a knife. Remove rim from pan. If desired, dust with confectioners' sugar.

1 piece: 326 cal., 24g fat (14g sat. fat), 108mg chol., 121mg sod., 15g carb. (14g sugars, 1g fiber), 5g pro.

6 SIMPLE TECHNIQUES, ONE FANCY CAKE!

This elegant cake comes together with just five ingredients and six steps— all basic techniques home bakers should know.

STEP 1: SEPARATING EGGS
Crack an egg in the middle. Then, over a bowl, tip the yolk back and forth between the shells, allowing the white to fall in the bowl.

STEP 2: MELTING CHOCOLATE
A double boiler uses slow, indirect heat to melt the chocolate, which makes it smooth and helps prevent the chocolate from burning.

STEP 3: BEATING YOLKS
Beating yolks thoroughly before beating in the chocolate gives the torte a rich texture.

STEP 4: WHIPPING EGG WHITES
Beating egg whites until stiff glossy peaks form is what will help your cake rise without baking soda or powder. Whip until the peaks hold, but be careful not to overbeat.

STEP 5: FOLDING IT ALL TOGETHER
Folding the beaten egg whites in by hand gives you more control and makes it easier to avoid overmixing.

STEP 6: TESTING AND DONE!
Ensure that your torte is thoroughly baked by testing with a toothpick.

Baking in a springform pan ensures the delicate torte releases much more easily than from a standard cake pan.

BAKING 101

PEAR OLIVE OIL CAKE

BLACKBERRY-ORANGE CAKE

My grandmother made luscious fruit pies and cobblers using blackberries from her garden. I decided to follow her lead and create a blackberry cake that's always lovely with a summer meal.
—Lisa Varner, El Paso, TX

PREP: 20 MIN. • **BAKE:** 40 MIN. + COOLING
MAKES: 10 SERVINGS

- ½ cup butter, softened
- 1 cup sugar, divided
- 1 large egg, room temperature
- 1 tsp. grated orange zest
- 1½ cups plus 1 Tbsp. all-purpose flour, divided
- ½ tsp. baking soda
- ⅛ tsp. salt
- ½ cup sour cream or plain yogurt
- 2 cups fresh blackberries
  Confectioners' sugar, optional

1. Preheat oven to 350°. Grease and flour a 9-in. springform pan.
2. In a large bowl, cream the butter and ¾ cup sugar until light and fluffy, 5-7 minutes. Beat in egg and orange zest. In another bowl, whisk 1½ cups flour, baking soda and salt; add to the creamed mixture alternately with sour cream, beating well after each addition. Transfer to prepared pan.
3. In a bowl, toss blackberries with remaining 1 Tbsp. flour; arrange over batter. Sprinkle with remaining ¼ cup sugar. Bake until a toothpick inserted in center of cake portion comes out clean, 40-45 minutes.
4. Loosen sides from pan with a knife; remove rim from pan. Cool on a wire rack; serve warm or at room temperature. If desired, dust with confectioners' sugar before serving.
1 piece: 274 cal., 12g fat (7g sat. fat), 51mg chol., 177mg sod., 38g carb. (22g sugars, 2g fiber), 4g pro.

PEAR OLIVE OIL CAKE

This moist, flavorful seasonal cake complements any holiday meal. You can use apples instead of pears if you like.
—Andrea Potischman, Menlo Park, CA

PREP: 15 MIN. • **BAKE:** 55 MIN. + COOLING
MAKES: 12 SERVINGS

- 1¼ cups plus 2 tsp. packed brown sugar, divided
- ½ cup olive oil
- 3 large eggs, room temperature
- 2 Tbsp. 2% milk
- 2 tsp. vanilla extract
- 1 cup all-purpose flour
- ¾ cup almond flour
- 2 tsp. baking powder
  Dash salt
- 3 medium red pears, peeled and thinly sliced
- ¼ tsp. ground cinnamon
  Sweetened whipped cream, optional

1. Preheat oven to 325°. Grease a 10-in. springform pan. Place pan on a baking sheet. In a large bowl, beat 1¼ cups brown sugar, oil, eggs, milk and vanilla until well blended. In another bowl, whisk flours, baking powder and salt; gradually beat into the sugar mixture.
2. Transfer to prepared pan. Arrange pears over top; sprinkle with remaining 2 tsp. brown sugar and cinnamon. Bake until a toothpick inserted in center comes out clean, 55-60 minutes. Cool completely in pan on a wire rack. If desired, serve with whipped cream.
1 piece: 294 cal., 14g fat (2g sat. fat), 47mg chol., 121mg sod., 40g carb. (28g sugars, 2g fiber), 4g pro.

SPICED RUM FRUITCAKE

This fruitcake not only can be made weeks ahead, it actually tastes better that way! You can substitute Brazil nuts, pecans and hazelnuts for the walnuts—or use a combination of nuts.
—Jason Boor, Manchester, NY

PREP: 25 MIN. • **BAKE:** 1¼ HOURS + COOLING
MAKES: 1 LOAF (16 PIECES)

- ¾ cup all-purpose flour
- ½ tsp. baking powder
- ¼ tsp. salt
- 2 cups chopped walnuts
- 1 pkg. (8 oz.) pitted dates, chopped
- 1 cup maraschino cherries, halved
- ½ cup dried mangoes, chopped
- 3 large eggs, room temperature
- ¾ cup packed brown sugar
- 1 cup spiced rum, divided

1. Preheat oven to 300°. Line a 9x5-in. loaf pan with parchment, letting the ends extend up sides of pan; grease and set aside.
2. In a large bowl, mix the flour, baking powder and salt. Add the walnuts, dates, cherries and mangoes; toss to coat. In a small bowl, whisk the eggs, brown sugar and ½ cup rum until blended; stir into fruit mixture. Transfer to prepared pan.
3. Bake until a toothpick inserted in the center comes out clean, 1¼-1½ hours. Cool in pan on a wire rack 20 minutes. Slowly pour remaining ½ cup rum over cake. Cool completely. Wrap tightly and store in a cool, dry place overnight. Cut with a serrated knife.
1 piece: 256 cal., 11g fat (1g sat. fat), 35mg chol., 96mg sod., 35g carb. (25g sugars, 3g fiber), 4g pro.

MINIATURE PUMPKIN CAKE TOWERS

I make these pumpkin treats every autumn and they are gone in minutes. Perfect for fall, the warm spice combination is all wrapped up in pretty little cakes.
—Deb Lyon, Bangor, PA

PREP: 50 MIN. • **BAKE:** 20 MIN. + COOLING
MAKES: 10 SERVINGS

- 1 can (15 oz.) pumpkin
- 2 cups sugar
- ¾ cup canola oil
- 4 large eggs, room temperature
- 2 cups all-purpose flour
- 2 tsp. baking powder
- 2 tsp. ground cinnamon
- 1 tsp. ground nutmeg
- ½ tsp. salt
- ½ tsp. ground ginger

SPICED CREAM CHEESE FILLING
- 1 pkg. (8 oz.) cream cheese, softened
- ½ cup shortening
- ½ cup butter, softened
- 1 Tbsp. 2% milk
- 1 tsp. ground cinnamon
- 1 tsp. vanilla extract
- 3 cups confectioners' sugar
  Hot caramel ice cream topping, warmed

1. Preheat oven to 350°. In a large bowl, beat the pumpkin, sugar, oil and eggs until well blended. Combine the flour, baking powder, cinnamon, nutmeg, salt and ginger; gradually beat into pumpkin mixture until blended. Transfer batter to 2 greased 15x10x1-in. baking pans; spread evenly in pans.
2. Bake for 20-25 minutes or until a toothpick inserted in the center comes out clean. Cool on wire racks.
3. For filling, in a large bowl, beat the cream cheese, shortening and butter until light and fluffy. Beat in the milk, cinnamon and vanilla. Gradually beat in confectioners' sugar until smooth.
4. Using a 3-in. round cookie cutter, cut out 30 circles from cakes. Spread 1 cup of filling over 10 cake circles. Repeat. Top with the remaining cakes. Pipe remaining filling over tops. Store in the refrigerator. Garnish with ice cream topping when ready to serve.
1 cake tower: 830 cal., 46g fat (15g sat. fat), 134mg chol., 361mg sod., 100g carb. (76g sugars, 3g fiber), 8g pro.

CHEESECAKES & CUSTARDS

Sweet, creamy and utterly delicious, baked cheesecakes and custards are rich and decadent treats—and they're much easier to make than you might imagine! From simple traditional flans to rich bread pudding to multilayered cheesecake creations, these desserts are truly special.

· · · · · · · · · · · · · · · ·

TIPS FOR SUCCESSFUL CHEESECAKES

For best results, use regular cream cheese and sour cream. Do not substitute reduced-fat or fat-free products unless the recipe calls for it.

To avoid lumps, soften cream cheese at room temperature for 30 minutes before mixing.

The batter should be completely free of lumps before adding the eggs. Add the eggs all at once and beat on low speed just until blended. Do not overbeat. Overbeating will whip in too much air, making the cheesecake puff, collapse and split.

Use a springform pan with a tight latched seal. If the seal is loose (or just to be careful!), tightly wrap heavy-duty foil around the outside of the pan to prevent leaking.

Greasing the bottom and sides of the springform pan will help prevent the filling from cracking. The cake will pull away from the sides and contract as it cools.

After filling your pan, tap it gently on the countertop a couple of times to remove any air bubbles in the batter. Cheesecake batter should be smooth with very little air in it.

Bake cheesecakes in the center of the oven.

Open the oven door as little as possible while baking, especially during the first 30 minutes, as drafts can cause a cheesecake to crack.

Cheesecakes need to set and chill before slicing. After baking, let cool for 1 hour at room temperature, then refrigerate for 3 to 4 hours. Cover the cheesecake with foil and chill for at least 6 hours total before slicing it.

Slice the cheesecake when you remove it from the refrigerator, then let it stand for 30 minutes before serving it. Cheesecakes slice best when they are cold, but they are more flavorful when they warm to room temperature.

Cheesecakes keep (covered) in the refrigerator for up to 3 days. Individual slices can be frozen for up to 2 months.

ABOUT CUSTARDS

Baked custards are a flavored, delicate mixture of sweetened milk and eggs, and usually are baked in a water bath for gentle, even heating.

Custards are done cooking when a knife inserted near the center comes out clean and the top looks set. To preserve an unbroken top, use the wobble test (p. 360).

Unmold cooled custard by running a knife around the edge of the dish to loosen. If possible, lift the bottom edge of the custard with the tip of the knife to loosen the bottom. Invert onto a serving plate and gently lift off the baking dish. If custard doesn't immediately release, let it sit for 10 minutes.

Bread puddings combine a custard mixture with cubes or slices of bread. They may contain spices, fruits, nuts or chocolate. They can be served warm or cold, and may have accompanying sauce. They're done when a knife inserted near the center comes out clean.

ABOUT WATER BATHS

Even if your recipe doesn't specifically call for it, a water bath is a good technique to use when baking cheesecake or custard. Also called a *bain-marie*, a water bath helps custards bake gently and evenly, and the steam from the hot water creates a nice humid environment that will help prevent the custard or cheesecake from cracking.

To make a water bath, all you need is a large, deep pan—like a high-sided roasting pan—and hot water. Always use hot water, as cold water will change the oven temperature and affect the bake time.

You don't need a lot of water—just about an inch or so in the large pan. The most important thing is to make sure that you don't get water in your cheesecake or custard. Using too much water can be disastrous when you set the cheesecake in place, as the displaced water might run over the side of the springform pan.

An alternative is to set the cheesecake or custard in the larger pan first, and then add the water around it. This works, but be sure to pour the water in slowly, to avoid splashing.

Protect your cheesecake by wrapping the springform pan in foil or setting it within a larger round cake pan before placing it in the bath. Even if your springform pan seems secure, you don't want to risk any water seeping inside.

CHEESECAKE

CUSTARD

WHAT CAUSES CRACKS?

There are a few reasons a cheesecake may crack during the baking process.

- The batter was overbeaten.
- The cake was overbaked.
- The oven temperature was too high.
- Doneness was checked with a knife or toothpick.
- The cheesecake was cooled in a drafty area or the oven door was opened during baking.

If your cake made it through baking, it's still not guaranteed safe! As the cheesecake cools, it will contract, and if the cake sticks to the sides of the pan, the tension will make it tear. Let the cheesecake cool for about 10 minutes, then run a table knife or small spatula around the inside edge of the pan to loosen it. Let the cheesecake cool for a full hour, then put it in the refrigerator.

"FIXING" A CRACKED CHEESECAKE

The sad news is that a crack in your cheesecake can't be fixed. But even though you can't repair it, you can cover it up with fresh whipped cream, a layer of chocolate ganache (p. 428), fresh fruit, cookie crumbs or chopped nuts.

One option is to add a sweetened sour cream topping for a flawless finish. Combine ½ cup sour cream with 2 Tbsp. confectioners' sugar until smooth. Add the topping to the cheesecake for the last 10 minutes of baking time.

TESTING FOR DONENESS

If you're making a cheesecake that will be covered with topping, go ahead and use a probe thermometer—when it reads 150°, your cake is done. But for most cheesecakes, creme brulee and other baked custards, you don't want to mar the top of your creation. Breaking the surface of a cheesecake when it's still baking is inviting cracks. So instead, use the wobble test.

A cheesecake is done when the edges are slightly puffed and a 1-inch circle in the center jiggles slightly when you tap the pan with a spoon. (The retained heat will continue to cook the center as the cheesecake cools.) For cheesecake baked in a water bath, the top will look dull and just be set. An not-fully-baked cheesecake will ripple noticeably; look instead for a subtle wiggle. Test at the minimum recommended baking time, and as few times as necessary to avoid opening the oven door too often.

TROUBLESHOOTING CUSTARDS

Custard is curdled: The custard is overbaked. Bake only until a knife inserted about halfway to the center comes out clean or until it passes the wobble test (above), not until the center is completely set. If you're baking in a water bath, be sure to remove the custard from the bath as soon as it comes out of the oven; otherwise, it will continue to cook in the hot water.

Custard has bubbles on top: The eggs were overbeaten. Beat eggs only until they are blended, not foamy.

THE PERFECT GRAHAM CRACKER CRUST

The perfect graham cracker crust couldn't be simpler to make—it comes together with just three ingredients:

2¾ cups graham cracker crumbs

½ cup butter, melted

¼ cup sugar

You can either buy graham cracker crumbs or crush your own, but crushing your own gives you more control over your crust's texture. For a crust with more crunch—perhaps for a cheesecake that has a lot going on—use a coarser crumb. For simple, elegant cheesecakes, a fine crumb works well.

Place about 14 whole graham crackers in a resealable plastic bag, and seal it. Use a rolling pin or the bottom of a glass measuring cup to roll or tap the crackers into crumbs. Mix the crumbs in a large bowl with the melted butter and sugar until the crumbs are well-coated.

Transfer to your pie plate or springform pan and lightly press the mixture onto the bottom and up the sides. Use a flat-bottomed measuring cup or glass to firmly press the mixture into place. Either prebake at 350° for 10 minutes before filling or fill and bake as your recipe directs.

CREATIVE CRUMB CRUSTS

Crumb crusts are the go-to for cheesecakes but are also used for pies. To make a crumb crust, follow the procedure for making The Perfect Graham Cracker Crust (left), and experiment with different kinds of crumbs. Use these proportions for a 9-in. pie plate; half again or double the amounts for a deep springform pan for a cheesecake.

	TYPE OF CRUST	CRUMBS	SUGAR	BUTTER, MELTED
	CHOCOLATE WAFER	1¼ CUPS (20 WAFERS)	¼ CUP	¼ CUP
	VANILLA WAFER	1½ CUPS (30 WAFERS)	NONE	¼ CUP
	CREAM-FILLED CHOCOLATE	1½ CUPS (15 COOKIES)	NONE	¼ CUP
	GINGERSNAP	1½ CUPS (24 COOKIES)	NONE	¼ CUP
	MACAROON	1½ CUPS	NONE	¼ CUP

QUICK WORK WITH A FOOD PROCESSOR

• Crumb crusts are a snap to whir together with a food processor.

• If you don't have one, seal cookies in a resealable plastic bag and crush with a rolling pin or can. The bag makes a good way to store leftovers for the next time!

CHEESECAKES

LAYERED TURTLE CHEESECAKE

After receiving a request for a special turtle cheesecake and not finding a good recipe, I created my own. Everyone was thrilled with the results and this remains a favorite at the coffee shop where I work.
—Sue Gronholz, Beaver Dam, WI

PREP: 40 MIN. • **BAKE:** 1¼ HOURS + CHILLING
MAKES: 12 SERVINGS

- 1 cup all-purpose flour
- ⅓ cup packed brown sugar
- ¼ cup finely chopped pecans
- 6 Tbsp. cold butter, cubed

FILLING
- 4 pkg. (8 oz. each) cream cheese, softened
- 1 cup sugar
- ⅓ cup packed brown sugar
- ¼ cup plus 1 tsp. all-purpose flour, divided
- 2 Tbsp. heavy whipping cream
- 1½ tsp. vanilla extract
- 4 large eggs, room temperature, lightly beaten
- ½ cup milk chocolate chips, melted and cooled
- ¼ cup caramel ice cream topping
- ⅓ cup chopped pecans

GANACHE
- ½ cup milk chocolate chips
- ¼ cup heavy whipping cream
- 2 Tbsp. chopped pecans
  Additional caramel ice cream topping, optional

1. Preheat oven to 325°. Place a greased 9-in. springform pan on a double thickness of heavy-duty foil (about 18 in. square). Securely wrap foil around pan.

2. In a small bowl, combine the flour, brown sugar and pecans; cut in butter until crumbly. Press onto the bottom of prepared pan. Place pan on a baking sheet. Bake for 12-15 minutes or until set. Cool on a wire rack.

3. In a large bowl, beat cream cheese and sugars until smooth. Beat in ¼ cup flour, the cream and vanilla. Add eggs; beat on low speed just until blended.

4. Remove 1 cup of the batter to a small bowl; stir in melted chocolate. Spread chocolate batter over crust.

5. In another bowl, mix caramel topping and the remaining 1 tsp. flour; stir in the pecans. Drop by tablespoonfuls over the chocolate batter. Top with the remaining batter. Place springform pan in a large baking pan; add 1 in. of hot water to the larger pan.

6. Bake at 325° for 1¼-1½ hours or until center is just set and top appears dull. Remove springform pan from water bath; remove foil. Cool cheesecake on a wire rack for 10 minutes. Loosen the sides from pan with a knife; cool 1 hour longer. Refrigerate overnight.

7. For ganache, place chips in a small bowl. In a small saucepan, bring cream just to a boil. Pour over the chips; whisk until smooth. Cool the mixture slightly, stirring occasionally.

8. Remove sides of springform pan. Spread ganache over cheesecake; sprinkle with pecans. Refrigerate until set. If desired, drizzle with additional caramel topping before serving.

1 piece: 664 cal., 46g fat (25g sat. fat), 182mg chol., 330mg sod., 55g carb. (36g sugars, 2g fiber), 11g pro.

LAYERED TURTLE
CHEESECAKE

JAM-TOPPED MINI CHEESECAKES

Presto! We turned cheesecake into irresistible bite-sized snacks with these cute little treats. Feel free to swap in a favorite flavor of jam.
—*Taste of Home* Test Kitchen

PREP: 20 MIN. • **BAKE:** 15 MIN. + CHILLING
MAKES: 9 SERVINGS

- ⅔ **cup graham cracker crumbs**
- 2 **Tbsp. butter, melted**
- 1 **pkg. (8 oz.) cream cheese, softened**
- ⅓ **cup sugar**
- 1 **tsp. vanilla extract**
- 1 **large egg, room temperature**
- 3 **Tbsp. assorted jams, warmed**

1. Preheat oven to 350°. Combine the graham cracker crumbs and butter. Press onto the bottom of 9 paper-lined muffin cups. In another bowl, beat the cream cheese, sugar and vanilla until smooth. Add egg; beat on low speed just until combined. Spoon over crusts.
2. Bake 15-16 minutes or until centers are just set. Cool for 10 minutes before removing from pan to a wire rack to cool completely. Refrigerate for at least 1 hour.
3. Remove paper liners; top each cheesecake with 1 tsp. jam.
1 mini cheesecake: 198 cal., 13g fat (7g sat. fat), 53mg chol., 141mg sod., 19g carb. (14g sugars, 0 fiber), 3g pro.

. . . .
TEST KITCHEN TIP
The key to the creamiest cheesecake is to not overbake it. It's a good idea to check a few minutes earlier than the recommended time in case your oven runs hot.

NEW YORK CHEESECAKE WITH SHORTBREAD CRUST

NEW YORK CHEESECAKE WITH SHORTBREAD CRUST

Light, creamy and smooth, this traditional New York cheesecake will melt in your mouth. It features a shortbread crust and is topped with a triple berry sauce made with raspberries, blueberries and blackberries. This recipe takes time, but is not hard. It is well worth the effort.
—Karen Nielson, St. George, UT

PREP: 50 MIN. • **BAKE:** 1¼ HOURS + CHILLING
MAKES: 16 SERVINGS

- 1 cup all-purpose flour
- ¼ cup sugar
- 1 tsp. grated lemon zest
- ½ cup cold butter, cubed
- 2 large egg yolks
- 1 tsp. vanilla extract

FILLING
- 5 pkg. (8 oz. each) cream cheese, softened
- 1¾ cups sugar
- ½ cup heavy whipping cream
- 3 Tbsp. all-purpose flour
- 2 tsp. vanilla extract
- 2 tsp. lemon juice
- 1½ tsp. grated lemon zest
- 5 large eggs, room temperature, lightly beaten
- 2 large egg yolks, room temperature

TRIPLE BERRY SAUCE
- 1¼ cups sugar
- ¼ cup cornstarch
- 2 cups cranberry juice
- 1 tsp. lemon juice
- 2 cups fresh or frozen unsweetened raspberries, divided
- 1 Tbsp. butter
- 1 cup fresh or frozen blueberries
- 1 cup fresh or frozen blackberries or boysenberries

1. Preheat the oven to 325°. Place a greased 9-in. springform pan on a double thickness of heavy-duty foil (about 18 in. square). Wrap foil securely around pan. Place on a baking sheet.
2. In a small bowl, mix flour, sugar and lemon zest; cut in butter until crumbly. Add egg yolks and vanilla, tossing with a fork until the mixture pulls together. Press onto bottom and 1½ in. up sides of the prepared pan. Bake until lightly browned, 12-16 minutes. Cool on a wire rack.
3. Beat cream cheese and sugar until smooth. Beat in cream, flour, vanilla, lemon juice and zest. Add the eggs and egg yolks; beat on low speed just until blended. Pour into the crust. Place springform pan in a larger baking pan; add 1 in. of hot water to larger pan.
4. Bake until the center is just set and top appears dull, 1¼-1½ hours. Remove springform pan from water bath. Cool cheesecake on a wire rack 10 minutes. Loosen sides from pan with a knife; remove foil. Cool 1 hour longer. Refrigerate overnight, covering when completely cooled. Remove rim of pan.
5. In a small saucepan, combine sugar and cornstarch. Gradually add the cranberry and lemon juices. Stir in 1 cup raspberries. Bring to a boil; cook and stir until thickened, about 2 minutes. Remove from the heat; stir in butter.
6. Strain the sauce; discard seeds. Cool to room temperature. Stir in the blueberries, blackberries and remaining 1 cup raspberries. Serve with cheesecake.
1 piece: 494 cal., 36g fat (21g sat. fat), 200mg chol., 295mg sod., 37g carb. (28g sugars, 0 fiber), 8g pro.

DOUBLE CHOCOLATE ESPRESSO CHEESECAKE

Every slice of this creamy cheesecake is a standout. The classic pairing of chocolate and coffee is sure to please partygoers.
—Cheryl Perry, Hertford, NC

PREP: 35 MIN. • **BAKE:** 1 HOUR + CHILLING
MAKES: 16 SERVINGS

- 1½ cups crushed vanilla wafers (about 45)
- ¼ cup butter, melted
- 2 Tbsp. sugar
- ¼ tsp. instant espresso powder

FILLING

- 4 pkg. (8 oz. each) cream cheese, softened
- 1½ cups sugar
- 1 cup sour cream
- 1 cup 60% cacao bittersweet chocolate baking chips, melted
- ½ cup baking cocoa
- ¼ cup half-and-half cream
- 1 Tbsp. all-purpose flour
- 5 large eggs, room temperature, lightly beaten
- 1½ tsp. instant espresso powder
- 1 tsp. vanilla extract

TOPPING

- 1 cup coffee liqueur
- 1 Tbsp. half-and-half cream
- 1 cup heavy whipping cream
- 2 Tbsp. confectioners' sugar
- ½ cup 60% cacao bittersweet chocolate baking chips, chopped
- 16 chocolate-covered coffee beans

1. Preheat the oven to 350°. Place a greased 9-in. springform pan on a double thickness of heavy-duty foil (about 18 in. square). Securely wrap foil around pan.
2. In a large bowl, combine the wafer crumbs, butter, sugar and espresso powder. Press onto the bottom and 1 in. up the sides of prepared pan.
3. In a large bowl, beat the cream cheese, sugar, sour cream, melted chocolate, cocoa, cream and flour until smooth. Add eggs; beat on low speed just until combined. Stir in the espresso powder and vanilla. Pour into crust. Place springform pan in a large baking pan; add 1 in. of hot water to larger pan.
4. Bake until center is just set and top appears dull, 60-70 minutes. Remove springform pan from water bath. Cool on a wire rack for 10 minutes. Carefully run a knife around the edge of pan to loosen; cool 1 hour longer. Refrigerate overnight. Remove sides of pan.
5. In a small saucepan, combine liqueur and cream. Bring to a boil; cook until liquid is reduced by half. Meanwhile, in a large bowl, beat whipping cream until it begins to thicken. Add confectioners' sugar; beat until stiff peaks form.
6. Drizzle cheesecake with coffee syrup; garnish with whipped cream, chocolate and coffee beans.
1 piece: 610 cal., 40g fat (23g sat. fat), 170mg chol., 259mg sod., 52g carb. (41g sugars, 2g fiber), 9g pro.

CUT LIKE A PRO

A hot knife is the secret to cutting nice tidy slices of cheesecake. Dip the blade of a sharp knife in hot water, then wipe dry on a towel and cut. Repeat each time for pretty slices with a clean edge.

CONTEST-WINNING BLUEBERRY SWIRL CHEESECAKE

1. Preheat the oven to 350°. In a small saucepan, combine blueberries, sugar and lemon juice. Cook and stir over medium heat for 5 minutes or until the berries are softened. Combine cornstarch and water until smooth; stir into the blueberry mixture. Bring to a boil; cook and stir for 2 minutes or until thickened. Remove from the heat; cool to room temperature. Transfer to a blender; cover and process until smooth. Set aside.

2. For crust, in a small bowl, combine the crumbs and sugar; stir in the butter. Press onto the bottom of a greased 9-in. springform pan. Place pan on a baking sheet. Bake at 350° for 10 minutes. Cool on a wire rack.

3. In a large bowl, beat cream cheese and sugar until smooth. Beat in the sour cream, flour and vanilla. Add eggs; beat on low speed just until combined. Pour filling over crust. Drizzle with 3 Tbsp. blueberry mixture; cut through batter with a knife to swirl.

4. Return pan to baking sheet. Bake for 40-45 minutes or until center is almost set. Cool on a wire rack for 10 minutes. Carefully run a knife around the edge of pan to loosen; cool 1 hour longer. Refrigerate cheesecake overnight. Serve with the remaining blueberry sauce. Refrigerate leftovers.

1 piece: 424 cal., 28g fat (16g sat. fat), 129mg chol., 262mg sod., 38g carb. (30g sugars, 1g fiber), 7g pro.

- - - - - - - - - - - - - - - - - -

DID YOU KNOW?

The first mention of a cheesecake in culinary history was in ancient Greece. However, the familiar New York-style cheesecake, made with cream cheese, is credited to Arnold Reuben—who also created the Reuben sandwich!

CONTEST-WINNING BLUEBERRY SWIRL CHEESECAKE

This is my favorite blueberry recipe, which I often make for family get-togethers. I know your clan will love it, too!
—Cathy Medley, Clyde, OH

PREP: 40 MIN. • **BAKE:** 40 MIN. + CHILLING
MAKES: 12 SERVINGS

- 1½ cups fresh blueberries
- ¼ cup sugar
- 1 Tbsp. lemon juice
- 2 tsp. cornstarch
- 1 Tbsp. cold water

CRUST
- 1 cup graham cracker crumbs (about 16 squares)
- 2 Tbsp. sugar
- 2 Tbsp. butter, melted

FILLING
- 3 pkg. (8 oz. each) cream cheese, softened
- 1 cup sugar
- 1 cup sour cream
- 2 Tbsp. all-purpose flour
- 2 tsp. vanilla extract
- 4 large eggs, room temperature, lightly beaten

5 SIMPLE SWIRLS

Step up your cheesecake skills in minutes with these gorgeous (and easy!) designs.

SPIRAL
Use a piping bag to pipe dots of jam in a swirl pattern, then drag a clean toothpick or wooden skewer through the dots to achieve a glorious whirly effect. This technique works best with jams or thick sauces.

HERRINGBONE
Begin by piping straight lines of jam, caramel or even festively dyed cheesecake filling onto your batter. Then drag a toothpick across the batter in opposite direction of your lines, starting with alternating sides of the pan for each pass.

FLOWER
Pipe the sauce of your choice in a clover-shaped pattern in the center of the batter. Repeat the shape until you reach the outer edge of the springform pan. Then pull a skewer through the center of each petal. Finish it off by piping dots of sauce in the spaces between the largest petals; pull the toothpick or skewer through the dots.

MARBLE
For recipes that have two flavors of batter, use the primary flavor as the base; pour most of it into the springform pan and level it. Drizzle the secondary flavor over top. With a skewer, swirl the batter. Add a few final dollops of the primary flavor on top and marble with the skewer again.

TWO-TONE
If you have more than one flavor you'd like to swirl into your cheesecake, add small dollops of sauces, fruit fillings or jams to your batter with a piping bag or teaspoon. Use a toothpick to swirl every which way until you achieve the desired look.

BAKING 101

MAPLE PUMPKIN CHEESECAKE

For our first Thanksgiving with my husband's family, I wanted to bring a special dish and decided I couldn't go wrong with a dessert that combines cheesecake and pumpkin pie.
—Jodi Gobrecht, Bucyrus, OH

PREP: 30 MIN. • **BAKE:** 1¼ HOURS + CHILLING
MAKES: 14 SERVINGS

- 1¼ cups graham cracker crumbs
- ¼ cup sugar
- ¼ cup butter, melted
- 3 pkg. (8 oz. each) cream cheese, softened
- 1 can (14 oz.) sweetened condensed milk
- 1 can (15 oz.) solid-pack pumpkin
- ¼ cup maple syrup
- 1½ tsp. ground cinnamon
- 1 tsp. ground nutmeg
- ½ tsp. salt
- 3 large eggs, room temperature, lightly beaten

TOPPING
- 2 cups sour cream
- ⅓ cup sugar
- 1 tsp. vanilla extract

1. Preheat oven to 325°. In a small bowl, combine the cracker crumbs, sugar and butter. Press onto the bottom of a greased 9-in. springform pan. Place on a baking sheet. Bake for 12 minutes. Cool on a wire rack.

2. In a large bowl, beat cream cheese and milk until smooth. Beat in the pumpkin, syrup, cinnamon, nutmeg and salt. Add eggs; beat on low speed just until combined.

3. Pour over crust. Place pan on baking sheet. Bake at until the center is almost set, 70-75 minutes. Combine the topping ingredients; spread over cheesecake. Bake 5 minutes longer.

4. Cool on a wire rack for 10 minutes. Carefully run a knife around the edge of the pan to loosen; cool 1 hour longer. Refrigerate overnight. Remove sides of pan. Refrigerate leftovers.

1 piece: 465 cal., 30g fat (19g sat. fat), 140mg chol., 361mg sod., 38g carb. (32g sugars, 2g fiber), 9g pro.

EASY NUTELLA CHEESECAKE

A creamy chocolate-hazelnut spread tops a crust made of crushed Oreo cookies to make this irresistible baked cheesecake.
—Nick Iverson, Denver, CO

PREP: 35 MIN. • **BAKE:** 1¼ HOURS + CHILLING
MAKES: 16 SERVINGS

- 2½ cups lightly crushed Oreo cookies (about 24 cookies)
- ¼ cup sugar
- ¼ cup butter, melted

FILLING
- 4 pkg. (8 oz. each) cream cheese, softened
- ½ cup sugar
- 2 jars (26½ oz. each) Nutella
- 1 cup heavy whipping cream
- 1 tsp. salt
- 4 large eggs, room temperature, lightly beaten
- ½ cup chopped hazelnuts, toasted

1. Preheat oven to 325°. Pulse cookies and sugar in a food processor until fine crumbs form. Continue processing while gradually adding butter in a steady stream. Press the crumb mixture onto bottom of a greased 10x3-in. springform pan. Securely wrap bottom and sides of springform in a double thickness of heavy-duty foil (about 18 in. square).

2. For filling, beat cream cheese and sugar until smooth. Beat in Nutella, cream and salt. Add the eggs; beat on low speed just until blended. Pour over crust.

3. Bake until a thermometer inserted in the center reads 160°, about 1¼ hours. Cool cheesecake for 1¼ hours on a wire rack. Refrigerate overnight, covering when completely cooled.

4. Gently loosen sides from pan with a knife; remove rim. Top cheesecake with chopped hazelnuts.

1 piece: 900 cal., 62g fat (22g sat. fat), 129mg chol., 478mg sod., 84g carb. (71g sugars, 4g fiber), 12g pro.

BAKING 101

CHERRY FUDGE TRUFFLE COCONUT CHEESECAKE

Cherries and chocolate come together in this dazzling coconut cheesecake. It's a holiday showstopper!
—Jeanne Holt, St. Paul, MN

PREP: 40 MIN.
BAKE: 1 HOUR 20 MIN. + CHILLING
MAKES: 16 SERVINGS

- 1²⁄₃ cups crushed Oreo cookies (about 17 cookies)
- ²⁄₃ cup sweetened shredded coconut, toasted
- ¼ cup butter, melted

FILLING
- 4 pkg. (8 oz. each) cream cheese, softened, divided
- 1 cup sugar
- ¾ cup cream of coconut
- 1 tsp. coconut extract
- 3 large eggs, room temperature, lightly beaten
- ¼ cup chopped maraschino cherries
- 1 cup 60% cacao bittersweet chocolate baking chips, melted and cooled
- ⅓ cup cherry preserves, finely chopped

TOPPING
- ½ cup 60% cacao bittersweet chocolate baking chips, melted and cooled
- 1 cup sweetened whipped cream
- ⅓ cup sweetened shredded coconut, toasted
- 16 maraschino cherries with stems, patted dry

CHERRY FUDGE TRUFFLE COCONUT CHEESECAKE

1. Preheat oven to 375°. Grease a 10-in. springform pan and place on a double thickness of heavy-duty foil (about 18 in. square). Wrap foil securely around pan. Place on a baking sheet.
2. In a small bowl, mix crushed cookies and coconut; stir in butter. Press onto bottom and ½ in. up sides of prepared pan. Bake for 10 minutes. Cool on a wire rack. Reduce oven setting to 325°.
3. In a large bowl, beat 3 pkg. cream cheese and sugar until smooth. Beat in cream of coconut and extract. Add eggs; beat on low speed just until blended. Stir in chopped cherries. Pour 3 cups batter into crust.
4. In another bowl, beat the remaining 8 oz. cream cheese until smooth. Beat in the cooled chocolate and cherry preserves. Drop by tablespoonfuls over coconut batter. Carefully spoon the remaining coconut batter over top.
5. Place the springform pan in a larger baking pan; add 1 in. hot water to larger pan. Bake until center is just set and top appears dull, 80-85 minutes.
6. Remove springform pan from water bath. Cool cheesecake on a wire rack for 10 minutes. Loosen sides from pan with a knife; remove the foil. Cool 1 hour longer. Refrigerate overnight, covering when completely cooled.
7. Remove rim from pan. Top the cheesecake with melted chocolate, whipped cream, toasted coconut and cherries before serving.

1 piece: 545 cal., 37g fat (22g sat. fat), 108mg chol., 290mg sod., 52g carb. (44g sugars, 2g fiber), 6g pro.

SUNNY CITRUS
CHEESECAKE

SUNNY CITRUS CHEESECAKE

This beautiful layered cheesecake takes a bit longer to make, but the end result is so worth it! Citrus is the perfect ending for an Easter meal and those bright flavors really shine in this dessert. To save time, I'll make this cheesecake a week in advance and freeze it without the sour cream topping. Thaw in the refrigerator overnight and spread with the topping before serving.
—Sue Gronholz, Beaver Dam, WI

PREP: 35 MIN. + COOLING
BAKE: 1 HOUR 25 MIN. + CHILLING
MAKES: 16 SERVINGS

- 1   cup all-purpose flour
- ⅓   cup sugar
- 1   tsp. grated lemon zest
- ⅓   cup cold butter, cubed

FILLING
- 4   pkg. (8 oz. each) cream cheese, softened
- 1⅓   cups sugar
- 2   Tbsp. all-purpose flour
- 1   tsp. vanilla extract
- 4   large eggs, room temperature, lightly beaten
- ¼   cup lime juice
- 1   Tbsp. grated lime zest
- 3   drops green food coloring
- ¼   cup lemon juice
- 1   Tbsp. grated lemon zest
- 6   drops yellow food coloring, divided
- ¼   cup orange juice
- 1   Tbsp. grated orange zest
- 2   drops red food coloring

TOPPING
- ¾   cup sour cream
- 1   Tbsp. sugar
- ¼   tsp. lemon extract
     Optional: Orange slices, lime slices and lemon slices

1. Preheat the oven to 325°. Place a greased 9-in. springform pan on a double thickness of heavy-duty foil (about 18 in. square). Wrap foil securely around pan. Place on a baking sheet.
2. In a small bowl, mix flour, sugar and zest; cut in butter until crumbly. Press onto bottom of prepared pan. Bake until the edges are lightly browned, 25-30 minutes. Cool on a wire rack.
3. In a large bowl, beat cream cheese and sugar until smooth. Beat in flour and vanilla. Add the eggs; beat on low speed just until blended. Divide batter into thirds. To 1 portion, add lime juice, lime zest and green food coloring. Pour batter over crust.
4. Place springform pan in a larger baking pan; add 1 in. of hot water to larger pan. Bake until center is just set and top appears dull, about 25 minutes.
5. Meanwhile, to another portion of batter, add lemon juice, lemon zest and 3 drops yellow food coloring. Carefully remove pan from oven. Gently spoon lemon filling over the lime layer. Return to oven; bake until center is just set and top appears dull, about 25 minutes.
6. To the remaining batter, add orange juice, orange zest, red food coloring and the remaining 3 drops yellow food coloring. Carefully remove pan from oven. Gently spoon orange filling over the lemon layer.
7. Return to oven; bake until the center is just set and the top appears dull, 30-35 minutes. Carefully remove pan from oven.
8. In a small bowl, whisk the topping ingredients. Gently spoon over the cheesecake in small dollops; spread carefully. Return to the oven; bake 5 minutes longer.
9. Remove springform pan from water bath. Cool cheesecake on a wire rack 10 minutes. Loosen sides from pan with a knife; remove foil. Cool 1 hour longer. Refrigerate overnight, covering when completely cooled. Remove rim from pan. If desired, top with orange, lime and lemon slices. Refrigerate leftovers.
1 piece: 394 cal., 27g fat (16g sat. fat), 117mg chol., 231mg sod., 33g carb. (25g sugars, 0 fiber), 6g pro.

PEPPERMINT CHIP CHEESECAKE

I love to make cheesecakes and often give them to friends as gifts or donate them to local fundraisers. This one is always very popular.
—Gretchen Ely, West Lafayette, IN

PREP: 20 MIN. • **BAKE:** 50 MIN. + CHILLING
MAKES: 12 SERVINGS

- 1 pkg. (10 oz.) chocolate-covered mint cookies, crushed
- 3 Tbsp. butter, melted

FILLING
- 3 pkg. (8 oz. each) cream cheese, softened
- ¾ cup sugar
- 5 tsp. cornstarch
- 3 large eggs, room temperature, lightly beaten
- 1 large egg yolk, room temperature, lightly beaten
- ½ cup heavy whipping cream
- 2 tsp. peppermint extract
- 1¼ tsp. vanilla extract
- 3 to 4 drops green food coloring, optional
- 1 cup miniature semisweet chocolate chips
- ½ cup chocolate-covered mint cookies, crushed, optional

1. Preheat oven to 325°. In a small bowl, combine the cookie crumbs and butter. Press onto the bottom and 1 in. up the sides of a greased 9-in. springform pan.
2. Beat the cream cheese, sugar and cornstarch until smooth. Add eggs and egg yolk; beat on low speed just until combined. Stir in the cream, extracts and, if desired, food coloring. Fold in chocolate chips. Pour into crust. Place pan on a baking sheet.
3. Bake until the center is almost set, 50-60 minutes. Cool on a wire rack for 10 minutes. Carefully run a knife around the edge of pan to loosen; cool 1 hour. Refrigerate overnight, covering when cooled. Top with additional crushed cookies if desired. Refrigerate any leftovers.

1 piece: 391 cal., 25g fat (15g sat. fat), 113mg chol., 166mg sod., 39g carb. (30g sugars, 2g fiber), 5g pro.
NOTE: This recipe was tested with Keebler Grasshopper Fudge Mint Cookies.

OLD-WORLD RICOTTA CHEESECAKE

I reconstructed this dessert based on an old recipe that had been in the family for years but was never written down. The subtle cinnamon flavor of the zwieback crust and the dense texture of the ricotta cheese are reminiscent of the cheesecake I enjoyed as a child.
—Mary Beth Jung, Hendersonville, NC

PREP: 20 MIN. • **BAKE:** 1 HOUR + CHILLING
MAKES: 12 SERVINGS

- 1⅔ cups zwieback, rusk or plain biscotti crumbs
- 3 Tbsp. sugar
- ½ tsp. ground cinnamon
- ⅓ cup butter, softened

FILLING
- 2 cartons (15 oz. each) ricotta cheese
- ½ cup sugar
- ½ cup half-and-half cream
- 2 Tbsp. all-purpose flour
- 1 Tbsp. lemon juice
- 1 tsp. finely grated lemon zest
- ¼ tsp. salt
- 2 large eggs, room temperature, lightly beaten

TOPPING
- 1 cup sour cream
- 2 Tbsp. sugar
- 1 tsp. vanilla extract

1. Combine zwieback crumbs, sugar and cinnamon; mix in the butter until mixture is crumbled. Press onto bottom and 1½ in. up sides of a greased 9-in. springform pan. Refrigerate the crust until chilled.
2. Preheat oven to 350°. Beat all filling ingredients except eggs until smooth. Add eggs; beat on low until combined. Pour into the crust. Place the pan on a baking sheet.
3. Bake until the center is set, about 50 minutes. Remove from oven; let stand 15 minutes, leaving oven on. Combine topping ingredients; spoon around edge of cheesecake. Carefully spread topping over filling. Bake for 10 minutes longer.
4. Loosen sides from pan with a knife; cool 1 hour. Refrigerate 3 hours or overnight, covering when completely cooled. Remove the rim from pan. Refrigerate leftovers.

1 piece: 260 cal., 14g fat (9g sat. fat), 83mg chol., 191mg sod., 25g carb. (16g sugars, 0 fiber), 7g pro.

RED VELVET CHEESECAKE

RED VELVET CHEESECAKE

This cheesecake will become a fixture on your holiday menu. The red velvet filling is spiked with cocoa, baked in a chocolate cookie crust, and topped with fluffy cream cheese frosting.

—Karen Dively, Chapin, SC

PREP: 30 MIN. • **BAKE:** 1 HOUR + CHILLING
MAKES: 16 SERVINGS

17 chocolate cream Oreo cookies, crushed
¼ cup butter, melted
1 Tbsp. sugar
FILLING
3 pkg. (8 oz. each) cream cheese, softened
1½ cups sugar
1 cup sour cream
½ cup buttermilk
3 Tbsp. baking cocoa
2 tsp. vanilla extract
4 large eggs, room temperature, lightly beaten
1 bottle (1 oz.) red food coloring
FROSTING
3 oz. cream cheese, softened
¼ cup butter, softened
2 cups confectioners' sugar
1 tsp. vanilla extract

1. Preheat the oven to 325°. Place a greased 9-in. springform pan on a double thickness of heavy-duty foil (about 18 in. square). Securely wrap foil around pan.
2. In a small bowl, combine the cookie crumbs, butter and sugar. Press onto the bottom of prepared pan.
3. In a large bowl, beat the cream cheese, sugar, sour cream, buttermilk, cocoa and vanilla until smooth. Add the eggs; beat on low speed just until combined. Stir in food coloring. Pour over the crust. Place springform pan in a large baking pan; add 1 in. of hot water to larger pan.
4. Bake until the center is just set and the top appears dull, 60-70 minutes. Remove springform pan from water bath. Cool on a wire rack for 10 minutes. Carefully run a knife around the edge of the pan to loosen; cool 1 hour longer. Refrigerate overnight, covering when completely cooled. Remove the sides of the pan.
5. For frosting, in a small bowl, beat cream cheese and butter until fluffy. Add the confectioners' sugar and vanilla; beat until smooth. Frost top of cheesecake. Refrigerate until serving.
1 piece: 463 cal., 29g fat (17g sat. fat), 131mg chol., 276mg sod., 46g carb. (39g sugars, 1g fiber), 7g pro.

BROWN SUGAR & CHOCOLATE SWIRL CHEESECAKE

Searching for a dessert superstar? This chocolate swirl cheesecake is the one that people ask for again and again.
—Jeanne Holt, St. Paul, MN

PREP: 30 MIN. • **BAKE:** 50 MIN. + CHILLING
MAKES: 16 SERVINGS

- ¾ cup cinnamon graham cracker crumbs (about 4 whole crackers)
- ¾ cup finely chopped walnuts, divided
- 1 Tbsp. sugar
- 3 Tbsp. butter, melted

FILLING
- ½ cup heavy whipping cream
- 1 cup semisweet chocolate chips
- 4 pkg. (8 oz. each) cream cheese, softened
- ¾ cup packed brown sugar
- ½ cup sour cream
- 3 Tbsp. all-purpose flour
- 1 tsp. vanilla extract
- ¼ tsp. salt
- ¼ cup maple syrup, divided
- 3 large eggs, room temperature, lightly beaten

TOPPING
- 2 cups sweetened whipped cream

1. Preheat oven to 350°. Wrap a double thickness of heavy-duty foil (about 18 in. square) around a greased 9-in. springform pan; set aside. Combine cracker crumbs, ½ cup walnuts and sugar; stir in butter. Press onto bottom and 1 in. up sides of the prepared pan; place on a baking sheet. Bake crust for 10 minutes. Cool on a wire rack.
2. In a small saucepan, bring cream just to a boil. Pour over the chocolate; whisk until smooth. Cool.
3. Beat cream cheese until smooth. Add next 5 ingredients and 2 Tbsp. maple syrup; beat until well blended. Add eggs; beat on low speed until combined. Pour into prepared crust, reserving 3 Tbsp. of batter.
4. Mix the reserved cheesecake batter into cooled chocolate; drop spoonfuls over filling. Cut through the batter and chocolate with a knife to swirl.
5. Place springform pan in a larger baking pan; add 1 in. of hot water to larger pan. Bake until center is just set but still jiggles when shaken, 50-65 minutes. Remove springform pan from water bath. Cool on a wire rack 10 minutes. Loosen sides from pan with a knife; remove foil. Cool 1 hour longer. Refrigerate overnight, covering when completely cooled.
6. Remove rim from pan. Serve with whipped cream. Sprinkle with remaining walnuts; drizzle with the remaining syrup.

1 piece: 936 cal., 75g fat (40g sat. fat), 267mg chol., 613mg sod., 57g carb. (47g sugars, 2g fiber), 14g pro.

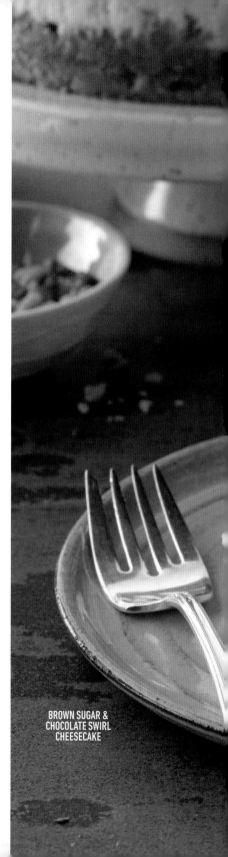

BROWN SUGAR & CHOCOLATE SWIRL CHEESECAKE

GINGER TEA
PUMPKIN CUSTARD

CUSTARDS & MORE

GINGER TEA PUMPKIN CUSTARD

I created this recipe when I was first attending photography school. I realized I didn't have any of my usual spices, so out came the ginger tea. The result was wonderful and subtle. Even though I missed my kitchen at home, it was nice to have this comforting custard.
—Rhonda Adkins, Great Falls, MT

PREP: 15 MIN+ STANDING
BAKE: 35 MIN+ CHILLING
MAKES: 4 SERVINGS

- 1 cup whole milk
- 1 ginger tea bag
- 1 cinnamon sticks (3 in.)
- 1 whole star anise
- 2 large eggs
- 1½ cups canned pumpkin
- ⅔ cup sugar
- ⅛ tsp. salt
  Whipped cream and maple syrup

1. Preheat the oven to 325°. In a small saucepan, heat milk, tea bag, cinnamon sticks and star anise until bubbles form around sides of pan. Remove from heat; steep, covered, 10 minutes. Strain milk mixture. In a large bowl, whisk eggs, pumpkin, sugar and salt until blended but not foamy. Slowly stir in the hot milk mixture.
2. Place 4 greased 8-oz. ramekins in a baking pan large enough to hold them without touching. Pour egg mixture into cups. Place pan on oven rack; add very hot water to pan to within ½-in. of top of the ramekins.
3. Bake 35-40 minutes or until centers are set. Remove ramekins from water bath immediately to a wire rack; cool for 10 minutes. Refrigerate until cold. Serve with whipped cream and syrup.
1 serving: 234 cal., 5g fat (2g sat. fat), 99mg chol., 140mg sod., 44g carb. (40g sugars, 3g fiber), 6g pro.

CHOCOLATE BREAD PUDDING

This is a fun recipe because the chocolate makes it different from traditional bread pudding. It's a rich, comforting dessert.
—Mildred Sherrer, Fort Worth, TX

PREP: 15 MIN. + STANDING
BAKE: 30 MIN. • **MAKES:** 2 SERVINGS

- 2 oz. semisweet chocolate
- ½ cup half-and-half cream
- ⅔ cup sugar
- ½ cup 2% milk
- 1 large egg
- 1 tsp. vanilla extract
- ¼ tsp. salt
- 4 slices day-old bread, crusts removed and cut into cubes (about 3 cups)
  Optional: Confectioners' sugar and whipped cream

1. Preheat the oven to 350°. In a small microwave-safe bowl, melt chocolate; stir until smooth. Stir in the cream; set aside.
2. In a large bowl, whisk the sugar, milk, egg, vanilla and salt. Stir in chocolate mixture. Add bread cubes and toss to coat. Let stand for 15 minutes.
3. Spoon into 2 greased 2-cup souffle dishes. Bake until a knife inserted in the center comes out clean, 30-35 minutes.

BAKING 101

4. Sprinkle with confectioners' sugar and top with a dollop of whipped cream.
1 serving: 622 cal., 17g fat (9g sat. fat), 145mg chol., 656mg sod., 105g carb. (79g sugars, 2g fiber), 12g pro.

DID YOU KNOW?
If you've heard both "bread pudding" and "bread & butter pudding," there's actually a difference. In bread & butter pudding, the bread is spread with butter before the liquid is added—the bread can be cut into cubes or layered in a baking pan in whole slices.

CHOCOLATE-RASPBERRY CREME BRULEE

Just when I thought nothing could beat the specialness of creme brulee, I created this decadent version that stars rich chocolate and sweet raspberries. Cracking through the top reveals a smooth and rich custard everyone enjoys.

—Jan Valdez, Chicago, IL

PREP: 25 MIN. • **BAKE:** 40 MIN. + CHILLING
MAKES: 10 SERVINGS

 8 oz. semisweet chocolate, chopped
 4 cups heavy whipping cream
½ cup plus 2 Tbsp. sugar, divided
 8 large egg yolks, beaten
 1 Tbsp. vanilla extract
30 fresh raspberries
 2 Tbsp. brown sugar
    Additional fresh raspberries, optional

1. Preheat oven to 325°. Place chocolate in a large bowl. In a large saucepan, bring cream and ½ cup sugar just to a boil. Pour over chocolate; whisk until smooth. Slowly stir hot cream mixture into egg yolks; stir in vanilla.
2. Place 3 fresh raspberries in each of 10 ungreased 6-oz. ramekins or custard cups. Evenly divide the custard among ramekins. Place in a baking pan; add 1 in. of boiling water to the pan. Bake, uncovered, for 40-50 minutes or until centers are just set (custard will jiggle). Remove ramekins from water bath; cool 10 minutes. Cover and refrigerate for at least 4 hours.
3. Combine brown sugar and remaining 2 Tbsp. sugar. If using a creme brulee torch, sprinkle the custards with sugar mixture. Heat sugar with the torch until caramelized. Serve immediately. If broiling the custards, place ramekins on a baking sheet; let stand at room temperature for 15 minutes. Sprinkle with sugar mixture. Broil 8 in. from the heat until the sugar is caramelized, 4-7 minutes. Refrigerate until firm, 1-2 hours. If desired, top with additional fresh raspberries.
1 serving: 549 cal., 46g fat (27g sat. fat), 294mg chol., 44mg sod., 32g carb. (27g sugars, 2g fiber), 6g pro.

LEMON PUDDING CAKE

My husband, Lloyd, loves this cake because it tastes like lemon meringue pie. The cake is no-fuss and makes just enough for the two of us.

—Dawn Fagerstrom, Warren, MN

PREP: 15 MIN. • **BAKE:** 40 MIN.
MAKES: 2 SERVINGS

 1 large egg, separated, room temperature
½ cup sugar
⅓ cup whole milk
 2 Tbsp. all-purpose flour
 2 Tbsp. lemon juice
 1 tsp. grated lemon zest
⅛ tsp. salt
    Optional: Confectioners' sugar, lemon slices and whipped cream

1. Preheat oven to 325°. In a bowl, beat egg yolk. Add sugar, milk, flour, lemon juice, zest and salt; beat until smooth. Beat egg white until stiff peaks form; gently fold into lemon mixture. Pour into 2 ungreased 6-oz. custard cups (cups will be very full).
2. Place the cups in an 8-in. square baking pan. Pour boiling water into pan to a depth of 1 in. Bake until a knife inserted in the center comes out clean and top is golden, 40-45 minutes. If desired, top with confectioners' sugar, lemon slices and whipped cream.
1 serving: 288 cal., 4g fat (2g sat. fat), 112mg chol., 200mg sod., 60g carb. (51g sugars, 0 fiber), 5g pro.

HAZELNUT POTS DE CREME

White chocolate and toasted ground hazelnuts make a heavenly combination in this rich, silky custard. Guests are sure to rave about the elegant individual treats served in ramekins.
—Elise Lalor, Issaquah, WA

PREP: 30 MIN. • **BAKE:** 25 MIN. + CHILLING
MAKES: 6 SERVINGS

- 2 cups heavy whipping cream
- 1 cup ground hazelnuts, toasted
- 4 oz. white baking chocolate, chopped
- 6 large egg yolks
- ⅓ cup sugar
- 2 Tbsp. hazelnut liqueur, optional
    Chocolate curls

1. Preheat the oven to 325°. In a small saucepan, heat cream, hazelnuts and chocolate until bubbles form around sides of pan and chocolate is melted, stirring occasionally.
2. In a small bowl, whisk egg yolks and sugar. Remove cream mixture from heat; stir a small amount of the hot cream mixture into the egg mixture. Return all to the pan, stirring constantly. Stir in hazelnut liqueur if desired. Strain, discarding hazelnuts.
3. Transfer to six 6-oz. ramekins. Place in a baking pan; add 1 in. of boiling water to pan. Bake, uncovered, 25-30 minutes or until the centers are just set (mixture will jiggle). Remove ramekins from water bath; cool for 10 minutes. Cover and refrigerate at least 2 hours. Garnish servings with chocolate curls.
1 serving: 555 cal., 48g fat (24g sat. fat), 318mg chol., 58mg sod., 27g carb. (22g sugars, 1g fiber), 7g pro.

SWEET ORANGE CROISSANT PUDDING

BAKING 101

SWEET ORANGE CROISSANT PUDDING

Time-crunched cooks will definitely appreciate the make-ahead convenience of this delightful dish. Feel free to replace the orange marmalade with any jam or jelly that suits your taste.
—Mary Gabriel, Las Vegas, NV

PREP: 15 MIN. + CHILLING
BAKE: 40 MIN. + COOLING
MAKES: 8 SERVINGS

- 4 croissants, split
- 1 cup orange marmalade, divided
- 3 large eggs
- 1¼ cups whole milk
- 1 cup heavy whipping cream
- ½ cup sugar
- 1 tsp. grated orange zest, optional
- ½ tsp. almond extract

1. Spread the croissant bottoms with 3 Tbsp. marmalade; replace tops. Cut each croissant into 5 slices; place in a greased 11x7-in. baking dish.
2. Whisk together the next 4 ingredients, orange zest if desired, and extract. Pour over croissants. Refrigerate pudding, covered, overnight.
3. Remove from refrigerator 30 minutes before baking. Preheat oven to 350°. Place dish in a larger baking dish. Fill larger dish with 1 in. boiling water.
4. Bake, uncovered, until a knife inserted in center comes out clean, 40-45 minutes. Remove pan from water bath; cool on a wire rack 10 minutes. Brush remaining 4 Tbsp. marmalade over top. Cut and serve warm.
1 serving: 416 cal., 20g fat (11g sat. fat), 143mg chol., 287mg sod., 55g carb. (42g sugars, 1g fiber), 7g pro.

CHALLAH BREAD PUDDING

When my mother-in-law told me that she liked bread pudding, I went on a mission to create a version that was so good she'd ask me for the recipe. It worked! This can be served for breakfast, brunch or dessert.
—Marsha Ketaner, Henderson, NV

PREP: 25 MIN. • **BAKE:** 45 MIN.
MAKES: 16 SERVINGS

- 1 cup sugar
- 1 cup packed brown sugar
- 7 large eggs
- ½ cup butter, melted
- 2 cans (12 oz. each) evaporated milk
- 2 cups half-and-half cream
- 1½ Tbsp. vanilla extract
- 1 tsp. ground nutmeg
- 1 tsp. ground cinnamon
- ¼ tsp. ground cloves
- ¼ tsp. ground ginger
- 10 cups torn challah or egg bread (about 20-oz. loaf)
- 1 cup raisins
- 2 medium tart apples, peeled and chopped
- 1 cup chopped walnuts
- ¼ cup cold butter, cubed
  Vanilla ice cream, optional

1. Preheat oven to 350°. In a large bowl, whisk the first 11 ingredients until blended. Gently stir in bread; let stand 15 minutes or until bread is softened. Stir in raisins, apples and walnuts. Dot with cold butter.
2. Transfer to a greased 13x9-in. baking dish. Bake until puffed, golden, and a knife inserted near the center comes out clean, 40-45 minutes. Serve warm, with ice cream if desired.
¾ cup: 498 cal., 24g fat (11g sat. fat), 152mg chol., 300mg sod., 59g carb. (40g sugars, 2g fiber), 12g pro.

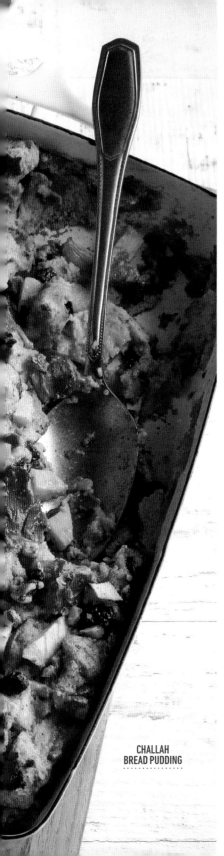

CHALLAH
BREAD PUDDING

CARAMEL APPLE CREME BRULEE

Here's the cream of the apple dessert crop. Fruit, caramel and cinnamon flavors enhance rich, velvety custard. Served warm or chilled, it's a classic end to a meal.
—Cheryl Perry, Hertford, NC

PREP: 35 MIN. • **BAKE:** 1 HOUR + CHILLING
MAKES: 6 SERVINGS

- 3 medium tart apples, peeled and thinly sliced
- 6 Tbsp. caramel ice cream topping
- ¼ cup sugar plus 4 Tbsp. sugar, divided
- ¼ cup plus 2 Tbsp. packed brown sugar, divided
- ½ tsp. ground cinnamon
- 2 cups heavy whipping cream
- 5 large egg yolks, beaten
- 1 tsp. vanilla extract

1. Preheat oven to 325°. Place apples in a microwave-safe dish; cover with water. Cover and microwave on high for 3-4 minutes or until tender. Drain apples and pat dry on paper towels. Arrange apples in the bottoms of six 6-oz. ramekins or custard cups. Top with caramel topping; set aside.
2. In a small saucepan, combine ¼ cup sugar, ¼ cup brown sugar and cinnamon; stir in the cream. Heat over medium heat until bubbles form around sides of pan. Remove from the heat; stir a small amount of hot mixture into the egg yolks. Return all to the pan, stirring constantly. Stir in vanilla.
3. Pour the mixture into the prepared ramekins. Place ramekins in a baking pan; add 1 in. of boiling water to pan. Bake, uncovered, until centers are just set (mixture will jiggle), 55-60 minutes. Remove the ramekins from the water bath; let cool for 20 minutes. Cover and refrigerate overnight.

4. If using a creme brulee torch, sprinkle the remaining 4 Tbsp. sugar evenly over the custards. Heat the sugar with the torch until caramelized. Serve immediately.
5. If broiling, place ramekins on a baking sheet; let stand at room temperature for 15 minutes. Sprinkle the remaining 4 Tbsp. sugar evenly over the custards. Broil 8 in. from the heat for 4-7 minutes or until the sugar is caramelized. Refrigerate for 1-2 hours or until firm.
1 serving: 504 cal., 33g fat (20g sat. fat), 280mg chol., 114mg sod., 50g carb. (33g sugars, 1g fiber), 4g pro.

SIMPLE SOFT BAKED CUSTARD

BAKING 101

The creamy texture of this soft-set custard is so inviting, you could call it comfort food. It has a pleasant vanilla flavor complemented by nutmeg.
—Mary Ann Pearce, Sparks, NV

PREP: 10 MIN. • **BAKE:** 35 MIN.
MAKES: 2 SERVINGS

- 1 large egg
- 1 cup whole milk
- 3 Tbsp. sugar
- ¾ tsp. vanilla extract
- ⅛ tsp. salt
  Dash ground nutmeg

1. Preheat oven to 350°. In a bowl, beat egg. Add the milk, sugar, vanilla and salt; stir well. Pour the mixture into 2 ungreased 6-oz. custard cups. Sprinkle with nutmeg.
2. Place cups in a baking pan. Fill pan with hot water to a depth of 1 in. Bake, uncovered, for 35-40 minutes or until a knife inserted in the center comes out clean.
1 serving: 189 cal., 7g fat (3g sat. fat), 123mg chol., 239mg sod., 25g carb. (24g sugars, 0 fiber), 7g pro.

CARAMEL CUSTARD

CLASSIC CREME BRULEE

My favorite dessert is creme brulee, so I quickly learned how to successfully make this on my own. Recently I was at a party where the guests finished off their own desserts broiling the sugar on their portions with a small torch. What a clever idea!
—Joylyn Trickel, Helendale, CA

PREP: 30 MIN. • **BAKE:** 45 MIN. + COOLING
MAKES: 8 SERVINGS

- 4   cups heavy whipping cream
- 9   large egg yolks
- ¾   cup sugar
- 1   tsp. vanilla extract
  Brown sugar

1. Preheat oven to 325°. In a large saucepan, combine the cream, egg yolks and sugar. Cook and stir over medium heat until mixture reaches 160° or is thick enough to coat the back of a metal spoon. Stir in vanilla.
2. Transfer to eight 6-oz. ramekins or custard cups. Place cups in a baking pan; add 1 in. of boiling water to pan. Bake, uncovered, for 25-30 minutes or until centers are just set (mixture will jiggle). Remove ramekins from water bath; cool for 10 minutes. Cover and refrigerate for at least 4 hours.
3. One hour before serving, place the custards on a baking sheet. Sprinkle each with 1-2 tsp. brown sugar. Broil 8 in. from the heat for 4-7 minutes or until sugar is caramelized. Refrigerate any leftovers.
1 serving: 551 cal., 50g fat (29g sat. fat), 402mg chol., 53mg sod., 22g carb. (22g sugars, 0 fiber), 6g pro.

CARAMEL CUSTARD

My husband and I have enjoyed this simple dessert many times, especially after a Tex-Mex meal. In fact, I've made it so often I don't even look at the recipe anymore.
—Linda McBride, Austin, TX

PREP: 15 MIN. • **BAKE:** 40 MIN.
MAKES: 8 SERVINGS

- 1½   cups sugar, divided
- 6   large eggs
- 3   cups whole milk
- 2   tsp. vanilla extract

1. Preheat oven to 350°. In a large heavy saucepan, cook and stir ¾ cup sugar over low heat until sugar is melted and golden. Pour into eight 6-oz. custard cups or ramekins, tilting to coat the bottom of each ramekin; let stand for 10 minutes.
2. Beat the eggs, milk, vanilla and the remaining ¾ cup sugar until blended but not foamy. Pour over the caramelized sugar.
3. Place the ramekins in two 8-in. square baking pans. Pour very hot water in pans to a depth of 1 in. Bake until a knife inserted in the center comes out clean, 40-45 minutes. Remove from pans to cool on wire racks.
4. To unmold, run a knife around the rim of each ramekin and invert onto a dessert plate. Serve warm or chilled.
1 serving: 259 cal., 7g fat (3g sat. fat), 172mg chol., 92mg sod., 42g carb. (41g sugars, 0 fiber), 8g pro.

CINNAMON-SPICED PUMPKIN FLAN

I love pumpkin and decided to add it to a traditional recipe for flan. It's an interesting change of pace from the usual holiday pie.
—Alisha Rodrigues, Tetonia, ID

PREP: 20 MIN. • **BAKE:** 50 MIN. + CHILLING
MAKES: 12 SERVINGS

⅔ cup sugar
FLAN
2 cups half-and-half cream
6 large egg yolks
1 large egg
1 cup sugar
1 cup canned pumpkin
1 tsp. ground cinnamon
1 tsp. vanilla extract

1. Preheat oven to 325°. In a small heavy saucepan, spread sugar; cook, without stirring, over medium-low heat until it begins to melt. Gently drag the melted sugar to center of pan so sugar melts evenly. Cook, without stirring, until the melted sugar turns a medium amber color, about 8 minutes. Quickly pour into an ungreased 9-in. deep-dish pie plate, tilting to coat the bottom of the plate.

2. In a large saucepan, heat cream until bubbles form around the side of pan; remove from heat. In a large bowl, whisk the egg yolks, egg, sugar, pumpkin, cinnamon and vanilla until blended. Slowly stir in hot cream. Pour into the pie plate.

3. Place pie plate in a larger baking pan. Place pan on oven rack; add very hot water to pan to within ½ in. of top of pie plate. Bake for 50-60 minutes or until center is just set (mixture will jiggle). Immediately remove the flan from water bath to a wire rack; cool 1 hour. Refrigerate until cold, for about 5 hours or overnight.

4. Run a knife around the edge and invert onto a rimmed serving platter. Refrigerate leftovers.

1 piece: 204 cal., 7g fat (4g sat. fat), 128mg chol., 31mg sod., 32g carb. (30g sugars, 1g fiber), 3g pro.

OVER-THE-TOP BLUEBERRY BREAD PUDDING

This delicious southern treat boasts out-of-this-world flavor and eye appeal. You just may want to skip the main course and go straight to dessert. It's a favorite for our summer celebrations.
—Marilyn Haynes, Sylacauga, AL

PREP: 15 MIN. + STANDING • **BAKE:** 50 MIN.
MAKES: 12 SERVINGS

3 large eggs
4 cups heavy whipping cream
2 cups sugar
3 tsp. vanilla extract
2 cups fresh or frozen blueberries
1 pkg. (10 to 12 oz.) white baking chips
1 loaf (1 lb.) French bread, cut into 1-in. cubes
SAUCE
1 pkg. (10 to 12 oz.) white baking chips
1 cup heavy whipping cream

1. Preheat oven to 350°. In a large bowl, combine eggs, cream, sugar and vanilla. Stir in blueberries and baking chips. Stir in the bread cubes; let stand until bread is softened, about 15 minutes.

2. Transfer to a greased 13x9-in. baking dish. Bake, uncovered, until a knife inserted in the center comes out clean, 50-60 minutes. Let stand for 5 minutes before serving.

3. For sauce, place baking chips in a small bowl. In a small saucepan, bring cream just to a boil. Pour over baking chips; whisk until smooth. Serve with bread pudding.

1 serving: 869 cal., 54g fat (33g sat. fat), 195mg chol., 344mg sod., 89g carb. (65g sugars, 1g fiber), 11g pro.
Over-the-Top Raspberry Bread Pudding: Substitute raspberries for the blueberries.

BAKING 101

BAKING 101

PUMPKIN PECAN CUSTARD

My family loves pumpkin pie, but this is a delicious, creamy, healthier alternative— and we don't miss the crust at all.
—Abby Booth, Coweta, OK

PREP: 20 MIN. • **BAKE:** 35 MIN. + CHILLING
MAKES: 8 SERVINGS

- 1   can (15 oz.) pumpkin
- 1   can (12 oz.) reduced-fat evaporated milk
- ¾ cup egg substitute
- ⅓ cup packed brown sugar
- 1½ tsp. vanilla extract
- 1   tsp. ground cinnamon
- ½ tsp. ground ginger
- ¼ tsp. ground cloves
- ⅛ tsp. salt

TOPPING
- 3   Tbsp. all-purpose flour
- 3   Tbsp. brown sugar
- ½ tsp. ground cinnamon
- 2   Tbsp. cold butter
- ½ cup chopped pecans

1. Preheat oven to 325°. In a large bowl, combine the first 9 ingredients. Transfer to eight 6-oz. ramekins or custard cups. Place in a baking pan; add 1 in. boiling water to pan. Bake, uncovered, for 20 minutes.

2. Meanwhile, for topping, in a small bowl, combine the flour, brown sugar and cinnamon. Cut in the butter until crumbly. Stir in pecans. Sprinkle over custards. Bake 15-20 minutes longer or until a knife inserted in the center comes out clean.

3. Remove the ramekins from water bath; cool for 10 minutes. Cover and refrigerate at least 4 hours.

½ cup: 213 cal., 9g fat (3g sat. fat), 11mg chol., 160mg sod., 27g carb. (21g sugars, 3g fiber), 7g pro. **Diabetic exchanges:** 2 starch, 1½ fat.

EASY LIFTING

Compared to a full-size springform pan for cheesecake, it can be tricky to remove hot ramekins from a hot water bath after baking. The solution: jar lifters or canning tongs. The rounded nonslip edges make it easy to lift the ramekins without the risk of splashes or burning yourself.

BILTMORE'S BREAD PUDDING

BILTMORE'S BREAD PUDDING

Here's one of our classic dessert recipes. A golden caramel sauce enhances the rich bread pudding.
—The Biltmore Estate, Asheville, NC

PREP: 30 MIN. • **BAKE:** 40 MIN.
MAKES: 12 SERVINGS

- 8 cups cubed day-old bread
- 9 large eggs
- 2¼ cups 2% milk
- 1¾ cups heavy whipping cream
- 1 cup sugar
- ¾ cup butter, melted
- 3 tsp. vanilla extract
- 1½ tsp. ground cinnamon

CARAMEL SAUCE

- 1 cup sugar
- ¼ cup water
- 1 Tbsp. lemon juice
- 2 Tbsp. butter
- 1 cup heavy whipping cream

1. Preheat oven to 350°. Place bread cubes in a greased 13x9-in. baking dish. In a large bowl, whisk the eggs, milk, cream, sugar, butter, vanilla and cinnamon. Pour evenly over bread.
2. Bake, uncovered, for 40-45 minutes or until a knife inserted in the center comes out clean. Let stand 5 minutes before cutting.
3. Meanwhile, in a small saucepan, bring the sugar, water and lemon juice to a boil. Reduce heat to medium; cook until sugar is dissolved and mixture turns a golden amber color. Stir in butter until melted. Gradually stir in cream. Serve with bread pudding.
1 piece: 581 cal., 39g fat (23g sat. fat), 273mg chol., 345mg sod., 49g carb. (37g sugars, 1g fiber), 9g pro.

BAKING 101

385

PASTRIES & MORE

The word "pastry" conjures visions of intricate, delicate creations lining the shelves in a professional European bakery. But there's no reason to be nervous at the prospect of making pastries at home. These delectable, indulgent treats are beautiful to look at and even better to taste!

. . . .

PASTRY DOUGHS

Conveniently enough for today's home cook, two of the three most commonly used types of pastry doughs—phyllo dough and puff pastry—are readily available in the supermarket!

PHYLLO DOUGH

This tissue-thin pastry dough is traditionally used in Greek and Middle Eastern cuisine. The word phyllo comes from the Greek word for "leaf." As the sheets bake, they become crispy and flaky. The dough is made with flour, water, vinegar and a little oil, and must be worked until it develops enough gluten to be rolled into extremely thin sheets and layered with melted butter. Luckily, commercially prepared phyllo dough results in a product that is as good as homemade. Phyllo dough can be used as a substitute for strudel dough or other pastry wrappers.

It's best to thaw frozen phyllo dough overnight in the refrigerator or at room temperature for 2 hours. Wait until it's completely thawed before attempting to unwrap and separate the sheets—otherwise, they can crack. Once thawed, phyllo dough is very vulnerable to drying, so it's vital to keep it protected.

Always have all other ingredients assembled and ready to go before unwrapping your phyllo dough. Cover unwrapped and unrolled dough with a damp kitchen towel. Work with 1 sheet at a time and keep the rest covered until ready to use. Work on a smooth, dry surface—the dough tears easily.

PUFF PASTRY

Also called "roll-in" or "laminated" dough, puff pastry is a rich French pastry dough that consists of many layers of dough separated by layers of cold butter. The most famous use of puff pastry dough is the classic French croissant. The dough is made using a lengthy process of repeated layering, folding, chilling and rolling that can take a few days to complete— which makes the ready availability of commercially prepared puff pastry a true gift to home cooks. The recipes in this book call for frozen puff pastry, found in the freezer section in the grocery store.

As puff pastry bakes, the water contained in the butter creates steam, helping the dough expand and crisp up. Thaw puff pastry for about 8 hours in the refrigerator. If you do need to thaw at room temperature, put the thawed dough back in the refrigerator for 15-20 minutes before you use it; warm butter in the dough will result in a less crisp finished pastry.

Handle the dough as little as possible to avoid stretching and tearing. When cutting puff pastry, use a very sharp knife for the cleanest edge possible. Compressing the layers at the edge rather than cutting them cleanly will prevent the steam from escaping and will prevent the dough from rising evenly. Likewise, if you're using an egg wash, brush it on only the top of the dough, not on the edges. If the edges are coated, they will stick together, blocking the steam's escape and preventing the pastry from rising.

STORING PHYLLO DOUGH

- Unopened phyllo dough lasts in the refrigerator for up to 3 weeks or in the freezer for up to 3 months.

- Once opened, keep the dough in the refrigerator and use within 3 days.

- Once baked, phyllo dough keeps in an airtight container for 3 days, or in the freezer for 3 months.

- Freeze unfilled pastries for up to 2 months. Thaw them at room temperature 15-20 minutes before using; heat in the oven for a few minutes to restore their crispness.

STORING PUFF PASTRY

- Once opened, wrap puff pastry tightly in plastic; keep in the refrigerator up to 3 days or in the freezer up to 1 month.

- Baked and filled pastries are best served the day they are made; they don't hold up well in the refrigerator.

- Baked unfilled pastries may be frozen for up to 6 weeks.

PÂTE À CHOUX

Otherwise known as choux pastry or even cream puff pastry, this dough is similar to popover batter—steam creates the rise in the dough, puffing it up during baking and creating a crisp, hollow shell just waiting to be filled. This is the pastry used to make cream puffs and eclairs; it can be simply dropped onto a baking sheet in rounded spoonfuls or piped out using a pastry bag with a large round tip. cream

puffs and eclairs are baked at a high temperature, which makes the dough expand rapidly.

Bake cream puffs and eclairs in the lower third of the oven. Don't crowd the baking sheet; leave 3 inches of space around each pastry. This dough needs room to expand during baking and it needs air circulation so the steam can evaporate. The pastries are done when they are golden brown and have a dry, crisp exterior.

STORING CREAM PUFFS & ECLAIRS

• These pastries are best served the day they're made, as the filling may make them soggy if they sit for too long.

• If preparing ahead of time, store unfilled pastries in an airtight container in the refrigerator and fill them before serving.

• For longer storage, arrange unfilled pastries in a single layer on a baking sheet and freeze. Transfer to airtight freezer containers and freeze for up to 2 months. Thaw at room temperature 15-20 minutes before using. If necessary, reheat pastries in the oven a few minutes to restore their crispness.

A NOTE ABOUT COFFEE CAKES

Many different varieties of recipes—yeast breads, quick breads, skillet cakes and some variations on pound cakes and sheet cakes—all lay claim to the name "coffee cake." The only common thread seems to be that the finished sweet is an ideal pairing for a hot beverage and is a welcome treat for midmorning breaks and late-night snacks. For this book, we have collected a variety of coffee cakes in this chapter (see p. 408), organizing them by their intended use rather than separating them according to their individual cooking methods.

MERINGUES

Meringue is sweetened egg white foam; the ratio of sugar to egg white determines whether the meringue will be hard or soft. Soft meringues are commonly used as a topping for pies or as the base for various buttercream frostings (p. 432), while hard meringues are baked to make cookies and pastry shells. As meringues bake, the moisture in the egg white evaporates, leaving a sweet, crisp shell that dissolves on the tongue. Meringues should be perfectly dry but without any color.

Always make meringue on dry days. Meringues absorb the moisture in the air, so on humid days they'll become limp or sticky. Always use clean, dry beaters and metal or glass bowls. Specks of egg yolk, oil or grease will prevent the egg whites from reaching their maximum volume. After stiff peaks form, check to make sure the sugar is dissolved by rubbing a dab of the meringue between your fingers. It should feel silky-smooth.

TROUBLESHOOTING

PHYLLO DOUGH
Dough is crumbly: The dough was kept in the freezer too long or dough was not thawed completely before using.

Dough is brittle: The dough became too dry. Keep it covered while not using.

PUFF PASTRY
Dough did not bake up puffy: The cut edges were brushed with an egg wash, preventing the layers from rising.

Sides did not rise evenly: Dough was torn or cut with a dull knife.

Dough baked unevenly: Pastry was overhandled before baking.

CREAM PUFFS & ECLAIRS
Dough is dry: The water was boiled too long, causing too much liquid to evaporate.

Bottoms are soggy: Puffs were filled too soon. Fill no sooner than 2 hours before serving.

Puffs are not crisp: Puffs are underbaked. They should be golden brown, crisp and dry.

BREAKFAST ROLLS & PASTRIES

BEST CINNAMON ROLLS

Surprise a neighbor with a batch of oven-fresh cinnamon rolls slathered in cream cheese frosting. These breakfast treats make Christmas morning or any special occasion even more memorable.
—Shenai Fisher, Topeka, KS

PREP: 40 MIN. + RISING
BAKE: 20 MIN. + COOLING
MAKES: 16 ROLLS

BEST CINNAMON ROLLS

1   pkg. (¼ oz.) active dry yeast
1   cup warm whole milk (105° to 115°)
½   cup sugar
⅓   cup butter, melted
2   large eggs, room temperature
1   tsp. salt
4   to 4½ cups all-purpose flour
FILLING
¾   cup packed brown sugar
2   Tbsp. ground cinnamon
¼   cup butter, melted, divided
FROSTING
½   cup butter, softened
¼   cup cream cheese, softened
½   tsp. vanilla extract
⅛   tsp. salt
1½   cups confectioners' sugar

1. Dissolve yeast in warm milk. In another bowl, combine sugar, butter, eggs, salt, yeast mixture and 2 cups flour; beat on medium speed until smooth. Stir in enough remaining flour to form a soft dough (dough will be sticky).
2. Turn onto a floured surface; knead until smooth and elastic, 6-8 minutes. Place dough in a greased bowl, turning once to grease the top. Cover and let rise in a warm place until doubled, about 1 hour.

3. Mix brown sugar and cinnamon. Punch down dough; divide in half. On a lightly floured surface, roll 1 portion into an 11x8-in. rectangle. Brush with 2 Tbsp. butter; sprinkle with half the brown sugar mixture to within ½ in. of edges. Roll up jelly-roll style, starting with a long side; pinch seam to seal. Cut into 8 slices; place in a greased 13x9-in. pan, cut side down. Cover with a kitchen towel. Repeat with second portion of dough, remaining 2 Tbsp. butter and

remaining filling. Let rise in a warm place until doubled, about 1 hour.
4. Bake at 350° until golden brown, 20-25 minutes. Cool on wire racks.
5. For frosting, beat the butter, cream cheese, vanilla and salt until blended; gradually beat in the confectioners' sugar. Spread over tops. Refrigerate any leftovers.
1 roll: 364 cal., 15g fat (9g sat. fat), 66mg chol., 323mg sod., 53g carb. (28g sugars, 1g fiber), 5g pro.

BAKED LONG JOHNS

Because you don't have to fry these doughnuts, you can feel good about having them for breakfast!
—Nicki Lazorik, Mellen, WI

PREP: 15 MIN. • **BAKE:** 20 MIN. + COOLING
MAKES: 8 SERVINGS

BAKING 101

- 2 cups all-purpose flour
- ½ cup sugar
- 2 tsp. baking powder
- ½ tsp. salt
- ¼ tsp. ground cinnamon
- 2 large eggs, room temperature
- ¾ cup fat-free milk
- 1 Tbsp. butter, melted
- 1 tsp. vanilla extract

GLAZE

- ¾ cup semisweet chocolate chips
- 1 Tbsp. butter
- 4½ tsp. fat-free milk

1. Preheat oven to 325°. In a small bowl, combine flour, sugar, baking powder, salt and cinnamon. In another bowl, whisk the eggs, milk, butter and vanilla. Stir into dry ingredients just until moistened.
2. Transfer to eight 4½x2½x1½-in. loaf pans coated with cooking spray. Bake for 18-22 minutes or until golden brown. Immediately remove from pans to a wire rack to cool completely.
3. In a microwave, melt chocolate chips and butter. Add milk; stir until smooth. Dip tops of doughnuts in glaze. Return to wire rack; let stand until set.
1 doughnut: 291 cal., 9g fat (5g sat. fat), 61mg chol., 298mg sod., 48g carb. (23g sugars, 2g fiber), 6g pro.

ALMOND BEAR CLAWS

3. Place dough onto a well-floured surface; roll into a 21x12-in. rectangle. Starting at a short side, fold dough in thirds, forming a 12x7-in. rectangle. Give dough a quarter turn; roll into a 21x12-in. rectangle. Fold into thirds, starting with a short side. Repeat, flouring work surface as needed. (Do not chill dough between each rolling and folding.) Cover and chill 4-24 hours or until firm.

4. For filling, in a bowl, beat the egg white until foamy. Gradually add confectioners' sugar and almond paste; beat until smooth. Cut dough in half widthwise. Roll each portion into a 12-in. square; cut each square into three 12x4-in. strips. Spread about 2 Tbsp. filling down center of each strip. Fold long edges together over filling; seal edges and ends. Cut into 3 pieces.

5. Place on parchment-lined baking sheets with folded edge facing away from you. With scissors, cut strips 4 times to within ½ in. of folded edge; separate slightly. Repeat with remaining dough and filling. Cover and let rise in a warm place until doubled, about 1 hour.

6. Lightly beat water and the remaining egg; brush over dough. Sprinkle with sugar and almonds. Bake at 375° for 15 minutes or until golden brown. Remove from pans to wire racks to cool.

1 pastry: 352 cal., 19g fat (11g sat. fat), 73mg chol., 207mg sod., 38g carb. (10g sugars, 1g fiber), 6g pro.

DID YOU KNOW?

Almond paste is a mixture of ground blanched almonds, sugar and glycerin. It should be firm but pliabe when used in a recipe. If it is hard, heat it for 2-3 seconds in the microwave. Once opened, wrap tightly and keep in the refrigerator.

ALMOND BEAR CLAWS

These bear claws are absolutely melt-in-your-mouth delicious! It's impossible to resist the delicate pastry, rich almond filling and pretty fanned tops sprinkled with sugar and almonds.
—Aneta Kish, La Crosse, WI

PREP: 45 MIN. + CHILLING • **BAKE:** 15 MIN.
MAKES: 1½ DOZEN

- 1½ **cups cold butter, cut into ½-in. pieces**
- 5 **cups all-purpose flour, divided**
- 1 **pkg. (¼ oz.) active dry yeast**
- 1¼ **cups half-and-half cream**
- ¼ **cup sugar**
- ¼ **tsp. salt**
- 2 **large eggs, room temperature, divided use**
- 1 **large egg white**
- ¾ **cup confectioners' sugar**
- ½ **cup almond paste, cubed**
- 1 **Tbsp. water**
  Sugar or coarse sugar
  Sliced almonds

1. In a bowl, toss butter with 3 cups flour until well coated; refrigerate. In a large bowl, combine yeast and the remaining 2 cups flour.

2. In a saucepan, heat cream, sugar and salt to 120°-130°. Add to the yeast mixture with 1 egg. Beat until smooth. Stir in the butter mixture just until moistened.

HEAVENLY CHEESE DANISH

This tempting cheese Danish is baked to flaky perfection and made to shine with a simple egg wash. It tastes just as decadent as any breakfast pastry you'd find in a bakery or coffee shop.

—Josephine Triton, Lakewood, OH

PREP: 50 MIN. + CHILLING • **BAKE:** 15 MIN.
MAKES: 16 ROLLS

- 2 pkg. (¼ oz. each) active dry yeast
- ½ cup warm water (105° to 115°)
- 4 cups all-purpose flour
- ⅓ cup sugar
- 2 tsp. salt
- 1 cup cold butter, cubed
- 1 cup 2% milk
- 4 large egg yolks, room temperature

ASSEMBLY
- 3 tsp. ground cinnamon, divided
- 12 oz. cream cheese, softened
- ⅓ cup sugar
- 1 large egg, separated, room temperature
- 1 Tbsp. water
- 2 Tbsp. maple syrup

1. Dissolve yeast in warm water. In another bowl, mix flour, sugar and salt; cut in butter until crumbly. Add milk, egg yolks and yeast mixture; stir to form a soft dough (dough will be sticky). Cover and refrigerate 8-24 hours.
2. To assemble, punch down dough; divide into 4 portions. On a lightly floured surface, pat each portion into a 9x4-in. rectangle; sprinkle each with ¾ tsp. cinnamon. Cut each rectangle lengthwise into four 9x1-in. strips. Twist each strip, then loosely wrap it around itself to form a coil; tuck end under and pinch to seal. Place 3 in. apart on greased baking sheets.
3. Beat cream cheese, sugar and egg yolk until smooth. Press an indentation in center of each coil; fill with 1 rounded Tbsp. cream cheese mixture. Cover; let rise in a warm place until doubled, about 45 minutes.
4. Whisk egg white with water; brush over rolls. Bake at 350° until golden brown, 15-20 minutes. Remove to wire racks; brush with syrup. Serve warm. Refrigerate leftovers.
1 Danish: 359 cal., 21g fat (12g sat. fat), 111mg chol., 468mg sod., 37g carb. (12g sugars, 1g fiber), 7g pro.

MAPLE-WALNUT STICKY BUNS

Mmm! These ooey-gooey goodies will have everyone licking maple syrup from their fingers—and reaching for seconds. The yeast dough chills overnight.

—Nancy Foust, Stoneboro, PA

PREP: 45 MIN. + CHILLING • **BAKE:** 30 MIN.
MAKES: 2 DOZEN

- 1 pkg. (¼ oz.) active dry yeast
- 1 cup warm water (105° to 115°)
- ½ cup mashed potatoes (without added milk and butter)
- 1 large egg, room temperature
- 2 Tbsp. shortening
- 2 Tbsp. sugar
- 1 tsp. salt
- 3 to 3½ cups all-purpose flour

TOPPING
- 1 cup maple syrup
- ¾ cup coarsely chopped walnuts

FILLING
- ⅓ cup sugar
- 1½ tsp. ground cinnamon
- 3 Tbsp. butter, softened

1. In a small bowl, dissolve yeast in warm water. In a large bowl, combine potatoes, egg, shortening, sugar, salt, the yeast mixture and 1 cup flour; beat on medium speed until smooth. Stir in enough of the remaining flour to form a soft dough.
2. Turn onto a floured surface; knead until smooth and elastic, 6-8 minutes. Place dough in a greased bowl, turning once to grease the top. Cover and refrigerate overnight.
3. Pour syrup into a greased 13x9-in. baking dish; sprinkle with walnuts. In a small bowl, mix sugar and cinnamon.
4. Punch down dough; turn onto a lightly floured surface. Roll into a 24x8-in. rectangle. Spread with butter to within ½ in. of edges; sprinkle with cinnamon sugar. Roll up jelly-roll style, starting with a long side; pinch seam to seal. Cut into 24 slices.
5. Place in prepared baking dish, cut side down. Cover with a kitchen towel; let rise in a warm place until doubled, about 30 minutes. Preheat oven to 350°.
6. Bake 30-35 minutes or until golden brown. Cool 5 minutes before inverting buns onto a platter.
1 bun: 159 cal., 5g fat (1g sat. fat), 13mg chol., 114mg sod., 26g carb. (12g sugars, 1g fiber), 3g pro.

TAHITIAN BREAKFAST TREATS

This is a healthy take on the Tahitian coconut breakfast treat, firi firi, which is typically fried. My version of this doughnut-like treat is baked and rolled in a spicy sugar mix.
—Sue Falk, Sterling Heights, MI

PREP: 35 MIN. + RISING • **BAKE:** 10 MIN.
MAKES: 8 SERVINGS

- 1 pkg. (¼ oz.) active dry yeast
- ¼ cup warm water (105° to 115°)
- ½ cup warm coconut milk (105° to 115°)
- ½ cup sweetened shredded coconut
- ⅓ cup sugar
- ½ tsp. salt
- 2 to 2½ cups all-purpose flour

SPICED SUGAR
- ½ cup sugar
- 1 tsp. ground cinnamon
- ½ tsp. ground ginger
- ½ vanilla bean
- ¼ cup butter, melted

1. Add yeast to warm water and stir to dissolve; allow to sit until yeast has bubbled, 5-7 minutes. Add yeast mixture to warm coconut milk.
2. In a large bowl, combine coconut, sugar, salt, the yeast mixture and 1 cup flour; beat on medium speed until smooth. Stir in enough of the remaining flour to form a stiff dough (dough will be sticky).
3. Turn onto a floured surface; knead until smooth and elastic, 6-8 minutes. Place in a greased bowl, turning once to grease the top. Cover and let rise in a warm place until doubled, about 1½ hours.
4. Punch down dough. Turn onto a lightly floured surface; divide into 8 portions. Roll each into a 12-in. rope. Curl ends in opposite directions to form a figure 8. Tuck each end under where it meets center of roll and pinch lightly to seal. Place rolls 2 in. apart on a parchment-lined baking sheet. Cover with a kitchen towel; let rise in a warm place until almost doubled, about 30 minutes.
5. Preheat oven to 375°. Bake until light brown, 10-12 minutes. Meanwhile, place sugar, cinnamon and ginger in a shallow bowl. Split vanilla bean lengthwise. Using the tip of a sharp knife, scrape seeds from the center; stir into sugar mixture. Brush warm pastries with melted butter; roll in the sugar mixture to coat.

1 pastry: 251 cal., 8g fat (6g sat. fat), 8mg chol., 191mg sod., 42g carb. (18g sugars, 1g fiber), 4g pro.

BOHEMIAN KOLACHES

In Eastern Europe, a kolache is typically shaped into a circle, which is a symbol of good luck, prosperity and eternity. My mother-in-law gave me this recipe.
—Maxine Hron, Quincy, IL

PREP: 30 MIN. + RISING • **BAKE:** 10 MIN.
MAKES: ABOUT 28 ROLLS

- 2 pkg. (¼ oz. each) active dry yeast
- ½ cup sugar, divided
- 2 cups warm 2% milk (105° to 115°)
- 5¾ to 6½ cups all-purpose flour
- 4 large egg yolks, room temperature
- 1 tsp. salt
- ¼ cup butter, softened
- 2 cups canned prune, poppy seed, cherry or lemon pie filling
- 1 large egg white, beaten

1. In a small bowl, dissolve yeast and 1 Tbsp. sugar in warm milk; let stand 10 minutes. In a large bowl, combine 2 cups flour, remaining sugar, egg yolks, salt, butter and the yeast mixture. Mix until smooth. Add enough remaining flour to make a stiff dough.

2. Turn out onto a floured surface; knead until smooth and elastic, 6-8 minutes. Add additional flour if necessary. Place dough in greased bowl, turning once to grease top. Cover; let rise in a warm place until doubled in bulk, about 1 hour.
3. Punch dough down and allow to rise again. Roll out on floured surface to ½-in. thickness. Cut with large glass or a 2½-in. cutter. Place on greased baking sheets; let rise until doubled, about 45 minutes.
4. Preheat oven to 350°. Firmly press an indentation in the center of each roll and fill with a heaping tablespoon of filling. Brush dough with egg white. Bake for 10-15 minutes or until rolls are light golden brown.

1 kolache: 164 cal., 3g fat (2g sat. fat), 37mg chol., 116mg sod., 29g carb. (9g sugars, 1g fiber), 4g pro.

BREAKFAST DANISH CRISPS

This treasured recipe has been in our family for nearly 50 years. The tender, flaky treats are a perfectly light and airy partner to ice-cold milk or strong morning coffee.
—F. H. Steele, Clovis, NM

PREP: 40 MIN. + RISING
BAKE: 15 MIN./BATCH
MAKES: ABOUT 1½ DOZEN

1	pkg. (¼ oz.) active dry yeast
¼	cup warm water (105° to 115°)
1	cup warm 2% milk (105° to 115°)
2	cups sugar, divided
½	cup plus 6 Tbsp. butter, softened, divided
1½	tsp. grated lemon zest
1	tsp. salt
½	tsp. ground mace
2	large eggs, room temperature
5½	to 6 cups all-purpose flour
3	tsp. ground cinnamon

1. In a large bowl, dissolve yeast in the warm water. Add the milk, ½ cup sugar, ½ cup butter, lemon zest, salt, mace, eggs and 2 cups flour; beat well. Stir in enough of the remaining flour to form a soft dough.

2. Turn onto a floured surface; knead until smooth and elastic, 6-8 minutes. Place in a greased bowl, turning once to grease top. Cover; let rise in a warm place until doubled, about 1 hour.

3. Punch dough down. On a lightly floured surface, roll out dough into a large rectangle, about ¼ in. thick. Spread with 2 Tbsp. butter. Sprinkle with ⅓ cup sugar. Fold dough in half lengthwise; roll to ¼-in. thickness. Spread with 2 Tbsp. butter; sprinkle with ⅓ cup sugar.

4. Fold in half widthwise; roll to an 18x10-in. rectangle. Spread with remaining butter. Combine cinnamon and the remaining sugar; sprinkle half over dough to within ¼ in. of edges. Roll up tightly, starting with a short side; pinch to seal. Cut into ½-in. slices.

5. Place on greased baking sheets (4 to 6 slices per sheet). Cover with waxed paper and flatten with palm of hand. Sprinkle with the remaining cinnamon-sugar mixture. Let stand in a warm place for 30 minutes.

6. Bake at 400° for 12-15 minutes. Immediately remove from pans to wire racks.

1 crisp: 322 cal., 10g fat (6g sat. fat), 49mg chol., 236mg sod., 53g carb. (23g sugars, 1g fiber), 5g pro.

BREAKFAST
DANISH CRISPS

STRAWBERRY-PECAN YEAST ROLLS

These treats are so good! The strawberry filling, creamy glaze and crunchy nuts balance the sweet yeast rolls so perfectly. My family loves to eat them as much as I enjoy making them.

—Annie Thomas, Michigan City, MS

PREP: 40 MIN. + RISING
BAKE: 25 MIN. + COOLING • **MAKES:** 2 DOZEN

- 4 to 4½ cups all-purpose flour
- 1 pkg. (¼ oz.) active dry yeast
- 1 tsp. salt
- 1½ cups 2% milk
- 1 Tbsp. canola oil
- 1 Tbsp. honey
- 1 large egg, room temperature

FILLING
- ¼ cup butter, softened
- ⅔ cup strawberry preserves
- 1 Tbsp. sugar
- ½ tsp. ground cinnamon

GLAZE
- 3 oz. cream cheese, softened
- 1¾ cups confectioners' sugar
- ¼ tsp. almond extract
- 1 to 2 Tbsp. 2% milk
- ½ cup chopped pecans

1. In a large bowl, combine 2 cups flour, yeast and salt. In a small saucepan, heat milk, oil and honey to 120°-130°. Add to dry ingredients; beat just until moistened. Add egg; beat until smooth. Stir in enough of the remaining flour to form a soft dough.

2. Turn onto a floured surface; knead until smooth and elastic, 6-8 minutes. Place in a greased bowl, turning once to grease top. Cover and let rise in a warm place until doubled, about 1 hour.

3. Punch dough down; turn onto a lightly floured surface. Divide in half; roll each portion into a 15x10-in. rectangle. Spread butter to within ½ in. of edges; spread with strawberry preserves. Combine sugar and cinnamon; sprinkle over preserves.

4. Roll up jelly-roll style, starting with a long side; pinch seams to seal. Cut each roll into 12 slices. Place cut side down in 2 greased 15x10x1-in. baking pans. Cover and let rise until almost doubled, about 30 minutes.

5. Bake at 350° until golden brown, 25-30 minutes. Cool for 20 minutes. For glaze, in a small bowl, beat the cream cheese, confectioners' sugar and extract until smooth. Add enough milk to reach desired consistency; drizzle over rolls. Sprinkle with pecans.

1 roll: 202 cal., 6g fat (3g sat. fat), 20mg chol., 139mg sod., 33g carb. (16g sugars, 1g fiber), 4g pro.

OVERNIGHT CHERRY DANISH

These rolls with cherry-filled centers melt in your mouth and store well, unfrosted, in the freezer.

—Leann Sauder, Tremont, IL

PREP: 1½ HOURS + CHILLING
BAKE: 15 MIN. • **MAKES:** 3 DOZEN

- 2 pkg. (¼ oz. each) active dry yeast
- ½ cup warm 2% milk (105° to 115°)
- 6 cups all-purpose flour
- ⅓ cup sugar
- 2 tsp. salt
- 1 cup cold butter, cubed
- 1½ cups warm half-and-half cream (70° to 80°)
- 6 large egg yolks, room temperature
- 1 can (21 oz.) cherry pie filling

ICING
- 3 cups confectioners' sugar
- 2 Tbsp. butter, softened
- ¼ tsp. vanilla extract
  Dash salt
- 4 to 5 Tbsp. half-and-half cream

1. In a small bowl, dissolve yeast in warm milk. In a large bowl, combine flour, sugar and salt. Cut in butter until crumbly. Add yeast mixture, cream and egg yolks; stir until mixture forms a soft dough (dough will be sticky). Refrigerate, covered, overnight.

2. Punch down dough. Turn onto a lightly floured surface; divide into 4 portions. Roll each portion of dough into an 18x4-in. rectangle; cut each rectangle into 4x1-in. strips.

3. Place 2 strips side by side; twist together. Shape into a ring and pinch ends together. Place rings 2 in. apart on greased baking sheets. Repeat with remaining strips. Cover with kitchen towels; let rise in a warm place until doubled, about 45 minutes.

4. Preheat oven to 350°. Using the end of a wooden spoon handle, make a ½-in.-deep indentation in the center of each Danish. Fill each with about 1 Tbsp. pie filling. Bake 14-16 minutes or until lightly browned. Remove from pans to wire racks to cool.

5. In a bowl, beat confectioners' sugar, butter, vanilla, salt and enough cream to reach desired consistency. Drizzle over Danish.

1 Danish: 218 cal., 8g fat (5g sat. fat), 55mg chol., 188mg sod., 33g carb. (16g sugars, 1g fiber), 3g pro.

PEAR-BERRY BREAKFAST TARTS

When my kids were small, I could never get the pancakes on the table before they got cold. Then I got the idea for these breakfast tarts. It's a simple recipe for any busy family.
—Joan Elbourn, Gardner, MA

PREP: 45 MIN. + CHILLING • **BAKE:** 20 MIN.
MAKES: 10 SERVINGS

- ½ cup butter, softened
- 1 cup sugar, divided
- 2 large eggs, room temperature
- 2½ cups all-purpose flour
- 2 tsp. baking powder
- 2 cups chopped peeled pears (about 2 large)
- 2 Tbsp. cornstarch
- 2 Tbsp. water
- ½ cup fresh raspberries
- 1 large egg white
- 3 to 5 Tbsp. 2% milk, divided
- 1⅓ cups confectioners' sugar
  Food coloring, optional

1. Cream butter and ½ cup sugar until light and fluffy, 5-7 minutes. Add eggs, 1 at a time, beating well after each addition. In another bowl, whisk flour and baking powder; gradually beat into the creamed mixture to form a dough. Divide dough in half; shape each into a rectangle. Wrap and refrigerate 1 hour.
2. Meanwhile, in a small saucepan over medium heat, combine the pears and remaining sugar. Cook and stir until the sugar is dissolved and pears are softened, 6-8 minutes. In a small bowl, mix cornstarch and water until smooth; stir into the pear mixture. Return to a boil, stirring constantly; cook and stir 1-2 minutes or until thickened. Remove from heat; cool. Stir in raspberries.

3. Preheat oven to 350°. On a lightly floured surface, roll half the dough into a 15x8-in. rectangle. Cut into ten 4x3-in. rectangles. Transfer to parchment-lined baking sheets; spoon about 2 Tbsp. filling over each pastry to within ½ in. of edges. Roll the remaining dough into a 15x8-in. rectangle; cut into ten 4x3-in. rectangles and place over filling. Press edges with a fork to seal. Whisk egg white and 1 Tbsp. milk; brush over pastries. Bake until golden brown and filling is bubbly, 20-25 minutes.

4. Remove from baking sheets to wire racks to cool. For icing, mix confectioners' sugar and enough of remaining milk to reach desired consistency; tint with food coloring if desired. Spread or drizzle on pastries.
1 tart: 379 cal., 11g fat (6g sat. fat), 62mg chol., 193mg sod., 67g carb. (39g sugars, 2g fiber), 5g pro.

PEAR-BERRY BREAKFAST TARTS

PUFF PASTRY & PHYLLO DOUGH

DELICIOUS ALMOND BRAIDS

Similar to an almond crescent, this coffee cake is light and flaky with a rich almond center. It's so versatile you can serve it for dessert, breakfast or brunch. It tastes like it came from a high-end bakery, but puff pastry dough makes it easy.
—Gina Idone, Staten Island, NY

PREP: 25 MIN. • **BAKE:** 30 MIN. + COOLING
MAKES: 2 BRAIDS (6 SERVINGS EACH)

1   pkg. (7 oz.) almond paste
½   cup butter
½   cup sugar
1   large egg, room temperature
2   Tbsp. all-purpose flour
1   pkg. (17.3 oz.) frozen puff pastry, thawed

GLAZE
¾   cup plus 1 Tbsp. confectioners' sugar
2   Tbsp. 2% milk
½   tsp. almond extract
¼   cup sliced almonds, toasted

1. Preheat oven to 375°. Place the almond paste, butter and sugar in a food processor; cover and pulse until chopped. Add egg and flour; process until smooth.

2. Place puff pastry sheets onto a greased baking sheet. Spread half of the filling mixture down the center third of 1 pastry sheet. On each side, cut 8 strips about 3½ in. into the center. Starting at 1 end, fold alternating strips at an angle across filling. Pinch ends to seal. Repeat with the remaining pastry and filling.

3. Bake 30-35 minutes or until golden brown. Remove braids to a wire rack to cool completely.

4. Combine the confectioners' sugar, milk and almond extract. Drizzle over braids; sprinkle with almonds. Cut into slices to serve.

1 piece: 430 cal., 25g fat (8g sat. fat), 38mg chol., 197mg sod., 49g carb. (22g sugars, 4g fiber), 6g pro.

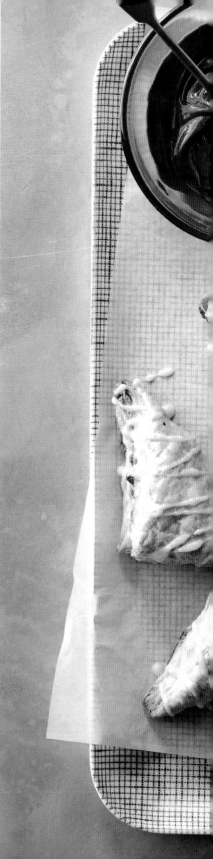

NUTELLA
HAND PIES

BAKING
101

NUTELLA HAND PIES

These pint-sized Nutella hand pies made with puff pastry are too good to keep to yourself, and they're so easy to make!
—*Taste of Home* Test Kitchen

TAKES: 30 MIN. • **MAKES:** 9 SERVINGS

- 1 large egg
- 1 Tbsp. water
- 1 sheet frozen puff pastry, thawed
- 3 Tbsp. Nutella
- 1 to 2 tsp. grated orange zest

ICING
- ⅓ cup confectioners' sugar
- ½ tsp. orange juice
- ⅛ tsp. grated orange zest
  Additional Nutella, optional

1. Preheat oven to 400°. In a small bowl, whisk egg with water.
2. Unfold puff pastry; cut into 9 squares. Place 1 tsp. Nutella in center of each; sprinkle with orange zest. Brush edges of pastry with the egg mixture. Fold 1 corner over filling to form a triangle; press edges to seal. Transfer to an ungreased baking sheet.
3. Bake until pastry is golden brown and cooked through, 17-20 minutes. Cool slightly.
4. In a small bowl, mix confectioners' sugar, orange juice and orange zest; drizzle over pies. If desired, warm additional Nutella in a microwave and drizzle over tops.
1 hand pie: 190 cal., 10g fat (2g sat. fat), 21mg chol., 100mg sod., 24g carb. (8g sugars, 2g fiber), 3g pro.

ROASTED GRAPE
& SWEET CHEESE
PHYLLO GALETTE

ROASTED GRAPE & SWEET CHEESE PHYLLO GALETTE

Faced with an abundant grape crop, I needed to come up with creative ways to use them. This became a quick and easy way to make an impressive dessert. It's fun to work with phyllo dough, and it bakes up golden and flaky. A layer of orange-kissed cream cheese is topped with roasted grapes. I drizzle with a bit of honey and a sprinkle of coarse sugar to finish it off. You can use other berries for this.
—Kallee Krong-McCreery, Escondido, CA

PREP: 25 MIN. • **BAKE:** 35 MIN. + COOLING
MAKES: 10 SERVINGS

1 pkg. (8 oz.) cream cheese, softened
2 Tbsp. orange marmalade
1 tsp. sugar
8 sheets phyllo dough (14x9-in. size)
4 Tbsp. butter, melted
1 cup seedless grapes
1 Tbsp. honey
2 tsp. coarse sugar

1. Preheat oven to 350°. In a large bowl, beat cream cheese, marmalade and sugar until smooth; set aside.
2. Place 1 sheet of phyllo dough on a parchment-lined baking sheet; brush with butter. Layer with remaining phyllo sheets, brushing each layer. (Keep the remaining phyllo covered with a damp towel to prevent it from drying out.) Spread the cream cheese mixture over phyllo to within 2 in. of edges. Arrange grapes over cream cheese.
3. Fold the edges of the phyllo over filling, leaving center uncovered. Brush folded phyllo with any remaining butter; drizzle with honey and sprinkle with coarse sugar. Bake until phyllo is golden brown, 35-40 minutes. Transfer galette to a wire rack to cool completely. Refrigerate leftovers.

1 piece: 177 cal., 13g fat (8g sat. fat), 35mg chol., 148mg sod., 15g carb. (9g sugars, 0 fiber), 2g pro.

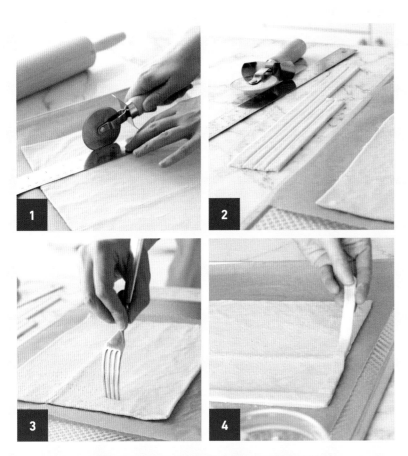

HOW TO MAKE A PUFF PASTRY GALETTE

With puff pastry, you can build clean, geometric edges for a galette, rather than the rustic, folded-over look.

STEP 1
On a parchment-lined baking sheet, unfold puff pastry sheet. Form a 10-in. square; use a rolling pin if necessary. Cut a 10x2-in. rectangle with a long sharp knife or pastry wheel.

STEP 2
From the 10x2-in. strip, cut two 10x½-in. strips and two 7x½-in. strips. Remove and discard scraps

STEP 3
Prick the remaining 10x8-in. pastry base all over with a fork.

STEP 4
Brush water ½ in. around edges of pastry base. Place the 10x½-in. and 7x½-in. strips along edges to form sides. Press lightly. Fill as directed.

DUTCH APPLE PIE TARTLETS

These adorable mini apple pie pastries make a delightful addition to a dessert buffet or snack tray. The recipe calls for convenient frozen phyllo shells, so they're surprisingly easy to prepare. The lemon curd filling adds a unique flavor twist.
—Mary Ann Lee, Clifton Park, NY

PREP: 15 MIN. • **BAKE:** 20 MIN.
MAKES: 2½ DOZEN

BAKING 101

- 1 cup finely chopped peeled apple
- ¼ cup lemon curd
- 2 pkg. (1.9 oz. each) frozen miniature phyllo tart shells

TOPPING
- ½ cup all-purpose flour
- 3 Tbsp. sugar
- ½ tsp. ground cinnamon
- ¼ cup cold butter
  Confectioners' sugar

1. In a small bowl, combine apples and lemon curd. Spoon into tart shells.
2. In another bowl, combine the flour, sugar and cinnamon; cut in butter until mixture resembles fine crumbs. Spoon over apple mixture. Place tartlets on an ungreased baking sheet.
3. Bake at 350° for 18-20 minutes or until golden brown. Cool on wire racks for 5 minutes. Dust with confectioners' sugar. Serve tartlets warm or at room temperature. Refrigerate leftovers.
Note: You can use a jar of lemon curd from the supermarket for this, or make your own. See the recipe on p. 433.
1 tartlet: 57 cal., 3g fat (1g sat. fat), 6mg chol., 22mg sod., 7g carb. (3g sugars, 0 fiber), 1g pro. **Diabetic exchanges:** ½ starch, ½ fat.

CHOCOLATE
BANANA
BUNDLES

BAKING
101

PUFF PASTRY DANISHES

Even though they're simple, these jam-filled pastries are right at home in a holiday brunch spread. They were my dad's favorite, so the recipe will always be close to my heart.
—Chellis Richardson, Jackson Center, OH

PREP: 30 MIN. • **BAKE:** 15 MIN.
MAKES: 1½ DOZEN

- 1 pkg. (8 oz.) cream cheese, softened
- ¼ cup sugar
- 2 Tbsp. all-purpose flour
- ½ tsp. vanilla extract
- 2 large egg yolks
- 1 Tbsp. water
- 1 pkg. (17.3 oz.) frozen puff pastry, thawed
- ⅔ cup seedless raspberry jam or jam of choice

1. Preheat oven to 425°. Beat the first 4 ingredients until smooth; beat in 1 egg yolk.
2. Mix water and the remaining egg yolk. On a lightly floured surface, unfold each sheet of puff pastry; roll into a 12-in. square. Cut each into nine 4-in. squares; transfer squares to parchment-lined baking sheets.
3. Top each square with 1 Tbsp. cream cheese mixture and 1 rounded tsp. jam. Bring 2 opposite corners of pastry over filling, sealing with yolk mixture. Brush tops with remaining yolk mixture.
4. Bake until pastry is golden brown, 14-16 minutes. Serve Danishes warm. Refrigerate leftovers.
1 pastry: 197 cal., 12g fat (4g sat. fat), 33mg chol., 130mg sod., 20g carb. (3g sugars, 2g fiber), 3g pro.

CHOCOLATE BANANA BUNDLES

Banana and chocolate is such an irresistible combo that I make this quick dessert often. You can also top these tasty bundles with the butter and brown sugar mixture left over from coating the bananas, or sprinkle on a dash of sea salt.
—Thomas Faglon, Somerset, NJ

TAKES: 30 MIN. • **MAKES:** 4 SERVINGS

- 2 Tbsp. butter
- ¼ cup packed brown sugar
- 2 medium ripe bananas, halved lengthwise
- 1 sheet frozen puff pastry, thawed
- 4 oz. semisweet chocolate, melted
  Vanilla ice cream, optional

1. Preheat oven to 400°. In a large cast-iron or other heavy skillet, melt butter over medium heat. Stir in brown sugar until blended. Add bananas; stir to coat. Remove from heat; set aside.
2. Unfold the sheet of puff pastry; cut into 4 rectangles. Place a halved banana in the center of each square. Overlap 2 opposite corners of puff pastry over banana; pinch tightly to seal. Place on parchment-lined baking sheets.
3. Bake 20-25 minutes or until golden brown. Drizzle with chocolate. Serve warm, with ice cream if desired.
1 serving: 596 cal., 31g fat (12g sat. fat), 15mg chol., 249mg sod., 78g carb. (35g sugars, 8g fiber), 7g pro.
Caramel Banana Bundles: Omit chocolate. Drizzle with caramel ice cream topping.

BAKLAVA

Baklava is a traditional Middle Eastern pastry made with phyllo dough, nuts and honey. This dessert is very rich, so one pan goes a long way.
—Judy Losecco, Buffalo, NY

PREP: 30 MIN. • **BAKE:** 40 MIN.
MAKES: 4 DOZEN

- 1½ lbs. finely chopped walnuts
- ½ cup sugar
- ½ tsp. ground cinnamon
- ⅛ tsp. ground cloves
- 1 lb. butter, melted, divided
- 2 pkg. (16 oz. each, 14x9-in. sheet size) frozen phyllo dough, thawed

SYRUP
- 2 cups sugar
- 2 cups water
- 1 cup honey
- 1 Tbsp. grated lemon or orange zest

1. In a small bowl, combine the walnuts, sugar, cinnamon and cloves; set aside. Brush a 15x10x1-in. baking pan with some of the butter. Unroll 1 package phyllo dough; cut stack into a 10½x9-in. rectangle. Repeat with the remaining package of phyllo. Discard scraps.

2. Line bottom of prepared pan with 2 sheets of phyllo dough (sheets will overlap slightly). Brush with butter. Repeat layers 14 times. (Keep dough covered with a damp towel until ready to use to prevent it from drying out.)

3. Spread with 2 cups of the walnut mixture. Top with 5 layers of phyllo dough, brushing with butter between each sheet. Spread with the remaining walnut mixture. Top with 1 layer of phyllo dough; brush with butter. Repeat 14 times. Cut into 2½-in. squares; cut each square in half diagonally. Brush the remaining butter over top. Bake at 350° for 40-45 minutes or until pastry is golden brown.

4. In a large saucepan, bring syrup ingredients to a boil. Reduce heat; simmer for 10 minutes. Strain and discard zest; cool to lukewarm. Pour syrup over warm baklava.

1 piece: 271 cal., 16g fat (5g sat. fat), 21mg chol., 162mg sod., 30g carb. (17g sugars, 1g fiber), 5g pro.

Pistachio Almond Baklava: Omit walnuts. In a food processor, combine 4 cups unsalted pistachios and 3 cups unsalted unblanched almonds; cover and process until finely chopped. Proceed as directed in step 1.

Chocolate Baklava: For nut mixture, combine 1 pound finely chopped walnuts, 1 package (12 oz.) miniature semisweet chocolate chips, ¾ cup sugar, 1½ tsp. ground cinnamon and 1 tsp. grated lemon zest. Layer and bake as directed.

HONEY-NUT SWIRLS

Puff pastry creates a quick and easy dough for pretty pinwheel-type cookies featuring two types of nuts. The flaky treats are hard to resist.
—Sally Sibthorpe, Shelby Township, MI

PREP: 25 MIN. • **BAKE:** 10 MIN.
MAKES: 2 DOZEN

- 1 sheet frozen puff pastry, thawed
- 1 cup finely chopped walnuts
- 1 cup finely chopped pistachios
- 3 Tbsp. brown sugar
- 2 Tbsp. butter, softened
- 2 Tbsp. honey
- 1 tsp. ground cinnamon
- ¼ tsp. salt
- 2 Tbsp. heavy whipping cream
- 2 Tbsp. turbinado (washed raw) sugar or sugar

1. Preheat oven to 375°. On a lightly floured surface, unfold the puff pastry. Roll into a 12x9-in. rectangle.

2. In a small bowl, combine the walnuts, pistachios, brown sugar, butter, honey, cinnamon and salt. Spread over the pastry to within ½ in. of edges. Roll up jelly-roll style, starting with a long side. Cut roll into ½-in. slices.

3. Place slices 2 in. apart on parchment-lined baking sheets. Brush with heavy cream and sprinkle with sugar. Bake for 10-12 minutes or until lightly browned. Remove to wire racks.

1 cookie: 141 cal., 10g fat (2g sat. fat), 4mg chol., 88mg sod., 12g carb. (5g sugars, 2g fiber), 3g pro.

EASY APPLE STRUDEL

My family always loves it when I make this wonderful dessert. Old-fashioned strudel was too fattening and time-consuming, but this revised classic is just as good. It's best served warm from the oven.
—Joanie Fuson, Indianapolis, IN

PREP: 30 MIN. • **BAKE:** 35 MIN.
MAKES: 6 SERVINGS

- ⅓ cup raisins
- 2 Tbsp. water
- ¼ tsp. almond extract
- 3 cups coarsely chopped peeled apples
- ⅓ cup plus 2 tsp. sugar, divided
- 3 Tbsp. all-purpose flour
- ¼ tsp. ground cinnamon
- 2 Tbsp. butter, melted
- 2 Tbsp. canola oil
- 8 sheets phyllo dough (14x9-in. size)
  Confectioners' sugar, optional

1. Preheat oven to 350°. Place raisins, water and extract in a large microwave-save bowl; microwave, uncovered, on high for 1½ minutes. Let stand for 5 minutes. Drain. Add chopped apples, ⅓ cup sugar, flour and cinnamon; toss to combine.
2. In a small bowl, mix melted butter and oil; remove 2 tsp. mixture for brushing top. Place 1 sheet of phyllo dough on a work surface; brush lightly with some of the butter mixture. (Keep the remaining remaining phyllo covered with a damp towel to prevent it from drying out.) Layer with 7 additional phyllo sheets, brushing each layer with some of the butter mixture. Spread apple mixture over phyllo to within 2 in. of 1 long side.
3. Fold the short edges over filling. Roll up jelly-roll style, starting from the side with a 2-in. border. Transfer to a baking sheet coated with cooking spray. Brush with reserved butter mixture; sprinkle with remaining 2 tsp. sugar. With a sharp knife, cut diagonal slits in top.
4. Bake until pastry is golden brown, 35-40 minutes. Cool on a wire rack. If desired, dust with confectioners' sugar before serving.

1 piece: 229 cal., 9g fat (3g sat. fat), 10mg chol., 92mg sod., 37g carb. (24g sugars, 2g fiber), 2g pro.

BLOOD ORANGE CARAMEL TARTE TATIN

I had never had blood oranges until moving to California. Their season is pretty short, so I use them in everything I possibly can while I can. The perfect combination is that sweet orange flavor combined with brown sugar. Whenever I have a gathering to attend, my friends demand I bring this dessert.
—Pamela Butkowski, Hermosa Beach, CA

PREP: 20 MIN. • **BAKE:** 20 MIN. + COOLING
MAKES: 6 SERVINGS

- ½ cup butter, cubed
- ½ cup packed brown sugar
- 1 tsp. vanilla extract
- 1 medium blood orange, thinly sliced
- 1 sheet frozen puff pastry, thawed
  Vanilla ice cream, optional

1. Preheat oven to 400°. In an 8-in. cast-iron or other ovenproof skillet, melt butter over medium heat; stir in brown sugar and vanilla until dissolved. Arrange orange slices in a single layer over brown sugar.
2. On a lightly floured surface, unfold puff pastry. Roll to a 9-in. square; place over oranges, tucking in corners.
3. Bake until tart is golden brown and filling is heated through, 20-25 minutes. Cool for 10 minutes before inverting onto a serving plate. Serve warm, with ice cream if desired.

1 piece: 416 cal., 26g fat (12g sat. fat), 41mg chol., 262mg sod., 43g carb. (19g sugars, 3g fiber), 3g pro.

LEMONY WALNUT-RAISIN GALETTE

This flaky, buttery pastry dessert has a filling of fruit, walnuts, coconut and cinnamon. There's a lot to love! For even more appeal, dollop sweetened whipped cream on top of each serving.

—Ellen Kozak, Milwaukee, WI

PREP: 30 MIN. • **BAKE:** 30 MIN.
MAKES: 10 SERVINGS

- 1 medium lemon
- 1 cup finely chopped walnuts
- 1 cup raisins
- 1 cup apricot spreadable fruit
- ⅔ cup unsweetened finely shredded coconut
- 2 tsp. ground cinnamon
- 8 sheets phyllo dough (14x9-in. size)
- ⅓ cup butter, melted
  Sweetened whipped cream, optional

1. Preheat oven to 350°. Cut unpeeled lemon into 8 wedges; remove seeds. Place wedges in a food processor; process until finely chopped. Transfer to a large bowl; stir in walnuts, raisins, spreadable fruit, coconut and cinnamon.
2. Place 1 sheet of phyllo dough on a parchment-lined baking sheet; brush with butter. Layer with remaining phyllo sheets, brushing each layer. (Keep remaining phyllo covered with a damp towel to prevent it from drying out.)
3. Spoon filling onto center of phyllo, leaving a 2-in. border on all sides. Fold edges of phyllo over the filling, leaving center uncovered. Brush folded edges with butter. Bake 30-35 minutes or until golden brown. Using parchment, carefully slide galette onto a wire rack to cool slightly. If desired, serve with whipped cream.

1 piece: 324 cal., 18g fat (8g sat. fat), 16mg chol., 125mg sod., 41g carb. (23g sugars, 3g fiber), 4g pro.

BAKING 101

PEPPERMINT PUFF PASTRY STICKS

PEPPERMINT PUFF PASTRY STICKS

I wanted to impress my husband's family with something you'd expect to find in a European bakery, and these chocolaty treats are what I came up with. The flaky pastry melts in your mouth.

—Darlene Brenden, Salem, OR

PREP: 15 MIN.
BAKE: 15 MIN./BATCH + COOLING
MAKES: 3 DOZEN

- 1 sheet frozen puff pastry, thawed
- 1½ cups crushed peppermint candies
- 10 oz. milk chocolate candy coating, coarsely chopped

1. Preheat oven to 400°. Unfold pastry sheet. Cut in half to form 2 rectangles. Cut each rectangle crosswise into 18 strips, about ½ in. wide. Place strips on ungreased baking sheets. Bake until pastry is golden brown, 12-15 minutes. Remove from pans to wire racks to cool completely.
2. Place crushed candies in a shallow bowl. In a microwave, melt candy coating; stir until smooth. Dip each cookie halfway in coating; allow excess to drip off. Sprinkle with peppermint candies. Place on waxed paper; let stand until set. Store cookies in an airtight container.

1 cookie: 89 cal., 4g fat (2g sat. fat), 0 chol., 24mg sod., 13g carb. (7g sugars, 1g fiber), 1g pro.

COFFEE CAKES

CHERRY-GO-ROUND
This fancy coffee cake is surprisingly easy. It makes a great gift.
—Kathy McCreary, Wichita, KS

PREP: 30 MIN. + CHILLING • **BAKE:** 20 MIN.
MAKES: 2 COFFEE CAKES (12 PIECES EACH)

- 1 pkg. (¼ oz.) active dry yeast
- ¼ cup warm water (105° to 115°)
- 1 cup warm whole milk (105° to 115°)
- ½ cup sugar
- ½ cup butter, softened
- 1 large egg, room temperature
- 1 tsp. salt
- 4½ to 5 cups all-purpose flour

FILLING
- 2 cans (16 oz. each) pitted tart cherries, well drained and roughly chopped
- ½ cup all-purpose flour
- ½ cup packed brown sugar
- ½ cup chopped pecans

ICING
- 1 cup confectioners' sugar
- ¼ tsp. vanilla extract
- 1 to 2 Tbsp. whole milk

1. In a large bowl, dissolve the yeast in warm water. Add the milk, sugar, butter, egg, salt and 2 cups flour. Beat until smooth. Stir in enough remaining flour to form a soft dough.

2. Turn the dough onto a lightly floured surface; knead until smooth and elastic, 6-8 minutes. Place in a greased bowl, turning once to grease top. Cover and refrigerate overnight.

3. Line 2 baking sheets with parchment; set aside. Punch dough down. Turn onto a lightly floured surface; divide in half. Roll each dough portion into a 14x7-in. rectangle. Spread cherries over dough to within ½ in. of edges. Combine the flour, brown sugar and pecans; sprinkle over cherries.

4. Roll up jelly-roll style, starting with a long side; pinch seams and tuck ends under. Place seam side down on prepared baking sheets; pinch ends together to form a ring. With kitchen scissors, cut from the outside edge two-thirds of the way toward center of ring at 1-in. intervals. Separate strips slightly and twist to allow the filling to show. Cover and let rise until doubled, about 1 hour.

5. Bake at 350° until golden brown, 20-25 minutes. Remove from pans to wire racks.

6. In a small bowl, combine the confectioners' sugar, vanilla and enough milk to reach desired consistency; drizzle over warm coffee cakes.

1 piece: 223 cal., 6g fat (3g sat. fat), 21mg chol., 149mg sod., 38g carb. (18g sugars, 1g fiber), 4g pro.

CHERRY-GO-ROUND

CHERRY-ALMOND
COFFEE CAKE

BLUEBERRY KUCHEN

In the summer, we can get beautiful, plump blueberries, which I use in this easy-to-make dessert. I like to freeze extra blueberries so I have them available any time I want this treat.
—Anne Krueger, Richmond, BC

PREP: 10 MIN. • **BAKE:** 40 MIN.
MAKES: 12 SERVINGS

BAKING 101

- 1½ cups all-purpose flour
- ¾ cup sugar
- 2 tsp. baking powder
- 1½ tsp. grated lemon zest
- ½ tsp. ground nutmeg
- ¼ tsp. salt
- ⅔ cup 2% milk
- ¼ cup butter, melted
- 1 large egg, room temperature, beaten
- 1 tsp. vanilla extract
- 2 cups fresh or frozen blueberries

TOPPING
- ¾ cup sugar
- ½ cup all-purpose flour
- ¼ cup butter, melted

1. Preheat oven to 350°. In a bowl, combine the first 6 ingredients. Add the milk, butter, egg and vanilla. Beat for 2 minutes or until well blended.
2. Pour into a greased 13x9-in. baking dish. Sprinkle with blueberries. In a bowl, combine sugar and flour; add butter. Toss with a fork until crumbly; sprinkle over blueberries. Bake for 40 minutes or until lightly browned.
1 piece: 271 cal., 9g fat (5g sat. fat), 37mg chol., 189mg sod., 45g carb. (28g sugars, 1g fiber), 3g pro.

CHERRY-ALMOND COFFEE CAKE

Every Christmas morning, I bake a coffee cake that's rich and creamy like a cheesecake. My family loves cherries on top, but personalize it with any kind of fruit preserves.
—Sue Torn, Germantown, WI

PREP: 15 MIN. • **BAKE:** 50 MIN. + COOLING
MAKES: 12 SERVINGS

- 2½ cups all-purpose flour
- 1 cup sugar, divided
- ¾ cup cold butter, cubed
- ½ tsp. baking powder
- ½ tsp. baking soda
- ¼ tsp. salt
- 1 cup sour cream
- 2 large eggs, room temperature, divided use
- 1 tsp. almond extract
- 1 pkg. (8 oz.) cream cheese, softened
- 1 cup cherry preserves
- ½ cup sliced almonds

1. Preheat oven to 350°. In a large bowl, mix flour and ¾ cup sugar; cut in butter until crumbly. Reserve ½ cup crumb mixture for topping. Add baking powder, baking soda and salt to the remaining crumb mixture. Stir in sour cream, 1 egg and the extract until blended.
2. Spread onto bottom of a greased 9-in. springform pan. In a small bowl, beat cream cheese and the remaining ¼ cup sugar until smooth. Add the remaining egg; beat on low speed just until blended. Pour into pan; spoon preserves over top. Sprinkle with the reserved crumb mixture and almonds.
3. Bake until top is golden brown, 50-60 minutes. Cool on a wire rack 15 minutes. Loosen sides from pan with a knife; remove rim from pan. Serve warm or cold. Refrigerate leftovers.
1 piece: 468 cal., 24g fat (14g sat. fat), 96mg chol., 298mg sod., 56g carb. (34g sugars, 1g fiber), 6g pro.

CINNAMON COFFEE CAKE

I love the excellent texture of this old-fashioned streusel-topped coffee cake. Always a crowd-pleaser, its lovely vanilla flavor enriched by sour cream may remind you of brunch at Grandma's!

—Eleanor Harris, Cape Coral, FL

PREP: 20 MIN. • **BAKE:** 1 HOUR + COOLING
MAKES: 20 SERVINGS

1	cup butter, softened
2¾	cups sugar, divided
4	large eggs, room temperature
2	tsp. vanilla extract
3	cups all-purpose flour
1	tsp. baking soda
1	tsp. salt
2	cups sour cream
2	Tbsp. ground cinnamon
½	cup chopped walnuts

1. Preheat oven to 350°. In a large bowl, cream butter and 2 cups sugar until light fluffy, 5-7 minutes. Add 1 egg at a time, beating well after each addition. Beat in vanilla. Combine flour, baking soda and salt; add alternately with the sour cream, beating just enough after each addition to keep the batter smooth.
2. Spoon a third of batter into a greased 10-in. tube pan. Combine cinnamon, nuts and remaining sugar; sprinkle a third over batter in pan. Repeat layers 2 more times. Bake for 60-65 minutes or until a toothpick inserted in center comes out clean. Cool for 15 minutes before removing from pan to a wire rack to cool completely.

1 piece: 340 cal., 16g fat (9g sat. fat), 83mg chol., 299mg sod., 44g carb. (28g sugars, 1g fiber), 5g pro.

MAPLE BACON WALNUT COFFEE CAKE

The sleepyheads will roll out of bed when they smell this sweet and savory coffee cake baking. Nuts and bacon in the crumbly topping blend with maple syrup, nutmeg and cinnamon.

—Angela Spengler, Niceville, FL

PREP: 25 MIN. • **BAKE:** 35 MIN. + COOLING
MAKES: 24 SERVINGS

2½	cups all-purpose flour
1	cup packed brown sugar
½	tsp. salt
⅓	cup cold butter
2	tsp. baking powder
½	tsp. baking soda
½	tsp. ground cinnamon
¼	tsp. ground nutmeg
2	large eggs, room temperature
1½	cups buttermilk
½	cup maple syrup
⅓	cup unsweetened applesauce
5	bacon strips, cooked and crumbled
½	cup chopped walnuts

1. Preheat oven to 350°. Combine flour, brown sugar and salt. Cut in butter until crumbly. Set aside ½ cup for topping. Combine baking powder, baking soda, cinnamon and nutmeg; stir into the remaining flour mixture.
2. Whisk the eggs, buttermilk, syrup and applesauce until well blended. Gradually stir into the flour mixture until combined.
3. Spread into a 13x9-in. baking pan coated with cooking spray. Sprinkle with reserved topping, then bacon and walnuts. Bake until a toothpick inserted in the center comes out clean, 35-40 minutes. Cool on a wire rack.

1 piece: 160 cal., 5g fat (2g sat. fat), 27mg chol., 183mg sod., 25g carb. (14g sugars, 1g fiber), 3g pro. **Diabetic exchanges:** 1½ starch, 1 fat.

CRANBERRY CRUMBLE COFFEE CAKE

This delicious coffee cake doesn't last long! People are always delighted to find the ruby cranberry sauce swirled inside.
—Jeani Robinson, Weirton, WV

PREP: 20 MIN. • **BAKE:** 70 MIN. + COOLING
MAKES: 12 SERVINGS

- ¼ cup chopped almonds
- 1 cup sugar
- ½ cup butter, softened
- 1 tsp. vanilla extract
- 2 large eggs, room temperature
- 2 cups all-purpose flour
- 1¼ tsp. baking powder
- ½ tsp. baking soda
- ¼ tsp. salt
- 1 cup sour cream
- 1 cup whole-berry cranberry sauce

TOPPING
- ¼ cup all-purpose flour
- ¼ cup sugar
- ¼ cup chopped almonds
- ¼ tsp. vanilla extract
- 2 Tbsp. cold butter

1. Preheat oven to 350°. Sprinkle the almonds over the bottom of a greased 9-in. springform pan; set aside. In a bowl, cream the sugar, butter and vanilla; beat on medium for 1-2 minutes. Add eggs, 1 at a time, beating well after each addition.

2. Combine dry ingredients; add to batter alternately with sour cream. Mix well. Spread 3 cups over almonds. Spoon cranberry sauce over batter. Top with the remaining batter.

3. For topping, combine flour, sugar, almonds and vanilla; cut in butter until crumbly. Sprinkle over batter.

4. Bake until a toothpick inserted in the center of the cake comes out clean, 70-75 minutes. Cool in pan on a wire rack for 15 minutes; remove sides of pan. Serve warm.

1 piece: 368 cal., 17g fat (9g sat. fat), 74mg chol., 266mg sod., 49g carb. (27g sugars, 2g fiber), 5g pro.

MAPLE TWIST COFFEE CAKE

If you like the flavor of maple, you'll want to add this recipe to your keeper file. The coffee cake makes a pretty addition to a Christmas morning spread.
—Deanna Richter, Elmore, MN

PREP: 45 MIN. + RISING • **BAKE:** 20 MIN.
MAKES: 16 SERVINGS

- 1 pkg. (¼ oz.) active dry yeast
- ¾ cup warm whole milk (105° to 115°)
- ¼ cup butter, softened
- 3 Tbsp. sugar
- 1 large egg, room temperature
- 1 tsp. maple flavoring
- ½ tsp. salt
- 2¾ to 3 cups all-purpose flour

FILLING
- ½ cup sugar
- ⅓ cup chopped walnuts
- 1 tsp. ground cinnamon
- 1 tsp. maple flavoring
- ¼ cup butter, melted

GLAZE
- 1 cup confectioners' sugar
- 2 Tbsp. butter, melted
- 1 to 2 Tbsp. whole milk
- ½ tsp. maple flavoring

1. In a large bowl, dissolve yeast in warm milk. Add the butter, sugar, egg, maple flavoring, salt and 1½ cups flour. Beat until smooth. Stir in enough remaining flour to form a soft dough.

2. Turn onto a floured surface; knead until smooth and elastic, 6-8 minutes. Place in a greased bowl, turning once to grease top. Cover and let rise in a warm place until doubled, about 1 hour. Meanwhile, in a small bowl, combine the sugar, walnuts, cinnamon and maple flavoring; set aside.

3. Punch dough down. Turn onto a lightly floured surface; divide into thirds. Roll each portion into a 12-in. circle; place 1 circle on a greased baking sheet or 12-in. baking pan. Spread with a third of the butter; sprinkle with a third of the filling. Repeat layers twice. Pinch edges of dough to seal.

4. Carefully place a glass in the center of the circle. With scissors, cut from outside edge just to the glass, forming 16 wedges. Remove glass; twist each wedge 5 or 6 times. Pinch ends to seal and tuck under. Cover and let rise until doubled, about 30 minutes.

5. Bake at 375° until golden brown, 18-20 minutes. In a small bowl, combine the glaze ingredients; set aside. Carefully remove coffee cake from pan by running a metal spatula under it to loosen; transfer to a wire rack. Drizzle with glaze.

1 piece: 236 cal., 10g fat (5g sat. fat), 33mg chol., 134mg sod., 34g carb. (17g sugars, 1g fiber), 4g pro.

MAPLE TWIST
COFFEE CAKE

SWEDISH CREAM
APPLE RINGS

SWEDISH CREAM APPLE RINGS

My mother made these coffee cake classics for every important holiday—Thanksgiving, Christmas and Easter. Now, I carry on the tradition. As I make them, I remember my mom, who was a lot like this recipe: full of surprises. The overnight rise lets you make the dough in advance so your morning won't be so hectic.

—Heather Hood, Hillsboro, OR

PREP: 20 MIN. + CHILLING
BAKE: 25 MIN. + COOLING
MAKES: 2 RINGS (10 PIECES EACH)

1   pkg. (¼ oz.) active dry yeast
¼   cup warm water (105° to 115°)
4   cups all-purpose flour
¼   cup sugar
½   tsp. salt
¾   cup cold butter, cubed

1   cup heavy whipping cream (105° to 115°)
¼   cup evaporated milk (105° to 115°)
3   large egg yolks, room temperature

FILLING

2   cups finely chopped peeled apples
½   cup raisins
¼   cup cinnamon-sugar

GLAZE

2   cups confectioners' sugar
1   tsp. vanilla extract
2   to 3 Tbsp. 2% milk

1. In a small bowl, dissolve yeast in warm water. In a large bowl, combine the flour, sugar and salt. Cut in butter until crumbly. Add the yeast mixture, cream, milk and egg yolks; stir until mixture forms a soft dough. Cover and refrigerate overnight.

2. In a small bowl, combine the filling ingredients. Punch down dough; divide in half. On a lightly floured surface, roll out 1 portion into a 13x7-in. rectangle. Sprinkle with half of filling.

3. Roll up jelly-roll style, starting with a long side. Pinch seam to seal. Place seam side down on a greased baking sheet; pinch ends together to form a ring. Repeat with the remaining dough and filling. Cover and let rise in a warm place, about 45 minutes.

4. Bake at 375° until golden brown, 25-30 minutes. Remove from pans to wire racks to cool. Combine the confectioners' sugar, vanilla and enough milk to reach a drizzling consistency. Drizzle over warm rings.

1 piece: 290 cal., 12g fat (8g sat. fat), 61mg chol., 123mg sod., 41g carb. (21g sugars, 1g fiber), 4g pro.

ALMOND COCONUT KRINGLES

My mom was famous for her kringle. She made it from memory, and when she passed away, we didn't have a recipe to carry on her tradition. We searched through her recipe box and found what we believe was her starting point. The dough remains the same, but I adjusted the filling ingredients until it was just right. Try this tender, flaky pastry with its almonds and coconut filling, and you'll be hooked the way we are!
—Deborah Richmond, Trabuco Canyon, CA

PREP: 1 HOUR + CHILLING
BAKE: 25 MIN. + COOLING
MAKES: 4 KRINGLES (9 SERVINGS EACH)

- 2 cups all-purpose flour
- 1 cup cold butter, cubed
- 1 cup sour cream

FILLING
- 1¼ cups butter, softened
- 1 cup packed brown sugar
- 3 cups sliced almonds, toasted
- 1½ cups sweetened shredded coconut, toasted

GLAZE
- 1 cup confectioners' sugar
- 1 Tbsp. butter, softened
- 1 tsp. vanilla extract
- 4 to 6 tsp. 2% milk

1. Place flour in a large bowl; cut in cold butter until crumbly. Stir in sour cream. Wrap and refrigerate overnight.
2. Preheat oven to 375°. For filling, in a small bowl, cream softened butter and brown sugar until light and fluffy, 5-7 minutes. Stir in the almonds and coconut.
3. Divide dough into 4 portions. On a lightly floured surface, roll 1 portion into a 12x10-in. rectangle. (Keep the remaining dough refrigerated until ready to use.) Spread 1 cup filling lengthwise down the center. Fold in sides of pastry to meet in the center;

pinch seam to seal. Repeat with remaining dough and filling. Transfer to 2 ungreased baking sheets. Bake for 23-27 minutes or until lightly browned. Remove to wire racks to cool completely.
4. Meanwhile, for the glaze, combine confectioners' sugar, butter, vanilla and enough milk to reach desired consistency; drizzle over pastries.
1 piece: 244 cal., 18g fat (10g sat. fat), 35mg chol., 98mg sod., 18g carb. (11g sugars, 1g fiber), 3g pro.

CREAM-FILLED CINNAMON COFFEE CAKE

When guests stay over for the holidays, they ask that I make this cinnamon coffee cake for breakfast. You can prepare it in advance to make the morning super easy.
—Arlene Wengerd, Millersburg, OH

PREP: 25 MIN. • **BAKE:** 20 MIN. + COOLING
MAKES: 12 SERVINGS

- ½ cup butter, softened
- 1 cup sugar
- 2 large eggs, room temperature
- 1 tsp. vanilla extract
- 1½ cups all-purpose flour
- ½ tsp. baking soda
- ½ tsp. salt
- 1 cup sour cream

TOPPING
- ½ cup sugar
- ½ cup chopped pecans
- 2 tsp. ground cinnamon

FILLING
- 1 Tbsp. cornstarch
- ¾ cup 2% milk
- ¼ cup butter, softened
- ¼ cup shortening
- ½ cup sugar
- ½ tsp. vanilla extract
  Caramel ice cream topping, optional

1. Preheat oven to 350°. In a large bowl, cream butter and sugar until light and fluffy, 5-7 minutes. Add eggs, 1 at a time, beating well after each addition. Beat in vanilla. Combine the flour, baking soda and salt; add to creamed mixture alternately with sour cream, beating just until combined.
2. Pour batter into 2 greased and waxed parchment-lined 9-in. round baking pans. Combine the topping ingredients; sprinkle over batter. Lightly cut through with a knife to swirl.
3. Bake until a toothpick inserted in the center comes out clean, 20-25 minutes. Cool for 10 minutes; remove from pans to wire racks to cool completely.
4. In a small saucepan, combine the cornstarch and milk until smooth. Bring to a boil; cook and stir until thickened, 1-2 minutes. Cover; refrigerate until chilled. In a small bowl, cream butter, shortening and sugar until light and fluffy, 5-7 minutes. Add vanilla and milk mixture; beat on medium speed until smooth and creamy, about 10 minutes.
5. Place 1 cake layer on a serving plate; spread with filling. Top with remaining layer. Store in the refrigerator. If desired, serve with caramel topping.
1 slice: 419 cal., 24g fat (11g sat. fat), 67mg chol., 268mg sod., 49g carb. (35g sugars, 1g fiber), 4g pro.

RICH FRUIT KUCHENS

This classic is such a part of our reunions, we designate a special place to serve it. We all flock to the "Kuchen Room" for this.
—Stephanie Schentzel, Northville, SD

PREP: 40 MIN. + CHILLING • **BAKE:** 35 MIN.
MAKES: 4 COFFEE CAKES (8 SERVINGS EACH)

- 1 ⅛ tsp. active dry yeast
- ½ cup warm water (105° to 115°)
- ½ cup warm milk (105° to 115°)
- ½ cup sugar
- ½ tsp. salt
- ½ cup canola oil
- 1 large egg, room temperature, lightly beaten
- 3½ cups all-purpose flour, divided

CUSTARD
- 4 large eggs, lightly beaten
- 2 cups heavy whipping cream
- 1½ cups sugar
- 8 to 10 cups sliced peeled tart apples or canned sliced peaches, drained, or combination of fruits

TOPPING
- ½ cup sugar
- ½ cup all-purpose flour
- 1 tsp. ground cinnamon
- ¼ cup cold butter

1. In a large bowl, dissolve yeast in warm water. Add the milk, sugar, salt, oil, egg and 2½ cups flour; beat until smooth. Stir in enough remaining flour to form a soft dough. Place in a greased bowl, turning once to grease top. Do not knead. Cover and refrigerate overnight.
2. The next day, for custard, whisk the eggs, cream and sugar in a large bowl until combined; set aside. Divide dough into 4 portions. Preheat oven to 350°.
3. On a lightly floured surface, roll each portion into a 10-in. circle. Press each circle onto the bottom and up the sides of an ungreased 9-in. pie plate. Arrange 2 to 2½ cups of fruit in each crust. Pour 1 cup custard over fruit.
4. For topping, combine the sugar, flour and cinnamon in a small bowl. Cut in butter until mixture resembles coarse crumbs. Sprinkle ⅓ cup over each coffee cake. Cover edges of dough with foil. Bake 35-40 minutes or until golden brown and custard reaches 160°.
1 piece: 242 cal., 11g fat (5g sat. fat), 58mg chol., 69mg sod., 32g carb. (19g sugars, 1g fiber), 3g pro.

GINGERBREAD COFFEE CAKE

At our house, we love gingerbread that's not too sweet. If you want to sweeten it, add a confectioners' sugar drizzle.
—Barbara Humiston, Tampa, FL

PREP: 20 MIN. • **BAKE:** 20 MIN. + COOLING
MAKES: 8 SERVINGS

- 1 cup all-purpose flour
- ½ cup plus 1 Tbsp. sugar, divided
- 1¾ tsp. ground cinnamon, divided
- 1 tsp. ground ginger
- ¼ tsp. salt
- ¼ tsp. ground allspice
- ¼ cup cold butter
- ¾ tsp. baking powder
- ½ tsp. baking soda
- 1 large egg, room temperature
- ½ cup buttermilk
- 2 Tbsp. molasses

ICING (OPTIONAL)
- ¾ cup confectioners' sugar
- 1 Tbsp. 2% milk
- ½ tsp. vanilla extract
- 2 Tbsp. finely chopped crystallized ginger

1. In a large bowl, mix flour, ½ cup sugar, ¾ tsp. cinnamon, ginger, salt and allspice; cut in butter until crumbly. Reserve ⅓ cup for topping.
2. Stir baking powder and baking soda into remaining flour mixture. In a small bowl, whisk the egg, buttermilk and molasses. Add to flour mixture; stir just until moistened. Transfer batter to a greased 8-in. round baking pan.
3. Add remaining sugar and cinnamon to reserved topping; sprinkle over batter. Bake at 350° for 20-25 minutes or until a toothpick inserted in center comes out clean. Cool completely in pan on a wire rack.
4. If desired, mix confectioners' sugar, milk and vanilla; drizzle over cooled coffee cake. Sprinkle with ginger.
1 piece: 195 cal., 7g fat (4g sat. fat), 39mg chol., 283mg sod., 31g carb. (19g sugars, 1g fiber), 3g pro.

POTECA CAKE

Rock Springs is home to 56 nationalities. This recipe showcases our region's Slavic heritage. It's one of my favorite holiday treats.

—Rachelle Stratton, Rock Springs, WY

PREP: 25 MIN. + CHILLING
BAKE: 1 HOUR + COOLING
MAKES: 12 SERVINGS

- 1 cup butter, cubed
- ½ cup 2% milk
- 3 large egg yolks, room temperature, beaten
- 2 pkg. (¼ oz. each) active dry yeast
- ¼ cup warm water (105° to 115°)
- 2½ cups all-purpose flour
- 1 Tbsp. sugar
- ¼ tsp. salt

FILLING
- 2 cups ground walnuts
- 2 cups chopped dates
- ¼ cup 2% milk
- 3 Tbsp. plus 1 cup sugar, divided
- ½ tsp. ground cinnamon
- 3 large egg whites, room temperature
  Confectioners' sugar, optional

POTECA CAKE

1. In a small saucepan, melt butter with the milk; cool. Stir in egg yolks until blended. In a small bowl, dissolve yeast in warm water. In a large bowl, combine flour, sugar and salt; add butter mixture and yeast mixture. Beat on medium speed for 3 minutes (dough will be sticky). Cover and refrigerate overnight.

2. In a small saucepan over medium heat, combine the nuts, dates, milk, 3 Tbsp. sugar and cinnamon. Cook and stir until mixture forms a paste. Transfer to a large bowl.

3. Beat egg whites until soft peaks form. Gradually beat in the remaining sugar, 1 Tbsp. at a time, on high until stiff peaks form. Fold into nut mixture.

4. Cut dough in half; on a floured surface, roll 1 portion of dough into a 20-in. square. Spread with half the filling. Roll up tightly jelly-roll style. Place seam side up in a greased 10-in. tube pan. Repeat with second portion; place seam side down over the first roll (layers will bake as 1 loaf).

5. Bake at 350° until golden brown, 60-70 minutes. Cool for 10 minutes before removing from pan to a wire rack to cool completely. If desired, sprinkle with confectioners' sugar.

1 piece: 509 cal., 26g fat (11g sat. fat), 92mg chol., 182mg sod., 66g carb. (41g sugars, 4g fiber), 8g pro.

. . . .

DID YOU KNOW?

Poteca is a Slovenian name for a nut roll, which goes by other names in other Slavic countries. Nut rolls are traditionally served as part of Christmas and Easter celebrations.

GERMAN CHOCOLATE RING

This recipe is modeled after German chocolate cake, which is my favorite. I enjoy making and eating this sweet-tasting bread!
—Anne Frederick, New Hartford, NY

PREP: 30 MIN. + RISING
BAKE: 20 MIN. + COOLING
MAKES: 24 SERVINGS

- 1¼ cups sweetened shredded coconut, divided
- 1 cup semisweet chocolate chips, divided
- ¾ cup chopped pecans
- 3 large eggs, room temperature, divided use
- 4½ to 5 cups all-purpose flour
- ½ cup sugar
- 1 tsp. salt
- 1 pkg. (¼ oz.) active dry yeast
- 1 cup 2% milk
- 5 Tbsp. butter, divided

1. In small bowl, combine 1 cup coconut, ¾ cup chocolate chips, chopped pecans and 1 egg; set aside. In a large bowl, combine 1 cup flour, sugar, salt and yeast. In small saucepan, heat milk and 4 Tbsp. butter to 120°-130°; add to the flour mixture, beating until smooth. Add remaining eggs and enough remaining flour to form a soft dough.
2. Turn onto a lightly floured surface. Knead 6-8 minutes or until smooth and elastic. Place in greased bowl, turning once to grease top. Cover; let rise in warm place until doubled, about 1 hour.
3. Punch dough down; turn onto lightly floured surface. Roll dough into a 18x10-in. rectangle. Melt remaining butter and brush over dough; spread with reserved chocolate mixture.
4. Roll up dough jelly-roll style, starting with a long side; pinch seam to seal. Place seam side down on a greased baking sheet. Pinch ends together to form a ring.
5. With scissors, cut from outside edge to two-thirds of the way toward center of ring at 1-in. intervals. Separate strips slightly; twist each strip to allow filling to show. Cover and let rise until doubled, about 1 hour.
6. Bake at 350° for 20-25 minutes or until golden brown. Sprinkle with remaining chocolate chips; let stand for 5 minutes. Spread melted chips; sprinkle with remaining coconut. Carefully remove from pan to a wire rack to cool.

1 piece: 222 cal., 10g fat (5g sat. fat), 34mg chol., 149mg sod., 30g carb. (11g sugars, 2g fiber), 4g pro.

CAST-IRON APPLE NUTMEG COFFEE CAKE

In an effort to practice my baking I used the morning's last bit of coffee to make a coffee cake—literally. It is super moist and crumbly and tastes like you dunked your cake right into a cup of hot joe. You can add pecans to the apples if you want some crunch.
—Darla Andrews, Boerne, TX

PREP: 25 MIN. • **BAKE:** 20 MIN. + COOLING
MAKES: 8 SERVINGS

- 3 Tbsp. butter, cubed
- 2 cups chopped peeled Gala apple
- ½ cup packed brown sugar, divided
- ¼ cup brewed coffee
- ⅔ cup canola oil
- ½ cup sugar
- 1 large egg plus 1 large egg white, room temperature
- 2 tsp. vanilla extract
- 1½ cups all-purpose flour
- 2 tsp. ground cinnamon
- ½ tsp. salt
- ½ tsp. baking soda
- ¼ tsp. ground nutmeg

DRIZZLE
- ⅓ cup brewed coffee
- ¼ cup heavy whipping cream
- 1½ cups confectioners' sugar

1. Preheat oven to 375°. In a 10-in. cast-iron or other ovenproof skillet, melt butter over low heat. Add apple and ¼ cup brown sugar. Cook and stir until crisp-tender, about 5 minutes. Stir in coffee; remove from heat.
2. In a large bowl, beat oil, sugar, egg, egg white, vanilla and remaining ¼ cup brown sugar until well blended. In another bowl, whisk flour, cinnamon, salt, baking soda and nutmeg; gradually beat into the oil mixture. Gently spread over the apple mixture.
3. Bake until a toothpick inserted in the center comes out clean, 18-22 minutes. Cool on a wire rack 10 minutes.
4. Meanwhile, for drizzle, in a small saucepan, bring coffee and cream to a boil; cook until liquid is reduced to ¼ cup, 10-12 minutes. Remove from heat; stir in confectioners' sugar. Let stand 10 minutes. Drizzle over cake.

1 piece: 532 cal., 27g fat (6g sat. fat), 43mg chol., 284mg sod., 71g carb. (51g sugars, 1g fiber), 4g pro.

ASSORTED PASTRIES

PEACH CREAM PUFFS

On a sizzling day, we crave something light, airy and cool. Nothing says summer like cream puffs stuffed with peaches and whipped cream.
—Angela Benedict, Dunbar, WV

PREP: 55 MIN. + COOLING
BAKE: 25 MIN. + COOLING
MAKES: 16 SERVINGS

- 1   cup water
- ½   cup butter, cubed
- ⅛   tsp. salt
- 1   cup all-purpose flour
- 4   large eggs, room temperature

FILLING
- 4   medium peaches, peeled and cubed (about 3 cups)
- ½   cup sugar
- ½   cup water
- ½   cup peach schnapps liqueur or peach nectar
- ½   tsp. ground cinnamon
- ¼   tsp. ground nutmeg

WHIPPED CREAM
- 2   cups heavy whipping cream
- ½   cup confectioners' sugar
- 3   Tbsp. peach schnapps liqueur, optional
    Additional confectioners' sugar

1. Preheat oven to 400°. In a large saucepan, bring water, butter and salt to a rolling boil. Add flour all at once and beat until blended. Cook over medium heat, stirring vigorously until mixture pulls away from sides of pan and forms a ball. Transfer dough to a large bowl; let stand 5 minutes.

2. Add eggs, 1 at a time, beating well after each addition until smooth. Continue beating until the mixture is smooth and shiny.

3. Cut a ½-in. hole in tip of a pastry bag. Transfer dough to bag; pipe sixteen 2-in. mounds 3 in. apart onto parchment-lined baking sheets.

4. Bake on a lower oven rack for 25-30 minutes or until puffed, very firm and golden brown. Pierce the side of each puff with the tip of a knife to allow steam to escape. Cool completely on wire racks.

5. Meanwhile, in a large saucepan, combine filling ingredients; bring to a boil, stirring occasionally. Reduce heat; simmer, uncovered, 25-30 minutes or until the mixture is slightly thickened and the peaches are tender. Cool the mixture completely.

6. In a bowl, beat cream until it begins to thicken. Add confectioners' sugar and, if desired, peach schnapps; beat until soft peaks form.

7. Cut top third off each cream puff. Pull out and discard soft dough from inside tops and bottoms.

8. To serve, spoon 2 Tbsp. whipped cream into each bottom; top with 2 Tbsp. filling and 2 Tbsp. additional whipped cream. Replace tops. Dust with additional confectioners' sugar.

1 cream puff with ¼ cup whipped cream and 2 Tbsp. filling: 256 cal., 18g fat (11g sat. fat), 103mg chol., 94mg sod., 21g carb. (14g sugars, 1g fiber), 3g pro.

PEACH CREAM PUFFS

CREME DE MENTHE CREAM PUFF TREE

CREME DE MENTHE CREAM PUFF TREE

A tower of creme de menthe-flavored puffs makes an eye-catching centerpiece for your dessert table. Guests will have this luscious pyramid deconstructed quickly!
—Agnes Ward, Stratford, ON

PREP: 1½ HOURS + CHILLING
BAKE: 25 MIN. + COOLING
MAKES: 60 SERVINGS

- 1¼ cups water
- ⅔ cup butter, cubed
- 1¼ cups all-purpose flour
- 5 large eggs, room temperature
FILLING
- 2 cups heavy whipping cream
- ⅓ cup green creme de menthe
GLAZE
- ⅓ cup butter, cubed
- 2 oz. unsweetened chocolate, chopped
- 2 cups confectioners' sugar
- 1½ tsp. vanilla extract
- 3 to 6 Tbsp. hot water
  Additional confectioners' sugar, optional

1. Preheat oven to 400°. In a large saucepan, bring water and butter to a boil. Add flour all at once and stir until a smooth ball forms. Remove from the heat; let stand for 5 minutes.
2. Add eggs, 1 at a time, beating well after each addition. Continue beating until mixture is smooth and shiny. Drop by rounded teaspoonfuls 2 in. apart onto greased baking sheets.
3. Bake for 20-25 minutes or until golden brown. Remove to wire racks. Cut a small slit in the side of each puff to allow steam to escape. Cool puffs.

4. For filling, in a large bowl, beat cream until soft peaks form. Fold in creme de menthe. Pipe about 1 Tbsp. into each puff. Refrigerate for up to 2 hours.
5. For the glaze, in a small saucepan, combine butter and chocolate. Cook and stir over low heat until melted. Remove from heat. Using a whisk, stir in the confectioners' sugar, vanilla and enough water to make consistency for dipping. Stir until smooth and no lumps appear.
6. To assemble tree: Separate puffs according to size and shape, choosing the flattest ones for the bottom layer and the smallest ones for the top. Dip the bottoms of the 21 flattest puffs into glaze. On a 10-in. round serving platter, place puffs in concentric circles forming a solid circle.
7. For the second layer, dip bottoms of 15 puffs into the glaze, then position on top of the base layer. Continue building tree, using about 11 puffs in third layer, about 6 puffs in fourth layer, about 4 puffs in fifth layer and 1 puff on top.
8. Drizzle the remaining glaze over tree, thinning with hot water if necessary.
9. Loosely cover tree with plastic wrap and refrigerate for up to 2 hours. If desired, dust with confectioners' sugar just before serving.

1 mini cream puff: 96 cal., 7g fat (4g sat. fat), 37mg chol., 31mg sod., 7g carb. (4g sugars, 0 fiber), 1g pro.

TEST KITCHEN TIP

You can use more or less flour to create a sturdier or lighter cream puff. As long as there is at least as much flour as there is liquid, you can adjust all the way up to a 2:1 flour-to-liquid ratio. More flour results in a sturdier cream puff shell suitable for wetter or heavier fillings, such as jam.

MAPLE WHOOPIE PIES

In New York, we have a huge maple syrup industry. I took a basic whoopie pie and gave it a twist using our beloved maple flavor.
—Holly Balzer-Harz, Malone, NY

PREP: 40 MIN.
BAKE: 10 MIN./BATCH + COOLING
MAKES: ABOUT 2 DOZEN

- ⅓ cup butter, softened
- ¾ cup sugar
- 1 large egg, room temperature
- 1 tsp. vanilla extract
- 1 tsp. maple flavoring
- 2¼ cups all-purpose flour
- 1¼ tsp. baking powder
- 1 tsp. salt
- ½ cup heavy whipping cream
- ½ cup maple syrup
- ½ cup chopped pecans

FILLING
- ½ cup butter, softened
- ½ cup shortening
- 1 tsp. maple flavoring
- 4 cups confectioners' sugar
- ¼ cup heavy whipping cream
- 2 Tbsp. maple syrup

1. Preheat oven to 375°. In a large bowl, cream butter and sugar until light and fluffy, 5-7 minutes. Beat in egg, vanilla and flavoring. In another bowl, whisk flour, baking powder and salt; add to the creamed mixture alternately with cream and syrup, beating well after each addition. Stir in pecans.
2. Drop by rounded tablespoonfuls 2 in. apart onto greased baking sheets. Bake until the edges are light brown and the tops spring back when lightly touched, 8-10 minutes. Remove from pans to wire racks to cool completely.
3. For filling, in a large bowl, beat butter, shortening and flavoring until creamy. Beat in confectioners' sugar alternately with cream and syrup until smooth. Spread filling on bottoms of half of the cookies; cover with remaining cookies. Store in airtight containers.

1 whoopie pie: 306 cal., 15g fat (7g sat. fat), 35mg chol., 183mg sod., 41g carb. (32g sugars, 1g fiber), 2g pro.

BANANA CREAM ECLAIRS

To surprise my banana-loving family, I made these for a reunion, where they stood out among the usual fare. They're special treats that look and taste delicious.
—Ruby Williams, Bogalusa, LA

PREP: 40 MIN. • **BAKE:** 25 MIN. + COOLING
MAKES: 16 SERVINGS

- 1 cup water
- ½ cup butter, cubed
- ¼ cup sugar
- ½ tsp. salt
- 1 cup all-purpose flour
- 4 large eggs, room temperature

FILLING
- 2½ cups heavy whipping cream
- 3 Tbsp. sugar
- 1 tsp. vanilla extract
- 3 to 4 medium firm bananas

GLAZE
- ½ cup confectioners' sugar
- 2 Tbsp. baking cocoa
- 2 Tbsp. butter, melted
- 1 tsp. vanilla extract
- 1 to 2 Tbsp. boiling water
- ½ cup finely chopped pecans

1. In a large saucepan, bring the water, butter, sugar and salt to a boil. Add the flour all at once and stir until a smooth ball forms. Remove from the heat; let stand for 5 minutes. Add eggs, 1 at a time, beating well after each addition. Continue beating until dough is smooth and shiny.
2. Insert a ¾-in. round tip into a pastry bag; add dough. Pipe 3-in. strips about 3 in. apart on a greased baking sheet. Bake at 400° for 25-30 minutes or until golden brown. Remove to wire racks. Immediately split puffs open; remove tops and set aside. Discard soft dough from inside. Cool puffs.
3. For the filling, in a large bowl, beat cream until it begins to thicken. Add sugar and vanilla; beat until stiff peaks form. In another bowl, mash bananas; gently fold in the whipped cream. Spoon into eclairs; replace tops.
4. In a small bowl, combine the confectioners' sugar, cocoa, butter and vanilla. Add enough water to make a thin glaze. Spread over eclairs. Sprinkle with pecans. Refrigerate leftovers.

1 eclair: 323 cal., 25g fat (14g sat. fat), 123mg chol., 176mg sod., 22g carb. (14g sugars, 1g fiber), 4g pro.

PECAN APPLE STRUDEL

This is one of my favorite recipes to make during autumn. The aroma of homemade strudel baking on a cool, crisp day is absolutely wonderful.
—Helen Lesh, Forsyth, MO

PREP: 20 MIN. + CHILLING
BAKE: 55 MIN. + COOLING • **MAKES:** 3 LOAVES

- 1 cup cold butter, cubed
- 2 cups all-purpose flour
- 1 cup sour cream
- ¼ tsp. salt

FILLING
- 2 cups dry bread crumbs
- ¼ cup butter, melted
- 4 medium tart apples, peeled and chopped
- 2 cups sugar
- 1 cup golden raisins
- ½ cup chopped pecans
- 2 tsp. ground cinnamon
  Confectioners' sugar, optional

1. In a large bowl, cut butter into flour until mixture resembles coarse crumbs. Stir in sour cream and salt. Shape the dough into a ball; cover and refrigerate overnight.

2. For filling, combine bread crumbs and butter. Add apples, sugar, raisins, pecans and cinnamon; set aside.

3. Preheat oven to 350°. Divide dough into thirds; turn onto a floured surface. Roll each into a 15x12-in. rectangle. Spoon filling evenly onto dough; spread to within 1 in. of edges. Roll up from a long side; pinch seams and ends to seal.

4. Carefully place each loaf seam side down on an ungreased baking sheet. Bake 55-60 minutes or until lightly browned. Cool completely on wire racks. Dust with confectioners' sugar if desired.

1 piece: 192 cal., 9g fat (5g sat. fat), 21mg chol., 136mg sod., 26g carb. (15g sugars, 1g fiber), 2g pro.

OLD-FASHIONED WHOOPIE PIES

OLD-FASHIONED WHOOPIE PIES

Who can resist soft chocolate sandwich cookies filled with a layer of fluffy white frosting? Mom has made these for years. They're a treat that never lasted very long with my two brothers and me around.
—Maria Costello, Monroe, NC

PREP: 35 MIN. + CHILLING
BAKE: 10 MIN./BATCH + COOLING
MAKES: 2 DOZEN

½ cup baking cocoa
½ cup hot water
½ cup shortening
1½ cups sugar
2 large eggs, room temperature
1 tsp. vanilla extract
2⅔ cups all-purpose flour
1 tsp. baking powder
1 tsp. baking soda
¼ tsp. salt
½ cup buttermilk

FILLING
3 Tbsp. all-purpose flour
    Dash salt
1 cup 2% milk
¾ cup shortening
1½ cups confectioners' sugar
2 tsp. vanilla extract

1. Preheat oven to 350°. In a small bowl, combine cocoa and water. Cool for 5 minutes. In a large bowl, cream shortening and sugar until light and fluffy, 5-7 minutes. Beat in the eggs, vanilla and cocoa mixture. Combine dry ingredients; gradually add to creamed mixture alternately with buttermilk, beating well after each addition
2. Drop by rounded tablespoonfuls 2 in. apart onto greased baking sheets. Bake until firm to the touch, 10-12 minutes. Remove to wire racks to cool.
3. For the filling, in a small saucepan, combine the flour and salt. Gradually whisk in milk until smooth; cook and stir over medium-high heat until thickened, 5-7 minutes. Remove from heat. Cover and refrigerate until completely cool.
4. In a small bowl, cream shortening, sugar and vanilla until light and fluffy, 5-7 minutes. Add the milk mixture; beat until fluffy, about 7 minutes. Spread filling on half the cookies; top with the remaining cookies. Store the whoopie pies in refrigerator.

1 whoopie pie: 244 cal., 11g fat (3g sat. fat), 19mg chol., 116mg sod., 33g carb. (20g sugars, 1g fiber), 3g pro.

. . . .
TEST KITCHEN TIP

There are plenty of different filling ideas you could try with this recipe. We recommend swapping the classic frosting for a raspberry or cream cheese filling. You can also try mixing in chocolate chips or crushed peppermint (perfect for the holidays!) to add a bit of bite.

ICINGS, FROSTINGS & FILLINGS

What makes the perfect finishing touch to your homemade treat? Decorating it with the perfect frosting or glaze. Learn how to make some of our favorite classic icings and fillings, and decorate like a pro by following our tips. Plus, we share a guide to some of the other delicious icings, glazes and fillings you can find throughout the book.

. . . .

BUTTERCREAM

MERINGUE BUTTERCREAM

WHIPPED CREAM

CREAM CHEESE

GANACHE

GLAZE

FAVORITE FROSTINGS

Whipped Cream Frosting:
Mix 1 cup heavy whipping cream, 3 Tbsp. confectioners' sugar and any flavoring you desire (cinnamon, vanilla extract, lemon zest, etc.). Beat until stiff peaks form. Treats frosted with whipped cream should be kept refrigerated and served quickly; the frosting doesn't hold for long.

Buttercream: Buttercream ranges from classic simple buttercream (p. 280) to more complex **meringue buttercreams** (p. 431, p. 432) that are more stable—ideal for desserts made ahead, like wedding cakes.

Ganache: This luscious chocolaty frosting (right) is a go-to for all kinds of baking and is deceptively easy to make.

Glaze: Combine confectioners' sugar with a liquid, such as water, melted butter, milk, or orange juice to reach a drizzling consistency. Glaze dries to a shiny layer.

Cream Cheese: This tangy and substantial frosting (p. 431) is a classic—perfect with carrot cake and other cakes with rustic textures and bold flavors.

ABOUT CHOCOLATE GANACHE

A decadent combination of cream and melted chocolate, ganache is a staple in a baker's repertoire, with its gorgeous shine and fudgelike texture.

There are a few different forms of ganache, and all are simple to make. Cooled at room temperature, **pourable ganache** has a smooth and velvety texture. **Spreadable ganache** has a thicker consistency, so it can easily be piped onto cakes or cupcakes. Light and fluffy **whipped ganache** makes a great frosting for cupcakes or cakes.

For best results, use good-quality chocolate. You can also make ganache using white baking chips or chopped white chocolate. If you make white ganache, you can add food coloring to create your own array of colors.

If your ganache becomes too stiff to use, heat it in the microwave 10 seconds at a time until it's the right consistency. Let the cake cool completely before adding the ganache.

HOW TO MAKE GANACHE:

You'll need:

- 1 cup semisweet chocolate chips or finely chopped chocolate
- ⅔ cup heavy whipping cream

Place chocolate in a heat-proof bowl. Gently heat cream in a heavy saucepan. Once it just reaches a simmer, pour it over the chocolate. Avoid overboiling—too hot, and it can overheat the fat in the chocolate, causing it to separate.

Cover the bowl and let it sit for up to 10 minutes. (Mix too soon, and the cream will cool too quickly; the ganache could become grainy.) Whisk until smooth. If your ganache does become grainy, add more liquid and re-whisk until it becomes smooth. You can also whisk it over your stove's lowest heat setting—just enough heat to remelt the chocolate.

Cool at room temperature until the mixture reaches 85-90° and is slightly thickened, about 40 minutes. For spreadable ganache, chill, stirring occasionally, until it is the desired consistency. For whipped ganache, let it cool, then use a mixer to whisk the ganache until it has a fluffy texture and paler brown color.

SIMPLE CAKE FINISHES

Peaks: Press the flat side of a tablespoon into the frosting and pull straight up, forming a peak. Repeat over entire cake.

Waves: Use the back of a tablespoon to make a twisting motion in one direction. Move the spoon over a bit and make another twist in the opposite direction. Repeat.

Spiral Effect: Set cake on a lazy Susan or rotating stand. Hold spatula flat against the top of the cake; press slightly. Rotate platform, gradually drawing the spatula outward.

Nut Edge: Place plastic wrap or waxed paper under the edges of cake. Sprinkle nuts onto the plastic. Lift wrap and press nuts into the frosting. Use a clean spatula to lift one side of the cake at a time to remove wrap.

Ruffled Effect: Pipe frosting in a zigzag motion to create a ruffled look.

Ombre Effect: Divide the frosting into 3-4 portions; use gel food coloring to dye each portion a progressively darker shade. Start with the darkest shade at the bottom of the cake, adding the next lighter color in a band above the last. When each shade has been applied, use an offset spatula or a cake smoother to smooth the surface.

PEAKS

WAVES

SPIRAL EFFECT

NUT EDGE

RUFFLED EFFECT

OMBRE EFFECT

PIPING PRIMER

- For small projects, a DIY piping bag—made by cutting off one corner of a resealable plastic bag or rolling parchment into a cone—will do. But we recommend using either disposable or reusable piping bags as you take on more ambitious projects. Disposable bags are best for beginners as their thin plastic allows for easy manipulation. Reusable bags make more sense if you bake often.

- Choose small piping tips for writing messages or creating delicate detailed designs. Use large tips for filling pastries, piping retaining walls for cakes, and for frosting cupcakes.

- The two-part coupler enables you to change tips while frosting without switching bags. The first piece inserts into the interior of the bag. The outside ring, which holds the pastry tips, is then screwed on from the outside.

- To fill the bag, place it in a tall drinking glass and fold the top down over the sides of the glass to make a cuff. Once the bag is two-thirds full, uncuff it, push the frosting down and twist the bag closed. Wrap the twist with a rubber band or masking tape.

- Grasp the top of the bag with your dominant hand; guide with your nondominant hand. Squeezing with one hand helps you apply even pressure.

- When making a layer cake with a filling that needs to be contained (a bright contrasting color of frosting or a filling like lemon curd) pipe a retaining wall in your middle layers. Use a large, plain round tip to pipe a wide rim of frosting around the edge of the layer, then add the filling inside the wall.

ABOUT ROYAL ICING

Royal icing hardens when cooled, making it a great choice for decorated cookies. The secret ingredient in royal icing is meringue powder. This egg white substitute helps the icing achieve its glossy consistency. You can buy meringue powder at many grocery and craft stores or online.

HOW TO MAKE ROYAL ICING

You'll need:

- 2 cups confectioners' sugar
- 2 Tbsp. plus 2 tsp. water
- 4½ tsp. meringue powder
- ¼ tsp. cream of tartar
- Food coloring, optional

In a small bowl, combine confectioners' sugar, water, meringue powder and cream of tartar. Beat on low speed just until combined, then beat on high for 4-5 minutes until stiff peaks form. Tint with food coloring if desired.

TIPS FOR WORKING WITH ROYAL ICING

- To prevent lumpy icing—and clogging your piping tip—sift the confectioners' sugar before mixing it in.

- Adjust the icing's consistency by adding either more confectioners' sugar or more water. Use a thicker icing for piping, and a thinner icing for flooding open spaces.

- Gel food coloring works best to tint royal icing. For a bright white effect, use a few drops of blue; natural icing appears cream-colored when it dries.

- Keep unused icing covered at all times with a damp cloth.

- Lightly tap freshly iced cookies on a flat surface to bring any air bubbles to the top. Use a toothpick to pop each bubble, then reblend the icing.

- To prevent smearing, allow 24 hours of air-drying before moving the iced cookies. If time is tight, place cookies under a fan on the lowest setting.

DIPPING

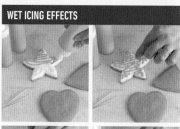

WET ICING EFFECTS

PIPED DESIGNS

ROYAL ICING TECHNIQUES

DIPPING
The easiest way to decorate cookies is to dip them. Prepare a thin royal icing, place it in a shallow bowl, then dip the top of your cutout cookies into the icing.

WET ICING EFFECTS
While the dipped icing is still wet, fill a piping bag or decorating bottle with a colored icing. For a marbled effect, pipe on the colored frosting on in a twisty pattern, then use a toothpick and swirl the colored and white icing together. For a swirled (or heart-shaped) effect, pipe on dots of colored icing and run the toothpick through them. For a herringbone pattern, pipe straight lines of colored frosting and run the toothpick through the lines perpendicularly.

PIPED DESIGNS
For more intricate designs, first let the base layer dry completely.

Using a slightly stiffer royal icing (just use more confectioners' sugar) pipe on your design. White on white is great for winter. Make flowers, dots or other patterns in any color using the same tools.

To fill in selected areas of a cookie (or to create the sharpest possible edge), first pipe a border using a stiffer mixture of icing. Then use a thinner icing to "flood" the open area. The border will act as a barrier, preventing the thinner icing from flowing where you don't want it to go.

ICINGS & FROSTINGS

BEST VANILLA BUTTERCREAM

Why is this recipe crowned the best vanilla buttercream frosting? With its powerfully decadent vanilla bean flavor and delightfully creamy texture, your family and friends will scrape every last bit of this frosting off their plates.
—Margaret Knoebel, Milwaukee, WI

PREP: 30 MIN. + COOLING • **MAKES:** 5 CUPS

    6 oz. white baking chips
    ¼ cup heavy whipping cream
    1 Tbsp. vanilla bean paste
    1 Tbsp. vanilla extract
    6 large egg whites, room
       temperature
 1½ cups sugar
    ½ tsp. cream of tartar
    ½ tsp. salt
    2 cups unsalted butter, cubed

1. In a microwave, melt baking chips with cream until smooth, stirring every 30 seconds. Stir in vanilla paste and extract. Set aside to cool slightly. Meanwhile, in a heatproof bowl of a stand mixer, whisk egg whites, sugar, cream of tartar and salt until blended. Place over simmering water in a large saucepan over medium heat. Whisking constantly, heat the mixture until a thermometer reads 160°, 8-10 minutes.
2. Remove from heat. With whisk attachment of stand mixer, beat on high speed until cooled to 90°, about 7 minutes. Gradually beat in butter, a few tablespoons at a time, on medium speed until smooth. Beat in cooled baking chip mixture until blended.
2 Tbsp.: 144 cal., 11g fat (7g sat. fat), 27mg chol., 43mg sod., 10g carb. (10g sugars, 0 fiber), 1g pro.

CREAM CHEESE FROSTING

This smooth, versatile frosting has a delicate vanilla flavor. The woman who made the wedding cake for our daughter, Leanne, and her groom, Billy Waters, used this recipe. It's also excellent on carrot cake.
—Sharon Lugdon, Greenbush, ME

TAKES: 10 MIN. • **MAKES:** ABOUT 3 CUPS

    1 pkg. (8 oz.) cream cheese,
       softened
    ½ cup butter, softened
    2 tsp. vanilla extract
    ⅛ tsp. salt, optional
 3¾ to 4 cups confectioners' sugar

In a large bowl, beat cream cheese, butter, vanilla and, if desired, salt until fluffy. Gradually beat in enough confectioners' sugar to achieve desired consistency. Store in the refrigerator.
2 Tbsp: 234 cal., 9g fat (6g sat. fat), 27mg chol., 109mg sod., 38g carb. (35g sugars, 0 fiber), 1g pro.

FLUFFY WHITE FROSTING

For a heavenly light and fluffy frosting, you can't top this variation of classic 7-minute frosting.
—Georgia Bohmann, West Allis, WI

TAKES: 20 MIN. • **MAKES:** 4 CUPS

    4 large egg whites
 1⅓ cups sugar
    1 Tbsp. water
    ½ tsp. cream of tartar
    1 tsp. vanilla extract

1. In a heatproof bowl of a stand mixer, whisk egg whites, sugar, water and cream of tartar until blended. Place over simmering water in a large saucepan over medium heat. Whisking constantly, heat the mixture until a thermometer reads 160°, 3-5 minutes.
2. Remove from heat; add vanilla. With the whisk attachment of a stand mixer, beat on high speed until stiff glossy peaks form, about 7 minutes. Use immediately. Store frosted cake, uncovered, in refrigerator.
2 Tbsp.: 35 cal., 0 fat (0 sat. fat), 0 chol., 7mg sod., 8g carb. (8g sugars, 0 fiber), 0 pro.
Fluffy Cherry Frosting: Reduce water to ¼ cup and add 2 Tbsp. maraschino cherry juice. Use ¼ tsp. cherry or vanilla extract.

OLD-FASHIONED ERMINE FROSTING

This old-timey frosting brings back memories of being in the kitchen with my grandmother. It was her go-to for cakes when she didn't have cornstarch or cream cheese.

—Rashanda Cobbins, Milwaukee, WI

PREP: 10 MIN. • **COOK:** 10 MIN. + CHILLING
MAKES: 5 CUPS

- ½ cup all-purpose flour
- 2½ cups whole milk
- 1¾ cups sugar
- ½ tsp. salt
- 1¾ cups butter, softened
- 1½ tsp. vanilla extract

1. In a small heavy saucepan, whisk flour and milk until smooth. Cook and stir over medium heat until thickened and bubbly, 5-7 minutes. Remove from heat. Stir in sugar and salt until dissolved; transfer to a small bowl. Press plastic wrap onto surface. Refrigerate until cold.
2. In a large mixing bowl, beat butter until light and fluffy, about 5 minutes. Gradually beat in cooled milk mixture. Beat in vanilla. Switch to the whisk attachment; continue beating on medium speed until frosting is stiff and fluffy. Frost cake immediately.

2 Tbsp.: 60 cal., 4g fat (3g sat. fat), 11mg chol., 50mg sod., 5g carb. (5g sugars, 0 fiber), 0 pro.

CLASSIC CHOCOLATE FROSTING

This fast fudgelike frosting is so fantastic. It even makes cakes from a box mix taste like homemade! This recipe makes enough to frost 24 cupcakes or the top of a 13x9-in. sheet cake—and it can be easily doubled.
—Karen Ann Bland, Gove, KS

PREP: 10 MIN. + COOLING • **MAKES:** 1½ CUPS

- 1⅔ cups confectioners' sugar
- ¾ cup heavy whipping cream
- 4 oz. unsweetened chocolate, chopped
- 2 tsp. vanilla extract
- 6 Tbsp. butter, softened

1. In a saucepan, combine the confectioners' sugar and cream. Bring to a boil, stirring constantly. Remove from heat; stir in chocolate until melted and smooth. Stir in vanilla. Cool until mixture is thickened, about 25 minutes, stirring occasionally.
2. In a bowl, cream butter. Gradually beat in chocolate mixture until blended. Cover and refrigerate until ready to use.
1 Tbsp.: 90 cal., 6g fat (4g sat. fat), 18mg chol., 32mg sod., 9g carb. (8g sugars, 0 fiber), 0 pro.

SWISS MERINGUE BUTTERCREAM

Swiss buttercream is rich, creamy and has a soft, silky texture—perfect for frosting cakes and cupcakes. It's less sweet than American buttercream, but still provides a sweet touch to any baked good.
—Margaret Knoebel, Milwaukee, WI

PREP: 30 MIN. + COOLING • **MAKES:** 5 CUPS

- 6 large egg whites, room temperature
- 1½ cups sugar
- ½ tsp. salt
- 2 cups unsalted butter, cubed
- 1 Tbsp. vanilla extract

1. In a heatproof bowl of a stand mixer, whisk egg whites, sugar and salt until blended. Place over simmering water in a large saucepan over medium heat. Whisking constantly, heat mixture until a thermometer reads 160°, 8-10 minutes.
2. Remove from heat. With whisk attachment of stand mixer, beat on high speed until cooled to 90°, about 20 minutes. Gradually beat in butter, a few tablespoons at a time, on medium speed until smooth. Whisk in vanilla.
2 Tbsp.: 114 cal., 9g fat (6g sat. fat), 24mg chol., 39mg sod., 8g carb. (8g sugars, 0 fiber), 1g pro.
Chocolate Swiss Buttercream: add 6 oz. melted semisweet baking chocolate after all the butter has been added to the buttercream.

FILLINGS

HOMEMADE LEMON CURD

Lemon curd is a scrumptious spread for scones, biscuits or other baked goods. You can find it in larger grocery stores alongside the jams and jellies or with the baking supplies, but we like making it from scratch.
—Mark Hagen, Milwaukee, WI

PREP: 20 MIN. + CHILLING • **MAKES:** 1⅔ CUPS

- 3 large eggs
- 1 cup sugar
- ½ cup lemon juice (about 2 lemons)
- ¼ cup butter, cubed
- 1 Tbsp. grated lemon zest

In a small heavy saucepan over medium heat, whisk eggs, sugar and lemon juice until blended. Add butter and lemon zest; cook, whisking constantly, until mixture is thickened and coats the back of a metal spoon. Transfer to a small bowl; cool 10 minutes. Refrigerate, covered, until cold.

2 Tbsp.: 110 cal., 5g fat (3g sat. fat), 52mg chol., 45mg sod., 16g carb. (16g sugars, 0 fiber), 2g pro.

RASPBERRY CURD

Sweet and flavorful raspberries are perfect and refreshing during the summertime. This recipe can also be made in the winter with frozen berries.
—*Taste of Home* Test Kitchen

PREP: 5 MIN. • **COOK:** 10 MIN. + CHILLING
MAKES: ¾ CUP

- 1⅔ to 2 cups fresh or frozen unsweetened raspberries
- ½ cup sugar
- 1 Tbsp. cornstarch

- 2 Tbsp. butter
- 3 large egg yolks

1. Sieve raspberries through a strainer, pressing with the back of a spoon; reserve ½ cup plus 1 Tbsp. juice. Discard seeds in seive.
2. In a saucepan, combine sugar and cornstarch; add the raspberry juice and butter. Cook and stir until thick and bubbly.
3. In a small bowl, beat egg yolks until well blended. Stir in half the raspberry mixture. Return all to saucepan; bring to a gentle boil. Cook and stir 2 minutes.
4. Place into small jars; place plastic wrap on surface of curd. Cover and chill. Store in the refrigerator.

2 Tbsp.: 58 cal., 1g fat (0 sat.fat), 46mg chol., 2mg sod., 11g carb (9g sugars, 1g fiber), 1g pro.

ESPRESSO FILLING

Coffee lovers will go crazy for cakes made with this heavenly filling. It's rich, decadent and irresistible!
—Megan Byers, Wichita, KS

TAKES: 15 MIN. • **MAKES:** 2¼ CUPS

- 2 Tbsp. instant espresso powder
- 1½ tsp. hot water
- 1½ cups mascarpone cheese
- 1 cup confectioners' sugar, sifted
- ¾ cup heavy whipping cream
- 1½ tsp. vanilla extract

In a small bowl, mix espresso powder and water until smooth; cool. In a large bowl, beat the mascarpone cheese, confectioners' sugar, cream, vanilla and espresso mixture on medium speed until creamy and slightly thickened (do not overmix). Spread between cake layers.

2 Tbsp.: 222 cal., 21g fat (12g sat. fat), 60mg chol., 24mg sod., 7g carb. (6g sugars, 0 fiber), 3g pro.

OTHER FROSTINGS, SAUCES & FILLINGS

REFERENCE

Baking can seem like a precise science, but there is wiggle room when it comes to the ingredients and pans you use. With this handy collection of facts and figures, you can keep the math to a minimum and get on with the mixing!

. . . .

WEIGHTS FOR COMMON INGREDIENTS

FLOUR

INGREDIENT	1 CUP	½ CUP	⅓ CUP	¼ CUP
ALL-PURPOSE FLOUR	4.25 oz. 120 g	2.125 oz. 60 g	1.4 oz. 40 g	1.1 oz. 30 g
BREAD FLOUR	4.25 oz. 120 g	2.125 oz. 60 g	1.4 oz. 40 g	1.1 oz. 30 g
CAKE FLOUR	4.25 oz. 120 g	2.125 oz. 60 g	1.4 oz. 40 g	1.1 oz. 30 g
SELF-RISING FLOUR	4 oz. 112 g	2 oz. 58 g	1.3 oz. 37 g	1 oz. 28 g

NUTS

INGREDIENT	1 CUP	½ CUP	⅓ CUP	¼ CUP
ALMONDS, SLICED	1.5 oz. 42 g	0.75 oz. 21 g	0.5 oz. 14 g	0.375 oz. 10 g
ALMONDS, SLIVERED	2 oz. 58 g	1 oz. 28 g	0.6 oz. 19 g	0.5 oz. 14 g
ALMONDS, WHOLE	5 oz. 142 g	2.5 oz. 71 g	1.6 oz. 47 g	1.25 oz. 36 g
CASHEWS, CHOPPED OR WHOLE	4 oz. 112 g	2 oz. 56 g	1.3 oz. 37 g	1 oz. 28 g
PECANS, CHOPPED	4 oz. 112 g	2 oz. 56 g	1.3 oz. 37 g	1 oz. 28 g
PECANS, HALVED	3.5 oz. 99 g	1.75 oz. 50 g	1.2 oz. 33 g	0.875 oz. 25 g
PISTACHIOS, CHOPPED OR WHOLE	2.125 oz. 60 g	1.1 oz. 30 g	0.7 oz. 20 g	0.5 oz. 14 g
WALNUTS, CHOPPED	4 oz. 112 g	2 oz. 58 g	1.3 oz. 37 g	1 oz. 28 g
WALNUTS, WHOLE	2.25 oz. 64 g	1.125 32 g	0.75 oz. 21 g	0.6 oz. 16 g

SUGARS

INGREDIENT	1 CUP	½ CUP	⅓ CUP	¼ CUP
BROWN SUGAR, LIGHT OR DARK	7.5 oz. 212 g	3.875 oz. 106 g	2.5 oz. 71 g	1.875 oz. 36 g
CONFECTIONERS' SUGAR	8 oz. 228 g	4 oz. 114 g	2.7 oz. 76 g	2 oz. 58 g
GRANULATED SUGAR (REGULAR WHITE SUGAR)	7 oz. 198 g	3.5 oz. 99 g	2.3 oz. 66 g	1.75 oz. 50 g
TURBINADO, DEMERARA OR RAW SUGAR	7.75 oz. 220 g	3.875 oz. 110 g	2.6 oz. 73 g	1.9 oz. 55 g

OTHER INGREDIENTS

INGREDIENT	1 CUP	½ CUP	⅓ CUP	¼ CUP
CHOCOLATE CHIPS	6 oz. 170 g	3 oz. 85 g	2 oz. 57 g	1.5 oz. 43 g
COCOA	3 oz. 85 g	1.5 oz. 43 g	1 oz. 28 g	0.75 oz. 21 g
COCONUT, SHREDDED, UNSWEETENED	3 oz. 85 g	1.5 oz. 43 g	1 oz. 28 g	0.75 oz. 21 g
COCONUT, SHREDDED, SWEETENED	4 oz. 113 g	2 oz. 57 g	1.3 oz. 38 g	1 oz. 28 g
GRAHAM CRACKER CRUMBS	3.5 oz. 99 g	1.75 oz. 49 g	1.2 oz. 33 g	0.875 oz. 25 g
HONEY	12 oz. 340 g	6 oz. 170 g	4 oz. 113 g	3 oz. 85 g
MINI MARSHMALLOWS	1.5 oz. 43 g	0.75 oz. 22 g	0.5 oz. 14 g	0.375 oz. 11 g
OATS, TRADITIONAL ROLLED	3.5 oz. 99 g	1.75 oz. 49 g	1.2 oz. 33 g	0.875 oz. 25 g
OATS, QUICK-COOKING	3.125 oz. 89 g	1.5 oz. 45 g	1 oz. 30 g	0.8 oz. 22 g
PEANUT BUTTER	9.5 oz. 270 g	4.75 oz. 135 g	3.2 oz. 90 g	2.375 oz. 68 g
RAISINS	5.5 oz. 156 g	2.75 oz. 78 g	1.8 oz. 52 g	1.375 oz. 39 g

TEMPERATURE CONVERSIONS

To convert Fahrenheit to Celsius: Subtract 32. Divide result by 9. Multiply result by 5.

To convert Celsius to Fahrenheit: Divide by 5. Multiply result by 9. Add 32.

COMMON BAKING TEMPERATURE CONVERSIONS:

275°F	=	140°C	Gas Mark 1
300°F	=	150°C	Gas Mark 2
325°F	=	170°C	Gas Mark 3
350°F	=	180°C	Gas Mark 4
375°F	=	190°C	Gas Mark 5
400°F	=	200°C	Gas Mark 6
425°F	=	220°C	Gas Mark 7
450°F	=	230°C	Gas Mark 8

WEIGHT CONVERSIONS

To approximately convert ounces and pounds to grams: Multiply ounces by 28.35 to determine grams. Divide pounds by 2.2 to determine kilograms

To approximately convert grams to ounces or pounds: Divide grams by 28.35 to determine ounces. Divide grams by 453.59 to determine pounds.

COMMON WEIGHT CONVERSIONS:

½ oz.	=	15 g
1 oz.	=	30 g
2 oz.	=	55 g
3 oz.	=	85 g
4 oz. (¼ lb.)	=	115 g
8 oz. (½ lb.)	=	225 g
16 oz (1 lb.)	=	455 g

MEASURE EQUIVALENTS

TEASPOON & TABLESPOON MEASURES

Dash or Pinch	=	less than ⅛ tsp.
1½ tsp.	=	½ Tbsp.
3 tsp.	=	1 Tbsp. = ½ fluid oz.
4½ tsp.	=	1½ Tbsp.
2 Tbsp.	=	⅛ cup = 1 fluid oz.
4 Tbsp.	=	¼ cup = 2 fluid oz.
5⅓ Tbsp.	=	⅓ cup = 5 Tbsp. + 1 tsp.
8 Tbsp.	=	½ cup = 4 fluid oz.
10⅔ Tbsp.	=	⅔ cup = 10 Tbsp. + 2 tsp.
12 Tbsp.	=	¾ cup = 6 fluid oz.
16 Tbsp.	=	1 cup = 8 fluid oz. = ½ pint

CUP MEASURES

⅛ cup	=	2 Tbsp. = 1 fluid oz.
¼ cup	=	4 Tbsp. = 2 fluid oz.
⅓ cup	=	5⅓ Tbsp.
½ cup	=	8 Tbsp. = 4 fluid oz.
⅔ cup	=	10⅔ Tbsp.
¾ cup	=	12 Tbsp. = 6 fluid oz.
1 cup	=	16 Tbsp. = 8 fluid oz. = ½ pint
2 cups	=	1 pint = 16 fluid oz.
4 cups	=	2 pints = 1 quart = 32 fluid oz.

PINTS, QUARTS, GALLONS & POUNDS

½ pint	=	1 cup = 8 fluid oz.
1 pint	=	2 cups = 16 fluid oz.
1 quart	=	4 cups = 32 fluid oz.
4 quarts	=	16 cups = 1 gallon

BAKEWARE SUBSTITUTIONS

Some pan substitutions are more common than others.

Here are some quick and easy swaps, based on standard kitchen equipment.

IF YOU DON'T HAVE THIS	USE THIS INSTEAD
One 9x5-in. loaf pan	Three 5¾x3-in. mini loaf pans
One 8x4-in. loaf pan	Two 5¾x3x2-in. mini loaf pans
One 9-in. round baking pan	One 8-in. square baking pan
Two 9-in. round baking pans	One 13x9-in. baking pan
One 10-in. fluted tube pan	One 10-in. tube pan or two 9x5-in. loaf pans
One 11x7-in. baking pan	10-in. cast-iron skillet
One 13x9-in. baking pan	Two 9-in. round baking pans; two 8-in. square baking pans; one 12-in. skillet
24 muffin cups	48 mini muffin cups; 12 jumbo muffin cups

To use a **glass or nonstick pan,** reduce the baking temperature by 25°.

To use a **shallower pan,** reduce baking time by 25%.

To use a **deeper pan,** increase baking time by 25%.

HOW TO CONVERT A RECIPE TO ANY SIZE PAN

When making a substitution, match the volume of the pan called for in the recipe as closely as possible. To find a pan's volume, first find its area, then multiply that by the height. For best results, use a similar-shaped pan as the original.

To save on math, here are the volumes of the most common baking pans. Note that "volume" here refers to the total volume of the pan when filled to the rim, not the amount of batter it should contain. (See "Guidelines for Filling Pans," p. 440, for recommended fill levels.)

SQUARE/ RECTANGLE

PAN DIMENSIONS	VOLUME
8x8x2 in.	8 cups
9x9x1½ in.	8-9 cups
9x9x2 in.	10 cups
11x7x2 in.	6 cups
13x9x2 in.	14 cups
15x10x1 in. (jelly-roll)	10 cups

ROUND

PAN DIMENSIONS	VOLUME
8x1½ in. round	4-5 cups
8x2 in. round	5-6 cups
9x1½ in. round	6 cups
9x2 in. round	7-8 cups
10x2 in. round	10-11 cups
8x3 in. (springform)	12 cups
9x2½ in. (springform)	11 cups
9x3 in. (springform)	13 cups
10x2½ in. (springform)	13 cups

LOAF PANS

PAN DIMENSIONS	VOLUME
8x4x2½ in.	5 cups
8½x4½x2½ in.	6 cups
9x5x3 in.	8-9 cups

GUIDELINES FOR FILLING PANS

Unless your recipe directs otherwise:

• Fill round, square and rectangular cake pans half to two-thirds full.

• Fill deep pans (tube pans) half full.

• Fill loaf pans and muffin tins two-thirds full.

• Fill souffle dishes and steamed pudding molds to within 1 in. of rim.

• Fill jelly-roll pans at least half full or to within ¼ in. of the rim.

INGREDIENT SUBSTITUTIONS

DRY INGREDIENTS

FOR BAKING SODA:

• Use four times the amount of baking powder as the baking soda your recipe calls for. Baking powder contains its own acid (cream of tartar) while baking soda needs a separate acid to help it rise; consider reducing or replacing an acidic ingredient, such as using regular whole milk in place of buttermilk.

• Use an equal amount of potassium bicarbonate. Since it doesn't contain sodium, consider adding an extra pinch of salt.

FOR BAKING POWDER:

• Use ¼ teaspoon baking soda, ½ teaspoon cream of tartar and ¼ teaspoon cornstarch as a substitute for 1 teaspoon baking powder.

• Use ¼ teaspoon baking soda and add ½ teaspoon lemon juice to the wet ingredients for each 1 teaspoon baking powder your recipe calls for.

FOR CAKE FLOUR:

Use all-purpose flour, removing 2 tablespoons per cup and replacing it with 2 tablespoons of cornstarch. Sift several times to combine.

If you don't have cornstarch, use all-purpose flour; remove 2 tablespoons per 1 cup to reduce the protein and gluten in your recipe.

FOR BREAD FLOUR:

Use an equal amount of all-purpose flour. Bread flour has a higher protein content, which results in a chewier texture that works well with a yeast rise. But all-purpose flour can accomplish similar results.

FOR SELF-RISING FLOUR:

For each 1 cup of self-rising flour, combine 1 cup all-purpose flour, 1½ teaspoons baking powder and ¼ teaspoon salt.

WET INGREDIENTS

FOR EGGS:
• Use ¼ cup unsweetened applesauce in place of each egg. If you have only sweetened applesauce, reduce some of the sugar in your recipe.

• Use ¼ cup mashed banana in place of each egg.

• Use 3 tablespoons of mayonnaise in place of each egg.

FOR BUTTER:
• Use an equal amount of margarine.

• Use an equal amount of shortening. Consider increasing quantities of flavoring agents (like salt and extracts), as shortening doesn't have much flavor.

• Add ¾ cup of olive oil or vegetable oil for every 1 cup of butter, or use an equal amount of coconut oil. Oils work best in more liquid batters.

FOR HEAVY CREAM:
• Add ¼ to ⅓ cup cooled melted butter to ¾ cup whole milk to replace 1 cup of heavy cream. Cream is heavier than milk, so to make a substitute you need to add in some extra fat.

• For a dairy-free option, use coconut cream. When chilled, it yields a thick, solid cream. It will impart a slight coconut flavor.

• Use an equal amount of half-and-half cream. If desired, add a little cooled, melted butter for more richness.

FOR MILK:
• If you have almond, soy, cashew, oat or some other nondairy milk on hand, use it in place of dairy milk in equal amounts. Be prepared for slight texture or flavor tweaks—nondairy milk (especially almond) typically has less fat and is not quite as creamy as regular milk.

• Use ½ cup evaporated milk mixed with ½ cup water for every 1 cup of milk in your recipe.

• Use an equal amount of half-and-half, or dilute ½ cup heavy cream with ½ cup water for each 1 cup of milk.

FOR BUTTERMILK:
• For each 1 cup of buttermilk, substitute 1 tablespoon acid (white vinegar or lemon juice) plus enough milk to measure 1 cup.

• Use an equal amount of plain yogurt.

• Mix powdered buttermilk in with your dry ingredients and water in place of the liquid buttermilk in with your wet ingredients.

FOR EVAPORATED MILK:
• At its core, evaporated milk is milk with some of the water evaporated out. Add milk to a heavy bottomed pot, then simmer until it's reduced by 50-60%. Let cool, then use in your recipe as needed.

• Use an equal amount of whole milk in place of evaporated milk. The texture may be different, but the recipe will still work.

• Use an equal amount of half-and-half or heavy cream. (It will make a richer end product due to a much higher fat content.)

FOR CONDENSED MILK:
• Make your own sweetened condensed milk by combining milk and sugar on the stove or in the microwave.

> **In the microwave:** Whisk together ½ cup milk and ⅓ cup sugar in a microwave-safe bowl; heat for 1-2 minutes at a time until mixture is bubbly with a bit of froth. Allow it to cool in the refrigerator.

> **On the stovetop:** In a saucepan, whisk together 2 cups milk and 1 cup sugar. Heat on medium to dissolve the sugar. Reduce temperature just before milk boils; simmer until the milk reduces, about 35 minutes. Allow mixture to cool, then place it in the refrigerator to thicken.

• For a dairy-free option, substitute canned cream of coconut cup for cup. It has a thick, sweet taste; be prepared for a coconutty flavor.

FOR SOUR CREAM:
• Use an equal amount of plain Greek yogurt.

• Use a little less buttermilk than you would sour cream, to make sure the consistency is right.

FOR YOGURT:
• Use an equal amount of sour cream to replace plain Greek yogurt.

• In flavor and chemistry, buttermilk is a good substitute for plain yogurt. Consider increasing the amount of flour or reduce the called-for amount of yogurt to compensate for the thinner consistency.

FOR CREAM CHEESE:
• Use an equal amount of mascarpone cheese. If desired, add a squeeze of lemon juice to imitate the tangy flavor of cream cheese.

• Blend 1 cup each of ricotta cheese and yogurt in a food processor to create 2 cups of cream cheese substitute.

FOR BROWN SUGAR:
• For each cup of brown sugar, use 1 cup white sugar and 1 tablespoon molasses; mix in a stand mixer until thoroughly combined.

• Use an equal amount of white sugar. The result will be crisper, but it will still work. (See "Playing with Ingredients: Chocolate Chip Cookies," p. 123, for an example.)

• Use an equal amount of raw or turbinado sugar; it gives the same molasses flavor as brown sugar. The large crystals in turbinado sugar should dissolve well in wetter batters; for thicker batters, grind it in a food processor to help achieve a better texture.

FOR CORN SYRUP:
• Maple-flavored syrups (not pure maple syrup) are made of corn syrup and are a good replacement; use an equal amount.

• Use an equal amount of honey.

• Use half as much agave nectar as the corn syrup called for.

FOR MOLASSES:
• Use dark maple syrup (the darker the better) as a direct replacement for molasses. Consider reducing the amount of sugar in your recipe.

• Use ¾ cup of brown sugar for each 1 cup of molasses. You may need to add a little extra liquid to maintain the proper texture.

RECILPE INDEX

BAKING METHODS